ITIL
Intermediate
Certification Companion
Study Guide

ITIL®
Intermediate
Certification Companion
Study Guide
Intermediate ITIL Service
Capability Exams

Helen Morris

Liz Gallacher

A Wiley Brand

Senior Acquisitions Editor: Kenyon Brown
Development Editor: Kim Wimpsett
Technical Editors: Jim Tebby and David E. Jones
Production Editor: Dassi Zeidel
Copy Editor: Liz Welch
Editorial Manager: Mary Beth Wakefield
Production Manager: Kathleen Wisor
Executive Editor: Jim Minatel
Book Designers: Judy Fung and Bill Gibson
Proofreader: Amy J. Schneider
Indexer: Ted Laux
Project Coordinator, Cover: Brent Savage
Cover Designer: Wiley

Cover Image: ©Getty Images Inc./Jeremy Woodhouse

We dedicate this book to our long-suffering partners, Gary Cleaver and John Callaghan, who kept us supplied with food, drink, and encouragement while we slaved over our laptops every evening and weekend writing this book.

Acknowledgments

We thank our colleagues across many organizations over the years who have assisted us in our attempts to put best practices into practice. In particular, Liz Gallacher would like to thank Dave Cousin, who encouraged her to follow her instincts and gave her the opportunity to do just that in two major projects.

We thank the teachers who shared their passion for service management during our ITIL V2 Manager courses all those years ago: Ben Weston, Andrew Jacobs, and Mark Haddad, who taught Helen, and Dave Wheeldon and Lloyd Robinson, who taught Liz. Our commitment to focusing our careers in IT service management can be traced back to those few intense weeks.

We thank all the students we have taught for sharing their experiences with us and the clients who have had faith in us and our ability to put theory into practice. Our understanding of service management grows and develops with every organization we work with.

We thank all the ITIL trainers, wherever they are, spreading the service management message every week of the year.

We thank Dave Jones and Jim Tebby for checking the content of this book and for the helpful suggestions they made.

About the Authors

Liz Gallacher is a service management consultant and trainer with 30 years of practical experience. She placed in the top 5 percent of candidates in the ITIL Manager certificate and was invited to join the ISEB V2 Managers Certificate Examiners panel. She holds the ITIL Expert certification and is a certified ISO/IEC 20000 consultant.

Liz provides consultancy and training on all aspects of IT service management, focusing on the ITIL framework and the ISO/IEC2000 standard. She has designed and implemented improvement initiatives covering many areas of service management for a variety of organizations, large and small. Her experience over the past 30 years has been a mixture of consultancy, training, and implementation, including setting up service desks for many large organizations, working with clients to design their service management processes, and evaluating and implementing service management toolsets that met their requirements. She also advises organizations seeking certification against the ISO/IEC 20000 standard, performing gap analyses, advising and mentoring improvement plans, and so on.

Liz has worked for global organizations, central and local government departments, the U.K. National Health Service, and many others. She has set up service management organizations from scratch. In each case, she designed and documented the processes, procured the service management toolset, recommended the organizational structure, drafted job descriptions, and recruited several hundred staff over a number of projects. She then trained the staff and devised appropriate marketing campaigns to publicize the new service desks to the customer base.

She has implemented service improvement initiatives for several clients, combining improvements in processes and tools with customer awareness coaching for IT staff. For a national railway infrastructure organization, she implemented a 24x7x365 service desk to replace 18 other sources of support, delivering a service that was assessed by the Gartner and Maven organizations to be "world class" and "highly efficient."

She has provided consultancy on many aspects of service management, including service-level management, change management, request fulfillment, and incident and problem management. She has compiled detailed service catalogs.

For many clients, Liz has gathered toolset requirements, evaluated products, and recommended the purchase of products that matched the requirement. She has also specified the tool configuration to support the processes, delivered the required reporting, and overseen the implementation. She has also delivered user training.

Liz has developed and delivered customized training for clients covering particular aspects of service management. She has also coauthored classroom and distance-learning courses covering the ITIL framework. She delivers ITIL foundation and intermediate training and consultancy worldwide, with courses in 22 countries so far, as well as the United Kingdom. With Helen Morris, she has devised an innovative blended approach to mentoring and supporting clients remotely.

Helen Morris provides quality training and consultancy to organizations, assisting with delivery of IT service management. She specializes in providing cultural change support and training to organizations to enable the full exploitation of the benefits from implementing service management best practices.

Helen has 25+ years of experience in service management, including operational management of service desks, technical support teams, and service level management. She holds the ITIL Expert qualification and has delivered service management training for many years. She now delivers ITIL foundation and intermediate training in the United Kingdom, Europe, and the United States. She has coauthored and recorded distance-learning courses covering the ITIL framework. Helen is also a certified ISO/IEC 20000 consultant.

Helen is an experienced trainer, consultant, and service delivery manager focused on providing customer satisfaction and business benefits. Many of her assignments involve an initial assessment against best practices, recommendations for improvement, and target setting. She leads programs to achieve significant improvements in customer satisfaction, quality of service, reduced costs, and better control.

Helen has presented at a number of international service management conferences, and she blogs regularly on service management topics. With Liz Gallacher, she has devised a unique approach to mentoring, providing assistance and resources to clients while encouraging them to develop the skills they need without the need for expensive on-site consultancy.

As an experienced consultant, Helen has led a number of successful service management improvement programs, working with organizations to develop their service management strategy and being a key player in the implementation of the strategy within the organizations. She has delivered strategic improvements in customer satisfaction, service delivery, and regulatory standards.

Helen managed the support environment for a Microsoft partner and supported the launch of Windows 95, implementing an improvement initiative to achieve the required customer satisfaction targets. Throughout this period, Helen was also leading a team to achieve and maintain successful ISO 9001 compliance within the division. This included extensive process reengineering in the support division to ensure an efficient and effective process to support the customer satisfaction targets.

An assignment with a blue-chip telecommunications company allowed Helen to implement strategies for introducing best practices into the service delivery management team as the lead for the rollout of ITIL. This formed part of the company initiative to achieve BS15000 (a precursor to ISO 20000), in which Helen was a key player, specializing in incident and problem management.

Many of Helen's assignments have involved assessing and restructuring the support environment to provide improvements in cost efficiency and customer satisfaction. This has often required working across a broad spectrum of the business to achieve an agreed-on approach within the organization. Helen was the lead consultant in delivering the service improvement program for an outsource provider; she provided support services and networks for a large number of blue-chip and financial institutions, delivered by a service support function of more than 120 personnel. Helen achieved and maintained an improvement in service levels from 80 percent to 95 percent (target) within three months across all service areas.

Helen and Liz co-wrote the successful Sybex *ITIL Foundation Study Guide* and the *ITIL Lifecycle Exams Companion Guide*.

Contents at a Glance

Contents

Introduction

IT service management is an increasingly important area of study for all IT professionals. IT managers are realizing that, whatever the technology in use, the requirements to manage that technology efficiently and effectively and to deliver services that are aligned to the business requirement have never been more important.

The internationally recognized ITIL framework is the best-known approach to IT service management. The popularity of ITIL has spread around the world, with an enthusiastic take-up in India, the Middle East, and China in particular. For most IT staff members, the certification is now regarded as an essential addition to their résumés, with many job ads specifying the foundation qualification as a mandatory requirement. This book takes the next step, from the foundation qualification to the intermediate capability level. The content focuses on the practical application of process best practices.

The capability modules can teach organizations and individuals how to manage ITIL processes and gain a better understanding of how to implement the processes that will enable them to deliver and support services to customers.

It also covers issues relating to the people, relationships, procedures, and infrastructure technology required to ensure that the organization or program can provide the high-quality and cost-effective IT services that are required to meet organizational needs.

To achieve any of the intermediate level ITIL qualifications, the foundation certificate is a prerequisite. An accredited course, provided by an accredited training organization, is also mandatory, although this may be a classroom course, or an accredited e-learning course. This book is intended to supplement such a course, not replace it. As experienced classroom tutors and authors of several eLearning courses, we support this mandatory requirement. However, we believe that a real need exists for additional material beyond what these courses provide. For those who do attend classes, it is a common comment that there is too much material to cover in the time allowed. The guidance specifies that students should complete an accredited course and at least 21 hours of activity in addition to the course. Purchasing the official core volumes is a considerable investment, which may be unaffordable. By providing every key aspect of the intermediate capability syllabuses, this book overcomes these difficulties. This book is an economical alternative to purchasing the core volumes; it provides more depth than slides or videos. Concepts that were confusing in the course can be studied in depth at the student's own pace. The many practice questions help reinforce understanding.

ITIL Intermediate Certification Companion Study Guide provides intermediate-level training for IT practitioners. Readers will gain an overview of the ITIL processes, roles, and functions. They will gain specialized knowledge in one or more processes, with focus on the day-to-day execution of ITIL practices and how they interact.

The book covers the full syllabus for the four capability courses. These four examinations include the following:

Operational Support and Analysis (OSA)   Focuses on the practical application of OSA practices in order to enable event, incident, request, problem, access, technical, IT operations, and application management.

The content is based mainly on the best practice guidance contained in the ITIL Service Operation publication.

Planning Protection and Optimization (PPO)   Focuses on practical PPO practices in order to enable capacity, availability, IT service continuity, information security, and demand management.

The content of the course is based mainly on the best practice guidance contained in the ITIL Service Design publication.

Release, Control, and Validation (RCV)   Focuses on the practical application of RCV practices in order to enable the successful planning, testing, and implementation of new services that meet the organization's or users' needs.

The content of the course is based mainly on the best practice guidance contained in the ITIL Service Transition publication.

Service Offerings and Agreements (SOA)   Focuses on the practical application of SOA practices in order to enable portfolio, service level, service catalog, demand, supplier, and financial management.

The content of the course is based mainly on the best practice guidance contained in the ITIL Service Strategy and ITIL Service Design publications.

This book covers the full syllabus for each of the four ITIL Capability courses. However, we want to call your attention to a large amount of overlap in the syllabi for these courses, which will be apparent to any student attending the classroom courses. Only students studying multiple courses will see the duplication. As a result, you might see some content, such as Review Questions, for example, repeated in chapters and the online test bank. We have attempted to mix up the order of the questions, where possible. In the mandatory classroom/online courses, which students will be undertaking along with this companion Study Guide, such overlap in each syllabus will be obvious, and, indeed, will probably be welcomed by many students.

Interactive Online Learning Environment and Test Bank

The interactive online learning environment and test bank that accompanies *ITIL Intermediate Certification Companion Study Guide: Intermediate ITIL Service Capability Exams* provides a test bank with study tools to help you prepare for the certification exam—and increase your chances of passing it the first time! The test bank includes the following:

Sample Tests   All the questions in this book are provided, including the **Assessment Test**, which you'll find at the end of this introduction, and the **Chapter Tests** that include the review questions at the end of each chapter. Use these questions to test your knowledge of the study guide material. The online test bank runs on multiple devices.

Flashcards   Questions are provided in digital flashcard format (a question followed by a single correct answer). You can use the flashcards to reinforce your learning and provide last-minute test prep before the exam.

Other Study Tools   A glossary of key terms from this book and their definitions is available as a fully searchable PDF.

Go to http://www.wiley.com/go/sybextestprep to register and gain access to this interactive online learning environment and test bank with study tools.

How to Contact the Authors

The authors are experienced trainers and consultants and use practical examples and explanations to help the students grasp the content. We provide support to all our students; emails seeking further explanation or clarification will be answered within 24 hours in most cases. You can contact us at enquiry@helix-services.com.

ITIL Capability Intermediate Exam Objectives

The following tables map each of your study requirements to the chapters of this book. We organized the contents of each chapter to be read in an order that will make your study easy. The syllabus for each intermediate capability exam is most applicable to those who are looking to gain specialized knowledge in one or more processes, with focus on the day-to-day execution of ITIL practices and how they interact.

 Mock exams are not included in this book. The complex multiple-choice format of these exams means that exam guidance is difficult to convey in a purely written format. Students should use their classroom tutor or the "ask-the-tutor" function of their eLearning course provider to obtain guidance as to the most effective approach to these exams, and to explore any difficulties they experience in choosing the best answer.

Part 1: Operational Support and Analysis

Topic	Chapter
Introduction to Operational Support and Analysis	1
Incident and Problem Management	2
Event Management, Request Fulfillment, and Access Management	3
The Service Desk	4
Technical Management, Application Management, and IT Operations Management	5
Technology and Implementation Considerations for Operational Support and Analysis	6

Part 2: Planning, Protection, and Optimization

Topic	Chapter
Introduction to Planning, Protection, and Optimization	7
Capacity, Availability, and Information Security Management	8
IT Service Continuity Management and Demand Management	9
Technology and Implementation Considerations for Planning, Protection, and Optimization	10

Part 3: Release, Control, and Validation

Topic	Chapter
Introduction to Release, Control, and Validation	11
Change Management and Service Asset and Configuration Management	12
Service Validation and Testing and Change Evaluation	13
Release and Deployment Management and Knowledge Management	14
Technology and Implementation Considerations for Release, Control, and Validation	15

Part 4: Service Offerings and Agreements

Topic	Chapter
Introduction to Service Offerings and Agreements	16
Service Portfolio Management and Service Catalog Management	17
Service Level Management and Supplier Management	18
Business Relationship Management and Financial Management for IT	19
Technology Considerations for Service Offerings and Agreements	20

Exam units are subject to change at any time without prior notice and at ITIL's sole discretion. Please visit ITIL's website (www.itil-officialsite.com) for the most current listing of units.

Assessment Test

1. Which of the following is a source of best practice?

    A. Suppliers

    B. Technologies

    C. Standards

    D. Advisers

2. Which is the *correct* definition of a service?

    A. A means of delivering value to customers to facilitate outcomes customers want to achieve without the ownership of specific cost and risks

    B. A means of delivering outcomes to customers to facilitate the value that customers pay for without owning the service assets

    C. A means of delivering resources to customers to facilitate capabilities that customers want to acquire without the ownership of specific risks

    D. A means of delivering results to customers to facilitate achievement of contractual obligations without incurring financial penalties

3. What are customers of IT services who do *not* work in the same organization as the service provider known as?

    A. Strategic customers

    B. External customers

    C. Valued customers

    D. Internal customers

4. What should be documented as part of every process?

    A. The process owner, process policy, and set of process activities

    B. The service owner, service level agreement, and set of process procedures

    C. The policy owner, operational level agreement, and set of process steps

    D. The service manager, service contract, and set of work instructions

5. Which of the following is *most* concerned with the design of new or changed services?

    A. Change management

    B. Service transition

    C. Service strategy

    D. Service design

6. Which one of the following is *not* a responsibility of the service transition stage of the service lifecycle?

   A. To ensure that a service can be managed and operated in accordance with constraints specified during design

   B. To design and develop capabilities for service management

   C. To provide good-quality knowledge and information about services

   D. To plan the resources required to manage a release

7. Which of the following is the purpose of service operation?

   1. To coordinate and carry out the activities and processes required to deliver and manage services at agreed levels to the business

   2. The successful release of services into the live environment

   A. 1 only

   B. 2 only

   C. Both of the above

   D. Neither of the above

8. Which of the following is the *best* description of a business case?

   A. A decision support and planning tool that projects the likely consequences of a business action

   B. A portable device designed for the secure storage and transportation of important documents

   C. A complaint by the business about a missed service level

   D. The terms and conditions in an IT outsource contract

9. Which of the following statements about service asset and configuration management is/are *correct*?

   1. A configuration item (CI) can exist as part of any number of other CIs at the same time.

   2. Choosing which CIs to record will depend on the level of control an organization wishes to exert.

   A. 1 only

   B. 2 only

   C. Both of the above

   D. Neither of the above

10. Which of the following *best* defines availability?

    A. How quickly a service or component can be restored after failure

    B. The ability of a third-party supplier to meet the terms of its contract

    C. The ability of a service desk to restore service to configuration items (CIs) and infrastructure components

    D. The ability of a service, component, or CI to perform its agreed function when required

11. The definitive media library is the responsibility of which of the following?

    A. Facilities management

    B. Access management

    C. Request fulfillment

    D. Service asset and configuration management

12. What is the underlying cause of one or more incidents defined as?

    A. A known error

    B. A workaround

    C. A problem

    D. A root cause

13. Where would all the possible service improvement opportunities be recorded?

    A. CSI register

    B. Known error database

    C. Capacity management information system

    D. Configuration management database

14. Which is *not* a defined area of value?

    A. Customer preferences

    B. Business policies

    C. Customer perceptions

    D. Business outcomes

15. Which is the correct list of the 4 Ps of service design?

    A. Process, product, partners, people

    B. People, process, product, performance

    C. Problem, product, performance, people

    D. Process, problem, partners, performance

16. Which one of the following do technology metrics measure?

    A. Components

    B. Processes

    C. The end-to-end service

    D. Customer satisfaction

17. What would be the next step in the continual service improvement (CSI) model?

   1. What is the vision?

   2. Where are we now?

   3. Where do we want to be?

   4. How do we get there?

   5. Did we get there?

   A. What is the return on investment (ROI)?

   B. How much did it cost?

   C. How do we keep the momentum going?

   D. What is the value on investment (VOI)?

18. Which one of the following does service metrics measure?

   A. Functions

   B. Maturity and cost

   C. The end-to-end service

   D. Infrastructure availability

19. In which document would you expect to see an overview of actual service achievements against targets?

   A. Operational level agreement (OLA)

   B. Capacity plan

   C. Service level agreement (SLA)

   D. SLA monitoring chart (SLAM)

20. In which document will the customers' initial service targets be documented before the service level agreement (SLA) is produced?

   A. Operational level agreement (OLA)

   B. Service level requirements (SLR)

   C. Service catalog

   D. Configuration management database (CMDB)

21. The remediation plan should be evaluated at what point in the change lifecycle?

   A. Before the change is approved

   B. Immediately after the change has failed and needs to be backed out

   C. After implementation but before the postimplementation review

   D. After the postimplementation review has identified a problem with the change

22. Which two documents are *most* likely to be updated by the change advisory board (CAB)?

    A. Change schedule and service level agreements (SLAs)

    B. Service catalog and service pipeline

    C. Projected service outage (PSO) and change schedule

    D. Projected service outage (PSO) and service level agreements (SLAs)

23. Which of the following is the *best* reason for categorizing incidents?

    A. To establish trends for use in problem management and other IT service management activities

    B. To ensure that service levels are met and breaches of agreements are avoided

    C. To enable the incident management database to be partitioned for greater efficiency

    D. To identify whether the user is entitled to log an incident for this particular service

24. Which of the following should be documented in an incident model?

    1. Details of the service level agreement (SLA) pertaining to the incident

    2. Chronological order of steps to resolve the incident

    A. 1 only

    B. 2 only

    C. Both of the above

    D. Neither of the above

25. Which process is responsible for eliminating recurring incidents and minimizing the impact of incidents that cannot be prevented?

    A. Service level management

    B. Problem management

    C. Change management

    D. Event management

26. With which process is problem management likely to share categorization and impact coding systems?

    A. Incident management

    B. Service asset and configuration management

    C. Capacity management

    D. IT service continuity management

27. Which of the following processes contributes *most* to quantifying the financial value of IT services to the business?

    A. Service level management

    B. Financial management for IT services

    C. Demand management

    D. Risk management

28. Which process is responsible for recording the current details, status, interfaces, and dependencies of all services that are being run or being prepared to run in the live environment?

   A. Service level management

   B. Service catalog management

   C. Demand management

   D. Service transition

29. Which process includes business, service, and component subprocesses?

   A. Capacity management

   B. Incident management

   C. Service level management

   D. Financial management

30. Which process would ensure that utility and warranty requirements are properly addressed in all service designs?

   A. Availability management

   B. Capacity management

   C. Design coordination

   D. Release and deployment management

31. Which process is responsible for ensuring that appropriate testing takes place?

   A. Knowledge management

   B. Release and deployment management

   C. Service asset and configuration management

   D. Service level management

32. The experiences, ideas, insights, and values of individuals are examples of which level of understanding within knowledge management?

   A. Data

   B. Information

   C. Knowledge

   D. Governance

33. Which of the following identifies the purpose of service transition planning and support?

    A. Provide overall planning for service transitions and coordinate the resources they require

    B. Ensure that all service transitions are properly authorized

    C. Provide the resources to allow all infrastructure elements of a service transaction to be recorded and tracked

    D. Define testing scripts to ensure that service transactions are unlikely to ever fail

34. Which one of the following would *not* involve event management?

    A. Intrusion detection

    B. Recording and monitoring environmental conditions in the datacenter

    C. Recording service desk staff absence

    D. Monitoring the status of configuration items

35. Which process is responsible for dealing with complaints, comments, and general inquiries from users?

    A. Service level management

    B. Service portfolio management

    C. Request fulfillment

    D. Demand management

36. Which of the following is the *best* description of a centralized service desk?

    A. The desk is co-located within or physically close to the user community it serves.

    B. The desk uses technology and other support tools to give the impression that multiple desk locations are in one place.

    C. The desk provides 24-hour global support.

    D. There is a single desk in one location serving the whole organization.

37. Which one of the following activities does application management perform?

    A. Defining where the vendor of an application should be located

    B. Ensuring that the required functionality is available to achieve the required business outcome

    C. Deciding who the vendor of storage devices will be

    D. Agreeing on the service levels for the service supported by the application

38. Which of the following statements about the service owner is *incorrect*?

   A. Carries out the day-to-day monitoring and operation of the service they own

   B. Contributes to continual improvement affecting the service they own

   C. Is a stakeholder in all of the IT processes that support the service they own

   D. Is accountable for a specific service within an organization

39. Which rules should be followed when defining an RACI authority matrix?

   A. More than one person is accountable.

   B. At least one person is consulted.

   C. Only one person is accountable.

   D. Only one person is responsible.

40. What areas can benefit from service automation?

   1. Monitoring

   2. Pattern recognition

   3. Wisdom

   4. Prioritization

   A. 1, 2, and 3

   B. 1, 2, and 4

   C. 1, 3, and 4

   D. 2, 3, and 4

Answers to Assessment Test

1. **C.** Standards are a source of best practice. Technologies (Option B), suppliers (Option A), and advisers (Option D) are all enablers of best practice.

2. **A.** This is the book definition where value is delivered to facilitate outcomes without ownership of costs and risks. The incorrect answers are themed around this but incorrect in terms of their order and/or goals.

3. **B.** The fact that they belong to a different organization from the service provider makes them an external customer. Those named in Option D (internal customers) belong to the same organization as the service provider. Options A and C (strategic and valued customers) may or may not belong to other organizations.

4. **A.** The process must have an owner to ensure that it is followed, a policy to guide its activities, and the detailed activities themselves. Option B has only process procedures, which are valid. In Option C, the process does not require an OLA. In Option D, only the work instructions might be included for each process.

5. **D.** Service design oversees the design of new or changed services. The other three options would only be involved at some point. Design would be done under change management (Option A), would receive input from service strategy (Option C), and would provide output to service transition (Option B).

6. **B.** Service transition will ensure that changes adhere to time, cost, and quality objectives, thus delivering value to the business. Option A is an objective of service level management. Option C is an objective of service operation, and Option D relates to service catalog management.

7. **A.** Only statement 1 is a purpose of service operation. Service operation manages the services at agreed levels through its processes and functions. Statement 2 is a purpose of service transition.

8. **A.** A business case will contain costs, benefits, and risks that will allow an organization to make an informed decision on the viability of an action. Option B describes a briefcase! Option C describes a concern that may be raised in a service review meeting. Option D describes something that might be assessed in a business case but not the case itself.

9. **C.** Both statements are true. In the case of statement 1, a monitor may be a CI in its own right but could be (when joined with a base unit) part of a PC configuration item. The second statement is also true. For example, the level of detail an organization chooses to record about its hardware may be dictated by the level of control required by industry regulation.

10. **D.** This is the book definition. Option A describes an element of maintainability. Option B is serviceability. Option C just focuses on the service desk and technology, *not* services, and so is incorrect.

11. D. The storage of the definitive media library's logical list of media as CIs in the CMS defines the key to it being the responsibility of service asset and configuration management. The other three could be involved but only in a more minor role. Facilities management (Option A) may be responsible for a fire safe, allowing the physical store of the actual media. Access management (Option B) may be involved in granting rights to use the DML. Request fulfillment (Option C) might be the route to accessing the components in the DML for users and customers.

12. C. That's the book definition of a problem.

13. A. The CSI register contains all improvement opportunities to be considered. Option B (the known error database), as indicated by the name, contains known errors. Option C is wrong as the capacity management information system contains the business, service, and component data to allow the capacity management process to function. Option D (the CMDB) contains CI information.

14. B. Perception of value is defined by customer preferences (Option A)—that is, what they want; customer perceptions (Option C)—that is, if they think it's valuable it is; and delivering on outcomes (Option D)—that is, it enables them to complete their task. Business policies are not part of this calculation.

15. A. The balance of service design is achieved through the balance of process, product, partners, and people.

16. A. Technology metrics are one of the three categories used by CSI. Components are measured by them. The other two types are process (Option B) and service (Option C). Customer satisfaction doesn't fit into any of the three.

17. C. The final stage of the process is "How do we keep the momentum going?"

18. C. Service metrics measure elements that cover the total service. Of the other two types of metrics available (technology and process), the performance of a function (Option A) might be measured through compliance to a process or other process success metrics. Maturity (Option B) is a process metric. Infrastructure availability (Option D) is a technology metric.

19. D. The SLAM chart shows progress against service targets, in a simple, pictorial form. Option A (OLA) is the internal supporting targets for the SLA. Option B (capacity plan) shows the future needs and plans for capacity within the organization. Option C (SLA) contains the targets that the SLAM chart uses as its targets.

20. B. The service level requirements documents the customers actual needs for the service, which can be verified by the service provider and perhaps amended by negotiation before arriving at a signed SLA. Option A (OLA) is the internal supporting targets for the SLA. The service catalog (Option C) would be used as the basis to start the discussion of the service level requirements. Option D (the CMDB) is not used as part of this process.

21. A. The remediation plan will be required if the change fails, so it should be assessed in advance of the change being approved. If the remediation plan is not considered sufficient, the risk is greatly increased, as it may be impossible to restore to the previous state if the change fails, so the proposed change may need to be rejected. Option B is incorrect because it is too late to evaluate the plan when it is about to be used. Option C is incorrect because the plan may not have been used if the change was successful. Option D is incorrect because the remediation plan is for backing out of the change immediately if it fails. A problem identified at the postimplementation review would require a second change to be authorized to overcome the issue.

22. C. The PSO and change schedule are effectively the customer and service provider view of changes taking place. They may be updated as a result of CAB decisions. Other documents mentioned in incorrect answers are not within the CAB remit to change—namely the SLA, service pipeline, and service catalog.

23. A. The reason we categorize anything (incidents included) is to make management easier. Spotting recurring incidents by category will facilitate easier raising of problems. Simply categorizing an incident does not make it certain that the SLA will not be breached (Option B). The partitioning of the incident management database (Option C) is not a consideration when deciding on incident categories. Categorization could, in some circumstances, be used to decide if a user can log an incident (Option D), but the question asks for the *best* reason.

24. B. Only statement 2 is true. Statement 1 is impractical. An organization could have an incident model for restoring a printing service. The printing service may actually support multiple SLA targets, so there would be little sense in including them in the model. The incident itself would be the guide for restoration targets. The incident model tells us how to deal with the type of incident so the chronological order of steps would be mandatory to include.

25. B. This is an objective of problem management.

26. A. Sharing of categorization and impact codes makes matching incidents to problems and known errors a much easier, often automatic task. Problem management will use the CMDB (Option B) in its process but will not share categories. Capacity management (Option C) will share data with problem management but not codes and categories. ITSCM (Option D) might share information for risk assessment (including impact codes) with problem management but is very unlikely to share categories.

27. B. Financial management will use cost models, ROI analysis, and so forth to understand the financial value of the service. Service level management (Option A) may understand the nonfinancial value of a service from customer satisfaction. Demand management (Option C) will identify trends that may lead to maintaining the value of a service by increasing capacity. Risk management (Option D), though not an ITIL process, may also measure value of a service in terms of risk reduction, but this is again nonfinancial.

28. B. The service catalog will record interfaces and dependencies through its business and technical components. Service level management (Option A) uses the catalog to understand the dependencies. Demand management (Option C) and service transition (Option D) will use the catalog but do not record details in it.

29. A. These are the three subprocesses of capacity management.

30. C. Design coordination is responsible for both utility (fitness for purpose) and warranty (fitness for use). Availability (Option A) and capacity (Option B) are both concerned with warranty only. Release and deployment (Option D) is a service transition process and so not worthy of consideration as the correct answer.

31. B. Build and test is the second phase of the release and deployment process. The other processes have only minor involvement in testing.

32. C. Knowledge is a collection of experience and ideas and is the element required to understand how an activity should be performed. Data (Option A) becomes more valuable once it is processed into information (Option B). This information becomes the basis for knowledge. Governance (Option D) concerns policy and control and is not relevant here.

33. A. Service transition planning and support almost does a project management role within service transition, meaning planning and resource coordination are in scope. Option B describes the role of change management. Recording and tracking (Option C) is done by service asset and configuration management, whereas test scripts (Option D) are part of release and deployment management.

34. C. Service desk staff absence would be recorded via an HR system outside of the scope of ITIL. All other areas could be monitored under the event management process.

35. C. Complaints, compliments, and general inquiries come under the request fulfillment process handled almost exclusively at the service desk. Service level management (Option A) may deal with complaints but at a customer level and would not usually entertain general inquiries. Such interactions are way outside of the scope of service portfolio management (Option B) and demand management (Option D).

36. D. A single centralized service desk supports the whole organization. Option A describes a local service desk. Option B is a virtual service desk, and Option C describes a follow-the-sun model of service desk.

37. B. Application management is responsible for the functionality and utility. Option A is incorrect, since defining where vendors are located is likely to be a policy defined and managed by supplier management. Option C is more likely to be advised on by technical management. Option D is incorrect, since agreeing on service levels is the domain of service level management.

38. A. The service owner will be aware of the monitoring and operation of their service but not actually be directly involved in the activity. The other three activities are all part of the role of service owner.

39. C. Only one person should be accountable for a process. This immediately makes Option A incorrect. Nobody needs to be consulted (Option B) about an activity; for example, logging a service desk call doesn't need another person to be consulted. Option D is incorrect since multiple people may be responsible.

40. B. Technology and automation can help to monitor (Option 1), for example, free disc space on a server. Pattern recognition (Option 2) can also be automated, for example, spotting repeat incidents through the service desk toolset. Prioritization (Option 4) can also be automated through a tool, for example, when an incident is logged against a certain type of service. Wisdom (Option 3) cannot be automated.

Intermediate
Certification Companion

Study Guide

Operational Support and Analysis

Chapter

1

Introduction to Operational Support and Analysis

THE FOLLOWING ITIL OPERATIONAL SUPPORT AND ANALYSIS CAPABILITY INTERMEDIATE EXAM OBJECTIVES ARE DISCUSSED IN THIS CHAPTER:

✓ The value to the business of OSA activities

✓ The context of OSA activities within the service lifecycle

✓ How OSA activities support the service lifecycle

✓ Optimizing service operation performance

✓ Generic roles associated with all service management processes

Service operation's main aim is to deliver and manage services at agreed levels to business users and customers. The service operation stage is when the service is actually delivered, and it's often a much longer stage than the previous stages of strategy, design, and transition. It is the most visible part of the lifecycle to the business. We will cover the purpose, objectives, and scope of the service operation processes and their context within the service lifecycle. We'll examine the value provided to the business and discuss the fundamental concepts and definitions involved in these processes.

Understanding the Purpose, Objectives, and Value of the Operational Support and Analysis Processes

The outputs from service strategy, design, and transition becomes visible in service operation. It is in the operational stage that the service—which was originally considered in strategy, put together in design, and rolled out in transition—actually delivers the benefit that the business requires and the service was designed to deliver. It is also a much longer stage of the lifecycle than the first three stages; the service should continue to meet the defined business requirement for months or even years.

Most IT staff are involved (to a greater or lesser extent) in the service operation stage. They may contribute to other lifecycle stages, but their main focus is the delivery of the operational services.

Service operation is a critical stage of the service lifecycle. After all, the best strategy will fail if the service is badly managed, and good design is of limited value if the service is not run effectively. Transition can be successful only if the environment into which the service is being transitioned is ready to receive it and takes responsibility for managing it. Finally, service improvements will not be possible without reliable metrics from monitoring performance and other data. Service operation gathers the measurements used for *baselines* and for measuring success of improvements, so consistent, systematic measurements are a key element of service operation.

The staff working in this stage of the service lifecycle need to have *processes* and support tools in place to enable them to do their job—monitoring tools that allow them to have an overall view of service operation and delivery so they can detect failures and resolve them quickly. They also need service management tools to ensure that the correct workflow takes place for each process and the necessary information is easily accessible. This may entail monitoring elements of the service supplied by external providers.

Because services may be provided, in whole or in part, by one or more *partner/supplier* organizations, the service operation view of the end-to-end service needs to encompass external aspects of service provision, including managing cross-organizational workflows.

Process   A *process* is defined as "a set of coordinated activities designed to accomplish a specific objective. A process takes one or more defined inputs and turns them into defined outputs."

The processes included in Operational Support and Analysis are as follows:

Event Management   This process is concerned with having useful notifications about the status of the IT infrastructure and services. Event management sets up rules to ensure that events are generated so that they can be monitored, captured, and acted upon if necessary.

Incident Management   The purpose of incident management is to return normal IT service to users as quickly as possible. This may prompt the question, how do we define *normal service*? It is the level of service specified, and agreed to, in the service level agreement (SLA). The goal is to minimize the adverse impact of incidents on the business, and thus on service quality and business productivity. The objective of incident management is to ensure that the best possible levels of business-aligned service quality are maintained.

Problem Management   The responsibility of problem management is to manage the lifecycle of problems, which includes monitoring and reviewing the process in addition to managing problems to their conclusion. Problem management is about the prevention and reduction of incidents, solving and removing their root cause. At the very least, if an incident cannot be prevented, then the impact to the business should be reduced through the provision of workarounds provided through the known error database.

Request Fulfillment   The objectives of the request fulfillment process are to log and fulfill standard requests for users in a simple, efficient way. For a request to qualify, a predefined approval and qualification process must exist. Request fulfillment also provides information to users about the availability of services and how to obtain them. Users can request and receive the service or the software/hardware they require to use the service. Request fulfillment is also the channel for general information, complaints, and comments.

Access Management   Access management is responsible for putting the policies of availability and information security management into day-to-day practice. It is essential to control access to protect an organization's data and intellectual property while at the same time enabling authorized users to have the access they need. Access management is not responsible for ensuring that this access is available at all agreed times—this responsibility is provided by the *availability management* process.

The Purpose of Operational Support and Analysis Processes

The purpose of the service operation stage of the service lifecycle is to deliver the service at the level that was agreed to through the *service level management* process. This includes performing all the activities required to deliver the service as well as managing the technology used to deliver the service (such as applying updates and backing up data). These are the activities performed by the processes of operational support and analysis.

Service operation must deliver the service effectively but also has to ensure that the cost of that delivery is within the operational costs that formed part of the original business case. Should a service be operating at a higher cost than was originally envisaged, the benefits that were planned, such as cost savings, may never be realized.

Service operation staff members must view the service as a whole and be given the tools they need to evaluate whether the delivery meets the standard required. It is a common error to have staff members concentrate on individual aspects of a service or to ignore those parts of the service provided by third parties, losing sight of the end-to-end service as it appears to the customer. Technology can be used to spot deviations from expected service or *response levels* very quickly, allowing remedial action to be put in place immediately.

The Objectives of Operational Support and Analysis Processes

The objectives of service operation and its processes follow on from its purpose. Service operation is what the customer sees and experiences. Their perception of the quality of the service provision is based on their experience, not on the design or implementation of the service, which may or may not have been done well. It is important to remember that service operation is far more than just managing the components that make up the service. It is in service operation that it all comes together … or all falls apart! So the first objective is to maintain business satisfaction and confidence in IT through effective and efficient delivery and support of the service as agreed in the SLA; this ensures that the business receives the level of service it expects. The second objective supports the first; it is to minimize the impact of service *outages* on day-to-day business activities—by finding, preventing and resolving *incidents* and *problems* that could impact the business. Some service outages are inevitable; service operation will work to reduce both the number and impact of outages. The service operation process of problem management aims to reduce the recurrence of incidents that disrupt business activities, whereas incident management aims to resolve those incidents that do occur as quickly as possible.

Service operation is also responsible for controlling *access* to IT services. The final objective is to protect the services from unauthorized access. The access management process ensures that only authorized users can have access to the services provided.

The Scope of Operational Support and Analysis Processes

The scope of service operation, described in the ITIL framework, includes the "processes, functions, organization, and tools" that are used to deliver and support the agreed services. The processes are responsible for performing the critical day-to-day activities that ensure the service meets the business requirement and enables the business to achieve its objectives. They also collect the performance data that will be required by continual service improvement to identify and track improvement opportunities.

The Technology   Delivering IT services depends on the use of appropriate technology such as networks, desktops, servers, databases, and monitoring tools. Service operation is responsible for managing the technology that delivers the services.

The People   Despite automation, service operation depends on the actions of the support staff members to ensure that the service runs as it should. Their management of the technology and processes is the key to successful service delivery.

The Value Operational Support and Analysis Processes Deliver to the Business

Service operation is responsible for running the new service and for fixing any unforeseen flaws. The service must run efficiently if the cost of the service is to be less than the benefit to the business. The ITIL framework offers guidance on the best practices that can be used in the various lifecycle stages, and following this advice can deliver real benefits. In the area of service operation, the following benefits can be achieved from following best practices:

- Financial savings from reduced downtime as a result of the implementation of the service operation processes of problem and incident management. Problem management will reduce the frequency of failures so that less time (and therefore money) is wasted by the business not being able to work. It will ensure that skilled IT staff members concentrate their efforts on identifying and removing the *root cause* of the incident, thus preventing recurrence. Meanwhile, efficient incident management ensures that the service is restored as soon as possible, often by service desk staff members using defined *workarounds*. This both speeds up the service restoration and reduces costs, the latter because the more expensive IT staff members are not called on to resolve simple incidents.

- Service operation includes the production of management information regarding the efficiency and effectiveness of the service delivery. This is used by other processes to target, justify, and implement continual service improvement initiatives. Technology may be used to automate this report generation, reducing the cost of production.

- By carrying out the access management activities, service operation ensures that the business is able to meet the goals and objectives of the organization's security policy by ensuring that IT services will be accessed only by those authorized to use them; services are protected from unauthorized access in accordance with the organization's security policy.

- Service operation also provides quick and effective access to standard services through request fulfillment. This improves the productivity of users by enabling quick access to the services and equipment they need for optimum efficiency while maintaining control over expenditure. Technology may be used to provide users with a self-service facility such as resetting passwords, ordering standard items, or logging incidents through a web portal. This offers an efficient and cost-effective means of providing these services.

- By using technology to automate routine tasks, based on the information provided by the event management process, service operation reduces the number of staff members required to operate the service. This means, as the number of users grows and the complexity of the services increases, the number of people needed to support the users remains broadly the same. This reduces costs and frees up technical staff members to concentrate on identifying improvements and new opportunities. Automation also delivers a more reliable and consistent service.

- Service operation also provides the operational results and data that is then used by other ITIL processes as evidence of the need for service improvements (answering the "where are we now?" question) or to justify investment in service improvement activities. It also provides the data required to answer the "Did we get there?" question.

How Service Operation Provides Business Value

Each stage in the service lifecycle provides value to the business, but as we have said already, it is service operation where the actual value is seen from a customer viewpoint. In addition to the day-to-day running of the services, service operation needs to meet other challenges if it is to continue to deliver business value. These challenges center on the reluctance to invest in this stage of the lifecycle. Service operation needs to deliver the service within the projected cost in order to deliver the *return on investment (ROI)*, but once the project has been delivered, there may be little or no budget allocated for the costs of ongoing management of services, such as to fix design flaws or unforeseen requirements, because this is outside the original project scope.

Most organizations never undertake a formal review of operational services for design and value. Incident and problem management are expected to resolve issues, but if the design is fundamentally flawed, this may not be identified.

Service operation may struggle to be awarded the necessary budget for tools or improvement actions (including training) that would improve efficiency because they are not directly linked to the functionality of a specific service. Attempts to optimize the service or to use new tools to manage it more effectively are seen as successful only if the service has been very problematic in the past; otherwise, any action is perceived as "fixing services that are not broken."

The Context of Service Operation, the Operational Support and Analysis Processes, and the Service Lifecycle

Service operation needs to be considered within the context of the whole service lifecycle. Each area of the *lifecycle* addresses a particular set of challenges that need to be addressed for successful service management, and each stage has an impact on all the others. The service lifecycle diagram in Figure 1.1 shows the five areas of the lifecycle.

FIGURE 1.1   The ITIL service lifecycle

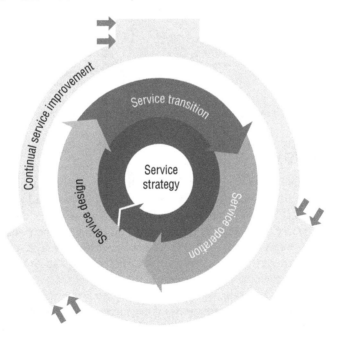

Stages of the lifecycle work together as an integrated system to support the ultimate objective of service management, which is to deliver business value. Every stage is interdependent, as shown in Figure 1.2. In particular, note the interdependence of service operation to each of the other lifecycle stages.

FIGURE 1.2   Integration across the ITIL service lifecycle

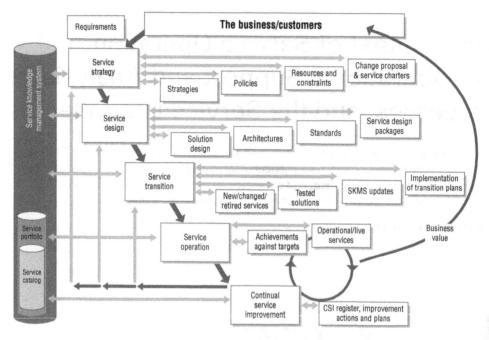

Service Strategy

Service strategy is at the core of the service lifecycle. It is the role of strategy to understand the organizational objectives and customer needs. People, processes, and products should support the strategy. ITIL service strategy asks why something is to be done before thinking of how. It helps service providers to set objectives and to set expectations of performance for serving customers and markets. It also helps to identify, select, and prioritize opportunities. Service strategy ensures that providers understand and can handle the costs and risks associated with their service portfolios.

The complete list of service strategy processes includes strategy management for IT services, *service portfolio* management, financial management for IT services, *demand* management, and *business relationship management*. These processes impact service operation in the following ways:

- The success or otherwise of the services provided in service operation in meeting the business requirement would confirm whether the service strategy management processes have been effective.

- Service portfolio management provides service operation with advance notice of future requirements through the pipeline, whereas the service catalog defines what is to be provided by service operation (in other words, it defines service operation's scope).

- If demand management has been successful, service operation will be able to cope with the level of demand for the service, and any fluctuations in that demand, and will have techniques available to affect the levels of demand where required.

- Both financial management and business relationship management are strategic processes that take place during the service operation lifecycle stage; managing budgets and liaising with the business at a senior level are ongoing activities that touch all areas of the lifecycle.

Service Design

Service design turns strategic ideas into deliverables. The design must always consider the strategy, to ensure that services are designed with the business objectives in mind. Design considers the whole IT organization and how it will deliver and support the services, turning the service strategy into a plan for delivering the business objectives. Requirements from service operation processes, people, and tools must be taken into account to ensure that the design will work in the operational environment. Remember, design includes changes to existing services.

The complete list of service design processes includes design coordination, *service catalog management*, service level management, *availability management, capacity management, IT service continuity management, information security management*, and *supplier management*. Through these processes, design ensures that both the *utility* and the *warranty* of the new or changed service is considered in design, covering the continuity of the service, its achievement of service levels, and conformance to security standards and regulations.

- Design coordination is responsible for ensuring that the service operation requirements are included in the design and that an operations plan exists.

- The service catalog, as stated previously, defines the scope of service operation because it provides information about all operational services.

- Service operation provides the monitoring and metrics needed to manage the delivery of the availability and capacity targets and identify areas of concern.

- The reporting against service level targets and any actions required to deliver a service improvement plan take place as part of service operation.

- IT service continuity plans are tested regularly as part of operations, and any invocation of the plan would be to ensure that service operation is able to continue to deliver the required services to the business.

- Information security provides the policies that access management implements in service operation.

- Supplier management is dependent on the metrics from live operational services to know whether the suppliers are providing the contracted services.

Service Transition

Service transition provides guidance for developing and improving *capabilities* for introducing new and changed services into supported environments. The value of a service is identified in strategy, and the service is designed to deliver that value. Service transition ensures that the value is realized; it does so by enabling the necessary changes to take place without unacceptable risks to existing services. It enables the implementation of new services, and the modification of existing services, to ensure that the services provided deliver the service strategy of achieving the business objectives and that the benefits of the service design are fully realized. Service transition also introduces the *service knowledge management system*, which ensures that knowledge is stored and made available to all stages of the service lifecycle and that lessons are learned and decisions are backed with factual data, leading to improved efficiency and effectiveness over time.

The complete list of service transition processes includes *transition planning and support*, change management, service asset *and configuration management*, *release* and *deploymentmanagement*, *service validation and testing*, *change evaluation*, and *knowledge management*. Each process has a role to play to ensure that beneficial changes can take place and, as a consequence, the service can be introduced and will work as transitioned.

- Service asset and configuration management provides service operation with detailed knowledge of how configuration items are combined to deliver the service, showing the relationships and dependencies between these items.

- Release and deployment management ensures that the components of changes are delivered into the live environment without disrupting the existing services.

- Service validation and testing provides quality assurance, establishing that the service design and release will deliver into service operation a new or changed service or service offering that is fit for purpose and fit for use in line with the strategy and design.

- Change evaluation checks the actual performance and outcomes of the new or changed service in service operation against the predicted performance and outcomes. Successful completion of the change evaluation ensures that the service can be formally closed and handed over to the service operation functions and *continual service improvement (CSI)*.

- Knowledge management provides knowledge base articles that can be of great use to incident, problem, and request processes.

Service Operation

Service operation, the subject of this section, describes best practice for managing services in supported environments. It includes guidance on achieving *effectiveness*, *efficiency*, stability, and security in the delivery and support of services to ensure value for the customer, the users, and the service provider. Without this, the services would not deliver the value required, and the achievement of business objectives would become difficult or impossible.

The service operation stage is therefore critical to delivering the design and, in doing so, achieving the service strategy. Service operation provides detailed guidance for delivering the service within the agreed service levels by tackling issues both proactively through problem and event management and reactively through incident management. It provides those delivering the service with guidance on managing the availability of services, controlling demand, optimizing capacity utilization, scheduling operations, and avoiding or resolving service incidents and managing problems. It includes advice on shared services, utility computing, web services, and mobile commerce. By delivering the services to the agreed levels, service operation enables the business to use the services to achieve its business objectives.

Service operation also describes the four service operation functions: the *service desk*, *technical management*, *IT operations management*, and *application management*. Each function is responsible for managing its own area of delivery across all stages of the lifecycle.

Continual Service Improvement

The final stage of the lifecycle is continual service improvement (CSI). CSI ensures that the service provider continues to deliver value to customers by ensuring that the strategy, design, transition, and operation of the services is under constant review. Feedback from any stage of the service lifecycle can be used to identify improvement opportunities for any other stage of the lifecycle. This ensures that opportunities for improvement are recognized, evaluated, and implemented when justified. These may include improvements in the quality of the service or the capabilities of the service provider. It may be developing ways of doing things better, or doing them at the same level but more efficiently. Improvements may be major or small and incremental. CSI enables every new operation to incorporate lessons from previous operations.

CSI ensures that feedback from every lifecycle stage is captured, analyzed, and acted on. Service operation is the source of information regarding the performance of services, and so the service operation lifecycle stage is an important source of information for CSI. Many of the improvement initiatives driven by CSI will directly affect service operation processes, products, and people; improvements to other lifecycle stages may lead indirectly to improved operational performance.

The CSI approach to improvement is based on establishing a baseline and checking to see whether the improvement actions have been effective. It uses the *Plan-Do-Check-Act (PDCA)* cycle, together with service measurement, demonstrating value with metrics, and conducting maturity assessments. The seven-step improvement process provides a framework for these approaches.

Optimizing Service Operation Performance

Service operation is optimized in two ways. First, there are the long-term incremental improvements. Service operation processes, technologies, functions, and outputs are analyzed over time and a decision made about whether improvement is needed and, if so, how best to implement it through service design and transition. The improvements are logged in the CSI register and designed and transitioned into service. Typical examples include the deployment of a new set of tools, changes to process designs, and reconfiguration of the infrastructure.

Second, there are the short-term ongoing improvements; these are the improvements made to working practices within the processes, functions, and technologies that underpin service operation. They are generally smaller improvements that are implemented without any change to the fundamental nature of a process or technology. Examples include tuning, workload balancing, personnel redeployment, and training.

Generic Roles and Responsibilities in Service Management Processes

There are many different ways to organize an IT department, and no two service providers are identical, so the exact configuration of roles within each organization will differ. Often two or more roles may be combined; in other organizations, a single role may be split. ITIL provides guidelines, not prescriptive rules, so each organization should consider what would best fit their own requirements.

We will first clarify what is meant by the term *role*. The official glossary defines it as follows:

> A set of responsibilities, activities, and authorities assigned to a person or team. A role is defined in a process or function.

Within each of the processes we will cover throughout the service lifecycle, there are a number of roles. The role may be carried out by an individual or a team, and one person may have multiple roles. The person responsible for the availability management of the infrastructure may often also be fulfilling the capacity management role. It may be that capacity management is divided between a number of people, with one considering network capacity, another responsible for storage, and so on.

It is important to remember that although roles may be shared, or combined, there can be only one process owner for each process and one service owner for each service.

Often a job title may be the same as a role description; service level manager is one such example. Job titles are for each organization to decide, and it may be the case that the job of service level manager includes the role of service level manager, along with one or more other roles, such as supplier manager, within that particular organization.

It is also often true that one task carried out by an individual may touch several processes. A technician may submit a request for change to overcome a capacity issue that has been identified by problem management. The action may have been identified as desirable as part of a service improvement plan (SIP), which has been logged on the CSI register. The technician's action therefore involves several processes: problem, change, capacity, service level management, and continual service improvement.

Every process has its own specific roles. Here we will be looking at the generic roles that appear in all lifecycle stages.

Service Owner

With every service interacting with so many processes, there is a danger that the service itself may no longer receive the required attention. To avoid this, ITIL recommends that each service should have a single service owner. This clarifies who is accountable for the service and ensures that there is a focus on the business processes that the service supports.

Whatever technology is used to deliver the service and regardless of whether aspects of the technology are provided in-house or are outsourced, the service owner remains accountable for delivering the service. This role is responsible to the customer for the service being developed, implemented, and maintained, but it is also accountable to the IT director or service management director for its delivery.

As we will examine, ITIL recommends that each process should have an identifiable owner. Each process may affect many services, and it is the service owner of each who will ensure the service is delivered effectively and efficiently, whatever process is being carried out. Service owners will often own more than one service. For each service, they will carry out the following responsibilities:

- Ensuring that the service is delivered and supported to the required standards by working with all IT groups and process owners
- Ensuring that the customer's requirements are understood and that the tasks required to deliver them are implemented by working with the business relationship manager
- Communicating with the customer as required on all issues regarding the delivery of the service
- Using the service portfolio management process to define new service models and to evaluate the impact of any changes to existing services
- Ensuring that the service undergoes continual service improvement by identifying possible improvements and, with the customer's agreement, putting these forward as requests for change
- Ensuring that appropriate monitoring and reporting is taking place to enable an accurate view of the level of service being delivered
- Ensuring that the required levels of performance and availability are delivered
- Developing a thorough understanding of the components that make up the service and ensuring that the potential impact of their failure is realized
- Representing the service across the organization and attending service review meetings with the business

- Representing the service within IT and at change advisory board (CAB) meetings and internal service reviews

- Being the escalation (notification) point for major incidents affecting the service

- Working with service teams to negotiate service level agreements that meet the customer requirements and operational level agreements that support the service provision at the agreed level

- Maintaining the service catalog entry

- Working with the CSI manager to identify improvements to be added to the CSI register and participating in the review and prioritization of these and their eventual implementation

As the owner of the service, this role is concerned with the impact of any process affecting the service. This means service owners should be considered stakeholders in these processes, with whatever level of involvement is appropriate.

For example, the service owner plays a crucial part in the major incident process and will attend or possibly run any crisis meetings. They will also be involved in investigating the root cause of problems affecting their service. The service owner will represent the service at CAB meetings and will be involved in discussions regarding if and when a release should go ahead. They will want to ensure that the service portfolio and catalog entries and configuration data held on their service is accurate.

As explained earlier, a close relationship should exist between the service level management process and the service owner who acts as the contact point for the service. The service owner will also liaise with the owners of the more technical processes, such as availability and capacity, to ensure that the data collected by these processes indicates that the performance and reliability of these services meets the agreed standard.

The service owner is responsible for ensuring that the IT service continuity management (ITSCM) plan for their service is practical and that every element of the plan is in place. They will work with the ITSCM manager to make sure that all aspects are considered. They will often attend rehearsals of the plan to observe it in action to confirm that nothing has been forgotten.

The service owner understands the costs involved in delivering the service and will work with the supplier manager and other managers to ensure that costs are controlled and value for money is achieved. In organizations where the business is charged for IT services, they will ensure that the recovery of costs takes place as agreed.

Finally, the service owner ensures that the service follows the information security management policies.

Process Owner

As we have seen, the service owner is the focus for one particular service across all process areas. The process owner, in contrast, is accountable for a single process, whatever the service it affects.

The process owner must ensure that the process works efficiently and effectively. Although the role may often be carried out by the same person who fulfills the process manager role, in larger organizations this is less likely. A global company may have a change management process owner and a number of process managers carrying out the process in different countries, for example. The process owner is accountable for ensuring the process is fit for its purpose and is being carried out correctly by the process managers and practitioners. The role therefore has both a design and an enforcement aspect.

The process owner is accountable for the following:

- Developing the process strategy, policies, and standards
- Assisting with designing the process and amending it as required to implement improvements that make it more effective or efficient
- Assisting with designing the metrics for the process and ensuring that these provide the necessary information to judge the effectiveness and efficiency of the process
- Ensuring that the process is documented, that this documentation is available to those who require it, and that it is updated as needed
- Where the process has changed, ensuring that the process documentation is updated and the changes communicated to the process practitioners (those who actually carry out the process steps)
- Auditing the process activities to ensure adherence to the correct process
- Ensuring that the required resources are available to carry out the process and that the staff members involved have been trained to carry it out
- Communicating to the process practitioner the importance of adhering to the documented process and explaining the implications for IT and the business of nonadherence
- As part of continual service improvement, reviewing the process strategy and the effectiveness of the process itself to identify possible improvements
- Where improvements to effectiveness or efficiency are identified, having these included in the CSI register and working with the CSI manager to review, prioritize, and implement them as appropriate

The process owner role is critical to the success of the process. In organizations where no such single point of ownership exists, those carrying out the process may decide to drop or amend steps in the process, and there is no one with the overall authority to prevent this. In global organizations, this can mean the process may develop regional variations. In addition to the danger of losing focus on the purpose of the process, this may invalidate the reporting from the process, because each area may be inputting data differently.

Without a process owner, there is no one with the responsibility of ensuring consistency in applying the process, and there is no one to ensure that the process output still matches the process objectives. Process documentation may not be updated, because the responsibility for its upkeep would be unclear. Finally, there would be no one to assess the process and identify improvements.

Process Manager

The process owner is accountable for the success of the process but may often not be responsible for actually carrying it out. The responsibility for managing the day-to-day implementation of a process belongs to the process manager. In large or geographically spread-out organizations, there may be several process managers responsible for managing the implementation of the same process, each with a regional or infrastructure responsibility.

The process manager is accountable for the following:

- Liaising with the process owner to ensure that the process is implemented across all lifecycle stages as the process owner intended
- Ensuring the right numbers of staff are assigned to the various roles within the process and that they understand what is required of them
- Working with other process managers and service owners to ensure the services are delivered as required
- Monitoring the process metrics to confirm the process is working as designed
- As part of continual service improvement, reviewing the process performance to identify possible improvements
- Where improvements are identified, having them included in the CSI register and working with the CSI manager and process owner to review, prioritize, and implement them as appropriate

The role of process manager is important, because it is the process manager who ensures that the process is carried out correctly day-to-day. The process owner may be distant from where the process occurs (working in the head office while the process takes place in branch offices, for example). The process manager, or managers, will ensure that the staff members understand what is required of them and have been provided with the right resources and training to carry out the tasks. Because process managers are close to the process execution, they are in an ideal position to identify issues and possible improvements. The success of any improvement initiatives will depend heavily on the enthusiastic involvement of the process manager in ensuring that staff members adopt the improved process.

Process Practitioner

Depending on the process, there may be one or more people carrying out the process activities. In a small organization or for a simple process, this may be a single person, who is also likely to be the process manager. For a large organization or for a complex process, there may be many people, each carrying out parts of the process. The people involved in carrying out the process activities are the process practitioners.

The process practitioner is usually responsible for the following:

- Completing process activities to the required standard
- Understanding the importance of the process and their role within it, and how they contribute to delivering the service
- Working with all the process stakeholders to ensure the process inputs, outputs, and interfaces are working properly so that the process delivers the desired result
- Producing evidence that the process activities have been carried out correctly, in the form of records
- Identifying necessary improvements to the process or supporting tool

The process practitioner role is responsible for actually delivering the process activities. Under the guidance of the process manager (unless these roles are combined), the practitioner is responsible for carrying out the process as designed, consistently and efficiently. It may be tempting to believe that the practitioner has nothing to contribute other than carrying out the activities; this is far from the truth. As a practitioner, the staff member will experience firsthand any issues with the process, such as tools that do not support the process effectively, bottlenecks in the process flow, or ambiguities in the documentation. The process manager and process owner should therefore seek out the views of practitioners when attempting to identify possible improvements.

Each role has its own purpose. Even where the roles are carried out by the same person, that person should attempt to consider each aspect of the roles. The practitioner has the advantage of daily interaction with the process but may be too close to it to see it objectively; the process manager is judged on the outcome of the process and so has a particular focus on the resources required to deliver these effectively and efficiently. They will monitor the process metrics closely to ensure that the outputs are being delivered on time and within budget. The manager will see only their own part of the process delivery, however. The process owner has the advantage of seeing the overall picture, comparing the delivery of the process in different locations and under different process managers. By understanding the strengths and weaknesses of each perspective, a complete picture of the process delivery can be achieved, and improvement initiatives can be gathered from each level.

Summary

This chapter covered the value, purpose, and objectives of the operational support and analysis processes and how they deliver value to the organization. We looked at the processes within the context of the service lifecycle and considered the fundamentals of the operational support and analysis processes. We covered which processes from other lifecycle stages require service operation action. We also considered the generic roles applicable to the processes, including that of service owner, with which the processes have a significant interaction.

It is important to remember that the generic roles will apply across all lifecycle stages and service management processes.

In the following chapters, we will be examining the service operation processes of incident management, problem management, access management, request fulfillment, and event management.

Exam Essentials

Understand the value of operational support and analysis processes.   These processes form the core of the service operational activities and how the service operation lifecycle stage adds value to the business.

Understand the place of operational support and analysis processes in the service lifecycle.   Understand the impact each of the other lifecycle stages has on service operation. Know the inputs from these other stages into service operation processes and the outputs from service operation into the rest of the lifecycle.

Understand the responsibility of service operation to deliver the services in line with the SLAs that have agreed with the business.   The transition stage should have validated the SLA targets through testing and piloting the service; it is the responsibility of service operation to continue to meet the SLA targets during the operational stage of the service lifecycle.

Understand the role played by operational support and analysis processes in ensuring that the services deliver business value.   By delivering the services efficiently and to agreed service targets, service operation ensures that the business benefits from the service as planned.

Understand the key processes of service operation.   Be able to name the five service operation processes: incident management, request fulfillment, access management, problem management, and event management.

Understand the generic roles associated with the processes of service operation.   Be able to name and explain the significance of the roles associated with all the processes in service operation.

Review Questions

You can find the answers to the review questions in the appendix.

1. Service operation includes which of the following activities?

   A. Testing the service

   B. Rolling out the service

   C. Deciding whether to retire the service

   D. Optimizing the service

2. Many processes from other lifecycle stages also take place during the service operation stage. Which of the following processes does not fall into this category?

   A. IT service continuity management

   B. Availability management

   C. Service level management

   D. Design coordination

3. Which of the following is the correct list of service operation functions described in ITIL?

   A. Technical management function, facilities management function, service desk function

   B. Infrastructure management function, desktop support function, application management function, service desk function

   C. Technical management function, operations management function, application management function, service desk function

   D. Infrastructure management function, service desk function, application development function

4. Which of these activities is facilities management *not* responsible for?

   A. Maintaining air-conditioning to the required level in the server rooms

   B. Defining the infrastructure requirements to support the services

   C. Ensuring that the power supply at disaster recovery sites meets the requirement

   D. Testing the UPS and generators

5. Match the activities to the functions.

   1. Activity: Console management

   2. Activity: Identifying functional and manageability requirements for application software

   3. Activity: Providing a single point of contact

   4. Activity: Designing and managing the infrastructure

   a. Function: Service desk

   b. Function: Technical management

   c. Function: Application management

   d. Function: Operations management

     A. 1d, 2a, 3c, 4b

     B. 1d, 2c, 3a, 4b

     C. 1a, 2b, 3c, 4d

     D. 1b, 2c, 3d, 4a

6. The service desk is *not* responsible for which of the following?

     A. Providing a first point of contact

     B. Resolving straightforward incidents

     C. Preventing incidents from recurring

     D. Providing updates to users

7. The service desk carries out two processes. What are they?

   1. Incident management

   2. Design coordination

   3. Request fulfillment

   4. Change management

     A. 2 and 4

     B. 1 and 3

     C. All of the above

     D. 3 and 4

8. Which of the following are generic roles for all processes?

   1. Service owner

   2. Process owner

   3. Process manager

   4. Process practitioner

     A. 1 and 2

     B. 2 and 3

     C. All of the above

     D. 2, 3, and 4

9. Which of these is a correct description of the responsibilities of a service owner?

   A. Ensuring the service is delivered according to the customer's requirements

   B. Managing the process activities

   C. Carrying out process activities

   D. Facilities management, operations control

10. Which of the following is a responsibility of a process practitioner?

   A. Managing the delivery of service

   B. Ensuring process policies are correctly documented

   C. Carrying out the work instructions for the process

   D. Managing the resources for the process

Chapter

2

Incident and Problem Management

THE FOLLOWING ITIL OPERATIONAL SUPPORT AND ANALYSIS CAPABILITY INTERMEDIATE EXAM OBJECTIVES ARE DISCUSSED IN THIS CHAPTER:

✓ **Incident management and problem management are discussed in terms of their**

- Purpose
- Objectives
- Scope
- Value to the business, and to the service lifecycle
- Policies, principles and basic concepts
- Process activities, methods and techniques and how they relate to the service lifecycle
- Triggers, inputs, outputs and interfaces
- Information management within the process
- Roles
- Challenges and Risks
- Using critical success factors and key performance indicators to check the effectiveness and efficiency of the process

This book is a study guide to assist you in achieving the ITIL Intermediate Capability certificates; it supports the mandatory accredited courses for these qualifications, which may be classroom courses or distance-learning. The first section of the book covers the Operational Support and Analysis qualification. The syllabus for this course includes the day-to-day operation of each process and the detail of the process activities, methods and techniques, and its information management. More detailed guidance covering the managerial and supervisory aspects of service operation processes is covered in the service lifecycle intermediate qualifications. Each process is considered from the operational perspective. The first section of this book, comprising Chapters 1 to 6, covers operational support and analysis. That means at the end of this section you should understand incident and problem management principles, techniques and relationships, and their application to the support and operation of effective service solutions.

Incidents and Problems: Two Key Service Management Concepts

The two processes of *incident* and *problem* management are among the most important of all the ITIL processes. They are often the first to be implemented by an organization that has decided to adopt the ITIL framework. The differentiation between incident management and problem management is an important distinction, and an organization that has adopted both of these processes has made a major advance toward improving their services and their service management.

Both these processes are carried out by every IT service provider, whether they are called by these names or not. All service providers fix faults as quickly as possible when they occur (incident management) and try to ascertain why the fault occurred so that it can be prevented from happening again (problem management). Many organizations do not differentiate between the two processes, however, and problem management in particular may not be carried out in a consistent fashion. A failure to appreciate the difference between problems and incidents may result in delayed service restoration following an incident and in allowing incidents to recur, causing business disruption each time.

ITIL provides guidance for the best approach to these two key processes. Effective incident management will improve *availability*, ensuring that users are able to get back to work quickly following a failure. Problem management will improve the overall quality and availability of services (and as such works in conjunction with continual service improvement [CSI]); it also makes best use of skilled IT staff, who are freed from resolving repeat incidents and are able to spend time preventing them instead.

Incident Management

In ITIL terminology, an *incident* is defined as an unplanned interruption to an IT service, a reduction in the quality of an IT service, or a failure of a Configuration Item (CI) that has not yet impacted an IT service (for example, failure of one disk from a mirror set). We can easily think of examples of "unplanned interruptions to an IT service"—a server crash, hardware failures, and so on. A good example of the second part is the failure of a disk in a storage device with a RAID (redundant array of independent disks) configuration. This is treated as an incident, although the storage device is still usable. The point is that the failure of one disk means that the storage is no longer protected from the failure of another disk. If another disk fails, then the device will fail and the data on it will be inaccessible.

This is an important definition; because the incident is an interruption to service, restoring the service or improving the quality of the service to agreed levels resolves the incident. Note that incident resolution does not necessarily include understanding why the fault occurred or preventing its *recurrence*; these are matters for problem management. By understanding this distinction, you can see that resolving an incident does not need the skill that resolving a problem requires. If the service can be restored by a simple reboot, then the user can be instructed to do this by the service desk staff without involving the more skilled (and therefore more expensive) second-line technicians.

From the user and business perspectives, the focus is on being able to get back to work, and there is less interest in the cause of the failure. Repeat occurrences will impact their work and increase the number of calls to the service desk. An investigation of the cause and the permanent resolution of the underlying problem will be required, but this can take place without impacting the users.

The incident management process is responsible for progressing all incidents from when they are first reported until they are closed. Some organizations may have dedicated incident management staff, but the most common approach is to make the service desk responsible for the process.

Sometimes the resolution of an incident is possible only by understanding the cause and fixing the underlying fault. A hardware or network failure due to a failed hardware component where there is no resilience will need to have the component replaced or repaired before service can be restored. In the majority of incidents, however, service can be restored to the individual user without a permanent problem resolution.

The Purpose of Incident Management

The purpose of *incident management* is to restore normal service operation as quickly as possible and minimize the adverse impact on business operations, thus ensuring that agreed levels of service quality are maintained. *Normal service operation* is defined as an operational state where services and CIs are performing within their agreed service and operational levels.

As explained, by focusing on service restoration, incident management enables the business to return to work quickly, thus ensuring that the impact on business processes and deadlines is reduced.

The Objectives of Incident Management

The objectives of the incident management process are as follows:

- Use standardized methods and models for managing incidents. This means that incidents should be handled in a consistent way regardless of service, technology, or support group. This enables the business and the service provider management to have clear expectations of how any particular incident will be handled.

- Increase visibility and communication of incidents. This allows the business to track the progress of the incidents they report and ensures that all IT staff have access to the information relating to an incident.

- Enhance business perception of IT. All IT service providers will suffer incidents, but the way in which they respond can enhance their reputation; a well-designed incident management process should enhance the reputation of IT in the business by demonstrating a professional, effective approach.

- Align activities with business needs by ensuring that incidents are prioritized based on their importance to the business.

- Maintain user satisfaction.

All incidents must be efficiently responded to, analyzed, logged, managed, resolved, and reported on. By carrying out these tasks in an efficient and effective manner and by ensuring that affected customers are updated as required, the IT service provider aims to improve customer satisfaction, even though a fault has occurred. At all times during the incident management process, the needs of the business must be considered; business priorities must influence IT priorities.

The Scope of Incident Management

Incident management encompasses all incidents: all events have a real or potential impact on the quality of the service. Incidents will mostly be logged as the result of a user contacting the service desk, but event management tools may report an incident following an alert (see the discussion of event management in Chapter 3, "Event Management, Request Fulfillment, and Access Management"); often there will be a link between the event system and incident management tool so that events meeting certain criteria can automatically generate an incident log. Third-party suppliers may notify the service desk of a failure, or technical staff may notice that an error condition has arisen and log an incident.

 As discussed, not all events are incidents; many are informational or a confirmation that a component is functioning correctly.

Requests may be logged and managed at the service desk, but it is important to differentiate between these requests and incidents; in the case of requests, no service has been impacted. Incident and problem management seek to reduce the number of incidents over time, whereas the IT service provider may want to handle increasing numbers of requests through the service desk and the request fulfillment process as a quick, efficient, and customer-focused method of dealing with them.

The Value of Incident Management to the Business and to the Service Lifecycle

Efficient incident management delivers several benefits to the business. For example, it reduces the cost of incident resolution by resolving incidents quickly, using less-skilled staff. Where incidents need to be escalated, the resolution is faster (because the relevant information required will have been gathered by first-line staff and an initial diagnosis will have been made). Faster incident resolution means a faster return to work for the affected users, who are once again able to exploit the functionality of the service to deliver business benefits. Effective incident management improves the overall efficiency of the organization because nonproductive users are a cost to the company.

Incident *prioritization* is based on an assessment of impact and urgency based on business priorities, which ensures that resources are allocated to maximize the business benefit. The data gathered by the service desk about the numbers and types of incidents can be analyzed to identify training requirements or potential areas for improvement.

As highlighted in the discussion of the service desk in Chapter 4, "The Service Desk," incident management is one of the most visible processes, as well as one that all users understand the need for. So, it is one of the easier areas to improve, because an improved incident resolution service has easily understood benefits for the business.

The incident management process also delivers value to the other areas of the service lifecycle. By concentrating on reducing downtime, it helps service level management ensure that the availability targets are met. Additionally, by ensuring that straightforward incidents are resolved at first line, it assists financial management by ensuring that the more expensive staff are used more efficiently. It captures details of issues regarding capacity and security. It gathers useful data on the performance of third parties for supplier management, and on issues caused by changes. It highlights areas for CSI; the data gathered by incident can also show the effectiveness of improvement initiatives.

Incident Management Policies

Next we consider some of the policies that support effective incident management.

Incidents and their status must be communicated in a timely and effective way.   Users must be kept informed of the progress of incidents that affect them, and the information they are given must make sense to them—most users don't understand technical jargon, so this should not be used. This policy shows that incident management is not solely about resolving the incident—the business needs information about the status of open incidents so that it can make decisions about what to do to minimize the business impact. This is one of the key responsibilities of the service desk.

Incidents must be resolved in timeframes that that are acceptable to the business.   We should remember that IT is the servant of the business. Service level management will determine what timeframes are acceptable, and must ensure that the necessary *operational level agreements* and *underpinning contracts* (UCs) are in place to support them. You should be familiar with these concepts from your foundation studies. Further information regarding service level management can be found in Chapter 18, "Service Level Management and Supplier Management." Achieving the resolution within the required timescales requires the allocation of sufficient and appropriate resources to work on the incident, with access to the necessary tools, technology, and incident, *known error*, and configuration information.

Customer satisfaction must be maintained at all times.   Customer satisfaction is not only about meeting *SLA* targets. Users and customers will be dissatisfied even if IT meets or exceeds all of its incident-related targets if support staff are rude or patronizing. Even if targets are missed, keeping the customer informed can result in an improved level of customer satisfaction.

Incident processing and handling should be aligned with overall service levels and objectives.   Incidents should not be handled to suit the convenience or priorities of IT; incident management activities should support service levels and objectives by prioritizing those activities based on actual business need.

All incidents should be stored and managed in a single management system.   Using a single system provides a definitive recognized source for incident information and supports reporting and investigation efforts. Status and detailed information on the incident should be recorded and updated on a timely basis in incident records.

All incidents should be categorized in a standard way.   Standardized *categorization* enables useful analysis and reporting; it speeds up troubleshooting by making it easier to find other occurrences of a fault within the incident database or the *known error database*. It makes identification of trends easier. To be effective, there must be a well-defined and communicated set of incident classification categories. The service management tools can be programmed to discourage the entry of nonstandard categories.

Incident records should be audited on a regular basis.   The incident database is a rich source of information about what is happening in the infrastructure and about the difficulties being experienced by the business. However, its usefulness depends on it being accurate and complete. We have already considered the importance of consistency in data entry; this policy ensures that the guidelines for such data are being followed by auditing incident records for accuracy and completeness. Any issues discovered should be noted and acted on.

All incidents should use a common format.   Staff should record the information that the service provider has deemed to be necessary in a standard format. This helps both the management of a live incident and later reporting and analysis.

Use a common and agreed-upon set of criteria for prioritizing and escalating.   This ensures that customer needs are handled consistently across all services and components, rather than bring dependent on the opinion of whoever logs the incident.

Principles and Basic Concepts for Incident Management

ITIL describes a number of principles and basic concepts to keep in mind when implementing the incident management process. They are covered in the following sections.

Timescales

Time is of the essence in incident management because every incident represents some loss or deterioration of service. Every aspect of the process needs to be optimized to produce the fastest end result. Service level agreements (SLAs), operational level agreements (OLAs), and underpinning contracts will define how long a support group or third party has to complete each step, with measurable targets. When an incident is passed to a support group for investigation, a clock starts ticking; that group has a defined length of time to complete its work, defined in the OLA. If the incident is passed to a third party, the timescales set in the underpinning contracts would apply. These OLA and contract *target* timescales support the achievement of the SLA target.

Service management tool sets should be configured to capture how long it takes to log and escalate an incident, how many incidents are resolved within the first few minutes without requiring escalation, and how long support teams take to respond to and to fix incidents. These times should be monitored, and steps should be taken to identify bottlenecks or underperforming teams so that improvement actions can be taken. These tools can be used to automate timescales and escalate the incident as required based on predefined rules.

Incident Models

Many incidents have happened before and may well happen again. For this reason, many organizations will find it helpful to predefine "standard" *incident models* and apply them to appropriate incidents when they occur. A model is a predefined way of carrying out a commonly required task. ITIL recommends models for a number of processes such as incident, request, and change. An incident model describes the steps needed to investigate and resolve a particular type of incident. The benefit of these models is that they speed up the resolution of incidents. Most service management tools have the capability to store multiple models; when one of these incidents occurs, the incident is logged using the appropriate pre-prepared model. The incident can then be handled using the model. The tool may also automate many of the model steps, such as automatic assignment to the correct support group and escalations.

Incidents that require specialized handling can be treated in this way (for example, security-related incidents can be routed to information security management and capacity, or performance-related incidents can be routed to capacity management). Using incident models will help ensure consistency of approach and will speed up resolution.

The contents of a typical incident model should include the following:

- The steps required to handle the incident, including their timescales and the chronological order with any dependencies

- Details of who is responsible for each step, and the escalation contacts

- Any precautions to be taken such as backing up data, or steps to comply with health and safety related guidelines such as isolating equipment from the power supply

- In the case of security- and capacity-related incidents, any steps to be taken to preserve evidence

Major Incidents

All incidents should get resolved as quickly as possible, but some incidents are so serious, with such an impact on the business, that they require extra attention. The first step is to agree on exactly what is defined as a *major incident*. Some organizations will define all priority one incidents as major; others may restrict priority one incidents to those whose impact will be felt by the external customers. In this definition, an incident with a major impact within the organization would not normally be classed as major. An incident that (for example) prevents customers from ordering goods from the organization's website and that is therefore affecting both revenue and reputation would be included. The definition must align with the priority scheme to avoid confusion.

The purpose of defining an incident as a major incident is so that it can receive special focus. Specific actions to be undertaken are defined in advance so that when the major incident occurs, everyone knows what they are expected to do. Typical actions might include the following:

- Notification of key contacts within the service provider organization and the business as soon as the major incident is declared

- Regular updates posted through agreed channels—intranet, key users, and so on

- A recorded greeting put on the service desk number to inform callers that the incident has occurred and is being dealt with to reduce the number of calls being handled by the desk

- The appointment of a major incident manager (this may be the service desk manager) and the appointment of a separate team to focus on resolving the incident

Where the service desk manager is managing the incident, another manager may be appointed to head up the team; they would then report progress to the incident manager. This is necessary to avoid a situation where the two roles, that of managing the situation and keeping stakeholders informed and that of pursuing a solution, are in conflict.

As with any incident, some major incidents can be resolved without understanding the cause (perhaps by restarting a server); some require the underlying cause to be understood. In the second case, problem management would become involved. It is essential, however, that the focus of incident management remains on restoring service as quickly as possible.

As we discuss in Chapter 4, a major responsibility of the service desk is communicating with the users; this is particularly true in the case of major incidents. Regular updates should be provided. The service desk staff members are also accountable for ensuring that the incident record is kept up-to-date throughout the incident, although it may be the technicians in other teams who actually enter the information. An accurate record is essential during the incident so that there is no confusion; it will also be used after the incident is resolved, as part of the major incident review. Regular updates showing the steps taken and whether they were successful will allow improvements to be identified for future events.

Incident Status

Incident management tracks incidents through their lifecycle, moving from when the incident is identified through diagnosis and resolution and finally closure, using status codes. Incident management will remind resolving groups of the associated target times, making sure no incident is forgotten or ignored.

Most service management tool sets will allow a number of statuses to be defined for each incident to facilitate progress tracking. Typical statuses include the following:

Open The incident has been identified and logged. It may be being worked on by a service desk analyst, or the service desk may be considering which second-line team it should be escalated to. Incidents resolved by the first-line team may move directly from Open to Closed, because the service desk analyst obtains the user confirmation that the incident has been satisfactorily resolved.

Assigned This may mean the incident has been sent to a support team but not allocated to a particular individual.

Allocated or In Progress This is usually defined as when a support technician has been allocated the call.

On Hold This status is sometimes used when the user is not available or has not the time to test the resolution. It is used to "stop the target clock," because the service provider cannot do anything further to resolve the incident without the user.

On Hold status should be used with caution; support staff may be tempted to use it when they are too busy to work on the incident or when they are awaiting the actions of a third-party supplier. This is not its purpose, and using it in this way distorts reporting against OLAs and UCs, because the failure to provide the support and meet the target is hidden by the fact that the clock is stopped.

Resolved   This status indicates that the technician has completed their work, but it has not been confirmed by the user that this was successful. It is common to use the service management's email facility to automatically email the user when an incident is resolved, asking for a response within a certain timescale if the user is still not happy. If no reply is received, the incident is automatically closed.

- If the user is unhappy, the call is put back into In Progress, and further work is carried out to resolve it.

- The service desk should attempt to contact users to obtain permission to close calls before the automated closure, especially for high-impact incidents, where the user may not be aware of the resolution.

Closed   This status confirms that the incident is over to the user's satisfaction. The incident management process has no further involvement, although problem management may now investigate the underlying cause.

Expanded Incident Lifecycle

The expanded incident lifecycle is used by the service design availability management process and within CSI. The expanded lifecycle breaks down each step of the process so that they can be examined to understand the reasons for the failed targets. For example, the diagnosis of the incident may ascertain very quickly that the resolution requires the restoration of data, which takes three hours; this information would be used to pinpoint where improvements should be made. Delays in any step of the lifecycle can be analyzed, and improvements can be implemented to speed up resolution. Implementing a knowledge base or storing spare parts on-site are two typical measures that are taken to shorten the diagnosis and repair steps.

Incident Management Process Activities, Methods, and Techniques

This section takes a high-level look at each of the activities in incident management. Refer to Figure 2.1, which shows the process flow.

FIGURE 2.1 Incident management process flow

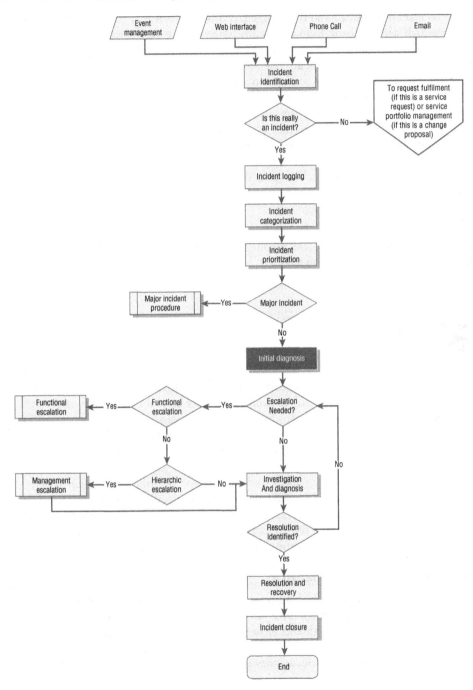

Step 1: Incident Identification and Logging

First, the incident is identified and then logged. Many incidents will be reported to the service desk, which will log them. But not all calls to the service desk are related to incidents; some will be service requests, which are handled by the request fulfillment process. As the diagram in Figure 2.1 shows, these are re-routed.

It is essential that incidents are resolved in the shortest possible time, because each represents business disruption. Whenever possible, therefore, we should be trying to identify that an incident has occurred before the user notices or, failing that, before they have reported it to the service desk. Chapter 3 describes how event management monitoring tools can be used to identify failures. The event management process should link directly to incident management so that any incidents spotted are worked on immediately and resolved quickly. Where event management is not in place, incidents will be identified by users contacting the service desk.

Where an automated response to an incident is used, such as restarting a server following a failure, an incident should still be logged for future analysis.

All incidents must be logged, no matter how they are identified.

The *incident record* contains all the information concerning a particular incident; details of when it was logged, assigned, resolved, and closed may be required for service level management reporting. Details of symptoms and the affected equipment may be used by problem management. Steps taken to resolve the incident may be used to populate a knowledge base. It is essential that all relevant information is added to the record as it progresses through its lifecycle.

A good integrated service management tool makes good recordkeeping much easier, because it can automatically populate the record with user details (from Active Directory or a similar tool) and equipment and warranty details (based on the CI number). The completeness of the information in the record can be improved by automatic date and time stamping of each update and identification of who made the update.

Step 2: Incident Categorization

Incidents are categorized during the logging stage. This can be helpful in guiding the service desk agent to the correct known error entry or the appropriate support team for escalation. A simple category structure should be used, however; too complex a scheme leads to incidents all being logged as "other" or "miscellaneous" because the agent does not want to spend the time considering which category is correct. This makes later analysis very difficult. A multilevel scheme, as shown in Figure 2.2, achieves granularity without facing the service desk agent with a long list to choose from. Incidents should be re-categorized during investigation and on resolution, if the original choice was incorrect.

FIGURE 2.2 Multilevel incident categorization

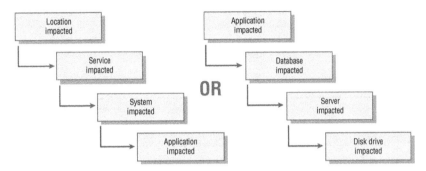

The process step that checks whether the call is actually a request is there to identify and filter out any requests that have been misreported as incidents.

Step 3: Incident Prioritization

Incidents need to be prioritized to ensure that the most critical incidents are dealt with first. It is often said that all users believe that their own incident is the highest priority, so it is important to agree during service level negotiations which criteria should be used to decide priority.

The ITIL framework recommends that two factors be considered: business impact and urgency (how quickly the business needs a resolution). Business impact can be assessed by considering a number of factors: the number of people affected, the criticality of the service, the financial loss being incurred, damage to reputation, and so on. Dependent on the type of organization, other factors such as health and safety (for a hospital or a railway company or similar organization) and potential breach of regulations (such as for financial institutions) may be considered.

During the life of an incident, it may be necessary to adjust the priority of an incident if the assessment of the impact changes or a resolution becomes more urgent.

Deciding the priority must be simple, because the incident has to be logged quickly. Employing service desk staff with good business knowledge and ensuring they are trained to be aware of business impact will help ensure a realistic assessment of business impact. Table 2.1 shows a simple but effective way to determine priority.

TABLE 2.1 Impact and urgency: A matrix for determining an incident's priority

Impact	Urgency		
	High	Medium	Low
High	1	2	3
Medium	2	3	4
Low	3	4	5

Table 2.2 shows how the determination of priority made using the matrix in Table 2.1 can in turn be employed to set a target resolution time for the incident.

TABLE 2.2 Target resolution

Priority code	Description	Target resolution time
1	Critical	1 hour
2	High	8 hours
3	Medium	24 hours
4	Low	48 hours
5	Planning	Planned

Many organizations struggle with applying the prioritization rules when the user reporting the fault is very senior. Some organizations address this issue by formally recognizing the needs of VIPs for fast service and defining a special service level (e.g., gold service) for them within the SLA, documented in the service catalog. It is vital that this VIP list is discussed and agreed on with the customer—that it is not simply a list produced by IT of people they assume need a different level of service.

Step 4: Initial Diagnosis

The initial diagnosis step refers to the actions taken at the service desk to diagnose the fault and, where possible, to resolve it at this stage. The service desk agent will use the known error database provided by problem management, incident models (covered earlier), any other diagnostic tools to assist in the diagnosis, and possible resolution. Where the service desk is unable to resolve the incident, the initial diagnosis will identify the appropriate support team for escalation.

Part of this stage is the gathering of information to assist the second-line technician in resolving the incident quickly. Again, sufficient time is required for this step; "saving" time by passing the incident to a second-line technician quickly but with insufficient or sparse details is not helpful. The second-line technician will need to contact the customer to obtain the information, adding delay and frustration. Support teams should provide guidance to the service desk about the type and level of information they should be gathering.

Step 5: Incident Escalation

The ITIL framework describes two forms of escalation that may take place during *incident management*: *functional escalation* and *hierarchic escalation*.

Functional escalation takes place when the service desk is unable to resolve the incident; this may be realized immediately because of the type of incident such as a server failure or because the service desk agent may have spent the maximum time allowed under the organization's guidelines attempting to resolve the incident without success. It then needs to be passed to another group with a greater level of knowledge. The second-line support group that receives this escalated incident will also have a time limit for resolution, after which the incident gets escalated again to the next support level. Sometimes, as with the service desk, it is obvious that the incident will require a high level of technical knowledge, and in such a case the incident would be immediately escalated, without any attempt by second-line support staff to resolve it.

To avoid unnecessary delays, the service desk must know the correct group to escalate an incident to; therefore, the service desk staff needs sufficient technical knowledge to be able to identify which incident goes to which team. Operational level agreements will specify the responsibilities of each group. There may be occasions where cooperation between support groups is required or where the incident should be referred to third parties such as hardware maintenance companies. The OLAs and UCs should specify what happens in this situation.

Incident ownership remains with the service desk. Incidents may be escalated to support groups or third parties, but the service desk retains ownership of the incident, tracking progress, keeping users informed, and obtaining the user's agreement to its eventual closure.

The second type of escalation is hierarchic escalation, which usually takes place for high priority or major incidents, or incidents which have exceeded resolution targets. This escalation consists of informing the appropriate level of management about the incident so that they are aware of it. This ensures that the management is able to make any decisions that are required regarding prioritization of work, involving suppliers, and so on. In the case of a major incident, the IT director may be expected to brief the business directors about the progress of the incident; even if this is not the case, business managers may go directly to senior IT managers when a serious incident has occurred, so it is essential that the IT managers be thoroughly briefed themselves.

It is also sometimes necessary to use hierarchic escalation when the incident is not progressing as quickly as it should or if there is disagreement among the support groups regarding to whom it should be assigned.

A good service management tool will be able to automatically escalate incidents, based on the SLA targets, updating the record with details. For example, a tool could be set to notify a team leader when 90 percent of the SLA target time had passed and to inform the team leader's line manager when the incident breached the target.

Step 6: Investigation and Diagnosis

The major activity that takes place for every incident is investigation and diagnosis. The incident will have undergone the initial diagnosis step covered earlier; this identifies whether the service desk can resolve the incident because the incident has been seen before. The investigation and diagnosis stage here is different; it involves trying to ascertain what has happened and how the incident can be resolved.

The incident record should be updated to record what actions have been taken, and an accurate description of the symptoms, and the various actions taken, is required to prevent duplication of effort; it will also be useful when the incident is reviewed, perhaps as part of problem management. Typical investigation and diagnosis actions would include gathering a full description of the issue and its impact and urgency, creating a timeline of events, identifying possible causes such as recent changes, interrogating knowledge sources such as the known error database, and so on.

It is important to recognize that the primary focus here is to identify what actions need to be taken to enable the service to be restored. Its focus is not full root cause analysis, which will only be undertaken by the problem management process, if needed.

Step 7: Resolution and Recovery

Potential incident resolutions should be tested to ensure that they resolve the issue completely with no unintended consequences. This testing may involve the user. Other resolution actions might include the service desk agent or technician remotely taking over the user's equipment to implement a resolution or to show the user what they need to do in the future. Once the incident is resolved, it returns to the service desk for closure.

Step 8: Incident Closure

When the incident has been resolved and the service restored, the service desk will contact the user to verify that the incident may be closed. This is an important step, because the fault may appear resolved to the IT department, but the user may still be having difficulties, especially if there were actually two incidents, with the symptoms of one being hidden by the other. The second incident would become apparent only after the first was resolved. The service desk may contact the user directly, or an email could be sent with a time limit when the incident will be closed, as described earlier.

If the underlying cause of the incident is still unknown, despite the fact it has been resolved, a problem record may be raised to investigate the underlying cause and to prevent a recurrence. As previously stated, the incident category needs to be checked and amended, if necessary. Finally, a user satisfaction survey may be carried out.

Incident Management Triggers, Inputs, and Outputs

Let's now look at the triggers, inputs, and outputs for the incident management process.

Triggers

The incident management process is triggered by the notification of an incident. As already discussed, this could be from users, support staff or suppliers, or from the event management process.

Inputs

Information inputs that are needed by incident management include the following:

- Communication of events from event management.
- Information about CIs from the configuration management system (CMS). This information includes things like the location of hardware and its configuration, CI status, and the version numbers of software.
- Known errors and their workarounds from the known error database. This database contains details of workarounds that enable the rapid resolutions of some recurring incidents.
- Incidents and their symptoms.
- Recent changes and releases. Many incidents are related to changes that have unexpected side effects; the schedule of change provides information about recent and planned changes that can help with the diagnosis of incidents. Information about planned changes may also be useful, especially if they are intended to implement a fix to a recurrent fault.
- Operational and service level objectives. Information in SLAs provide resolution targets for incident management and also guidance on the impact and urgency of incidents affecting the service.
- Customer feedback.
- Criteria for prioritizing and escalating incidents.

Outputs

Information outputs from incident management include the following:

- Resolved incidents and records of the resolution actions
- Updated incident records with accurate incident detail and history

- Updated incident classification once the cause is known; this is used by problem management
- New problem records where the underlying cause of the incident has not been identified
- Validation that problem resolution has been effective in stopping recurring incidents
- Feedback on incidents related to changes and releases
- Identification of affected CIs
- Customer satisfaction feedback
- Feedback on the effectiveness of event management activities
- Incident and resolution history details to assist in assessing overall service quality

Interfaces between Incident Management and the Lifecycle Stages

Incident management is a key process that is carried out by all service providers. There are several links between this process and other service operation processes as well as with processes within the service design and service transition stages.

Service Operation

There is a strong interface between incident management and problem management. Access management issues may also cause incidents, and incidents may be logged as a result of alerts generated by the event management process.

Problem Management   As you will learn when we discuss problem management in the rest of this chapter, incident management and problem management have many links. Incident management provides the data on repeat incidents that problem management uses to identify underlying problems. The permanent resolution of these problems helps incident management by reducing the number of incidents that occur. The incident impact and urgency information helps problem management prioritize between problems.

Problem management provides known error information, which enables incident management to restore service.

Access Management   Incident management raises incidents following security breaches or unauthorized access attempts. This information can be used by access management to investigate access breaches. Failure to ensure users are granted the necessary access they require to do their job may result in incidents being reported when the user is greeted with an error message when attempting to carry out a task.

Event Management   Incident management may raise incidents following defined alert conditions reported by event management. Examples could include failure of a device to respond to a "ping" or a threshold for response time or disk usage being breached, indicating a failure. Some service management tools may be configured to automatically raise an incident record in certain circumstances, and even to assign it to the correct resolving group.

Service Design

Several of the service design processes interface directly with the incident management process. These processes are among those we discuss in other chapters, where many of the process activities take place in the service operation lifecycle stage. Service level management interfaces with incident management because SLAs will contain incident resolution targets; the other service design processes may result in incidents if the processes fail to prevent a security breach, a lack of capacity, or unplanned downtime.

Service Level Management   As we have seen, numerous links exist between incident and service level management (SLM). Incidents have target response and resolution times; these targets are set in the SLAs. Incident management in turn provides the management information from the service management toolset to enable SLM to report on the success achieved in meeting these targets. Incident reporting enables SLM to identify failing services and to implement service improvement plans for them (in conjunction with CSI).

Information Security Management, IT Service Continuity Management, Capacity Management, and Availability Management   Incident management collects data on the number of security-related incidents and capacity issues. It provides the data on downtime that availability management uses to calculate availability reports, and analysis of incident records helps availability management understand the weak points in the infrastructure that need attention. An efficient incident lifecycle also improves overall availability. Particularly in the case of major incidents, incident management may need to invoke an IT service continuity plan.

Service Transition

The service transition processes of service asset and configuration management (SACM) and change management interface with incident management. SACM provides useful information to the incident process, and changes may be the cause of incidents or the means by which incidents are resolved.

Service Asset and Configuration Management   Incident management uses SACM data to understand the impact of an incident, because it shows the dependencies on each CI. It provides useful information regarding who supports particular categories of CI. By logging each incident against a CI and checking that the user of the CI is as recorded in the CMS, incident management helps keep the CMS accurate.

Change Management   Changes are often implemented to overcome incidents. Incidents may often be caused by changes. An important input into incident investigation is the change schedule; asking the question "What changed just before this incident occurred?" can often highlight the cause of incidents. In the case of a major incident caused by a change, the decision may be made to back out the change. Information identifying how many incidents were caused by changes should be fed back to change management to improve future changes.

Information Management within the Incident Management Process

Next we look at information management for the incident management process. As we discussed when considering the value of this process to the service lifecycle, incident management is responsible for the collection of significant quantities of information; this information is used for the management of incidents, but is also an input into many other processes. Efficient and effective incident management is also dependent on information from other processes. Let's look at the common sources of information used in this process.

Incident Management Tools

These tools are used to log every incident, whether these are reported by users to the service desk, reported by technical staff, or created as a result of an alert condition detected by event management tools. These tools will contain the incident and problem history, incident categories, and any actions taken to resolve the incidents. These tools will also contain the diagnostic scripts which first-line analysts use to either resolve the incident immediately or, if that is not possible, to ensure that sufficient information is gathered to help second- or third-line analysts resolve it faster.

Incident Records

Each incident will have an associated incident record. The incident record needs to contain sufficient information to enable the incident to be tracked and resolved, details about downtime, time to resolve, and so forth to enable service level reporting against incident targets and information that will be used by problem management to analyze and ascertain the root cause. Typical information contained within the incident record would include the following:

- Unique reference number
- Classification/categorization
- Date and time stamp of creation and any updates, including diagnosis and resolution actions
- Name of the person creating or updating the incident record
- Name and contact details of affected user(s)
- Description of symptoms
- Incident category, impact, urgency and priority
- Links to other incidents, problems, changes, or known errors
- Closure details, including closure category

Service Catalog

The service catalog is an important information source for the incident management process; in addition to the details it provides regarding service level targets and delivery objectives, it includes information about the service expressed in terms that the customer and users understand. This information can be useful when communicating with the customers about the service.

Configuration Management System

Incident management also requires access to the CMS. Service desk staff will use this to identify the affected CIs. This will assist in ascertaining the impact of the incident. It may also highlight when several, apparently separate incidents are actually all symptoms of the same fault. For example, when a router fails, users may report incidents regarding printing, email access, and issues with particular applications, which are all caused by the same network CI failure.

Known Error Database

The known error database (KEDB) is supplied by problem management to incident management. We will look at this in more detail in the following section. The KEDB provides workarounds for incidents, even where the underlying cause has yet to be resolved. The objective of incident management is to restore service as soon as possible; these workarounds enable this restoration to be achieved quickly.

Roles within Incident Management

The ITIL framework specifies that each process have an owner carrying out generic ownership responsibilities and a manager focused on the management of the activities of the practitioners.

In addition to the generic responsibilities of the process owner, manager, and practitioner outlined in Chapter 1, "Introduction to Operational Support and Analysis," each process has specific roles identified in the ITIL framework. Here we consider the specific incident management roles; later in this chapter we will look at the roles identified for problem management.

For incident management there are normally three practitioner roles: first-line, second-line, and third-line analyst. The first-line analyst role is usually combined with the service desk analyst role. The others correspond to the levels of functional escalation, which means they reflect the levels of skill and seniority or experience in the supported technologies. Third-line analysts are often associated with the technical or application management functions.

Remember that these are roles, not job titles. Each organization will define the job titles and descriptions for the people who fulfill these roles.

Incident Management Process Owner

The incident management process owner's responsibilities include not only the generic process owner duties but also additional specific incident management tasks. They will design and document the desired workflows for different incident types and ensure that these are configured in the service management tool. They also identify common incidents and create incident models for these, predefining the steps to be taken to log and resolve them.

The incident management process owner will also liaise with the process owners for problem, event, and access management, and for request fulfillment, to ensure that these processes are integrated with incident management.

Incident Management Process Manager

As with the incident management process owner, the incident management process manager's responsibilities include not only the generic process manager duties but also additional specific incident management tasks. These will include monitoring and developing the incident management process to ensure that it is efficient and effective and interfaces as required with the other processes, making recommendations for improvements where required. The manager must also ensure that the tool used supports the process and provides the required management information. The role is also responsible for day-to-day management of the first- and second-line staff involved in incident management, and for managing major incidents when they occur. This role is often assigned to the service desk manager/supervisor in smaller organizations, but larger enterprises may have sufficient incident volumes to justify a separate role. Whoever carries out this role must be given sufficient authority to ensure that the incidents are managed effectively, regardless of which team is responsible for resolution.

First-Line Analyst

This role is usually carried out by the service desk analysts. Duties include the logging of all incidents into the service management tool, and resolving them at first contact whenever possible. Should the first-line analyst be unable to resolve the incident, they are responsible for escalating it to the correct second-line support team or third party.

The first-line analyst requires sufficient business knowledge to be able to prioritize incidents according to business impact and urgency, and sufficient technical knowledge to correctly classify the incidents and identify the correct support team.

When incidents are assigned to second- and third-line teams, or external suppliers, the first-line analyst, as part of the service desk, retains ownership of the incident records. This entails monitoring the status of the incidents, and progress-chasing them as required, so as to ensure resolution service level targets are met. Where necessary, the analyst will escalate the incident in accordance with the incident management escalation policies. The analyst will also keep affected users informed of the progress achieved. When the incidents are resolved, the analyst will contact the user to obtain agreement for the incident to be closed.

Second-Line Analyst

Some organizations may employ a second generalist support team. This group will not provide specialist in-depth support; instead the staff will have a deeper technical knowledge than the first-line analysts, and since they will not be required to answer support calls, they will have more time to pursue a resolution. This has the advantage of ensuring that less complicated incidents can be resolved relatively quickly and at a lower cost than those requiring more specialist third-line support. First-line staff may have a short time in which to achieve a resolution—typically 5–10 minutes before assigning the incident, because spending too much time on resolution at first-line will impact the ability to answer telephone support calls within the agreed targets. Second-line analysts are able to spend longer—typically 10–30 minutes to achieve a resolution.

This arrangement can ensure a quick resolution while also making best use of the more expensive technical experts who are able to concentrate on the most difficult incidents and in investigating the underlying causes through problem management. Ideally, second-line groups should be located close to the service desk; this will facilitate the sharing of knowledge and enable secondment of staff between the teams. The second-line analysts can assist the service desk during busy periods, and provide training to the first-line analysts.

A large second-line analyst team will usually have their own manager; smaller groups may have a supervisor. In some cases both teams will report to the same incident manager.

Third-Line Analyst

Third-line support is provided by technical specialists; these may be internal groups or third-party suppliers. Typical groups include network, server, and desktop support teams. Other third-line groups include those providing database support and hardware and environmental equipment maintenance engineers.

Application management will usually be provided by different teams, according to the different applications or application types. Some applications may be managed by external suppliers. In organizations where the development and management of applications are both carried out by the same team, care must be taken to ensure that the support of existing applications is not given a lower priority than the development of new applications.

Challenges and Risks

In this section of our examination of the incident management process, we look at the challenges and risks associated with this process.

Challenges

Incident management faces a number of challenges. First is the challenge of detecting incidents as early as possible. Comprehensive monitoring of the infrastructure plays a significant role here, but there are other things to be done—for example, implementing user education and encouraging users to always report incidents as they occur.

A common challenge is that of persuading technical staff to log incidents that they encounter. Their automatic response is to fix the issue and move on, which is good, but information about trouble spots will not be captured.

A poor or nonexistent problem management process will mean that the incident management workload will continue to rise because underlying errors are not being found and corrected.

The lack of a CMS that holds accurate information about CIs and their relationships is another challenge. A comprehensive CMS would support the prioritization of incidents by linking CIs to services, and provide valuable diagnostic information.

Finally, integrating the process with SLM would help the process correctly assess the impact and priority of incidents, and help define escalation procedures.

Risks

The risks faced by incident management include the failure to meet these challenges. Other risks include insufficient resources in terms of numbers and capabilities of support staff, meaning that the process will be overwhelmed by incidents that cannot be handled within the agreed timescales.

Another risk is a backlog of incidents resulting from inadequate support tools. It is generally agreed that successful service management in general, and incident management in particular, need good tools. Inadequate tools also produce the risk of inadequate information.

Finally, there is the risk of failing to meet agreed resolution times because the support staff are not properly incentivized by OLA targets that align with process objectives.

Critical Success Factors and Key Performance Indicators

Next we look at some examples of critical success factors (CSFs) for incident management and the key performance indicators (KPIs) that measure whether the CSFs are being achieved.

The first CSF is to resolve incidents as quickly as possible, thus minimizing impacts to the business. Two of the key performance indicators that measure this include the mean time to achieve resolution and the breakdown of incidents at each stage. The percentage of incidents resolved at first-line or resolved remotely are also key indicators that this critical success factor is being achieved.

Another example of a critical success factor for incident management is to maintain user satisfaction with IT services. The KPIs that measure its success include the average user/customer survey score (total and by question category) and the percentage of satisfaction surveys answered versus total number of satisfaction surveys sent.

A third CSF is to maintain the quality of IT services, measured by the number of incidents reported, and the backlog of incidents awaiting resolution remaining steady or declining.

Another example of a CSF for incident management is to ensure that standardized methods and procedures are used for efficient and prompt response, analysis, documentation, ongoing management, and reporting of incidents to maintain business confidence in IT capabilities. The key indicators that this is being achieved include a low and reducing number of incidents that are incorrectly assigned or categorized.

How Incident Management Can Support Continual Improvement

Continual improvement is dependent on the collection and analysis of data to identify areas requiring improvement (supporting the "Where are we now?" activity) and to judge the effectiveness of improvement initiatives (supporting the "Did we get there?" activity). The incident management process collects data useful to the analysis undertaken by CSI, in particular data showing incident trends. This data can be analyzed to ensure its accuracy, to identify issues, and to spot where the achievement of agreed service levels is under threat.

The incident management process also supports the presentation activity undertaken by CSI. It provides the data used in the CSI reports, and by showing the business impact of incidents, it assists in the prioritization of improvements.

Problem Management

According to ITIL official terminology, a *problem* is defined as an underlying cause of one or more incidents. *Problem management* is the process that investigates the cause of incidents and, wherever possible, implements a permanent solution to prevent recurrence. Until such time as a permanent resolution is applied, it will also attempt to provide a workaround to enable the service to be restored and the incident to be resolved.

It is important to understand the differences between incidents and problems and to realize that an incident *never* becomes a problem; they are separate entities, or records that are related to each other.

A Mechanical Incident, Problem, and Workaround

One morning, as you leave your house to go to work, you find that your car will not start. You have an *incident*.

You have little mechanical knowledge, but you do know how to apply a *workaround*—to use jumper cables. You do this, the car starts, and your incident is over.

Every morning for a week, the same thing happens, and each time you apply the workaround to overcome the incident and restore service. The underlying *problem* could have several possible causes: a faulty battery, a mechanical fault preventing the engine from charging the battery, a light in the trunk left permanently on, and so on. The problem investigation has to be carried out by someone with a greater mechanical knowledge than you.

On the weekend, you take the car to a mechanic, who diagnoses the root cause and applies a permanent resolution (replaces the battery, fixes the wiring, or whatever is required). Your car will now start each morning!

Many organizations make the mistake of thinking that problem management is not essential. Until and unless problem management is undertaken, incidents will recur, inconveniencing the business and occupying support staff time. Problem management will reduce incidents, freeing up more time to undertake more problem management. It is a virtuous circle; the more time spent on it, the more time is freed up by it.

Let's start by defining a problem. The definition used by ITIL is "the underlying cause of one or more incidents."

The use of the word problem is often misunderstood. Outside of service management we might hear a total network failure described as a major problem. But service management would describe it as an incident, possibly a major incident. If we did not know why the network had failed, then we would also have a problem. If we did know why the failure occurred, then there would be no problem. So, a problem is a mystery—the mystery of why an incident occurred.

Purpose

The purpose of the problem management process is to document, investigate, and remove causes of incidents. It also provides another useful benefit: by providing workarounds, it reduces the impact of incidents that occur. It proactively identifies errors in the infrastructure that could cause incidents and provides a permanent resolution, thus preventing the incidents.

Objectives

Problem management aims to identify the root cause of incidents, to document known errors, and to take action to remedy them. Problem management has three simple objectives:

- First, it must prevent problems and resulting incidents from happening.

- Second, it should eliminate recurring incidents. This is a key objective; there are few things that will do more damage to a service provider's reputation than recurring incidents.

- The third objective is to minimize the impact of incidents that can't be prevented. The underlying fault can't always be fixed, or it may take some time to have a fix implemented, but problem management could identify a fast, reliable way of restoring service should an incident occur.

Scope

The scope of problem management includes diagnosing the root cause of incidents and taking the necessary action in conjunction with other processes (such as change management and release and deployment management) to permanently remove them.

Problem management is also responsible for compiling information about problems and any associated workarounds or resolutions. By identifying faults, providing workarounds, and then permanently removing them, problem management reduces the number and impact of incidents. It has a strong relationship with knowledge management, because it is responsible for maintaining a known error database and could also be said to be part of continual service improvement.

There are important similarities and differences between the two principal service operation processes. The same service management tool will usually be used to track both incidents and problems, and a good tool will facilitate the linking of incident occurrences to specific problem records. Similar categories and prioritization classifications may be used. However, problem management may be a process of which the business is unaware. Once a workaround has been applied and an incident resolved, the user may think no more about it. Meanwhile, the IT service provider uses problem management to prevent recurrence. An effective workaround can take some of the pressure off support staff, allowing them to take the time to investigate the underlying cause without being chased for a resolution, since the service has been restored.

As we have said, an incident is an unplanned interruption to an IT service or reduction in the quality of an IT service. Sometimes an incident cannot be resolved until the cause is known and remedied; a server fails and will not restart, for example, because of a hardware fault.

The Value of Problem Management to the Business and to the Service Lifecycle

The value of problem management derives from the fact that it will diminish the impact of incidents on the organization. Permanent fixes will tend to reduce the number of incidents, and workarounds enable fast resolution of recurring incidents. Together these mean higher availability of the services with all that it implies:

- Problem management improves the productivity of IT staff because they spend less time investigating and resolving incidents.
- Problem management identifies the underlying causes of incidents and is therefore able to devise an effective fix or workaround that always works. If the underlying cause is not known or is misunderstood, then there is a risk that any fix or workaround won't work.
- The process reduces the impact of recurring incidents, which reduces associated costs.

Policies, Principles, and Basic Concepts

Next we consider the policies, principles, and basic concepts that underpin problem management.

Policies

The ITIL Service Operation publication suggests three policies that support problem management.

The first policy states that "problems should be tracked separately from incidents." The focuses of the two processes are very different, especially in regard to problem management's proactive activities.

The second policy states that "all problems should be stored and managed in a single management system." It is not a good idea for each technical team, for example, to have its own database of problems. There are many reasons why a single management system is essential. For example, the investigation of problems requires the use of scarce technical resources. In order to make best use of those resources, we should prioritize their activities by, in this context, prioritizing problems—how can you do that if information about problems is scattered across many databases or spreadsheets?

The final problem management policy states that "all problems should subscribe to a standard classification schema that is consistent across the business enterprise." The standard classification of problems provides faster access to investigation and diagnostic data, and enables more effective analysis, particularly by proactive problem management. Notice that this policy says "across the business enterprise." In the case of a global enterprise, problems should be categorized in the same manner wherever in the world they manifest themselves.

Principles and Concepts

Problem management principles and concepts include reactive and proactive approaches, problem models, known errors, and workarounds.

Reactive and Proactive Aspects   Unlike incident management, which is entirely reactive (you cannot resolve an incident until it has occurred), problem management has both reactive and proactive features.

- Problem management will react to incidents and attempt to identify a workaround and a permanent resolution.

- Problem management will also proactively try to identify potential incidents and take action to prevent them from ever happening. This might include analysis of incident trends, such as intermittent but increasingly frequent complaints about poor response times, to identify a potential capacity issue. By working with capacity management, we can take proactive measures to provide sufficient capacity and avoid any major breaks in service. Event management reports may also be analyzed to the same end, in this case, prevent an incident before the user is aware of any issue.

- Problem management may assist in a major incident review, trying to identify how to prevent a recurrence.

The process steps for managing problems that are raised in reaction to incidents and those that are proactively identified are broadly similar. The main difference is the trigger for the process. Reactive activities take place as a result of an incident report and help prevent the incident from recurring or provide a workaround if avoidance is impossible; these activities complement the incident management process.

Proactive problem management analyzes incident records to identify underlying causes of incidents. It may be that analysis of previous incidents reveals a trend or pattern that was not apparent when each incident occurred. For example, users may complain of poor response periodically; it is only when all these complaints are analyzed that it becomes apparent that the poor response is always reported against the same module or from the same location. This would trigger a problem record to be raised to identify the common cause linking all these incidents.

Reactive and proactive problem management activities normally take place as part of service operation, but problem management is also closely related to continual service improvement. Where improvement opportunities are identified as a result of problem management, they should be entered into the CSI register.

Problem Models Most problems are unique and can't be investigated in a predetermined way. But sometimes there are underlying issues that cannot be resolved—they are too difficult, the resolution is too costly, or they are outside our scope of action. For example, a badly designed application may, over time, experience intermittent incidents, each of which has a different specific cause and results in a different problem. A problem model might guide the investigation of problems in that application. For example, it might describe how to collect and interpret relevant diagnostic information.

Incidents vs. Problems As we have said, problem management and incident management are very closely related. Although incident management is not concerned with discovering the underlying causes of the incidents it investigates, sometimes it is necessary to do that in order to resolve the incident. Where that is the case, then problem management should get involved. Potentially, problem management could get involved whenever an incident occurred that had no corresponding problem or known error record, but that would probably be overkill. Every organization should define criteria for determining when to involve problem management that are appropriate to its specific circumstances. It is very common, usual even, for problem management to be involved in the handling of major incidents.

Known Errors When we examine the problem management process in detail, we will see that the process attempts to identify and document known errors, usually when the cause of the problem is known, and a workaround is available, but the permanent fix has yet to be applied. Known error records are used to document root causes and workarounds and allow quicker diagnosis and resolution if further incidents do occur. This is not the only source of known errors. Some will come from application development. It's often the case that a new application will go live in spite of known bugs in the software, when these have been considered not worth delaying the rollout for. Where this is the case, these should be documented in the known error database so that it is available should there be an incident during live operation. These bugs might be discovered in development or during testing in service transition. These bugs, or defects identified during testing, are generally referred to as *development known errors*.

Workaround A workaround is defined as a means of reducing or eliminating the impact of an incident or problem for which a full resolution is not yet available—for example, by restarting a failed configuration item. Workarounds for problems are documented in known error records.

Process Activities, Methods, and Techniques

The first consideration in the problem management process is to decide when and in which circumstances a problem record should be raised.

Sometimes it is helpful to raise a problem record while the incident is still open. Each organization will decide its own criteria for when a problem record should be raised. For example, a problem record may be raised when the support teams are sure that the incident has been caused by a new problem, because the incident appears to be part of a trend, or because there is no match with existing known errors. The incident may have been resolved by the service desk or support teams without knowing the cause, and so there is a risk that the fault may recur. This is particularly true in the case of a major incident; the underlying cause needs to be identified as soon as possible to prevent future disruption to the business. (The problem diagnosis activity may take place in parallel with the incident resolution and may continue after the successful resolution, until the underlying cause is identified and removed.) It is also possible that suppliers may inform their customers of problems that they have identified.

As stated earlier, problem management is not an optional activity; it is fundamental to providing a consistent service, in line with SLA commitments. By providing workarounds to enable resolution of incidents with the first-line staff, better use is made of the more skilled and therefore more expensive second- and third-line staff, who are freed up to use their skills in problem investigation.

Process Activities

Now we are going to examine the problem management process step by step. Refer to Figure 2.3 as we discuss each activity.

Step 1: Detecting Problems

The first step in the process is to identify that a problem exists. As we discussed previously, problem records may be raised either reactively in reaction to incidents or proactively. In addition to the triggers identified earlier, a problem may be identified as a result of alerts received as part of event management. The event monitoring tools may identify a fault before it becomes apparent to users and may automatically raise an incident in response.

As Figure 2.3 shows, problems can be identified in a number of ways but they are all handled by a single problem management process and logged in a single database. A major source is the service desk acting for the incident management process. Any incident whose cause is unknown could trigger a problem investigation. In practice, few organizations will do that because of the very large number of problems that result. Most organizations are quite selective about the problems they log and investigate. This is supplemented by regular analyses of incident data searching for recurring incidents that might have been missed. Potential problems can also be identified by event management and suppliers, and of course proactive problem management itself identifies problems.

FIGURE 2.3 The problem management process

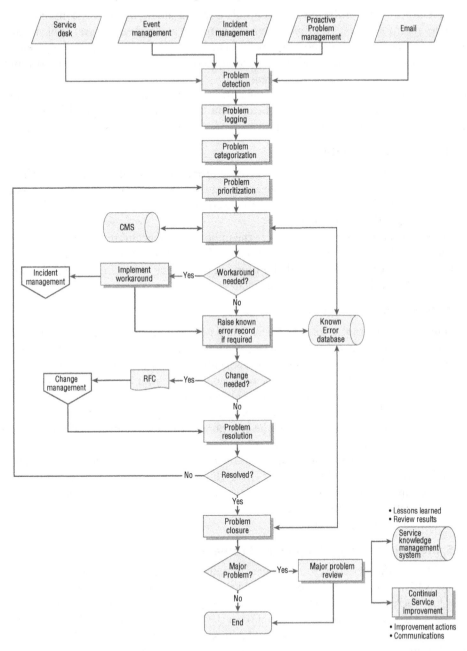

Step 2: Logging Problems

Having identified that a problem exists, a problem record should be logged, containing all the relevant information and time-stamped to provide a complete picture. Typical data would include details of who reported it and when, details of the service and equipment used, and a description of the incident and actions taken. The incident record number and the priority and category would also be required.

Where possible, use the service management tool to link problem records with the associated incident records. Remember that the incident has not "become" a problem; the incident must continue to be managed to resolution whether the problem is resolved or not.

Step 3: Categorizing Problems

The problem is then categorized using the same approach as incident management, which allows incidents and problems to be more easily matched. For example, it might be possible to relate a number of types of incident to a single common problem, which would bring a lot of extra diagnostic information.

The problem manager should emphasize the importance of accurate categorization to the service desk. The use of incident models can be helpful here because they standardize the way common incidents are recorded. Enforcing categorization on incident resolution, as mentioned earlier, will also help ensure incident categories are accurate.

Step 4: Prioritizing Problems

As with incidents, the priority of a problem should be based on the impact to the business of the incidents that it is causing and the urgency with which it needs to be resolved. The problem manager should also consider how frequently the incidents are occurring. It is possible that a "frozen screen" that can be resolved with a reboot is not a high-priority incident; if it is occurring 100 times a day, the combined impact to the business may be severe, so the problem needs to be allocated a high priority. The impact to the business must always be considered, so factors such as the cost of resolving the incident, and the time this is likely to take, will be relevant when assessing priority.

Analyzing factors such as number affected, the duration of the downtime, and the business cost is known as pain value analysis. This technique can be useful in determining the business impact of a problem. Of course, circumstances change, new information is learned, and further incidents may occur, so the priority of a problem should be kept under review and changed if appropriate.

Step 5: Investigating and Diagnosing Problems

The next stage in the process is to investigate and diagnose the problem. The purpose of this stage is first to discover the root cause and then to determine a workaround and permanent fix. There may not be the resources to investigate every problem, so the priority level assigned to each will govern which ones get the necessary attention. It is important to allocate resources to problem investigation, because until the problem is resolved, the incident will recur, and resources will be spent on incident resolution.

Usually the task of investigating and diagnosing the problem is passed to the appropriate technical or application team. If it is unclear where the problem originates, it might be necessary to establish a team of technical specialists to investigate it. Sometimes it will be necessary to escalate a problem to a supplier.

The ITIL framework suggests a number of different problem-solving techniques, which are helpful in approaching the diagnosis logically. The CMS can be useful in providing CI information to help identify the underlying cause. It will also help in identifying the point of failure, where several incidents are reported; the CMS may identify that all the affected CIs are linked to the same CI. The KEDB may also provide information about previous, similar problems and their causes. Where a test environment exists, this can be used to re-create the fault and to try possible solutions.

Step 6: Identifying a Workaround

Although the aim of problem management is to find and remove the underlying cause of incidents, this may take some time; meanwhile, the incident or incidents continue, and the service is affected. When a user suffers an incident, the first priority is to restore the service so that they can continue working. A priority of the process, therefore, is to provide a workaround to be used until the problem is resolved. A workaround is a means of reducing the impact of an error. This can be in the form of a circumvention, which is a way of working that avoids triggering incidents, or it may be a way of resolving incidents should they occur. At this point, a known error record should be raised and stored in the known error database.

The workaround does not fix the underlying problem, but it allows the user to continue working by providing an alternative means of achieving the same result. The workaround can be provided to the service desk to enable them to resolve the incidents while work on a permanent solution continues. The problem record remains open, because the fault still exists and is continuing to cause incidents. The details of the workaround are documented within the problem record, and a reassessment of its priority may be carried out.

It is possible that IT or business management may decide to continue to use the workaround and suspend work on a permanent solution if one is not justified. A problem affecting a service that is due to be replaced, for example, may not be worth the effort and risk involved in implementing a permanent solution.

Of course, it is not always possible to devise a workaround and sometimes a workaround is not acceptable to the business—the fault must be fixed.

Step 7: Raising a Known Error Record

When problem management has identified and documented the root cause and workaround, this information is made available to support staff as a *known error*. Information about all known errors, including which problem record it relates to, is kept in the *known error database (KEDB)*. When repeat incidents occur, the support staff can refer to the KEDB for the workaround.

There may be times when a workaround is available although the root cause is not yet known (for example, a reboot restores the service, although we do not know what causes the error). On other occasions, we may know the cause but not have a workaround because a change has to be implemented to fix the fault.

Sometimes a known error record is raised before a workaround is available and sometimes even before the root cause has been fully identified. This may be just for information purposes;

a workaround may be available that has not been fully proven. Rather than have a rigid rule about when a known error record should be raised, a more pragmatic approach is advisable; a known error should be raised as soon as it becomes useful to do so.

Step 8: Resolving Problems

When problem management has identified a solution to the problem, it should be implemented to resolve the underlying fault and thus prevent any further incidents from disrupting the service. Implementing the resolution may involve a degree of risk, however, so the change management process will ensure the risk and impact assessment of the RFC is satisfactory before allowing the change. The error might be in an application that is scheduled to be phased out in the near future so the business may choose to accept the likely disruption temporarily rather than accept the cost and risk of a fix. Ultimately, the decision whether to go ahead with the resolution despite the risk is a business decision; the business damage being done by the problem may mean the business is prepared to accept the risk in order to have the fix implemented.

Problem Closure

When a permanent solution to the problem has been identified, tested, and implemented through the change management process, the problem record can be updated and closed. Any open incidents caused by the problem can be closed too. The KEDB should be updated to show that the problem is resolved, so any future incidents will not have been caused by it; however, the information contained within the problem record may prove useful in addressing a future, similar problem.

Major Problem Review

Every major problem should be the subject of a formal review in order to learn from the experience. Each organization must determine what, for it, constitutes a major problem. The review should be carried out in the immediate aftermath of events, when memories are fresh. It is led by the problem manager but should include the participation of everyone who played a role in the events under review.

The review is not only concerned with the failure that first triggered the major problem but also with everything that happened and was done afterward. It takes a holistic view, in other words.

Specifically, the review asks

- What did we do that was right? What did we do that made things worse?
- What could we do better in future?
- What can we do to prevent it from happening again?
- Are there any proposals for improvement? These could involve making changes to processes or technology, they could require specific training for support or other staff, or they could require action by suppliers or changes to contracts.

A major problem review also has a significant role to play in rebuilding customer confidence, which will probably have suffered due to the major problem. The conduct of the review and the resulting report should keep this in mind. It might be useful to include a representative from the business in the review.

Figure 2.4 illustrates the way incident, problem, and change management activities are linked. It is largely self-explanatory. Note that an incident is closed when service is restored but a problem is only closed when a fix has been applied and is confirmed to be effective. Sometimes problem management cannot supply a workaround, so the incident stays open until the permanent fix is implemented.

FIGURE 2.4   How incidents, problems, and changes are linked

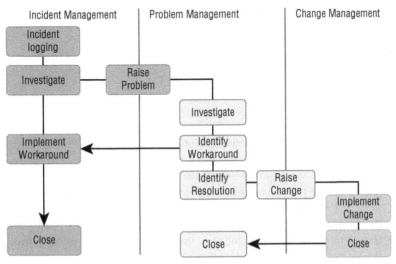

Problem Analysis Methods and Techniques

There are a number of different approaches to the analysis of problems. Choosing the most appropriate one to use will depend on the situation, the tools available, and the preferences of the individuals concerned. Here we examine some of the more common techniques:

Chronological Analysis   This technique is one that many use without thinking about it as a technique at all; it is a logical approach to document what happened and when. By drawing up a timeline, we can see what events might have triggered the incidents, and we also can discount possible causes if they do not fit the timeline. For example, there may be an inclination to blame a recent change for the incidents, but the timeline may prove that the incidents started occurring before the change was implemented.

Pain Value Analysis   This technique is used to assess impact. A simple calculation of the number of occurrences does not in itself tell us the impact to the business of a particular problem; some incidents may occur frequently but not affect the business achieving its aims. Pain value analysis uses a formula to calculate the level of pain the incidents/problems cause to the organization. The formula will take into account factors such as the number of people affected, how much downtime has resulted, and an assessment of the business cost. By estimating the pain value, the incidents/problems can be prioritized and addressed in the order that matches the true business impact.

Kepner-Tregoe Analysis   This technique was devised by Charles Kepner and Benjamin Tregoe. It helps avoid the tendency to jump to a conclusion regarding the cause before the problem is understood, which leads to wasted effort and time. The technique involves a structured, logical approach to problem analysis that narrows down the potential causes to those that fit the properties of the problems being experienced. The steps are

- Define
- Describe
- Establish possible causes
- Test
- Verify

The Kepner-Tregoe method begins by defining and describing the problem, in particular in terms of where and when it happens, and also where and when it does *not* happen. For example, the instances of poor response only occur on Tuesday mornings and only in one satellite office; any possible cause would have to fit this pattern (perhaps related to the work done in that office that is only carried out on Tuesday mornings). Other suggested causes that would not explain why the fault only occurs where and when it does can be discounted. So using this technique allows possible causes to be established, tested, and verified.

Brainstorming   This technique is often used when the cause of the problem is unclear; it helps ensures that all possible causes are considered, not just the most obvious or common. It also helps break down the tendency of each group to concentrate on their own area of expertise, when the solution may require knowledge of how different technologies interact. All the relevant people are gathered together, usually in a face-to-face meeting. Brainstorming requires the facilitator to record every suggestion of possible causes without allowing the meeting to divert into a discussion or argument about the suggestions until all have been recorded. This approach helps the less obvious possible causes to surface. Once all the suggestions have been made, they are then discussed and evaluated during the meeting, where the presence of representatives from the various groups enables a fuller evaluation than a single support team would provide. Brainstorming sessions, if effectively facilitated, can be useful by breaking down the tendency to focus on the familiar and encouraging innovative theories.

5-Whys   This is a simple technique that enables us to drill down to the root cause. First we ask why an event happened—the simple answer might be because a hardware failure occurred. By then asking why the failure occurred, and so on, we can arrive at the true root cause. Five rounds of asking why is usually enough; sometimes the root cause may be apparent sooner. For example:

Description: My car fails to start. Why? Answer: Because the battery is dead. Why is the battery dead? Answer: The lights were left on. Why were the lights left on? Answer: The alarm that should alert me to the fact that my lights are still on when I take my keys out of the ignition failed to sound. Why didn't the alarm sound? Answer: A loose connection between the alarm and the dashboard—this is the root cause. Without arriving at the root cause and fixing the connection, the incident would have occurred again. This is a simple and fast technique.

Fault Isolation   This approach involves understanding the series of steps that should have taken place in correct operation and checking each one in sequence. For example, connecting to a website requires the PC, browser software, Wi-Fi connection, modem, broadband link, and remote website all to be working. By testing each one in turn—is the PC working, can the site be accessed using a different browser, is it connected to the router, can other sites be accessed, and so forth—we can ascertain where the fault lies.

Affinity Mapping   This technique is useful for workshops where there is a great deal of data to process. Unless managed properly, such workshops can result in only the loudest voices being heard, and good suggestions can be lost. This approach allows large numbers of ideas stemming from brainstorming to be sorted into groups, based on their natural relationships, for review and analysis.

The process starts with recording each idea on cards or sticky notes and sticking these to a wall or table. Next sort all the cards into groups and look for ideas that seem to be related. Each resulting group is then given a name that identifies these similarities. The group is then analyzed to see if a common cause can be identified.

Hypothesis Testing   This method uses educated guessing as part of a brainstorming session to compile a list of possible root causes and then tests each hypothesis. For example, one suggested hypothesis to explain incidents concerning poor response is that it is the fault of the latest application release; this could be tested by installing the release elsewhere and seeing whether slow response results, and backing out of the release on other CIs to ascertain whether the incidents stop occurring.

Technical Observation Post   This method is used for intermittent incidents, for which the cause is unknown. Some issues can only be fully understood when we observe them occurring. Specialist support staff are gathered together to focus on monitor events in real time, focusing on the specific issue. A commonly quoted example of this is the "urban myth" to explain a loss of service occurring each evening being caused by the office janitor unplugging IT equipment to plug in a vacuum cleaner. It is only when the janitor is observed doing this that the cause is identified.

Ishikawa Diagram   The Ishikawa diagram, sometimes called the Fishbone or Cause and Effect diagram, is named after the Japanese quality control expert Kaoru Ishikawa. This technique is a useful way of documenting and visually representing possible causes and effects. As with some of the other methods discussed, it is often used as part of a brainstorming workshop, where the participants suggest possible causes. It is also similar to the 5-Whys approach, since it drills down to the circumstances that might have led to the fault. The main goal is represented by the spine of the diagram, and main causes are represented as bones. Secondary causes are then added as bones, branching off from the higher level and so on. Figure 2.5 shows the beginning of such a diagram, where the four main causes of network downtime are identified. Figure 2.6 shows how each of these is broken down in turn to possible causes, and, in turn, these are broken down.

FIGURE 2.5 Sample of starting an Ishikawa diagram

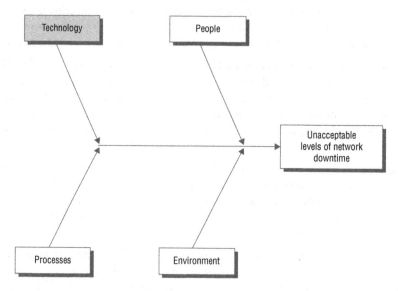

FIGURE 2.6 Sample of a completed Ishikawa diagram

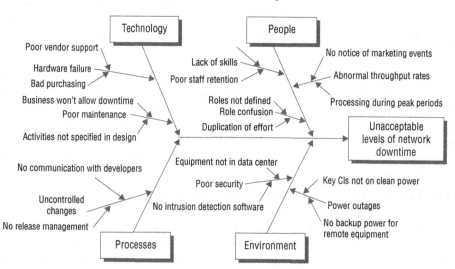

Pareto Analysis   This is a technique for separating the most important potential causes of failures from more trivial issues. It identifies the most common causes of failures, those few causes that are responsible for 80 percent of the occurrences. This is done by creating a table showing the causes and what percentage of all faults are as a result of each cause. The causes are then ranked to identify those having the highest percentage. Table 2.3 shows an example of this technique in use, including a cumulative percentage, and the bar chart in Figure 2.7 shows that the network controller, file corruption, and addressing conflicts are responsible for 80 percent of the failures and should therefore be targeted first.

TABLE 2.3   Pareto cause ranking chart

Network failures

Causes	Percentage of total	Computation	Cumulative (%)
Network controller	35	0 + 35%	35
File corruption	26	35% + 26%	61
Addressing conflicts	19	61% + 19%	80
Server OS	6	80% + 6%	86
Scripting error	5	86% + 5%	91
Untested change	3	91% + 3%	94
Operator error	2	94% + 2%	96
Backup failure	2	96% + 2%	98
Intrusion attempts	1	98% + 1%	99
Disk failure	1	99% + 1%	100

Error Detection in Development Environments

During the testing of new applications, systems, or releases in service transition, it is inevitable that some faults will be discovered. Those considered serious will be resolved before the service is deployed into the live environment. However, if the benefits of deployment outweigh the inconvenience of a fault, the error will be documented and scheduled to be resolved in the next release. These known deficiencies, and any associated workarounds, should be logged in the KEDB, and this information formally handed over to service operation. This avoids wasted time investigating reported incidents in operation that are already documented.

FIGURE 2.7   Important vs. trivial causes

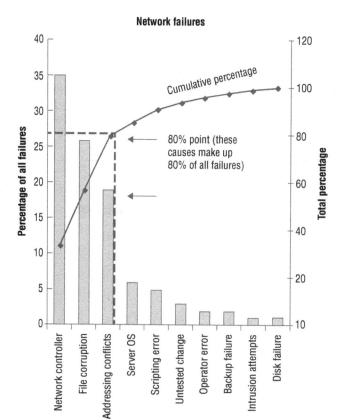

Triggers, Inputs, Outputs, and Interfaces

Let's now look at the triggers, inputs, outputs, and interfaces for the problem management process.

Triggers

Triggers for problem management will vary between organizations. They include triggers for both reactive and proactive problem management:

Reactive problem management triggers include the identification of a cause of one or more incidents by the service desk, resulting in a problem record being created. The incidents may have been resolved, but the cause is unknown; undertaking problem management should enable the underlying cause to be identified and removed, preventing any recurrence. Sometimes it is obvious that an incident has been caused by a major problem, so a problem record will be created immediately.

Another trigger for reactive problem management is the result of incident analysis by a technical support group showing an underlying problem. Event monitoring tools may raise incidents automatically, and these may require a problem record to be created. Finally, a supplier may inform the service provider that a problem exists that has to be resolved.

Proactive problem management triggers include analysis of incidents that have occurred, leading to a decision to create a problem record to investigate what is causing them to occur. An analysis of trends may identify one or more underlying causes. By removing the cause, recurrence can be prevented.

Another possible proactive trigger may result from continual service improvement. Steps taken to improve the quality of a service may result in the need for a problem record to identify further possible improvement actions.

Trend analysis depends on meaningful and detailed categorization of incidents/problems as well as regular reporting of patterns and repeat occurrences of incidents. This can be helped by regular reporting on the "Top Ten" incidents.

Inputs

The incident database is a vital source of information for problem management. It contains information about current incidents and problems and is the basis of proactive problem management.

The configuration management system (CMS) provides information about the hardware and software components that underpin the IT services. It is essential for problem investigation and diagnosis. The CMS also helps IT to prioritize problems appropriately by showing the links between components and services.

Problem management must assess whether a business case exists for the change request; financial information is needed for this. SLAs should be consulted to ascertain the business requirements. Input from change management will provide feedback on progress and whether the changes are successful.

Finally in this list comes feedback from customers. Building and maintaining customer satisfaction is an essential objective of all service management activity, including problem management.

Outputs

Outputs from problem management include the obvious outputs such as resolved or updated problem records, requests for change, workarounds, and known error records. In addition, the process will output various reports. For example, a problem report may be discussed at a service review meeting. Reports of issues are referred to design teams and other processes. When these reports include recommendations for improvement, they may be logged in the CSI register.

Interfaces

As we discussed in the earlier part of this chapter, when discussing incident management the major relationship that problem and incident management have is with each other. Problem management does interface with other processes, however.

Problem management uses the financial management for IT services process to assess the financial impact of possible solutions or workarounds. This information can be used to decide whether a permanent resolution is financially justified.

Problem management interfaces with several of the service design processes; for example, availability management has a similar aim: to prevent downtime. The proactive activities undertaken by availability management are directly related to proactive problem management; availability attempts to proactively identify risks that could result in a loss of service and to take preventive action. Problem management can supply information to availability management about the success of any measures taken.

Some performance problems can be caused by capacity issues. Capacity management will be involved in resolving these issues and also taking proactive measures to prevent capacity issues. Again, problem management can supply information about the success of any measures taken.

If a significant problem is causing or will cause major disruption to the business, it may be necessary to invoke the IT service continuity management (ITSCM) plan until the issue is resolved. The ITSCM plan also attempts to proactively identify risks that could result in a major loss of service and to take preventive action.

The service level management (SLM) process interfaces with problems in a different way. SLM is dependent on problem management to identify the root cause of incidents and resolve them in order to prevent downtime that could cause a service level target to be breached.

Problem management interfaces with several of the service transition processes. As discussed, changes may be the cause or solution to problems. Service asset and configuration management provides invaluable information to enable common factors to be identified across multiple incidents. Release and deployment is involved in contributing to problem management's known error database, which is also related to knowledge management. The last interface with service design is with knowledge management. The workarounds developed by problem management are examples of the service knowledge that is the core concern of knowledge management. The KEDB can be the basis of the service knowledge management system (SKMS).

Finally, problem management and continual service improvement have similar objectives; problem management activities can also be seen as CSI activities. The aims of CSI and problem management are closely allied. Both seek to drive out errors and improve service quality. As stated earlier, actions identified to resolve or prevent problems may be entered into the CSI register. The seven-step improvement process can be used by CSI or problem management to identify and resolve underlying problems.

Information Management in the Problem Management Process

This section explores the sources of information used in problem management.

Configuration Management System

The CMS provides problem management with details of the IT components and their relationships with each other. This information helps in evaluating the impact of a problem and the resultant incidents, as it will show which services depend on the correct operation of a particular device. It also helps in problem diagnosis; if some devices are exhibiting a fault while others are not, it will provide the information required to identify common attributes in failing items—such as whether they are all connected to the same part of the infrastructure, or whether they have all recently had a new software release installed. It can provide useful historical data to help identify trends as part of proactive problem management.

Known Error Database

The KEDB stores information about incidents/problems and associated workarounds to enable repeat occurrences to be resolved quickly. Each known error record should describe the symptoms so that repeat occurrences can be matched with the known error and details of workaround or resolution actions.

Ideally, the service management tool should record how often the known error information is used to identify the frequency of the fault and therefore the urgency for its permanent resolution. However, it should be noted that if an effective workaround exists, and a permanent resolution would be costly, risky, or time-consuming, it may be decided that the benefit of a permanent resolution for the problem far outweighs the benefits, and the problem will be tolerated.

An effective KEDB must be fast and effective at finding the correct known error to match specific symptoms, or staff will not refer to it. Care needs to be taken to avoid duplication of information, poorly described symptoms, and out-of-date records. The problem manager should act as a gatekeeper to the KEDB, vetting the quality of all suggested entries and archiving records when a permanent resolution is implemented.

Roles in Problem Management

As discussed earlier in this chapter in relation to the incident management roles, the ITIL framework specifies that each process should have an owner carrying out generic ownership responsibilities as well as a manager focused on the management of the activities of the practitioners.

In this section, we consider the specific problem management roles that are carried out in addition to the generic responsibilities of the process owner, manager, and practitioner outlined in Chapter 1. As before, these roles are not job titles, and each organization will define appropriate job titles and job descriptions that fit its requirements.

Problem Management Process Owner

The problem management process owner's responsibilities include not only handling the generic process owner duties but also the specific problem management tasks of designing the desired workflows for different problem types, as well as ensuring that these are configured in the service management tool. The process owner also identifies common problems and creates models that define the steps to be taken to log and resolve those problems.

The problem management process owner will also liaise with the process owners for incident, event, and access management and for request fulfillment, to ensure that these processes are integrated with problem management.

Problem Management Process Manager

There should be a designated person to act as a single point of coordination for the problem management process; in larger organizations, this might be a team rather than an individual, whereas smaller organizations may combine this responsibility with other roles. As with the problem management process owner, the problem management process manager's responsibilities include not only the generic process manager duties but also additional specific problem management tasks. These will include the following:

- Supporting the problem management tools and processes
- Working with the various support teams in addition to third-party suppliers to ensure that problems are resolved within SLA targets
- Ownership and maintenance of the KEDB, including the role of database gatekeeper
- Conducting major problem reviews and ensuring that any required actions identified are carried out
- Formal closure of all problem records
- Coordinating interfaces between problem management and other service management processes

Problem Analyst

Problems will usually be assigned to the same technical teams who are assigned incidents to resolve. This may also include suppliers or support contractors. These various support resources come together to undertake problem resolution activities under the coordination of the problem manager. Their responsibilities typically include

- Reviewing incident data to enable problem resolution or root cause identification
- Analyzing problems for correct prioritization and classification
- Coordinating actions of others groups as necessary to assist with analysis and resolution actions
- Raising RFCs to resolve problems
- Monitoring the resolution of known errors
- Informing incident management staff on the best available workaround for incidents
- Updating the KEDB
- Assisting with the handling of major incidents and identifying their root causes

Serious problems may require a dedicated problem management team to focus on overcoming that particular problem. The problem resolver must ensure that the correct staff resources are made available and that the necessary escalation and communication up the management chain of all organizations concerned takes place.

Challenges and Risks

In this final section of our examination of the problem management process, we'll look at the challenges and risks associated with this process.

Challenges

We've seen that problem management is dependent on the incident management process. This poses a number of challenges:

- The incident process must be mature enough to correctly identify possible problems and to gather sufficient information to enable problem management to diagnose the cause. A critical challenge is ensuring that the two processes have formal interfaces and common working practices.

- Problem resolution staff must have the skills and capabilities for problem solving.

- Ideally, a single tool should be used for problem and incident management. The tool should have the ability to relate incidents to problems and enable the determination of relationships between CIs to assist in problem diagnosis.

- A good working relationship between the second- and third-line staff working on problem support activities and first-line staff must be developed. Each must understand their role in the investigation of problems and that it is very much a team effort.

- Staff working on problem resolution must understand the impact of problems on the business. Understanding the business and the role of IT in supporting it is a common challenge across the lifecycle.

- The next challenge is the integration of activities with the CMS, which holds essential information about configuration items, their relationships, and their history.

- The final challenge is having staff with the necessary technical knowledge to investigate and diagnose problems. This requires the staff to be available to work on the problem. It can be difficult to release staff from other work to do problem management.

Risks

The risks facing problem management include

- Failing to meet any of the challenges listed in the preceding section is a risk.

- There may be simply too many problems to handle due to insufficient resources or because the criteria for raising problems are too loose.

- There may be a lack of information from incident management or from a CMS.

- The focus of operational level agreements may be on incident resolution, and so staff do not realize the importance of problem management.

Critical Success Factors and Key Performance Indicators

The next topic that we'll discuss is that of the CSFs for effective problem management and the KPIs that will show whether these CSFs are being achieved. The ITIL Service Operation publication provides three examples of CSFs for problem management. The first is "Minimize the impact to the business of incidents that cannot be prevented." This CSF is concerned with workarounds and their effectiveness, so we need KPIs to evaluate this. The first KPI example is the "number of errors added to the Known Error Database." This involves measuring the success of the process in identifying workarounds. Identifying these workarounds is only of benefit if they are being used. This is where the second example of a KPI comes in: "% of incidents resolved by the Service Desk." The assumption here is that the fix rate of the service desk will increase in line with an increasing number of known errors logged. The second CSF is "Maintain quality of IT services through elimination of recurring incidents." This involves measuring the effectiveness of the process of eliminating the underlying causes of incidents through the provision of permanent fixes. Two possible KPIs are "the size of the problem backlog" and "the number of repeat incidents." You should be able to devise other KPIs that support these CSFs.

The third example CSF found in the ITIL Service Operation publication is "Provide overall quality and professionalism of problem handling activities to maintain business confidence in IT capabilities." This CSF is very much about the process itself rather than its direct impact on the quality of the IT services. Many possible KPIs would be relevant to this; let's consider just three examples:

The Percentage of Major Problem Reviews Completed   A best practice problem management process would conduct a formal review of every major problem. This KPI indicates whether that is being done. A KPI that told us whether the reviews were being conducted in a timely manner would also be valuable.

The Average Cost per Problem   This refers to the cost of investigation and diagnosis; it would tell us whether problem management is efficient.

The Backlog of Outstanding Problems and the Trend   How effective is the process? This is an example of a KPI that might be used when the process is first established but that might be discarded once the process is mature and has eliminated the backlog.

Summary

This chapter explored the first two processes in the service operation stage, incident management and problem management. We covered the following:

- Purpose
- Objectives
- Scope
- Value
- Policies, principles, and basic concepts
- Process activities, methods, and techniques
- Triggers, inputs, outputs, and interfaces
- Information management
- Roles
- Challenges and risks
- Critical success factors and key performance indicators

We examined how each of these processes supports the other, and the importance of these processes to the business and to the IT service provider.

We examined the following key ITIL concepts:

- Incident
- Major incident
- Impact
- Urgency
- Priority
- First-line support
- Second-line support
- Third-line support
- Functional escalation
- Hierarchic escalation
- Problem
- Workaround
- Known error
- Known error database (KEDB)
- Ishikawa diagram
- Kepner-Tregoe analysis
- Pain value analysis
- Pareto analysis
- Proactive problem management
- Root cause analysis
- Technical observation

Exam Essentials

Understand the purpose and objectives of incident management in reducing downtime by resolving incidents quickly.   Be able to describe the scope and basic concepts such as major incidents, incident models, and the importance of timely resolution. Identify sources of incident reports other than users reporting them to the service desk; suppliers, support staff, or event management alerts are all possible sources. Understand that incident management is a reactive process. Be able to list and explain the interfaces that incident management has with other processes, especially problem management and service level management.

Understand that the aim of incident management is to restore service, not to identify the cause.   This focus on service restoration means that less skilled staff are required to resolve incidents than problems. Be able to describe the differences between an incident, a problem, and a service request.

Explain how priority is calculated using business impact and urgency.   Understand what these terms mean.

Explain the different roles involves in incident management.   Be able to differentiate between generic and specific roles.

Be able to explain the concept of incident and problem models and their use.   Be able to describe the lifecycle of an incident and the use of the different statuses assigned to each stage. Be able to list the key information that would be recorded in an incident record. Be able to describe the difference between the two types of escalation (hierarchic and functional) and when each is used.

Understand the purpose, objectives, scope, basic concepts, process activities, and interfaces of problem management.   Understand that a problem is the unknown, underlying cause of one or more incidents and that the aim of problem management is to find the cause of incidents and remove it to prevent recurrence. Be able to describe the relationship between problem management and other processes.

Explain the different roles involves in problem management.   Be able to differentiate between generic and specific roles.

Understand the concepts of a workaround and a known error.   Be able to explain why some problems might not be resolved when it is not cost-effective to implement the fix, and when a workaround exists. Be able to explain how the known error database is used.

Understand the various problem analysis methods.   Be able to describe the different approaches and how they are used.

Review Questions

You can find the answers to the review questions in the appendix.

1. Which is the best description of an incident?

    A. An event that has significance and impacts the service

    B. An unplanned interruption to an IT service or reduction in the quality of an IT service

    C. A fault that causes failures in the IT infrastructure

    D. A user error

2. When should an incident be closed?

    A. When the technical staff members are confident that it will not recur

    B. When desktop support staff members say that the incident is over

    C. When the user confirms that the service has been restored

    D. When the target resolution time is reached

3. Which of the following is *not* a satisfactory resolution to an incident?

    A. A user complains of poor response; a reboot speeds up the response.

    B. A user complains of poor response; second-line support runs diagnostics to be able to monitor it the next time it occurs.

    C. The service desk uses the KEDB to provide a workaround to restore the service.

    D. The service desk takes control of the user's machine remotely and shows the user how to run the report they were having difficulty with.

4. Incident management aims to restore normal service operation as quickly as possible. How is *normal service operation* defined?

    A. It is the level of service that the user requires.

    B. It is the level of service that the technical management staff members say is reasonable.

    C. It is the level of service defined in the SLA.

    D. It is the level of service that IT believes is optimal.

5. A service management tool has the ability to store templates for common incidents that define the steps to be taken to resolve the fault. What are these called?

    A. Major incidents

    B. Minor incidents

    C. Incident models

    D. Incident categories

6. Which incidents should be logged?

   A. Major incidents

   B. All incidents that resulted from a user contacting the service desk

   C. Minor incidents

   D. All incidents

7. What factors should be taken into consideration when assessing the priority of an incident?

   A. Impact and cost

   B. Impact and urgency

   C. Urgency and severity

   D. Severity and cost

8. What of the following are types of incident escalation defined by ITIL?

   1. Hierarchical

   2. Management

   3. Functional

   4. Technical

   A. 1 and 4

   B. 1 and 3

   C. 1, 2, and 4

   D. All of the above

9. What is the best definition of a problem?

   A. An incident that the service desk does not know how to fix

   B. The result of a failed change

   C. The cause of one or more incidents

   D. A fault that will require a change to resolve

10. Problem management can produce which of the following?

    1. Known errors

    2. Workarounds

    3. Resolutions

    4. RFCs

    A. 1 and 4

    B. 1 and 3

    C. 1, 2, and 4

    D. All of the above

Chapter

3

Event Management, Request Fulfillment, and Access Management

✓ **Event management, request fulfillment, and access management are discussed in terms of their**

- Purpose

- Objectives

- Scope

- Value

- Policies

- Principles and basic concepts

- Process activities, methods, and techniques

- Triggers, inputs, outputs, and interfaces

- Information management

- Process roles

- Critical success factors and key performance indicators

- Challenges

- Risks

Event management is the process that deals with modern infrastructure management's requirement for the use of event monitoring tools. These tools are able to monitor large numbers of configuration items simultaneously, identifying any issues as soon as they arise and notifying the appropriate tool or team. The process of event management is responsible for managing events throughout their lifecycle. Event management is one of the main activities of IT operations.

Request fulfillment is the process for handling requests for standard services, equipment, or information. ITIL uses the expression *service request* to describe all those repeat, low-risk change/information requests that occur in any environment.

Access management is the process of granting *authorized* users the right to use a service while preventing nonauthorized users from gaining access. It is also sometimes referred to as *rights management* or *identity management*. Access requirements can change frequently, and service operation is responsible for granting access quickly, in line with the needs of the business, while ensuring that all requests are properly authorized.

Event Management

To begin, let's consider some definitions from the ITIL Service Operation publication. These should be familiar from *ITIL Foundation Exam Study Guide* (Sybex, 2012).

An *event* can be defined as any change of state that has significance for the management of a configuration item (CI) or IT service. Remember, an event is not necessarily an indication that something is wrong; it can merely be a confirmation that the system is working correctly. Many events are purely informational. Informational events could include notification of a user logging onto an application (significant because the use of the application may be metered) or a transaction completing successfully (significant because the notification of the successful completion may trigger the start of the next transaction).

An event that notifies staff of a failure or that a *threshold* has been breached is called an *alert*. An alert could be, for example, notification that a server has failed or a warning that the memory or disk usage on a device has exceeded 75 percent. If you consider these concepts in a non-IT environment, a car console may issue an event to say that the system has successfully connected to a Bluetooth device, or it might raise an alert (together with a beep or flashing light) to warn that a threshold has been breached and the car is now low on gas.

Effective service operation is dependent on knowing the status of the infrastructure and detecting any deviation from normal or expected operation. Event management monitors services for any occurrences that could affect their performance. It also provides information to other processes, including incident, problem, and change management.

There are two types of event monitoring tools:

- *Active monitoring tools* monitor configuration items or IT services by automated regular checks to discover the current status. The tool sends a message and expects a positive response within a defined time, such as sending a ping to a device. This is called *polling* of devices, and it is done to check that they are working correctly. Support staff will be notified of a failure to respond. Some tools will have *automated responses* to such situations, perhaps automatically restarting a device or rerouting data to avoid the faulty CI so that the service is not affected.

- *Passive monitoring tools* do not send out polling messages. They detect events generated by CIs and *correlate* them; that is, they identify related events. They rely on an alert or notification to discover the current status. Such notifications could include error messages.

Purpose

The purpose of event management is to detect events, understand what they mean, and take action if necessary.

Many devices are designed to communicate their status, and event monitoring will gather these communications and act on any that need action. Some communications report operational information, such as "backup of file complete," "print complete," and so on. These events show that the service is operating correctly. They can be used to automate routine activities such as submitting the next file to be backed up or the next document to be printed. They may also be used to monitor the load across several devices, issuing automated instructions to balance the load depending on the events received. If the event is an alert, such as "backup failed," "printer jam," or "disk full," the necessary corrective steps will be taken. An incident should be logged in the case of a failure.

Objectives

Event management has the following objectives:

- It enables all significant changes of state for a CI or service to be detected. Event management should determine the appropriate control actions for each event and ensure that they are communicated as necessary.

- The process provides the trigger for the automatic execution of many service operation processes and operations management activities. For example, a notification of a failure in the infrastructure would trigger the incident management process. By providing information when thresholds have been breached (for example, when a service has failed to respond within the agreed time), an event enables service level management to compare the actual operating performance against the SLA. The actual performance can also be compared to what was expected and planned for during the design stage.

- It triggers automated processes or activities in response to certain events. This may include automatically logging an incident in the service management tool in the event of a failure.

- Finally, the data gathered by event management forms the basis for service assurance and reporting and for comparing performance before and after a service improvement has been implemented.

Scope

Event management can be applied to any aspects of service management that need to be controlled and that could benefit from being automated. For example, the service management toolset automatically logs incidents in response to emails or events being received, escalates incidents when thresholds have been reached, and notifies staff of certain conditions (for example, a priority one incident being logged).

Configuration items can be monitored by event management tools. This monitoring can be for two different reasons:

- Some CIs will be monitored to make sure they are constantly available. An example of this is where action needs to be taken as soon as a CI such as a network device fails to respond to a ping.

- Other CIs may need to be updated frequently. This updating can be automated using event management, and the CMS can be automatically updated to show the new state.

Tracking licenses is another possible use for event management tools; licenses can be tracked to make sure there is no illegal use of an application by checking to see that the number of people using the software does not exceed the licenses held. This may also save money; if IT can show that there is less demand for concurrent use than was thought, the number of licenses can be reduced.

Monitoring for and responding to security events, such as detecting intruders, is another use; the tools can also be used to detect a denial-of-service attack or similar event.

Another use is the monitoring of *environmental conditions*. This might be for detecting a sudden increase in temperature in the server room or for other environmental changes.

Using Event Management to Preempt a Major Incident

A large transport organization installed event monitoring across its infrastructure, including monitoring the server room environments. A screen showing current events was installed at the service desk. On the second day after this was implemented, its value was proved. The service desk called the head office 150 miles away to ask the staff there to check the server room, because there were environmental alerts showing on the screen. The head office staff entered the server room to find that the air conditioning had failed and the room was extremely warm. Had the temperature increased much more, the servers would have failed, causing major disruption to the services. The head office staff members were able to avert the incident by using fans to lower the temperature until the air-conditioning engineer arrived to fix the fault.

Value

Event management offers many benefits to a business:

- Organizations can carry out extensive monitoring without requiring a lot of staff. Using staff to monitor when errors may occur only occasionally would not be making best use of their skills.

- Errors would be identified faster, enabling an automated response, which would reduce downtime and its resultant costs to the business.

- Near-capacity situations would be identified before it is too late, allowing time to take action.

- Event monitoring removes the need for repeated checks to be carried out on devices; it reduces effort by requiring responses only to exceptions.

- Event management, like other automation, takes place constantly, whereas staff may have other duties and may therefore miss something. It is also less error prone.

- Event management provides historical data to enable the identification of trends and potential problems.

Policies

Next, let's consider suggested policies for event management.

The first policy states that event notifications should go to only those who have responsibility for acting on them. This means that a target audience must be identified for every event that we have chosen to handle—it is not acceptable to send a notification to everyone and hope that someone will do something.

The second policy relates to the centralization of event management. This ensures that notifications are handled consistently, that none are missed, and that none are handled by more than one person or team. It implies that a single rules engine will be used to process notifications, and of course that set of rules should be subject to change management.

The third policy provides guidance and constraints for the designers of new applications. There should be a common set of standards for events generated by applications. This will ensure consistency across applications and, of course, reduce the time to engineer event handling in new applications.

The fourth policy is that the handling of events should be automated as much as possible. The advantages of automation in general are well known: reduced costs and fewer errors, among others.

The fifth policy mandates the use of a standard classification scheme for events to ensure that similar types of events are handled in a consistent way.

The last policy states that all recognized events should, at the very least, be logged. This will provide a source of valuable information that might have a number of uses, for example, in problem investigation. A more sophisticated analysis of logged events might identify patterns of events that can be used to predict failures before they actually occur.

Principles and Basic Concepts

It is important to understand the difference between the two similar activities of monitoring and managing events. These are similar processes, but with specifically different emphasis.

Monitoring and Event Management

We need to monitor events, but monitoring covers more than events. Monitoring can be used, for example, to make sure devices are operating correctly, even without any events being generated. Monitoring actually looks for conditions that do not generate events.

Event management is about having useful notifications about the status of the IT infrastructure and services. Event management sets up rules to ensure that events are generated so they can be monitored, captured, and acted on if necessary. Action is the key to event management.

The particular notifications themselves may be vendor specific. However, they are likely to use *Simple Network Management Protocol (SNMP)*, an Internet standard protocol for managing devices on IP networks. Devices that typically support SNMP include routers, switches, servers, workstations, printers, modem racks, and more. Because SNMP is an open standard, it makes interaction between different products simpler. Events must generate useful notifications. The time taken to create meaningful descriptions, with suggested actions, will save effort later.

Event management can be enormously useful in managing large and complex infrastructures. It is often the case, however, that the full value of these tools is not realized. This is usually because there has been insufficient time spent making sure they are configured correctly to only notify staff of events for which they actually need notification. Failing to specify the correct thresholds, for example, will mean that far too many breaches are reported, causing staff to ignore them because they are seldom significant. Of course, this means that significant events may be missed. If events are not filtered properly, the service management tool would be flooded with multiple spurious events, which would make it difficult to use its ability to automatically raise incidents.

Another important definition is that of an alert: An alert is a warning that a threshold has been reached, something has changed, or a failure has occurred. Alerts are often created and managed by system management tools and the event management process. Creating an alert when a disk or mailbox is nearly full is one such example.

Informational, Warning, and Exception Events

Some events indicate a failure that must be fixed, whereas others simply flag that something has happened and should be recorded. These are two types of event: the first is an *exception* and the second *informational*. There is a third type—a *warning* event. A warning event signifies unusual but not necessarily exceptional behavior. Warning events require further analysis to determine whether any action is required. Events will be handled according to their type.

Here are some examples of each type of event:

- Informational
    - A scheduled workload has completed.
    - A user has logged in to use an application.
    - An email has reached its intended recipient.

- Warning
  - A server's memory utilization reaches within 5 percent of its highest acceptable performance level.
  - The completion time of a transaction is 10 percent longer than normal.
- Exception
  - A user attempts to log on to an application with an incorrect password.

Notice that not all of these examples relate to a failure. (Failures would be alerts.) Some simply contain information, but information that for some reason it is important to record. For example, the business might want to maintain a record of who is using an application for audit purposes.

There are no definitive criteria for determining the type of an event; it depends very much on the specific situation of the organization. For example, an event might be that a previously unknown device has been detected on the network. Some organizations allow their staff to attach their own laptops to the corporate network, in which case the event would be informational. In a highly secure organization, it would almost certainly be treated as an exception.

Filtering

The next topic we'll examine is event filtering. We don't have complete control over the notifications that are generated by the configuration items. Hardware manufacturers determine which notifications will be generated, and they may not have provided their customers with the ability to switch them off. A common experience when first beginning to monitor networks is that the monitoring tool is swamped by unrecognized and therefore unneeded notifications.

Filtering prevents the event management system from being overwhelmed by discarding notifications of events that have no significance to the organization.

There are four possible approaches to the problem:

- The first approach is to integrate event management into each service management process. What this means is that each process will identify the events that it is interested in.
- The second approach is to include event management requirements into the design of new services.
- A third approach is to use trial and error—evaluate notifications on a case-by-case basis and adjust the filtering accordingly.
- The final approach is to plan the introduction of event management within a formal project.

These approaches are not mutually exclusive; many organizations will adopt some hybrid of them.

Designing for Event Management

Successful event management in service operation requires analyzing and planning for what will be required. This should happen in the service design phase, although it will continue to be adjusted in service operation. Many organizations attempt and abandon event management, or they fail to achieve real value from it because this crucial design phase has been neglected.

The following questions should be asked when designing a service or planning the introduction of new technology:

- What needs to be monitored?
- What type of monitoring is needed?
- Why are we monitoring?
- When should events be generated?
- What information should be communicated?
- Who are messages intended for?
- Who will respond to the event?

When event management is first established, these questions should be asked about the existing services and infrastructure. Stakeholders who must be consulted include the business, process owners, and operations management staff. Each of these groups will have monitoring requirements, and each could be involved in handling events when they occur.

Instrumentation

Instrumentation refers to specific ways to monitor and control the infrastructure and services. A number of practical issues need to be addressed when designing an event management system:

- How will events be generated? In the case of bought-in components, of course, this question is really, How *are* events generated?
- How will they be classified? This is not straightforward, and classifications can change over time.
- How will they be communicated and escalated? How exactly will the events get to the appropriate function? For example, how will an exception event trigger the incident management process? Ideally, this will be automated by integrating the event and incident management tools so that an incident will be logged automatically. Of course, this can only happen if the two tools have the necessary functionality.
- What data must be included in the event notification? What data will be needed for the event management system itself to interpret and make sense of the event, and what data will be needed by the function that will respond to the event? If the event relates to an error, then it should include necessary diagnostic information such as error messages and codes. Again, for bought-in software, this question is really, What data is included?
- Another question to be asked relates to the type of monitoring to use. Should it be active or passive?
- Where will event data be stored? There is likely to be a significant amount of event data, so the question of storage is important. Associated with this is the question of how long the data should be retained. This decision must be made on a case-by-case basis in consultation with the relevant stakeholders. Policies relating to retention may also be developed where there are specific requirements from the business, for example, financial sector regulatory requirements.
- How will supplementary data be gathered? In some cases, the event data alone will not be sufficient to evaluate the event. For example, it might be necessary to integrate the event management system with a configuration management database (CMDB).

Correlation Engine

As events are detected, the event management system must interpret and make decisions about how to handle them. This is done by software known as a *correlation engine*. The correlation engine allows the creation of rule sets that it will use to process events.

Using a correlation engine will enable the system to determine the significance of each event and whether there is any predefined response to an event. Patterns of events are defined and programmed into correlation tools for future recognition. The correlation engine can translate component-level events into service impacts and business impacts, as shown in Figure 3.1.

FIGURE 3.1 Correlation engine

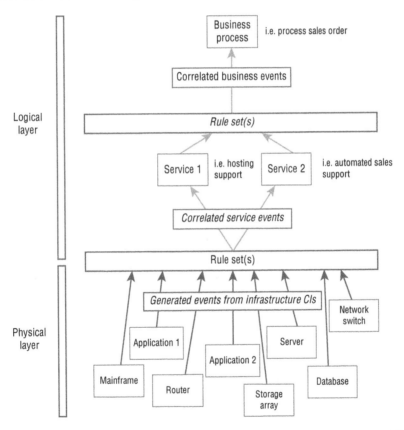

Process Activities, Methods, and Techniques

Next, we'll take a look at the event management process. The process steps are shown in Figure 3.2.

FIGURE 3.2 Event management process flow

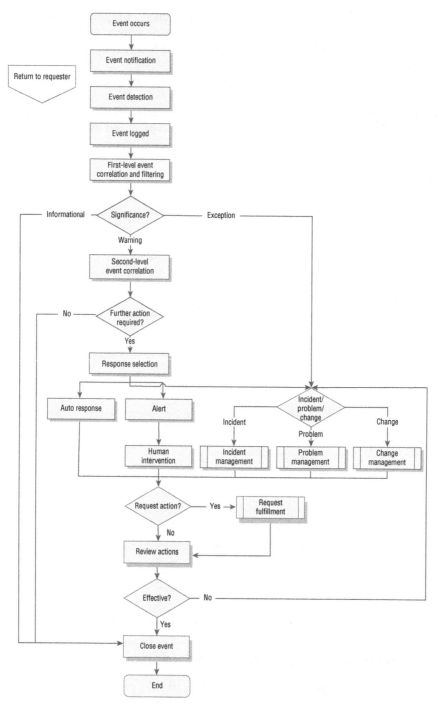

The initial sequence of activities in the event management process is as follows:

- An event occurs.
- The event notification is sent.
- The event is detected by the event management system and logged.
- First-level correlation and filtering takes place.

At this point, the event type (exception, warning, or informational) has been identified. No further processing is required for informational events. For exception events, one or more of the service management processes will be triggered. If the event concerns something that has broken and requires restoring to normal service levels, an incident should be raised. A problem record may be updated if another example of a fault under investigation occurs. The automated response to an event may include raising a change. Some events, such as a "toner low" message, may require a service request to be handled by the request fulfillment process.

Warning events will then enter second-level correlation, which identifies how to proceed. In some cases, the event will be treated as informational or as an exception. Other cases will trigger either an automated response or an alert for human intervention, as detailed in the following section.

Event Notification

Let's look at the initial process activities in a little more detail. Event notification refers to the communication of information about an event. You've already seen that some components will generate notifications independently, whereas others have to be prompted by polling.

Event Detection and Logging

Some events will be detected directly by the event management tool. Other events will be detected by a software agent running on the device being monitored. This agent then generates a notification that can be detected by the event management tool. All events are logged.

Correlation and Filtering

In first-level correlation, a decision about whether any further action is required is made, including whether the event has any significance to the organization. Correlation will determine whether an event is informational, a warning, or an exception. We discussed filtering earlier; this is necessary to stop staff from being overwhelmed with events that do not require any action, or multiple reports of the same fault.

Informational events are closed at this point. Exception events will trigger one of the other service management processes. Warning events will go forward to second-level correlation.

Next, we consider the criteria that might be used by the second-level correlation engine to interpret an event:

- The number of similar events might be significant. For example, an event might notify us of an unsuccessful attempt to access our network. If this is just a single instance, we might treat it as informational, but if there have been 500 such attempts in the last 5 minutes, we might judge that we are the target of an organized attempt to break in.

- The number of devices generating similar events might be significant. It might indicate a widespread virus infection, for example.

- The data supplied with the event might indicate its significance.

- Events related to device utilization might be compared with a defined threshold.

The correlation engine determines whether the event requires some action or whether it can be treated as informational and closed.

Actions Taken

Response selection covers a number of possible options. These include the following:

Automation   Some events indicate conditions that can be resolved automatically without human intervention. For example, if a file server is detected to be nearly full, then a script could be run that would free up space by archiving old data.

Human Intervention   Some events will require human intervention—an alert from a smoke detector, for example. It's important that the alert be directed to the right person and that the individual knows what to do.

Incident   Exception events will normally trigger the incident management process. Ideally, the event and incident management systems will be integrated so that an incident record can be raised automatically. A word of warning, however: this should be implemented only when you are happy that the filtering of events is working correctly. If this is not the case, your incident management system will be flooded with thousands of spurious incidents!

Problem   The problem management process might be triggered if the organization has a policy of always investigating the root causes of incidents that impact key services. Event management can support such a policy by automatically raising a problem record when it detects such an incident.

Change   Change management can be triggered in two circumstances:

- First, if a previously unknown device is detected, an RFC should be raised, which can be progressed as appropriate by change management to have the device either added to the CMS or removed if required.

- The second circumstance is if a change is needed. For example, a server might need to be allocated more storage from a storage area network (SAN).

Remember, sometimes it will be necessary to trigger a combination of these responses.

Review and Closure

There could be thousands of events each day, so it's unlikely that every one of them could be reviewed. It's sensible to review only what the service provider considers to be significant events. It is probably unnecessary to review events that have triggered other service management processes except to ensure that the triggers were effective.

Most events are neither opened nor closed but just logged in management systems or system logs. Many others can be closed automatically. For example, when a script is triggered to respond to an issue, the script itself could check that the corrective action has worked and generate an event to that effect.

Triggers, Inputs, Outputs, and Interfaces

We'll now consider the event management process triggers, inputs, outputs, and interfaces.

Triggers

Any type of change in state can trigger event management, and an organization should define which of these state changes need to be acted on. Some examples are shown here:

- Exceptions to any level of CI performance defined in the design specifications or standard operating procedures.

- A breach of a threshold in an OLA could also generate an event.

- Any exceptions to a process, such as a failure to complete a process within the target time. An exception could also be a routine change that has been assigned to a build team or a business process that is being monitored by event management.

- The completion of an automated task or job could trigger the issuing of an event, as could a status change in a server or database CI.

- A user accessing a particular application or database could also cause an event to be issued if this is information that the business or the IT department wanted to know about. For example, IT may wish to track how often a service is being used to decide on the number of licenses required, or the business may wish to know how often a customer service representative needs to refer to the knowledge base to answer a query, as this might indicate a training requirement.

- The more usual trigger for an event, such as a situation in which a device, database, or application has reached a predefined threshold of performance.

Inputs

Inputs to event management usually come from service design and service transition. They include the examples listed here:

- Operational and service level requirements associated with events and their actions.

- Alarms, alerts, and thresholds for recognizing events.

- Event correlation tables, rules, event codes, and automated response solutions that will support event management activities.

- Roles and responsibilities for recognizing events and communicating them to those who need to handle them.

- Operational procedures for recognizing, logging, escalating, and communicating events.

- SLAs, which can be used by the correlation engine to determine the significance of an event or to identify a performance threshold.

- Rule sets that are provided by technical or application management staff based on the monitoring and management requirements. For example, the capacity management process would define the capacity thresholds that should generate an event.
- The roles and responsibilities of all those involved.
- Procedures for logging and escalating events as required.

Outputs

Outputs from event management are usually passed to other service management processes, such as incident management, change management, and request fulfillment. They include the examples listed here:

- Events that have been communicated and escalated to those responsible for further action
- Incident, problem, change, or request records required as a result of an event
- Event logs describing what events took place and any escalation and communication activities taken to support forensic, diagnosis, or further CSI activities
- Events that indicate an incident has occurred
- Events that indicate the potential breach of an SLA or OLA objective
- Events and alerts that indicate completion status of deployment, operational, or other support activities
- Populated service knowledge management system (SKMS) with event information and history

The most obvious output of the process is the events themselves. These should have been communicated and escalated to the appropriate people. Another output is a chronological event log describing what events took place and any escalation and communication activities taken. This may be useful information if further investigation is required or to spot possible improvement opportunities.

Some events output by event management will indicate that an incident has occurred, and others will warn of the potential breach of an SLA or OLA objective. Of course, as we have said, not all events show that something is wrong, and many events will just indicate successful completion of deployment or operational activities. The data output from event management can be used to populate the SKMS with the event information and history.

Interfaces between Event Management and the Lifecycle Stages

Finally, let's consider the interfaces event management has with the other lifecycle stages and their associated processes. Event management can interface with any process that requires monitoring and control, especially those that don't require real-time monitoring but do require some form of intervention following an event or group of events. First we'll consider how the process can even help the business directly.

Business Processes

The information provided by event monitoring may be used to help manage unusual occurrences with business processes.

Using Event Management to Preempt a Major Incident

Some years ago, a camera was mistakenly priced on a website at $59.99, when it should have been $599.99. Word spread through social media and thousands of orders were placed, which the company had to honor to avoid bad publicity. It took some time before anyone noticed, and then it was only when a staff member received an email from a friend. Event monitoring could have alerted the company to the unusual sales pattern very quickly, thus limiting the financial damage. Another similar example was an ATM that was filled with $20 notes in the $5 note holder. Queues formed as people withdrew cash from the machine, which was delivering four times the amount requested. In that situation, event management was in place, and the unusual pattern of multiple $5 withdrawals was spotted, and the machine was remotely closed down.

Service Design

Event management interfaces with a number of service design processes. Examples include the following:

- Service level management is the first such interface. Event management can be used to detect any potential impact on SLAs early so that action can be taken to resolve the fault to minimize that impact.

- Information security management may use event monitoring to monitor for unusual activity. This may be multiple login attempts or unusual activity for a business process, such as unusual spending on a credit card, which alerts the bank to a possible stolen card.

- Capacity and availability management define what events are significant, what the thresholds should be, and how to respond to them. Event management then responds to these events, improving the performance and availability of services.

Service Transition

Event management tools may also be used to support service transition processes:

- The service asset and configuration management process uses events to determine the current status of any CI. A discrepancy with the authorized baselines in the CMS will highlight a potential unauthorized change.

- Event management can determine the lifecycle status of assets. For example, an event could signal that a new asset has been successfully configured and is now operational.

- Knowledge management stores information obtained by event management in knowledge management systems. For example, patterns of performance information correlated with business activity is input into future design and strategy decisions.

- Event management interfaces with change management to identify conditions that may require a response or action.

Service Operation

Event management is a service operation process, and it interfaces with the other processes in that lifecycle stage:

- There is an obvious interface with incident and problem management because many alerts are results of failures and require an incident to be raised.

- By catching and logging each such occurrence, event management provides vital information to problem management about when and where the incidents are occurring.

- Finally, event management can be used by access management to detect unauthorized access attempts and security breaches.

Information Management

There are several elements that should be considered as key in the management of information for event management:

Messages (Simple Network Management Protocol [SNMP] messages) are a standard way of communicating technical information on the status of an individual component or set of components of IT infrastructure.

Databases that form the basis of information about an IT device (for example, information about the operating system; the basic input/output [BIOS] version; configuration parameters) are useful sources of information for event management. But the systems in place must be able to interrogate these databases and then compare them to a norm, which is crucial to the success of the process in generating events.

Vendors' own monitoring systems are often key sources for information.

Correlation engines provide considerable information, as described earlier in this chapter.

There is no standard event record for all types of event. It can cover many areas, but there is normally a requirement for the following data sets:

- Device

- Component

- Type of failure

- Date/time

- Parameters in exception

- Unique identifier to allow for tracking of the event across the event management infrastructure and correlation into the other ITSM processes like incident, problem, and change

- Value

Process Roles

In Chapter 1, "Introduction to Operational Support and Analysis," we explored the generic roles applicable to all processes throughout the service lifecycle. These are relevant to the event management process, but specific additional requirements also apply. Remember that these are not "job titles"; they are guidance on the roles that may be needed to successfully run the process.

It is unusual to find a specific "event manager" role in an organization, as events are often managed in a number of different areas in the IT environment. But it is important to ensure that there is a consistent approach to the management of events across the organization, as well as coordination of the tools and effort, to avoid duplication.

Event Management Process Owner

The event management process owner's responsibilities may include

- Carrying out the generic process owner role for the event management process (see Chapter 1)

- Planning and managing support for event management tools

- Ensuring the integration of this process with other processes in the operational lifecycle stage by working with other process owners

Event Management Process Manager

The event management process manager's responsibilities may include

- Carrying out the generic process manager role for the event management process (see Chapter 1)

- Planning and managing support for event management tools

- Coordinating the interfaces between this and other service management processes

Event Management Process Practitioner: Other Roles

There may not be a specific identification of a "practitioner" role in the event management process, but the activities are carried out by a number of other roles.

The Role of Service Desk Staff

The service desk may not be involved unless the event requires action that falls within the scope of service desk duties—for example, notifying the user of a completed action. Event management is normally carried out by the operations bridge, if this exists, but in some organizations the service desk and the operations bridge may have been combined.

If an event has been identified as an incident, then this may be handled through the service desk in the normal course of the process. This will include communication to the user, and support teams, of progress.

The Role of Technical and Application Management Staff

Technical and application management may play several important roles, as follows:

- During service design, they will participate in the design of the tools, configuration of the correlation engines, and classification of events. If automation is required, this will also be developed during design.

- During service transition, they will be involved in testing to ensure events are being generated and that the responses are appropriate.

- During service operation, these teams will provide the expert knowledge and support for the systems under their control. It is important to ensure that the appropriate procedures are executed and defined.

- Technical and application management may also be involved in resolution if an event is classified as an incident.

- There is also a responsibility for these teams to provide expertise and training to the appropriate level for the service desk and operations management to support the process.

The Role of IT Operations Management Staff

If IT operations management is separate from the service desk and technical or application management functions, it is common for event management to be carried out by this group. They will carry out monitoring and first-line support activity for events.

If there is an operations bridge, then this is the area that will carry out the monitoring of the alerts set up by the event management process. The operations bridge can initiate and coordinate, or even perform, the responses required.

Critical Success Factors and Key Performance Indicators

The next topics for discussion are critical success factors (CSFs) and key performance indicators (KPIs). Before we look at the CSFs and KPIs relevant to event management, let's take a minute to understand what these terms mean.

- A CSF is a high-level statement of what a process must achieve if it is to be judged a success. Normally, a process would have only three or four CSFs. A CSF cannot be measured directly—that's what KPIs are for.

- A KPI is a metric that measures some aspect of a CSF. Each CSF will have three or four associated KPIs.

Here are some examples of CSFs and KPIs for event management:

- Critical success factor: "Detect all changes of state that have significance for the management of CIs and IT services." Possible associated KPIs for this CSF include the following (notice that the first KPI is trying to gauge the success in detecting faults while the second is trying to measure the scope of the event management implementation):

  - Number and ratio of events compared with the number of incidents

  - Number and percentage of each type of event per platform or application versus total number of platforms and applications underpinning live IT services

- Critical success factor: "Ensure that all events are communicated to the appropriate functions that need to be informed or take further control actions." Associated KPIs might be as follows:
  - Number and percentage of events that required human intervention and whether this was performed
  - Number of incidents that occurred and percentage of them that were triggered without a corresponding event
- Critical success factor: "Provide the means to compare actual operating performance and behavior against design standards and SLAs." The following KPIs would enable the CSF to be assessed:
  - Number and percentage of incidents that were resolved without impact to the business (indicates the overall effectiveness of the event management process and underpinning solutions)
  - Number and percentage of events that resulted in incidents or changes
  - Number and percentage of events caused by existing problems or known errors (this may result in a change to the priority of work on that problem or known error)

Challenges

The following challenges could be encountered in event management:

- Lack of funding for tools and the effort needed to implement them successfully
- Establishing the correct level of filtering to avoid being flooded by events or having insufficient useful information
- Installing monitoring agents across the entire infrastructure
- Lack of time and funding for training to acquire the necessary skills to design and interpret events

Risks

The following risks are associated with event management; in many cases the risks are the result of failing to meet the challenges listed earlier.

- Failing to obtain adequate funding
- Failing to apply the correct level of filtering
- Failing to maintain momentum in deploying the necessary monitoring agents across the IT infrastructure

If any of these risks are not addressed, they could adversely impact the success of event management.

Request Fulfillment

There is no absolute definition as to what will be classed as a request because this may vary from organization to organization. Many may, in fact, be small changes, falling under the definition of standard changes because they require a change to the configuration management system, such as equipment relocation or the installation of additional software. Service requests occur frequently, at a low cost, with an understood and acceptable low risk. Examples of service requests that are not standard changes could include a password reset or information requests. Service requests are usually handled by a service desk, without a requirement for an RFC to be submitted.

The definition used by ITIL is "a formal request from a user for something to be provided—for example, a request for information or advice, to reset a password or to install a workstation for a new user."

Service requests relate to small-scale, clearly defined, and acceptable low-risk activities, such as the provision of a single workstation or supply of a toner cartridge. An important feature of what ITIL calls service requests is that they represent things that the service provider will be asked for repeatedly. They are all opportunities to provide the user with something they have asked for, and the request fulfillment process is used to handle them.

Many service requests require a change—the installation of a workstation, for example. If you think back to your Foundation studies, you may remember standard changes, which are low-risk, simple, preauthorized changes. The only changes that can be handled by the request fulfillment process are those for which a standard change exists. Be careful here, though—not all standard changes are implemented through request fulfillment, and not all service requests involve standard changes. Requests for information or advice also fall within the scope of request fulfillment.

Purpose and Objectives

Request fulfillment is the process responsible for managing the lifecycle of all service requests from the users. The process has five objectives:

- To maintain customer and user satisfaction through efficient and professional handling of all service requests. You've learned that ensuring satisfaction involves meeting not only objective targets, but also the human aspects—treating requesters with respect, keeping them informed of progress, and so on.

- To provide a way for the user to make a request. This is normally through a web portal but the service desk could be used.

- To provide a way for users to find out what standard services are available to them and how they can request them. It can be surprising that, particularly in a large organization, users aren't aware of everything the service provider can do for them.

- To source and deliver the tangible components of service—hardware, software, licenses, and so on.

- To assist with general information, complaints, or comments. The process should not only provide a means to submit a question, it should also ensure that the user gets a satisfactory response.

Request fulfillment provides an efficient way to supply standard equipment to users once an item has been assessed and accepted as compatible with the infrastructure. The provision of such equipment can be preapproved and handled as a standard change. It can be added as a service within the service catalog, and all future requests of this type can be handled through this process. This encourages users to request the standard equipment and software because it is the easiest and fastest to obtain. This is beneficial to IT because the equipment has been assessed as supportable and compatible with the infrastructure.

 Real World Scenario

Improving Efficiency by Providing a Standard Request Fulfillment Process

A hospital IT department handled requests for hardware and software from the hospital staff. Users would ask for equipment or software that they had seen advertised in magazines or at their local PC store. Often this equipment and software offered no benefit over the standard equipment and software in use in the rest of the organization. Each request was handled by the IT staff, who approached several suppliers to find the best price and then informed the requester of the cost so that they could create a purchase order. The money saved by sourcing the cheapest supplier did not cover the cost of the IT staff time it used. The process might be repeated several times a week for very similar requests because each was handled separately. When the purchase order was created, the item would be ordered, and when it was delivered, the support staff would install it. Because each item could be different, the staff had to ensure that they were following the installation directions for the particular model or software. The IT department then had to support all these different items and manage the warranty agreements. Occasionally incidents would be caused because these nonstandard items were incompatible with a change. The whole process was expensive and took up considerable IT time. The process was slow, often taking three or four weeks from request to fulfillment, so users would sometimes circumvent it by buying and installing items themselves!

A new standard request fulfillment process was introduced to address these issues. Following discussion with the business, the IT department agreed on some standard software and a number of standard devices—a standard laptop and one for "power" users, a standard desktop PC, and a standard office printer. A small stock of each of these was bought and put in storage. Users now ordered from this short list, at a set price, supplying the purchase order at the time of order. The item was taken from stock and installed the same day, while the purchase order was used to replenish the stock. The new arrangement suited everybody; the user was happy to forgo the ability to order any item in return for same-day installation, the IT staff had a simpler range of items to support, the IT management was happy to have a less labor-intensive process, and the finance department was pleased that the IT department was able to negotiate a good price from a single supplier in return for a steady stream of orders.

In addition to these benefits, the simpler process meant that the service desk was able to handle the request, assigning the installation to the desktop support team and ordering the replacement. The simple process was suited to user self-service and became one of the first services offered to users on the new self-service portal.

Scope

The scope of request fulfillment will vary from one organization to another; it can include any requests that can be standardized and used where the organization has agreed to use it. Each request should be broken into agreed activities, each with a documented procedure. The procedures are then used to build the request models.

ITIL calls all these *service requests*; they are all opportunities to provide the user with something they have asked for, such as information, advice, a standard change, or access to an IT service (such as resetting a password or providing standard IT services for a new user), and as mentioned in the introduction, the request fulfillment process is used to handle them.

The ITIL Service Operation publication suggests that other sorts of requests, such as requests for building maintenance, may be handled together with IT requests. Take a moment to consider the advantages of this approach:

- Similar handling for both
- Expands single point of contact
- De-skills the (usually service desk) job

It will be up to each organization to decide and document which service requests it will handle through the request fulfillment process and which will have to go through other processes, such as business relationship management (BRM) processes for dealing with requests for new or changed services.

Value to the Business

The request fulfillment process benefits the business in a number of ways.

First, it improves the productivity of the business by giving its staff quick and effective access to the services they need to do their jobs. By providing a straightforward means of having its requests fulfilled, business staff can remain productive. Centralization encourages consistency and efficiency. Bureaucracy and delay is reduced, thus reducing the cost of fulfillment. Second, the process provides an efficient way to handle requests, again reducing bureaucracy. A formal process implies the centralization of sourcing and purchasing, enabling the service provider to standardize the hardware and software used and reducing support costs. Central purchasing through approved suppliers can also reduce costs through economies of scale.

The standardized nature of request fulfillment means that it is an obvious candidate for self-help. Although not essential, automating the process with a *self-help* front end enables the requester to interface directly with the process and thus speeds up the fulfillment process. Typically, users can access a list of possible requests on a company external website or intranet. This ensures that the user provides all the necessary information and can be informed as to expected lead times (defined in the SLA).

Automation can simplify the logging of requests. It can also automate the fulfillment process, without the intervention of the service desk if there is a direct interface into the necessary systems. An example of such automated fulfillment is when you request and receive a password reset from an Internet shopping site such as Amazon without any human intervention. Financial approval of requests can also be automated, with the request being sent to the appropriate budget holder for approval or rejection before fulfillment.

Next, we consider the policies, principles, and basic concepts of the request fulfillment process. Let's start with policies.

Policies

In this section, we'll consider some of the policies that support effective request fulfillment.

Policy: Process flows should be defined for each service request.   A process flow should be defined for the entire lifecycle of each service request. This will ensure that requests are satisfied effectively, efficiently, and consistently. Service designers should include new requirements for standard services in their design efforts.

Policy: Process should be owned by a centralized function.   A centralized function should own all service requests. This does not mean that there should be a single function for fulfilling the requests. Rather, the central function will be a single point of contact to monitor progress of requests and take action should progress be slow. This central function will also provide requesters with updates on progress where appropriate. Often the service desk takes this role.

Policy: A standard change process should be used when a change to a configuration item is involved.   If a request involves a change to a configuration item, then it must be implemented by a standard change. In other words, request fulfillment must follow normal change management procedures.

Policy: All service requests should be handled by a single system.   Service requests should be handled by a single system. The parallel here is with incident management and the service desk.

Policy: All service requests must be authorized.   All requests must be authorized before they are fulfilled. Many requests incur costs, such as the purchase of hardware or a software license, and those costs must be authorized.

Policy: All service requests should be prioritized according to business criteria.   The activity needed to fulfill a request must align with the needs and objectives of the business. In other words, each request must be prioritized using business criteria. Here is another parallel with incident management.

Policy: Users must be able to submit requests and obtain updates easily. Users must have a clear means of submitting a request and of getting an update on progress. This could be the single point of contact that is provided by the service desk for incidents. For request fulfillment, the point of contact could be the service desk or the web portal.

Principles and Basic Concepts

Many organizations use their existing incident management process (and tools) to handle service requests because key steps are often the same. In each case, the following questions need to be answered:

- Can the service desk deal with this?
- Would this impact negatively on incident handling?
- If not the service desk, who can deal with this?
- What are the timescales/agreed service levels?
- Is the user satisfied?

Separation of Requests and Incidents

Some organizations separate requests from incidents because incidents are unplanned and unwanted; a major aim of service management is to reduce the number of incidents through improved design, problem management, and continual service improvement. In contrast, there may be a policy of increasing the number of items that can be dealt with through the request fulfillment process. The targets for incidents and requests may be very different: requests often have specified lead times, which are dependent on other factors (such as the user not being given access until they have attended a training course), whereas with incidents, the aim is to resolve each one as quickly as possible. Where there are a significant number of requests to be fulfilled, a separate process with a different record type should be used. This allows the service provided to be monitored and reported on in a more appropriate way than using incident reporting. Also, it is likely incidents will be given priority over requests, resulting in requests not meeting SLA targets because fixes take precedence. Similarly, if dealing with requests has an impact on incident resolution, the customer will be dissatisfied.

Request Models

The process needed to fulfill a request will vary depending on exactly what is being requested, but it can usually be broken down into a set of activities that have to be performed. For each request, these activities should be documented into a *request model*. In this case, a request model defines how to handle a particular, frequently occurring request.

The model should define the sequence of actions that must be performed, who will perform them, and the required timescales for each of the steps as well as for the fulfillment of the complete request. Any *escalation* paths that may be required should also be included.

Menu Selection

The effectiveness of request fulfillment is hugely enhanced if it is supported by a software tool, and probably a tool that is web based. Such a tool should feature a menu of available services from which the user is able to select. The provision of all the required information can be enforced by using mandatory fields and providing drop-down lists of possible options. In addition, the tool should set the user expectations by showing lead times, costs, and so on.

Where organizations are already offering a self-help IT support capability to the users, it makes sense to combine this with a request fulfillment system as described.

Specialist web tools that offer this type of "shopping basket" experience can be used together with interfaces directly to the back-end integrated ITSM tools used to manage the request fulfillment activities.

Request Status Tracking

The request owner must be able to track requests through their lifecycle and report progress to the requester where appropriate. Each organization will choose the appropriate statuses for its needs, but let's consider the most common statuses that are used:

- *Draft* indicates that a request is being prepared for submission. For whatever reason, at the moment the requester is unable or unwilling to submit the request.

- *In Review* indicates a request that has been authorized but is now under review by the relevant fulfillment team. They could be planning a desktop installation, for example.

- *Suspended* indicates that fulfillment activity has been suspended. This may be because the fulfillment group is waiting for action or information from the requester.

The other common statuses—*Waiting Authorization*, *Rejected*, *Canceled*, *In Progress*, *Completed*, and *Closed*—are self-explanatory.

Prioritizing and Escalating Requests

All service requests should be prioritized based on a standard set of criteria. This can be done by considering the impact and urgency of a request, as with incident management. Alternatively, an organization might have set lead times for different request types.

A variety of reasons exist for escalating a request. Perhaps the obvious one is that a request might not be fulfilled within agreed timescales. Escalation might also be required if the process is being misused by the business. For example, the relocation of up to five workstations might be a service request but more than five would require the submission of a change request. Some managers in the business might try to get around this limitation by submitting several requests, each for five workstations but amounting to a large number in total. The request owner should be on the alert for this and escalate in the agreed manner.

Approval

As you've seen, many requests will incur a cost that must be approved. Some requests will have a standard charge—a software license or a standard workstation, for example. In other cases, the fulfillment group must establish the cost in the context of what exactly has to be done, as with an equipment move, for example. The role within the business responsible for approving the spend should be identified within the request model. Financial approval can be automated, and it may take place before the request is seen by the service desk. Requests for standard cost items may be routed to the approver before arriving at the desk.

Sometimes other types of approval are needed. These may include *compliance* with the organization's policies, especially in regard to information security, or *technical approval* to confirm that the request will work with the infrastructure. Request fulfillment must have the ability to define and check such approvals where needed. Procedures for obtaining required approvals should be included as part of the request fulfillment models to save time in processing the service request.

Coordination of Fulfillment Activity and Closure of the Request

A request, including fulfillment, can be handled in many ways. Some requests can be automated—password resets, for example. When human intervention is needed, the request can be fulfilled by a dedicated fulfillment group, the technical support teams, suppliers, or a combination of these. Remember, though, that ownership of requests should remain with one team—usually the service desk, unless a dedicated request team exists.

The service desk should monitor and chase progress and keep users informed throughout, regardless of the actual fulfillment source.

When the service request has been fulfilled, it must be referred back to the service desk for closure. The service desk should go through a closure process that checks to see whether the user is satisfied with the outcome.

Process Activities, Methods, and Techniques

We are now going to review the process flow shown in Figure 3.3. Although you do not need to know the process flow in detail for the exam, an understanding of what is involved in fulfilling service requests will help you grasp its objectives.

First we will look at the process flow and then discuss the high-level activities.

Figure 3.3 shows the complete request fulfillment process flow. You can see that it includes logging, categorizing, and prioritizing a request as you would an incident. It also includes some activities that are specific to this process. The request is logged and validated, categorized, and prioritized. Any necessary authorizations are then obtained, and the request is reviewed to ascertain who will fulfill it. The appropriate request model is then executed, and finally, the request is closed, with the requester's agreement. We'll look at each of these steps in turn.

FIGURE 3.3 Request fulfillment process flow

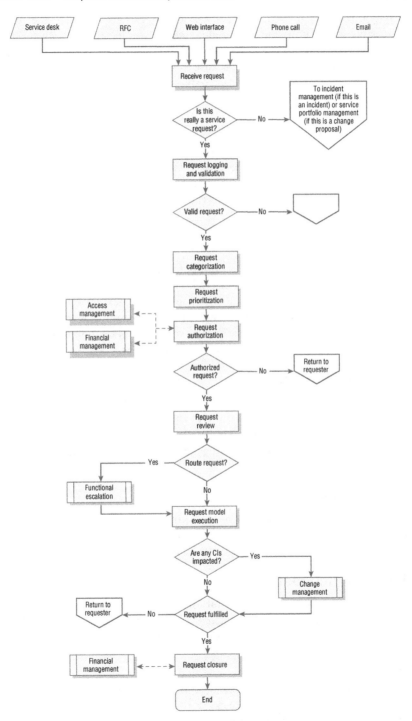

Receiving the Request

The first activity is receiving the request. Most service requests are received either from the web portal or at the service desk, but they could come in by other routes, such as email or even as requests for change (RFCs). From the point of view of the service provider, the preferred route is through the web portal because this will reduce the calls to the service desk. Not all incoming requests will be service requests; they could be incidents or change requests, in which case they must be routed to the appropriate process.

Logging the Request

When a request is received, it should be logged and allocated a unique reference number, and all necessary information should be recorded. The web portal should be designed to help the requester provide the necessary information. The request record should be updated as necessary as the request proceeds through its lifecycle with date- and time-stamping to maintain a track of what happened and when.

Validating the Request

The request is examined to confirm that it is valid; this includes making sure the request is within the scope of the IT services being offered. The web portal may help by restricting what can be logged to the available types of service requests. These tools ensure that the source of the request is valid and that only valid types of request are issued. Any requests that are invalid should be returned to the requester with an explanation; for example, the requested service might not be provided by the service provider.

Categorizing the Request

Categorizing the request will enable future analysis and reporting. As with the categorization of incidents, some thought should be given to the system employed. Requests can be categorized in a number of ways. For example, they can be categorized by activity, such as password reset or software installation. Another example is categorizing by the function that will fulfill the request.

Prioritizing the Request

Prioritization will be in line with business need, taking into account the impact and urgency of the request. A model like the one described in Chapter 2, "Incident and Problem Management," for the prioritization of incidents could also be used here.

Authorizing the Request

We discussed the need for all requests to be authorized as one of the request policies. The degree of rigor needed here depends very much on the type of request. Requests that cannot be authorized should be returned to the requester with an explanation of rejection.

Fulfilling the Request

After a request has been authorized, it is reviewed by the service desk and the appropriate fulfillment function is determined. In some cases, this will be the service desk itself; in others it might be a dedicated fulfillment team or even a supplier.

The request is then fulfilled by performing the actions specified in the appropriate request model. The request model can take a number of forms. In many organizations, it will simply be described in a written document; in others, a workflow tool will be used.

Completion and Closure of the Request

When the request has been fulfilled, it can be closed. Usually there will be a two-stage closure. The first stage simply records that, so far as the service provider is concerned, the fulfillment actions are complete. The second stage is the final closure, which should be performed only after consulting the requester.

If the service performed is chargeable, then at this point the appropriate charging mechanism is triggered. This might be sending a bill or registering a recharge. The service desk should check that the request documentation is up-to-date and that it is correctly categorized before final closure. Any updates to the CMS need to have been completed. This is also the time to conduct a satisfaction survey.

Triggers, Inputs, Outputs, and Interfaces

ITIL requires that every process should have a trigger and inputs to and outputs from the process activities. Each process will also have interfaces with a number of other processes.

Trigger

As previously explained, the request fulfillment process is triggered when a user submits a request. As you have seen, this may be delivered directly to the service desk or via the web portal where users can choose from a list of possible requests.

Inputs

The main input to the process is a request from the user. As you've seen, this can come by a variety of routes, each with its own format of information. Another significant input is the authorization form that may be required for some requests. Some requests may be logged as RFCs. Some requests will be for information, whereas others are for standard goods or services to be supplied.

Outputs

The following list includes examples of outputs from the process:

- Requests that have been authorized or rejected and those that are canceled.
- Some requests may be rerouted as incidents. For example, a user requests a new laptop because their current machine keeps crashing. This could be rerouted to resolve the fault and thus save unnecessary expenditure on new equipment.
- Status reports may be output from the process.
- Where a standard change is required, an *RFC* must be created.
- Some requests may be routed as changes because they are asking for nonstandard products or applications and need to be approved for use within the organization.

- The request should be updated as it is fulfilled.

- When the request is completed, the output will be a fulfilled request, which should then be closed.

- The final output is the update to the CMS when standard changes have been made.

Interfaces

Examples of primary interfaces with request fulfillment are as follows:

Financial Management for IT Services   Some requests may be chargeable, and financial approval may be required.

Service Catalog Management   The services that can be requested should be listed in the *service catalog.*

Release and Deployment Management   This will interface with request fulfillment when the request concerns the automatic deployment of new or upgraded components. In such cases, the release is predefined, built, and tested and then deployed on request.

Service Asset and Configuration Management   The CMS will need to be updated following any changes that may have been made as part of fulfillment activities. Where appropriate, software license checks and updates will also be necessary.

Change Management   When a change is required to fulfill a request, it will need to be logged as an RFC and progressed through change management.

Incident and Problem Management   As discussed, requests may be handled using the incident management process. Where appropriate, it will be necessary to relate service requests issued by IT to any incidents or problems that created the need for the requests.

Access Management   This process may be involved with request fulfillment activities to ensure that those making requests are authorized to do so in accordance with the information security policy. Request fulfillment can act as the input to the access management process in relation to the creation and deletion of accounts.

Information Management

The process of request fulfillment is heavily dependent on information from formal service requests, and these can include the following:

- What service is being requested.

- Who requested and authorized the service.

- Which process will be used to fulfill the request.

- Who it was assigned to and what action was taken.

- The date and time when the request was logged as well as the date and time of all actions taken.

- Closure details.

- RFCs: In some cases the request fulfillment process will be initiated by an RFC. This is typical where the service request relates to a CI.

- The service portfolio, to enable the scope of agreed service requests to be identified.

- Security policies that prescribe any controls to be executed or adhered to when providing the service—for example, ensuring that the requester is authorized to access the service, or that the software is licensed.

Each organization will have to define their own requirements, as the process of request fulfillment will vary from organization to organization.

Process Roles

There are a number of roles that need to be performed in support of the request fulfillment process, which are not job titles, but each organization needs to understand their requirements and allocate roles appropriately.

Request Fulfillment Process Owner

The request fulfillment process owner's responsibilities may include

- Carrying out the generic process owner's role for the request fulfillment process (see Chapter 1)

- Designing request workflows and models

- Working with other process owners to ensure an integrated approach across all processes

Request Fulfillment Process Manager

The request fulfillment process manager's responsibilities may include

- Carrying out the generic process manager's role for the request fulfillment process (see Chapter 1)

- Planning and managing support for request fulfillment tools and processes

- Coordinating interfaces between this and other service management processes

- Handling staff, customer, and management concerns, requests, issues, and inquiries

- Ensuring that request fulfillment activities operate within service level targets

- Proactively seeking improvements in the process

- Managing the gathering of customer and user feedback on the process

- Managing resources and resourcing levels

- Ensuring that service requests are carried out in a timely manner and according to any required authorization

- Representing request fulfillment at CAB

- Reviewing process records for accuracy and consistency

Request Fulfillment Process Practitioner/Analyst

This role is responsible for the day-to-day activities and ensures that service requests are completed to a high level of customer satisfaction. The role includes the following:

- Providing a single point of contact and end-to-end responsibility to ensure service requests are properly carried out

- Triaging service requests at point of contact to allocate resources

- Communicating service requests to other process areas involved in the process

- Ensuring service requests are appropriately logged

The initial handling of service requests is commonly carried out at the service desk, but the eventual fulfillment will be undertaken by the appropriate service operational staff, or suppliers, as required. Often there is no need for additional or specific roles to be identified. In certain circumstances, where the workload justifies it, a dedicated team may be created to carry out the process.

Critical Success Factors and Key Performance Indicators

There are several possible CSFs for request fulfillment, each of which will have KPIs to show whether the CSF is being achieved. Before we look at the CSFs and KPIs, let's take a minute to understand what these terms mean:

- A CSF is a high-level statement of what a process must achieve if it is to be judged a success. Normally, a process would have only three or four CSFs. A CSF cannot be measured directly; that's what KPIs are for.

- A KPI is a metric that measures some aspect of a CSF. Each CSF will have three or four associated KPIs.

   Here are some examples of CSFs and KPIs for request fulfillment:

- Critical success factor: "Requests must be fulfilled in an efficient and timely manner that is aligned to agreed service level targets for each type of request."

   Possible associated KPIs for this CSF are as follows:

   - The mean elapsed time for handling each type of service request

   - The number and percentage of service requests completed within agreed target times

   The first KPI relates to the requirement to fulfill requests in a timely manner and the second to meeting agreed targets. You may be able to think of other KPIs.

- Critical success factor: "Only authorized requests should be fulfilled."

   This could be measured by the following KPIs:

   - The percentage of service requests fulfilled that were appropriately authorized

   - The number of incidents related to security threats from request fulfillment activities

- Critical success factor: "User satisfaction must be maintained."

  The following examples would be relevant KPIs for this CSF:

  - The level of user satisfaction with the handling of service requests (as measured in some form of satisfaction survey)

  - The total number of incidents related to request fulfillment activities

  - The size of the current backlog of outstanding service requests

Challenges

There are some common challenges encountered when implementing and running a request fulfillment process:

- Ensuring that the scope of the process is clearly defined by documenting the type of requests that will or will not be handled by this process and which requests need to go to change management.

- Providing an effective portal that will encourage users to submit requests there rather than calling the service desk. Clear targets must be agreed with the business for each type of request. These targets will be documented in the service level agreement.

- Reaching agreement with the business on where, when, and how authorization should be sought. It's important to adhere to normal budgetary controls in place within the organization.

- Agreeing on the costs for fulfilling requests, specifying whether they are to be recharged, and ensuring that service requests do not violate the information security policy.

- Providing the required level of information regarding the types of available requests in an easily accessible format, usually as part of the service catalog.

- Providing a documented request model with a predefined process flow for each of the services being requested to ensure that all requests follow a predefined standard fulfillment procedure.

- Making sure all service requests made through the web portal are processed in a timely manner and in accordance with agreed SLA targets to ensure customer satisfaction. Regular customer satisfaction surveys should be carried out.

Risks

Five common risks are faced by the request fulfillment process:

- A poorly defined or communicated scope will mean that users and IT staff will be unclear as to what the process will and won't handle.

- A poorly defined or implemented web portal will not be used. Users will continue to call the service desk and a major benefit of the process will be lost.

- Poorly designed or insufficiently resourced back-office fulfillment activities will mean that the process will not operate effectively or efficiently. Targets will not be met, backlogs will build up, and customer satisfaction will plummet.

- Inadequate monitoring capability will prevent metrics from being gathered, and as a result, performance won't be managed.

- Users may be reluctant to use a web-based tool if it is a new concept to the organization.

Access Management

Access management is the process of granting authorized users the right to use a service while preventing nonauthorized users from gaining access. It is also sometimes referred to as rights management or identity management.

Purpose

As part of your Foundation training, you will have covered the process of information security management and its role in defining security policies. The process for implementing many of these policies is access management. This process provides users who have the required authorization with the ability to use the services they require. Ensuring that only authorized individuals are given access to data is a concern of every IT service provider; failure to carry this out correctly can be damaging and possibly breach legal or regulatory requirements. Consider the damage that could be done to an organization discovered to have allowed unauthorized access to medical or banking records because of poor access management processes.

Organizations need to ensure that access is managed not only when a new member of staff is appointed and set up with access to the systems and services, but also when the staff member leaves. A challenge many organizations face is keeping up-to-date with changing access requirements as a staff member moves between departments. Often new access rights are requested, but it's never determined whether the existing access rights are still required in the new position; therefore, the individual may amass significant rights over a period of years if this step is not carried out. It is dependent, in part, on the business informing the IT service provider of staff moving between departments; the IT provider should routinely query whether existing access is still required when additional access is requested.

There may also be occasions when access is restricted—for example, during an investigation into suspected wrongdoing to prevent any evidence from being destroyed. Such requests would normally be made by senior management or human resources department.

Objectives

The objectives of the access management process are to do the following:

- Manage access to services, carrying out the policies defined within information security management (see Chapter 15, "Technology and Implementation Considerations for Release, Control, and Validation").

- Ensure that all requests for access are verified and authorized. This may include requests to restrict or remove access.

- Ensure that requests are dealt with efficiently, balancing the requirement for authorization and control with the need to be responsive to business requirements.

- Ensure (once access rights are granted) that the rights that have been granted are used in accordance with security policies. This might include, for example, Internet access for personal use. Although some personal use may be allowed, there are likely to be categories of websites that may not be accessed.

Scope

The scope of access management, as we have said, is the efficient execution of information security management policies. Carrying these out ensures that the *confidentiality*, integrity, and availability (CIA) of the organization's data and intellectual property are protected. Confidentiality here means that only authorized users are able to see the data. Integrity means that the data is kept safe from corruption or unauthorized change. Access management ensures that users are given the right to use a service. This does not guarantee that it will always be available during service hours, which is the responsibility of availability management.

A request for access will often be made through the request management process. Some organizations will maintain a specialized team to carry out requests, but more commonly they are carried out by other functions. Technical and application management functions are involved, and a significant part of the process may be handled within the service desk. There should be a single coordination point to ensure consistency.

Value

The access management process provides a number of benefits to the business:

- First, by controlling access to services, it protects the confidentiality of the organization's information. Customer confidentiality, for example, is a significant concern for many organizations.

- A second benefit is that staff members have the right level of access to perform their roles.

- A third benefit is that the process provides a means of tracking the use of services by users.

- Sometimes there may be a need to revoke access rights quickly—for example, if a user is suspected of criminal behavior. The process enables this to be done.

- Finally, the process will support regulatory and legal compliance not only by managing access, but also by being able to demonstrate that access is managed.

Policies

The *ITIL Service Operation* publication describes five useful policies for access management.

- The first policy is a formal statement of things we have already mentioned, especially that the management of access to services is led by the policies and controls defined by information security management. An implication of this is that if an unusual request for access is received, and it doesn't appear to fall within the guidelines laid down by information security management, then the request should be escalated to information security management. It cannot be granted at the discretion of access management.

- Another policy is that the use of services should be logged and tracked. *Tracked* here implies that access should be monitored in real time and events triggered as appropriate. There are also implications here for service designers—services must have the means of logging activity built into them.

- The third policy is that the process must keep the access rights up-to-date. In particular, it should modify rights as individuals change roles or leave the organization.

- The fourth policy is related to the second. It says that the process should maintain an accurate history of successful and unsuccessful attempts to access services. This information would be useful, for example, for later examination by auditors.

- The final policy is that escalation procedures should be defined for any events that threaten security.

Principles and Basic Concepts

We're now going to examine a number of basic access management concepts.

Access   Refers to the level and extent of a service's functionality or data that a user is entitled to use.

Identity   Refers to the information about a user that distinguishes them as an individual, makes them uniquely identifiable, and verifies their status within the organization.

Rights or Privileges   Refer to the settings whereby a user is provided access—for example, read, write, execute, change, and delete.

Service Groups   Provide a means of simplifying the task of allocating rights. The idea behind service groups is that there are groups of users who will require exactly the same rights to the same set of services. Instead of rights being granted individually, a service group is created that has the required set of rights. Users are linked to the service group and will inherit the rights of the group.

Directory Services   Refer to specific types of tools that are used to manage access and rights.

Process Activities, Methods, and Techniques

It is important to understand the steps and activities in the process, as shown in Figure 3.4, the access management process flow. We are going to look at each step of the process.

FIGURE 3.4 Access management process flow

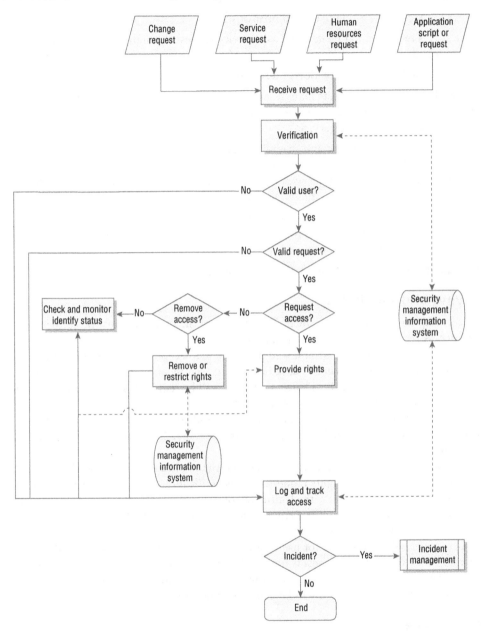

Request Access

A request for access can be made in a number of ways:

- The access request could be handled as a service request through the request fulfillment portal.

- It may result from the completion of a request form.

- If the change of access affects many users, a request for change will probably be used. For example, the transition of a new service will mean updating the access rights of everyone who will use the service.

- Another route is through an automated process. For example, each year a college or university will enroll possibly thousands of new students, and each of them must be granted access to student IT services. This is often done automatically by the student registration system when the student actually registers.

- The request may also come automatically from the HR system when a new member of staff is recorded or the status of an existing employee changes, such as when someone resigns or is transferred or promoted.

    All requests, whether or not they are valid, are logged.

Verifying and Validating

The access request must then be verified. The identity of the requester must be confirmed, and the access requirement must be judged as legitimate.

Usually, an existing user's username and password are accepted as proof of identity. In more secure environments, biometric data or physical identification devices can be used.

For new users, some physical evidence of identity will be required, such as official proof of identity (such as a passport or driver's license).

New users include not only new permanent staff members but also temporary and third-party users such as visitors, contract staff, and vendors. The organization will define how a request will be verified.

The second aspect of verification is checking that the request is legitimate—that is, the user is authorized to have the rights requested. This verification must be independent of the requester. A user cannot verify the legitimacy of their own request. Often a request will be verified by a line manager or HR. Requests that come by way of a RFC will have been authorized through the change management process.

Some services will be available for use by anyone who requests them; there should be a policy that defines this. If the request is not valid, then it will be logged and returned to the requester. An incident may be raised to investigate why an invalid request was created, if thought necessary. A valid request will be actioned appropriately.

Provide Access

The task of providing rights is often delegated to a specialist technical or application team that has the necessary knowledge and skills. This task can be automated by using access management tools that interface with multiple applications. This is only possible, of course, if the design of the applications included this as a requirement.

Access rights are associated with a role: a payroll clerk has the right to use the payroll system. Users can occupy multiple roles, each of which brings a set of rights, and sometimes these conflict with some enterprise policy such as the separation of duties. For example, it is usual practice to ensure that a person who places an order with a supplier is not able to authorize payment. Where a role conflict occurs, access management should escalate the issue to the appropriate stakeholder, who will be someone in the business area concerned. (For example, if the roles are within the finance department, the issue would be referred to the appropriate stakeholder in that department; if the roles are within the IT department, the appropriate IT manager would be consulted.)

Monitor Access

Once the access has been granted, the status of the user should be monitored to ensure that they still have a valid requirement for the access. In practice, this can be difficult to achieve. Access management should be notified of staff who leave so that their access can be revoked, and many organizations have robust procedures to ensure that this is done. Many organizations encounter difficulty in tracking the changing roles and accompanying access requirements of users, especially those who have been in the organization for many years. In this situation, new access requirements are added to existing rights, with no verification that the existing rights are still required. Consideration should be given to adding questions about existing access requirements to the access request form. The HR department needs to be made aware of the importance of supplying information regarding changing job roles to access management in order to protect the organization's data. Access management should understand these different types of staff changes and determine how it will become aware of them. Ideally, this will be automated by an interface with the HR system. The failure to respond to changes in status is a common security issue. It leads, for example, to computer accounts remaining available for use even though the users have left the organization.

The tracking access activity might trigger a security incident if, for example, an unsuccessful attempt to access a service is made by a valid user.

Remove Access

The last activity that we'll look at is removing or restricting a user's rights. There are a number of circumstances when this might be necessary. Although in many cases the modification is permanent, such as in the case of dismissal or promotion, there may be situations where this is only temporary. For example, in some organizations, a user's computer account is suspended when they go on leave.

Access should be permanently revoked when a user leaves an organization; again, the HR department needs to understand the importance of informing access management quickly in this situation.

Access management has to ensure that rights are not improperly used, which will require that access is logged and tracked. The degree of oversight required is determined when the service is designed and the appropriate logging mechanisms are provided. Should possible misuse be detected, the process must respond appropriately. This will usually entail raising a security incident and alerting stakeholders. In this situation, access may be temporarily revoked during the investigation, with access being restored if the misuse is deemed to have been an innocent mistake or permanently revoked if it is found to be deliberate. The access management process may be required to provide a record of access, perhaps in the context of the investigation of criminal behavior.

Triggers, Inputs, Outputs, and Interfaces

Next let's consider the triggers for the process, its inputs and outputs, and the interfaces it shares with other processes.

Triggers

Access management is triggered by a request for a user or users to access a service or group of services. This could originate from a number of circumstances.

The first possible trigger is an RFC, especially where a large number of access changes are required, perhaps as part of a rollout or project.

Another possible trigger is a service request. This is usually initiated through the service desk, or input directly into the request fulfillment system, and executed by the relevant technical or application management teams.

A request from human resources is another possible trigger. In this situation, HR management personnel make the request through the service desk. These requests are usually as a result of hiring, promoting, relocating, termination, or retirement.

The final trigger may be a request from the manager of a department, who could be performing a human resources role or who could have made a decision to start using a service for the first time.

Inputs

The inputs to the process are those that relate to the triggers, such as these:

- Authorized RFCs and authorized requests to grant or terminate access rights
- The security policies of the enterprise
- Any information about the identity of users

Other inputs are the operational and service level requirements for granting access to services, performing access management administrative activities, and responding to events related to access management.

Outputs

The access management process has the following outputs:

- The provision of access to IT services in accordance with information security policies
- The access management records showing when access has been granted or denied and the reasons for the denial
- Timely communications concerning inappropriate access or abuse of services

Interfaces

The access management process interfaces with a number of other service management processes.

A key interface is the one with information security management. As already stated, access management acts under the guidance and instruction of information security management and plays an essential part in ensuring that the requirements of the information security policies are met.

Many requests for access will come from the change management process in the form of authorized requests for change or even standard changes.

It is through the service level management process that access requirements and criteria are agreed on with the business on a service-by-service basis.

The relationship of the process with IT service continuity management is interesting. Access requirements may need to be varied should the continuity plan be invoked. Also, there may be a need to grant temporary access when the plan is being tested.

Request fulfillment provides a route for users to submit access requests.

Information Management

Information is critical to the success of access management and is part of the definition of identity.

Identity

Examples of things that may be included in the identity of a user are

- Name
- Address
- Contact details, such as telephone number and email address
- Physical documentation, such as driver's license, passport, or marriage certificate
- Numbers that refer to a document or an entry in a database, such as employee number, tax number, government identity number, driver's license number
- Biometric information, such as fingerprints, retinal images, voice recognition patterns, DNA
- Expiration date (if relevant)

Access management should provide access to IT services or organizational information to any legitimate users. These could include permanent employees or contractors temporarily engaged by the organization, vendor personnel such as account managers or support staff, or customers.

It is normally the responsibility of the organization to verify a user's identity before they join the organization and are granted access to IT systems or services. But IT will need to verify that the correct person is associated with the information provided. The higher the level of organizational security, the more information will be required to verify an individual.

Temporary access is just as important to manage as permanent access. Any identification will be captured and filed as part of an employee record.

Users, Groups, Roles, and Service Groups

It is often helpful to group numbers of users together to make the management of access rights more effective. The term *user profile* or *user template* can be used to describe these.

Many organizations have a standard set of services that users can access and may use this for grouping users together. But it must be flexible enough for the individual requirements to be catered for, as well as providing sufficient control. A catalog of user roles may be useful to help the definition of user groups.

However, the data profiles of all groups or users must be subject to the relevant legislation or governance—for example, the Data Protection Act (UK), or state-specific legislation in the US. This should be specified as part of the information security management policy.

Process Roles

These are the roles and responsibilities carried out by the access management process. As with all service management processes, the roles defined for an organization will depend on its needs.

Access Management Process Owner

The access management process owner's responsibilities may include

- Carrying out the generic process owner role for the access management process (see Chapter 1)

- Designing access request workflows

- Working with other process owners to ensure an integrated approach to the management of access request across the lifecycle

Access Management Process Manager

The access management process manager's responsibilities may include

- Carrying out the generic process manager role for the access management process (see Chapter 1)

- Planning and managing support for access management tools and processes

- Coordinating interfaces between access management and other service management processes

Access Management Process Practitioner/Other Roles

Access management is the operational execution of the information security management and availability management processes. As a consequence, the practitioner roles are most likely to be defined by these design processes, based on the content of the information security policy. These roles can be identified as follows.

The Role of Service Desk Staff

The service desk will often be the first point of contact to validate a request for access to a service. This may be done using a service request, which may require validation of the correct level of authorization, and also the identity of the user requesting the access.

Once validated, the request may be passed to the appropriate team for action. Depending on the security levels required by the organization, this may be at the service desk or require a higher level of technical access.

Incidents relating to the process of access management will also be handled by the service desk.

The Role of Technical and Application Management Staff

Technical and application management may play several important roles:

- During service design, they will ensure that access management requirements are part of the capability of the service design. This should include detection and monitoring of access to the service, and the approach to management of any access-related issues or incidents.

- During service transition, they will be involved in and responsible for the testing of the access to the service.

- During service operation, these teams will typically manage the access for systems under their control.

- Technical and application management will also be involved in the resolution of access-related incidents and problems.

- In the situation where the service desk has been granted the rights to manage access for particular services, technical and application management must ensure that appropriate training is given.

The Role of IT Operations Management Staff

If there is an operations management function, it is common practice for the access management activities to be delegated to this group. This will include providing or revoking access to services or systems, and there will need to be clear instructions for the management of such access.

If the operations bridge also exists, it may have the responsibility for managing the monitoring for access events.

Critical Success Factors and Key Performance Indicators

The ITIL Service Operation publication suggests three CSFs for access management.

The first is "Ensuring that the confidentiality, integrity, and availability of services are protected in accordance with the information security policy." The KPIs show whether the CSFs are being achieved. The first KPI is the percentage of incidents that involved inappropriate security access or attempts at access to services. You can see that this is measuring actual consequences of poor access management. The second KPI is the number of audit findings that discovered incorrect access settings for users who have changed roles or left the company. This is measuring the potential for security lapses caused by poor access management.

The second CSF for access management is "Provide appropriate access to services in a manner that's timely enough to meet business needs." The example KPI for this is the percentage of requests for access that were provided within established SLAs and OLAs.

The last CSF for access management is "Provide timely communications about improper access or abuse of services." This and the suggested KPI of a reduction in the average duration of access-related incidents (from time of discovery to escalation) are about ensuring that any issues are dealt with expeditiously.

Challenges

For access management to be successful, it must overcome a number of challenges. It must be able to do the following:

- Verify the identity of both the user and the approving person or body.
- Verify that a user qualifies for access to a specific service.
- Link multiple access rights to an individual user.
- Determine the status of the user at any time, such as to assess whether they are still employees.
- Manage changes to a user's access requirements.
- Restrict access rights to unauthorized users.
- Keep a database of all users and the rights that they have been granted.

Meeting these challenges requires a considerable effort.

Risks

Finally, we consider the risks faced by access management. Failure to meet any of the challenges described in the preceding section is a risk, of course. There are five additional risks:

- The first risk is a lack of appropriate supporting technologies, causing a reliance on error-prone manual involvement.
- A second risk is controlling access from "backdoor" sources such as application interfaces.
- A third risk is managing and controlling access to services by external third-party suppliers. Third parties may need access for a variety of legitimate reasons, but the access is often occasional and unplanned, which makes it difficult to manage.

- Lack of management support for the process is a risk for all service management processes. A particular issue here is that management often sees security controls as obstructing them and their staff from accomplishing their tasks and therefore does not support them.
- There is a risk that access controls will hinder the ability of users to conduct business.

Summary

This chapter explored the next processes in the service operation stage, event management, request fulfillment, and access management.

We covered the use of event monitoring to manage large numbers of items and how automated responses to particular events may improve the delivery of services. We also explained the role of events in automating processes.

We discussed the key ITIL concepts of events and alerts and how event management can improve availability by preempting failures or reducing the time taken to identify them. Finally, for this process, we considered the technical and staff challenges of implementing the event management process, and the roles included in the process.

We also explored the process of request fulfillment. We discussed the key ITIL concepts of service requests and how the request fulfillment process can save time and money in expediting simple user requirements.

We examined the process in depth, covering its purpose, objectives, scope, and value. We considered its policies, principles, activities, and basic concepts and how its success might be measured. We also discussed what factors might work against a successful implementation. The chapter also explored the appropriate roles for the process.

This chapter also covered access management's purpose, objectives, scope, and value. We discussed policies, principles, and basic concepts; process activities, methods, and techniques; triggers, inputs, outputs, and interfaces; critical success factors and key performance indicators; and challenges and risks.

You learned about the key ITIL concepts of access, identity, rights, and service groups.

We discussed the importance of access management in preventing unauthorized access to data and some of the issues that arise in monitoring access rights. This included exploration of the roles and responsibilities of staff involved in managing this activity.

We examined the following key ITIL concepts:

- Active monitoring
- Alert
- Event
- Identity
- Information security management

- Information security policy
- Monitoring
- Passive monitoring
- Request model
- Threshold

Exam Essentials

Understand the purpose, objectives, and scope of event management.   Describe events (a change of state that has significance for the management of a CI) and alerts (a failure or breach of a threshold) and the difference between them. Be able to give examples of each.

Understand the role of event management in automation.   Describe passive and active monitoring and the difference between them. Be able to give examples of each. Understand the importance of filtering events and explain how effective event management can reduce downtime. Be able to explain automatic responses to certain types of events.

Know how event management benefits the customer and the IT department.   Understand the efficiency benefits to be gained by being able to have a small number of staff monitor huge numbers of CIs and services. Understand how improved availability through reduced downtime benefits the business.

Understand how event management can be used to monitor business events and environmental conditions.   Be able to explain how the process of event management can be applied beyond the technical IT environment.

Understand the purpose, objectives, and scope of request fulfillment.   Request fulfillment provides an efficient means of delivering defined standard services to customers, with low-risk requests and a defined fulfillment process. It can include IT and non-IT requests and be accessed through a self-help web portal.

Know how request fulfillment benefits the customer and the IT department.   Request fulfillment provides the customer with an easy, efficient means of requesting defined standard services and enables the requests to be fulfilled by service desk and second-line staff with minimum bureaucracy.

Understand the use of request models.   Because requests have a predefined fulfillment process, they are very well suited to the use of request models, which can be programmed into the service management toolset.

Understand the need for technical and financial approval.   Although some requests are preauthorized, there may be occasions when authorizations are required. The usual corporate financial controls still apply, so the budget holder may need to approve, for example, the purchase of equipment. Technical authorization may be necessary as a confirmation that the request is compatible with the user's existing equipment.

Understand the use of a web portal and menu selection in implementing an efficient user interface.   Request fulfillment can be greatly enhanced by providing the equivalent of an online shop, complete with "Add to Cart" facility. Users are familiar with this approach through Internet shopping, and it reduces the need for data entry at the service desk.

Understand the purpose, objectives, and scope of access management.   Explain the relationship between access management and information security management. Access management is not just granting access—it is also restricting or removing it as required.

Understand the main process activities of access management.   Explain the following access management activities: requesting access, validating and verifying a request, providing a request and monitoring how it is used, and finally, where necessary, removing it.

Understand and recognize the roles and responsibilities for each process.   This includes not only the generic roles applicable in all cases but also the specific relating to each process.

Review Questions

You can find the answers to the review questions in the appendix.

1. For which of these situations would implementing automation to support event management by using event management be appropriate?
    1. Hierarchical escalation of incidents
    2. Speeding up the processing of month-end sales figures
    3. Notification of an "intruder detected" to local police station
    4. Running backups
        A. 3 and 4 only
        B. All of the above
        C. 2 and 3 only
        D. 1, 3, and 4 only

2. Event management can be used to monitor which of the following?
    1. Environmental conditions
    2. System messages
    3. Staff rosters
    4. License use
        A. 1 and 2 only
        B. 2 and 3 only
        C. 1, 2, and 4 only
        D. All of the above

3. Which of the following are types of event monitoring?
    1. Passive
    2. Virtual
    3. Active
    4. Standard
        A. 1 and 2 only
        B. 2 and 3 only
        C. 1 and 3 only
        D. All of the above

4. The request fulfillment process is suitable for which of the following?
    A. All requests, including RFCs
    B. Only requests that have been approved by the CAB
    C. Emergency requests for change, because the process will ensure a fast implementation
    D. Common, low-risk requests with a documented fulfillment procedure

5. Requests are most likely to be fulfilled by which of the following?

1. Service desk staff

2. Second-line staff

3. Service level manager (SLM)

4. Business relationship manager (BRM)

   A. 1 and 2

   B. All of the above

   C. 1 and 3

   D. 2 and 3

6. Which of the following statements is *incorrect*?

   A. Requests need to be authorized by the CAB.

   B. Requests need to be authorized by the budget holder when an expense will be incurred.

   C. Requests need to be authorized by technical management when technical compatibility is an issue.

   D. Requests that involve a change should be primarily preauthorized standard changes.

7. Which of the following is the best description of access management?

   A. Access management enables authorized access to services and data. Information security management prevents nonauthorized staff from gaining access.

   B. Access management grants authorized users the right to use a service while preventing nonauthorized users from gaining access.

   C. Access management is responsible for setting security policies.

   D. Access management decides what services users should have access to.

8. Why is effective access management important for an organization?

1. Because there may be legal requirements to require control over access to data.

2. Because poor access management may lead to data that should have been protected being made available to unauthorized individuals, leading to negative press that could damage the reputation of the organization.

3. Because effective access management will reduce costs.

4. Because without it, potential customers may hesitate to deal with the organization, concerned that their data will not be protected.

5. Because otherwise, deciding what access to allow will be an IT rather than a business decision.

   A. 1, 2, and 4 only

   B. 1, 4, and 5 only

   C. All of the above

   D. 1, 2, 4, and 5 only

9. Which of the following is *not* a challenge for access management?

   A. Verifying identity

   B. Validating access requests

   C. Tracking access rights when users change names (such as upon marriage) or have the same name as another user

   D. Tracking changes in requirements as users change jobs

10. When might access management reduce or remove access?

1. If the user is on long-term leave

2. If the user has left the organization

3. If the user is under investigation for wrongdoing

4. If the user has changed jobs within the organization

   A. All of the above

   B. 1, 3, and 4 only

   C. 2, 3, and 4 only

   D. 1, 2, and 3 only

Chapter

4

The Service Desk

THE FOLLOWING ITIL OPERATIONAL
SUPPORT AND ANALYSIS INTERMEDIATE
EXAM OBJECTIVES ARE DISCUSSED IN
THIS CHAPTER:

✓ **The service desk role**

✓ **Objectives**

✓ **Organizational structures**

✓ **Staffing options**

✓ **Efficiency and effectiveness metrics**

✓ **Issues and safeguards when outsourcing**

This chapter and Chapter 5, "Technical Management, Application Management, and IT Operations Management," cover how the IT service provider organizes to deliver the services to the required standard. The four functions defined in the ITIL guidance are the service desk, technical management, application management, and IT operations management.

A *service desk* is described in the ITIL framework is a functional unit consisting of a dedicated number of staff members responsible for dealing with a variety of service activities, usually via telephone calls, web interface, or automatically reported infrastructure events. We will cover this function in detail because it plays a critical role in customer and user satisfaction. Although the service desk staff members do not have the same level of in-depth technical knowledge as the staff members in the other functions, their role is just as important.

The service desk function is the most visible of the four functions; every hour of every day they come into contact with business users at all levels. A poor service desk can result in a poor overall impression of the IT department, while an efficient, customer-focused team can ensure customer satisfaction even when the service is operating below the agreed service level.

An essential feature of a service desk is that it provides a single point of contact (SPOC) for users needing assistance. It provides a single day-to-day interface with IT, whatever the user requirement. It provides a variety of services:

- Handles incidents, resolving as many as possible where the resolution is straightforward and within the service desk authority level
- Owns incident records that are escalated to other support groups for resolution
- Reports potential problems to the problem management process
- Handles service requests
- Provides information to users
- Communicates with the business about major incidents, upcoming changes, and so on
- Provides an interface for users regarding the progress of requests for change, if required
- Tracks the performance of third-party maintenance providers, ensuring that they provide the agreed service as defined for the incident and request processes
- Monitors incidents and service requests against the targets in the SLA and provides reporting from the service desk tool to show the level of service achieved
- Updates the CMS as required
- Captures data regarding downtime due to incidents to be used by availability management

Role

The provision of a single point of contact is accepted in many industries as being central to good customer service. Without a service desk, users would have to try to identify which IT support team they should approach. This could be confusing for the business, leading to a delay in having their issue resolved. Technical staff members would waste time dealing with issues outside their specialist area or issues that could be dealt with by more junior staff members.

Providing a good service desk leads to a number of benefits:

- Increased focus of customer service
- Increased customer satisfaction
- Easier provision of support through the single point of contact
- Faster resolution of incidents and fulfillment of requests at the service desk, without the need for further escalation
- Reduced business impact of failures because of faster resolution
- More effective use of specialist IT staff members
- Accurate data (taken from the service desk tool) regarding the numbers and nature of incidents.

Objective

As we have said already, the main objective of the service desk is to provide a single point of contact. A desk that concentrates solely on this objective, logging and escalating every incident or request, is not a service desk; it is a call center. Service desks differ from call centers because of their next most important objective: focusing on restoring service as quickly as possible in the event of a failure. This may not mean a complete resolution of the incident; it may mean instead the provision of a workaround, to enable the user to continue working. Fulfilling a request, resetting a password, or answering a "How do I . . . ?" query all help the user get back to work as soon as possible.

The service desk also has the following responsibilities:

- Logging all incidents and requests with the appropriate level of detail
- Categorizing incidents and requests for future analysis
- Agreeing on the correct priority with the user based on impact and urgency (utilizing SLAs wherever possible for consistency)
- Investigating, diagnosing, and resolving incidents whenever possible
- Deciding upon the correct support team to escalate the incident should the service desk be unable to resolve it

- Monitoring progress of the incident by support teams
- Communicating progress to the users
- Confirming closure of resolved incidents with the user
- Owning the incident on behalf of the user to ensure that it is progressed to resolution
- Carrying out surveys to ascertain the level of customer and user satisfaction

These activities are covered in more depth in Chapter 2, "Incident and Problem Management," on incident management and Chapter 3, "Event Management, Request Fulfillment, and Access Management," on the request fulfillment processes.

Service Desk Organizational Structures

The best structure for the service desk is dependent upon the size and structure of the organization. A global organization will have different needs from one with all its employees based in the same location. Here we look at the most common structures; the best option may be a combination of them. This will have been determined in service strategy.

Local Service Desk

This option provides a service desk co-located with the users it serves; an organization with three offices would have three local service desks. There are advantages with this approach in that the service desk is local, so it understands the local business priorities. For organizations with offices spread across different countries, local service desks provide support in the language of the local users, work in the same time zone, have the same public holidays, and so on. This structure can also be useful when different locations have specialized support needs. The basic principle of a single point of contact is retained because, from the user perspective, they have only one number to call and are unaware of any other desks that may exist.

This is an expensive option because each new office location would require a new service desk too. Each desk needs sufficient staff to allow for annual leave, training, and sickness. At quiet times, there would be several service desk staff members spread across the various desks waiting for calls. There are potential issues with incidents and requests being logged in different languages; this makes incident analysis and problem identification difficult. Sharing knowledge is also more difficult: an incident that could be resolved by one service desk might be escalated by another because the resolution has not been shared between the desks. Resilience may be another issue. With local distributed desks, there may be the option of each desk providing cover for the others, but in reality this may be difficult to achieve.

To overcome these issues, IT management must ensure that information is shared effectively. Procedures need to be put in place to ensure that issues affecting more than one location are managed effectively without duplication of effort, each service desk assuming that another desk is responsible. Figure 4.1 shows the local structure.

FIGURE 4.1   Local service desk

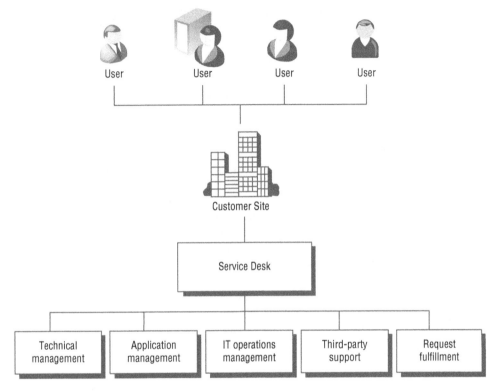

Centralized Service Desk

A more common structure for service desks is that of a centralized service desk. In this model, all users contact the same service desk. This has the benefit of providing economies of scale because there is no duplication of provision. Specialist technology, such as intelligent call distribution or an integrated service management tool, may be justified for a centralized service desk but not when implementing this technology across many sites. There are no issues with confusion regarding ownership of major incidents, and knowledge sharing becomes much more straightforward. Offering a service at times of low demand is more cost effective when only one service desk needs to be staffed.

Staff members on a centralized desk will gain more experience with particular incidents, which a local service desk may encounter only occasionally, leading to an increased ability to resolve these issues immediately. Where the centralized desk is supporting users in many countries, the language issue may be resolved by the following:

- Employing staff members with language skills and using technology to allocate calls requiring support in a particular language to staff members who have that language ability. Staff members would then log the call in the main language.

- Standardizing on one language; callers would need to report incidents in that language, and support would be provided in it. This option depends on the type of organization and whether its users may reasonably be expected to be able to converse in the language.

- Local super users may be required to support users without the necessary language ability and to log calls on their behalf.

To provide support to a global organization, a 24/7 service may be required. Where the resolution requires a physical intervention (unjamming a printer, for example), the service desk would require local support staff who could be assigned calls and be responsible for updating the incident records or could assist in the resolution of an issue at a remote site.

Consideration should also be given to maintaining service continuity because an event that affects a centralized service desk would impact support across the entire organization. A plan to provide the service from another location, possibly using different staff members, in the event of a disaster must be developed and tested in conjunction with IT service continuity management. There should also be plans in place to ensure the service desk's tool resilience in the event of disruption to the network or a power failure. This centralized structure is shown in Figure 4.2.

FIGURE 4.2   Centralized service desk

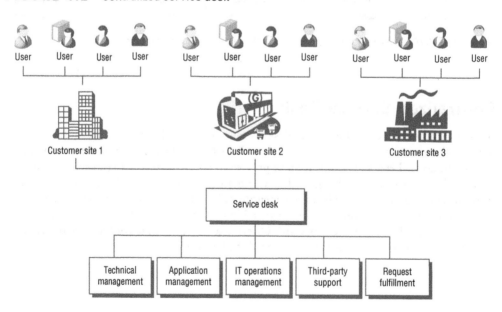

Virtual Service Desk

The third organizational option described by ITIL is that of a virtual service desk. This option consists of two or more service desk locations that operate as one desk. Calls and emails are distributed across the staff members as if they were in one centralized location. This ensures that the workload is balanced across all the desks. To the user, the virtual service desk appears as a single entity; the users may be completely unaware that this is not the case in reality. The virtual service desk retains the single-point-of-contact principle.

The considerations we discussed earlier regarding knowledge sharing and clear ownership apply even more in this scenario, as does the need for all calls to be logged immediately. Users will become very frustrated if they call the service desk and explain an issue in detail only to find when they call for a second time that the service desk analyst can find no record of their first call. This is, of course, true for all service desks, but the difficulty of locating a "lost call" is increased in the virtual environment, where team members are not located together.

The ability to route calls to analysts with particular language knowledge or to adopt one language for all users can be considered, as with a centralized desk. Calls must be logged on one common system, using one language, because the next analyst to handle the incident may be in another location.

The virtual service desk structure allows for a variety of ways of working. Many call centers use home-based staff members, who log on to the service desk telephone system and are allocated calls. Extra staff members from other teams can supplement the core service desk staff members at busy times, without the users being aware. Many of us have had the experience of calling a local company only to have the call answered offshore outside normal hours or during busy times.

Offshoring support (providing support from another geographical location where staff members' costs may be lower) can be cost effective but requires careful management to ensure consistency of service. Managers need to be culturally sensitive because users may become irritated by staff members behaving in a way that they find unfamiliar.

 **Real World Scenario**

Offshore Support Difficulties

A large insurance company in the United Kingdom decided to offshore its service desk. Overseas staff members were recruited carefully, with tests to validate their language and technical skills. After some months, an analysis of telephone traffic showed that many customers were hanging up as soon as they realized that their call was being answered offshore. Focus groups of users were interviewed to try to understand why this was happening.

The answer was not the level of technical support but a combination of the lack of local knowledge and cultural issues. The offshore staff members had been coached in customer service and were putting the recommendations into effect, explaining to the user what they were doing, thanking the user after every piece of information was provided, and so on. The users were not used to this level of service and expressed a wish that "the service desk staff members just got on with the task and stopped talking about it!"

One benefit of a virtual structure is that it has built-in resilience; should one location go offline because of a major disruption affecting that location, the service would continue with little or no impact.

Figure 4.3 shows the virtual service desk structure.

FIGURE 4.3 Virtual service desk

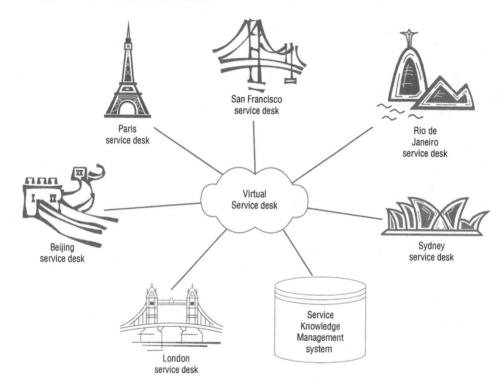

Follow the Sun

The fourth structure described within ITIL is known as *follow the sun*. This is a form of virtual service desk, but with this structure, the allocation of calls across the various desks is based on time of day rather than workload.

Follow the sun enables a global organization to provide support around the clock, without needing to employ staff members at night to work on the service desk. A number of service desks will each work standard office hours. The calls will be allocated to whichever desk or desks are open at the time the calls are made. Typically, this might mean a European service desk will handle calls until the end of the European working day, when calls will then be allocated to a desk or desks in North America. When the working day in North America finishes, calls are directed to another desk or desks in the Asia-Pacific region before being directed back to the European desk at the start of the next European working day.

This option is an attractive one for many global organizations, providing 24-hour coverage without the need for shift or on-call payments. The requirements for effective call logging, a centralized database, and a common language for data entry referred to earlier for the virtual structure apply equally here. Procedures for handoff between desks are also required to ensure that the desk that is taking over knows, for example, the status of any major incidents.

To the user, the single point of contact still applies; they have one number to call, no matter who answers it or where the service desk analyst may be located.

Specialized Service Desk Groups

Another possible variant on the previous structures is to provide specialist support for particular services. In this structure, a user may call the usual service desk number and then choose an option depending on the issue they have. Typically, the message would say, "Press 1 if the call is regarding system X, press 2 if it is regarding system Y, or hold for a service desk analyst if your call is in regard to anything else."

Although this approach can be useful, especially where in-depth knowledge is required to resolve a call, it is not popular with users when it expands to numerous options to choose from followed by yet more options.

There is a danger that the user does not always know what support they need and may choose the wrong option, leading to delay and frustration. For example, a printer may not print because of a hardware fault, a network issue, an application malfunction, or a user error. The user will not know which option to choose.

This specialist support option works best for a small number of complex services that require a level of both business and technical knowledge beyond what can reasonably be expected of a service desk analyst. Another possible reason to use this option is when the service contains confidential data. In this situation, the organization may wish to limit access to a small number of specialist support staff.

Service Desk Single Point of Contact

Building a single point of contact is an important part of the service desk communication. Regardless of the combination of options chosen to fulfill an organization's overall service desk structure, individual users should be in no doubt about whom to contact if they need assistance or where they can access self-help support. A single telephone number (or a single number for each group if separate desks are chosen) should be provided and well publicized, as well as a single email address and a single web service desk contact page.

There are several ways to help publicize the service desk telephone number and email address and make them easily available when users are likely to need them, such as including the service desk telephone number on hardware CI labels attached to the components the user is likely to be calling about and printing service desk contact details on telephones.

For PCs and laptops a customized background or desktop with the service desk contact details could be provided, possibly including information such as IP address and OS build number.

Other common ways of communicating the service desk details include printing the service desk number on giveaway materials (pens, pencils, mugs, mouse mats, etc.), publicizing it on internet/intranet sites, and including it on calling cards or satisfaction survey cards left with users when a desk visit has been necessary. Repeating the details on all correspondence sent to users (together with call reference numbers) and placing the details on notice boards or physical locations that users are likely to regularly visit (entrances, canteens, refreshment areas, etc.) is an important part of maintaining the corporate presence of the service desk.

Service Desk Staffing

The service desk will usually use a service management tool and other technical resources to enable it to carry out its tasks and will follow defined processes (especially incident management and request fulfillment). Although these tools and processes are important, the people aspect of the service desk is critical. The interactions with the customers and users require good communication skills in addition to technical knowledge. Knowing the answer is only part of the job; explaining it in terms that users understand is essential.

Recruiting and retaining good service desk staff members is the key to customer satisfaction. This function often acts as an entry level to the other functions, providing staff members with an understanding of all the services, the technology that supports them, and the business impact of failure. This provides an excellent basis for future technical specialization.

Service desk staff members require a mix of technical knowledge and interpersonal skills. The technical knowledge may not be in depth, but it covers all the services provided by the IT service provider. The service desk analyst can be said to know a little about a lot of services rather than a lot about a few.

The ability to correctly prioritize incidents based on business impact and urgency requires that the service desk analyst has a good level of awareness about the business processes. Added to this knowledge is the requirement to be patient, helpful, assertive when dealing with support teams or third parties who are failing to meet targets, well-organized, and calm under pressure.

As we have discussed in the previous section of this chapter, "Service Desk Organizational Structures," service desks are organized differently depending upon the particular requirements of the organization. The skill level required may also vary; the service desk may be tasked with resolving a high proportion (75 percent to 80 percent) of incidents, or it may be limited to logging and escalating them for resolution by another team.

An organization must ensure that the correct number of staff are available at any given time to match the demand being placed upon the desk by the business. There is often a variety in the volumes of calls received by the service desk. An organization planning a new desk should attempt to predict the call arrival rate and profile and staff accordingly. Statistical analysis of call arrival rates of the current volumes or similar volumes will provide a good basis for understanding the requirements.

A common pattern of calls will be a peak in the mornings, with maybe another peak later in the day, around the early part of the afternoon. Each organization will be different, but it is common to find that there will be a recurring pattern. Staffing can then be adjusted to meet the demand.

A number of factors should be considered when choosing staffing levels, including customer service expectations and business requirements such as budget and call response times.

Self-help tools and automation of service request handling (e.g., password resets) will also have an impact on staffing levels, as will the size, relative age, design, and complexity of the IT infrastructure and service catalog. For example, staffing may be influenced by the number and type of incidents or the extent of customization deployed instead of standard off-the-shelf software.

There are clearly some factors that have a direct impact on the staffing levels of the service desk, such as the number of customers and users speaking a different language, the skill levels of the staff, and the types of calls handled. The duration of time required for call types (e.g., simple queries, specialist application queries, hardware, etc.) and whether or not local or external expertise is required for the volume and types of incidents and service requests are also factors.

Other factors will be the hours the service desk is taking calls, the after-hours support requirements, time zones to be covered, and locations to be supported (particularly if service desk staff also conduct desk-side support, given the travel time between locations). Understanding the pattern of requests (e.g., daily, end of the month) and the service level targets in place (response levels) will also have an impact, as will the type of responses required. There are a variety of contact mechanisms in use: telephone, email/voicemail/video, online chat, texting, and online access/control. The skill levels and the level of training required for staff to support the processes and procedures will identify the requirements for development of the service desk.

These are factors to be considered before making any decision on staffing levels. These factors should also be reflected in the levels of documentation required. Service desks are often victims of their own success because the better the service, the more the business will use it.

A number of tools are available to help determine the appropriate number of staff for the service desk. These workload modeling tools are dependent on detailed local knowledge of the organization, such as call volumes and patterns and service and user profiles. Industry standards suggest 1,000 users equals 104 calls/day, but this may not fit all organizations.

The skill levels for the service desk will be dependent on the nature of the requirements of the business. A basic call logging service where staff need only very basic technical skills will be able to handle a large volume of calls but will achieve a low resolution rate. A technical service desk staffed by the organization's most technically skilled staff members will have a high resolution rate but will not be able to handle a large volume, due to the time that needs to be spent on each call.

The required skills level will often depend on target resolution times (agreed with the business and captured in service level agreements), the complexity of the systems supported, and the business budget. There is a strong correlation between response and resolution targets and costs. Generally speaking, the shorter the target times, the higher the cost because more resources are required.

There is no rule about the way a service desk should be set up, but often organizations will start with a call logging approach, with technical skills second and third in line, and build up expertise at the service desk over time. A way of improving the first-line skill set is to consider the physical location of the second- and third-line support teams. Closer proximity will enable and foster information exchange and enable the utilization of the more technical support personnel to provide support and backup for peak periods for the service desk. It should be remembered, however, that second-line staff often have duties outside the service desk. In addition, having to deal with routine calls may be demotivating for more experienced staff. A further potential drawback is that the service desk focuses on resolving incidents, whereas second-line staff skills should be focused on removing the root cause instead. If second-line staff spend time on the service desk, they will have less time available for problem management.

It is worth noting that although successful problem management will improve service desk performance by providing known error resolutions, in the longer term it may lead to a reduced first-time fix rate at the service desk. This is because, as recurrent faults are permanently fixed, the service desk is dealing with more complex and individual calls. A falling fix rate therefore does not necessarily mean that the service desk service is deteriorating.

Once the required skill levels have been identified, it is important to ensure that personnel with the correct balance of skills are on duty so that consistency is maintained.

Service desks will need necessary ongoing training and awareness programs to cover interpersonal skills, such as telephony, communication, active listening, and customer care skills. Business awareness and specific knowledge of the organization's business areas, drivers, structure, and priorities are critical for effective support.

Service awareness of all the organization's key IT services for which support is being provided is also essential for the effective support of the organization. Depending on level of support provided, some diagnostic skills may be required, and the ability to use support tools and techniques will be important. All service desk staff are required to be trained on new systems and technologies prior to their introduction.

The service desk will need to be aware of the processes and procedures in the IT department, most particularly incident, request, change, and service asset and configuration management, but an overview of all ITSM processes and procedures is also valuable. Another useful skill is typing to ensure quick and accurate entry of incident or service request details.

To ensure that the service desk continues to perform as required, skill requirements and levels should be evaluated periodically and training records maintained. Careful formulation of staffing rotations or schedules should be maintained so that a consistent balance of staff experience and appropriate skill levels are present during all critical operational periods. It is important to have the correct blend of skills available.

Training

It is vital that all service desk staff are adequately trained before they are called upon to staff the service desk. This should include organizational induction and business awareness programs to ensure the staff are conversant with the organization they will support.

When starting on the service desk, new staff should initially "shadow" experienced staff (that is, sit with them and listen in on calls) before starting to take calls themselves with a mentor listening in and able to intervene and provide support where necessary. Mentoring is a useful technique to maintain training as the service desk personnel gain experience, and a mentor can be allocated for each service desk person as they progress through their career.

Service desk staff need training to keep their knowledge up-to-date and stay aware of new developments, services, and technologies. The timing of such events is critical so normal duties are not disrupted.

It is important to invest in the service desk to maintain a professional team. Traditionally, the service desk suffers from a high turnover of staff, but this can be mitigated by having staff progress into the organization rather than taking their knowledge away to a new company.

Staff Retention

It is very important that all IT managers recognize the importance of the service desk and the staff who work on it. High staff turnover is expensive because new staff have to be recruited and trained before they are fully effective. It is one of the common challenges in running a service desk. Any significant loss of staff can be disruptive and lead to inconsistency of service, so efforts should be made to make the service desk an attractive place to work.

Recognition of the importance of the service desk is vital, with reward packages, team-building exercises, and staff rotation to other activities (projects, second-line support, etc.). Good documentation and cross-training can support this approach.

The service desk can often be used as a stepping-stone into other, more technical or supervisory/managerial roles. However, care is needed to ensure that proper succession planning takes place so that the desk does not lose key expertise in any area at one time.

Super Users

The introduction of super users throughout the user community to act as liaison points with IT in general and the service desk in particular can be beneficial, particularly for specific application expertise. As they understand how the services support the business processes, they may be able to provide guidance regarding when and how the services should be used.

Super users can be given some additional training and used as a conduit for communications in both directions. It is important to note that super users should log all calls they deal with and not just those they pass on to IT. They will need access to, and training on how to use, the incident logging tools. This will ensure that valuable history regarding incidents and service quality is not lost.

They can also be used to cascade information from the service desk outward throughout their local user community, which can be useful in disseminating service details to all users very quickly.

It is important to ensure that the super users have the time and interest to perform the role. This will require commitment and support from their management.

Measuring Service Desk Performance

Metrics should be established so that service desk performance can be evaluated at regular intervals. This is important to assess the health, maturity, efficiency, and effectiveness of the service desk and recognize opportunities to improve its operations.

Metrics should not be viewed in isolation, and it is important to remember that metrics may drive behavior; for example, isolated measures of call closure may result in poor quality of customer/user satisfaction, because the driver for the support analyst is to close the call, not ensure that the customer is satisfied with the result.

Typical service desk metrics include call-handling statistics and first-line resolution rates. The first-line resolution rate is the figure often quoted by organizations as the primary measure of the service desk's performance. It's also used for comparison with the performance of other service desks, but care is needed when making any comparisons to ensure that there is a "like-for-like" comparison in terms of the nature of the support delivered and the technical capability of the desk.

Other service desk metrics include average times to achieve a particular target, for example, the average time to resolve an incident (when resolved at first line).

It may be important to understand the average time to escalate an incident (where first-line resolution is not possible). This will show that the service desk staff are efficient and recognize their limitations, and it will identify where the user will be best served by the escalation of a call to more expert resources.

Service desks are bound by service targets. The user experience of IT is often only based on their contact with the service desk and measured with the service desk service targets. So the percentage of customer or user updates conducted within target times, as defined in SLA targets, may be the only measure on which the users base their perception of the whole IT department.

The average time to review and close a resolved call will demonstrate the efficiency of the service desk in handling their workload.

The number of calls broken down by time of day and day of week, combined with the average call-time metric, is critical in determining the staff required. There are no hard and fast rules about staffing levels for a service desk, so this analysis is vital to understand each organization's individual requirements.

Further general details on metrics and how they should be used to improve the quality of service is included in the *ITIL Continual Service Improvement* core volume.

As well as tracking the "hard" measures of the service desk's performance, it is important to assess "soft" measures. These are expressed by how well the customers and users feel their calls have been answered, whether they feel the service desk operator was courteous and professional, and whether the operator instilled confidence in the user.

The only successful approach to soft measures is to obtain them from the users themselves. A common method for understanding service desk issues is through a call-back telephone survey, in which an independent service desk operator or supervisor calls back a small percentage of users shortly after their incident has been resolved to ask their opinion of the support they have received. Some ITSM tools have an automatic survey function—for example, every tenth resolved call will receive the survey.

This can be done as part of a wider customer/user satisfaction survey covering all of IT, or it can be specifically targeted at the service desk issues alone.

Care should be taken to keep the number of questions to a minimum so that users will have the time to cooperate. Survey questions should be designed so that the user or customer knows what area or topic the questions address and which incident or service they are referring to. To allow adequate comparisons of service over a given time period, the same percentage of calls should be selected in each period, and they should be rigorously carried out despite any other time pressures.

The service desk must act on low satisfaction levels and any feedback received.

Surveys are a complex and specialized area, requiring a good understanding of statistics and survey techniques, but it is not necessary to understand these as part of your studies of the ITIL Service Operation publication.

Table 4.1 lists some typical examples of surveys.

TABLE 4.1   Survey techniques and tools

Technique/Tool	Advantages	Disadvantages
After-call survey Callers are asked to remain on the phone after the call and then asked to rate the service.	High response rate because the caller is already on the phone. Caller is surveyed immediately after the call, so they can easily recall their experience.	People may feel pressured into taking the survey, resulting in a negative service experience. The surveyor is seen as part of the service desk being surveyed, which may discourage open answers.
Outbound telephone survey Customers and users who have previously used the service desk are contacted sometime after their experience.	Higher response rate because the caller is interviewed directly. Specific categories of users or customers can be targeted for feedback (e.g., people who requested a specific service, or people who experienced a disruption to a particular service).	This method could be seen as intrusive if the call disrupts the users' or customers' work. The survey is conducted sometime after the user or customer used the service desk, so their perception may have changed.

TABLE 4.1   Survey techniques and tools *(continued)*

Technique/Tool	Advantages	Disadvantages
Personal interviews Customers and users are interviewed personally by the person doing the survey. This is especially effective for customers or users who use the service desk extensively or who have had a very negative experience.	The interviewer is able to observe nonverbal signals as well as listen to what the user or customer is saying. Users and customers feel a greater degree of personal attention and a sense that their answers are being taken seriously.	Interviews are time consuming for both the interviewer and the respondent. Users and customers could turn the interviews into complaint sessions.
Group interviews Customers and users are interviewed in small groups. This is good for gathering general impressions and for determining whether there is a need to change certain aspects of the service desk (e.g., service hours or location).	A larger number of users and customers can be interviewed. Questions are more generic and therefore more consistent between interviews.	People may not express themselves freely in front of their peers or managers. People's opinions can easily be changed by others in the group during the interview.
Postal/email surveys Survey questionnaires are mailed to a target set of customers and users. They are asked to return their responses by email or regular mail.	Either specific or all customers or users can be targeted. Postal surveys can be anonymous, allowing people to express themselves more freely. Email surveys are not anonymous but can be created using automated forms that make it convenient and easy for users to reply and increase the likelihood surveys will be completed.	Postal surveys are labor intensive to process. The percentage of people responding to postal surveys tends to be small. Misinterpretation of a question could affect the result.
Online surveys Questionnaires are posted on a website, and users and customers are encouraged via email or links from a popular site to participate in the survey.	The potential audience of these surveys is fairly large. Respondents can complete the questionnaire in their own time. The links on popular websites are good reminders without being intrusive.	The type and percentage of respondents cannot be predicted.

Service Desk Environment

The environment where the service desk is to be located should be carefully chosen. It is important to remember that the staff will often be expected to remain in a single location for long periods of time, and so, where possible, the facilities should be provided to take the working conditions into consideration.

If the organization can provide a location where the entire function can be positioned with sufficient natural light and overall space to allow adequate desk and storage space and room to move around if necessary, this will make the working environment much more acceptable.

Service desk staff should have easy access to the correct equipment to support their responsibilities, such as consoles, monitoring displays, and message boards to quickly gain a picture of any key operating or service events or issues that may be taking place. Because the service desk is often busy, potentially handling many different conversations at once, a quiet environment with adequate acoustic control so that one telephone conversation is not disrupted by another is essential.

The service desk can be a very stressful place to work, and thoughtful use of space, furniture, and assistive technology such as cordless or noise-cancelling headsets can be beneficial. Many organizations have discovered that the provision of pleasant surroundings and comfortable furniture to lighten the mood helps with the management of stress. Consider the use of a separate restroom and refreshment area nearby so that staff can take short breaks when necessary, without being away for too long. Breakout areas that encourage relaxation can be very helpful in maintaining service desk morale.

Placing the service desk at the heart of the department, not hidden away, will encourage collaborative working with second- and third-line colleagues.

Outsourcing the Service Desk

Outsourcing the service desk, or any other area of IT, is a strategic business decision. The decision to outsource the service desk does not mean that the IT department has abdicated all responsibility for the service desk service that will be provided; the organization is ultimately accountable for the outcomes of the decision. There are some safeguards that are needed to ensure that the outsourced service desk works effectively and efficiently with the organization's other IT teams and departments and that end-to-end service management control is maintained. Some of these are specific to outsourcing the service desk; others are generic concerns whatever is being outsourced.

Common Tools and Processes

In an outsourced environment, the service desk tools must not only support the outsourced service desk, they must support the customer organization's processes and business requirements as well. Some of the challenges of outsourcing involve access to tools—from in-house staff needing access to the outsourcer's tools and data to the outsourced support teams needing access to in-house tools and data.

The service desk will need access to several different types of data to be effective:

- All incident records and information
- Problem records and information
- Known error data
- Change schedule
- Sources of internal knowledge (especially technical or application experts)
- SKMS
- CMS
- Alerts from monitoring tools

There may be security issues in allowing staff from another organization such access. Integrating different tools can be challenging, but integrating processes of two very different organizations, with different maturity levels and different cultures, is very complex. Outsourcing is dependent on successful integration between the organizations.

It is important for the organization to understand the capability of the outsource partner. It may be incorrectly assumed that service management quality and maturity in an external outsource partner can be guaranteed by stating requirements in the procurement process for "ITIL conformance" or "ISO/IEC 20000 certification." These statements may indicate that a potential supplier uses the ITIL framework in its delivery of services to customers, or that it has achieved standards certification for its internal practices. This is not a guarantee that its approach to outsourcing is managed in the same way.

SLA Targets

When considering outsourcing arrangements, there may be issues with operational level agreements (OLAs) and underpinning contracts (UCs) in a mixed-sourced environment, which can be complex and, if not well handled, could impact service.

The important fact is that the user must receive a seamless service even when there are a number of outsourced organizations involved in the delivery of the service. It is essential that OLAs and UCs with internal and external providers of the component parts of the service are agreed and realistic and are actually achieved.

Good Communications

In this complex situation, good communication will happen only if it is planned; the OLAs and UCs can specify how this should be done.

It is essential that the service desk can communicate with the users and the support and fulfillment teams. This is more difficult if they are not co-located, and it can be very challenging if the service desk is offshored as well as outsourced.

Training in the customer organization's tools and methods of operation will help, especially if the service desk staff attend identical training as the end users do so they understand the capability of the users.

Offshored service desks need to concentrate on achieving good communication with the users, despite possible cultural and language issues. Training programs can help, especially understanding idiomatic use of the language in the customer market.

Ownership of Data

Another important factor for an outsourced environment is that the management of data be well defined because some cross-access is essential while other data has to be kept confidential.

Ownership of all data relative to users, customers, affected CIs, services, incidents, service requests, changes, and so on must remain with the organization that is outsourcing the activity, but both organizations will require access to it. Data that is related specifically to performance of employees of the outsourcing company (the company carrying out the work on behalf of the main organization) will remain the property of that company.

All reporting requirements and issues around ownership of data must be specified in the underpinning contract with the company providing the outsourcing service.

Summary

In this chapter, we explored the service desk function and how it contributes to service operation. We considered the role, objectives, and structures relating to the service desk, and potential staffing options. We also reviewed service desk performance metrics and the issues relating to in- or outsourcing the service desk.

We examined the following key ITIL concepts:

- Call center
- Follow the sun
- Single point of contact
- Super user

Exam Essentials

Understand the role and importance of the service desk function.   Be able to explain the difference between a call center and a service desk, and its role in the incident management and request fulfillment processes and any other processes that the service desk will interface with.

Be able to list and explain the skills and attributes that are required for service desk staff. Understand why the skills and attributes of business awareness, technical awareness, and customer focus are required for the role.

Be able to describe the different service desk structures.   Be able to describe the service desk structures of local, central, virtual, and follow the sun. Understand when each might be used, and the advantages and disadvantages of each option.

Understand the safeguards required when outsourcing the service desk.   Be able to explain the importance of the ultimate accountability for the service remaining with the organization, and the need to retain ownership of data. Understand the issues regarding shared tools, and the need for common processes.

Review Questions

You can find the answers to the review questions in the appendix.

1.   The service desk is *not* responsible for which of the following?
    A.   Providing a first point of contact
    B.   Resolving straightforward incidents
    C.   Preventing incidents from recurring
    D.   Providing updates to users

2.   The service desk carries out two processes. What are they?
    1.   Incident management
    2.   Design coordination
    3.   Request fulfillment
    4.   Change management
        A.   2 and 4
        B.   1 and 3
        C.   All of the above
        D.   3 and 4

3.   Which of the following should service desk staff members possess?
    1.   Detailed application knowledge
    2.   Interpersonal skills
    3.   Technical ability
    4.   Business knowledge
        A.   2 and 3
        B.   1 and 2
        C.   All of the above
        D.   2, 3, and 4

4.   Which of the following is *not* a service desk structure described in ITIL?
    A.   Virtual
    B.   Matrix
    C.   Follow the sun
    D.   Local

5.   Which of the following information sources should be available to the service desk staff?
    1.   Change schedule
    2.   Configuration management system covering the infrastructure and applications supported

3. Known error database

4. Incident diagnostic scripts

    A. 1 and 2

    B. All of the above

    C. 3 and 4

    D. 1, 2, and 3

6. Which of the following are valid performance indicators for the service desk?

  1. Percentage of incidents closed without escalation to another team

  2. Percentage of incidents correctly categorized at logging

  3. Number of hardware incidents logged

  4. Customer satisfaction survey scores

    A. All of the above

    B. 1, 2, and 3

    C. 3 and 4

    D. 1, 2, and 4

7. Which of these is a DIRECT benefit of having a service desk?

    A. Customer service level requirements are documented.

    B. Technical support staff do not spend time resolving simple incidents.

    C. Requests for change are authorized before implementation.

    D. All the information in the CMS is kept up to date.

8. Which of the following is/are potential benefit(s) of utilizing designated super users?

  1. Super users can deal with simple queries without the need for logging incidents, reducing the workload of the service desk.

  2. Super users can provide a point of coordination with the business, especially when information needs to be communicated, such as during major incidents.

  3. Super users understand the business context in which IT services are used.

  4. Super users can approach support teams directly as required, saving the time that would otherwise be spent logging the incident at the service desk.

    A. 2 and 3

    B. All of the above

    C. 1, 2, and 3

    D. 3 and 4

9. Which is the BEST description of a virtual service desk?

    A. The desk is based in the same location as the user community it serves.

    B. The desk uses telephony to give the impression that multiple desks in multiple locations are actually a single desk.

    C. The desk provides 24 hour global support, with calls being diverted to different countries, dependent on the time of day.

    D. Service desk staff answer calls during the working day with calls are diverted to on-call support staff outside those times.

10. Which of the following statements are correct when an organization outsources the service desk?

1. The supplier of the outsourced service desk is accountable for the level of service provided.

2. The supplier of the outsourced service desk is responsible for the level of service provided.

3. The senior management of the organization is accountable for the level of service provided.

4. The outsourcer determines what service will be provided.

    A. 2, 3, and 4 only

    B. 2 and 3 only

    C. 1 and 2 only

    D. 1, 2, and 4 only

Chapter

5

Technical Management, Application Management, and IT Operations Management

---

THE FOLLOWING ITIL OPERATIONAL SUPPORT AND ANALYSIS CAPABILITY INTERMEDIATE EXAM OBJECTIVES ARE DISCUSSED IN THIS CHAPTER:

✓ **Technical management**

- ■ Technical management role
- ■ Objectives
- ■ Activities
- ■ Organization
- ■ Metrics
- ■ Documentation

✓ **Application management**

- ■ Application management role
- ■ Objectives
- ■ Activities
- ■ Organization
- ■ Metrics
- ■ Documentation

✓ **IT operations management**

- ■ Activities
- ■ Organization

This chapter continues to explore how the IT service provider organizes to deliver the services to the required standard. The service operation stage is when the service is actually being delivered, and often it takes much longer than the previous stages of strategy, design, and transition. We will cover the purpose, objectives, and scope for the remaining functions of technical management, application management, and IT operations management along with the value they provide to the business.

When applied to an IT environment, operations management covers the aspect of the business that maintains and optimizes the IT services on a daily basis. In smaller organizations, this concept of separation in such detail may seem confusing; it may just be that everyone supporting the infrastructure is involved with the operations management function as well as the technical management function. It is important to remember that these are functions, not specific organizational structures.

ITIL Functions

ITIL describes four main functions that are responsible for carrying out all the lifecycle processes. These are technical management, application management, IT operations management, and the service desk. We have reviewed the service desk (see Chapter 4, "The Service Desk"), so now we will move on to the remaining functions. The IT operations management function is further divided into IT operations control and facilities management. We will cover each of these in turn and then look at where the responsibilities of each function overlap. It is important to remember that ITIL is not prescriptive and does not specify an organizational structure or specific names for teams within an organization. The responsibilities of the functions described here should be carried out, but each organization will have its own structure.

Technical Management

Whatever the name given to the team or teams in any particular organization (infrastructure support, technical support, network management, and so on), the function referred to in the ITIL framework as *technical management* is required to manage and develop the IT infrastructure. This function covers the groups or teams that together have the technical expertise and knowledge to ensure that the infrastructure works effectively in support of the services required by the business.

Role

The technical management function has a number of responsibilities:

- It is responsible for managing the IT infrastructure. This would include ensuring that the staff members performing this function have the necessary technical knowledge to design, test, manage, and improve IT services.

- Although we discuss this function under service operation, the function provides appropriately skilled staff members to support the entire lifecycle. Technical management staff members would be involved in drawing up the technical strategy and ensuring that the infrastructure can support the overall service strategy. Technical management staff members would also carry out the technical design of new or changed services and would be involved in planning and implementing their transition to the operational environment.

- Once the service is live, technical management provides technical support, resolving incidents, investigating problems, responding to alerts, and specifying any changes or updates required to have the service operate efficiently. Technical management staff members will identify service improvements and work with the CSI manager to design, test, and implement these improvements.

It is the responsibility of the manager or managers of this function to ensure the correct number of staff members, with the correct skills to carry out the required tasks. Specifying the numbers and skill levels required is discussed as part of the lifecycle stage strategy and detailed as part of the lifecycle stage of service design. Transition tests that the staff members are able to support the service as designed, and CSI identifies any improvements or training requirements. The technical manager must decide whether to employ new staff members with the correct skills, train existing staff members, or use short-term contract resources to meet a particular requirement. Larger organizations may have a team of subject matter experts that can be called on when required by subsidiary departments, without the need for those skills to be developed across the organization.

Most of the everyday operational support activities will be undertaken by the operations support staff members, but it is the responsibility of technical management, as the experts in the technology, to guide and support the operations staff members.

Objectives

The objectives of technical management are as follows:

- Providing the appropriate technical infrastructure to support the business processes. This should take account of the availability and capacity requirements, providing a stable resilient infrastructure at an affordable cost.

- Planning and designing the technical aspects of any new or changed service.

- Implementing these technical aspects and supporting them in the live environment, using the technical expertise that the function possesses to ensure that any issues that arise are swiftly resolved.

Generic Technical Management Activities

Technical management is involved in two types of activity. This includes activities that are generic to the technical management function as a whole. The other type of activity is linked to the processes that are performed by all three of the functions (technical, application, and IT operations management).

In this section, we will explore the activities that enable technical management to execute its role.

Technical management is responsible for identifying the knowledge and expertise required to manage and operate the IT infrastructure and to deliver IT services. This process starts during the service strategy stage, is expanded in detail in service design, and is executed in service transition and service operation. Ongoing assessment and updating of these skills is done during CSI. In this way, technical management operates throughout the service lifecycle.

This function is also responsible for documenting the technical skills that exist in the service provider organization as well as skills that need to be developed. This will include the development of skills inventories and the performance of technical training needs analyses. Following this, it will be technical management that initiates training programs to develop and refine the skills in the appropriate technical resources and maintains training records for all technical resources.

The technical management function should have the appropriate skills to design and deliver training for users, the service desk, and other groups. Although training requirements must be defined in service design, they are executed in service operation. If there is no capability to deliver training, technical management will be responsible for identifying organizations that can provide it.

Technical management takes responsibility for managing the acquisition of skills that cannot be developed internally—for example, by recruiting or contracting additional resources. They also are responsible for acquisition of additional skills when an insufficient number of people are available to perform the required technical management activities.

This function will also be involved in procuring skills for specific activities when the required skills are not available internally or in the open market, or when it is more cost efficient to hire specialists.

During the service strategy and design stages, technical management will define the standards to be used in the design of new architectures and participate in the definition of technology architectures. As the repository of technical expertise, the function will also be responsible for research and development solutions that can help expand the service portfolio or be used to simplify or automate IT operations, reduce costs, or increase levels of IT service.

Additional activities for technical management include involvement in the design and build of new services. Technical management will contribute to the design of the technical architecture and performance standards for IT services. In addition, it will be responsible for specifying the operational activities required to manage the IT infrastructure on an ongoing basis.

Technical management will be participating in projects, not only during service design and service transition, but also for CSI or operational projects, such as operating system upgrades, server consolidation projects, and physical moves.

Modeling and workload forecasting are often done with technical management resources so that availability and capacity management for IT services meet the levels of service required by the business. This will also require assessing risk, identifying critical service and system dependencies, and defining and implementing countermeasures.

Technical management activities should include designing and performing tests for the functionality, performance, and manageability of IT services to support service transition activities. The function may also be engaged in managing suppliers; many technical management departments or groups are the only ones who know exactly what is required of a supplier and how to measure and manage them. For this reason, many organizations rely on technical management departments to manage contracts with suppliers of specific CIs. If this is the case, it is important to ensure that these relationships are managed as part of the SLM and supplier management processes.

It is obvious that as a function with service operation responsibilities, technical management will play a large role in the operational processes. For example, it will take the lead in defining and managing event management standards and tools. Technical management should test event mechanisms during service transition and will also monitor and respond to many categories of events during service operation.

It is crucial that technical management departments or groups are integral to the performance of incident management. They receive incidents through functional escalation and provide second- and higher-level support. They are also involved in maintaining categories and defining the escalation procedures that are executed in incident management. They can provide scripts to ensure that correct incident details are captured and workarounds to assist the service desk in first-line resolution.

Technical management as a function provides resources that contribute to the execution of the problem management process. It provides technical expertise and knowledge that is used to diagnose and resolve problems. It also maintains relationships with the suppliers and their support teams that are used to escalate and follow up on technical issues, changes, incidents, and problems. They play an important part in defining coding systems that are used in incident and problem management (e.g., incident categories) and supporting problem management in validating and maintaining the known error database.

But as you have already seen, it is not only operational processes that gain value from this function; other lifecycle stages, such as service transition, will also benefit. Technical management will support the change management process where reliance on technical knowledge and expertise may be needed to evaluate changes and will assist with the deployment of releases.

In cooperation with application management, technical management will provide information for, and operationally maintain, the CMS and its data. This will be done to ensure that the correct CI attributes and relationships are created from the deployment of services and the ongoing maintenance over the life of CIs.

Technical management is involved in the CSI activities, identifying opportunities for improvement, particularly in highlighting areas for improvement and then helping evaluate alternative solutions.

System and operating documentation needs to be maintained and kept up-to-date and properly utilized. This includes ensuring that all management, administration, and user manuals are up-to-date and complete and that technical staff are familiar with their contents. This needs to be done by those who have sufficient technical expertise, and the resources will often be provided through technical management.

Technical management will also be responsible for updating and maintaining data used for reporting on technical and service capabilities (e.g., capacity and performance management, availability management, problem management) as well as for assisting financial management for IT services to identify the cost of technology and IT human resources used to manage IT services.

Many technical management departments, groups, or teams define the operational activities performed as part of IT operations management as well as performing the operational activities as part of an organization's IT operations management function.

Technical Management Organization

Technical management is not normally provided by a single department or group. It is usual to find one or more technical support teams or departments providing technical management and support for the IT infrastructure. In all but the smallest organizations, where a single combined team or department may have to cover everything, separate teams or departments may be needed for each type of infrastructure being used.

Because technical management consists of a number of technological areas—each of which may require a specific set of skills to manage and operate it—there may be a number of teams. Some skill sets are related and can be performed by generalists, whereas others are specific to a component, system, or platform.

The principle of technical management organizational structure is that people are grouped according to their technical skill sets and that these skill sets are determined by the technology that needs to be managed.

Technical Design and Technical Maintenance and Support

In the ITIL framework, technical management teams include both specialist technical architects and designers (who are primarily involved during service design) and specialist maintenance and support staff (who are primarily involved during service operation).

Many organizations see them as two separate teams or even departments. The challenge of a separated approach is that good design needs input from the people who are required to manage the solution, and good operation requires involvement from the people who designed the solution. In other words, support staff should be involved during the design or architecture of a solution.

If possible, it is advisable to introduce measures to support the technical function approach, so designers should be held accountable for their portion of the design flaws that create operational outages, and support staff should be held accountable for their contribution to the technical architecture.

Measuring Technical Management Performance

The performance metrics for technical management will largely depend on which technology is being managed, but some generic metrics are listed next.

Measurement of Agreed Outputs

The following outputs could be measured:

- Transaction rates and availability for critical business transactions
- Service desk training
- Problem resolutions recorded into the KEDB
- User measures of the quality of outputs as defined in the SLAs

Process Metrics

Technical management teams execute many service management process activities that could be measured:

- Response time to events and event completion rates
- Incident resolution times for second- and third-line support
- Problem resolution statistics
- Number of escalations and reason for those escalations
- Number of changes implemented and backed out

Technology Performance

These metrics are based on service design specifications and will typically be contained in OLAs or standard operating procedures (SOPs). Actual metrics will vary by technology but are likely to include the following:

- Utilization rates (memory or processor for server, bandwidth for networks)
- Availability of systems, network, devices, and other resources
- Accuracy of information and data that is being presented
- Performance (e.g., response times or queuing rates)

Mean Time between Failures of Specified Equipment

This metric is used to ensure that good purchasing decisions are being made and that the equipment is being properly maintained (the latter when compared with maintenance schedules).

Measurement of Maintenance Activity

The following metrics provide information on maintenance activity:

- Maintenance performed per schedule
- Number of maintenance windows exceeded
- Maintenance objectives achieved (number and percentage).

Training and Skills Development

These metrics ensure that technical staff members have the skills and training to manage the technology that is under their control:

- Achieved skills performance levels

- Number of calls and escalations to third-party or other internal subject matter experts for additional help and support

- Percentage of incidents caused by technical staff skills issues

The areas of measurement include agreed outputs and process metrics. It will be important to measure technology performance, including the mean time between failures for specific equipment. Understanding the success of maintenance activity is equally important for this function. Because technical management will be responsible for training, it is important to measure the effectiveness of training and skills development.

Technical Management Documentation

Technical management is involved in drafting and maintaining several documents as part of other processes (e.g., capacity planning, change management, and problem management). There will be some documents that are specific to the technical management groups or teams, such as technical documentation for CIs (e.g., technical manuals and administration manuals).

During the design lifecycle phase, technical management will be part of the creation of maintenance schedules for the infrastructure. They will also maintain a skills inventory in line with the processes, architectures, and performance standards, which will enable the identification of training requirements. It is important to remember that skills inventories provide information about the capability of the department for the delivery of service as well as identifying technical training needs.

IT Operations Management

In business, the term *operations management* is used to mean the department, group, or team of people responsible for performing the organization's day-to-day operational activities, such as running the production line in a manufacturing environment or managing the distribution centers and fleet movements within a logistics organization. It is useful to consider IT operations management in the same way.

We will now explore the IT operations management function and how it contributes to service operation. We will look at the IT operations management role and how to balance requirements. We will review the objectives, organization, metrics, and documentation relating to the function and how it supports service operation as a lifecycle stage.

The role of IT operations management is to carry out all the day-to-day activities that are required to deliver and support the services provided. The applications and technical management functions are the subject matter experts in their respective fields and define what operational activities are to take place; operations management's role is to make sure these are done.

The service design stage defined the required service levels, and the transition phase carried out tests to ensure that they were achievable; operations management is responsible for ensuring that these service levels are met consistently. Although the primary focus is on stability and availability, operations management will seek to continually improve by implementing changes that will help protect the live service or by reducing costs and opportunities for human error by implementing automation of routine tasks wherever possible.

The quality of the service delivered to the business depends on operations management. This role is divided into two parts: IT operations control and facilities management.

IT Operations Control

This part of operations management oversees the IT infrastructure. In larger organizations, this may be carried out as part of an operations bridge or network operations center (NOC). In these organizations, there are dedicated staff members monitoring operational events on consoles and reacting to them as necessary, often in a separate area from the rest of IT. In smaller organizations, the line between technical management and operations control may be more blurred, with operations control carried out by the technical management team, who monitor the systems from their desks, perhaps with one or two wall-mounted plasma screens. Whichever arrangement is chosen depends on what suits the organization, but it is important that there are clearly defined expectations to ensure that the operations control tasks are carried out to the level required.

The operations control tasks are as follows:

- The centralized monitoring and management of system events, as discussed, sometimes referred to as *console management.*

- The scheduling and management of batch jobs to carry out routine tasks such as database updates.

- Carrying out backups of data and ensuring that this data can be restored if and when required. This may include the backup of entire systems or the restoration of individual files that a user may have corrupted.

- Although most printing is now carried out directly by the users, there may be certain requirements for centralized printing; pay slips will need to be printed in a secure environment to ensure confidentiality, and large print volumes may make centralized printing more efficient. The printing and distribution of these and other electronic output is an operations control task.

- Management of the output from any control activities should also be undertaken, such as distribution.

- Operations control may also undertake maintenance activities, under the guidance of the technical or application management functions; this could include archiving data, applying system packs, updating virus signatures, and so on.

Facilities Management

The other part of IT operations management is *facilities management.* Staff members involved in this will be responsible for the physical IT environment. This would include the following:

- Ensuring that the necessary power is supplied (including any requirements for its quality, such as the prevention of power spikes) at operational and recovery sites.

- Operating and maintaining uninterruptible power supply (UPS) devices and generators. Facilities management is responsible for ensuring that these are available and for testing to ensure that they will work as designed in the event of a power failure. This role may cover just a server room in a smaller organization or one or more data centers for larger ones.
- Ensuring the maintenance of satisfactory air-conditioning/cooling for rooms housing IT equipment, whether this is a server room or a complete data center for either operational or recovery sites.

Many organizations have undertaken data center or server consolidation projects in recent years to take advantage of technical advances. The facilities management function would be responsible for managing any such projects. In the case where the data center management is carried out by a third party, it would be the responsibility of facilities management to ensure that the external service provider was carrying out the required tasks to the agreed standard and managing any exceptions utilizing the supplier management process.

To be effective, operations management needs to understand the technology and how it supports the services provided, although this level of knowledge will be less than that provided by the technical and application management functions. There is a risk that operations staff members do not interact with the business as part of their work and so may fail to appreciate the business impact of failures or to understand the business importance of services, thinking of them in purely technical terms. It is essential that they have adequate understanding of the business aspect; the information showing how technology supports the business is available in the service knowledge management system (SKMS), but specific training may be required to ensure that they have the necessary appreciation of the impact technology has on the business.

The importance of stability of services has been already mentioned; one way of maintaining that stability is to ensure that routine tasks are carried out consistently, no matter which staff members are on shift. This requires that properly documented procedures and technical manuals are available to operations staff members.

The performance of the operations management function should be measured against clear objectives based on the performance of the service, not merely of the technology. Delivering the service to the required level, within the agreed cost, is essential, so operations management should be able to demonstrate the effectiveness of what they do but also prove that they are operating at maximum efficiency. Operations management should always strive to optimize the use of existing technology and exploit new technical advances to provide the required level of service at the best cost.

Objectives

The objectives of IT operations management include continuing to provide stable services to enable the business to obtain the business benefits identified as part of the strategy, documented in design, built and tested in transition, delivered in operation, while also investigating possible improvements to enable the services to be provided more cost-effectively.

Service operation's other objectives are to overcome any failures that do occur as quickly as possible in order to minimize the impact to the business and to maintain service quality as new services are introduced.

Figure 5.1 illustrates that IT operations management is seen as a function in its own right but that, in the majority of organizations, staff from technical and application management groups form part of this function.

FIGURE 5.1   Service operation functions

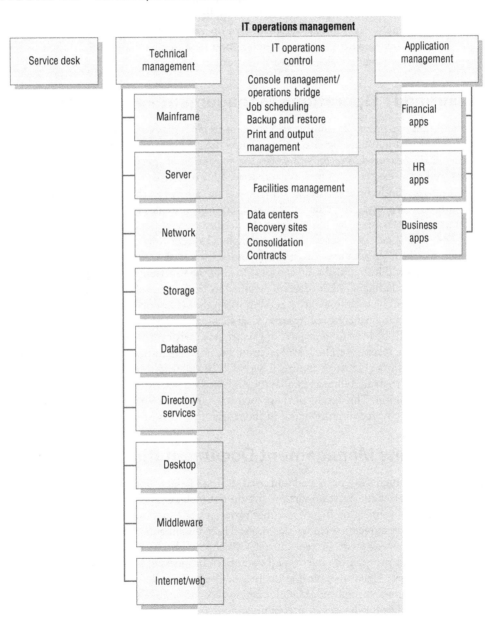

Some technical and application management departments or groups will manage and execute their own operational activities, whereas others will delegate these activities to a dedicated IT operations department.

Each organization is different and has its own requirements, so there is no single method for assigning activities because it depends on the maturity and stability of the infrastructure being managed. For example, technical and application management functions that are fairly new and unstable tend to manage their own operations. Groups where the technology or application is stable, mature, and well understood tend to have standardized their operations more. This will enable delegation of these activities.

Measuring IT Operations Management Performance

As with all lifecycle processes and functions, measurement plays an important part in understanding and maintaining effectiveness and efficiency. IT operations management performance is measured in terms of its effective execution of specified activities and procedures as well as its execution of process activities. This is an area in which numerous examples of measures might be applied, but they should be tailored to the needs of the individual organization in measuring the true value that operations provides in business terms.

Examples of key metrics used to measure the performance of the IT operations function can include the percentage of scheduled jobs completed successfully on time or the number of exceptions to scheduled activities and jobs. Quantification of the number of data or system restores required will help understand the workload of the function, as will equipment installation statistics, including number of items installed by type, successful installations, and so on. This in turn will be used to identify and report on the cost of operational activities.

IT operations management executes many service management process activities. Its ability to do so will be measured as part of the process metrics where appropriate, and some examples are response times, resolution times, implementation timescales for changes and releases, and their success or failure. There will be financial process measures and measures relating to availability and capacity, all based on activities carried out by the IT operations function. The details of these measures are best considered as part of the processes and are covered in more detail in the relevant process areas across the lifecycle.

IT Operations Management Documentation

A number of documents are produced and used during IT operations management. In this section we summarize the most important and do not include reports that are produced by IT operations management on behalf of other processes or functions.

The first set of documents includes the SOPs. These documents represent the routine work for every device, system, or procedure. SOPs should also include specific security administration procedures covering all operational aspects of service, system, data, and physical security. They also outline the procedures to be followed if an exception is detected or if a change is required. SOP documents could also be used to define standard levels of performance for devices or procedures.

In some organizations, instead of listing detailed performance measures, the SOP documents are referred to in the OLA. A clause is inserted to refer to the performance standards in the SOP and how they will be measured and reported.

Any activity that is conducted as part of IT operations should be recorded in an operations log because they can be used to confirm the successful completion of specific jobs or activities or that an IT service was delivered as agreed. They are the basis for reports on the performance of the IT operations management teams and departments. The format of these logs is as varied as the number of systems and operations management teams or departments. They may also be used to support problem management, enabling research into the root cause of incidents.

Where required, IT operations will be responsible for managing shift patterns. Not all organizations will have a 24-hour operation, but where one does exist, shift schedules are used to outline the exact activities that need to be carried out during the shift. They will also list all dependencies and activity sequences. There will probably be more than one shift schedule; each team will have a version for its own systems. It is important that all schedules are coordinated before the start of the shift. This is usually done with the help of scheduling tools by a person who specializes in shift scheduling.

Shift reports are similar to operations logs, but they have additional functions to record major events and actions that occurred during the shift and to form part of the handover between shift leaders. They will be used to report exceptions to service maintenance objectives and identify uncompleted activity that might impact performance in the next service hours.

Operations schedules are similar to shift schedules but cover all aspects of IT operations at a high level. This schedule can include reviews of the "forward schedule of change" document and an overview of all planned change actions as well as information about maintenance, routine jobs, and additional work. It can also include information about upcoming business or vendor events. The operations schedule may be used as the basis for a daily operations meeting. It may also be used for IT operations managers to track progress and detect exceptions.

Applications Management

The final function described in the ITIL framework is *application management*. This function shares many features with the technical management function, although in this case it is the application software that is supported and managed throughout its lifecycle rather than the infrastructure. Application management and application development are not the same, and it is important to understand the differences between them:

- Application *management* is involved in every stage of the service lifecycle, from ascertaining the requirements through design and transition and then to operation and improvement.

- Application *development* is mostly involved in single, finite activities, such as designing and building a new service. We discuss this in more detail later in this chapter.

As with technical management, the application management function may be called something different in many organizations. Whichever teams of staff members are responsible for managing and supporting operational software applications is the application management function. As with technical management, this function may be split across a number of teams.

Application management may carry out some tasks as part of application development projects, such as design or testing. This is not the same as the work of application development itself.

Role

The application management function is involved in all applications. Even when the function has recommended purchase of the application from an external supplier, there is still a requirement for management activities to take place. These activities are similar to those of the technical management function:

- The application management function is responsible for managing the IT applications. This includes ensuring that the staff members performing this function have the necessary technical knowledge to design, test, manage, and improve the applications that form part of the IT services.

- It is the custodian of technical knowledge and expertise related to managing applications.

- Although we discuss this function under service operation, it provides appropriately skilled staff members to support the entire lifecycle. Application management staff members would be involved in drawing up the application strategy. They would carry out the design of new or changed applications and would be involved in planning and implementing their transition to the operational environment. Once the service is live, application management provides support, resolving incidents, investigating problems, and specifying changes or updates required to have the service operate efficiently. Application management staff members will identify service improvements and work with the CSI manager to design, test, and implement them.

Application management staffing and training responsibilities are the same as those identified for technical management, and the function similarly interacts with the other stages of the lifecycle.

Application management also performs other specific roles:

- Application support ensures that the operations management staff members are given the correct training to enable the applications to be run efficiently. They also contribute to the training for users so that the users can competently use the new or changed applications to support their business functions.

- As part of service design, application management may carry out a training needs analysis covering the service operation staff members and provide the required training, but this role is a continuous one, providing day-to-day support to the operations staff members.

Objectives

The objectives of application management are to do the following:

- Identify functional and manageability requirements for application software.
- Help in the design of applications.
- Assist in their deployment.
- Support the applications in the live environment.
- Identify and implement improvements.

To be successful, application management must ensure that applications are well designed, taking account of both the utility and warranty aspects of service design. They must be able to deliver the right functionality at a reasonable cost if the business benefit is to be realized. The provision of the correct numbers of appropriately skilled staff members is essential so that these skills may be applied to resolve any application failures.

Application Management Principles

Application management is responsible for choosing whether to buy an application that supports the required business functionality or build the application specifically for the organization's requirements. The decisions are often made at a senior management level, perhaps by a chief technical officer (CTO) or steering committee, but they are dependent on information from a number of sources. This is covered as part of service design, but from an application management function perspective, there are a number of considerations that will require application management expertise and input.

Application management will explore the capability of existing applications to deliver the required functionality and, if it requires customization, consider the implications and cost to the organization. They will assist by providing application sizing and workload forecasts and specifying manageability requirements, ongoing operational costs, and the requirements for reporting or integration into other applications.

Another important aspect is identifying what skills will be required to support the solution and the impact of administration and security requirements.

Once a decision has been made to build, then a further decision has to be made on whether the development will be outsourced or built using in-house employees. To achieve this, there must be recognition of the management of the requirements, the acceptance criteria, and management of the operational environment.

This will require a clear understanding of the operational model, which is the specification of the operational environment in which the application will eventually run when it goes live. The operational model should be used for testing and transition prior to live operation.

Application Management Lifecycle

There are many names for the lifecycle in which applications are developed and managed, including the software lifecycle (SLC) and software development lifecycle (SDLC), both of which are used by application development teams and their project managers. Examples of these lifecycle approaches are structured systems analysis and design methodology (SSADM), dynamic systems development method (DSDM), and rapid application development (RAD).

Although these are important for any organization, ITIL is primarily interested in the overall management of applications as part of IT services, whether the applications are developed in-house or purchased from a third party.

In Figure 5.2, you can see the six steps in the lifecycle, which applies to both developed and purchased software.

FIGURE 5.2 Application management lifecycle

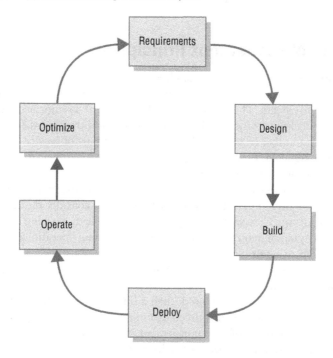

The SDL is a valid approach used by developers, especially third-party software companies. So there should be alignment between the development view of applications and the ongoing lifecycle management of those applications.

The basic lifecycle is used even for large third-party applications, like email, in that whatever the size of the application, it will need requirements, design, customization, operation, and deployment. Optimization is achieved through better management, improvements to customization, and upgrades.

The application management lifecycle is not an alternative to the service management lifecycle. Applications are part of services and have to be managed as such. Applications require a specialized focus at each stage of the service management lifecycle.

In the next sections, we'll review each step of the application management lifecycle.

Requirements

Obviously, as the name suggests, the requirements stage is the stage during which the requirements for a new application are gathered, based on the business needs of the organization. As you would expect, this stage is active primarily during the service design stage of the service lifecycle.

There are six types of requirements for any application, whether it is developed in-house, outsourced, or purchased.

The first is the functional requirements, which are specifically required to support a particular business function. Then we have the manageability requirements; the application is looked at from a service management perspective, and these requirements address the need for a responsive, available, and secure service and deal with issues such as deployment, operations, system management, and security. Next come the usability requirements that address the needs of the end user and result in features of the system that facilitate its ease of use. Architectural requirements are needed if a change to existing architecture standards is required.

Most applications will not be stand-alone, so an important factor is to identify the interface requirements. These are needed where there are dependencies between existing applications or tools and the new application.

Finally, but not because they are less important, there are service level requirements. These specify how the service should perform, the quality of its output, and any other qualitative aspects measured by the user or customer.

Design

The design stage includes the design of the application itself and the design of the environment, or the operational model that the application has to run on, as the requirements are translated into specifications.

Architectural considerations for the application (design of the application architecture) and architectural considerations for the operation model (design of the system architecture) are strongly related and need to be aligned. Architectural considerations are the most important aspect of this stage because they can have an impact on the structure and content of both the application and the operational model.

In the case of purchased software, it is unlikely that an organization will be allowed direct input to the design of the software because it has already been built. However, it is important that application management be able to provide feedback to the software vendor about the functionality, manageability, and performance of the software. This should be a part of the continual improvement of the software. A good vendor will be responsive to improvements but should ensure that there is a balance between being responsive and changing the software so much that it is disruptive or that it changes some basic functionality.

The design stage for purchased software should include the design of any customization that is required. It is important to evaluate the capability of future versions of the software to support importing and maintaining the customization. It is common to discover that with each successive upgrade, the actual time for release gets longer in order to reapply existing customization to the product.

Build

In this stage, both the application and the operational model are made ready for deployment. Application components are coded or acquired and then integrated and tested.

Testing is an integral component of both the build and deploy stages because it is a validation of the activity and output of those stages, even if different environments and staff are used. Testing in the build stage focuses on whether the application meets its functionality and manageability specifications. The test environment allows for testing the combination of application and operational models.

For purchased software, this will involve the actual purchase of the application, any required middleware, and the related hardware and networking equipment. If customization is required, a pilot implementation by the relevant application management team or department will need to be done. The creation of tables, categories, and so on that will be used should be tested for success before full implementation.

Deploy

In the deploy stage, both the operational model and the application are deployed. The operational model is incorporated into the existing IT environment, and the application is installed on top of the operational model using the release and deployment management process, as described in the ITIL Service Transition publication.

Testing takes place during this stage as well, although here the emphasis is on ensuring that the deployment process and mechanisms work effectively—for example, testing whether the application still performs to specification after it has been downloaded and installed. Specialized support for a new or changed IT service for a period of time after it is released is known as early life support (ELS). Support activities during this period can include review of KPIs, service levels, and monitoring thresholds and provision of additional resources for incident and problem management. ELS is covered in detail in the ITIL Service Transition publication.

Operate

In the operate stage, the IT services organization operates the application as part of delivering a service required by the business.

It is important to understand that applications are not a service. It is common in many organizations to refer to applications as services, but applications are only one component of many needed to provide a business service. The performance of the application in relation to the overall service is measured continually against the service levels and key business drivers.

The operate stage is not exclusive to applications but exists for any product, technology, or service provision.

Optimize

During this stage, the results of the service level performance measurements are analyzed and acted on. This is when possible improvements are discussed and developments are initiated if necessary. The two main strategies in this stage are to maintain and/or improve the service levels and to lower cost. This could lead to a repeat of the lifecycle or to justified retirement of an application.

An important thing to remember about the application management lifecycle is that the same application can reside in different stages of the lifecycle at the same time. This obviously requires strong version, configuration, and release control; for example, when the next version of an application is being designed and the current version is being deployed, the previous version might still be in operation in parts of the organization.

Some stages might take longer or seem more significant than others, but they are all crucial.

It is critical that information be passed along by those handling the application in one stage of its existence to those handling it in the next stage. Good communication is essential as an application works its way through the stages of the lifecycle. It is also important that an organization monitor the quality of the application management lifecycle. Understanding the characteristics of every stage in the application management lifecycle is vital to improving the quality of the whole. Methods and tools used in one stage might have an impact on others, whereas optimization of one stage might have a negative impact on the whole.

Application Management Generic Activities

The exact nature of the role will vary depending on the applications being supported, but application management teams or departments will be needed for all key applications. There are a number of generic activities, which we will briefly explore in this section.

Similar to technical management, the generic activities include the identification and provision of knowledge and expertise to manage and support the application and management of training to use or support the application.

Further activities will include recruiting or contracting resources with skills that cannot be developed internally. Resources will also need to be recruited when there are not enough people to perform the required application management activities.

Application management is responsible for designing and delivering end-user training. Training may be developed and delivered by either the application development or application management groups or by a third party, but application management is responsible for ensuring that training is conducted as appropriate. It is important to understand the staffing requirements and the most cost-effective way to provide them. This may include outsourcing for specific activities where the required skills are not available internally or in the open market or where it is more cost-efficient to do so.

During the definition of application architectures (as part of the service strategy processes), application management should help to define standards used in the design of new architectures. They should also play a major part in researching and developing solutions that can help expand the service portfolio or can be used to simplify or automate IT operations, reduce costs, or increase levels of IT service.

Application management should participate in the design and building of new services. All application management teams or departments will contribute to the design of the technical architecture and performance standards for IT services. They will also be responsible for specifying the operational activities required to manage applications on an ongoing basis.

In addition, application management may be used to participate in projects, not only during the service design process, but also for CSI or operational projects.

They will have responsibility for designing and performing tests for the functionality, performance, and manageability of IT services (bearing in mind that testing should be controlled and performed by an independent tester).

The design activity will include designing applications to meet the levels of service required by the business. Availability and capacity management depend on application management for design expertise and guidance to assess the appropriate level of resources that will meet business demand for applications. This means that modeling and workload forecasting are often done together by technical and application management resources.

Application management, like technical management, will be vital in providing assistance in assessing risk, identifying critical service and system dependencies, and defining and implementing countermeasures.

Many application management departments or groups are relied on to manage contracts with suppliers of specific applications because they will have the required understanding and knowledge. If this is the case, it is important to ensure that these relationships are managed as part of the SLM and supplier management processes.

The application management function will be heavily involved in all of the operational processes, and they should be involved in the definition of event management standards and especially in the instrumentation of applications for the generation of meaningful events. The function will also be expected to provide resources that contribute to the execution of the problem management process. It is their technical expertise and knowledge that is used to diagnose and resolve problems. It is also their relationship with the vendors that is used to escalate and follow up with vendor support teams or departments. Other activities relating to incident and problem management include defining coding systems that are used in incident and problem management (e.g., incident categories) and providing resources to support problem management and the application development teams in validating and maintaining the known error database. Application management also provides scripts to the service desk to ensure good-quality incident capture and workarounds to facilitate first-time fixes.

Service transition will also make use of application management to support change management with technical application knowledge and expertise to evaluate changes. Many changes may be built by application management teams. They will also participate in release and deployment management activities. Application management is frequently the driver of the release and deployment management process for the applications they manage.

An important part of the function is assistance in defining, managing, and maintaining attributes and relationships of application CIs in the CMS and ensuring that they provide input into, and maintenance of, software configuration policies. They will also help in identifying opportunities for improvement and assist in the evaluation of alternative solutions.

Application management will be responsible for coordinating with development teams to ensure that a mechanism is in place to store and maintain documentation related to applications. This includes ensuring that all design, management, and user manuals as well as SOPs are up-to-date and complete and properly utilized on an ongoing basis. Application management also ensures that application management staff and users are aware of application documentation and familiar with its contents.

Another key area for this function is collaborating with technical management on performing training needs analysis and maintaining skills inventories for those teams involved in supporting the applications.

The application management function is involved throughout the service lifecycle. They will assist financial management for IT services to identify the cost of the ongoing management of applications.

Many application management departments, groups, or teams also perform operational activities as part of an organization's IT operations management function, and they will be involved in defining the operational activities related to applications that will be performed as part of IT operations management.

Application bug tracking and patch management (coding fixes for in-house code, transports/patches for third-party code) are also part of the role, as is involvement in application operability and supportability issues such as error code design, error messaging, and event management hooks.

As part of service design, and in support of capacity and availability management processes, the function will be engaged in application sizing and performance, volume metrics, and load testing.

They will be involved in developing release policies and, of course, identification of enhancements to existing software, from both a functionality and manageability perspective.

Although all application management departments, groups, or teams perform similar activities, each application or set of applications has a different set of management and operational requirements. Each application was developed to meet a specific set of objectives, usually business objectives. For effective support and improvement, the group that manages an application needs to have a comprehensive understanding of the business context and how the application is used to meet the business objectives. The business objectives will depend on a number of factors, such as the application's purpose. An understanding of the business objectives is often achieved by business analysts who are close to the business and responsible for ensuring that business requirements are effectively translated into application specifications. Business analysts should recognize that business requirements must be translated into both functional and manageability specifications. Another consideration is the functionality of the application. Each application is designed to work in a different way and to perform different functions at different times.

Not all applications run on the same platform, so technical management and application management will need to work together as they support the environment and the applications. Even applications that have similar functionality operate differently on different databases or platforms. Similarly, the type or brand of technology used will have an impact. These differences have to be understood to manage the application effectively.

Even though the activities to manage these applications are generic, the specific schedule of activities and the way they are performed will be different. For this reason, application management teams and departments tend to be organized according to the categories of applications they support.

For example, in larger organizations where a number of different applications are used for various aspects of financial management, there may be several departments, groups, or teams managing these applications (e.g., applications for debtors and creditors and age analysis, general ledger).

This approach can be used for several applications, such as messaging and collaboration applications, HR applications, manufacturing support applications, and applications for business functions such as sales and marketing, call centers, web portals, and online shopping.

Application Development vs. Application Management

As discussed earlier, application management and application development have separate aims and responsibilities. These two groups may work closely together or they may be quite separate, with different reporting structures and a different interface with the business. Application development, as we said earlier, is normally a finite activity to develop an application, and the team moves on to the next requirement when finished. Application management, on the other hand, remains involved throughout the lifecycle of the application. Here is a summary of the differences between them:

- Development focuses on the utility aspects, and most of its work is carried out on applications developed in-house. Management activities consider both warranty and utility and are carried out whether the application is internally developed or purchased.

- Development is concerned with functionality and does not consider how the application is to be operated or managed, whereas application management is concerned with how this functionality is to be delivered consistently.

- Development is often carried out as part of a project, with defined deliverables, costs, and handoff dates. This differs from application management, whose activities are ongoing throughout the service lifecycle and whose costs may not be separately identified.

- Developers may not have an understanding of what is required to manage and operate an application because they do not support the applications they have developed, instead moving on to the next development project. Similarly, application management staff members may have little involvement in development and therefore have less understanding of how applications are developed.

- Development staff members follow software development lifecycles. Application management staff members are often involved only in the operation and improvement stages of the service lifecycle.

Figure 5.3 shows the various roles of the application management and application development teams; the application development team is primarily concerned with the functionality of the application, whereas the application management team considers how the application infrastructure will support the application and how it will be built, deployed, and monitored in operation.

FIGURE 5.3   Role of teams in the application management lifecycle

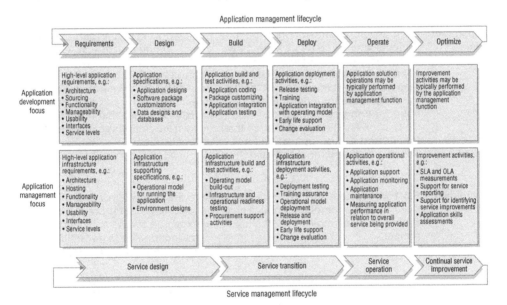

There is a growing tendency to end the division between the two teams because it is confusing for the business to understand. Ideally, this will mean a broadening of the development role to include considering how applications will operate, and it will mean more involvement in development for staff members who will be managing the application, as shown in Table 5.1.

TABLE 5.1   Application development vs. application management

	Application development	Application management
Nature of activities	One-time set of activities to design and construct application solutions.	Ongoing set of activities to oversee and manage applications throughout their entire lifecycle.
Scope of activities	Performed mostly for applications developed in-house.	Performed for all applications, whether purchased from third parties or developed in-house.
Primary focus	Utility focus. Building functionality for their customer. What the application does is more important than how it is operated.	Both utility and warranty focus. What the functionality is as well as how to deliver it. Manageability aspects of the application, i.e., how to ensure stability and performance of the application.
Management mode	Most development work is done in projects where the focus is on delivering specific units of work to specification, on time, and within budget. This means that it is often difficult for developers to understand and build for ongoing operations, especially because they are not available for support of the application once they have moved on to the next project.	Most work is done as part of repeatable, ongoing processes. A relatively small number of people work on projects. This means that it is very difficult for operational staff to get involved in development projects because that takes them away from their ongoing operational responsibilities.
Measurement	Staff are typically rewarded for creativity and for completing one project so that they can move on to the next project.	Staff are typically rewarded for consistency and for preventing unexpected events and unauthorized functionality (e.g., "bells and whistles" added by developers).
Cost	Development projects are relatively easy to quantify because the resources are known and it is easy to link their expenses to a specific application or IT service.	Ongoing management costs are often mixed in with the costs of other IT services because resources are often shared across multiple IT services and applications.
Lifecycles	Development staff focus on software development lifecycles, which highlight the dependencies for successful operation but do not assign accountability for these.	Staff involved in ongoing management typically control only one or two stages of these lifecycles— operation and improvement.

Measuring Application Management Performance

Performance metrics for application management will largely depend on which applications are being managed, but some generic metrics are included here.

Measurement of Agreed Outputs

The following metrics could be used to measure agreed outputs:

- Percentage of users able to access the application and its functionality
- Percentage of reports and files that are transmitted accurately and on time to the users
- Percentage of availability for critical business transactions
- Number of capacity- and performance-related incidents compared to business transaction volumes
- Percentage of service desk staff with appropriate support skills
- Number of recorded problem resolutions in the KEDB
- User measures of the quality of outputs as defined in the SLAs

Process Metrics

Application management teams execute many service management process activities. Their ability to do so will be measured as part of the process metrics, such as the following examples:

- Response time to events and event completion rates
- Incident resolution times for second- and third-line support
- Problem resolution statistics
- Number of escalations and reason for those escalations
- Number of changes implemented and backed out
- Number of unauthorized changes detected
- Number of releases deployed, total and successful, including releases for which adherence to the release policies of the organization are ensured
- Security issues detected and resolved
- Actual application transaction volumes and demand loads against capacity plan forecasts (where the team has contributed to the development of the plan)
- Tracking against service improvement plans (SIPs)
- Expenditure against budget

Application Performance

Application performance metrics are based on service design specifications and technical performance standards set by vendors and will typically be contained in OLAs or SOPs. Actual metrics will vary by application but are likely to include the following measures as part of the suite of performance measures applied to application performance.

Response Times

Application availability is helpful for measuring team or application performance but is not to be confused with service availability, which requires the ability to measure the overall availability of the service and may use the availability figures for a number of individual systems or components. The following metrics are used to measure team performance:

- Integrity and accuracy of data and reporting
- Measurement of maintenance activity

The following metrics are application availability metrics:

- Maintenance performed per schedule
- Number of maintenance windows exceeded
- Maintenance objectives achieved (number and percentage)
- Measurement of project activity

Application management teams are likely to work closely with application development teams on projects, and appropriate metrics should be used to measure this, including these:

- Time spent on projects
- Customer and user satisfaction with the output of the project
- Cost of involvement in the project
- Training and skills development

These metrics ensure that staff members have the skills and training to manage the applications that are under their control and will also identify areas where training is still required:

- A measure of the achieved skills by individuals, to meet the required skill levels
- Number of calls and escalations to third-party or other internal subject matter experts for additional help and support
- Percentage of incidents caused by skills issues

Application Management Documentation

As you would expect, a number of documents are produced and used during application management. The following sections provide a summary of some of the most important but do not include reports or documents produced by application management on behalf of other processes or functions.

Application Portfolio

Used primarily as part of service design, the application portfolio is a list (more accurately a system or database) of all applications in use within the organization. It includes the following information:

- Key attributes of the application
- Customers and users
- Business purpose

- Level of business criticality

- Architecture (including the IT infrastructure dependencies)

- Developers, support groups, suppliers, or vendors

- The investment made in the application to date. In this respect, the application portfolio can be used as an asset register for applications.

The purpose of the application portfolio is to analyze the need for and use of applications in the organization, and it forms part of the overall IT service portfolio. It can be used to link functionality and investment to business activity and is therefore an important part of ongoing IT planning and control. Another benefit of the application portfolio is that it can be used to identify duplication and excessive licensing of applications.

The Application Portfolio and the Service Catalog

The application portfolio should not be mistaken for the service catalog, and it should not be advertised as a list of services to customers or users. An application by itself is not a service. Applications are service assets and only one of the many components used to provide IT services.

The application portfolio should be used as a planning document by managers and staff who are involved with the development and management of the organization's applications. Other interested parties (for example, IT staff who may be tasked with managing the applications or the platforms on which the applications run) should also have access to the application portfolio.

The service catalog will focus on listing the services that are available rather than simply listing applications.

Application Requirements

Two sets of documents contain requirements for applications: business requirements documents and application requirements documents.

Business Requirements Documents

Business requirements documents outline the utility and warranty conditions as well as any constraints for the required application. This includes the return on investment for the application as well as all related improvements to the business, and they outline what the business will do with the application. Business requirements documents also include the service level requirements as defined by the service customers and users.

Application Requirements Documents

Application requirements documents are based on the business requirements and specify exactly how the application will meet them. They gather information that will be used to commission new applications or changes to existing applications. They can be used, for example, for the following purposes:

- To design the architecture of the application (specification of the different components of the system, how they relate to one another, and how they will be managed)

- To specify a request for proposal (RFP) for a commercial off-the-shelf (COTS) application

- To initiate the design and building of an application in-house.

Requirements documents are usually owned as part of a project and as such are subject to document control for the project as part of the overall scope of the project.

Four different types of application requirements need to be defined:

- Functional requirements describe the things an application is intended to do and can be expressed as services, tasks, or functions the application is required to perform.

- Manageability requirements are used to define what is needed to manage the application or to ensure that it performs the required functions consistently and at the right level. Manageability requirements also identify constraints on the IT system. They drive design of the operational models and performance standards used in IT operations management.

- Usability requirements are normally specified by the users of the application and refer to its ease of use. Special requirements for disabled users also need to be specified here.

- Test requirements specify what is required to ensure that the test environment is representative of the operational environment and that the test is valid (i.e., that it actually tests what it is supposed to).

Use Cases

Use cases are developed within service design and maintained by application management. For purchased software, the team that develops the functional specifications usually maintains the use case for that application. Use cases document the intended use of the application with real-life scenarios to demonstrate its boundaries and its full functionality. They can also be used as modeling and sizing scenarios.

Design Documentation

There is not a single design document. Design documentation is any documentation produced by application development or management. Because these documents are generally owned and managed by the development teams, application management should ensure that design documentation contains the following items:

- Sizing specifications
- Workload profiles and utilization forecasts
- Technical architecture
- Data models
- Coding standards
- Performance standards
- Software service asset and configuration management definitions
- Support requirements
- Environment definitions and building considerations (if appropriate)
- For third-party developed applications, documents that take the form of application specifications and are owned and managed by application management

Manuals

Application management is responsible for the management of manuals for all applications. Although these are generated by the application development teams or third-party suppliers, application management is responsible for ensuring that the manuals are relevant to the operational versions of the applications.

Three types of manuals are generally maintained by application management:

- Design manuals contain information about the structure and architecture of the application. These are helpful for creating reports or defining event correlation rules. They could also help in diagnosing problems.

- Administration or management manuals describe the activities required to maintain and operate the application at the levels of performance specified in the design stage. These manuals will also provide detailed troubleshooting, known error and fault descriptions, and step-by-step instructions for common maintenance tasks.

- User manuals describe the application functionality as it is used by an end user. These manuals contain step-by-step instructions on how to use the application as well as descriptions of what should typically be entered into certain fields or what to do if there is an error.

Manuals and Standard Operating Procedures

Manuals should not be seen as a replacement for SOPs but as input into the SOPs. SOPs should contain all aspects of applications that need to be managed as part of standard operations. Application management should ensure that any such instructions are extracted from the manuals and inserted into separate SOP documentation for operations so that it is clear what needs to be done to maintain the application. It is also responsible for ensuring that these instructions are updated with every change or new release of the software.

Technical and Application Management Roles

The technical and application management roles defined in the ITIL Service Operation publication carry out the activities of these functions. If you understand what these functions do, then we don't think that the manager and analyst roles need any explanation.

A technical operator is a person who carries out routine day-to-day tasks related to the management of the infrastructure. If IT operations management exists as an organizational unit, then this role is carried out there.

IT Operations Management

Many IT operations groups work some sort of shift system, often providing 24-hour coverage. The staff are organized into shifts, each with a shift leader who has a supervisory role.

IT operations analysts are skilled, experienced staff who are able to determine the best way of carrying out operational duties. For example, they would determine the best way to schedule the batch work.

The IT operator carries out the tasks defined for IT operations management.

Summary

We looked at the technical management role and the objectives, activities organization, metrics, and documentation relating to the technical management function.

The applications management function also contributes to service operation. We looked at the applications management role and the objectives and principles, and how applications management relates to the service lifecycle. We reviewed the activities of the function and the organization, metrics, and documentation relating to those activities.

Finally, we looked at the roles for service operation and the structures applicable to the organization based on its functions and requirements.

We explored the following concepts and terminology:

- Application management
- Function
- IT operations
- IT operations control
- IT operations management
- Operations bridge
- Technical support
- Technical management

Exam Essentials

Explain the operations management function.   Understand the two areas of operations management: operations control and facilities management. Be able to list examples of the responsibilities of each of these areas, such as monitoring environmental conditions (IT facilities management) and console management (operations control).

Explain the technical management function.   Understand the role of the technical management function, and be able to articulate the responsibilities of the function and apply them to a specific scenario.

Understand the application management function.   Understand the role of the application management function, and be able to articulate the responsibilities of the function and apply them to a specific scenario.

Understand the overlap between technical and application management functions and operations management. Understand the role of the technical and application management functions in providing resources to the other lifecycle stages and in specifying the operational tasks that service operation staff members should carry out.

Explain the difference between the application management function and application development. Understand the individual roles of the application management and development functions, and be able to articulate the responsibilities of each and apply them to a specific scenario.

Review Questions

You can find the answers to the review questions in the appendix.

1. Which of these activities is facilities management not responsible for?

    A. Maintaining air-conditioning to the required level in the server rooms

    B. Defining the infrastructure requirements to support the services

    C. Ensuring that the power supply at disaster recovery sites meets the requirement

    D. Testing the UPS and generators

2. Match the activities to the functions.

    1. Activity: Console management

    2. Activity: Identifying functional and manageability requirements for application software

    3. Activity: Providing a single point of contact

    4. Activity: Designing and managing the infrastructure

    a. Function: Service desk

    b. Function: Technical management

    c. Function: Application management

    d. Function: Operations management

    A. 1d, 2a, 3c, 4b

    B. 1d, 2c, 3a, 4b

    C. 1a, 2b, 3c, 4d

    D. 1b, 2c, 3d, 4a

3. There are two elements to operations management. What are they called?

    A. Facilities management, operations development

    B. Facilities ownership, operations control

    C. Console management, facilities management

    D. Facilities management, operations control

4. Which of the following correctly identifies an objective of the technical management function?

    A. Planning and designing the technical aspects of any new or changed service

    B. Carrying out the backup and restore of files for users

    C. Planning and designing the applications of any new services

    D. Answering user calls and dealing with requests

5. Application management is responsible for the technical expertise in the support and management of applications. Which of these statements best reflects the objectives of application management?

1. Designing applications
2. Deciding which applications should be purchased
3. Agreeing to the support arrangement for application support
   - **A.** 1 only
   - **B.** 2 only
   - **C.** All of them
   - **D.** 1 and 3 only

6. What is the best description of the technical management function?
   - **A.** Refers to the groups, departments, or teams that provide first-line technical support to end users
   - **B.** Refers to the groups, departments, or teams that provide expertise and overall management of the software
   - **C.** Refers to the groups, departments, or teams that provide management expertise for the 24-hour shift team
   - **D.** Refers to the groups, departments, or teams that provide technical expertise and overall management of the IT infrastructure

7. What are the objectives of technical management?
1. To maintain the status quo to achieve stability of the organization's day-to-day processes and activities
2. Regularly scrutinize and improve service at reduced cost while maintaining stability
3. Swiftly apply operational skills to diagnose and resolve any IT operations failures that occur
4. Plan new deployment of applications delivered from service design
   - **A.** 2 and 3 only
   - **B.** 1, 2, and 3 only
   - **C.** 1, 2, and 4 only
   - **D.** None

8. What is the responsibility of application management?
1. To support business in defining and identifying requirements for application software
2. To oversee security breaches in application development
3. To assist in support and improvement of applications
4. To assist in deployment of applications
   - **A.** 2 and 3 only
   - **B.** 1, 3, and 4 only
   - **C.** 1, 2, and 3 only
   - **D.** All of them

9. Which of these statements is correct?

1. Technical management teams include both specialist technical architects and designers (who are primarily involved during service design).

2. Technical management teams include both specialist maintenance and support staff (who are primarily involved during service operation).

   A. Statement 1 only

   B. Statement 2 only

   C. Both statements

   D. Neither statement

10. The importance of stability of services has been mentioned repeatedly in this chapter; one way of maintaining that stability is to ensure that routine tasks are carried out consistently. Which function has this as a *primary* objective?

   A. Technical management

   B. IT operations management

   C. Application management

   D. Service desk

Chapter

6

Technology and Implementation Considerations for Operational Support and Analysis

THE FOLLOWING ITIL OPERATIONAL SUPPORT AND ANALYSIS CAPABILITY INTERMEDIATE EXAM OBJECTIVES ARE DISCUSSED IN THIS CHAPTER:

✓ **Service operation technology considerations:**

- The types of tools that would benefit service operation

- The generic requirements for service management tools

- The specific service operation process requirements for service management tools

- The use of tools and how they support the service lifecycle

✓ **Service operation and project management**

✓ **Assessing and managing risk in service operation**

✓ **Operational staff in design and transition**

✓ **Planning and implementing service management technologies**

✓ **Challenges, critical success factors and risks**

This chapter brings all technology and implementation requirements together to define the overall requirements of an integrated set of service management technology tools for service operation. The same technology, with some possible additions, should be used for the other phases of IT service management (ITSM)—service strategy, service design, service transition, and continual service improvement—to ensure consistency and allow an effective ITSM lifecycle to be properly managed.

Tools can help the service operation and other processes to work more effectively. They should allow large amounts of repetitive work to be carried out quickly and consistently. Tools also provide a wealth of management information, leading to the identification of weaknesses and opportunities for improvement.

The use of tools will help standardize practices and both centralize and integrate processes.

Often organizations believe that by purchasing or developing a tool, all of their problems will be solved, and it is easy to forget that we are still dependent on the process, the function, and, most important, the people. Remember, "a fool with a tool is still a fool," and therefore training in the process and tool is imperative.

We are going to consider the generic requirements for such tools and the particular requirements needed to support the service desk function and the service operation processes of request fulfillment and event, incident, problem, and access management. It is important that the tool being used should support the processes, not the other way around.

We also consider the challenges, critical success factors, and risks appropriate to the service operation lifecycle stage.

Service Management Tools

We will begin by considering the generic requirements for IT service management tools. In this section, we look at a number of these requirements, which we would expect any good integrated toolset to offer.

The first two requirements are self-help functionality and a workflow engine.

You should be able to recall from the discussion of the request fulfillment process that we discussed the option for dealing with requests or simple incidents via self-help functionality. This might be restricted to the logging of requests and incidents, or it could allow them to be tracked and updated throughout their lifecycle. The advantage to providing a self-help facility is that requests and incidents can be logged at any time and this process is not dependent on service desk staff being available to answer the phone. This helps the service desk manage high volumes of calls if the less urgent ones are handled via a self-help, self-logging site. Self-help request tools can assist with password resets by, for example, requiring the user to validate their identity by answering previously set questions before the reset takes place. Additionally, a self-help request tool could download approved versions of requested software.

The next generic requirement is for a workflow or a process engine that can automate the steps of the process (assigning, escalating, etc.). It can also release work orders when prerequisite steps have been completed.

 Remember, the ITSM toolset is essential for many of the service management processes and functions and as such should be included in the IT service continuity provision.

The next generic requirement is for an integrated configuration management system (CMS). The service management tool should be integrated with the CMS to allow the organization's configuration item (CI) information to be interrogated and linked to incident, problem, known error, and change records as appropriate.

Another generic requirement is for discovery, deployment, and licensing technology tools; these are extremely helpful in verifying the accuracy of the CMS, especially with regard to license use. It is also very helpful if only changes since the last audit can be extracted and reported on. The same technology can often be used to deploy new software to target locations; this is essential to enable patches, upgrades, and so on to be distributed to the correct users.

When implemented in conjunction with the self-help functionality previously mentioned, this facilitates the automation of the fulfillment of many service requests for software.

Another generic requirement is remote control. This allows the service desk analysts to take control of the user's desktop (under properly controlled security conditions) to do things such as conduct investigations and correct settings.

Some tools will store diagnostic scripts and other diagnostic utilities to assist with earlier diagnosis of incidents.

Good reporting is a requirement of any ITSM toolset. The tools hold enormous amounts of information about what is happening day to day. This data is helpful in planning ahead and tracking trends, but such reporting has to be flexible if it is to be useful. Standard reports and ad hoc reports should both be easily available.

Another generic requirement to consider is a dashboard facility. Dashboards are useful, both for day-to-day operations and for IT and business management to get a clear idea of real-time performance.

To facilitate greater business alignment, business applications and tools need to be able to interface with ITSM support tools to give the required functionality. An example of integration includes event management tools spotting unusual spending patterns on credit cards.

Software as a Service (SaaS) technologies offer hosted service management capabilities over the Internet. The advantages this offers include lower capital and start-up costs, faster implementation, and built-in service continuity.

However, it also means limited customization and changes to functionality, access restricted to the vendor's contracted hours of service availability, and licensing schemes that may become restrictive or expensive. There may also be limits on data storage size and possible security and access management constraints or risks. Finally, integration with other service management tools may be difficult or even impossible.

Each organization should review its requirements carefully so that it acquires the most appropriate toolset for its needs.

Tool Requirements for Service Operation Processes

In this section, we'll consider the requirements of each service operation process.

Event Management

The tool requirements for this process include an open interface with standard Simple Network Management Protocol (SNMP) agents to enable events from differing technologies to be managed together. The tool should be easy to deploy and should route all events to a single location. It should be able to be programmed to handle alerts differently, depending on symptoms and impact, and to escalate events if they are not responded to within a set time period. It is essential that the tool provide meaningful management information and a business user dashboard. It should also have a direct interface into the organization's incident management processes. Another possible capability would be the ability to use SMS messaging to escalate events to support staff.

Incident Management

Next, we will consider the specific tool requirements for incident management.

The first is the capability to log incidents quickly, often by using predefined "quick calls" for common incidents (also referred to as incident models), with preset categorization, prioritization, and assignment. Tracking and reporting of incidents must also be easy and efficient.

Another requirement is an integral CMS to allow automated relationships to be made and maintained between incidents, service requests, problems, known errors, workarounds, and all other CIs. The CMS should also be able to assist in determining priority, help investigation and diagnosis, and escalate to appropriate resolution teams within technical and application management.

A process flow engine is essential to allow processes to be predefined using target times to automate the workflow and escalation. So, for example, if a support team has not responded within 60 minutes to an incident assigned to them, the team leader is automatically informed.

An interface to event management should be in place, as previously discussed, to allow failures to be automatically raised as incidents, and a web interface can be set up to allow the use of self-help tools and self-logging of incidents and service requests.

An integrated known error database (KEDB) for recording and searching for diagnosed and/or resolved incidents and problems can help speed up future incident resolution.

Easy-to-use reporting facilities are needed to allow incident metrics to be produced, and diagnostic tools will help the service desk to resolve incidents at first contact. Reporting capabilities should enable efficient access to incident histories and summarizations of incidents by category, priority, status, and CIs impacted to provide data and support for reactive and proactive problem management activities.

Request Fulfillment

The specific requirements for request fulfillment include the ability to differentiate requests from incidents and the ability to link service requests to incidents or events that have initiated them. As previously mentioned, tools should include self-help capabilities to allow users to submit requests via a web-based, menu-driven selection process.

Otherwise, the facilities needed to manage service requests are similar to those for managing incidents. They include predefined workflow control of request models, the ability to set and automate priority levels, automated escalation, and effective reporting.

Problem Management

Having a good ITSM tool is essential for effective problem management. A specific tool requirement for problem management is an integrated service management tool that differentiates between incidents and problems—and allows them to be linked.

Integration with change management is also required to allow request, event, incident, and problem records to be related to requests for change that have caused problems and to RFCs created to resolve problems and incidents. There should be an integrated CMS to allow problem records to be linked to the components affected and the services impacted. Service asset and configuration management forms part of a larger service knowledge management system (SKMS), which includes links to many of the data repositories used in service operation.

An effective KEDB will be an essential requirement to allow easy storage and retrieval of known error data. The ability to be able to link to vendor KEDBs is also a requirement.

Good reporting facilities are needed to ease the production of management reports and to allow drill-down capabilities for incident and problem analysis.

Access Management

The final service operation process, access management, requires integration with a number of technologies.

The first requirement is the ability to link to the technology used by human resources to validate the identity of users and to track their status. Another requirement is the ability to link to directory services. This technology enables technology managers to assign names to resources on a network and then provide access to those resources based on the profile of the user. Directory services tools also enable access management to create roles and groups and to link them to both users and resources.

Access management will use features in applications, middleware, operating systems, and network operating systems.

Changes to access requirements may be logged via a service request or be part of a work order from change management, so integration with these systems is very useful.

Access management also requires links to incident management in the case of suspected security incidents from people requesting access they should not have or inappropriate use of access.

Service Desk Function

In this section, we'll consider the requirements of the service desk, because in addition to the technology requirements for each process, the service desk function has some specific requirements.

The first requirement is for a KEDB (already mentioned when we talked about the requirements of the incident and problem processes) to store details of previous incidents and problems and their resolutions so that recurrences can be more quickly diagnosed and fixed.

Diagnostic scripts should be developed, stored, and managed to allow service desk staff to pinpoint the cause of failures. This requires input from the technical and application management functions and suppliers who need to provide details of likely faults, the key questions to be asked, and details of the resolution actions to be taken.

We have already mentioned the importance of a self-help web interface so users can log their own incidents and requests and even obtain assistance, which will enable them to resolve their own difficulties. This should include the following features:

- FAQs
- Password change capabilities, including identity checking, without the need for service desk intervention
- Software fixes, downloads, and repairs
- Downloads of additional authorized software packages
- Advance notice of planned downtime

Finally, it is often helpful for the service desk analysts to be able to take control of the user's desktop to allow them to, for example, conduct investigations or correct settings. Facilities to allow this level of remote control will be needed.

In addition to an integrated ITSM tool, the service desk needs the facilities offered by modern telephony services:

- An automated call distribution (ACD) system to allow a single telephone number. These systems provide extensive statistical reporting, providing insight into the busy times, average length of call, and so on.

- Interactive voice recognition (IVR) selection. These systems, which provide users with one or more menu selections, should be used with care. They should not have too many levels of options or offer ambiguous options.

- Computer Telephony Interface (CTI) software enables the caller to be identified from their telephone number and the incident record to then be automatically populated with their details extracted from the CMS.

- Voice over IP (VoIP) technology can significantly reduce telephony costs when dealing with remote and international users.

- Other possible facilities include cordless headsets, the ability to record calls for training purposes, and the ability to listen in on calls.

Service Management Tool Choice

Many service management tools are available, each with its own strengths and weaknesses, which makes choosing the right one difficult. To help with the decision process, you should define some objective selection criteria.

One simple method is MoSCoW analysis. This involves creating a detailed list of all your requirements and classifying each one as *must have*, *should have*, *could have*, or *would like in the future*.

- *Must have* requirements are mandatory. Any tool that does not satisfy *all* of those requirements is rejected.

- *Should have* requirements are those that we expect but are not essential.

- *Could have* requirements are useful but not hugely important.

- *Would like in the future* requirements are those that we don't need right now but will need in the future. For example, we're choosing a tool for incident management right now, but we'd like it to have problem management capability later.

You can then devise a scoring system based on this analysis, which would enable you to rank alternatives. It is possible to weight your decision, making a scoring system to ensure that you are getting the service management tool that delivers against your requirements.

Remember, the ITSM toolset is essential, but you are unlikely to get all of the requirements on your wish list. If you manage to get 80 percent of your requirements and the tool has some ability to be customized to meet your needs, then it probably is the best fit you can find.

Service Operation and Project Management

The use of project management processes to manage changes is commonplace in other lifecycle stages, but there is often a disinclination to use these processes for operational changes. Service operation is generally viewed as "business as usual" and does include a project approach. In fact, project management processes are both appropriate and helpful for major infrastructure upgrades or the deployment of new or changed procedures; these significant tasks will benefit from the improved control and management of costs and resources delivered by project management. Using project management to manage these types of activity would deliver a number of benefits:

- A clear, agreed statement of the benefits to be delivered by the project.
- Greater visibility of tasks and their management, which enables other IT groups and the business to understand the contributions made by operational teams. This helps in obtaining funding for projects that have traditionally been difficult to cost justify.
- Greater consistency and improved quality of the deliverables.
- The achievement of objectives, leading to operational groups gaining credibility.

Assessing and Managing Risk in Service Operation

The overriding concern of service operation is to maintain stability; any threat to that stability has to be assessed and acted on urgently. An obvious example of a situation in which service operation needs to carry out a risk and impact assessment is the risk to stability from a potential change. Service operation staff must assess the possible impact of the change and share this assessment with the change advisory board (CAB).

Risks Resulting from Changes

A change might be implemented despite the existence of known errors that become apparent during testing but were not considered serious enough to delay the change. The existence of such known errors poses a risk to operational stability; until the errors are resolved, incidents resulting from them can recur. The impact of these incidents and the effectiveness of the appropriate workaround for each (including the speed at which it overcomes the fault) must be assessed. The results of this assessment will feed into the prioritization of the problem. Having a proven workaround mitigates the risk to a certain extent because, although the fault will occur when the service is operational and will therefore impact the business, a quick fix can reduce the impact of the incident.

Every incident, whether reported through the incident and problem processes, through a warning from the supplier, or by event management, will be assessed for impact and urgency to calculate its priority. This assessment is also an assessment of the risk it poses to the business. Finally, new projects that will result in delivery into the live environment are assessed because there is a risk that they may impact other services.

Other Sources of Risk

There are other risks to operational stability that would require a risk assessment. The first is an environmental risk. Environmental risks would include the sorts of risks that are assessed as part of IT service continuity planning, such as fire and flood. There may also be political and commercial risks and risks related to industrial relations. Examples of these are the risks faced by drug companies that carry out testing on animals and therefore may be subject to sabotage by those opposed to this practice, the risk of strikes affecting operation, or even the risk of a competitor engaging in a price war, which would drive down the income received.

Suppliers may also constitute a source of risk. Their failure to deliver could affect the delivery of the overall service. Their ability to provide a service might also be affected by their own internal risks. This is particularly a problem if they are the sole supplier for a particular element of the service. Taking on new suppliers also involves some risk; without a known track record of reliable delivery, there is a risk that their service may not be satisfactory. Another major area of risk involves security; security-related incidents or events may result in either theoretical or actual risks. Finally, every new customer or service to be supported is both an opportunity to be successful and a potential risk for failure.

Operational Staff in Design and Transition

All IT groups will be involved during service design and service transition to ensure that new components or services are designed, tested, and implemented to provide the correct levels of functionality, usability, availability, and capacity. Additionally, service operation staff must be involved during the early stages of service design and service transition to ensure that when new services reach the live environment, they are fit for purpose from a service operation perspective and are "supportable" in the future.

In this context, *supportable* means that they will not negatively impact other services, processes, schedules, or operational working practices. They must also be capable of being operated by the current staff, at an understood cost. The support structure, including both the internal support teams and the support provided by third-party suppliers, must be clear and understood. There should be no unexpected costs after the service goes live, and contractual obligations must be clear and straightforward.

Note that change is not just about technology. There is also organizational change to consider, and the possibility that staff or users may be hostile to the change. It is possible to reduce the risk of people resisting change through a program of communication and training. Further details about organizational change are included in the ITIL Service Transition publication.

Planning and Implementing Service Management Technologies

The final topic of this chapter is service management tools. A good service management tool can be very helpful for implementing processes based on the ITIL framework. Many organizations implement new tools to assist their implementation of new or improved processes. These organizations need to consider a number of factors if the new tool is to be helpful and appropriate.

Licenses

The first factor to be considered is the type of license. There are usually a number of options, at different costs. Where tools are licensed on a modular basis, careful planning is needed to ensure that the right access is obtained to enable people to carry out their work with no unnecessary modules being purchased. Here are some possible options:

Dedicated Licenses   For this option, each named person has their own license. Dedicated licenses are suitable for staff who require frequent and prolonged use of a particular module. For example, service desk staff would need a dedicated license to use an incident management module.

Shared Licenses   These licenses can be shared between individuals; there is, however, a possibility that a staff member may not be able to access the tool because the license is already in use. Shared licenses are suitable for regular users who do not require constant access, such as second-line support staff. Careful calculation is required to ascertain the correct ratio of users to licenses. These licenses are more expensive than dedicated licenses, but fewer are required.

Web Licenses   These allow access via a web browser. Web licenses are usually suitable for staff requiring remote access or only occasional access. They usually cost a lot less than other licenses (they may even be free with other licenses). It is possible to provide sufficient access for a large number of occasional users by purchasing a small number of such licenses, since the number of concurrent users and therefore the number of licenses required will be low. In this way overall costs can be reduced further.

On Demand   Access to tools is provided when required (on demand), and the supplier charges for the access based on the time spent using the application. This can be attractive to smaller organizations or if the tools in question are very specialized and used relatively infrequently. A variation to this is the use of a specialist tool as part of a consultancy assignment (e.g., specialist capacity management tools); in such cases, the license fees are likely to be included in the consultancy fee.

Agent/Activity A further variation in license options is software that is licensed and charged on an agent/activity basis. An example of this is simulation software (e.g., agent software that can simulate customer paths through a website to assess and report on performance and availability).

In all cases, it is essential that sufficient investigation be done to ensure that the costs are understood and agreed to and that the organization remains legal in respect to having sufficient licenses.

Deployment

Many ITSM tools, particularly discovery and event monitoring tools, will require some client/agent software deploying to all target locations before they can be used. This will need careful planning and execution and should be handled through formal release and deployment management. Some deployment considerations are listed here:

- There should be careful scheduling and testing, and the deployment must be tracked so that it is clear which CIs have the software and which have yet to receive it.

- The CMS should be updated as the deployment progresses.

- It is often necessary to reboot devices for the client software to be recognized, and this needs to be arranged in advance to minimize service interruption.

- Special arrangements may be needed for portable equipment, which may not be present on site during deployment.

- The devices receiving the software must be checked in advance to ensure that they have sufficient storage and processing capacity to host and run the new software.

- The network capacity needs to be checked to ensure that it is capable of transmitting everything required.

- The best time to deploy a tool depends on the maturity level. A tool that is deployed too early shifts the focus of the improvement initiative away from the requirement to change processes and ways of working, and the whole improvement exercise then becomes merely a tool implementation.

- Training in the tool prior to deployment is necessary if benefits are to be realized.

Remember, a tool is usually not enough to make things work better. However, if it supports processes and the user has been trained to use it, a good tool can help staff carry out new processes.

Here are some further aspects of the deployment that must be considered:

The Type of Introduction to Be Used A decision must be made whether a "Big Bang" introduction or some sort of phased approach is to be adopted. Because most organizations will have live services to keep running during the introduction, a phased approach is more likely to be necessary.

Transition between Tools   If an older tool is being replaced, consideration must be given to the best way to transition between the old tool and the new one. For example, the service desk should not be assigning an incident on a new tool to a team that has yet to transition from the old tool.

Data Migration   A decision needs to be made regarding what data needs to be migrated from the old tool to the new one. This may require reformatting, and so may need to be validated after migration, especially if the data is transferred electronically. A period of parallel running may be implemented instead, with the old tool being available in a read-only mode for an initial period alongside the new one so that historical data can be referenced if needed.

Complete details on the release and deployment management process can be found in the ITIL Service Transition publication.

Service Operation Challenges

The following main challenges facing service operation management are expanded on in this chapter:

- Lack of engagement with development and project staff
- Justifying of funding within service operations
- The differences between design and operational activities
- Ineffective service transition
- Ineffective service metrics
- The use of virtual teams
- Balancing of internal and external relationships

Engagement with Development and Project Staff

The first challenge in service operation is to ensure the correct level of cooperation and engagement between the service operation staff and the development and project teams.

The focus of the development and project teams is very different from that of service operation staff. Staff involved in projects and development will focus on the development of new applications or functionality and delivering it into the operational environment. Their work has a defined end point, which is when the application or functionality is delivered. Staff involved in service operation focus on the long-term operation of what has been delivered.

Project staff consider that the delivery of a service on time and to budget is paramount, whereas operations staff care less about meeting a specific date than they do about how well the service will run and what will be involved in supporting it.

Development and project staff may know very little about service management and regard it as relevant only to operations. The ITIL framework makes it clear that service management processes are involved from the very beginning of a service, as part of service strategy, right through to design and transition. Service operation should be involved throughout the development of a new or changed service to ensure that the deliverable is supportable at the end.

These two areas of IT often work quite separately, and there may even be animosity between them. Development staff may see operations staff as introducing unnecessary delay into their project, and operations staff may feel that projects are "dumped" on them with little appreciation or consideration about how they are to be operated in the live environment.

Ensuring that this division is overcome is challenging, but it will mean that operational aspects are considered early enough in the development activities that they can be incorporated into the design fairly easily. Failure to achieve this would constitute a risk to the successful transition and operation of the new service.

Justifying Funding

Service operation managers face the challenge of justifying funding for their area. They may meet with resistance to their funding requests because money spent in this sphere is often regarded as infrastructure costs, with no clear benefit arising from the investment.

Service operation managers should be able to show how investment in the operations area can save the organization money as well as improve the quality of the service being delivered. Here are some examples:

- Reduced software license costs through the better management of licenses
- Fewer incidents and problems and faster resolutions due to effective problem management, leading to reduced support costs
- Improved processes, leading to better use of existing resources and the elimination of duplication of activities
- Better customer retention from delivering higher levels of service consistently
- Improved utilization of existing infrastructure equipment and deferral of further expenditure as a result of better capacity management

Differing Service Design and Service Operation Focus and Priorities

The differences between design activities and operational activities will continue to present challenges:

- Service design may tend to focus on one service at a time, whereas service operation tends to focus on delivering and supporting all services at the same time. Operation managers need to work closely with service design and service transition to provide the operation perspective.

- Service design will often be conducted in projects, whereas service operation focuses on ongoing, repeatable management processes and activities. This may mean that operational staff are unavailable to participate in service design project activities, although as we just mentioned, their participation and engagement with development and project staff is essential if the new service is going to take account of operational issues.

- Once project staff have finished the design of one IT service, they could move on to the next project and not be available to provide support. Overcoming this challenge means ensuring that service operation staff are actively involved in design projects and participate in the early life support of services introduced in the operational environment.

- Success is measured differently for design and operation. Service design is measured by projects being on time and to budget, whereas service operation must ensure, through involvement in the design phase, that the service will operate as expected. If support and other costs are greater than expected in service operation, operational staff will blame the design, and service design staff will blame operations. Addressing this challenge requires service operation to be actively involved in the service transition stage of the lifecycle. The objective of service transition is to ensure that designed services will operate as expected. When the service operation manager is involved, operational aspects can be considered, allowing transition to understand and remedy issues before they become issues in the operational environment.

Other Challenges

Here is a list of other challenges:

- Ineffective service transition processes pose another challenge. Ensuring that service operation personnel are involved in validation and testing is required so that a decision to authorize changes is based on factual evidence. Good change management processes will ensure that changes that do not meet expectation are denied.

- Choosing meaningful metrics can be challenging. What can be measured easily may not actually be a useful indication of the level of service being provided. For example, measuring the time taken to answer the phone on the service desk may be easy but does not show whether the user then receives a good service. (The service design stage is responsible for ensuring that the appropriate metrics are included in the design of the service). Every service will produce its own measurements; interpreting them to understand the level of service being provided may not be straightforward, as the measurements may not be the same as others in use. Service level management can help to overcome this, but this requires involvement of operations staff.

Management of Staff

The management of staff will also present a number of challenges, some of which are described here:

- The use of virtual teams can also present challenges. Hierarchical management structures do not fit increasingly complex organizations, so matrix management has developed in response, where employees report to different sources for different tasks. This makes allocating accountability difficult. Knowledge management and the use of RACI (responsible, accountable, consulted, informed) matrices will help in this situation.

- One of the most significant challenges faced by service operation managers is balancing many internal and external relationships. Most IT organizations today are complex, with an increased use of value networks, partnerships, and shared services models. This increases the complexity of managing services, so investment in relationship management knowledge and skills is advisable to help deal with this challenge.

Critical Success Factors

Let's now consider some of the critical success factors for successful service operation:

- Visible ongoing management support, in relation to adherence to processes, appropriate ongoing funding of tools, and staff to support operational activities are essential for success.
- The support of the business is also important, to assist with formulating prioritization tables for incident management, ensuring that the users contact the service desk rather than approach support teams directly and providing the budget to fund operational activities.
- The existence of champions who lead others by their example and enthusiasm is another important factor. These may be senior managers, but champions can be at any level in the organization.
- Make sure sufficient staff resources are available to allow time to be spent implementing new processes and tools while ensuring that the day-to-day work does not suffer.
- Staff with the correct knowledge and skills is important. Staff need training and awareness of technical and service management aspects and may also require training in other areas, such as "soft skills," business awareness, and tool administration.
- Staff retention is important. Having invested in training, it is in the organization's interest to retain the trained staff, so it should try to develop career paths for these staff.

The final critical success factors that we consider are those surrounding the toolsets used:

- Using a tool that has been designed to support the processes described in ITIL makes the implementation and management of those processes much easier. Being able to link incidents and problems and to obtain information about configuration items and changes will support these processes, as will being able to report easily against KPIs.
- If a new tool is to be procured, evaluation against a set of defined criteria is required to ensure a good fit to requirements. The tools will also need to be configured and tested.
- The final critical success factor for tools is the ability to produce reports to show the effectiveness of the processes.

Service Operation Risks

In the last section of this chapter, we'll look at the risks service operation faces. These include the absence of the critical success factors—for example, the visible support of management is a CSF, and the absence of that support is a risk.

The ultimate risk is the loss of critical IT services and the resultant damage to the business. In addition to financial loss, there may be extreme cases where the IT services affected are used for critical health or safety purposes when poor service operation poses a health and safety risk.

Other risks are as follows:

Inadequate Funding and Resources   A clear business case needs to be made to secure adequate funding; inadequate funding will inevitably have an effect on the level of service that can be delivered. Once allocated, such funding must be reserved for its intended purpose and not spent on other items.

Loss of Momentum   Implementing best practice service management in service operation needs to become a permanent "business as usual" activity, not a short-term "flavor of the month." Without this clear message, staff may lose enthusiasm over time and revert to previous bad practices, seeing the move to best practice as purely temporary. An additional risk is that organizational changes may mean that the new best practice approach is dropped; again, this is the result of seeing the changes as temporary, to be replaced by the next initiative, rather than embedded.

Loss of Key Personnel   This may be a significant risk for less mature organizations in which the loss of one or two key staff members can have a severe impact. This can be mitigated by ensuring that staff are cross-trained, thus reducing dependencies on individuals. A more mature organization should have formalized knowledge transfer into processes, documents, and tools; this removes any dependency on a few knowledgeable people.

Resistance to Change or Suspicion Regarding Changes   This factor can be helped by education and training and better communication of the benefits of the changes. Often resistance to change is actually fear of change; providing staff with information as to how the changes will affect and possibly even benefit them in terms of job satisfaction and learning new skills may help allay these fears and thus reduce resistance.

Lack of Management Support   Middle managers may not see the overall vision or appreciate the hands-on benefits that more junior staff will gain. As stated previously, management support is a critical success factor for implementing best practice. Senior management must ensure that the middle managers understand both the benefits and the need for the changes, which deliver these benefits, to be visibly supported. Involving these managers in the appropriate stages and processes of service design and transition may help them understand the benefits.

Poor Design   The success of each lifecycle stage is due, at least in part, to the quality of the inputs into that stage. A poor-quality design output from the design stage will impact both transition and operation. The implementation will never be really successful, and redesign will ultimately be necessary.

Distrust Service management can be viewed with suspicion by both IT and the business. While IT staff dislike the new controls it imposes on their work methods, the business may take the cynical view that IT is seeking more money without delivering any improvements. Overcoming this distrust and cynicism mean ensuring that the benefits are clearly articulated to stakeholders and then actually delivered.

Differing Customer Expectations Different customer and user groups may have differing expectations. One group may pay more for a superior service, but this higher level is resented by other groups. Clear service level management, and the involvement of business relationship management if required, will help overcome these issues. The solution is not to simply deliver improved service levels upon request if they are not required or funded.

Summary

This brings us to the end of the chapter. We reviewed the service operation requirements relating to tools such as the integrated service management tool.

We explored the following topics:

- The types of tools that would benefit service operation in support of the processes and service desk function
- The generic requirements for service management tools

We looked at the involvement of operations staff in service design and service transition and aspects to consider when planning and implementing service management technologies within a company.

Exam Essentials

Understand the role of tools in supporting service operation. This includes understanding how to select tools that are appropriate for organizational needs.

Explain the generic requirements that service operation has for toolsets and why they are important. Understand the generic requirements that are applicable to service operation and how these tools will support the objectives of the lifecycle.

Understand the specific requirements for the individual service operation processes. Be able to identify the requirements for the individual processes from service operation to ensure maximum efficiency from the toolset.

Explain the selection technique known as MoSCoW. Know what the acronym stands for (Must/Should/Could/Would) and be able to explain the use of each concept in tool selection.

Explain how project management processes can help in the implementation of changes in service operation.   Understand the benefits of using project management processes to implement changes in service operation and the reasons why it might be resisted.

Know the risks that change poses to operational stability.   Understand how these risks might be managed.

Understand why service operation staff need to be involved in the design and transition stages.   In particular, understand what the concept of a service being supportable means and what is required for this to be the case.

Understand the license options available when implementing a new service management tool.   Be able to describe the different options and give examples of when each would be appropriate.

Understand the deployment options available when implementing a new service management tool.   Be able to describe the different options and give examples of when each would be appropriate.

Review Questions

You can find the answers to the review questions in the appendix.

1. Which of these statements about service management tools and technology is correct?

   A. Tools are useful but not essential.

   B. Tools assist good processes instead of replacing them.

   C. Tools can replace processes that do not function well.

   D. Tools define the processes we use by formalizing the steps in the design.

2. Which of these statements is/are correct?

   1. A CMS should be an integrated part of the service management tool.

   2. A service management tool without an SKMS is not a true service management tool.

   A. Statement 1 only

   B. Statement 2 only

   C. Both statements

   D. Neither statement

3. What is the first step when choosing a service management tool?

   A. Define the interfaces the tool will need to integrate with business tools.

   B. Understand the requirements for the tool.

   C. Decide how staff will be trained to achieve most from the tool.

   D. Research the available tools.

4. Which of these would be included in the generic requirements for a service management tool?

   1. Remote access capability

   2. Capability for integration with business tools

   3. Capability to link records such as incident and problem records

   4. Web-based access

   A. 1, 2, and 3

   B. 2, 3, and 4

   C. 1, 2, 3, and 4

   D. 1, 3, and 4

5. What is the MoSCoW technique used for?

   A. Categorization of requirements

   B. Categorization of incidents and problems

   C. Categorization of service desk components

   D. Design of the SKMS

6. Which of these is most likely to be part of a self-service portal?

1. The ability to reset passwords

2. The ability to log requests

3. The ability to authorize a change request

4. The ability to download approved software

    A. 1, 2, and 3

    B. 2, 3, and 4

    C. 1, 3, and 4

    D. 1, 2, and 4

7. Which of these considerations for reporting requirements for service management tools is important?

    A. Only industry-standard reports should be generated.

    B. No reporting capability should be integrated into the tool; it should be managed separately.

    C. There should be a good selection of generic reports.

    D. There should be a good selection of generic reports supported by easy generation of custom reports.

8. Management support is critical for successful service operation. What benefits are expected from management's commitment to technology and tools?

    A. Leadership, funding, and supporting commitment

    B. Higher first-time fix rate, reduced outages, and funding

    C. Improved customer satisfaction, reduced outages, and higher first-time fix rate

    D. Reduced outages, funding, and supporting commitment

9. Which of the following is *not* a benefit of using project management for complex operational changes?

    A. Provides a clear, agreed-to statement of the benefits to be delivered by the project.

    B. Project management would be funded by service transition and the project office, thus providing cost savings to service operation.

    C. Gives greater visibility of tasks and their management, which enables other IT groups and the business to understand the contributions made by operational teams. This helps in obtaining funding for projects that have traditionally been difficult to cost justify.

    D. Greater consistency and improved quality of the deliverables.

10. Which of the following is *not* a license option for service management tools?

    A. Dedicated

    B. Time limited

    C. Shared

    D. Web based

Planning, Protection, and Optimization

PART II

Planning, Protection, and Optimization

Chapter

7

Introduction to Planning, Protection, and Optimization

THE FOLLOWING ITIL PLANNING, PROTECTION, AND OPTIMIZATION CAPABILITY INTERMEDIATE EXAM OBJECTIVES ARE DISCUSSED IN THIS CHAPTER:

✓ The purpose, objectives, and value of service design

✓ The lifecycle in context

✓ Service design basics

✓ The interfaces of design coordination with other processes related to PPO

Planning, protection, and optimization (PPO) collects together a number of relevant practices from the core guidance related to service optimization and security and the related planning. This introduction to PPO includes the basic purpose and objective from service design and service strategy in support of PPO within a lifecycle context. This first chapter of the PPO section considers the core concepts of service design in terms of its purpose, objectives, and value as well as its relationship to the other ITIL lifecycle stages. We look at the basic concepts of service design, and, in particular, how the design coordination process interfaces with the PPO-related processes.

The Purpose, Objectives, and Value of Service Design

Service design takes the outputs from service strategy, the preceding stage of the service lifecycle, and uses them to ensure that the solution designs produced are consistent with the overall IT service provider strategy in support of the changing needs of the business. In other words, service design is about development of services that convert the objectives from service strategy into portfolios of services and service assets. It is also concerned with redesigning existing services. Service design is a critically important stage of the service lifecycle. It is in design that the intentions behind the service strategy start to be made reality. A poor service design will fail to deliver the strategy, could prevent a worthwhile return on investment, and could potentially damage the performance and reputation of the business. This stage is often rushed, however, in an attempt to meet project deadlines; such a course of action is foolish, however—time spent in design saves time spent in rework later.

The Purpose of Service Design

The purpose of the service design stage of the lifecycle is to design IT services, with the necessary supporting IT practices, processes, and policies, to realize the service provider's strategy. It is important to understand this point—design is not just about the technical design; it also considers the way it will be used and the processes required. Design should also include thinking about how the service will be transitioned; it should facilitate the introduction of the service into the supported environment in such a way as to ensure quality service delivery, customer satisfaction, and cost-effective service provision. So it is the job of design to make the strategy a practical reality. Importantly, design must consider *how* the service will work.

The Goals and Objectives of Service Design

Let's start by considering the goals and objectives of service design. Service design has to design services to satisfy business objectives and align with business needs. This includes consideration of the quality, compliance, risk, and security requirements ensuring the delivery of more effective and efficient IT and business solutions by coordinating all design activities for IT services. Ensuring consistency and business focus in the design is a key goal.

The objective of service design is to design IT services so effectively that minimal improvement during their lifecycle will be required. It is only when services are being used in the live environment that we can understand what is required of them. The use of the services will also change over time. It is essential, therefore, for service design to embed continual improvement in all its activities. This ensures that the solutions and designs become even more effective over time. Changing trends in the business that may offer improvement opportunities are identified and acted upon. Service design activities can be periodic or exception-based when they may be triggered by a specific business need or event.

Additional goals and objectives of service design include the following:

- Ensure that the services that are designed are adaptable to future requirements so that they can be easily expanded or reduced or developed to meet changing requirements.

- A service that is too expensive to run has no future, so the design should aim to reduce, minimize, or constrain the long-term costs of provision.

- Design an efficient and effective service management system, including the processes required for the design, transition, operation, and improvement of high-quality IT services.

- Alongside the processes, design must provide the supporting tools, systems, and information, especially the service portfolio, to manage services through their lifecycle.

- Design also needs to identify and manage risks so that they can be removed or mitigated before the services go live.

The final set of goals and objectives of service design includes these:

- Design the measurement methods and metrics for assessing the effectiveness and efficiency of the design processes and their deliverables. Design must consider how the effectiveness of a service could be measured, and ensure that the service is designed so that these metrics can be gathered.

- Produce and maintain all the IT plans, processes, policies, architectures, frameworks, and documents needed for the design of high-quality IT solutions that will meet current and future agreed-on business needs.

- Service design assists in the development of policies and standards in all areas of design and planning of the IT services and processes. By receiving and acting on feedback on design processes from other areas and incorporating this feedback into the processes in the future, design ensures continual improvement of these processes.

- Design should aim to develop skills and capability within IT by moving strategy and design activities into operational tasks, making effective and efficient use of all IT service resources.

- Design contributes to the improvement of the overall quality of IT service within the imposed design constraints. It reduces the need for reworking and enhancing services once they have been implemented in the live environment.

The Value Service Design Delivers to the Business

Adopting the best practice recommended by ITIL delivers significant business benefits. Good service design ensures both the quality and the cost-effectiveness of the service. Both aspects need to be delivered if the service is to be useful to the business. Good service design, using a standard, consistent approach, delivers a number of benefits, which we will consider in turn. These are:

A Reduced Total Cost of Ownership (TCO)   The design will consider the costs of various design options, and choose one that delivers what is required without unnecessary expenditure. In addition, because the design fits the business requirement, there will not be a large volume of changes, to align it more effectively with the business requirement. By considering aspects such as availability and capacity in the design, incidents will be minimized, and the support costs will be less.

Improved Quality of Service   Services that are well designed and meet the required outcomes of the customer will deliver a higher quality of service

Improved Consistency of Service   Designing services within the corporate strategy, architectures, and constraints will ensure that a consistent level of service is delivered.

Easy-to-Implement New or Changed Services   Well-designed services are easier to transition.

Improved Service Alignment   By involving service design from the beginning, we can ensure that the new or changed service is designed to match the business requirement and will be able to support the required service levels.

Improved Service Performance   The service will have been designed to meet the specific performance criteria, incorporating capacity, availability, and IT service continuity requirements into the design.

Improved IT Governance   This will be a result of ensuring that the necessary controls are built into the design.

Improved Effectiveness of Service Management and IT Processes   The design of processes is one of the five aspects of service design discussed in the Service Design Basics section later in this chapter; by considering processes as part of design, it is to be expected that they will be designed to deliver both quality and cost effectiveness.

Improved Information and Decision Making   The design includes designing measurements and metrics—enabling the service provider to be confident that they possess accurate information on which to base decisions. These measurements will also form the basis for assessing the service and identifying opportunities for continual improvement of both services and service management throughout the service lifecycle.

Improved Alignment with Customer Values and Strategies   If an organization has a policy of promoting concepts such as green IT, or a strategy of using cloud technologies, service design will ensure that the design of the new or changed service is aligned with these values and strategies.

Service design ensures IT services focus on supporting business processes and goals. This includes the following:

- Prioritizing IT activities based on business impact and urgency so that critical business processes and services receive the most attention

- Increasing business productivity by ensuring that IT processes are efficient and effective

- Supporting corporate governance requirements with appropriate IT governance and controls, ensuring compliance with regulatory and legislative requirements

- Exploiting the IT infrastructure and providing innovative solutions to create competitive advantage

- Improving service quality, customer satisfaction, and user perception

- Ensuring that all IT and information assets are appropriately protected and secure

The Context of Service Design and the Service Lifecycle

Service design needs to be considered within the context of the whole service lifecycle. You should be familiar with the concept of the service lifecycle, shown in Figure 7.1. Each stage addresses a particular set of challenges that need to be addressed for successful service management, and each stage has an impact on all the others.

Let's consider each lifecycle stage in turn.

FIGURE 7.1 The ITIL service lifecycle

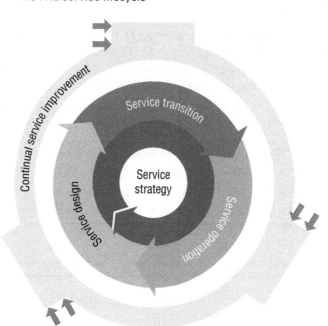

Service Strategy

Service strategy is at the core of the service lifecycle. It is the role of strategy to understand the organizational objectives and customer needs. People, processes, and products should support the strategy. ITIL service strategy asks why something is to be done before thinking of how. It helps service providers to set objectives; set expectations of performance serving customers and markets; and identify, select, and prioritize opportunities. Service strategy ensures that providers understand and can handle the costs and risks associated with their service portfolios.

The complete list of service strategy processes includes strategy management for IT services, service portfolio management, financial management for IT services, demand management, and business relationship management. We consider demand management in depth in Chapter 9, "IT Service Continuity Management and Demand Management," as part of planning, protection, and optimization.

Service Design

Service design, which is particularly relevant to planning, protection, and optimization, turns strategic ideas into deliverables. The design must always consider the strategy to ensure that services are designed with the business objectives in mind. Design considers the whole IT organization, and how it will deliver and support the services, turning the service strategy into a plan for delivering the business objectives. Remember: Design includes changes to existing services.

The complete list of service design processes includes those that address the warranty aspects of a service. These include availability management, capacity management, and information security management, which are covered in Chapter 8, "Capacity, Availability, and Information Security Management," and IT service continuity management, covered in Chapter 9 as part of planning, protection, and optimization. Other service design processes are covered in Part 4, "Service Offerings and Agreements," and include service catalog management (covered in Chapter 17, "Service Portfolio Management and Service Catalog Management") and service level management and supplier management (covered in Chapter 18, "Service Level Management and Supplier Management"). The final design process is design coordination, which we consider briefly later in this chapter. Through these processes, design ensures that both the utility and the warranty of the new or changed service is considered in design, covering the continuity of the service, its achievement of the agreed-to capacity and availability service levels, and its conformance to security standards and regulations.

Service Transition

Service transition provides guidance for developing and improving capabilities for introducing new and changed services into supported environments. The value of a service is identified in strategy, and the service is designed to deliver that value. Service transition ensures that the value is realized by enabling the necessary changes to take place without unacceptable risks to existing services. Service transition enables the implementation of new services, and the modification of existing services, to ensure that the services provided deliver the service strategy of achieving the business objectives and that the benefits of the service design are fully realized. Service transition also introduces the service knowledge management system, which ensures that knowledge is stored and made available to all stages of the service lifecycle, ensuring that lessons are learned and decisions are backed with factual data, thus leading to improved efficiency and effectiveness over time.

Part 3, "Release, Control, and Validation," covers the complete list of service transition processes. These include transition planning and support, covered briefly in Chapter 11, "Introduction to Release, Control, and Validation"; change management and service asset and configuration management, covered in Chapter 12, "Change Management and Service Asset and Configuration Management"; service validation and testing and change evaluation, covered in Chapter 13, "Service Validation and Testing and Change Evaluation"; and release and deployment management and knowledge management, covered in Chapter 14, "Release and Deployment Management and Knowledge Management." Each process has a role to play to ensure that beneficial changes can take place, and, as a consequence, the service can be introduced and will work as designed.

Service Operation

Service operation describes best practice for managing services in supported environments. It includes guidance on achieving effectiveness, efficiency, stability, and security in the delivery and support of services to ensure value for the customer, the users, and the service provider. Without this, the services would not deliver the value required, and the achievement of business objectives would become difficult or impossible.

The service operation stage is therefore critical to delivering the design and, in doing so, achieving the service strategy. Service operation provides detailed guidance for delivering the service within the agreed-to service levels by tackling issues both reactively and proactively through problem management, and reactively through incident management. It provides those delivering the service with guidance for managing the availability of services, controlling demand, optimizing capacity utilization, scheduling operations, and avoiding or resolving service incidents and managing problems. It includes advice on shared services, utility computing, web services, and mobile commerce. By delivering the services to the agreed levels, service operation enables the business to use the services to achieve its business objectives.

The service operation processes are covered in Part 1, "Operational Support and Analysis"; the complete list includes incident management and problem management in Chapter 2, "Incident and Problem Management," and event management, request fulfillment, and access management in Chapter 3, "Event Management, Request Fulfillment, and Access Management." Each process has a role to play to ensure the delivery of services within the agreed-to service levels. Service operation also describes the four service operation functions; the service desk (covered in Chapter 4, "The Service Desk") and technical management, IT operations management, and application management (covered in Chapter 5, "Technical Management, Application Management, and IT Operations Management"). Each function is responsible for managing its own area of delivery across all stages of the lifecycle.

Continual Service Improvement

The final stage of the lifecycle is continual service improvement (CSI). CSI ensures that the service provider continues to provide value to customers, by ensuring that the strategy, design, transition, and operation of the services is under constant review. Feedback from any stage of the service lifecycle can be used to identify improvement opportunities for that or any other stage of the lifecycle. It enables any individual to identify improvements, and every process should include an element of CSI. It enables every new design to incorporate lessons from previous designs. It ensures that opportunities for improvement are recognized, evaluated, and implemented when justified. These may include improvements in the quality of the service or the capabilities of the service provider. It may be developing ways of doing things better, or doing them to the same level, but more efficiently. Improvements may be major, or small and incremental. It enables every new operation to incorporate lessons from previous operations, and provides guidance on how to develop design capabilities for service management.

CSI ensures that feedback from every lifecycle stage and process is captured, analyzed, and acted on. The CSI approach to improvement is based on establishing a baseline and checking to see whether the improvement actions have been effective. It uses the Plan-Do-Check-Act (PDCA) cycle, together with measuring service, demonstrating value with metrics, and conducting maturity assessments. The seven-step improvement process provides a framework for these approaches.

Service Design Basics

The service design stage of the lifecycle starts with a set of new or changed business requirements. It ends with the development of a service solution designed to meet the documented needs of the business. The service solution, documented within its service design package, is then passed to service transition to evaluate, build, test, and deploy the new or changed service, after which service operation is responsible for delivering the service as designed. Service design has to take into consideration the environment in which the service will operate while still ensuring that the design is flexible, so that it can be changed easily since requirements may change later. Services must be designed to be both maintainable and cost-effective.

The benefits of using standardized and consistent approaches for service design include accurate estimates of the cost and resources required, a realistic assessment of the required budget, higher volumes of successful change, and the development of repeatable methods and reusable design assets. Time spent on good service design will be repaid by the delivery of designs that are "right the first time." This in turn will result in reduced time and money being spent on rework. Service design should manage stakeholder expectations so that they understand what is being delivered and the benefits they will receive; this will increase stakeholder confidence in a successful outcome.

Service Design and Business Change

The requirement for a change in IT service is usually the result of a business process change. Once the business requirements are clear, the service design can be done to meet the current and future agreed-to business requirements. Figure 7.2 shows the interaction between the business change process and IT.

FIGURE 7.2 The business change process

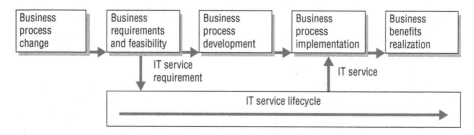

The Four Ps of Service Design

The implementation of IT service management as a practice is about preparing and planning the effective and efficient use of the four Ps: the people, the processes, the products (the services, technology, and tools), and the partners (the suppliers, manufacturers, and vendors). These are shown in Figure 7.3. Service design must consider each of the four Ps to ensure a robust design that meets requirements.

FIGURE 7.3 The four Ps

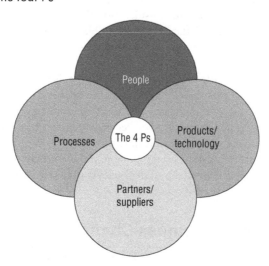

People

The best technical design will fail if the people who need to use it or support it are not adequately prepared. The people element of service design ensures that the human aspect is not forgotten. People are both a resource (you need the right number of people) and a capability (you need the right people with the right skills). Service designers must consider how many people will be required to support the new service (resource) and what skill set they will require to do so effectively (capability). The people who will be using the service will also need training in its use in order to gain the full benefit of the service.

Processes

The second element to be considered is that of processes. In addition to the service design processes described in the ITIL framework, the new service may require additional processes to be designed, such as an authorization or procurement process. As part of service design, processes should be documented, together with the interfaces between them and other processes. All existing processes across the lifecycle should be assessed to identify whether any changes to them are required to enable this new or changed service to become operational and be supportable.

Products

Products are not only the services that result from the service design stage itself but also the technology and tools that are chosen to assist in the design or to support the service later. So, for example, the service design may be for an online shopping service, and the other products may include a credit card processing application, an automatic stock reordering service when stock levels reach a threshold, monitoring tools that alert the service provider if user response time exceeds a set time, and so on.

Partners

Partners are those specialist suppliers—usually external third-party suppliers, manufacturers, and vendors—that provide part of the overall service. Ensuring that the correct supplier is chosen is essential, because failure by a supplier may cause the IT service provider to breach an agreed-on service level. External suppliers are managed through the supplier management process, which ensures that the necessary contracts are put in place and monitors the delivery by the supplier against the contract terms. Supplier management is covered in Chapter 19.

Holistic and Balanced Service Design

When a new service is being designed, or an existing design needs to be amended, concentrating on just the service solution will not be sufficient; other aspects need to be considered. The design process must take a holistic approach to designing new or changed services, because success depends not only on the technical solution but also the management and architectural environment in which that solution is to operate, the processes and skills that will be required to ensure that it runs effectively, and the metrics that need to be provided to monitor and manage it. In order for the service design processes to be effective, every essential element of design must be considered. A holistic approach considers all five aspects of design; we examine these aspects in "The Five Aspects of Service Design." An integrated approach, such as ITIL recommends, ensures that the development of the service, any changes to it during its lifecycle, and its eventual retirement are achieved without unforeseen consequences. It also ensures that the service delivers the required functionality and quality. Each design is the result of balancing the resources required, the time available, and the desired functionality. For example, a service with a high level of functionality will require a lot of resources, or a lot of time to develop.

A Structured Approach to Service Design

There are many activities to be completed within service design. Managing them all, and delivering to meet the time, budget, and quality criteria, is challenging, and it requires a formal and structured approach. This approach will facilitate the delivery of the new service at the right cost, utility, and warranty and within the right time frame.

An example of such an approach and its constituent stages is shown in Figure 7.4, together with the other major areas that will need to be involved along the way. This is a complex diagram; take the time to fully understand it

FIGURE 7.4   Aligning new services to business requirements

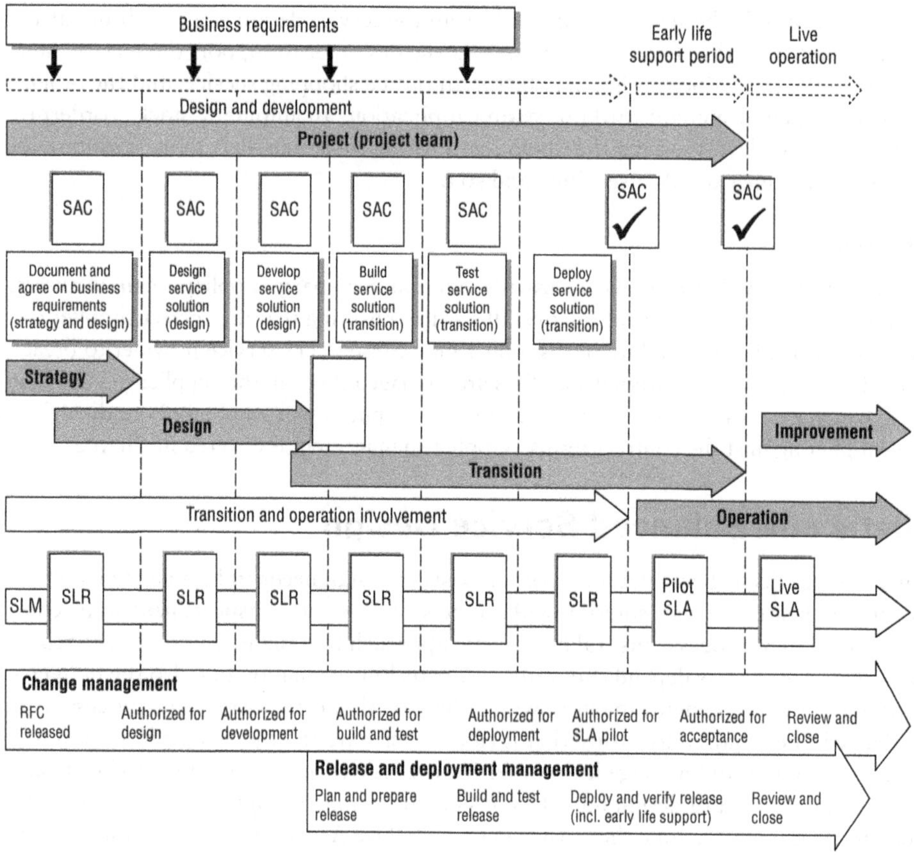

Figure 7.4 shows the lifecycle of a service from the initial or changed business requirement through the design, transition, and operation stages of the lifecycle.

First we see how the service moves through a design and development stage, into a pilot, and finally live running. The project team is involved during the first two stages, but not in the live operations stage. We can see the involvement of service level management and the change management process throughout, and the release and deployment management processes of service transition.

We can see how the business requirements feed into the service acceptance criteria. Documented requirements and service level requirements are produced during the strategy and design lifecycle stages.

As the solution is designed, developed, and built, the business requirements continue to feed into them, allowing for any changes to be incorporated (if this is agreed). The SLRs and SACs will be updated to fit the changed requirement. The SLRs are finalized and agreed by the business and the service provider. The service is then tested in transition against these criteria and deployed. It is important that there is effective transfer of knowledge at all stages between the operational staff and the project staff to ensure smooth progression through each of the stages illustrated.

The role of the project team within this activity of delivering new and changing IT services to the business and its relationship to design activities is also illustrated. This approach must be iterative and incremental to ensure that the service meets the evolving needs of the business as they develop during the business process development and the IT service lifecycle. Additional project managers and project teams may need to be allocated to manage the stages within the lifecycle for the deployment of the new service.

The Five Aspects of Service Design

As stated earlier, effective service design depends on a holistic approach to five key aspects. We need to ensure that each of the five aspects considers the desired business outcomes and planned results so that the final service when delivered meets the expectations of the customers and users. You may find the acronym STAMP helpful to remember these—Solutions, Tools, Architecture, Measurements, Processes:

- The design of the solution

- The service management system and tools that will be required to manage the service

- The management and technology architectures that the service will use

- The measurement systems, methods, and metrics that will be required

- The processes needed to support the service in operation

We have considered these five aspects before, as part of your Foundation studies. The key aspect is the design of new or changed service solutions to meet changing business needs. Every new solution must be checked to ensure that it conforms to the five aspects and will interface to other services successfully. Let's look at each aspect in turn; more information is available in the ITIL Service Design publication.

Designing Service Solutions

The first aspect is designing service solutions. The design of the service solution should include the following:

- Analyzing the agreed-to business requirements

- Reviewing the existing IT services and infrastructure to identify possible alternative solutions, or components that can be reused in the new design

- Designing the solution to include both the features and functionality required (i.e., the utility), and the nonfunctional warranty requirements

- Ensuring that the design will deliver the information required to enable the service or process to be adequately monitored, measured, and improved

- Addressing the requirements of any affected business processes, ensuring that the design takes account of dependencies, priorities, criticality, and the impact of the service

- Ensuring that the design will meet the acceptance criteria, including the service level requirements and service level targets (i.e., the warranty requirements), and that the design will provide the required service measures and metrics

- Understanding the timescales required and how the new service will impact existing services

- Planning the testing of the service, including any user acceptance testing (UAT)

- Integrating the new service into the overall service management system

The Design of the Management Information Systems and Tools

The design of the management information systems and tools is the second aspect of service design. These systems and tools will be essential to the management of the service throughout its lifecycle. Management information systems are usually part of a larger framework known as a management system. Examples include a quality management system, an information security management system, and the overall service management system.

The service management system may include the service portfolio, configuration management system (CMS), capacity management information system (CMIS), availability management information system (AMIS), security management information system (SMIS), and supplier and contract management information system (SCMIS).

Management and Technology Architectures

Architectural design can be thought of as the blueprint for the development and deployment of an IT infrastructure to satisfy the current and future needs of the business. In this context, architecture is defined as the fundamental organization of a system—that is, how its components relate to each other and to the environment, and the principles guiding its design and evolution. It can be thought of as encompassing service, application, data/information, and infrastructure architectures. Let's consider these different architectures in turn.

Service Architecture   This translates applications, infrastructure, organization, and support activities into a set of services. There may be changes in these architectures without changing the service itself. It includes the services themselves, their overall integration, and the management of those services.

Application Architecture   This maps business and functional requirements onto applications, and shows the interrelationships between applications.

Data/Information Architecture   This describes the logical and physical data assets of the enterprise and the data management resources. It shows how the information resources are managed and shared for the benefit of the enterprise.

IT Infrastructure Architecture   This describes the structure, functionality, and geographical distribution of the components that underpin the overall architecture and the technical standards applying to them.

Environmental Architecture   This describes all aspects, types, and levels of environment controls and their management.

Technology Architectures   These include applications and systems software; information, data, and databases; and infrastructure design.

Processes

The next aspect of service design is process design. A process is a structured set of activities designed to accomplish a specific objective. It takes one or more inputs and turns them into defined outputs. Process definitions should include the roles, responsibilities, tools, and management controls required to reliably deliver the outputs. The definition may also define or revise policies, standards, guidelines, activities, processes, procedures, and work instructions if they are needed.

Each process should be owned by a process owner, who should be accountable for the process and its improvement and for ensuring that a process meets its objectives. Service design should assist in the design of processes, to ensure consistency and enable integration between processes.

Measurement Systems and Metrics

The last of the five aspects of service design covers the design of measurement systems and metrics. To manage and control processes and services, you must monitor and measure them. Care should be exercised when selecting measurements and metrics and the methods used to produce them. This is because the metrics and measurements chosen will actually affect and change the behavior of people being measured, particularly where this relates to objectives, personal and team performance, and performance-related pay schemes. Therefore, you should only include measurements that encourage progression toward meeting business objectives or desired behavioral change.

Measurements should

- Be "fit for purpose," providing the information required.
- Be "fit for use"—not overengineered or underengineered.

- Be "right the first time" with minimal rework. If the basis of measurement is being continually tweaked, it will raise questions about the validity of the results and make it impossible to establish any trends.

- Reflect the perspective of the business and the customers.

- Reflect the ability of the delivered solutions to meet the identified and agreed-to requirements of the business.

Four types of metrics can be used to measure the capability and performance of processes: These measure

- Progress—that is, the milestones and deliverables in the capability of the process

- Compliance of the process to governance requirements and compliance of people to the use of the process

- Effectiveness of the process and its ability to deliver the right result

- Efficiency—the productivity of the process, its speed, throughput, and resource utilization.

The Service Design Package

Service design is responsible for creating plans for the design, transition, and subsequent operation of these five different aspects. These plans should cover the approach, timescales, and resource requirements; the organizational and technical impact; risks; commercial aspects; training requirements; and appropriate communication methods. The output from this planning is captured in the service design package (SDP), which is collated by the design coordination process, and is an output from that process. The SDP should contain everything necessary for the subsequent testing, introduction, and operation of the solution or service. This should include the production of a set of service acceptance criteria (SAC) that will be used to ensure that the service provider is ready to deliver and support the new or changed service in the live environment.

The Interfaces of Design Coordination with Other Processes Related to PPO

As you would expect, the principal interfaces to the adjacent stages of the lifecycle are through using information contained within the IT strategy and service portfolio for service strategy, and the handover of the design of service solutions within the SDP for service transition.

The interfaces between design coordination and other individual processes are many, because this is a key collaborative process for the lifecycle stage of service design. The design coordination process interfaces with all the service design processes, including availability, capacity, continuity, and security (the "warranty" processes) as well as demand management; we have covered these topics in Chapters 8 and 9. Other interfaces include the following:

- Service portfolio management, which supplies the service charter, business requirements, utility, and warranty requirements, risks, and priorities.

- Change management, which produces change requests and works with design coordination to define design policies and practices associated with changes. Large changes go through the service strategy and service portfolio management; smaller changes come to design coordination directly from change management. Design coordination provides updates on design milestones relating to changes, and change management authorizes next actions at defined points, ensuring that required actions have taken place and quality criteria have been met. Post-implementation reviews of changes provide valuable feedback on possible improvements for design coordination.

- Financial management for IT services, which provides budget information and details of the value proposition.

- Business relationship management, which provides information regarding the business's required outcomes, customer needs, and priorities.

- Transition planning and support, which receives the SDP from design coordination and plays a similar role in transition to design coordination's role in the design stage.

- Strategy management for IT services, which provides current and evolving service strategy information, thus ensuring that design coordination's guidelines and documentation remain aligned with the strategy over time.

- Release and deployment management, which plans and executes individual authorized changes, releases, and deployments. The planning and design for release and deployment is carried out during the service design stage. Design coordination integrates this planning with the other service design activities, and the plan forms part of the overall SDP.

- Service validation and testing, which plans and executes tests to ensure that the service matches its design specification. Planning and designing tests is carried out during the service design stage. Again, design coordination integrates this planning with the other service design activities, and the plan forms part of the overall SDP.

- Change evaluation, which determines the performance of a service change to ensure that it is able to meet the intended requirements. Design coordination ensures that the required resources are available to carry out the evaluation:

    - Service level management defines and agrees on the SLRs for new or changed services; this must be done in accordance with practices developed cooperatively with design coordination.

    - Supplier management works with design coordination to ensure that the contributions of suppliers to design activities are properly managed. Supplier management will then manage the suppliers and their performance during service design, with the assistance of design coordination.

Summary

This chapter was an introduction to planning, protection, and optimization. It covered relevant practices from the core guidance related to service optimization and security and the related planning. We looked at the basic purpose and objective from service design and service strategy in support of PPO within a lifecycle context and the core concepts of service design in terms of its purpose, objectives, value, and relationship to the other ITIL lifecycle stages. We looked at the basic concepts of service design and, in particular, how the design coordination process interfaces with the PPO-related processes.

Exam Essentials

Understand what is meant by the phrase "Holistic Service Design."   Be able to give examples of aspects to be considered using this approach.

Be able to explain the four separate areas of people, process, products, and partners that support components of every service.   Understand that design needs to address all four areas. Give examples.

Be able to list the typical contents of a service design package.   Understand why each item would be required, and how it would be used.

Know the purpose of service design.   The purpose is to design IT services, with the necessary supporting IT practices, processes, and policies, and to realize the service provider's strategy. Design is not just about the technical design; it also considers the way it will be used and the processes required.

Understand that services must be designed to be adaptable to future requirements.   The service should be easily expanded or developed, so that it can be easily expanded or developed to meet changing requirements.

Understand the relationship between service design and business change.   Understand that the design of appropriate and innovative IT services is necessary to meet current and future agreed-on business requirements, but that IT services alone will not produce a business outcome without business change taking place.

Be able to list and explain the five aspects of service design.   Be able to name and describe the five aspects of service design (the solution, management systems, architectures, processes, and metrics) and why they are important.

Understand how good design delivers financial and other benefits to the business.   By ensuring that the design fits the business requirement and is adaptable to changing requirements, the need to completely redesign the service is avoided, thus minimizing the total cost of ownership.

Review Questions

You can find the answers to the review questions in the appendix.

1. What are the 4 Ps of service design?
    A. People, principles, products, policies
    B. Process, policies, principles, projects
    C. Process, people, products, policies
    D. People, process, partners, products

2. Which three aspects must be balanced in a balanced design?
    A. Time, cost, complexity
    B. Resources, time, functionality
    C. Resources, utility, warranty
    D. Functionality, consistency, resources

3. What is meant by "holistic" service design?
    A. The design can be implemented without the users being affected.
    B. The design has taken into account all five aspects of design.
    C. The design is balanced between functionality, resources, and the required schedule.
    D. The design has been costed to show the total cost of ownership.

4. Which of the following is *not* a possible risk when designing a service?
    A. The design will be inflexible, and therefore unable to adapt to meet changing requirements.
    B. Insufficient time spent on warranty aspects may mean the service is not fit for use.
    C. Insufficient time spent on warranty aspects may mean the service is not fit for purpose.
    D. The delivery date may be missed.

5. The design for a service must include which of the following?
    1. Details of the underpinning contracts that will be required
    2. Details of the technology components required
    3. Details of the skills that support staff will need
    4. Details of the governance requirements for the service
        A. 1, 2, and 4 only
        B. 1 and 2 only
        C. 2 and 4 only
        D. All of the above

6. Once the desired service solution has been designed, service design must carry out three activities before the solution passes into the service transition stage. Which of the following is *not* one of these activities?

   A. Evaluate alternative solutions

   B. Develop the business case

   C. Procure the preferred solution

   D. Develop the solution

7. Which of the following is *not* a purpose of service design?

   A. To evaluate the financial impact of new or changed strategies on the service provider

   B. To ensure quality service delivery

   C. To ensure customer satisfaction

   D. To ensure cost-effective service provision

8. Which of the following is *not* one of the five aspects of service design?

   A. Designing service solutions

   B. Risk management

   C. Management and technology architectures

   D. Processes

   E. Measurement systems, methods, and metrics

9. Which of the following are valid inclusions in a service design package?

  1. Technical design documents

  2. Service level agreements

  3. Change schedule

  4. Acceptance criteria

  5. Business requirements

  6. Testing plans

  7. The CMS

   A. All of the above

   B. 1, 2, 3, 5, and 6 only

   C. 1, 2, 4, 5, and 6 only

   D. 1, 2, 4, and 5 only

10. Which process is responsible for creating the service design package?

   A. Transition planning and support

   B. Change management

   C. Service portfolio management

   D. Design coordination

Chapter

8

Capacity, Availability, and Information Security Management

THE FOLLOWING ITIL PLANNING, PROTECTION, AND OPTIMIZATION CAPABILITY INTERMEDIATE EXAM OBJECTIVES ARE DISCUSSED IN THIS CHAPTER:

✓ Capacity, availability management, and information security management are discussed in terms of their

- Purpose
- Objectives
- Scope
- Value
- Policies
- Principles and basic concepts
- Process activities, methods, and techniques
- Triggers, inputs, outputs, and interfaces
- Information management
- Process roles
- Critical success factors and key performance indicators
- Challenges
- Risks

The processes discussed in this chapter cover three of the four aspects of warranty; you should remember from your ITIL Foundation studies that in order for services to deliver value, they must provide both utility (the functionality required, described as fitness for purpose) and warranty (sufficient availability, capacity, service continuity, and security for the service to perform at the required level, described as fitness for use).

Capacity management ensures that the service, and the technology on which it is based, can support the patterns of business activity. Availability management ensures that the service is reliable and resilient, with any downtime kept to a level acceptable to the customer, that is, as agreed in the service level agreements. ITIL defines information security management as "the management process within the corporate governance framework, which provides the strategic direction for security activities and ensures objectives are achieved."

We are going to examine each of these processes in turn.

Capacity Management

ITIL states that capacity management is responsible for ensuring that the capacity of IT services and the IT infrastructure is able to meet agreed current and future capacity and performance needs in a cost-effective and timely manner. The capacity management process must therefore understand the likely changes in capacity requirements and ensure that the design and ongoing management of a service meet this demand. As we have just said, sufficient capacity is a key warranty aspect of a service that needs to be delivered if the benefits of the service are to be realized.

Capacity management is considered throughout the lifecycle; as part of strategy, the likely capacity requirements for a new service are considered as part of the service evaluation to ensure that the service is meeting a real need. In design, the service is engineered to cope with that demand and to be flexible enough to be able to adjust to meet changing capacity requirements. Transition ensures that the service, when implemented, is delivering according to its specification. The operational phase of the lifecycle ensures that day-to-day adjustments that are necessary to meet changes in requirements are implemented. Finally, as part of continual service improvement, capacity-related issues are addressed and adjustments are made to ensure that the most cost-effective and reliable delivery of the service is achieved.

Purpose of Capacity Management

The purpose of the capacity management process is to understand the current and future capacity needs of a service and to ensure that the service and its supporting services are able to deliver to this level. The actual capacity requirements will have been agreed on as part of service level management; capacity management must not only meet these, but also ensure that the future needs of the business, which may change over time, are met.

Objectives of Capacity Management

The objectives of capacity management are met by the development of a detailed plan that states the current business requirement, the expected future requirement, and the actions that will be taken to meet these requirements. This plan should be reviewed and updated at regular intervals (at least annually) to ensure that changes in business requirements are considered. Similarly, any requests to change the current configuration will be considered by capacity management to ensure that they are in line with expectations or, if not, that the capacity plan is amended to suit the changed requirement. Those responsible for capacity management will review any issues that arise and help resolve any incidents or problems that are the result of insufficient capacity. This helps ensure that the service meets its objectives. An essential objective is to make sure capacity is increased or decreased in a timely manner so that the business is not impacted.

As part of the ongoing management of capacity and its continual improvement, any proactive measures that may improve performance at a reasonable cost are identified and acted on. Advice and guidance on capacity and performance-related issues are provided, and assistance is given to service operations with performance- and capacity-related incidents and problems.

Scope of Capacity Management

The capacity management process has responsibility for ensuring sufficient capacity at all times, including both planning for short-term fluctuations, such as those caused by seasonal variations, and ensuring that the required capacity is there for longer-term business expansion. Changes in demand may sometimes actually be reductions in that demand, and this is also within the scope of the process. Capacity management should ensure that as demand for the service falls, the capacity provided for that service is also reduced or managed to ensure that unnecessary expenditure is avoided.

The process includes all aspects of service provision and therefore may involve the technical, applications, and operations management functions. Other aspects of capacity, such as staff resources, are also considered.

 **Real World Scenario**

Capacity Management

A retail organization that was struggling to maintain its market position decided to expand its online and telephone-ordering service through a major marketing campaign. As part of this initiative, the telephone-ordering service hours were to be extended to

24 hours, 7 days a week. The business was considering what this would mean in terms of increased call center staff, warehouse staff, and stock levels. The IT director was tasked with ensuring that the IT services would support this business initiative.

The IT director called together his managers involved in the capacity management process. Those in the technical management function had to ensure that the infrastructure would be able to cope with the expected increased demand. This included the telecoms infrastructure capacity, required for the extra call center staff, and the voice traffic that the staff would generate in addition to the increase in data traffic. The website's capacity to handle increased traffic and the ability of the applications to handle a high volume of orders, credit card processing, and so on were investigated by the technical and applications management functions. The technical solutions that were recommended as a result meant more equipment would be purchased. The operations management function investigated the impact on operational processes, such as increased time needed to carry out backups and the impact of 24/7 operations on planned maintenance. Included was the impact of the extra equipment on the UPS, air conditioning, and so on. Finally, the service desk manager calculated what increase in staff would be required to move to a 24/7 support operation and an increased user population during peak hours. This was calculated as requiring two new service desk analysts, and the building services department was asked to provide the extra office space for the new staff.

As the "Capacity Management" sidebar illustrates, an increase in capacity requirements may have repercussions across the infrastructure and on the IT staff resources required to manage it. Although staffing is a line management responsibility, the calculation of resource requirements in this area is also part of the overall capacity management process.

Capacity management also involves monitoring "patterns of business activity" to understand how well the infrastructure is meeting the demands on it and making adjustments as required to ensure that the demand is met. Proactive improvements to capacity may also be implemented, where justified, and any incidents caused by capacity issues need to be investigated.

Capacity management may recommend demand management techniques to smooth out excessive peaks in demand. These techniques are discussed in Chapter 9, "IT Service Continuity Management and Demand Management."

Capacity Management Value to the Business

Capacity management provides value to the business by improving the performance and availability of IT services the business needs; it does so by helping to reduce capacity- and performance-related incidents and problems. The process will also ensure that the required capacity and performance are provided in the most cost-effective manner.

All processes should be contributing in some way to the achievement of customer satisfaction, and capacity management does this by ensuring that all capacity- and performance-related service levels are met. Capacity management needs to be aware of new techniques and technologies as they become available, exploiting them to provide cost-justified performance improvements and support innovation.

Proactive capacity management activities will ensure that capacity aspects are considered during the design and transition of new or changed services. The capacity plan will ensure that business needs and future plans are taken into account when planning services.

As with availability management, capacity management will have the opportunity to improve the ability of the business to follow an environmentally responsible strategy by using green technologies and techniques.

Capacity Management Policies, Principles, and Basic Concepts

Capacity management is essentially a balancing act. It ensures that the capacity and performance of the IT services and systems match the evolving demands of the business in the most cost-effective and timely manner. This requires balancing the costs against the resources needed. Capacity management needs to ensure that the processing capacity that is purchased is cost justifiable in terms of business need. It ensures that the organization makes the most efficient use of those resources.

Capacity management is also about balancing supply against demand. It is important to ensure that the available supply of IT processing power matches the demands made on it by the business, both now and in the future. It may also be necessary to manage or influence the demand for a particular resource.

The policies for capacity management should reflect the need for capacity management to play a significant role across the service lifecycle.

It is important to ensure that capacity management is part of the consideration for all service level and operational level agreements, and of course any supporting contracts with suppliers. These agreements will capture the service requirements of the business, and capacity management should consider these for the current and future business needs.

Capacity Management Process Activities, Methods, and Techniques

Capacity management has three supporting subprocesses: business capacity management, service capacity management, and component capacity management. There are many similar activities that are performed by each of the subprocesses, but each has a very different focus. Business capacity management is focused on the current and future business requirements, whereas service capacity management is focused on the delivery of the existing services that support the business, and component capacity management is focused on the IT infrastructure that underpins service provision.

In Figure 8.1, you can see the full scope of the subprocesses, techniques, and activities for the capacity management process. We will look at each subprocess in turn.

FIGURE 8.1   Capacity management subprocesses

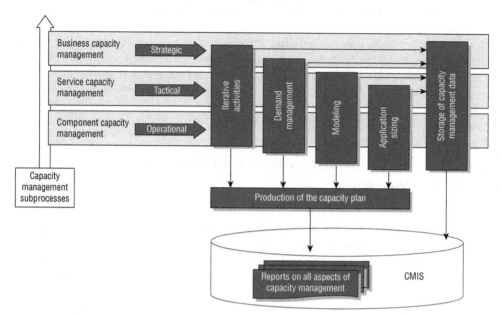

Business Capacity Management

The business capacity management subprocess is concerned with understanding the business plans and the implications of these on the IT infrastructure. This enables the necessary changes such as storage upgrades to be planned and implemented in time for the required capacity to be available when the business requires it. Capacity management will use existing utilization data for the current services and resources and extrapolate trends to predict future requirements. In addition, capacity management will plan the required capacity for new services due to come on-stream through the service strategy and service portfolio processes.

The capacity requirements are subject to change as the business changes. Business changes may require new services or changes to existing services or generate increased demand for those services. Some services will no longer be required, and this will free up spare capacity. These new requirements are identified by demand management, which analyzes patterns of business activity to understand how these patterns generate demand patterns for IT service. This information enables proactive capacity management to predict and satisfy future requirements.

Capacity management needs to be included in all strategic, planning, and design activities as early as possible if the services are going to be able to meet the level of demand and the performance targets set in the service level agreements. The process will model the capacity requirements for a number of different scenarios in order to understand the impact on capacity requirements. For example, such scenarios might include the impact of fewer or greater numbers of concurrent users than the original prediction.

Once the capacity requirements are understood, capacity management will recommend procurement of new capacity, if required, or other measures taken as necessary. It will also ensure that the actions taken are implemented through the change management process. It will also advise service level management what SLA performance targets are achievable.

Service Capacity Management

The service capacity management subprocess focuses on the management, control, and prediction of the end-to-end performance and capacity of the live, operational IT services usage and workloads. It ensures that the performance of all services, as detailed in service targets within SLAs and SLRs, is monitored and measured, and that the collected data is recorded, analyzed, and reported. Wherever necessary, proactive and reactive action should be instigated to ensure that the performance of all services meets their agreed-on business targets. Wherever possible, automated thresholds should be used to manage all operational services to ensure that situations where service targets are breached or threatened are rapidly identified. Service capacity management will monitor the workload to ensure that they do not exceed any specified limitations.

Service capacity management monitors changes in performance levels and assesses the impact of changes so that most issues can be predicted and acted on before the service is impacted.

Component Capacity Management

The component capacity management subprocess focuses on the management, control, and prediction of the performance, utilization, and capacity of individual IT technology components such as processors, memory, disks, network bandwidth, and network connections. It ensures that all components within the IT infrastructure that have finite resources are monitored and measured, and that the collected data is recorded, analyzed, and reported. Wherever possible, automated thresholds should be implemented to manage all components through the event management process to ensure that situations where service targets are breached or threatened by component usage or performance are rapidly identified, and cost-effective actions, such as load-balancing, are implemented to reduce or avoid their potential impact.

Capacity Management Tools

It is important to ensure that the tools used by capacity management conform to the organization's management architecture as well as integrate with other tools used for the management of IT systems and automation of IT processes.

Service operation monitoring and control activities provide a basis for the tools to support capacity management. The IT operations management function and the technical management departments (such as network management and server management) may carry out the bulk of the day-to-day operational duties. They will participate in the capacity management process by providing it with performance information.

Reactive and Proactive Activities

Capacity management has both reactive and proactive activities (as has availability management, which we will examine later in this chapter). In Figure 8.2, you can see the activities relating to both reactive and proactive capacity management and the interaction between the subprocesses.

FIGURE 8.2   Capacity management overview with subprocesses

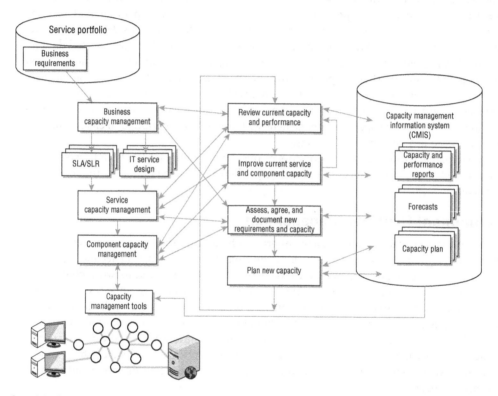

Capacity management should include the following proactive activities:

▪ Preempting performance issues by taking the necessary actions before the issues occur

▪ Producing trends of the current component utilization and using them to estimate the future requirements and for planning upgrades and enhancements

▪ Modeling and trending the predicted changes in IT services (including service retirements)

- Ensuring that upgrades are budgeted, planned, and implemented before SLAs and service targets are breached or performance issues occur
- Actively seeking to improve service performance wherever the cost is justifiable
- Producing and maintaining a capacity plan addressing future requirements and plans for meeting them
- Tuning (also known as optimizing) the performance of services and components

    Capacity management should include the following reactive activities:

- Monitoring, measuring, reporting, and reviewing the current performance of both services and components
- Responding to all capacity-related "threshold" events and instigating corrective action
- Reacting to and assisting with specific performance issues

Ongoing Activities

A number of ongoing activities form part of the capacity management process. These activities provide the basic historical information and triggers necessary for all the other activities and processes within capacity management (see Figure 8.3).

FIGURE 8.3   Ongoing iterative activities of capacity management

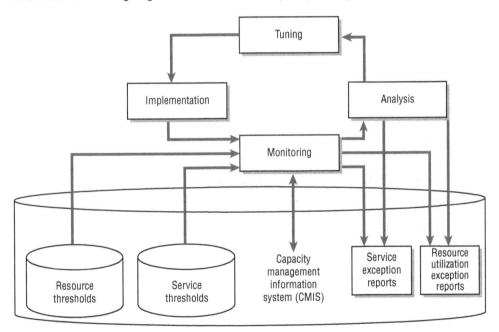

Each service, and all of its components, should be monitored, and compared against defined thresholds, to spot trends and identify potential issues. This enables the necessary action to be taken. Recommendations can also be made for the purchase of new capacity or the adoption of new technology.

Typical monitored data includes the following:

- Processor utilization

- Memory utilization

- I/O rates (physical and buffer) and device utilization

- Queue lengths

- Disk utilization

- Transaction rates

- Response times

- Batch duration

- Database usage

- Index usage

- Hit rates

- Concurrent user numbers

- Network traffic rates

Thresholds should be based on historical analysis of normal activity and set below the level at which the service is impacted to allow time for corrective action. If the thresholds are exceeded, alarms should be raised and exception reports produced.

The ongoing activities may include balancing services, balancing workloads, changing concurrency levels, and adding or removing resources. The monitoring reports and information about the actions recommended and taken are stored in the capacity management information system (CMIS).

Capacity Management Triggers, Inputs, and Outputs and Interfaces

Let's consider the triggers, inputs, and outputs for the capacity management process, and its interfaces with other service management processes. Capacity management is a process that has many active connections throughout the organization and its processes. It is important that the triggers, inputs, outputs, and interfaces be clearly defined to avoid duplicated effort or gaps in workflow.

Triggers

Many triggers will initiate capacity management activities:

- New and changed services requiring additional capacity

- Service breaches, capacity or performance events, and alerts, including threshold events

- Exception reports
- Periodic revision of current capacity and performance and the review of forecasts, reports, and plans
- Periodic trending and modeling
- Review and revision of business and IT plans and strategies
- Review and revision of designs and strategies
- Review and revision of SLAs, operational level agreements, contracts, or any other agreements
- Requests from service level management for assistance with capacity and/or performance targets and explanation of achievements

Inputs

A number of sources of information are relevant to the capacity management process:

- Business information
- Service and IT information
- Component performance and capacity information
- Service performance issue information
- Service information
- Financial information
- Change information
- Performance information
- CMS
- Workload information

Outputs

The outputs of capacity management are used within the process itself as well as by many other processes and other parts of the organization. The information is often reproduced in an electronic format as visual real-time displays of performance. The outputs are as follows:

- The capacity management information system
- The capacity plan
- Service performance information and reports
- Workload analysis and reports
- Ad hoc capacity and performance reports
- Forecasts and predictive reports
- Thresholds, alerts, and events
- Improvement actions

Interfaces

As we have already explained, capacity management has strong connections across the service lifecycle with a number of other processes. For example, all changes to service and resource capacity must follow all IT processes such as change, release, configuration, and project management.

The key interfaces are as follows:

- Availability management works with capacity management to determine the resources needed to ensure the required availability of services and components.

- Service level management provides assistance with determining capacity targets and the investigation and resolution of breaches related to service and component capacity.

- IT service continuity management is supported by capacity management through the assessment of business impact and risk, determining the capacity needed to support risk reduction measures and recovery options.

- Capacity management provides assistance with incident and problem management for the resolution and correction of capacity-related incidents and problems.

- By anticipating the demand for services based on user profiles and patterns of business activity, and by identifying the means to influence that demand, demand management provides strategic decision making and critical related data on which capacity management can act.

Information Management and Capacity Management

The CMIS is used to provide the relevant capacity and performance information to produce reports and support the capacity management process. The reports provide information to a number of IT and service management processes. These should include the reports described in the following sections.

Component-Based Reports

There is likely to be a team of technical staff responsible for each component, and they should be in charge of their control and management. Reports must be produced to illustrate how components are performing and how much of their maximum capacity is being used.

Service-Based Reports

Service-based reports will provide the basis of SLM and customer service reports. Reports and information must be produced to illustrate how the service and its constituent components are performing with respect to their overall service targets and constraints.

Exception Reports

Exception reports can be used to show management and technical staff when the capacity and performance of a particular component or service becomes unacceptable. Thresholds can be set for any component, service, or measurement within the CMIS. An example threshold may be that processor utilization for a particular server has breached 70 percent for three consecutive hours or that the concurrent number of logged-in users exceeds the specified limit.

In particular, exception reports are of interest to the SLM process in determining whether the targets in SLAs have been breached. Also, the incident and problem management processes may be able to use the exception reports in the resolution of incidents and problems; for example, slow response may be traced to lack of capacity. Excess capacity should also be identified. Unused capacity may represent an opportunity for cost savings.

Predictive and Forecast Reports

Part of the capacity management process is to predict future workloads and growth. To do this, future component and service capacity and performance must be forecast. This can be done in a variety of ways, depending on the techniques and the technology used. A simple example of a capacity forecast is a correlation between a business driver and component utilization. If the forecasts on future capacity requirements identify a requirement for increased resource, this requirement needs to be input into the capacity plan and included within the IT budget cycle.

Process Roles

In Chapter 1, "Introduction to Operational Support and Analysis," we explored the generic roles applicable to all processes throughout the service lifecycle. These are relevant to the capacity management process, but specific additional requirements also apply. Remember that these are not "job titles"; they are guidance on the roles that may be needed to successfully run the process.

Capacity Management Process Owner

The capacity management process owner's responsibilities typically include the following:

- Carrying out the generic process owner role for the capacity management process (see Chapter 1 for more detail)
- Working with managers of all functions to ensure acceptance of the capacity management process as the single point of coordination for all capacity- and performance-related issues, regardless of the specific technology involved
- Working with other process owners to ensure an integrated approach to the design and implementation of capacity management, availability management, IT service continuity management, and information security management

Capacity Management Process Manager

The capacity management process manager's responsibilities typically include the following:

- Carrying out the generic process manager role for the capacity management process (see Chapter 1 for more detail)
- Coordinating interfaces between capacity management and other processes, especially service level management, availability management, IT service continuity management, and information security management

- Ensuring adequate IT capacity to meet required levels of service
- Providing advice on matching capacity and demand and on optimizing the use of existing capacity
- Working with SLM to ascertain capacity requirements from the business
- Understanding the current usage and the maximum capacity of each component
- Modeling and sizing all proposed new services and systems
- Forecasting future capacity requirements
- Producing, reviewing, and revising the capacity plan, in line with the organization's business planning cycle
- Setting appropriate levels of monitoring of resources and systems
- Analyzing usage and performance data, and reporting on performance against targets contained in SLAs
- Raising incidents and problems when breaches of capacity or performance thresholds are detected, and assisting with the investigation and diagnosis of capacity-related incidents and problems
- Performing tuning to optimize and improve capacity or performance
- Implementing initiatives to improve resource usage—for example, demand management techniques
- Assessing new technology to improve performance and new techniques and products that could be used to improve the process
- Assessing all changes for their impact on capacity and performance and attending CAB meetings when appropriate
- Reporting on current usage of resources, trends and forecasts, and performance against targets contained in SLAs
- Testing performance of new services and systems
- Predicting the effects of future demand on performance service levels
- Determining achievable performance service levels that are cost-justified
- Acting as a focal point for all capacity and performance issues

Critical Success Factors and Key Performance Indicators for Capacity Management

The following list includes some sample critical success factors for capacity management and some key performance indicators for each.

- Critical success factor: "Accurate business forecasts"
    - KPI: Production of workload forecasts on time
    - KPI: Accuracy (measured as a percentage) of forecasts of business trends

- Critical success factor: "Knowledge of current and future technologies"
    - KPI: Timely justification and implementation of new technology in line with business requirements (time, cost, and functionality)
    - KPI: Reduction in the use of old technology, causing breached SLAs due to problems with support or performance
- Critical success factor: "Ability to demonstrate cost effectiveness"
    - KPI: Reduction in last-minute buying to address urgent performance issues
    - KPI: Reduction in the overcapacity of IT
- Critical success factor: "Ability to plan and implement the appropriate IT capacity to match business needs"
    - KPI: Reduction (measured as a percentage) in the number of incidents due to poor performance
    - KPI: Reduction (measured as a percentage) in lost business due to inadequate capacity

Challenges for Capacity Management

One of the major challenges facing capacity management is persuading the business to provide information on its strategic business plans. Without this information, the IT service provider will find it difficult to provide effective business capacity management. If there are commercial or confidential reasons this data cannot be shared, it becomes even more challenging for the service provider.

Another challenge is the combination of all of the component capacity management data into an integrated set of information that can be analyzed in a consistent manner. This is particularly challenging when the information from the different technologies is provided by different tools in differing formats.

The amount of information produced by business capacity management, and especially service capacity management and component capacity management, is huge, and the analysis of this information is often difficult to achieve.

It is important that the people and the processes focus on the key resources and their usage without ignoring other areas. For this to be done, appropriate thresholds must be used, and reliance must be placed on tools and technology to automatically manage the technology and provide warnings and alerts when things deviate significantly from the norm.

Risks for Capacity Management

The following list includes some of the major risks associated with capacity management:

- There is a lack of commitment from the business to the capacity management process.
- There is a lack of appropriate information from the business on future plans and strategies.
- There is a lack of senior management commitment to or a lack of resources and/or budget for the capacity management process.

- Service capacity management and component capacity management is performed in isolation because business capacity management is difficult or there is a lack of appropriate and accurate business information.

- The processes become too bureaucratic or manually intensive.

- The processes focus too much on the technology (component capacity management) and not enough on the services (service capacity management) and the business (business capacity management).

- The reports and information provided are too technical and do not give the information required by or appropriate for the customers and the business.

Availability Management

The availability of a service is critical to its value. No matter how clever it is or what functionality it offers (its utility), the service is of no value to the customer unless it delivers the warranty expected. Poor availability is a primary cause of customer dissatisfaction. Availability is one of the four warranty aspects that must be delivered if the service is to be fit for use. Targets for availability are often included in service level agreements, so the IT service provider must understand the factors to be considered when seeking to meet or exceed the availability target. This section covers how availability is measured; the purpose, objectives, and scope of availability management; and a number of key concepts.

Defining Availability

ITIL defines *availability* as the ability of an IT service or other configuration item to perform its agreed function when required. Any unplanned interruption to a service during its agreed service hours (also called the agreed *service time*, specified in the service level agreement) is defined as *downtime*. The availability measure is calculated by subtracting the downtime from the agreed service time and converting it to a percentage of the agreed service time.

It is important to note the inclusion of *when required* in the definition and the word *agreed* in the calculation. The service may be available when the customer does not require it; including time when the customer does not need the service in the calculation gives a false impression of the availability from the customer perspective. If customer perception does not match the reporting provided, the customer will become cynical and distrust the reports.

Calculating Availability: Two Examples

Example A: A service is available 24 hours a day, 7 days a week. One hour of downtime per week is calculated as follows:

168 hours − 1 hour downtime = 167/168 * 100 = 99.4% availability

Example B: If the service is available but used only 9 a.m. to 5 p.m., Monday through Friday (and these 40 hours are the service hours agreed to in the SLA), then the same 1 hour of downtime results in a different figure:

40 hours − 1 hour downtime = 39/40 × 100 = 97.5% availability

$$\text{Availability (\%)} = \frac{\text{Agreed service time (AST)} - \text{downtime}}{\text{AST}} \times 100$$

If the downtime occurred overnight, it would be included in the calculations in Example A but not those in Example B because there was no agreed service after 5 p.m.

It is important, therefore, to agree on exactly what the specified service hours are; they should be documented in the SLA. The basis for the calculation should be clear to the customer.

Keep in mind that the customer experiences the end-to-end service; the availability delivered depends on all links in the chain being operational when required. The customer will complain that a service is unavailable whether the fault is with the application, the network, or the hardware. The availability management process is therefore concerned with reducing service affecting downtime wherever it occurs. Again, it should be clearly stated in the availability reports whether the calculations are based on the end-to-end service or just the application availability. It is therefore essential to understand the difference between service availability and component availability.

Purpose of Availability Management

The purpose of the availability management process is to take the necessary steps to deliver the availability requirements defined in the SLA. The process should consider both the current requirements and the future needs of the business. All actions taken to improve availability have an accompanying cost, so all improvements made must be assessed for cost-effectiveness.

Availability management considers all aspects of IT service provision to identify possible improvements to availability. Some improvements will depend on implementing new technology; others will result from more effective use of staff resources or streamlined processes. Availability management analyzes reasons for downtime and assesses the return on investment for improvements to ensure that the most cost-effective measures are taken. The process ensures that the delivery of the agreed availability is prioritized across all phases of the lifecycle.

Objectives of Availability Management

The objectives of availability management are as follows:

- Producing and maintaining a plan that details how the current and future availability requirements are to be met. This plan should consider requirements 12 to 24 months in advance to ensure that any necessary expenditure is agreed on in the annual budget negotiations and any new equipment is bought and installed before the availability is affected. The plan should be revised regularly to take into account any changes in the business.

- Providing advice throughout the service lifecycle on all availability-related issues to both the business and IT, ensuring that the impact of any decisions on availability is considered.

- Managing the delivery of services to meet the agreed targets. Where downtime has occurred, availability management will assist in resolving the incident by utilizing incident management and, when appropriate, resolving the underlying problem by utilizing the problem management process.

- Assessing all requests for change to ensure that any potential risk to availability has been considered. Any updates to the availability plan required as a result of changes will also be considered and implemented.

- Considering all possible proactive steps that could be taken to improve availability across the end-to-end service, assessing the risk and potential benefits of these improvements, and implementing them where justified.

- Implementing monitoring of availability to ensure that targets are being achieved.

- Optimizing all areas of IT service provision to deliver the required availability consistently to enable the business to use the services provided to achieve its objectives.

Scope of Availability Management

As discussed, the availability management process encompasses all phases of the service lifecycle. It is included in the design phase because the most effective way to deliver availability is to ensure that availability considerations are designed in from the start. Once the service is operational, opportunities are continually sought to remove risks to availability and make the service more robust. The activities for these opportunities are part of proactive availability management. Throughout the live delivery of the service, availability management analyzes any downtime and implements measures to reduce the frequency and length of future occurrences. These are the reactive activities of availability management. Changes to live services are assessed to understand risks to the service, and measurements are put in place to ensure that downtime is measured accurately. This continues throughout the operational phase until the service is retired.

The scope of availability management includes all operational services and technology. Where SLAs are in place, there will be clear, agreed targets. There may be other services, however, where no formal SLA exists but where downtime has a significant business impact. Availability management should not exclude these services from consideration; it should strive to achieve high availability in line with the potential impact of downtime on the business. Service level management should work to negotiate SLAs for all such services in the future— without them, it is the IT service provider who is assessing the level of availability required—but this should be a business decision. Availability management should be applied to all new IT services and for existing services where SLRs or SLAs have been established. Supporting services must be included because the failures of these services impact the customer-facing services. Availability management may also work with supplier management to ensure that the level of service provided by partners does not threaten the overall service availability.

Every aspect of service provision comes within the scope of availability management. Poor processes, untrained staff, and ineffective tools can all contribute to causing or unnecessarily prolonging downtime. The availability management process ensures that the availability of systems and services matches the evolving needs of the business.

The role of IT within businesses is critical. The availability and reliability of IT services can directly influence customer satisfaction and the reputation of the business. Availability management is essential in ensuring that IT delivers the levels of service availability required by the business to satisfy its business objectives and deliver the quality of service demanded by its customers.

Customer satisfaction is an important factor for all businesses and may provide a competitive edge for the organization. Dissatisfaction with the availability and reliability of IT service can be a key factor in customers taking their business to a competitor.

Availability can also improve the ability of the business to follow an environmentally responsible strategy by using green technologies and techniques in availability management.

Availability Management Policies

The policies of availability management should state that the process is included as part of all lifecycle stages, from service strategy to continual service improvement. The appropriate availability and resilience should be designed into services and components from the initial design stages. This will ensure not only that the availability of any new or changed service meets the expected targets, but also that all existing services and components continue to meet all their targets.

Availability policies should be established by the service provider to ensure that availability is considered throughout the lifecycle. Policies should also be established regarding the criteria to be used to define availability and unavailability of a service or component and how each will be measured.

Availability management is completed at two interconnected levels:

- Service availability involves all aspects of service availability and unavailability. This includes the impact of component availability and the potential impact of component unavailability on service.

- Component availability involves all aspects of component availability and unavailability.

Availability Management Principles and Basic Concepts

Availability management must align its activities and priorities to the requirements of the business. This requires a firm understanding of the business processes and how they are underpinned by the IT service. Information regarding the future business plans and priorities and therefore the future requirements of the business with regard to availability is essential input to the availability plan. Only with this understanding of the business requirement can the service provider be sure that its efforts to improve availability are correctly targeted.

The response of the IT service provider to failure can improve the customer's perception of the service, despite the break in service. The service provider's actions can show an understanding of the impact of the downtime on the business processes, and an eagerness to overcome the issue and prevent recurrences can reassure the business that IT understands its needs.

Additionally, the process requires a strong technical understanding of the individual components that make up each service, their capabilities, and their current performance. Through this combination of business understanding and technical knowledge, the optimal design can be delivered to produce the required level of availability to meet current and future needs.

When designing a new service and discussing its availability requirements, the service provider and the business must focus on the criticality of the service to the business being able to achieve its aims. Expenditure to provide high availability across every aspect of a service is unlikely to be justified. The business process that the IT service supports may be a *vital business function (VBF)*, and identifying which services or parts of services are the most critical is therefore a business decision. For example, the ability of an Internet-based bookshop to be able to process credit card payments would be a vital business function. The ability to display a "customers who bought this book also bought these other books" feature is not vital. It may encourage some increased sales, but the purchaser is able to complete their purchase without it. Once these VBFs are understood, the design of the service to ensure the required availability can commence. Understanding the VBFs informs decisions regarding where expenditure to protect availability is justified.

Determining what the appropriate availability target of a service should be is a business decision, not an IT decision. However, availability comes at a price, and the service provider must ensure that the customer understands the cost implications of too high a target. Customers may otherwise demand a very high availability target (99.99% or greater) and then find the service unaffordable.

Where the cost of very high availability is justified, the design of the service will include highly reliable components, resilience, and minimal or no planned downtime.

Having considered the importance of availability to the business, in the following sections we examine some of the key availability management activities and concepts that the IT service provider may employ to cut downtime and thus deliver the required availability to the business, enabling it to achieve its business objectives.

Availability Concepts

Availability management comprises both reactive and proactive activities, as shown in Figure 8.4. The reactive activities include regular monitoring of service provisions involving extensive data gathering and reporting of the performance of individual components and processes and the availability delivered by them. Event management is often used to monitor components because this speeds up the identification of any issues through the setting of alert thresholds. It may even be possible to restart the failing service automatically, possibly before the break has been noticed by the customers. Instances of downtime are investigated, and remedial actions are taken to prevent a recurrence. The proactive activities include identifying and managing risks to the availability of the service and implementing measures to protect against such an occurrence. Where protective measures have been put in place to provide resilience in the event of component failure, the measures require regular testing to ensure that they work as designed to protect the service availability. All new or changed services should be subject to continual service improvement; countermeasures should be implemented wherever they can be cost justified. This cost justification requires an understanding of the vital business functions and the cost to the business of any downtime. It is ultimately a business decision, not a technical decision. Figure 8.4 also shows the availability management information system (AMIS); this is the repository for all availability management reports, plans, risk registers, and so on, and it forms part of the service knowledge management system (SKMS).

FIGURE 8.4   The availability management process

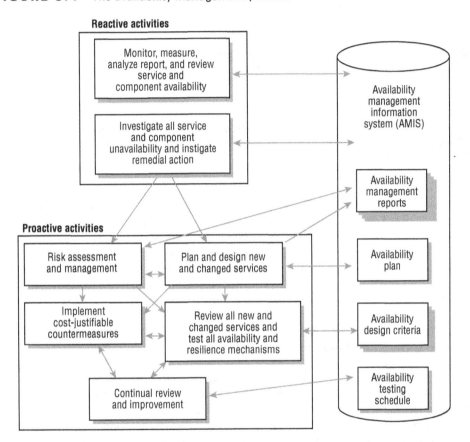

Business continuity management and IT service continuity management are outside the scope of availability management. A strong relationship exists between availability management and these processes, however, because every action taken to mitigate a risk to availability or to provide resilience will support ITSCM.

Reliability

The first availability concept we cover is *reliability.* This is defined by ITIL as "a measure of how long a service, component, or CI can perform its agreed function without interruption." We normally describe how reliable an item is by stating how frequently it can be expected to break down within a given time: "My car is very reliable. It has broken down only twice in five years." We measure reliability by calculating the *mean (or average) time between failures (MTBF)* or the *mean (or average) time between service incidents (MTBSI).*

MTBF is measured from when the configuration item starts working until it next fails. It is therefore a measure of uptime.

MTBSI is measured from when a system or IT service fails until it next fails. It therefore includes both the MTBF and the time taken to restore the service.

Reliability of a service can be improved first by ensuring that the components specified in the design are of good quality and from a supplier with a good reputation. Even the best components will fail eventually; however, the reliability of the service can be improved by designing the service so that a component failure does not result in downtime. This is another availability concept called *resilience.* By ensuring that the design includes alternate network routes, for example, a network component failure will not lead to service downtime because the traffic will reroute. Carrying out planned maintenance to ensure that all the components are kept in good working order will also help improve reliability.

Resilience through Redundancy

A good example of designing in resilience is that of a modern passenger aircraft. Although the engines are designed to be very reliable, with a long MTBF, an aircraft with a single engine could still suffer catastrophic failure if that engine developed a fault midflight. Aircraft are therefore designed to have several engines and to be able to fly and land with only one of them operational. This availability management approach delivers resilience by providing redundancy (the use of one or more additional configuration items to provide fault tolerance).

Maintainability

However reliable the equipment and resilient the design, not all downtime can be prevented. When a fault occurs and there is insufficient resilience in the design to prevent it from affecting the service, the length of the downtime that results can be affected by how quickly the fault can be overcome. This is called *maintainability* and is measured as the *mean time to restore service (MTRS).* It may be more cost-effective to concentrate on resilience measures for those items that have a long service restoration time. To calculate MTRS, divide the total downtime by the total number of failures.

Calculating MTRS

A service suffers four failures in a month. The duration of each was 1 hour, 2 hours, 1.2 hours, and 1.8 hours, resulting in a total downtime of 6 hours.

MTRS = 6 / 4 = 1.5 hours

$$\text{Maintainability (MTRS in hours)} = \frac{\text{Total downtime in hours}}{\text{Number of service breaks}}$$

Simple measures can be taken to reduce MTRS, such as having common spares available on site, and these measures can have a significant impact on availability.

ITIL recommends the use of MTRS rather than mean time to repair (MTTR) because repair may or may not include the restoration of the service following the repair. From the customer perspective, downtime includes all the time between the fault occurring and the service being fully usable again. MTRS measures this complete time and is therefore a more meaningful measurement.

These concepts are illustrated in Figure 8.5, which shows what ITIL calls the *expanded incident lifecycle*. This illustrates periods of uptime with incidents causing periods of downtime. MTRS is shown as the average of the downtime for the incident. MTBF is shown as the average of the uptime for the incident.

FIGURE 8.5   The expanded incident lifecycle

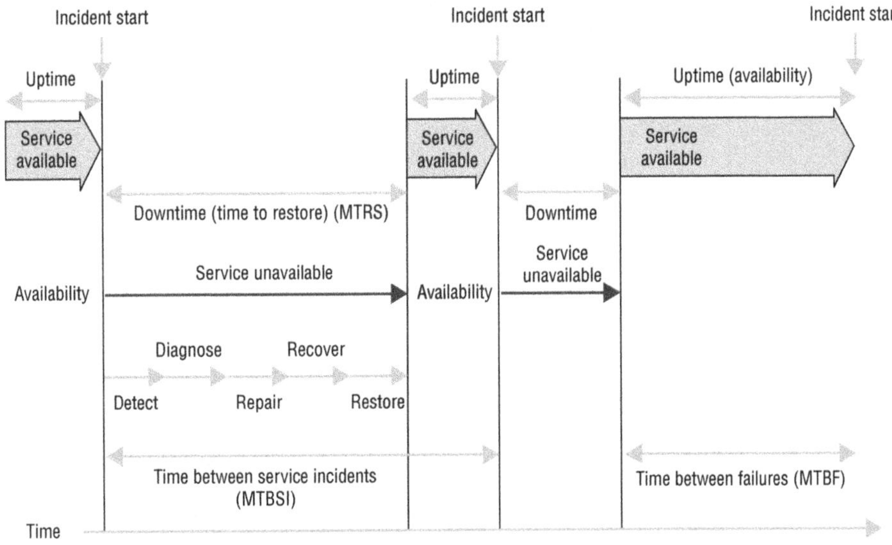

Each incident needs to be detected, diagnosed, and repaired, and the data needs to be recovered and the service restored. Any method of shortening any of these steps—speeding up detection through event management or speeding up diagnosis by the use of a knowledge base, for example—will shorten the downtime and improve availability. The figure also shows another concept: MTBSI, which calculates the average time from the start of one incident to the start of the next and is used as a measure of reliability.

Serviceability

Serviceability is defined as the ability of a third-party supplier to meet the terms of its contract. This contract will include agreed levels of availability, reliability, and/or maintainability for a supporting service or component.

In Figure 8.6, you can see the terms and measures used in availability management, which are combined when applied to suppliers providing serviceability.

FIGURE 8.6   Availability terms and measures

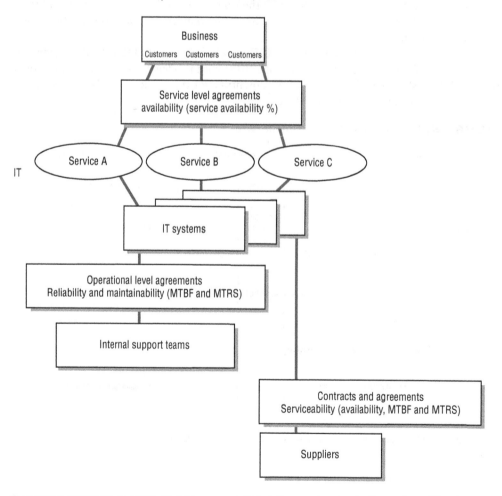

> **Availability Concepts: Reliability, Maintainability, and Serviceability**
>
> A large bakery had used a machine for making bread rolls for 15 years without any downtime. This machine was responsible for the production of all the bread rolls for a major fast-food company and was therefore very important to the business. The long period without failure showed that the machine was very *reliable*, possibly because of a *resilient* design. One day it failed. Because it had never failed before, there was consternation; there was no procedure in place for such an occurrence. Eventually a manual was located, but it was in German. The staff at the bakery tracked down the manufacturer in Germany (this was in the days before Google) and placed a call. An engineer arrived the following day (exactly two days since the fault occurred) and fixed the machine in 15 minutes. The mean time to repair was therefore short (15 minutes), but the mean time to restore service was 2 days and 15 minutes, which had a major impact on the ability of the company to satisfy its external customer, the fast-food chain. The weakness here was in the *serviceability* of the machine; there was no contract in place to ensure a response and fix in an appropriate time.

Measurement of Availability

The term *vital business function (VBF)* is used to reflect the part of a business process that is critical to the success of the business. The more vital the business function generally, the greater the level of resilience and availability that needs to be incorporated into the design of the supporting IT services. The availability requirements for all services, vital or not, should be determined by the business and not by IT.

Certain vital business functions may need special designs. These commonly include the following functions:

High Availability A characteristic of the IT service that minimizes or masks the effects of IT component failure to the users of a service.

Fault Tolerance The ability of an IT service, component, or configuration item to continue to operate correctly after failure of a component part.

Continuous Operation An approach or design to eliminate planned downtime of an IT service. Individual components or configuration items may be down even though the IT service remains available.

Continuous Availability An approach or design to achieve 100 percent availability. A continuously available IT service has no planned or unplanned downtime.

Within the IT industry, many suppliers commit to high availability or continuous availability solutions but only if specific environmental standards and resilient processes are used. They often agree to such contracts only after additional, sometimes costly, improvements have been made.

The availability management process depends heavily on the measurement of service and component achievements with regard to availability.

The decision on what to measure and how to report it depends on which activity is being supported, who the recipients are, and how the information is to be used. It is important to recognize the differing perspectives of availability from the business, users, and service providers to ensure that measurement and reporting satisfies these varied needs.

The business perspective considers IT service availability in terms of its contribution or impact on the vital business functions that drive the business operation.

The user perspective considers IT service availability as a combination of three factors. These are the frequency, the duration, and the scope of impact. For many applications, poor response times for the user are considered at the same level as failures of technology.

The IT service provider perspective considers IT service and component availability with regard to availability, reliability, and maintainability.

It is important to consider the full scope of measures needed to report the same level of availability in different ways to satisfy the differing perspectives of availability. Measurements need to be meaningful and add value. This is influenced strongly by the combination of "what you measure" and "how you report it."

Availability Management Process, Methods, and Techniques

We have explored the concepts and measures used in the availability management process. Figure 8.4 showed the key elements of the process, including the availability management information system. A number of different techniques can be used for availability management; we will examine them now.

Expanded Incident Lifecycle

We looked at the expanded incident lifecycle briefly earlier, in Figure 8.5, when considering availability concepts. This technique requires the analysis of the lifecycle of an incident from start to finish and the period between an incident and the next outage. Outages may not always be preventable; the availability management process seeks not only to avoid downtime, but also to minimize its duration and impact when it does occur. The duration of the downtime can be reduced by analyzing how long each step in the process takes, and then exploiting any opportunities to shorten that stage. Let's look at each of the incident stages in turn:

Incident Detection   This is time that elapses between the incident occurring and the IT service provider becoming aware of the failure. Event management tools can be very helpful in this regard, sending notification of failure, possibly before the users have become aware themselves. This enables the fault to be addressed quickly, thus reducing downtime and improving availability. Tools may have the capability to diagnose the fault and to automatically recover the service. Further information about event management is covered in Chapter 3, "Event Management, Request Fulfillment, and Access Management."

Incident Diagnosis   This is the time by which the cause of the fault has been identified. Faster diagnosis will reduce downtime and increase availability. Again, some monitoring tools can assist in gathering the necessary diagnostic data to help in problem resolution. This may occasionally delay the resolution of service, but it will enable the root cause of repeated failures to be identified and removed, thus reducing the overall downtime.

Incident Repair   This is the time at which the repair has been implemented. This may be impacted by the design of the component, so care should be taken in the service design stage to choose components that can be repaired quickly. It may also be impacted by the performance of internal teams or suppliers responsible for carrying out the repair actions. The relevant operational level agreements and underpinning contracts should be monitored by service level management and supplier management for breaches and service improvement plans put in place to prevent such breaches in the future.

Incident Recovery   This is the time at which component recovery has been completed. The backup and recovery requirements for the hardware, software, and data components should be identified as early as possible within the design cycle to enable appropriate recovery plans to be drawn up and tested. Wherever possible, recovery actions should be automated. Availability requirements should also contribute to determining what spare parts are kept within the definitive spares area. We discuss the storage of definitive spares in Chapter 12, "Change Management and Service Asset and Configuration Management," which describes a storage area set aside for the secure storage of spare components and assemblies that are maintained at the same revision level as the systems within the controlled test or live environment; these are used for testing new services in the transition stage and to replace faulty equipment in the operation stage.

Incident Restoration   This is the time at which normal business service is resumed. It is important that the ability to work normally is verified before the incident is closed. This may be verified by the service desk by talking to the service users. If the service is one used by the public, such as an ATM or web commerce site, visual checks of transaction throughput or user simulation scripts that validate the end-to-end service may be necessary.

By looking at each stage of the expanded incident lifecycle, we can identify delays and take action to reduce them in the future. For example, a downtime of an hour but with a repair action time of 5 minutes will identify delays such as time wasted before the fault was identified due to poorly configured event management tools, overlong diagnosis time, lack of skills, lack of documentation, and so forth. Availability management needs to work in close association with incident and problem management to ensure that repeat occurrences are eliminated.

Fault Tree Analysis

This approach uses Boolean logic, using AND and OR statements, to analyze the sequence of events that lead to a failure. These events may be characterized as basic, resulting, conditional, or trigger events. The AND statement means all the input events must occur simultaneously for the resultant event to take place (for example, when both the primary and fail-over lines must be down for the network to be down). OR is when the event occurs if any of the input events occurs. There is also an INHIBIT statement when the resulting event occurs only when the input condition is not met. Figure 8.7 gives an example of a fault tree and these statements.

FIGURE 8.7   Fault tree analysis example

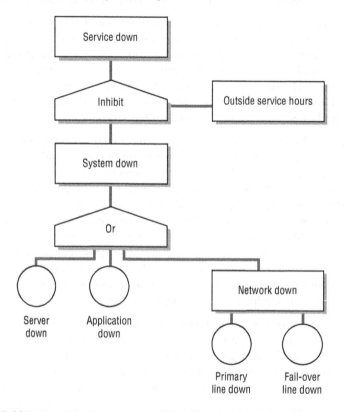

In Figure 8.7, the service is down if the network or the server or the application is down (an example of the OR statement). The network is down if both the primary and failover lines are down (an example of the AND statement). Finally the service would not be considered down if the fault(s) occurred outside service hours (an example of the INHIBIT statement).

Component Failure Impact Analysis

Component failure impact analysis (CFIA) is a technique that considers the importance of an individual component to the provision of service. It enables the impact on services of a failing component to be predicted, in particular any single points of failure (SPOFs). This, in turn, will indicate where resilience or risk reduction measures are required to protect availability. Combined with other techniques, this approach can provide useful information for the design of future services.

CFIA is a relatively simple technique that can be used to analyze all aspects of the IT infrastructure and applications, such as hardware, network, software, applications, data centers, and support staff. Additionally, it can identify impact and dependencies on IT support organization skills and staff competencies.

The technique involves identifying which elements of the IT infrastructure configuration are to be assessed, and then creating a grid with CIs on one axis and the IT services that have a dependency on the CI on the other, as shown in Figure 8.8.

FIGURE 8.8   Example of component failure impact analysis

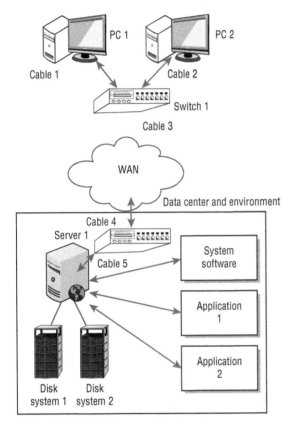

CI	Service 1	Service 2
PC 1	M	M
PC 2	M	M
Cable 1	M	M
Cable 2	M	M
Switch 1	X	X
Cable 3	X	X
WAN	X	X
Cable 4	X	X
Switch 2	X	X
Cable 5	X	X
Data center	X	X
Server 1	X	X
Disk 1	A	A
Disk 2	A	A
System S/W	X	X
Application 1	X	
Application 2		X

The next step is to perform the CFIA and populate the grid for each component with a blank where the failure of the CI does not impact the service, an "X" when the failure of the CI would bring down the service, an "A" when there is an alternative CI to provide the service, and an "M" when there is an alternative CI but it requires manual intervention to recover the service.

The completed grid will highlight the critical CIs. Actions can then be taken to provide resilience and protect availability.

Service Failure Analysis

Service failure analysis is used as a structured approach to the analysis of an interruption. Each time an interruption takes place, full analysis is undertaken as an assignment or project to identify a preventive action. It takes a holistic view looking for improvements in technology, the IT support organization, processes, procedures, and tools. Many of its activities are closely aligned with those of problem management. Both processes aim to identify root causes and encourage cross-functional teamwork, lateral thinking, and innovative, and often inexpensive, solutions.

SFIA should use a structured approach, as shown in Figure 8.9.

FIGURE 8.9   The structured approach to SFA

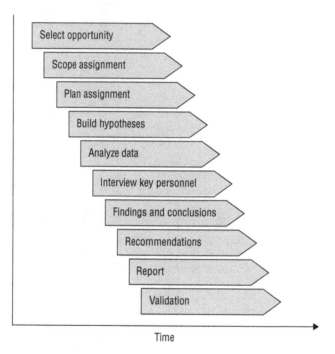

The report should categorize the recommendations under the following headings:

Detection   Actions to enable better event reporting to ensure that underlying IT service issues are detected early to enable a proactive response

Reduction   Actions to minimize the user impact from IT service interruption, possibly by reducing the duration of the impact

Avoidance   Actions to eliminate this particular cause of IT service interruption

Risk Analysis and Management

Risk analysis and management provides an analysis of the likelihood of business impact relating to availability risks (the likelihood of something happening). Business impact analysis and the identification of the potential impact of the business are vital parts of risk management. Identification of mitigation against risk is a key component of the design of services. Further information regarding techniques for risk management can be found in the relevant ISO standards, and other best practice frameworks such as the management of risk framework. One common approach to risk assessment is one described in ISO standard 31000. This assessment approach consists of three steps:

- *Risk identification* creates a comprehensive list of risks that could impact the service.
- *Risk analysis* involves developing a full understanding of the risks.
- *Risk evaluation* decides which risks require action and the relative priorities among them.

  Possible actions to address the risks may include the following:

- Avoiding the risk by deciding not to start or continue with the risky activity
- Deciding to take the risk in order to benefit from an opportunity
- Removing the risk
- Taking action to make the risk less likely to occur
- Lessening the impact of failure

Availability Management Triggers, Inputs, Outputs, and Interfaces

We will now review the triggers, inputs, and outputs of availability management and how the process interfaces with other service management processes.

Triggers

Many events may trigger availability management activity, including the following:

- New or changed business needs or new or changed services
- New or changed targets within agreements, such as service level requirements, service level agreements, operational level agreements, and contracts
- Service or component breaches, availability events, and alerts, including threshold events and exception reports
- Periodic activities such as reviewing, revising, or reporting against services
- Review of availability management forecasts, reports, and plans
- Review and revision of business and IT plans and strategies
- Review and revision of designs and strategies

- Recognition or notification of a change of risk or impact of a business process, a vital business function, an IT service, or a component
- Request from service level management for assistance with availability targets and explanation of achievements

Inputs

A number of sources of information are relevant as inputs to the availability management process. Some of these are as follows:

- Business information from the organization's business strategy, plans, and financial plans and information on its current and future requirements, including the availability requirements for new or enhanced IT services
- Service information from the service level management process, with details of the services from the service portfolio and the service catalog; from service level targets within service level agreements and service level requirements; and possibly from the monitoring of SLAs, service reviews, and breaches of the SLAs
- Financial information from financial management for IT services, the cost of service provision, and the cost of resources and components
- Change and release information from the change management process with a change schedule, the release schedule from release and deployment management, and an assessment of all changes for their impact on service availability
- Service asset and configuration management containing information on the relationships between the business, the services, the supporting services, and the technology
- Component information on the availability, reliability, and maintainability requirements for the technology components that underpin IT service(s)
- Technology information from the configuration management system
- Past performance from previous measurements, achievements, reports, and the availability management information system (AMIS)
- Unavailability and failure information from incidents and problems

Outputs

Availability management produces the following outputs:

- The availability management information system (AMIS)
- The availability plan for the proactive improvement of IT services and technology
- Availability and recovery design criteria and proposed service targets for new or changed services
- Service availability, reliability, and maintainability reports of achievements against targets, including input for all service reports
- Component availability, reliability, and maintainability reports of achievements against targets

- Revised risk assessment reviews and reports and an updated risk register

- Monitoring, management, and reporting requirements for IT services and components

- An availability management test schedule for testing all availability, resilience, and recovery mechanisms

- The planned and preventive maintenance schedules

- Contributions for the projected service outage (PSO) document to be created by change management in collaboration with release and deployment management

- Details of the proactive availability techniques and measures that will be deployed

- Improvement actions for inclusion within the service improvement plan

Availability Management Interfaces

As you would expect for this process, there are a number of interfaces across the lifecycle. In fact, availability management can be linked to the majority of the service management processes. However, the key interfaces that availability management has with other processes are as follows:

Service Level Management   This process relies on availability management to determine and validate availability targets and to investigate and resolve service and component breaches. It links to both the reactive and proactive elements of availability management.

Incident and Problem Management   As you have seen from the techniques used in availability measurement and management, these processes are assisted by availability management in the resolution of incidents and problems.

Capacity Management   This provides appropriate capacity to support resilience and overall service availability. Strong connections exist between the availability of a service and the capacity of the service. Patterns of business activity and user profiles are used to understand business demand for IT for business-aligned availability planning.

Change Management   As a result of investigations into outages, or improvements required by the business, change management supports the management of changes. This in turn is used in the creation of the projected service outage (PSO) document to project the availability-related issues during a change, with contributions from availability management.

IT Service Continuity Management   Availability management works collaboratively with this process on the assessment of business impact and risk and the provision of resilience, fail-over, and recovery mechanisms. A continuity invocation is the result of an availability management issue that cannot be resolved within the agreed time frames without additional resources as described in the recovery plan.

Information Security Management   Put simply, if the data becomes unavailable, the service becomes unavailable. Information security management defines the security measures and policies that must be included in the service design for availability and the design for recovery.

Access Management   Availability management provides the methods for appropriately granting and revoking access to services as needed. This should be carefully monitored because unauthorized or uncontrolled access can be a significant risk to service availability.

Information Management in Availability Management

The availability management process stresses the importance of an availability management information system. Although this is shown in the process diagram (Figure 8.4) as a single database or repository, it is far more likely that the information relating to availability is captured and resides in a number of different tools and systems. The challenge, for an availability manager, is to understand these disparate sources and create a single information source that enables the production of the availability plan.

Despite claims by suppliers of availability management tools, it is unlikely that the unique requirements of an individual customer can be met by a generic toolset. Customization, adaptation, and configuration to meet the customer requirements will always be required, and the information obtained must be managed so that it is fit for use and purpose. This information, covering services, components, and supporting services, provides the basis for regular, ad hoc, and exception availability reporting and the identification of trends within the data for the instigation of improvement activities.

The availability plan should have aims, objectives, and deliverables and should consider the wider issues of people, processes, tools, and techniques as well as have a technology focus. As the availability management process matures, the plan should evolve to cover the following:

- Actual levels of availability versus agreed levels of availability for key IT services. Availability measurements should always be business- and customer-focused and report availability as experienced by the business and users.

- Activities being progressed to address shortfalls in availability for existing IT services. Where investment decisions are required, options with associated costs and benefits should be included.

- Details of changing availability requirements for existing IT services. The plan should document the options available to meet these changed requirements. Where investment decisions are required, the associated costs of each option should be included.

- Details of the availability requirements for forthcoming new IT services. The plan should document the options available to meet these new requirements. Where investment decisions are required, the associated costs of each option should be included.

- A forward-looking schedule for the planned SFA assignments.

- Regular reviews of SFA assignments. These reviews should be completed to ensure that the availability of technology is being proactively improved in conjunction with the SIP.

- A technology futures section to provide an indication of the potential benefits and exploitation opportunities that exist for planned technology upgrades. Anticipated availability benefits should be detailed, where possible based on business-focused measures, in conjunction with capacity management. The effort required to realize these benefits where possible should also be quantified.

Covering a period of six months to a year, this plan is often produced as a rolling plan, continually updated to meet the changing needs of the business. At a minimum, it is recommended that publication is aligned with the capacity and business budgeting cycle and that the availability plan is considered complementary to the capacity plan and financial plan. Frequency of updates will depend on the nature of the organization and the rate of technological or business change.

The availability management information system can be utilized to record and store selected data and information required to support key activities such as report generation, statistical analysis, and availability forecasting and planning. It should be the main repository for the recording of IT availability metrics, measurements, targets, and documents, including the availability plan, availability measurements, achievement reports, SFA assignment reports, design criteria, action plans, and testing schedules.

 When considering the use of information in availability management, it is important to be pragmatic. If you define the initial tool requirements and identify what is already deployed and what can be used and shared, this will help to get started as quickly as possible. Where basic tools are not already available, it may be necessary to work with the other IT service and systems management processes to identify common requirements with the aim of selecting shared tools and minimizing costs. The AMIS should address the specific reporting needs of availability management not currently provided by existing repositories and integrate with them and their contents. After all, best practice does not include "reinventing the wheel"—if information is already available, there is no point in re-creating it in another form.

Availability Management Process Roles

As stated earlier in this chapter, Chapter 1 explored the generic roles applicable to all processes throughout the service lifecycle. These are relevant to the availability management process and are similar to the capacity management roles we discussed earlier in this chapter, but once again specific additional requirements also apply. Remember that these are not "job titles"; they are guidance on the roles that may be needed to successfully run the process.

Availability Management Process Owner

The availability management process owner's responsibilities typically include the following:

- Carrying out the generic process owner role for the availability management process (see Chapter 1 for more detail)
- Working with other managers to ensure acceptance of the availability management process as the single point of coordination for all availability-related issues, regardless of the specific technology involved
- Working with other process owners to ensure an integrated approach to the design and implementation of availability management, service level management, capacity management, IT service continuity management, and information security management

Availability Management Process Manager

The availability management process manager's responsibilities typically include the following:

- Carrying out the generic process manager role for the capacity management process (see Chapter 1 for more detail)

- Coordinating interfaces between availability management and other processes, especially service level management, capacity management, IT service continuity management, and information security management

- Ensuring that all existing and new services deliver the levels of availability agreed to by the business in SLAs

- Validating that the final design meets the minimum specified levels of availability

- Assisting with the investigation and diagnosis of all incidents and problems that cause availability issues or unavailability of services or components

- Participating in the IT infrastructure design, including specifying the availability requirements for hardware and software

- Specifying the requirements for new or enhanced event management systems for automatic monitoring of availability of IT components

- Specifying the reliability, maintainability, and serviceability requirements for components supplied by internal and external suppliers

- Monitoring and reporting actual IT availability achieved against SLA targets to ensure that agreed levels of availability, reliability, and maintainability are measured and monitored on an ongoing basis

- Proactively improving service availability wherever possible, and optimizing the availability of the IT infrastructure to deliver cost-effective improvements that deliver tangible benefits to the business

- Creating, maintaining, and regularly reviewing an availability management information system and a forward-looking availability plan aimed at improving the overall availability of IT services and infrastructure components, to ensure that existing and future business availability requirements can be met

- Ensuring that the availability management process, as well as its associated techniques and methods, are regularly reviewed and audited, and that all of these are subject to continual improvement and remain fit for purpose

- Creating availability and recovery design criteria to be applied to new or enhanced infrastructure design

- Working with financial management for IT services, ensuring that the levels of IT availability required are cost-justified

- Maintaining and completing an availability testing schedule for all availability mechanisms, ensuring that all availability tests and plans are tested after every major business change

- Assisting security and IT service continuity management with the assessment and management of risk

- Assessing changes for their impact on all aspects of availability, including overall service availability and the availability plan (this includes attending CAB meetings when appropriate)

Availability Management Critical Success Factors and Key Performance Indicators

This section includes some sample critical success factors for availability management. There are many more, and they can be obtained from the ITIL Service Operation publication, or from your own experience within your organization.

- Critical success factor: "Manage availability and reliability of IT service"
    - KPI: Reduction (measured as a percentage) in the unavailability of services and components
    - KPI: Increase (measured as a percentage) in the reliability of services and components
    - KPI: Effective review and follow-up of all SLA, OLA, and underpinning contract breaches relating to availability and reliability
- Critical success factor: "Satisfy business needs for access to IT services"
    - KPI: Reduction (measured as a percentage) in the unavailability of services
    - KPI: Reduction (measured as a percentage) of the cost of business overtime due to unavailable IT
- Critical success factor: "Availability of IT infrastructure and applications, as documented in SLAs, provided at optimum costs"
    - KPI: Reduction (measured as a percentage) in the cost of unavailability
    - KPI: Improvement (measured as a percentage) in the service delivery costs

Availability Management Challenges and Risks

We'll begin with looking at the key challenges for the process.

Challenges

The main challenge is to meet and manage the expectations of the customers and the business. The service levels should be publicized to all customers and areas of the business so that when services do fail, the expectation for their recovery is at the right level. It also means that availability management must have access to the right level of quality information on the current business need for IT services and its plans for the future.

Another challenge facing availability management is the integration of all of the availability data into an integrated set of information (AMIS). This can be analyzed in a consistent manner to provide details on the availability of all services and components. This is particularly challenging when the information from the different technologies is provided by different tools in different formats, which often happens.

Yet another challenge facing availability management is the investment needed in proactive availability measures. Availability management should work closely with ITSCM, information security management, and capacity management in producing the justifications necessary to secure the appropriate investment.

Risks

The following major risks are among those associated with availability management:

- A lack of commitment from the business to the availability management process
- A lack of appropriate information on future plans and strategies from the business
- A lack of senior management commitment to or a lack of resources and/or budget for the availability management process
- Labor-intensive reporting processes
- Processes that focus too much on the technology and not enough on the services and the needs of the business

Another risk is evident when the availability management information system is maintained in isolation and is not shared or consistent with other process areas, especially ITSCM, information security management, and capacity management. This interaction is particularly important when considering the necessary service and component backup and recovery tools, technology, and processes to meet the specified needs.

Information Security Management

Another of the key warranty aspects of a service is security, and it is this aspect that we will discuss in this final section of the chapter. A service that is insecure will not deliver value to the customer and indeed may not be used by the customer at all.

Central to *information security management (ISM)* is the identification and mitigation of risks to the security of the organization's information. The ISM process ensures that all security aspects are considered and managed throughout the service lifecycle.

> *Information* includes data stores, databases, and metadata (*metadata* is the term applied to a set of data that describes and provides information about other data).

Organizations operate under an overall corporate governance framework, and information security management forms part of this framework. In accordance with organization-wide governance, ISM provides guidance as to what is required, ensuring that risks are managed and the objectives of the organization are achieved.

Purpose of Information Security Management

The purpose of the information security management process is to align IT security with business security. IT and business security requires that the confidentiality, integrity, and availability of the organization's assets, information, data, and IT services always match the specified needs of the business.

Objectives of Information Security Management

The objective of information security management is to protect the interests of those relying on information. It should also ensure that the systems and communications that deliver the information are protected from harm resulting from failures of confidentiality, integrity, and availability.

For most organizations, the security objective is met when the following terms are fulfilled:

- Confidentiality, where information is observed by or disclosed to only those who have a right to know.
- Integrity, where information is complete, accurate, and protected against unauthorized modification.
- Availability, where information is available and usable when required and the systems that provide it can appropriately resist attacks and recover from or prevent failures.
- Business transactions, as well as information exchanges between enterprises or with partners, that can be trusted. This is referred to as authenticity and, where there is control of the denial of access, nonrepudiation.

Scope of Information Security Management

The scope of ISM includes all aspects of information security that are important to the business. It is the responsibility of the business to define what requires protection and how strong this protection should be. Risks to security must be recognized, and appropriate countermeasures should be implemented. These may include physical aspects (restricting access to secure areas through swipe cards) as well as technical aspects (password policies, use of biometrics, and so on). Information security is an integral part of corporate governance.

The information security management process should be the focal point for all IT security issues. A key responsibility of the process is the production of an information security policy that is maintained and enforced and covers the use and misuse of all IT systems and services.

Information security management needs to understand the total IT and business security environment. Important aspects that must be included in the policy are the business security policy and plans along with the current business operation and its security requirements. Consideration must also be given to future business plans and requirements. External factors, such as legislative and regulatory requirements, should also be included in the policy.

IT's obligations and responsibilities with regard to security should be contained within the service level agreements with their customers. The policy should also include reference to the business and IT risks and their management.

The information security management process should include the production, maintenance, distribution, and enforcement of an information security policy and supporting security policies. This will involve understanding the current and future security requirements of the business and the existing business security policy and plans.

The process will be responsible for implementation of a set of security controls that support the information security policy. This will support the management of risks associated with access to services, information, and systems. Information security management is responsible for the documentation of all security controls together with the operation and maintenance of the controls and their associated risks.

In association with supplier management, the process will also address the management of suppliers and contracts regarding access to systems and services.

Operationally, information security management will be involved in the management of all security breaches, incidents, and problems associated with all systems and services. It will also be responsible for the proactive improvement of security controls and security risk management and the reduction of security risks.

Information security management is also responsible for the integration of security aspects within all other IT service management processes. To achieve effective information security governance, the process must establish and maintain an information security management system (ISMS).

Information Security Management Value to the Business

Security has become a critical issue for organizations as their reliance on IT systems increases and more electronic media is used for confidential transactions within and between organizations.

Information security management ensures that an information security policy that fulfills the needs of the business security policy and the requirements of corporate governance is maintained and enforced. The information security policy provides assurance of business processes by enforcing appropriate security controls in all areas of IT. The process is responsible for the management of IT risk in line with business and corporate risk management processes and guidelines.

Information Security Management Policies

Information security management activities should be focused on and driven by an overall information security policy and a set of underpinning specific security policies.

The information security policy should have the full support of the top executive IT management. Ideally, the top executive business management should also be in support of and committed to the security policy. The policy should cover all areas of security, be appropriate, and meet the needs of the business. Email usage policies, antivirus policies, and remote access policies are examples of specific security policies.

The information security process is responsible for creating, managing, and maintaining an information security management system. The elements of the management system are shown in Figure 8.10. It begins with the identification of the customer requirements and business needs.

FIGURE 8.10   Elements of an ISMS for managing IT security

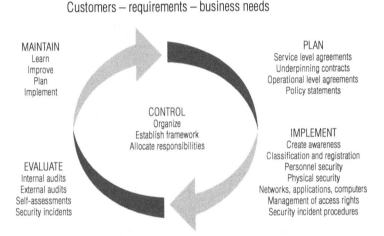

Customers – requirements – business needs

MAINTAIN
Learn
Improve
Plan
Implement

PLAN
Service level agreements
Underpinning contracts
Operational level agreements
Policy statements

CONTROL
Organize
Establish framework
Allocate responsibilities

IMPLEMENT
Create awareness
Classification and registration
Personnel security
Physical security
Networks, applications, computers
Management of access rights
Security incident procedures

EVALUATE
Internal audits
External audits
Self-assessments
Security incidents

Planning the system incorporates use of the details and targets captured in the various agreements and contracts. It also covers use of the various policies agreed to by the business and IT.

Implementation of the system requires awareness of the policies and the systems by all who are affected by them. This will need the engagement of all parts of the organization because the policies will cover everything from personnel security to the procedures for security incidents.

The next stage is evaluation, which requires internal and external audits of the state of system security, but there may also be self-assessments. Security incidents will also be evaluated as part of this stage of the management of the system.

Maintaining the system requires that the information security process capture the lessons learned so that improvements can be planned and implemented.

The overall approach is designed to maintain control and establish a framework for managing security throughout the organization. Part of this will be to allocate appropriate responsibilities for ensuring that the information security management system is maintained, within both the IT department and the rest of the organization.

IT Security Management Process Activities, Methods, and Techniques

In this section we are going to explore the process in detail. You should make sure you are familiar with all the aspects of the process and the management requirements for each. In Figure 8.11, you can see the information security management process and its techniques and activities.

FIGURE 8.11   Information security management process

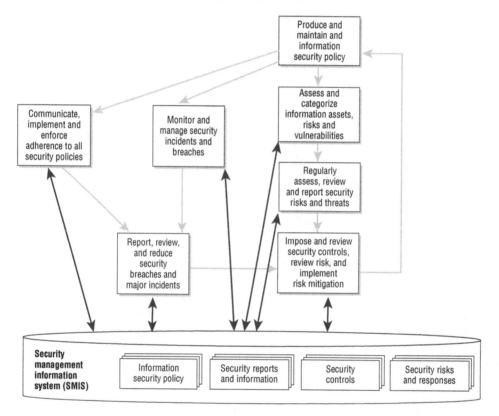

The information security management process ensures that the security aspects are appropriately managed and controlled in line with business needs and risks.

Process Activities

A key activity within the information security management process is the production and maintenance of an overall information security policy and a set of supporting specific policies. The process is also responsible for the communication, implementation, and enforcement of the security policies, including the provision of advice and guidance to all other areas of the business and IT on all issues related to information security.

Information security management is also responsible for the assessment and classification of all information assets and documentation. The process covers the implementation, review, revision, and improvement of a set of security controls as well as risk assessment and responses, including assessment of the impact of all changes on information security policies, controls, and measures. Where possible, if it is in the business's interest and the cost is justifiable, the process should implement proactive measures to improve information security.

Monitoring and management of all security breaches and major security incidents is a key part of the information security management process. This includes the analysis, reporting, and reduction of the volume and impact of security breaches and incidents.

The process is also responsible for scheduling and completing security reviews, audits, and penetration tests. The outputs from the process will be captured and recorded in the security management information system.

Security Strategy

The information security management process, together with the procedures, methods, tools and techniques, constitute the security strategy. It is the responsibility of the security manager to ensure that technologies, products, and services are in place, together with the published security policy. The security manager is also responsible for security architecture, authentication, authorization, administration, and recovery.

A key challenge for information security is to embed good security practices into every area of the business. Ensuring secure behavior depends on training and awareness. Security practices need to be easy to follow, if they are to be accepted. As technology changes, whether it is the trend toward bring your own device (BYOD) or computing in the cloud, new security challenges emerge. Information security management must understand these challenges and prepare to meet them.

Security Controls

Information security must be considered as an integral part of all services and systems. It needs to be continuously managed using a set of security controls that enforce the policy and minimize threats. These controls should be considered during the design of new services or changes to existing services; this is much easier and more cost effective than trying to apply them later when the service is live. Once the controls are in place, the day-to-day activities required will usually be carried out by access management. This process is covered in Chapter 3.

Security measures can be used at a specific stage in the prevention and handling of security incidents, as illustrated in Figure 8.12. The majority of such incidents are not technical threats, such as deliberate denial-of-service attacks or attempts to hack into the systems. Most breaches are the result of human errors and may even be accidental; they may involve other threats such as safety, legal, or health.

FIGURE 8.12   Security controls for threats and incidents

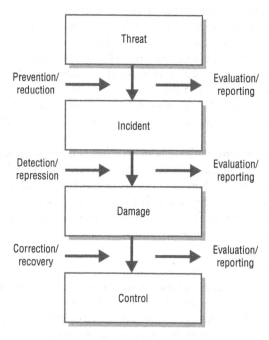

A threat can be anything that disrupts business processes or has negative impact on the business. First there is a risk of a threat actually occurring. Should this happen, it is termed a security incident. This may result in damage (to information or to assets) that has to be repaired or otherwise corrected. Each of these stages requires the appropriate measures to be taken. The choice of measures will depend on the importance attached to the information. These measures should all be documented in the information security management system. They include the following types:

Preventive   These security measures aim to prevent a security incident from occurring. An example of this type of measure is restricting access rights to a limited group of authorized people. This requires procedures to control access rights (granting, maintenance, and withdrawal of rights), authorization (identifying who is allowed access to which information and using which tools), identification and authentication (confirming who is seeking access), and access control (ensuring that only authorized personnel can gain access).

Reductive   These measures reduce the potential damage of a security breach. One example is ensuring that regular backups are taken in case of any data loss. Ensuring that tested contingency plans are in place is another reductive measure.

Detective   It is essential that any security breach is detected quickly; detective measures are concerned with discovering breaches as soon as possible. One example is the use of monitoring tools, linked to an alert procedure. Another example is virus-checking software, which will detect and virus infection.

Repressive   These security measures counteract any continuation or repetition of the security incident. One example is when an account or network address is temporarily blocked after numerous failed attempts to log on or when a card is retained when multiple attempts are made with a wrong PIN.

Corrective   These measures seek to repair any damage caused. Examples include restoring the backup, or backing out/rolling back to a previous stable situation.

Management of Security Breaches and Incidents

Whenever a serious security breach or incident occurs, it must be handled at the time, but also reviewed afterward to determine what went wrong, what caused it, and how it can be prevented in the future. This evaluation should not be restricted to serious security incidents, however; all breaches of security and security incidents need to be studied to understand the effectiveness or otherwise of the security measures as a whole. Every security incident must be logged as such to enable reporting and analysis. This analysis will also require other evidence, such as log files and audit files, in addition to the security incident record. Information security management should work with problem management to identify the root cause of these incidents and to take the required improvement actions to overcome weaknesses and prevent such incidents from recurring.

Information Security Management Triggers, Inputs, and Outputs

Let's consider the triggers, inputs, and outputs for the information security management process. Information security management is a process that has many active connections throughout the organization and its processes. It is important that the triggers, inputs, outputs, and interfaces be clearly defined to avoid duplicated effort or gaps in workflow.

Triggers

Information security management activity can be triggered by many events, including these:

- Changes in statutory or regulatory requirements
- New or changed corporate governance guidelines
- New or changed business security policy
- New or changed corporate risk management processes and guidelines
- New or changed business needs and new or changed services
- New or changed requirements within agreements, such as service level requirements, service level agreements, operational level agreements, and contracts
- Review and revision of business and IT plans and strategies
- Review and revision of designs and strategies

- Service or component security breaches or warnings, events, and alerts, including threshold events and exception reports

- Periodic activities such as reviewing, revising, and reporting, including reviewing and revising information security management policies, reports, and plans

- Recognition or notification of a change of risk or impact of a business process or vital business functions, an IT service, or a component

- Requests from other areas, particularly service level management, for assistance with security issues

Inputs

Information security management will need to obtain input from many areas:

- Business information from the organization's business strategy, plans and financial plans, and information on its current and future requirements

- Governance and security from corporate governance and business security policies and guidelines, security plans, and risk assessment and responses

- IT information from the IT strategy, plans, and current budgets

- Service information from the SLM process with details of the services from the service portfolio

- Risk assessment processes and reports from ISM, availability management, and ITSCM

- Details of all security events and breaches—from all areas of IT and IT service management, especially incident management and problem management

- Change information from the change management process

- The configuration management system containing information on the relationships between the business, the services, supporting services, and the technology

- Details of partner and supplier external access to services and systems from supplier management and availability management

Outputs

The following outputs are produced by the information security management process and used in all areas:

- An overall information security management policy, together with a set of specific security policies

- A security management information system (SMIS) containing all the information related to information security management

- Revised security risk assessment processes and reports

- A set of security controls with details of their operation and maintenance and their associated risks

- Security audits and audit reports

- Security test schedules and plans, including security penetration tests and other security tests and reports
- A set of security classifications and a set of classified information assets
- Reviews and reports of security breaches and major incidents
- Policies, processes, and procedures for managing partners and suppliers and their access to services and information

Information Security Management Interfaces

The key interfaces that information security management has with other processes are as follows:

Service Level Management   Information security management provides assistance with determining security requirements and responsibilities and their inclusion within SLRs and SLAs, together with the investigation and resolution of service and component security breaches.

Access Management   This process is responsible for following the security policies when granting and revoking access.

Change Management   Information security management (ISM) assesses every change for impact on security and security controls. ISM may also detect and report unauthorized changes that resulted from security breaches.

Incident and Problem Management   ISM assists with the resolution of security incidents and investigation of security problems. Incident management must be able to recognize and deal with security incidents.

IT Service Continuity Management   Information security management works with ITSCM on the assessment of business impact and risk, and the provision of resilience, failover, and recovery mechanisms. Security must also be considered when continuity plans are tested or invoked.

Service Asset and Configuration Management   An accurate CMS is a prerequisite for security classification of configuration items.

Availability Management   ISM ensures that the integrity of data is protected; without this assurance, the ability of the service to perform its agreed function is compromised.

Capacity Management   Security aspects must be considered when selecting and introducing new technology.

Financial Management for IT Services   This process should ensure that adequate funds are provided to finance security requirements.

Supplier Management   Security management works with supplier management to define contractual terms and conditions and enforce controls over supplier access to services and systems.

Legal and Human Resources Issues   As stated earlier, security breaches are often the result of human actions, accidental or deliberate. ISM activity should therefore be integrated with these corporate processes and functions.

Information Management in Information Security

All the information required by information security management should be contained within the security management information system (SMIS). This includes information regarding security controls, risks, breaches, processes, and reports, covering all IT services and components. The SMIS should be integrated and maintained in alignment with all other management information systems, particularly the service portfolio and the CMS. The SMIS provides the input to security audits and reviews and to the continual improvement activities. The SMIS also provides input to the design of new systems and services.

Information Security Process Roles

As you will recall, Chapter 1 explored the generic roles applicable to all processes throughout the service lifecycle. These are relevant to the information security management process and are similar to the capacity and availability management roles we discussed earlier in this chapter, but once again specific additional requirements also apply. Remember that these are not "job titles"; they are guidance on the roles that may be needed to successfully run the process.

Information Security Management Process Owner

The information security management process owner's responsibilities typically include the following:

- Carrying out the generic process owner role for the information security management process

- Working with the business to ensure proper coordination and communication between organizational (business) security management and information security management

- Working with managers of all functions to ensure acceptance of the information security management process as the single point of coordination for all information security-related issues, regardless of the specific technology involved

- Working with other process owners to ensure an integrated approach to the design and implementation of information security management, availability management, IT service continuity management, and organizational security management

Information Security Management Process Manager

The information security management process manager's responsibilities typically include the following:

- Carrying out the generic process manager role for the information security management process

- Coordinating interfaces between information security management and other processes, especially service level management, availability management, IT service continuity management, and organizational security management

- Developing and maintaining the information security policy and supporting specific policies, ensuring appropriate authorization, commitment, and endorsement from senior IT and business management

- Communicating and publicizing the information security policy to all appropriate parties
- Ensuring that the information security policy is enforced and adhered to
- Identifying and classifying IT and information assets (configuration items) and the level of control and protection required
- Assisting with business impact analyses
- Performing security risk assessment and risk management in conjunction with availability and IT service continuity management
- Designing security controls and developing security plans
- Developing and documenting procedures for operating and maintaining security controls
- Monitoring and managing all security breaches and handling security incidents, taking remedial action to prevent recurrence wherever possible
- Reporting, analyzing, and reducing the impact and volumes of all security incidents in conjunction with problem management
- Promoting education and awareness of security
- Maintaining a set of security controls and documentation, and regularly reviewing and auditing all security controls and procedures
- Ensuring that all changes are assessed for impact on all security aspects, including the information security policy and security controls, and attending CAB meetings when appropriate
- Ensuring that security tests are performed as required
- Participating in any security reviews arising from security breaches and instigating remedial actions
- Ensuring that the confidentiality, integrity, and availability of the services are maintained at the levels agreed to in the SLAs and that they conform to all relevant statutory requirements
- Ensuring that all access to services by external partners and suppliers is subject to contractual agreements and responsibilities
- Acting as a focal point for all security issues

Critical Success Factors and Key Performance Indicators for Information Security Management

The following list includes some sample critical success factors for information security management.

- Critical success factor: "The protection of business against security violations"
  - KPI: Decrease (measured as a percentage) in security breaches reported to the service desk
  - KPI: Decrease (measured as a percentage) in the impact of security breaches and incidents

- Critical success factor: "The determination of a clear policy, integrated with the needs of the business"
  - KPI: Decrease in the number of nonconformances of the information security management process with the business security policy and process
- Critical success factor: "Effective marketing and education in security requirements, and IT staff awareness of the technology supporting the services"
  - KPI: Increased awareness throughout the organization of the security policy and its contents
  - KPI: Increase (measured as a percentage) in completeness of supporting services against the IT components that make up those services
- Critical success factor: "Clear ownership and awareness of the security policies among the customer community"
  - KPI: Increase (measured as a percentage) in acceptable scores on security awareness questionnaires completed by customers and users

Challenges for Information Security Management

One of the biggest challenges is to ensure that there is adequate support from the business, business security, and senior management. It is pointless to implement security policies, procedures, and controls in IT if they cannot be enforced throughout the business. The major use of IT services and assets is outside IT, and so are the majority of security threats and risks.

If a business security process is established, then the challenge becomes alignment and integration. Once there is alignment, the challenge becomes keeping them aligned by management and control of changes to business methods and IT systems using strict change management and service asset and configuration management control. Again, this requires support and commitment from the business and from senior management.

Risks for Information Security Management

Information systems can generate many direct and indirect benefits—and as many direct and indirect risks. This means that there are new risk areas that could have a significant impact on critical business operations:

- Increasing requirements for availability and robustness
- Growing potential for misuse and abuse of information systems affecting privacy and ethical values
- External dangers from hackers, leading to denial-of-service and virus attacks, extortion, industrial espionage, and leakage of organizational information or private data
- A lack of commitment from the business

- A lack of senior management commitment
- The processes focusing too much on the technology issues and not enough on the IT services and the needs and priorities of the business
- Risk assessment and management performed in isolation and not in conjunction with availability management and ITSCM
- Information security management policies, plans, risks, and information becoming out of date and losing alignment with the corresponding relevant information and plans of the business and business security
- Security policies becoming bureaucratic and/or excessively difficult to follow, discouraging compliance
- Security policies adding no value to business

Summary

This chapter explored the processes of capacity, availability, and information security management. It covered the purpose and objectives for each process in addition to the scope.

We looked at the value of the processes. Then we reviewed the policies for each process and the activities, methods, and techniques, and the specific roles for each process.

Last, we reviewed triggers, inputs, outputs, and interfaces for each process and the information management associated with it. We also considered the critical success factors and key performance indicators and the challenges and risks for the processes.

We examined how each of these processes supports the other and the importance of these processes to the business and the IT service provider.

Exam Essentials

Understand the purpose and objectives of availability, capacity, and information security management. It is important for you to be able to explain the purpose and objectives of these processes. Availability management should ensure that the required availability is delivered to meet the targets in the service level agreement. Capacity management is concerned with the current and future capacity of services to the business. Information security management is concerned with the protection of information and data according to the security requirements of the business.

Understand the critical success factors and key performance indicators for the processes. Measurement of the processes is an important part of understanding their success. You should be familiar with the CSFs and KPIs for capacity, availability, and information security management.

Understand the definition of availability.   ITIL defines availability as the ability of an IT service or other configuration item to perform its agreed function when required. Any unplanned interruption to a service during its agreed service hours (also called the agreed service time, specified in the service level agreement) is defined as downtime. The availability measure is calculated by subtracting the downtime from the agreed service time and converting it to a percentage of the agreed service time.

Explain the different concepts of availability management.   You need to be able to differentiate between reliability, maintainability, and serviceability. *Reliability* is defined by ITIL as "a measure of how long a service, component, or CI can perform its agreed function without interruption." *Maintainability* is measured as the mean time to restore service (MTRS). *Serviceability* is defined as the ability of a third-party supplier to meet the terms of its contract. This contract will include agreed levels of availability, reliability, and/or maintainability for a supporting service or component.

Understand and differentiate between the methods and techniques of availability management.   A number of different techniques can be used for availability management. Ensure that you are familiar with each of them and can explain the purpose of each.

Explain the role of information management in availability management.   Information is key to the service lifecycle, so you need to understand the content of the availability management information system and its use throughout the lifecycle.

Understand the iterative activities of capacity management.   Capacity management has both proactive and reactive activities. These include monitoring, tuning, and analysis, which may be carried out as part of a proactive or reactive approach.

Understand the subprocesses of capacity management.   Business capacity management is concerned with the business requirements and understanding business needs. Service capacity management is concerned with the capacity of services to fulfill the needs of the business. Component capacity management is concerned with the technical aspect of capacity management and the capacity of individual service components.

Understand the approach to security management.   Plan, implement, evaluate, maintain, and control—ensure that you can explain how each of these stages supports the approach to the management of information security.

Understand the process of information security management.   Ensure that you are able to explain the various steps of the process and their relationship to the information security management system.

Review Questions

You can find the answers to the review questions in the appendix.

1. Which of the following are responsibilities of capacity management?

1. Negotiating capacity requirements to be included in the SLA

2. Monitoring capacity

3. Forecasting capacity requirements

4. Dealing with capacity issues

    A. 2, 3, and 4

    B. 1 and 2 only

    C. All of the above

    D. 1, 2, and 4

2. Capacity management includes three subprocesses. What are they?

    A. Service capacity, business capacity, component capacity

    B. System capacity, business capacity, component capacity

    C. Service capacity, business capacity, configuration capacity

    D. System capacity, business capacity, infrastructure capacity

3. Which of the following shows the correct description for the business capacity management subprocess?

    A. It considers the capacity of staff resources to support new services.

    B. It provides a view of the detailed information relating to the performance management of technical assets.

    C. It provides a view of the future plans and requirements of the organization.

    D. It provides a view of the service performance achieved in the operational environment.

4. True or False? Capacity management has both reactive and proactive activities.

    A. True

    B. False

5. Which of these statements is/are correct?

1. Risk management is a vital part of both capacity and information security management.

2. Both capacity management and information security management are cyclic processes.

    A. Statement 1 only

    B. Statement 2 only

    C. Both statements

    D. Neither statement

6. Which of these is the key purpose of the information security management process?

   A. Create and maintain an information security policy

   B. Deliver guidance to the operational processes on security issues

   C. Support supplier management in maintaining security concerns in contracts

   D. Manage the information security management information system

7. Which of these statements is/are correct?

   1. Plan is an element of the information security management system.

   2. Maintain is an element of the information security management system.

   A. Statement 1 only

   B. Statement 2 only

   C. Both statements

   D. Neither statement

8. Where does information security management keep information about security?

   A. ISDB

   B. IMSS

   C. KEDB

   D. SMIS

9. Which of the following concepts are key to availability management?

   1. Reliability

   2. Resilience

   3. Resistance

   4. Attainability

   5. Serviceability

   6. Maintainability

   7. Detectability

   A. 1, 2, 6, 7

   B. 2, 3, 5, 6

   C. 1, 4, 6, 7

   D. 1, 2, 5, 6

10. Availability management considers VBFs. What does VBF stand for?

   A. Viable business factors

   B. Vital business function

   C. Visibility, benefits, functionality

   D. Vital business facilities

Chapter

9

IT Service Continuity Management and Demand Management

THE FOLLOWING ITIL PLANNING, PROTECTION, AND OPTIMIZATION CAPABILITY INTERMEDIATE EXAM OBJECTIVES ARE DISCUSSED IN THIS CHAPTER:

✓ **IT service continuity management and demand management are discussed in terms of**

- ▪ Purpose
- ▪ Objectives
- ▪ Scope
- ▪ Value
- ▪ Policies
- ▪ Principles and basic concepts
- ▪ Process activities, methods, and techniques
- ▪ Triggers, inputs, outputs, and interfaces
- ▪ Information management
- ▪ Process roles
- ▪ Critical success factors and key performance indicators
- ▪ Challenges
- ▪ Risks

IT service continuity management is the process concerned with the management of service delivery in the event of a disaster to the business, and the prevention of disaster caused by IT services. It covers the protection of critical services and plans for recovery of these services.

Demand management covers the analysis of the business in terms of patterns of business activity, and the approach we need to take to meet and manage those demands for service.

IT Service Continuity Management

It is a fact that a service delivers value only when it is available for use. In addition to the activities carried out under the availability management process, there is a requirement for the IT service provider to ensure that the service is protected from catastrophic events that could prevent it from being delivered at all. Where they cannot be avoided, there is a requirement to have a plan to recover from any such disruption in a timescale and at a cost that meets the business requirement. Ensuring IT service continuity is an essential element of the warranty of the service.

It is important to understand that *IT service continuity management (ITSCM)* is responsible for the continuity of the IT services required by the business. The business should have a business continuity plan to ensure that any potential situations that would impact the ability of the business to function are identified and avoided. Where it is not possible to avoid such an event, the business continuity management process should have a plan, which is appropriate and affordable, to both minimize its impact and recover from it. Thus, ITSCM can be seen as one of a number of elements supporting a business continuity management (BCM) process, along with a human resources continuity plan, a financial management continuity plan, a building management continuity plan, and so on.

Purpose of IT Service Continuity Management

The purpose of the IT service continuity management process is to support the overall BCM process. It is not a replacement for business continuity, even though many organizations could not survive without their IT service provider. It is important that this process reflects the business continuity requirements. The service provider can then support these requirements by ensuring that, through managing the risks that could seriously affect IT services, the IT service provider can always provide the minimum agreed business continuity-related service levels.

To support and align with the BCM process, ITSCM uses formal risk assessment and management techniques to reduce risks to IT services to agreed acceptable levels. The service provider will plan and prepare for the recovery of IT services to meet these agreed levels.

Objectives of IT Service Continuity Management

A key objective of IT service continuity management is to produce and maintain a set of IT service continuity plans that support the overall business continuity plans of the organization. This will require complete and regular business impact analysis exercises to ensure that all continuity plans are maintained in line with changing business impacts and requirements.

A further objective is to conduct regular risk assessment and management exercises to manage IT services within an agreed level of business risk. This should be completed in conjunction with the business and the availability management and information security management processes.

As with all the service design processes, this process has an objective to provide advice and guidance to all other areas of the business and IT on all continuity-related issues.

IT service continuity should also ensure that appropriate continuity mechanisms are put in place to meet or exceed the agreed business continuity targets. This will require the assessment of the impact of all changes on the IT service continuity plans and supporting methods and procedures.

Working with availability management, the process should ensure that cost-justifiable proactive measures to improve the availability of services are implemented.

Service continuity management should also negotiate and agree on contracts with suppliers for the provision of the necessary recovery capability to support all continuity plans in conjunction with the supplier management process.

Scope of IT Service Continuity Management

When we consider the scope of IT service continuity management, it is important to understand that the process focuses on events that the business considers significant enough to be treated as a disaster. Less significant events will be dealt with as part of the incident management process.

Each organization will have its own understanding of what constitutes a disaster. The scope of IT service continuity management within an organization is determined by the organizational structure, culture, and strategic direction (both business and technology) in terms of the services provided and how these develop and change over time.

IT service continuity management first considers the IT assets and configurations that support the business processes. The process is not normally concerned with longer-term risks such as those from changes in business direction or other business-related alterations. Similarly, it does not usually cover minor technical faults (for example, noncritical disk failure) unless the possibility exists that the impact on the business could be major.

The IT service continuity management process includes the agreement of the scope of the ITSCM process and the policies adopted to support the business requirements. The process will also carry out business impact analysis to quantify the impact that the loss of IT service would have on the business.

It is important to establish the likelihood of potential threats taking place by carrying out risk assessment and management. This also includes taking measures to manage the identified threats where the cost can be justified. The approach to managing these threats will form the core of the ITSCM strategy and plans.

Essential to the process is the production of an overall IT service continuity management strategy that must be integrated into the business continuity management strategy. This should be produced by using both risk assessment and management and business impact analysis. The strategy should include cost-justifiable risk reduction measures as well as selection of appropriate and comprehensive recovery options.

As part of the strategy, there should be the requirement to produce an IT service continuity plan, which should integrate with the business continuity plan. These plans should be tested and managed as part of the ongoing operation. This will require regular testing and maintenance to ensure that they are in alignment with business continuity management.

IT Service Continuity Management Value to the Business

IT service continuity management is a vital part of the assurance and management of IT service provision for an organization because it supports the business continuity process. It can often be used to provide the justification for business continuity processes and plans by raising awareness of the impact of failures to the organization.

The process should be driven by business risk as identified by business continuity and ensure that the recovery arrangements for IT services are aligned to identified business impacts, risks, and needs.

IT Service Continuity Management Process, Methods, and Techniques

IT service continuity management is a repeating, cyclic process. As the needs of the organization change, so will the requirements for continuity and recovery, so the process must be continually reviewed and the output verified for effectiveness. The process is shown in Figure 9.1.

FIGURE 9.1   Lifecycle of IT service continuity management

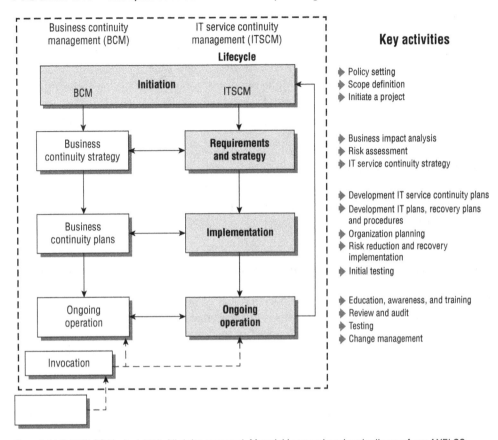

Initiation

The process is structured in four stages. The first is initiation, where the policies and scope of the continuity requirement are established in alignment with the business continuity requirements. It is during this stage that, if the scope requires it, a project management approach will be adopted. Ideally this stage will be led by the BCM team or approach, since this is the primary driver for the ITSCM requirements. At this stage it is important to focus on the vital business functions, as defined by the organization.

A policy to specify the management intent and objectives relating to continuity should be produced at this stage. The scope of ITSCM should be set, including the roles and responsibilities of all the stakeholders in the organization. The policy should be created based on the requirements of the organization and any regulatory, legislative, or insurance compliance issues that have been identified. This will include any standards in use in the organization, such as ISO/IEC 20000 or 27001.

If a project management approach is being used, it should cover the following:

- Allocating resources; consideration will need to be given to the setup and then the ongoing maintenance of the plans. The skills required for these two stages may be different, and external consultancy may be helpful to support the setup. But there should be sufficient training for permanent staff to carry on the plan.

- The structure of the team, which will be important for a project of this nature, since the responsibilities will cross over both IT and the business.

- Agreed outputs from the project; the plans for the achievement and final production of a continuity plan.

Requirements and Strategy

In the next stage, requirements and strategy, the activities of business impact analysis and risk assessment and management are carried out. This will allow the strategy for continuity to be developed.

Business Impact Analysis

Business impact analysis allows us to understand the impact to the business that loss of a particular service would have and in what circumstances. Impact could be financial, reputational, regulatory, risk to personal safety, loss of market share, political impact, additional costs, or loss of goodwill. This is not intended to be a comprehensive list; it will be necessary for the organization to identify the impact that is applicable to them. Consideration should also be given to the impact as the loss continues—often this will become more critical with time. Time will also be a factor in the speed to recovery, as will the required skills and capabilities to recover the minimum requirement for service delivery.

Impacts should be measured against particular scenarios—for example, understanding the impact of being unable to process orders from an online site. The differing perspectives of staff at all levels in the organization should be reviewed. It is unlikely that the organization will be able to afford to recover the whole enterprise as part of the process, but a partial recovery may be cost-justified. Understanding the minimum requirement for the business is important to producing the right level of recovery.

Risk Assessment

A second driver for the recovery strategy will be the likelihood of recovery being required. This will involve an assessment of the level of threat and the vulnerability of the organization if the threat situation occurs. A number of risk management approaches can be used, but it is important that the IT department use the approach recommended and used by the rest of the organization.

Conducting a formal risk assessment using a structured method will usually result in the production of a risk profile. This will include risks that are outside the accepted "risk tolerance" of the organization. Using the profile, it should be possible to plan to mitigate against these risks and ensure that the organization receives the appropriate assurance of risk management. IT has control over a number of different risk situations, such as the following:

- Loss of internal networks or systems
- Loss of external systems
- Loss of data
- Loss of network services
- Unavailability of key technical or support staff
- Failure of service providers (e.g., outsourced IT)

IT Service Continuity Strategy

Based on the risk assessment and business impact analysis, it should be possible to develop an IT service continuity strategy that supports the BCM strategy. The strategy should encompass a balance of risk reduction and recovery or continuity options. This will include the recovery options in response to the business impact analysis.

Risk response measures will be identified as part of availability management as well as through this process, but the eventual recovery options will have to be agreed to by the business to meet the continuity requirements. Recovery options include the following:

Manual Workarounds   A manual solution could be used temporarily for some situations—for example, use of a paper-based approach to call logging at the service desk.

Reciprocal Arrangements   Sharing the capability to continue to function with a competitor may seem counterintuitive, but in some cases this is legislated—for example, the sharing of networks in mobile phone companies to continue support for emergency services.

Gradual Recovery   This option, sometimes referred to as *cold standby*, provides a location with power and environmental controls, but without computing equipment or data. This solution is only suitable for noncritical services that can withstand an outage measured in days, not hours. The accommodation may be portable, and a dormant contract (invoked when the situation requires it) with computer equipment suppliers may be required to complete the capability.

Intermediate Recovery   Often referred to as *warm standby*, this option can be used to recover within a predetermined time to prevent impact to the business. This will have been agreed to by the business during the business impact analysis.

The most common approach is to use commercial facilities, offered by third-party recovery organizations. These are usually provided to a number of different subscribers, which allows for the cost to be spread across them, thus reducing the overall costs to each. The advantage of the recovery option is that it provides access to a location with basic computing capability within a very short timeframe. However, data will still need to be provided and configured on the equipment, so this is not an instantaneous solution.

There may be further financial considerations for the use of such a site if the outage requires sustained use of the recovery site past the original contractual agreement. Also, it is important to consider the risk of using a third-party location, if security is a key organizational factor.

Fast Recovery   This option, sometimes referred to as *hot standby*, provides a fast restoration of services and may be used as an extension to the previous option, intermediate recovery. Some organizations may provide their own facilities within the overall organizational estate that are not the normal center of operations. Others may have their own second locations on an alternative site to further the resilience of the recovery option.

Onsite servers or systems can be installed with organization data and may even be mirrored from the operational servers. In the event of a failure, this recovery option allows for a switchover to the backup site with little loss of service. This is usually achieved within a 24-hour period.

Immediate Recovery   This option, which may also be described as *hot standby*, *mirroring*, *load balancing*, or *split site*, provides for the immediate restoration of services with no significant loss of service to the business. This option can be applied to business-critical services or to organizations that require continuous operation. By providing equipment and data at a dual location, this option enables a seamless switchover to the recovery site. The second site can then be recovered while normal operation is maintained at the other. Located separately and far enough away to not be impacted by any incident taking place at the home site, it should be constantly manned and able to take on the normal operation of the organization. Because it would be impractical to have these staff simply waiting for a disaster, this type of facility is often part of the operational running of the organization. The additional capacity means that this is an expensive option but may be justified for business-critical processes. It will probably form part of a high-availability solution for specific vital business functions.

Whichever solution is adopted, consideration must be given to the supporting areas of the service provision, such as power, telecommunications, water, couriers, post, paper records, and reference material.

Implementation

Implementation of the strategy requires the development of the IT service continuity plans, including the recovery plans and procedures. This stage is where the risk reduction measures are implemented and the initial testing of the plans is carried out.

Develop IT Service Continuity Plans and Procedures

ITSCM plans provide the information required to support the continued provision or recovery of critical systems, services, and facilities within an acceptable time period for the business.

The plans should include reference to all the activities required to deliver services that are both *fit for purpose* and *fit for use* when they are invoked. The plans will also include the requirements for testing (performance, functional, operational, and acceptance testing) and validation of data integrity and consistency. These plans are more than just recovery plans—they should also include risk reduction measures and justification of the recovery solution selected. The plan will need to be accessed by all staff, and quickly in the case of invocation, so priority information should be easy to find and be clear and unambiguous.

Subsections of the plan may include the following:

Emergency Response   Interface to all emergency services and activities

Damage Assessment   Details of contact for damage assessors, plans, and processes

Salvage   Information on salvage contact, activities, and processes

Vital Records   Details of records and information vital to the operation of the business

Crisis Management and Public Relations Plan   Command and control of crisis situations and management of media and publicity

Accommodation and Services   Management of accommodation, facilities, and services required for continued operation

Security   Covering the security aspects on the home and recovery sites

Personnel   How personnel issues will be managed during a continuity event

Communication   How all aspects of communication will be managed throughout the continuity event

Finance and Administration   Details of alternative methods and processes for obtaining any necessary emergency funding

Not only will the ITSCM plan cover the information required to recover IT systems and services in a disaster situation once the plan has been invoked, but it will also cover how to return to normal working once the disaster has concluded.

The organizational structure will probably be different from the normal operational structures and should be detailed in the plan. Consideration should be given to the following:

Executive   The role of the executive and senior management with respect to organizational control, crisis management, and liaison with external services and media.

Coordination   Typically the next level of hierarchy down from the executive, these roles should be defined to manage the overall coordination of the recovery effort.

Recovery   Representation of the systems and services affected by the recovery from both business and IT. Each team will have specific duties and activities defined, and it is important that these roles be clearly defined in the continuity plans.

Risk Recovery/Reduction Arrangement Implementation

Risk reduction measures within the infrastructure are usually implemented in conjunction with availability management. But the specific requirements for continuity may require additional activity with respect to the standby arrangements. For example:

- Negotiating for third-party recovery facilities and entering into a contractual arrangement
- Preparing and equipping the standby accommodation
- Purchasing and installing standby computer systems

Initial Testing

It is a safe assumption that recovery plans that have not been fully tested are unlikely to work as expected, if at all. Testing is a critical part of the ITSCM process, since it is the only way of assuring that the recovery options, strategies, and business recovery plans and procedures will work in practice. It is the responsibility of the service provider to ensure that the IT services can be recovered within the agreed timescales and with the agreed functionality and performance after a disaster.

There are four basic types of test:

Walk-through   An initial approach to simulate the plan with the relevant people.

Full   Conducted after the plan has been produced and at regular intervals at least annually thereafter. The tests should involve the business units and wherever possible the actual standby arrangements. The end result is to test both the recovery plan and the recovery of business processes. To ensure objectivity, it is recommended that an outside observer be engaged and their report form part of the review of the test. The tests can be announced or unannounced; the first test is likely to be announced and well prepared. Any subsequent tests may be unannounced to check the actual capability of the recovery plans at specific times and with different stakeholders.

Partial   These are not a replacement for full tests but can be useful to check the plan for single services or specific elements of the plan.

Scenario   These can be used to test plans for specific scenarios, events, or situations. They can be used to verify that business continuity and IT service continuity plans integrate properly.

All tests should be undertaken against agreed test scenarios, which should be as realistic as possible. Obviously even the most comprehensive plans cannot cover every eventuality or fully predict the behaviors and attitudes of staff in the event of a serious disaster.

Ongoing Operation

During the operational stage, it will be important to ensure that adequate information is delivered to the organization through education, awareness, and training. The plans should be regularly reviewed and audited to ensure that they meet the ongoing requirements of the business. This will require an association with the change management process, and the plans and procedures for continuity should be subject to change procedures. Regular testing is part of this stage, and the results of testing will be fed back into the process.

Education, Awareness, and Training

The purpose of education, awareness, and training is to ensure that all staff are aware of the implications of business continuity and service continuity and how they are part of normal working. Everyone involved in the plan should be trained to fulfill their role in the plan.

Review and Audit

The ITSCM plan and all the deliverables (for example, contracts, agreements, roles, and responsibilities) must be reviewed regularly to ensure that they remain current. This is an important factor in the management of continuity; when the plan is invoked is not the time to find out it is obsolete.

Testing

It is important to establish a regular routine program of testing after the initial tests, preferably annually. This should be arranged in line with business continuity plans and business needs. After every business change, the plans need to be reviewed, updated, and retested to ensure IT continues to support business continuity and operational success following a disaster.

Change Management

The change management process should be used to assess all changes for their impact on continuity plans. Any alterations must be addressed as part of the overall implementation of the change. Any changes to services or business requirements should be assessed with a business impact analysis and risk assessment. The ITSCM plan must be under strict change control, since it is an important configuration item in its own right.

Invocation

It is important to ensure that there is a clearly understood mechanism and definition of when to invoke the continuity plans. This is not a stage of the process, as such, but it is a vital part of the process, because the establishment of the trigger for implementing the continuity plan is very important. The cost of invoking the plan and the consequent potential disruption to the business means that this is not a decision to be taken without justification. The decision to invoke needs to take into account the following:

- The extent of the damage and scope of the potential invocation.
- The likely length of the disruption and unavailability of premises and/or services.
- The time of day/month/year and the potential business impact. At year-end, the need to invoke may be more pressing to ensure that year-end processing is completed on time.

Invocation is going to be a time of high activity and stress for the organization as a whole, but particularly those who are involved in the actual recovery. Management should be aware of the issue of potential burn-out, and ensure that human resources are used appropriately. Other concerns include maintaining normal business activity and information security at the correct level and that data protection is assured.

Once a recovery has been completed and the business is operational from the recovery site, the next objective is to return to normal. Details of these activities should be covered in the plans. It may be that there is a specific contractual timeframe associated with use of the recovery facility. The return-to-normal plan is just as important as the recovery plans, and all staff need to be aware of the impact and activities involved.

IT Service Continuity Management Triggers, Inputs, and Outputs

We will now review the triggers, inputs, and outputs of IT service continuity management.

Triggers

Many events may trigger IT service continuity management activity, including new or changed business needs, new or changed services, and new or changed targets within agreements, such as service level requirements, service level agreements, operational level agreements, and contracts.

Major incidents that require assessment for potential invocation of either business or IT continuity plans are another trigger for the process, as are periodic activities such as the business impact analysis and risk assessment activities; maintenance of continuity plans; and other reviewing, revising, or reporting activities.

Assessment of changes and attendance at change advisory board meetings should be a part of the process scope, because it is here that there will be opportunity to review and revise business and IT plans and strategies in light of altering business needs, which may trigger changes to the process output. This will include the review and revision of designs and strategies, for both the business and the IT service provider.

Other triggers will include the recognition or notification of a change in the risk or impact of a business process or vital business function, an IT service, or a component. The results of testing the plans and lessons learned from previous continuity events will also provide triggers for the process.

Inputs

Many sources of input are required by the ITSCM process:

- Business information from the organization's business strategy, plans, and financial plans and information on their current and future requirements

- IT information from the IT strategy and plans and current budgets

- A business continuity strategy and a set of business continuity plans from all areas of the business

- Service information from the SLM process, with details of the services from the service portfolio and the service catalog and service level targets within SLAs and SLRs

- Financial information from financial management for IT services, the cost of service provision, and the cost of resources and components

- Change information from the change management process, with a change schedule and an assessment of all changes for their impact on all ITSCM plans

- A configuration management system (CMS) containing information on the relationships between the business, the services, the supporting services, and the technology

- Business continuity management and availability management testing schedules

- Capacity management information identifying the resources required to run the critical services in the event of a continuity event

- IT service continuity plans and test reports from supplier and partners, where appropriate

Outputs

The outputs from the ITSCM process are as follows:

- A new or revised ITSCM policy and strategy
- A set of ITSCM plans, including all crisis management plans, emergency response plans, and disaster recovery plans, together with a set of supporting plans and contracts with recovery service providers
- Business impact analysis exercises and reports, in conjunction with business continuity management and the business
- Risk assessment and management reviews and reports, in conjunction with the business, availability management, and information security management
- An ITSCM testing schedule
- ITSCM test scenarios
- ITSCM test reports and reviews
- Forecasts and predictive reports used by all areas to analyze, predict, and forecast particular business and IT scenarios and their potential solutions

IT Service Continuity Management Interfaces

IT service continuity should have interfaces to all other processes across the whole service lifecycle.

Important examples are as follows:

- Change management, because all changes need to be considered for their impact on the continuity plans. The plan itself must be under change management control.
- Incident and problem management require clear criteria that are agreed on and documented for the invocation of the ITSCM plans.
- Availability management undertakes risk assessment, and implementing risk responses should be closely coordinated with the availability process to optimize risk mitigation.
- Recovery requirements will be agreed and documented in the service level agreements. Different service levels that would be acceptable in a disaster situation could be agreed on and documented through the service level management process.
- Capacity management should ensure that there are sufficient resources to enable recovery to replacement systems following a disaster.
- Service asset and configuration management provides a valuable tool for the continuity process. The configuration management system documents the components that make up the infrastructure and the relationship between the components.
- A very close relationship exists between ITSCM and information security management. A major security breach could be considered a disaster, so when the service provider is conducting business impact analysis and risk assessment, security will be a very important consideration.

Process Roles

In Chapter 1, "Introduction to Operational Support and Analysis," we explored the generic roles applicable to all processes throughout the service lifecycle. These are relevant to the ITSCM process, but there are specific additional requirements that also apply. Remember that these are not "job titles"; they are guidance on the roles that may be needed to successfully run the process.

IT Service Continuity Management Process Owner

The IT service continuity management process owner's responsibilities, as well as the generic requirements, typically include these:

- Working with the business to coordinate business continuity and IT service continuity management

- Working with the managers of all functions to ensure that the IT service continuity management process is recognized as a single point of contact for the process and all continuity issues

- Ensuring that other processes include reference to ITSCM

IT Service Continuity Management Process Manager

The IT service continuity management process manager's responsibilities, including the generic requirements, typically include these:

- Coordinating interfaces between IT service continuity management and other processes, especially service level management, information security management, availability management, capacity management, and business continuity management

- Performing business impact analyses for all existing and new services

- Implementing and maintaining the IT service continuity management process

- Ensuring that all IT service continuity management plans, risks, and activities underpin and align with all business continuity management plans, risks, and activities, and are capable of meeting the agreed and documented targets under any circumstances

- Performing risk assessment and risk management to prevent outages where cost-justifiable and where practical

- Developing and maintaining the organization's IT continuity strategy

- Assessing potential service continuity issues and invoking the service continuity plan if necessary

- Managing the service continuity plan while it is in operation

- Performing postmortem reviews of service continuity tests and invocations, and instigating corrective actions where required

- Developing and managing the IT service continuity management plans

- Ensuring that all IT service areas are prepared and able to respond to an invocation of the continuity plans

- Maintaining a comprehensive IT testing schedule in line with business continuity and business change

- Undertaking quality reviews of all procedures and ensuring that they are incorporated into the testing schedule
- Communicating and maintaining awareness of IT service continuity management objectives
- Undertaking regular reviews, at least annually, of the continuity plans
- Negotiating and managing contracts with providers of third-party recovery services in conjunction with supplier management
- Assessing changes for their impact on service continuity and continuity plans
- Attending CAB meetings when appropriate

Information Management

ITSCM needs to record all of the information necessary to maintain a comprehensive set of ITSCM plans. This information base should include the following items:

- Information from the latest version of the BIA
- Comprehensive information on risk within a risk register, including risk assessment and risk responses
- The latest version of the BCM strategy and business continuity plans
- Details relating to all completed tests and a schedule of all planned tests
- Details of all ITSCM plans and their contents
- Details of all other plans associated with ITSCM plans
- Details of all existing recovery facilities, recovery suppliers and partners, recovery agreements and contracts, and spare and alternative equipment
- Details of all backup and recovery processes, schedules, systems, and media and their respective locations

All the preceding information needs to be integrated and aligned with all BCM information and all the other information required by ITSCM. Interfaces to many other processes are required to ensure that this alignment is maintained.

IT Service Continuity Management Critical Success Factors and KPIs

The following list includes some sample critical success factors for ITSCM.

- Critical success factor: "IT services are delivered and can be recovered to meet business objectives."
    - KPI: Increase in success of regular audits of the ITSCM plans to ensure that, at all times, the agreed recovery requirements of the business can be achieved
    - KPI: Regular and comprehensive testing of ITSCM plans achieved consistently

- KPI: Regular reviews, at least annual, of the business and IT continuity plans with the business areas

- KPI: Overall reduction in the risk and impact of possible failure of IT services

- Critical success factor: "Awareness throughout the organization of the business and IT service continuity plans"

  - KPI: Increase in validated awareness of business impact, needs, and requirements throughout IT

  - KPI: Increase in successful test results, ensuring that all IT service areas and staff are prepared and able to respond to an invocation of the ITSCM plans

IT Service Continuity Management Challenges and Risks

We'll begin with looking at the key challenges for the process and then look at the risks.

Challenges

A major challenge facing ITSCM is to provide appropriate plans when there is no BCM process. If there is no BCM process, then IT is likely to adopt the wrong continuity strategies and options and make incorrect assumptions about business criticality of business processes. Also, if BCM is absent, then the business may fail to identify inexpensive non-IT solutions and waste money on ineffective, expensive IT solutions.

In some organizations, the perception is that continuity is an IT responsibility, and the business assumes that IT will be responsible for disaster recovery and that IT services will continue to run under any circumstances.

The challenge, if there is a BCM process established, becomes one of alignment and integration. Following that, the challenge becomes one of keeping the ITSCM process and BCM process aligned by management and by controlling business and IT change. All documents and plans should be maintained under the strict control of change management and service asset and configuration management.

Risks

These major risks are among those associated with ITSCM:

- Lack of a business continuity management process

- Lack of commitment from the business to the ITSCM processes and procedures

- Lack of appropriate information on future business plans and strategies

- Lack of senior management commitment to or lack of resources and/or budget for the ITSCM process

- The risk that the processes focus too much on the technology issues and not enough on the IT services and the needs and priorities of the business

- The risk that the process is unlikely to succeed in its objectives if risk assessment and management are conducted in isolation and not in conjunction with availability management and information security management

- ITSCM plans and information becoming out of date and losing alignment with the information and plans of the business and BCM

Understanding Demand Management

An important process in planning and optimization is that of demand management, a process within the service strategy stage of the lifecycle.

So let's start with a reminder of what demand management is. Demand management is the process that seeks to understand, anticipate, and influence customer demand for services and the provision of capacity to meet these demands. It is a critical aspect of service management. Poorly managed demand is a source of risk for service providers because of the uncertainty in demand. Excess capacity generates cost without creating value.

Purpose

The purpose of demand management is to understand, anticipate, and influence customer demand for services and to work with capacity management to ensure that the service provider has capacity to meet this demand. Demand management works at every stage of the lifecycle to ensure that services are designed, tested, and delivered to support the achievement of business outcomes at the appropriate levels of activity.

Objectives

The objectives of demand management are as follows:

- The first objective is about understanding the demands that will be placed on the service by identifying and analyzing patterns of business activity.

- The second objective is concerned with understanding the different types of user profiles that will use the service and how the demand from each type differs from the others. An example of this would be a cell phone supplier who offers different tariffs to business users and schoolchildren because they put very different demands on the service provided.

- The third objective is to ensure that services are designed with appropriate capacity to meet the patterns of business activity that have been identified and are therefore able to meet the business outcomes.

- Another objective of demand management is to work with capacity management to ensure that adequate resources are available to meet the demand for services, maintaining a balance between the cost of service and the value that it achieves. Unused resources are an additional cost.

- Demand management seeks to anticipate and prevent or manage situations in which demand for a service exceeds the capacity to deliver it. Insufficient resources have an impact on the achievement of the business objectives.

- The process aims to gear the utilization of resources that deliver services to meet the fluctuating levels of demand for those services.

Scope

The scope of the demand management process is to identify and analyze the patterns of business activity that initiate demand for services and to identify and analyze how different types of business users influence the demand for services.

Value

The main value of demand management is to achieve a balance between the cost of a service and the value of the business outcomes it supports. The other service strategy processes define the linkage between (and the investment required for) business outcomes, services, resources, and capabilities. Demand management refines the understanding of how, when, and to what level these elements interact.

Policies, Principles, and Basic Concepts

Demand management is about matching supply to demand. Unlike a factory that produces products, which can continue to be produced and stockpiled in anticipation of increased demand later, when we supply a service, the demand has to be met immediately, not later. A call center that receives few calls on a Friday afternoon cannot start answering the following Monday morning's calls! Monday morning will be busy, but there is no way to use the quiet times to balance out that busy morning. Another way of saying this is that consumption produces demand and production consumes demand in a highly synchronized pattern. There is a real risk that insufficient capacity will mean that the demand cannot be met at the time it is needed.

Supply and Demand

A major part of demand management is to understand the potential demand and the impact of the demand on the service assets. This allows capacity management to manage service assets (and investments) toward optimal performance and cost. The aim is to adjust the productive capacity to meet the demand forecasts and patterns. Some types of capacity can be quickly increased as required and released when not in use. Offering price incentives to customers to use services at quieter times means that the arrival of demand can be influenced to some extent. However, we cannot stockpile the service output before demand actually materializes. This cycle of demand, which is then supplied, will function only while there is available capacity; as soon as capacity is no longer available, the service provider will not be able to supply enough of the services to satisfy customer demand.

This highly synchronized pattern of supply and demand can be seen in Figure 9.2. Each time a user consumes a service, demand is presented to the service provider, and this consumes capacity of the service assets. This, in turn, results in the service being supplied to meet the consumer's demand. The greater the consumption of the service, the higher the demand, the higher the consumption of capacity, and the more the service is supplied.

FIGURE 9.2   Tight coupling between demands, capacity, and supply

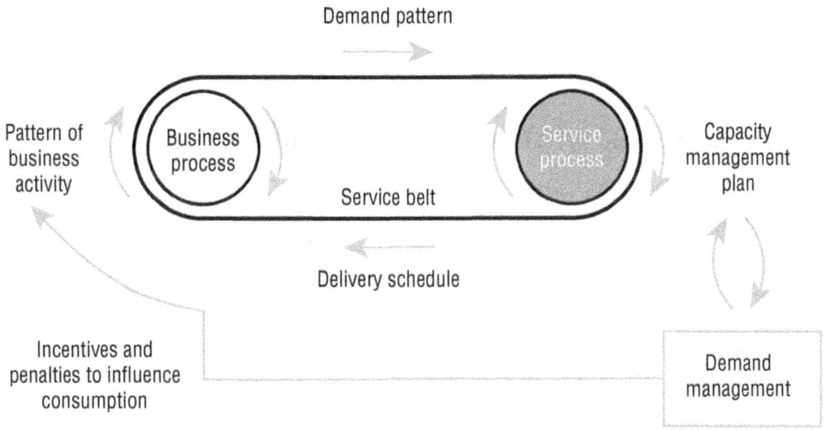

Gearing Service Assets

The balance of supply and demand is achieved by gearing the service assets to meet the dynamic patterns of demand on services. This means that the service provider does not just react to demand but proactively anticipates it, identifying the signals of increasing or decreasing demand and defining a mechanism to scale investment and supply as required.

This involves identifying the services using service portfolio management and quantifying the patterns of business activity. Next, the appropriate architecture to deal with the type and quantity of demand is chosen, and the capacity and availability planning processes ensure that the right service assets are available at the right time and are performing at the right levels. Performance management and tuning are carried out as required to deal with variations in demand. Gearing of service assets like this requires input from across the service lifecycle:

Service Strategy   Identifies the services, outcomes, and patterns of business activity and communicates the forecast demand to design teams.

Service Design   Service design confirms the availability and capacity requirements and validates that the service assets are designed to meet those requirements.

Service Transition   Service transition ensures that the new or changed service is tested and validated for the forecast utilization and patterns of business activity. Tests should also be carried out to check the ability to influence and manage demand.

Service Operation   The service operation functions should monitor service assets and service utilization levels to ensure that demand is within normal levels and, if not, initiate performance tuning or corrective action.

Continual Service Improvement   Continual service improvement will work with demand management to identify trends in patterns of business activity and to initiate changes to the capabilities of the service provider or changes to the behavior of customers where appropriate.

Process Activities, Methods, and Techniques

Demand management activities include identifying and implementing measures to influence and manage demand together with capacity management. This could be in situations where service demand exceeds capacity and where capacity increases are not feasible. Disincentives such as charging higher rates at peak times and imposing penalties can be used to lessen demand to what is deliverable. Where capacity exceeds demand (perhaps for a new service), incentives such as lower off-peak rates could be used.

If the peaks and troughs of demand can be smoothed out, the cost of providing the service is optimized because it can always deliver what is required without excessive wasted capacity.

Identify Sources of Demand Forecasting

Demand management is based on a good understanding of business activity and how that activity impacts the demand for services. Demand management must therefore identify any documents, reports, or information that can provide insight into these activities and assist in forecasting the levels of demand. These sources will be used to define, monitor, and refine the other components of demand management described in the following section.

The following potential sources of information can assist demand management in forecasting demand:

- Business plans
- Marketing plans and forecasts
- New product launch plans
- Sales forecasts

Patterns of Business Activity

Services are designed to enable business activities, which in turn achieve business outcomes. So every time a business activity is performed, it generates demand for services. Customer assets such as people, processes, and applications all perform business activities, and because of the way these assets are organized or because of the tasks they are completing, there will tend to be noticeable patterns in the way the activities are performed. These patterns of business activity (PBAs) represent the dynamics of the business and include interactions with customers, suppliers, partners, and other stakeholders.

PBAs must be properly understood, defined, and documented, and any changes to them must be properly controlled. Each PBA needs to have a documented PBA profile containing the following details:

Classification   PBAs are classified by type, which could refer to where they originate (user or automated), the type and impact of outcomes supported, and the type of workload supported.

Attributes   These may include frequency, volume, location, and duration.

Requirements   These could be performance, security, availability, privacy, latency, or tolerance for delays.

Service Asset Requirements   Design teams will draft a utilization profile for each PBA in terms of what resources it uses, when the resources are used, and how much of each resource is used. If the quantity of resources is known and the pattern of utilization is known, the capacity management process will be able to ensure that resources are available to meet the demand, provided it stays within the forecast range.

Figure 9.3 shows a number of different examples of patterns of business activity. Take a moment to look at them.

FIGURE 9.3   Examples of patterns of business activity

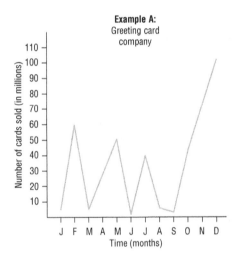

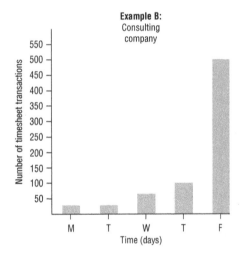

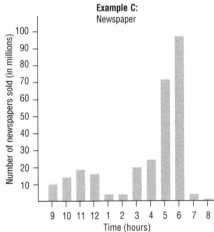

Each chart shows patterns of business activity (PBA). Each activity relies on IT services and each places a demand on the IT service provider's assets.

Example A – annual PBA: Greeting cards need to be designed, manufactured, and distributed for each major holiday. The fluctuation in sales will result in a fluctuation in demand for IT services.

Example B – weekly PBA: Consultants need access to a timesheet system to track their activities so that customers can be billed. Most consultants wait until the end of the week to complete their timesheets. Some consultants record their activities daily.

Example C – daily PBA: Journalists have to meet the deadline of 6 pm to submit their stories for publication. After the deadline, only high-impact corrections are made. The later in the day, the more critical the IT services become, and also the more utilized. Most journalists use the lunch hour to interview people for stories.

Example A shows the pattern of sales for a greeting card company in the United States. The pattern of card sales varies in line with major holidays or events; this in turn will lead to different levels of IT service utilization. The IT service provider must anticipate the business activity before each major holiday so the company can be sure to prepare and ship the greeting cards in time. In addition, the online ordering systems will be in high demand in the two weeks prior to the holiday. This high demand is not typical, so either the service provider will need to invest in spare capacity that will be idle at other times of the year or they will need to be able to balance the workload across multiple resources. In this way, processing lower-priority services will make way for the volumes of the higher-priority seasonal activity.

In example B, a consulting company relies on a timesheet service to bill consultants' time. Since most consultants complete their timesheets for the entire week at the end of the week, the service is more critical and is utilized more toward the end of the week. Consultants may need to be encouraged to log their time at the end of each day or the beginning of the next day.

Example C shows how journalists use a word processing and editorial service. From a quiet start early in the day, the service gets busier and busier as deadlines approach. This behavior is consistent with the nature of journalism, so trying to change it is unlikely to be successful. In these cases, measures will have to be taken to ensure that resources are available to match the PBA.

User profiles (UPs) are based on roles and responsibilities within organizations and may include business processes and applications. Many processes are automated and can consume services on their own. Processes and applications can have user profiles. Each UP can be associated with one or more PBAs.

Activity-Based Demand Management

Business processes are the primary source of demand for services. PBAs influence the demand patterns seen by the service providers. It is important to study the customer's business to identify, analyze, and classify such patterns to provide sufficient basis for capacity management. The service provider must visualize the customer's business activity and plans in terms of the demand for supporting services, as shown in Figure 9.4. Analyzing and tracking the activity patterns of the business process make it possible to predict demand patterns for services in the catalog that support the process. It is also possible to predict demand for underlying service assets that support those services.

Some of the benefits of analyzing PBAs are in the form of inputs to service management functions and processes:

- Service design can optimize designs to suit demand patterns.

- Capacity management translates the PBAs into workload profiles so that the appropriate resources can be made available to support the levels of service utilization.

- The service catalog can map demand patterns to appropriate services.

- Service portfolio management can approve investments in additional capacity, new services, or changes to services.
- Service operation can adjust allocation of resources and scheduling.
- Service operation can identify opportunities to consolidate demand by grouping closely matching demand patterns.
- Financial management for IT services can approve suitable incentives to influence demand.

FIGURE 9.4   Business activity influences patterns of demand for services.

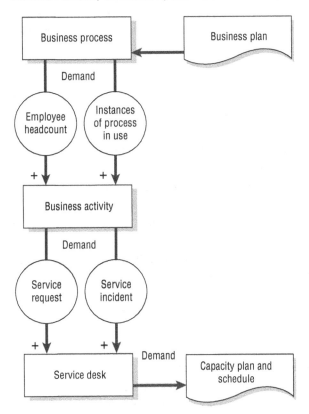

Develop Differentiated Offerings

The PBAs may show that different levels of performance are required at different times or with different combinations of utility. In these cases, demand and service portfolio management can work together to define service packages that meet the variations in PBAs.

One of the activities of demand management during service operation is to manage or influence the demand where services or resources are being overutilized. Typically this would occur in the following situations:

- Inaccurate patterns of business activity

- A change to the business environment

- An inaccurate resource forecast

There may be no spare budget to increase resources. Demand management could assist by differential charging or other means. It is important to note that any actions taken by demand management would be done in conjunction with the other processes, such as financial management, business relationship management, capacity management, and service level management.

Triggers

Triggers of demand management are as follows:

- A request from a customer for a new service or a change to an existing service. This will be initiated through business relationship management and service portfolio management and change management.

- A new service being created to meet a strategic initiative would be another trigger. This will be initiated through service portfolio management.

- The requirement to define a new service model and document its patterns of business activity and/or user profiles.

- Demand management would also be invoked if utilization rates are causing potential performance issues or a potential breach to an SLA.

- An exception has occurred to forecast patterns of business activity.

Inputs

Demand management has the following inputs:

- Initiatives to create a new service or to change an existing service. These inputs can come from service portfolio management or from change management.

- Service models need to be validated, and patterns of business activity associated with each service model will need to be defined. The customer portfolio, service portfolio, and customer agreement portfolio, all of which will contain information about supply and demand for services, are also inputs to demand management.

- Charging models will be assessed to ensure that under- or over-recovery does not occur with internal service providers or that pricing will be profitable for external service providers. Chargeable items will need to be validated to ensure that customers actually perceive them and use them as defined.

- Service improvement opportunities and plans will need to be assessed in terms of their impact on demand.

Outputs

The outputs of demand management include user profiles and documented patterns of business activity to be included in the service and customer portfolios. Other outputs are policies for management of demand when resources are overutilized and policies for how to deal with situations in which service utilization is higher or lower than anticipated by the customer. Finally, demand management will agree on and document the various options for differentiated offerings that can be used to create service packages.

Interfaces

Major interfaces with demand management are as follows:

- Strategy management for IT services will identify the key business outcomes and business activities that will be used to establish patterns of business activity and user profiles.

- Service portfolio management uses information from demand management to create and evaluate service models, to establish and forecast utilization requirements, and to identify the different types of users of the service. In addition, it will develop service packages based on the information about patterns of business activity and user profiles.

- Financial management for IT services forecasts the cost of providing the capacity to satisfy the demand and helps to identify charging measures to regulate demand in the event of overutilization.

- Business relationship management is the primary source of information about the business activities of the customer. Business relationship management will also be useful in validating the user profiles and differentiated service offerings before they are confirmed in the customer and service portfolios.

- Service level management will help to formalize agreements in which the customer commits to levels of utilization and the service provider commits to levels of performance. Actual levels of performance and utilization will be reviewed at the regular service level review meetings (using information from demand management and capacity management) and any deviations noted. Demand management will work with service level management to define policies for how to deal with variances in supply and demand.

- Capacity management works closely with demand management to define how to match supply and demand in the design and operation of services and to understand trends of utilization and how the services might be adjusted for future use. It also monitors the actual utilization of services.

- Availability management identifies the times when availability is the most important by analyzing patterns of business activity.

- IT service continuity management uses demand management information to analyze business impact and size recovery options.

- Change management works with demand management and capacity management to assess the impact of changes on how the business uses services.

- Service asset and configuration management identifies the relationship between the demand placed on services and the demand placed on systems and devices.

- Service validation and testing ensures that services deal with patterns of demand and validates the effectiveness of measures taken to prevent overutilization.
- Finally, event management provides information about actual patterns of service utilization versus the anticipated patterns of business activity for a service.

Process Roles

In Chapter 1, we explored the generic roles applicable to all processes throughout the service lifecycle. These are relevant to the demand management process, but specific additional requirements also apply. Remember that these are not "job titles"; they are guidance on the roles that may be needed to successfully run the process.

Demand Management Process Owner

The demand management process owner's responsibilities, in addition to the generic requirements, typically include:

- Working with other process owners to ensure there is an integrated approach to the design and implementation of demand management.

Demand Management Process Manager

The demand management process manager's responsibilities, in addition to the generic requirements, typically include these:

- Identifies and analyzes patterns of business activity
- Defines and analyzes user profiles
- Helps design services to meet the patterns of business activity and the ability to meet business outcomes
- Ensures that adequate resources are available at the appropriate levels of capacity to meet the demand for services
- Anticipates and prevents or manages situations where demand for a service exceeds the capacity to deliver it
- Gears the utilization of resources that deliver services to meet the fluctuating levels of demand for those services

Information Management

Effective demand management will use a number of different information sources. These include (but are not limited to)

- The service portfolio, which provides a view of the pipeline, catalog, and retired services
- The customer portfolio, showing details of the customers and the opportunities they may represent
- The project portfolio, to ensure that the projects include demand management as part of their considerations

- Business relationship management outputs, such as minutes from customer meetings
- Service level agreements to ensure the appropriate targets are being set and define limits for future agreements
- The configuration management system for information regarding the usage and configuration of service assets, customer assets, and business outcomes

Critical Success Factors and Key Performance Indicators

You'll recall from earlier discussions the definitions of critical success factors and key performance indicators. Here are some examples for demand management:

- Critical success factor: "The service provider has identified and analyzed the patterns of business activity and is able to use them to understand the levels of demand that will be placed on a service."
    - KPI: Patterns of business activity are defined for each relevant service.
    - KPI: Patterns of business activity have been translated into workload information by capacity management.
- Critical success factor: "The existence of a means to manage situations where demand for a service exceeds the capacity to deliver it."
    - KPI: Techniques to manage demand have been documented in capacity plans and, where appropriate, in service level agreements.
    - KPI: Differential charging (as an example of one such technique) has resulted in a more even demand on the service over time.

Challenges

Demand management faces the following challenges:

- Information about business activities may be hard to obtain if demand management was not included in the set of requirements.
- Customers may struggle to break down individual activities that make sense to the service provider. Business relationship management should be able to help.
- Lack of a formal service portfolio management process or service portfolio will hamper the understanding of the business requirements, relative value, and priority of services. This may mean that demand management information is only recorded on an ad hoc basis.

Risks

The risks of demand management are as follows:

- Lack of, or inaccurate, configuration management information makes it difficult to estimate the impact of changing demand on the service provider's infrastructure and applications.

- Service level management may be unable to obtain commitments from the business for minimum or maximum utilization levels. Without this commitment on utilization, it is difficult for demand management to commit to levels of service. As a result, higher levels of investments than are actually required are made to enable the service provider to keep ahead of demand, even when the service is not essential.

Summary

This chapter explored two processes, IT service continuity management and demand management. It covered the purpose and objectives for each process in addition to the scope.

We looked at the value of the processes. Then we reviewed the policies for each process and the activities, methods, and techniques.

Last, we reviewed triggers, inputs, outputs, and interfaces for each process and the information management associated with it. We also considered the critical success factors and key performance indicators and the challenges and risks for the processes.

We examined how each of these processes supports the other and the importance of these processes to the business and the IT service provider.

Through demand management, the service provider is able to anticipate and influence customer demand for services. Demand management techniques can moderate excessive demand or stimulate demand where there is overcapacity. Demand management endeavors to ensure that demand does not exceed the capacity to deliver and that there is no expensive unused capacity.

Exam Essentials

Understand the purpose and objectives of IT service continuity management and demand management. It is important for you to be able to explain the purpose and objectives of the IT service continuity management and demand management processes.

IT service continuity management should ensure that the required business continuity plan is delivered to meet the business needs.

Know the service strategy process of demand management. From a management-level viewpoint, know the purpose objectives, scope, principles, and activities of demand management.

Understand the interfaces with other processes. You need to be able to describe how the demand management process interfaces with the rest of the service lifecycle and the processes from the other lifecycle stages.

Understand the business value, challenges, and risks of each process.   You should be able to explain the value the business derives from the IT service continuity management and demand management processes and the challenges and risks involved in running them.

Understand the key activities of demand management.   Make sure you understand how demand management anticipates the level of demand and works with capacity management and other processes to meet it.

Explain and differentiate between the different stages of IT service continuity management. Initiation is the start of the process and the trigger received from business continuity management. Requirements and strategy are where a clear understanding of the business requirements and strategy are developed. Implementation is where the decisions in the strategy are realized. Ongoing operation is where the continuity plans are managed as part of the ongoing operation of the services.

Understand the critical success factors and key performance indicators for the processes. Measurement of the processes is an important part of understanding their success. You should be familiar with the CSFs and KPIs for both IT service continuity management and demand management.

Review Questions

You can find the answers to the review questions in the appendix.

1. Which of the following are responsibilities of IT service continuity management?
   1. Ensuring that IT services can continue in the event of a disaster
   2. Carrying out risk assessments
   3. Ensuring that the business has contingency plans in place in case of a disaster
   4. Ensuring that all IT staff know their role in the event of a disaster
      - **A.** 2, 3, and 4
      - **B.** 1, 2, and 4
      - **C.** 1 and 2 only
      - **D.** All of the above

2. IT service continuity management carries out a BIA in conjunction with the business. What does BIA stand for?
   - **A.** Business integrity appraisal
   - **B.** Business information alternatives
   - **C.** Benefit integration assessment
   - **D.** Business impact analysis

3. Which of the following statements about IT service continuity management (ITSCM) is TRUE?
   - **A.** ITSCM defines the service that can be provided in the event of a major disruption. The business can then plan how it will use the service.
   - **B.** ITSCM and business continuity management (BCM) have no impact on each other.
   - **C.** BCM defines the level of IT service that will be required in the event of a major disruption. ITSCM is responsible for delivering this level of service.
   - **D.** It is the responsibility of ITSCM to deliver a single continuity plan that will fit all situations.

4. Which of these are KPIs relating to IT service continuity management?
   1. KPI: Regular and comprehensive testing of ITSCM plans achieved consistently
   2. KPI: Regular reviews undertaken, at least annually, of the business and IT continuity plans with the business areas
   3. KPI: Overall reduction in the risk and impact of possible failure of IT services
   4. KPI: Number of incidents that result in a major incident
      - **A.** 1, 3, 4
      - **B.** 2, 3, 4

C. 1, 2, 3

D. 1, 2, 4

5. In which stages of the IT service continuity lifecycle does testing take place?

   A. Initiation and ongoing operation

   B. Initiation and implementation

   C. Implementation and ongoing operation

   D. Requirements and strategy and ongoing operation

6. What are patterns of business activity used to track?

   A. Usage of individual IT services by users

   B. Usage of individual IT services by departments

   C. Activity of the business to deliver business outcomes

   D. Value of services to the business

7. Demand management is about matching what to demand?

   A. Services

   B. Supply

   C. Strategy

   D. Service level agreements

8. Which of these information sources should be used by demand management?

   1. Business plans

   2. Marketing plans and forecasts

   3. Production plans (in manufacturing environments)

   4. Sales forecasts

   5. New product launch plans

   A. 1, 2, 3, 4, 5

   B. 1, 3, 5

   C. 2, 4

   D. 1, 2, 3, 4

9. User profiles (UPs) are based on what?

   A. Roles and responsibilities within organizations

   B. Processes within organizations

   C. Service level agreements

   D. Operational level agreements

10. Which of the following statements is incorrect?

A. From a strategic perspective, demand management is about matching supply to demand.

B. Demand management may use differential charging to try to influence the demand where services or resources are being overutilized.

C. Unlike goods, services cannot be manufactured in advance and stocked in a finished goods inventory in anticipation of demand.

D. Consumption consumes demand and production produces demand in a highly synchronized pattern.

Chapter

10

Technology and Implementation Considerations for Planning, Protection, and Optimization

---

THE FOLLOWING ITIL INTERMEDIATE EXAM OBJECTIVES ARE DISCUSSED IN THIS CHAPTER:

✓ The generic requirements for technology to assist service design

✓ The evaluation criteria for technology and tooling for process implementation

✓ The good practices for practice and process implementation

✓ The challenges, critical success factors, and risks related to implementing practices and processes

✓ How to plan and implement service management technologies

✓ The consideration for implementing technologies in supporting the processes within planning, protection, and optimization practice, in particular, designing technology architectures

This chapter brings all technology and implementation requirements together to define the overall requirements of an integrated set of service management technology tools to support the processes in planning protection and optimization. The same technology, with some possible additions, should be used for the lifecycle stages of IT service management (ITSM)—service strategy, service design, service transition, service operation, and continual service improvement—to give consistency and allow an effective ITSM lifecycle to be properly managed.

Tools can help the service management processes to work more effectively. They should allow large amounts of repetitive work to be carried out quickly and consistently. Tools also provide a wealth of management information, leading to the identification of weaknesses and opportunities for improvement.

The use of tools will help standardize practices and both centralize and integrate processes.

Often organizations believe that by purchasing or developing a tool, all of their problems will be solved, and it is easy to forget that we are still dependent on the process, the function, and, most important, the people. Remember, "a fool with a tool is still a fool," and therefore training in the process and tool is imperative.

We are going to consider the generic requirements for such tools. It is important that the tool being used support the processes, not the other way around.

Generic Requirements and Evaluation Criteria for Technology

We will begin by considering the generic requirements for technology to support service design, which for IT service management means IT service management tools. In this section, we look at a number of these requirements, which we would expect any good integrated toolset to offer.

The first two requirements are self-help functionality and a workflow engine.

You should be able to recall from the discussion of the release fulfillment process that we explored the option for dealing with requests or simple incidents via self-help functionality. This might be restricted to the logging of requests and incidents, or it could allow them to be tracked and updated throughout their lifecycle. The advantage to providing a self-help facility is that requests and incidents can be logged at any time, and this process is not dependent on service desk staff being available to answer the phone. This helps the service desk manage high volumes of calls if the less urgent ones are handled via a self-help, self-logging site. Self-help request tools can assist with password resets by, for example, requiring the user to validate their identity by answering previously set questions before the reset takes place. Additionally, a self-help request tool could download approved versions of requested software.

The next generic requirement is for a workflow or a process engine that can automate the steps of the process (assigning, escalating, etc.). It can also release work orders when prerequisite steps have been completed.

 Remember, the ITSM toolset is essential for many of the service management processes and functions and as such should be included in the IT service continuity provision.

The next generic requirement is for an integrated configuration management system (CMS).

The service management tool should be integrated with the CMS to allow the organization's configuration item (CI) information to be interrogated and linked to incident, problem, known error, and change records as appropriate.

Another generic requirement is for discovery, deployment. and licensing technology tools; these are extremely helpful in verifying the accuracy of the CMS, especially with regard to license use. It is also very helpful if only changes since the last audit can be extracted and reported upon. The same technology can often be used to deploy new software to target locations. This is essential to enable patches, upgrades, and so on to be distributed to the correct users.

When implemented in conjunction with the self-help functionality previously mentioned, the service management tool facilitates the automation of the fulfillment of many service requests for software.

Another generic requirement is remote control. This allows the service desk analysts to take control of the user's desktop (under properly controlled security conditions) to do things such as conduct investigations and correct settings.

Some tools will store diagnostic scripts and other diagnostic utilities to assist with earlier diagnosis of incidents.

Good reporting is a requirement of any ITSM toolset. The tools hold enormous amounts of information about what is happening day to day. This data is helpful in planning ahead and tracking trends, but such reporting has to be flexible if it is to be useful. Standard reports and ad hoc reports should both be easily available.

Another generic requirement to consider is a dashboard facility. Dashboards are useful, both for day-to-day operations and for IT and business management to get a clear idea of real-time performance.

To facilitate greater business alignment, business applications and tools need to be able to interface with ITSM support tools to give the required functionality. An example of integration includes event management tools spotting unusual spending patterns on credit cards.

Software as a Service (SaaS) technologies offer hosted service management capabilities over the Internet. The advantages this offers include lower capital and start-up costs, faster implementation, and built-in service continuity.

However, it also means limited customization and changes to functionality, access restricted to the vendor's hours of service availability, and licensing schemes that may become restrictive or expensive. There may also be limits on data storage size and possible security and access management constraints or risks. Finally, integration with other service management tools may be difficult or even impossible.

Each organization should review its requirements carefully so that it acquires the most appropriate toolset for its needs.

Good Practices for Practice and Process Implementation

In the following sections, we'll consider the basics of implementing good practices and processes. We need to take into account the requirements relating to the planning, protection, and optimization processes, and the approach to implementing service design. This should include

- Where do we start?

- How do we improve?

- How do we know we are making progress?

When looking at the implementation of any service management processes, including those of service design, the important factors to consider are the needs and desires of the customer and the business. The activities should be prioritized by

- Business needs and business impacts

- Risks to the services and processes

The activities will also be influenced by the service level requirements and agreements made in service level agreements.

Business Impact Analysis

One of the key inputs for understanding business needs, impacts, and risks is the output from a business impact analysis (BIA). BIA is used in a number of service design processes, particularly IT service continuity management (see Chapter 9, "IT Service Continuity Management and Demand Management"), where it is essential to help define the strategy for risk reduction and disaster recovery. BIA is normally used to identify the effect a disaster will have on the business, both on individual sections and on the business as a whole. It is used to identify the criticality of any particular business processes or activities, and also used to identify the times when this will be particularly affecting. BIA is also used for other processes—for example, availability management, capacity management, and information security management.

There are two areas for BIA. One is for business management, understanding the impact of loss on a business process or function. The second is to understand the BIA from the perspective of service loss. Both of these should be applied to identify the critical services and what constitutes a major incident on the services when a new service is being implemented. BIA will also assist in defining the acceptable level and duration of service outage, including the important periods to avoid. BIA can also assist with the understanding of financial loss and any security issues.

Service Level Requirements

As part of the service level management process (see Chapter 18, "Service Level Management and Supplier Management"), service level requirements for all services will be identified and the ability to deliver against the requirements will be assessed and agreed to in the service level agreements. This needs to be part of the approach to the design of services, and all processes in planning, protection, and optimization will have to be considered as part of the requirements capture.

Risks to the Services and Processes

It is important to ensure that business-as-usual processes are not adversely impacted by the implementation of the planning, protection, and optimization processes. This factor needs to be considered as part of the risk assessment during design, and it will be explored more fully during the transition lifecycle stage. Risk assessment and management form a key part of the planning, protection, and optimization processes—for example, availability management and IT service continuity management. Any solution created during service design must take risks into account.

Implementing Service Design

The process, policy, and architecture for the design of IT services will need to be documented and utilized to ensure that the appropriate services are provided to the business.

Best practice recommends that service design follow the continual service improvement approach and base the designs on the business requirements:

- Where do we start?
- How do we improve—the CSI approach:
  - What is the vision?
  - Where are we now?
  - Where do we want to be?
  - How do we get there?
  - Did we get there?
  - How do we keep the momentum going?

Challenges, Critical Success Factors, and Risks

When we consider the relationship between implementing good practices and planning, protection, and optimization processes, it is important to be aware of the challenges, critical success factors (CSFs), and risks associated with the implementation.

Challenges

Challenges will take many different forms, depending on the nature of the organization supported, but there are some common factors that will probably be applicable to all organizations in some aspect. These include

- Understanding business requirements and priorities
- Understanding organizational culture
- Effective communication to the business and service management staff
- Collaboration and engagement with all stakeholders
- Gaining commitment from management and staff
- Supplier management and contractual obligations
- Cost and budgetary constraints

These are common to most organizations, and the meeting of these challenges will be critical to the success of implementation of service management processes, including those for planning, protection, and optimization.

Critical Success Factors

As you are aware, *critical success factor* is a term used for an element that is necessary for an organization or project to achieve its mission. They can be used to identify the important elements of success. CSFs are measured by key performance indicators (KPIs) and should be set and measured as part of the service design lifecycle stage. The PPO processes will be critical in establishing the service requirements, and understanding the CSFs for each of the processes will provide a strong basis for the KPIs that will be used to demonstrate success in the service lifecycle stage.

Risks

As with challenges, some common risks are applicable to most organizations. They need to be appropriately identified and addressed to ensure successful service management implementation. Some examples include

- Meeting the identified CSFs
- Maturity of process
- Unclear business requirements
- Unrealistic business timeframes for service management design, transition, and operation
- Insufficient testing
- Lack of balance in focus on innovation or stability
- Lack of coordination among business, IT, and suppliers
- Insufficient resources, including cost and budget
- Lack of a holistic approach across the whole service management lifecycle

Service Management Tool Choice

Many service management tools are available, each with its own strengths and weaknesses, which makes choosing the right one difficult. To overcome this, you should define some objective selection criteria.

One simple method is MoSCoW analysis. This involves creating a detailed list of all your requirements and classifying each one as must have, should have, could have, or would like in the future.

- *Must have* requirements are mandatory. Any tool that does not satisfy *all* of those requirements is rejected.
- *Should have* requirements are those that we expect but are not essential.
- *Could have* requirements are useful but not hugely important.
- *Would like in the future* requirements are those that we don't need right now but will need in the future. For example, we're choosing a tool for incident management right now, but we'd like it to have problem management capability later.

You can then devise a scoring system based on this analysis, which would enable you to rank alternatives. It is possible to weight your decision, making a scoring system to ensure that you are getting the service management tool that delivers against your requirements.

Remember, the ITSM toolset is essential, but you are unlikely to get all of the requirements on your wish list. If you manage to get 80 percent of your requirements and the tool has some ability to be customized to meet your needs, then it probably is the best fit you can find.

Planning and Implementing Service Management Technologies

The final topic of this chapter is service management tools. A good service management tool can be very helpful for implementing processes based on the ITIL framework. Many organizations implement new tools to assist their implementation of new or improved processes. These organizations need to consider a number of factors if the new tool is to be helpful and appropriate.

Licenses

The first factor to be considered is the type of license. There are usually a number of options, at different costs. When tools are licensed on a modular basis, careful planning is required to ensure that the right access is obtained to enable people to carry out their work with no unnecessary modules being purchased. Here are some possible options:

Dedicated Licenses   For this option, each named person has their own license. Dedicated licenses are suitable for staff that require frequent and prolonged use of a particular module. For example, service desk staff would need a dedicated license to use an incident management module.

Shared Licenses   These licenses can be shared between individuals; there is, however, a possibility that a staff member may not be able to access the tool because the license is already in use. Shared licenses are suitable for regular users who do not require constant access, such as second-line support staff. Careful calculation is required to ascertain the correct ratio of users to licenses. These licenses are more expensive than dedicated licenses, but fewer are required.

Web Licenses   These allow access via a web browser. Web licenses are usually suitable for staff requiring remote access or only occasional access. They usually cost a lot less than other licenses (they may even be free with other licenses). It is possible to provide sufficient access for a large number of occasional users by purchasing a small number of such licenses, since the number of concurrent users and therefore the number of licenses required will be low. In this way, overall costs can be reduced further.

On Demand   Access to tools is provided when required (on demand), and the supplier charges for the access based on the time spent using the application. This can be attractive to smaller organizations or if the tools in question are very specialized and used relatively infrequently. A variation to this is the use of a specialist tool as part of a consultancy assignment (e.g., specialist capacity management tools); in such cases, the license fees are likely to be included in the consultancy fee.

Agent/Activity   A further variation in license options is software that is licensed and charged on an agent/activity basis. An example of this is simulation software (e.g., agent software that can simulate customer paths through a website to assess and report on performance and availability).

In all cases, it is essential that sufficient investigation be done to ensure that the costs are understood and agreed to and that the organization remains legal in respect to having sufficient licenses.

Deployment

Many ITSM tools, particularly discovery and event monitoring tools, will require some client/agent software deploying to all target locations before they can be used. This will need careful planning and execution and should be handled through formal release and deployment management. Some deployment considerations are listed here:

- There should be careful scheduling and testing, and the deployment must be tracked so that it is clear which CIs have the software and which have yet to receive it.
- The CMS should be updated as the deployment progresses.
- It is often necessary to reboot devices for the client software to be recognized, and this needs to be arranged in advance to minimize service interruption.
- Special arrangements may be needed for portable equipment, which may not be present on site during deployment.
- The devices receiving the software must be checked in advance to ensure that they have sufficient storage and processing capacity to host and run the new software.
- The network capacity needs to be checked to ensure that it is capable of transmitting everything required.
- The best time to deploy a tool is dependent on the maturity level. A tool that is deployed too early shifts the focus of the improvement initiative away from the requirement to change processes and ways of working, and the whole improvement exercise then becomes merely a tool implementation.
- Training in the tool prior to deployment is necessary if benefits are to be realized.

Remember, a tool is usually not enough to make things work better. However, if it supports processes and the user has been trained to use it, a good tool can help staff carry out new processes.

Here are some further aspects of the deployment that must be considered:

The Type of Introduction to Be Used   A decision must be made whether a "Big Bang" introduction or some sort of phased approach is to be adopted. Because most organizations will have live services to keep running during the introduction, a phased approach is more likely to be necessary.

Transition between Tools   If an older tool is being replaced, consideration must be given to the best way to transition between the old tool and the new tool. For example, the service desk should not be assigning an incident on a new tool to a team that has yet to transition from the old tool.

Data Migration   A decision needs to be made regarding what data needs to be migrated from the old tool to the new one. This may require reformatting, and so may need to be validated after migration, especially if the data is transferred electronically. A period of parallel running may be implemented instead, with the old tool being available in a read-only mode for an initial period alongside the new one so that historical data can be referenced if needed.

Complete details on the release and deployment management process can be found in the ITIL Service Transition publication.

Designing Technology Architectures

It is important for an IT organization to provide an infrastructure that will support the delivery of quality IT services, and this requires the correct approach to technology and technology architecture. *Architecture* is a term used in many different contexts. In this context it can be described as the fundamental organization of a system, embodied in its components, their relationships to each other and to the environment, and the principles guiding its design and evolution. *System* is used in the most general, not necessarily IT, sense to mean a collection of components organized to accomplish a specific function or set of functions.

The work of architectural design must assess and reconcile many types of needs, some of which may be in conflict with one another. The work should ensure that

- IT infrastructures, environments, data, applications, and external services serve the needs of the business, not just in terms of technology but also management of the technology
- The correct balance of innovation, risk, and cost is reached
- Compliance with standards, strategies, policies, regulations, and frameworks is achieved
- There is coordination between IT planners and designers and business planners and designers

The designs, plans, architectures, and policies should cover all aspects of IT, including roles and responsibilities, services, technology, architecture and frameworks, processes and procedures, partners and suppliers, and management methods. The work of architectural design must also cover all areas of technology, including the infrastructure, environment, applications, and data, and it should be closely linked to the overall business planning and design processes.

The complete enterprise architecture can be large and complex. Enterprise architecture is defined by Gartner as

> The process of translating the business's vision and strategy into effective enterprise change by creating, communicating and improving key requirements, principles and models that describe the enterprise's future state and enable its evolution toward it.

There are many proprietary and nonproprietary frameworks for the development of an enterprise architecture, as illustrated in Table 10.1.

TABLE 10.1   Enterprise architecture frameworks

Full framework name	Framework abbreviation
Architecture of integrated information systems framework	ARIS
Bredemeyer framework	Bredemeyer
Business transformation enablement program transformation framework	BTEP
Department of Defense architecture framework	DODAF
CSC catalyst	Catalyst
Computer integrated manufacturing open systems architecture	CIMOSA
Enterprise architecture framework	Gartner
Enterprise architecture planning	EAP
Extended enterprise architecture framework	E2AF
Federal Enterprise Architecture (FEA) reference models	FEA
Generalized enterprise reference architecture and methodology	GERAM
Integrated architecture framework	IAF
Pillars of Enterprise Architecture (EA)	Forrester
Reference model for open distributed processing	RM-ODP
Technical architectural framework for information management	TAFIM
Treasury enterprise architecture framework	TEAF
The Open Group Architecture Framework (TOGAF®) technical reference model	TOGAF
Zachman framework	Zachman

These frameworks include descriptions of all the relevant components and how they integrate. The enterprise architecture should be an integrated element of the business architecture and should include the following major areas:

- Service architecture
- Application architecture
- Data/information architecture
- IT infrastructure architecture
- Environmental architecture

The roles most likely to associated with the development of these architectures are often described as

- Business/organizational architect
- Service architect
- IT infrastructure architect

The real benefit and return on investment of the enterprise architecture comes not from the architecture itself, but from the ability of an organization to design and successfully implement projects and solutions in a rapid and consistent manner.

Technology Management

A strategic approach should be adopted with regard to the planning of an information technology and its management. Architectures need to be developed within the major areas of technology.

Technology Architectures

Architectures are needed in all areas of information technology. Where relevant, they need to be developed in the following areas:

- Applications and systems software
- Information, data, and database, including information security and confidentiality, data warehousing, and data mining
- Infrastructure design and architecture:
  - Central server, mainframe architectures, distributed regional servers, including local file and print servers
  - Data networks (LANs, MANs, WANs, VPNs, protocols etc.), Internet, intranet and extranet systems
  - Converged network technologies, including voice networks (PABXs, Centrex, handsets, mobiles, faxes, etc.)
  - Client systems (desktop PCs, laptop PCs, mobile access devices (handheld devices, mobile phones, palmtops, PDAs, scanners, etc.)
  - Storage devices, storage area networks (SANs), network-attached storage (NAS), including backup and recovery systems and services (servers, robots, etc.)

- Document storage, handling, and management
- Specialist areas of technology such as EPOS, ATMs, scanning devices, GPS systems, etc.
- Environmental systems and equipment, including their monitoring and management

This will result in a hierarchy of architectures, which will need to be integrated to construct a set of technology architectures for the organization.

Summary

In this chapter we reviewed the generic requirements for technology required to support the PPO processes and service design lifecycle stage. We explored some of the challenges and risks associated with their implementation, and considered the importance of an enterprise infrastructure. We discussed the overall requirements of an integrated set of service management technology tools to support the processes in planning protection and optimization.

Exam Essentials

Understand the role of tools in supporting service design.   This includes understanding how to select tools that are appropriate for organizational needs.

Explain the generic requirements that service design has for toolsets and why they are important.   Understand the generic requirements that are applicable to PPO processes and how these tools will support the objectives of the lifecycle.

Understand the specific requirements for the individual PPO processes.   Be able to identify the requirements for the individual processes from PPO to ensure maximum efficiency from the toolset.

Explain the selection technique known as MoSCoW.   Know what the acronym stands for (Must/Should/Could/Would) and be able to explain the use of each concept in tool selection.

Understand the risks in implementing technology.   Understand how these risks might be managed.

Understand the license options available when implementing a new service management tool.   Be able to describe the different options and give examples of when each would be appropriate.

Understand the deployment options available when implementing a new service management tool.   Be able to describe the different options and give examples of when each would be appropriate.

Review Questions

You can find the answers to the review questions in the appendix.

1. Which of these is most likely to be part of a self-service portal?
   1. The ability to reset passwords
   2. The ability to log requests
   3. The ability to authorize a change request
   4. The ability to download approved software
      - **A.** 1, 2, and 3
      - **B.** 2, 3, and 4
      - **C.** 1, 3, and 4
      - **D.** 1, 2, and 4

2. Management support is critical for successful service management. What benefits are expected from management's commitment to technology and tools?
   - **A.** Leadership, funding, and supporting commitment
   - **B.** Higher first-time fix rate, reduced outages, and funding
   - **C.** Improved customer satisfaction, reduced outages, and higher first-time fix rate
   - **D.** Reduced outages, funding, and supporting commitment

3. Which of the following is *not* a license option for service management tools?
   - **A.** Dedicated
   - **B.** Time limited
   - **C.** Shared
   - **D.** Web based

4. Which of these considerations for reporting requirements for service management tools is important?
   - **A.** Only industry-standard reports should be generated.
   - **B.** No reporting capability should be integrated into the tool; it should be managed separately.
   - **C.** There should be a good selection of generic reports.
   - **D.** There should be a good selection of generic reports supported by easy generation of custom reports.

5. Which of the following is *not* a benefit of using project management for complex operational changes?
   - **A.** It provides a clear, agreed statement of the benefits to be delivered by the project.
   - **B.** Project management would be funded by service transition and the project office, thus providing cost savings to service operation.

   C. It gives greater visibility of tasks and their management, which enables other IT groups and the business to understand the contributions made by operational teams. This helps in obtaining funding for projects that have traditionally been difficult to cost justify.

   D. It provides greater consistency and improved quality of the deliverables.

6. Which of these statements is/are correct?

  1. A CMS should be an integrated part of the service management tool.

  2. A service management tool without an SKMS is not a true service management tool.

   A. Statement 1 only

   B. Statement 2 only

   C. Both statements

   D. Neither statement

7. Which of these would be included in the generic requirements for a service management tool?

  1. Remote access capability

  2. Capability for integration with business tools

  3. Capability to link records such as incident and problem records

  4. Web-based access

   A. 1, 2, and 3

   B. 2, 3, and 4

   C. 1, 2, 3, and 4

   D. 1, 3, and 4

8. Which of these statements about service management tools and technology is correct?

   A. Tools are useful but not essential.

   B. Tools assist good processes instead of replacing them.

   C. Tools can replace processes that do not function well.

   D. Tools define the processes we use by formalizing the steps in the design.

9. What is the MoSCoW technique used for?

   A. Categorization of requirements

   B. Categorizing incidents and problems

   C. Categorization of service desk components

   D. Design of the SKMS

10. What is the first step when choosing a service management tool?

   A. Define the interfaces the tool will need to integrate with business tools.

   B. Understand the requirements for the tool.

   C. Decide how staff will be trained to achieve most from the tool.

   D. Research the available tools.

Release, Control, and Validation

Chapter 11

Introduction to Release, Control, and Validation

THE FOLLOWING ITIL RELEASE, CONTROL, AND VALIDATION CAPABILITY INTERMEDIATE EXAM OBJECTIVES ARE DISCUSSED IN THIS CHAPTER:

- ✓ The purpose, objectives, and scope of service transition

- ✓ Value to the business and how the RCV processes interact with processes within other lifecycle stages

- ✓ Development of an effective service transition strategy

- ✓ Defining service transition lifecycle stage

- ✓ The key initiatives that are important for effective preparation for service transition

- ✓ The approach and best practices in planning and coordinating service transition activities

- ✓ How service transition provides transition process support to stakeholders

In this chapter we will examine the concepts relating to the service transition lifecycle stage, including the purpose, objectives, and scope of the stage. You will be expected to be able to apply your understanding of these concepts in the examination. We will also consider the relationship of the release, control, and validation processes to the other lifecycle stages, and you should be able to analyze these relationships and demonstrate your understanding of their importance in the examination.

We will investigate the development and definition of a strategy relating to service transition and the key initiatives for the preparation of the lifecycle stage. Next we will explore the best practices for coordination of service transition and transition process support for stakeholders.

Service Transition Concepts

Service transition's main aim is to ensure that any modifications or transitions to the live operational environment—affecting new, modified, retiring, or retired services—meet the agreed expectations of the business, customers, and users.

Purpose

The purpose of service transition is to transition new, modified, retiring, or retired services that have been designed to deliver the strategy. Following transition, the services must meet the business expectations as established in the earlier lifecycle stages.

Objectives

The objectives of service transition include ensuring that changes to services happen as seamlessly as possible. The service releases are deployed into the supported live environment, where they can deliver the business value identified in service strategy. The new or changed service should be transitioned into the live environment without disrupting the other services and, as a result, without disrupting the business. Transition must strike a balance between avoiding risk to the live services and ensuring that the business can receive the new or changed service it requires without unnecessary delay or cost. Effective risk management is therefore also a key objective of this lifecycle stage.

A key aspect of service transition is communication. The business must know what to expect from the new or changed service in terms of its performance and use. If the business's expectations are not managed, it may judge a transition to have failed because it did not deliver the benefits or functionality that it was expecting but that had never been part of the design.

Having said that, however, transition must ensure that the expected business value is delivered. It is a common mistake to focus on the successful installation of hardware or software and fail to ensure that the business obtains the expected value from these.

An essential part of every transition is the accompanying knowledge transfer. A chief objective of service transition is to provide good-quality knowledge and information about services and service assets.

The requirements for successful service transition are as follows:

- Careful planning of resources

- Risk assessment and mitigation

- Control of service assets to ensure that their integrity is maintained

- Efficient repeatable mechanisms for building, testing, and releasing the service to increase the chances of success while reducing the cost and risks of transition

Service transition must understand the constraints under which the service will operate and ensure that the transitioned service can operate and be managed and supported successfully under these constraints.

Scope

The guidance given in the ITIL Service Transition publication is focused on improving an organization's capabilities for transferring new and changed services into supported environments. Its scope is wider than change management's scope; it covers planning the release, building it, testing it, and then evaluating and deploying it. Included within the scope of service transition are retiring services at the end of their useful life and transferring services between service providers, such as during an outsourcing or insourcing exercise or when a service is moved from one outsourced service provider to another. Service transition is all about ensuring that the requirements from service strategy, which were developed in service design, are effectively realized in service operation while controlling the risks of failure and subsequent disruption. A well-designed service can be damaged in the eyes of the business if it is poorly transitioned. If it fails to deliver the benefits reliably because the planning or testing was insufficient, it may be rejected by the business.

Service transition provides guidance on managing changes to services and service management processes, ensuring that the organization is protected from unplanned consequences of changes, while still enabling successful changes that deliver business benefits. These changes may be new services or improvements to existing services, such as expansion, reduction, change of supplier, acquisition or disposal of the user base or suppliers, or changed requirements.

Service transition also covers managing the end of a live service, including decommissioning equipment, discontinuing contracts or other service components, and so on.

The scope of service transition also includes managing the introduction of changes to the service provider's people, processes, products, or partners.

Transition includes managing the transfer of services to and from other service providers:

▪ Transfer to a new supplier by outsourcing the work or transfer between suppliers. Sometimes the transfer is from a supplier to in-house provision. This is called insourcing.

▪ Moving to a partnership or co-sourcing arrangement for some aspects of the service; this may involve multiple suppliers and is sometimes called multisourcing.

Although the service itself may not change, such transfers are not without risk, and careful planning is required to ensure that the transfer appears seamless to the business and nothing is forgotten.

Other transitions may be the result of setting up a joint venture with another organization or restructuring the organization by reducing staff (downsizing) or increasing staff (upsizing). Both of these are known as rightsizing, and the best solution will vary among organizations. Finally, work may be transferred to a location with cheaper labor costs. This is called offshoring. The organization may be involved in a merger or an acquisition.

Of course, in any organization, several of these transitions may be combined. All present risk as well as opportunity, and so must be carefully planned and executed.

The following two lists include the service transition processes. They can be categorized into two groups, based on the extent to which their activities take place within the service transition stage of the service lifecycle. The first group consists of processes that are critical during the service transition stage but influence and support all stages of the service lifecycle:

▪ Change management

▪ Service asset and configuration management

▪ Knowledge management

The second group consists of processes whose focus is strongly related to service transition:

▪ Transition planning and support

▪ Release and deployment management

▪ Service testing and validation

▪ Change evaluation

We will look at some of these processes later in this book (all except transition planning and support). Remember, almost all transition processes are active in other stages of the lifecycle, and transition is also impacted by processes from other lifecycle stages.

All the lifecycle processes should be linked closely together, and it is important to define the interfaces between processes when designing a service or improving or implementing a process.

Figure 11.1 shows all of the processes described in the ITIL Service Transition publication.

FIGURE 11.1   The scope of service transition

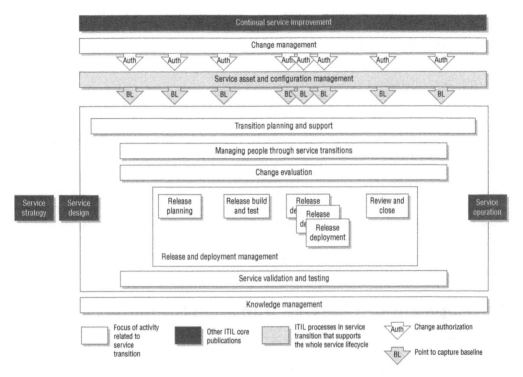

Processes that are largely within the service transition stage of the service lifecycle are shown within the central rectangle; the other stages of the service lifecycle that come before and after these processes are shown in the smaller, darker rectangles. The service transition processes that support the whole lifecycle are shown in the mid-color rectangles.

Not included in the diagram, but considered one of the release, control, and validation processes, is Request Fulfillment, from the Service Operation lifecycle stage. This process is covered in Chapter 3, "Event Management, Request Fulfillment, and Access Management."

Value to the Business

Selecting and adopting the best practice as recommended by ITIL will assist organizations in delivering significant benefits. Adopting and implementing standard and consistent approaches for service transition will benefit the business by making it easier for projects to estimate the cost, timing, resource requirement, and risks associated with service transition. This in turn enables a higher volume of successful change because less rework will be required. Other benefits include clear processes that are easy to adopt and follow and sharing assets across projects while avoiding clashes between transition projects that require the same asset (such as a test environment) at the same time. Avoiding such clashes will also reduce delay. Following the advice will also minimize the effort spent on managing the service transition test and pilot environments.

Good service transition ensures the following benefits:

- Better expectation setting for all stakeholders involved in service transition, including customers, users, suppliers, partners, and projects

- Increased confidence that the new or changed services can be delivered to specification without unexpectedly affecting other services or stakeholders

- Ensuring that new or changed services will be maintainable and cost-effective and improving the control of service assets and configurations

Use of the transition processes affects other lifecycle stages and promotes and supports an overall service management approach. For example, throughout the lifecycle we can observe interactions between change management and other processes such as service level management, availability and capacity from design, financial management from service strategy, and incident and problem management from service operation.

Transition does not just connect service design to service operation; it provides an interface and connection between all stages of the lifecycle.

Development of a Service Transition Strategy

To manage service transition activity appropriately, the organization should decide on their approach based on the size and type of the services provided, the number and frequency of releases required, and any specific requirements from the users.

The service transition strategy will cover the definition of the overall approach adopted by the organization to managing service transitions and allocating resources. Each organization will be different in its requirements, but the aspects to be considered should include the following:

- The purpose and objectives of service transition

- The organizational context of service transition, in relation to customers and contractual obligations from suppliers

- The scope, specifying the inclusions and exclusions

- Applicable standards or regulatory requirements either internal or external, including adherence to industry standards and contractual obligations

- Stakeholders and organizations involved in transition, which could include

  - Third parties, suppliers, service providers, and strategic partners

  - Customers and users

  - Service management

- Framework for service transition:
  - Policies, processes, and procedures for service transition, including service provider interfaces (SPIs)
  - Integration with program and project management methods and policies
  - Roles and responsibilities
  - Resource planning, and estimation, for transition
  - Training requirements for the transition
  - Change and release authorization
  - Knowledge usage, including experience, expertise, tools, historical data, and existing knowledge within the organization
- Transition criteria, including entry and exit for each release stage, stopping or restarting activity, success, and failure
- Requirements identification and content of the new or changed service, including
  - Services to be transitioned, along with the target locations, customers, and organizational units affected
  - Release definitions
  - SDP (which should include architectural design)
  - Environments to be used (locations, organizational, and technical)
  - Planning and management of environments (commissioning/decommissioning)
  - People, including the assignment of roles and responsibilities, authorization matrix, training, and knowledge transfer requirements
- Approach to transition:
  - Transition model
  - Plans for managing changes, knowledge, assets, and configurations
  - Baseline and evaluation points
  - Configuration audit and verification points
  - Identification of authorization points
  - Identification of change windows
  - Estimation, resource, and cost planning for transition
  - Preparation for the transition
  - Change authorization and change evaluation
  - Release and deployment activities
  - Error handling
  - Monitoring progress and reporting
  - Service performance and measurement, including key performance indicators and targets for improvements

- Deliverables for the transition activities (some mandatory, some optional documentation), which will include
  - Transition plans
  - Release policy and plans
  - Build, test, and deployment plans
  - Evaluation plans and reports
  - Transition closure report
- Schedule of milestones
- Financial requirements, which should include budgets and funding

Service Transition Lifecycle Stages

The lifecycle stages applicable to the transition of a new service should be defined and agreed to in the service design package. A useful approach would be a project management methodology, which would allow checks at the end of each stage, before proceeding to the next.

Typical stages might include

- Acquire and test new configuration items (CIs) and components
- Build and test
- Service release test
- Service operational readiness test
- Deployment
- Early life support
- Review and close service transition

For each stage, it is important to define the entry and exit criteria, which may be used as "quality gates" at specific stages through the transition.

Preparation for Service Transition

The service transition preparation activities include the following:

- Reviewing and accepting of inputs from the other service lifecycle stages
- Reviewing and checking the input deliverables—for example, the service design package, service acceptance criteria, and evaluation reports
- Identifying, raising, and scheduling requests for change (RFCs)
- Checking that configuration baselines are recorded in the configuration management system (CMS) before the start of service transition
- Checking transition readiness

All of these activities provide a point of reference and support a successful transition by ensuring that a baseline is in place to track progress. Tracking and tracing the progress will ensure that any variation or course change to the transition is identifiable and managed appropriately. Change evaluation will have a key role to play in the recommendation of authorization of a change, allowing the business to confirm their acceptance of, and readiness for, the transition.

Our basic requirement for readiness must be

- The agreement of the stakeholders who will be participating in, or be receiving, the transition
- That we have a suitable plan for the transition
- That it is going to provide the service as designed and documented in the service design package

The service design package will have been subject to evaluation as part of its sign-off, carried out by the change evaluation process. This interim report will be an important input into the preparation for our transition activity because it will identify the likelihood of successful implementation.

Planning and Coordinating Service Transition Activities

To coordinate the processes in the service transition stage, it is necessary to plan each transition to ensure that the work is completed effectively and efficiently. As part of the strategic approach to transition, it is important to identify the service transition model that will be used at this point. Each transition will have its own requirements, dependent on the desired outcome, and should have a specific plan. The plan should cover the following sections as a minimum:

- The work environment and infrastructure
- Schedule for the activities
- The activities and tasks to be undertaken
- Resource and budget allocation
- Issues and risks that can be identified at the start and will be added to as the plan is carried out
- Lead times and contingency for any specific actions or equipment

IT environments are complex and often distributed across a wide organizational structure. Managing the introduction of a new service or a change to an existing service is complicated and full of dependencies. It is vital to take an integrated approach to planning transitions. It is important to make sure that the overall plans are aligned and supportive of the individual plans for each stage of the transition. For example, the release and deployment plans need to consider that utilization of specific resources for testing may have very specific schedules.

If the transition relates to a new service or change to an existing service, it will require an overarching plan, which should include

- Milestone activities

- Release components, package release, build, test, deploy, evaluate, early life support

- Build and maintain services and IT infrastructure

- Measurement systems

Since there are likely to be a number of activities taking place at the same time, ITIL recommends adopting a project management approach. This allows for the coordination of all the activities as a program.

A number of project management methods can be used—for example, PRINCE2 or A Guide to the Project Management Body of Knowledge (PMBOK® Guide). But whatever the approach adopted, it is important to ensure that all the activities are coordinated. Larger releases such as those with a greater impact on the business, or perhaps involving a more complex approach, will probably be managed as projects in their own right.

Provide Transition Process Support

One of the key purposes of the ITIL Service Transition publication is the advice it provides to the stakeholders involved with the changes being carried out. This includes guidance to project managers (who may not have service management expertise) about the factors that are important for service management—for example, policies and processes that will enable the service transition to work effectively.

Transition planning and support provides assistance with the administration of the activities that are taking place, and should liaise with the program and project office.

Service management is heavily dependent on successful and meaningful communication, particularly when working on changes to the live environment. Service transition provides guidance on communication plans, which should cover the following:

- Objectives of the communication

- Defined stakeholders

- The content of the communication

- The frequency and format

- Measurement of whether the communication is successful

While the plans are being carried out, it is important to make sure there are sufficient monitoring and progress reports to establish the success of the plans.

Regularly monitoring progress will help identify if the plans are still appropriate for the business. Over the lifetime of a project, it is possible that business needs will have changed, and monitoring progress will help to identify whether any correction to the plan is needed.

Summary

In this chapter we looked at the introduction to service transition. We explored the purpose, objectives, and scope of service transition and its value to the business. We also identified the key elements supporting the stages of a transition. This included preparation for service transition, coordination for transition, and the support provided during transition for stakeholders.

Exam Essentials

Understand the purpose of service transition.   All lifecycle stages are important, but the purpose of service transition is to ensure that strategy and design are implemented correctly.

Be able to explain and expand on the objectives of service transition.   Ensure that the implementation of any and all new or changed services is seamless and effective for the business.

Understand and expand on the scope of service transition.   The scope of service transition is to improve an organization's capabilities for transferring new and changed services into supported environments, including all aspects of change, release, evaluation, and testing for new, modified, retiring, or retired services.

Be able to explain and justify the value of service transition to the business.   Transition is a key part of the lifecycle, enabling the services to be integrated seamlessly into the organization. Without this stage, testing and preparation may be overlooked, causing difficulties in delivery and support.

Understand and explain service transition preparation.   Transition requires considerable support and preparation to ensure readiness for support teams and other stakeholders. It is important to be able to articulate the needs of the stakeholders and ensure that they are met.

Understand the approach for planning transitions.   Recognize and be able to explain the approach for planning transitions, and the use of project management methodologies to support this activity.

Understand how service transition provides support to stakeholders.   Understand the role of evaluation and tracking in the management of transition to ensure operational stakeholder readiness.

Review Questions

You can find the answers to the review questions in the appendix.

1. Which of the following is *not* an objective of service transition?
   A. Set correct expectations on the performance and use of new or changed services.
   B. Provide good-quality knowledge and information about services and service assets.
   C. Document how service assets are used to deliver services and how to optimize their performance.
   D. Ensure that service changes create the expected business value.

2. Which of the following statements about service transition is/are correct?
   1. Transition turns strategy into deliverables.
   2. It is in the service transition stage that the design is used in the real world and the strategy is realized.
   3. The value of a service is identified in strategy, and the service is transitioned to deliver that value.
   4. Improvements identified by CSI may need to go through transition to be implemented.
      A. All of the above
      B. 1, 2, and 3 only
      C. 3 and 4 only
      D. 2, 3, and 4 only

3. Which of these situations is out of scope for service transition?
   1. Transferring between suppliers
   2. Producing a business case to justify outsourcing the service to an external supplier
   3. Moving to a partnership with several suppliers
   4. Setting up a joint venture with another organization
   5. Terminating a contract with a supplier
      A. None of the above
      B. 1, 3, and 4 only
      C. 1, 2, 3, and 4 only
      D. 1, 3, 4, and 5 only

4. True or False? The purpose of service transition is to ensure that new or changed services are designed according to the strategy.

    A. True

    B. False

5. Which of these options is *not* an aspect of successful service transition?

    A. Developing capacity plans to identify customer needs

    B. Assessing and mitigating risk

    C. Controlling service assets to ensure that their integrity is maintained

    D. Building efficient repeatable mechanisms for building, testing, and releasing the service

6. Which of these processes is considered to have a focus that is strongly related to service transition rather than in use across the service lifecycle?

    A. Change management

    B. Change evaluation

    C. Knowledge management

    D. Service asset and configuration management

7. Which of these statements is/are correct about the scope of service transition?

    1. Introduction of a new service is covered under service transition.

    2. Transfer of a service between providers is covered under service transition.

    A. Statement 1 only

    B. Statement 2 only

    C. Both statements

    D. Neither statement

8. Which of the following approaches are included in the management of transitional activity?

    1. Insourcing

    2. Outsourcing

    3. Co-sourcing

    4. Offshoring

    A. 1, 2, 3

    B. 2, 3, 4

    C. 1, 3, 4

    D. 1, 2, 3, 4

9. Which of these statements is correct about the service lifecycle?

   A. Service strategy describes the needs of the supplier as a priority for delivery.

   B. Service design controls the operational environment and optimizes service delivery.

   C. Service transition provides guidance for developing capabilities to introduce new services.

   D. Service operation exploits the business needs to describe and develop the strategy for improvement.

10. True or False? Service transition integrates with continual service improvement and will apply the PDCA approach to improving the processes in the transition lifecycle stage.

    A. True

    B. False

Chapter

12

Change Management and Service Asset and Configuration Management

THE FOLLOWING ITIL RELEASE, CONTROL, AND VALIDATION CAPABILITY INTERMEDIATE EXAM OBJECTIVES ARE DISCUSSED IN THIS CHAPTER:

✓ Change management and service asset and configuration management are discussed in terms of their:

- Purpose
- Objectives
- Scope
- Value
- Policies, principles, and basic concepts
- Process activities, methods, and techniques
- Triggers, inputs, outputs, and interfaces
- Information management
- Process roles
- Critical success factors and key performance indicators
- Challenges
- Risks

The Release, Control, and Validation capability syllabus covers the day-to-day operation of each process and the detail of the process activities, methods, and techniques and information management. The managerial and supervisory aspects of service transition processes are covered in the service lifecycle courses and in the Sybex *ITIL Intermediate Certification Companion Study Guide: Intermediate ITIL Service Lifecycle Exams*.

Change management ensures that the service, and the technology on which it is based, is able to continue to support the changing business requirement by implementing upgrades, moves, and problem and incident resolutions, while still protecting the live environment by carefully assessing the risk and impact of these changes. Service asset and configuration management provides many other processes, including change management, with information about where all the hardware, software, and other assets are and, crucially, the relationships between them.

We are going to examine each of these processes in turn.

Change Management

The one constant we can be sure of in IT management is that there will always be a need to change what we have. IT does not stand still, and whether changes are to take advantage of new technology, or because the business requirement has evolved, effective service management depends on being able to implement changes without disruption to the services being provided. Changes may be proactive, such as just described—improving or expanding the service—or may be as a reaction to errors or changing circumstances. We need to manage these changes, to minimize the risk to services, while ensuring that users and customers are fully prepared.

ITIL's change management guidance can be scaled to fit organizations of all sizes and of all types.

The Purpose of Change Management

The purpose of the *change management* process is to control the lifecycle of all changes, enabling beneficial changes to be made with minimum disruption to IT services.

The Objectives of Change Management

The objectives of change management are to facilitate the changes that the business requires, thus ensuring that services continue to align with the business needs. This means satisfying the customer's changing business requirements while avoiding incidents, disruption, and rework. Change management seeks to optimize overall business risk. Optimizing risk may mean avoiding a risk completely, but it also includes consciously accepting a risk because of the potential benefit.

Responding to requests for change entails an assessment of risk, impact, resource requirements, and business benefit. The risk of not implementing the change should also be considered as well as any risks that the change might introduce. It is essential to maintain the balance between the need for change and the impact of that change.

This means that the process is also responsible for managing the interfaces between the service lifecycle stages, ensuring the quality of the inputs and outputs.

Another objective of change management is to ensure that all changes are thoroughly understood. This means that they must be recorded, evaluated, prioritized, planned, tested, implemented, documented, and reviewed in a controlled manner. Change management also ensures that all changes to configuration items are recorded in the configuration management system.

The Scope of Change Management

Here we can see the ITIL definition of a change—"the addition, modification or removal of anything that could have an effect on IT services." This means that the scope of change management includes changes to all architectures, processes, tools, metrics, and documentation, as well as changes to IT services and other configuration items (CIs). Changing any of these could have an effect on the IT service, so change management ensures that we understand what we are changing and the potential impact of that change.

ITIL's definition of a change: "The addition, modification or removal of anything that could have an effect on IT services."'

The scope of change management is defined by each organization, but it usually includes changes to all CIs across the whole service lifecycle, including both physical and virtual assets. Changes to any of the five aspects of service design are also in scope, including changes to service solutions; management information systems and tools, technology, and management architectures required to provide the services; the processes needed to design, transition, operate, and improve the services; and the measurement systems, methods, and metrics used to measure it.

Each organization must decide exactly what lies outside the scope of its own change management process, such as those with wider impact—for example, changes to departmental organization, policies, or business operations. It should be noted that such changes would involve requests for change (RFCs) later to cater for the service changes that would follow as a consequence. Operational changes such as component repairs may also be excluded; however, if any identified CI is amended, removed, or replaced, this requires a change to the configuration management system information, and so such actions should be logged as changes.

Figure 12.1 illustrates a typical scope for the change management process for an IT department. It shows how the process interfaces with the business and suppliers at strategic, tactical, and operational levels. It shows the interfaces to internal service providers and also to those external service providers where there are shared assets that need to be under change management.

FIGURE 12.1   Scope of change management and release and deployment management for services

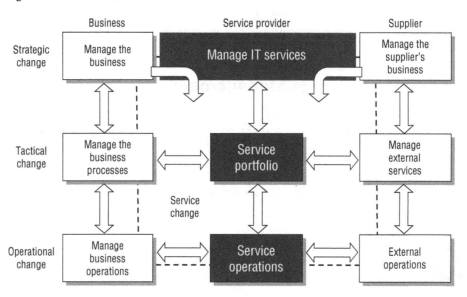

Service change management interfaces with business change management (to the left in the diagram), and with the supplier's change management (to the right). The supplier in this case may be an external supplier using their own change management process, or a project team using project change mechanisms.

The service portfolio defines current, planned, and retired services, and it therefore helps those involved to understand the potential impact of changes on current services. Changes may originate from different areas of the lifecycle—strategic changes come as proposals from service strategy and service portfolio management, whereas changes to a service come from service design, continual service improvement, service level management, and service catalog management. Corrective changes are also implemented to resolve faults and will originate from incident and problem management.

Remember: Change management is *not* responsible for coordinating the various service management processes to ensure the smooth implementation of projects. This is carried out by transition planning and support.

The Value of Change Management to the Business

Next, we consider the value that change management provides to the business. Consider your own organization. How would the business be impacted by poor IT change management? What benefits are gained by the introduction of good change management, and how would you explain this to the business?

Availability of a service is a key warranty aspect; without a reliable service, the business will not achieve the benefits the service is designed to deliver. Protecting this aspect, ensuring that changes do not disrupt the service, is a major benefit of implementing change management. Good change management enables the service provider to add value to the business by implementing beneficial changes while protecting existing services. It ensures that changes meet the business requirements while optimizing the costs of change. By providing auditable evidence of how changes are managed, the adherence of the organization to governance, legal, contractual, and regulatory requirements can be shown. This is also helpful where the service provider needs evidence of adherence to best practice processes in order to pass audits for ISO/IEC 20000 or ISO/IEC 38500 standards.

A robust change management process will ensure that risk involved in implementing changes is assessed and understood, and ensure that sufficient testing takes place before the change is implemented; this will reduce the numbers of failed changes, minimizing disruption and rework. By enforcing the process, the number of unauthorized changes should reduce, ensuring that only well-planned and understood changes are implemented. This, in turn, should reduce disruption and time spent resolving change-related incidents. By ensuring that changes are well managed, with the right balance of control without unnecessary bureaucracy, the service provider should be able to deliver accurate estimates of the time and cost required for a change and to track and implement changes promptly to meet business timescales. Change management ensures that risks associated with changes are understood and mitigated, where possible. Emergency changes are kept to a minimum and availability maximized.

Effective change management is essential for any organization as the reliance on complex IT services is becomes more widespread. Taking the time to analyze the impact of business change on IT and an IT change on the business is essential, as is communication with those affected and accurate records of actions taken. It enables the service provider to meet business needs and costs in a timely and controlled manner, and ensures that changes comply with governance standards; by controlling change, service providers are able to accurately predict costs and assess risks.

Despite the effort made, some disruption resulting from changes is inevitable; good communication with the business regarding forthcoming changes, and efficiently handling any incidents or problems caused by the change, should keep this to a minimum. Considerable cost savings and efficiencies can be gained from well-planned changes and releases.

Change Management Policies and Principles

This section discusses the policies and principles within change management that support its effective execution.

Policies and Principles

Laying down the principles behind the change process in one or more policy documents will help staff understand the seriousness with which this process is taken by senior management. In turn, this understanding will help build a culture where change management is taken seriously and the agreed process is followed. The adoption of this change management culture will increase the success rate of changes and releases, which will help build credibility for the process and reduce attempts to bypass it.

Ensuring adherence to best practice in this area can be challenging. Pressure to meet deadlines and cut costs encourages the cutting of corners by reducing testing and training. The existence of published policies will help such pressure to be resisted; this may even include a decision not to implement a required change, due to these policies having been ignored.

Let's look now at some of the possible policies supporting change management that an organization might adopt. The aim of these policies is to encourage zero tolerance for unauthorized changes. The process must align with business, project, and stakeholder change management processes to be effective. IT is not responsible for the business change process but should ensure that the IT process aligns to the business needs. Other policies include the following:

- All changes must create business value and the business benefits must be measured and reported.

- Prioritization of changes should follow the guidance laid down regarding innovation versus preventive versus detective versus corrective changes.

- Accountability and responsibilities for changes are laid down throughout the service lifecycle.

- Segregation of duty controls ensures that, for example, the person agreeing to the success of a test is not the person doing the testing.

- A single focal point for changes helps minimize conflicting changes and potential disruption to supported environments.

Other possible policies supporting change management that an organization might adopt include those covering these areas:

- Working with access management to ensure that people who are not authorized to make changes do not have access to supported environments

- Ensuring that people that have access rights to make changes only do so when the change has been authorized

- Working with other processes such as service asset and configuration management to detect unauthorized changes, and incident management to identify change-related incidents

- Ensuring that changes are implemented at suitable times by specifying change windows and then enforcing them

- Evaluating risk of all changes that impact service
- Measuring efficiency and effectiveness of the process

Design and Planning Considerations

The design of a robust change management process should include any legislative or regulatory requirements that exist within the organization. It should also consider the organizational roles and responsibilities required to ensure effective management of the process, along with the dependencies and relationships with other service management processes. Measurement is a key characteristic of any process, and suitable measures should be included to ensure that the process is working effectively. All of these aspects should be fully documented to ensure understanding of the complete process, including how changes are to be classified and authorized. Identification and classification of changes would include the change document identifiers to be used, the types of change documents required, templates for change documentation, and the expected content. The approach to prioritization of changes using impact and urgency should be specified with the roles, responsibilities, and accountabilities.

Other requirements to be considered in the design of change management processes are as follows:

- Organizational roles and responsibilities and accountabilities such as those for independent testing and formal evaluation of change
- Change authorization levels and escalation rules and the composition of the CAB and ECAB
- Details of how changes should be planned and communicated to stakeholders
- How changes may be grouped into releases or change windows and the detailed procedures for raising, assessing, evaluating, and verifying changes
- Identification of dependencies and clashes between changes
- The interfaces to other service management processes, especially the provision of information to service asset and configuration management
- The measurement and reporting of changes

The change management process should be planned in conjunction with release and deployment management and service asset and configuration management. This helps the service provider to evaluate the impact of the change on the current and planned services and releases.

Change Management Basic Concepts

A change request is a formal communication seeking an alteration to one or more configuration items. This may be an RFC document, or the request may be made by a call to the service desk or as a result of a project initiation document. Major changes may require a change proposal, created by the service portfolio management process. The procedures for different types of change should be appropriate for that type—minor changes should not require a lot of documentation. Similarly the levels of authorization required should be appropriate for that level of change.

Types of Change Request

There are three different types of service change:

- Many changes can be categorized as standard changes. These are low risk and relatively common and follow a defined procedure. As a result, they do not need to be assessed each time they are requested; instead these changes are preauthorized. Every standard change should have a change model defining how it should be handled. Many standard changes are triggered by request fulfillment and may be directly recorded and passed for action by the service desk. The crucial elements of a standard change include a defined trigger to initiate the change, a series of tasks that are well known, documented, proven, and preauthorized. Budgetary approval will be preauthorized or within the control of the change requester. Crucially, the risk involved in implementing the change is usually low and always well understood. Standard changes should be identified early on when building the change management process. This helps avoid unnecessarily high levels of administration.

- Emergency changes must be implemented with minimal delay—for example, to resolve a major incident or implement a security patch. These are normally defined as changes where the risk of *not* carrying out the change is greater than the risk of implementing it. Examples of emergency changes would be to overcome severe security flaws and major incidents where the service has already been seriously affected, or where imminent failure of the service is expected.

- All other changes are defined as normal changes.

Changes may be categorized as major, significant, and minor, depending on the cost and risk involved. This categorization may be used to identify an appropriate change authority.

As much use as possible should be made of devolved authorization, both through the standard change procedure and through the authorization of minor changes by change management staff.

Changes, RFCs, and Change Records

The terms *change*, *change record*, and *RFC* are often used inconsistently. The ITIL core guidance defines these terms as follows:

Change   The addition, modification, or removal of anything that could have an effect on IT services, including changes to architectures, processes, tools, metrics, and documentation, as well as changes to IT services and other configuration items.

Change Record   A record containing the lifecycle of a single change and referencing the affected CIs. One is created for every request received and can be stored in the configuration management system or elsewhere in the service knowledge management system.

RFC   A request for change—a formal proposal for a change to be made. It can be recorded on paper or electronically.

RFCs are only used to submit requests; they are not used to communicate the decisions of change management or to document the details of the change. A change record contains all the required information about a change, including information from the RFC, and is used to manage the lifecycle of that change.

Change Models and Workflows

Many organizations create change models to be applied to particular changes. A change model defines how to handle a particular type of change; this can then be programmed into the support tool to manage the change, ensuring that every such change is handled in this way. Models are useful for common changes, as well as those requiring specialized handling, such as emergency changes that may have different authorization and may have to be documented retrospectively, or any changes that require specific sequences of testing and implementation.

Change models are especially useful for standard changes, including those resulting from service requests.

The change model would normally include the steps to be carried out to handle the change, including resolving issues and unexpected events. The chronological order in which these steps should be taken with any dependences or concurrent steps would be included and the responsibility for each step defined. Timescales and thresholds for completion of the actions and any escalation procedures are also included. The support tools used can then automate many of these aspects.

Change Proposals

Major changes that involve significant cost, risk, or organizational impact will usually be initiated through the service portfolio management process. Before the new or changed service is chartered, it is reviewed for its potential impact. Authorization of the change proposal does not authorize implementation of the change but allows the service to be chartered so that service design activity can begin.

The proposal contains a high-level description of the change, including utility and warranty levels and the business outcomes it supports. The full business case and an outline schedule for design and implementation of the change are the remaining contents.

When the change proposal is authorized, the change schedule is updated to include the proposed change. RFCs will then be used in the normal way to request authorization for specific changes.

Change Authorities

It is unlikely that any one body will have the required knowledge to be able to assess all changes, especially in large, complex organizations. In this situation, change authorities should be identified for different categories of change. Each change must be authorized by a change authority, which can be a role, a person, or a group of people. The levels of authorization are dependent on the type, size, risk, and potential business impact of the change. Where changes affecting several sites in a large enterprise are planned, authorization may be needed by a higher-level change authority, such as a global CAB or the board of directors. All members of the change authority should assess the change based on impact, urgency, risk, benefits, and costs.

Depending on the culture of the organization, there may be many or few layers of authorization, and there may be delegated authority depending on specified parameters. Figure 12.2 shows an example of a change authorization model. Each organization should formally document its own change authorization hierarchy, which may be very different from the example shown here. All change authorities should be documented in the CMS.

FIGURE 12.2   Change authorization model

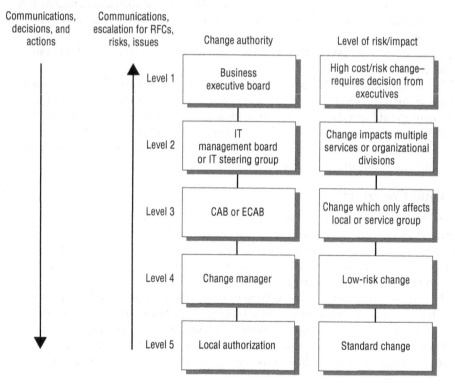

In Figure 12.2, if change assessment at level 2, 3, or 4 detects higher levels of risk, the authorization request is escalated to the appropriate higher level for the assessed level of risk. The use of delegated authority from higher levels to local levels must be accompanied by trust in the judgment of those lower levels. The level at which change is authorized should rest where accountability for accepting risk and remediation exist.

Change Advisory Board

The change advisory board (CAB) is a group of people who assist the change manager in deciding whether changes should be authorized. It can also have input to prioritization and scheduling decisions. The CAB may be the change authority for some change categories and play a merely advisory role for other categories. Depending on the organization, there may be a single CAB, or several, each responsible for dealing with changes for a particular geographic area, business unit, or other category. Some members will be permanent, involved in every assessment; others may be called on to participate in particular changes where they have specialist knowledge.

The members of the CAB or CABs must have sufficient knowledge and authority to understand the changes presented and to be able to assess the potential risks involved. The CAB representatives should be able to assess both technical and business risk. They will then make a recommendation to the appropriate change authority. Depending on the service management tool used, changes may be circulated for assessment prior to the CAB meeting. To ensure that the meeting is as efficient as possible, change proposals, RFCs, evaluation reports, the change schedule, and the projected service outage (PSO) document should be circulated in advance. The PSO identifies the effect of planned changes, maintenance activities, and test plans on agreed service levels.

The CAB will normally be chaired by the change manager. Potential members include

- Customer(s)
- User manager(s)
- User group representative(s)
- Business relationship managers
- Service owners
- Applications developers/maintainers
- Specialists and/or technical consultants
- Services and operations staff such as service desk, information security management, and capacity management
- Facilities staff where changes involve office moves
- Contractors' or third parties' representatives—e.g., in outsourcing situations
- Other parties as required

A standard CAB agenda is likely to include

- Change proposals from service portfolio management
- RFCs to be assessed, or that have already been circulated and assessed by CAB members
- Review of implemented changes
- Outstanding changes and changes in progress
- Evaluation reports from change evaluation
- Scheduling of changes and the required updates to the change schedule and projected service outage document
- Review of any unauthorized changes detected through service asset and configuration management
- Failed changes; unauthorized, backed-out changes; or changes applied without reference to the CAB
- Advance notice of RFCs expected for review at the next CAB

There may be situations where there is not enough time to wait until the next scheduled CAB to decide about a change. In this situation an emergency CAB (ECAB) may be convened. The ECAB consists of a small number of people who are empowered to make a decision quickly. The ECAB members are typically senior-level people, with representation from the business and technical staff. It is important that the criteria for declaring a change an emergency are clearly stated and agreed; emergency changes are inherently high-risk, since there is insufficient time for detailed evaluation and testing. As stated previously, a change would usually only be classified as an emergency if the consequences of not implementing it outweighed the risk involved.

Remediation

All changes must include a plan for dealing with failure; this plan must itself be tested. Understanding the remediation options helps in the assessment of risk of the change—if a simple backout is possible, the risk is reduced. Change plans should include decision points for when remediation is required, and sufficient time for it to be carried out.

ITIL definition of remediation: "Actions taken to recover after a failed change or release. Remediation may include back-out, invocation of service continuity plans, or other actions designed to enable the business process to continue."

Change Management Process Activities, Methods, and Techniques

In this section we'll examine the specific details of the methods and techniques for the change process. Managing changes effectively requires a number of activities to be addressed. These include

- Planning and controlling changes, ensuring that the schedule for implementing changes is appropriate
- Communicating the change to stakeholders with the right information at the right time
- Ensuring that those with authority to make authorize or decisions about changes are the most appropriate people with the necessary authority levels

We have already mentioned the importance of ensuring that remediation plans are in place. Measuring and controlling change is also essential to protect the live environment, as is understanding the impact of changes. Finally, providing management information through reporting helps to identify weaknesses in the process that may be addressed through continual service improvement.

Typical activities in managing individual changes include creating and recording the RFC, and then reviewing it so that incomplete or wrongly routed changes can be identified and filtered out. The change is assessed and evaluated, and the appropriate change authority identified. A decision is made regarding who should be involved in the CAB for this change. The change is evaluated in terms of its business justification, impact, cost, benefits, risks, and predicted performance and a request submitted to the change evaluation process. The change is then authorized or rejected and the stakeholders informed, especially the initiator. If approved, the implementation is planned, coordinated, reviewed, and closed. The documentation, such as baselines, evaluation reports, and lessons learned, is collated in the service knowledge management system (SKMS). When all actions are completed, the change is closed.

Figure 12.3 shows an example of a normal change such as a change to the service provider's services, applications, or infrastructure. You can see how the status of the change is altered. As the change progresses, information about it and the configuration items involved is updated.

Let's look at the main activities in more detail.

Log the Change

The process starts with the change initiator raising the request. The initiator will be the person or department that requires the change. The request receives an initial assessment to ascertain whether it is a major change, whether the information provided is complete, and whether the change required is clearly expressed. It may be necessary to refer the request to the initiator for clarification at this stage.

FIGURE 12.3 Example of a process flow for a normal change

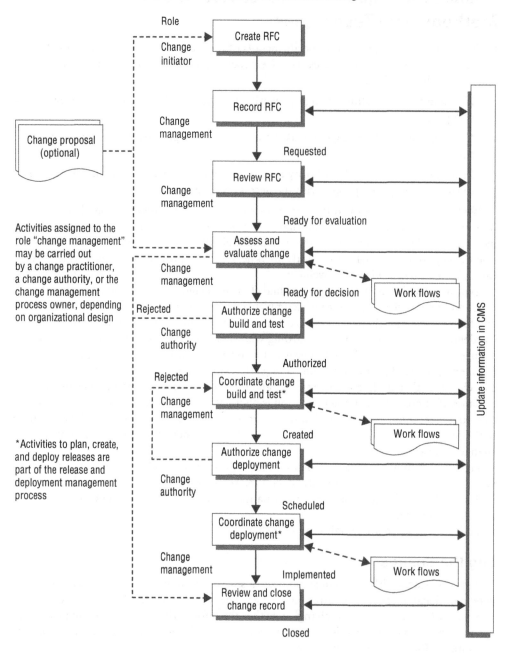

The change record will contain basic information, and this will be added to, as the change progresses. The level of documentation required will vary, according to the scale and complexity of the change. Table 12.1 shows examples of documentation required. Ideally, changes will be logged in an integrated service management tool. This should be able to link the changes with configuration items. Having this information easily available will help in assessing the likely impact of a change to one component of the system on other components. The tool will also enable an action log to be kept, so that it is clear what has been done as well as when it was done and by whom. The change record will contain basic information, and this will be added to as the change progresses.

TABLE 12.1   Example of contents of change documentation

Attribute on the change record	RFC/change record	Change proposal (if appropriate)	Related assets/CIs
Unique number			
Trigger (e.g., to purchase order, problem report number, error records, business need, legislation)			
Description	Detailed description	Description at a business level	
Identity of item(s) to be changed—description of the desired change	Detailed description	High-level description	Service (for enhancement) or CI with errors (corrective changes)
Reason for change, e.g., business case	Full justification, except if a change proposal exists	Full business case	
Effect of not implementing the change (business, technical, financial etc.)		Full business case	
Configuration items and baseline versions to be changed		Affected baseline/release	Details of CIs in baseline/release
Contact and details of person proposing the change			

TABLE 12.1   Example of contents of change documentation *(continued)*

Attribute on the change record	RFC/change record	Change proposal (if appropriate)	Related assets/CIs
Date and time that the change was proposed			
Change category, e.g., minor, significant, major	Proposed category	Used for major changes only	
Predicted timeframe, resources, costs, and quality of service	Full	Full business case and summary of expected implementation dates	
Change priority	Proposed priority		
Risk assessment and risk management plan	Full	High-level risk assessment for the overall proposal	
Backout or remediation plan	Full	High-level plan for the overall proposal	
Impact assessment and evaluation—resources and capacity, cost, benefits	Provisional	Full business case	
Would the change require consequential amendment of IT service continuity management (ITSCM) plan, capacity plan, security plan, and test plan?			Plans affected
Change decision body			
Decision and recommendations accompanying the decision			
Authorization signature (could be electronic)			

Attribute on the change record	RFC/change record	Change proposal (if appropriate)	Related assets/CIs
Authorization date and time			
Target baseline or release to incorporate change into			
Template change plan(s) to be used			
Scheduled implementation time (change window, release window, or date and time)		Summary of expected implementation dates	
Location/reference to release/implementation plan			
Details of change implementer			
Test results	Summary and pointer to details		
Change implementation details (success/fail/remediation)			
Actual implementation date and time			
Evaluation report	Summary and pointer to details		
Review date(s)			
Review results (including cross-reference to new RFC where necessary)	Summary		
Closure	Summary		

Some service management toolsets issue work orders to teams to carry out a task, such as to complete an impact assessment. This provides traceability of the progress of the change and will show where there are delays to the process. As the change progresses, the documentation and related configuration items are updated in the CMS. Estimates and actual costings may also be recorded for later analysis.

Assess and Evaluate the Change

Significant changes should undergo formal change evaluation. The decision as to the significance of a change should be made based on well-defined criteria. If deemed necessary, a formal request for evaluation should be submitted; if this is not required the evaluation will be carried out by the appropriate change authority.

Using generic assessment questions can be helpful when assessing impact. One such approach is known as the *seven Rs*, which involves assessing all change by answering seven questions:

- Who *raised* the change?
- What is the *reason* for the change?
- What is the *return* required from the change?
- What are the *risks* involved in the change?
- What *resources* are required to deliver the change?
- Who is *responsible* for the build, test, and implementation of the change?
- What is the *relationship* between this change and other changes?

Change management is responsible for ensuring that changes to all services receive the required evaluation and authorization, and are developed, tested, implemented, and reviewed. Final responsibility for a particular IT service lies with the service owner, who will have been involved in the change authority for that change.

Whoever is assessing a change—the CAB, ECAB, or any other change authority—must understand the potential business impact, the impact on the infrastructure, other services, SLA performance, and other service management aspects such as capacity, availability, and security aspects. Consideration must also be given to the resources required and the cost involved. The impact of implementing the change must be compared with the impact of not implementing it, which may prevent the business from achieving its aims.

Assessing the potential impact of a change is about assessing risk. No change is without risk, and the size of a change is not necessarily in line with the risk involved. The so-called "small change" may have a disastrous impact on the service, with repercussions on the brand image or reputation of the organization.

In this example, authorization for change build and test and for change deployment is required. For other changes there may be additional authorization steps, such as to authorize change design or change development.

Prioritize, Plan, and Schedule the Change

Prioritization is used to establish the order in which changes that have been put forward should be considered. As previously mentioned, this should be based on impact and urgency, although the requester may have a different assessment of these than the change manager and CAB.

Changes may be grouped into one release and designed, built, tested, and deployed together. This can save time, but care needs to be taken to ensure that the resulting release is not overly complex with many overlapping dependencies. Issues resulting from such a release may be difficult to diagnose as a result. Using regular change and release windows can be helpful and allow the service provider and the business to plan ahead.

Authorize Change Build and Test

Each change is authorized by the appropriate change authority as described earlier. Major changes may require multiple authorizations from change management at various points in its lifecycle, such as before design starts, later when the detailed release planning takes place, before build and test begins, before each deployment, and before agreeing to closure of the change.

Before each authorization the change should be evaluated to ensure that risks have been managed and that the predicted and the actual performance match the business requirements. Some organizations require a separate RFC for each of these steps; others use a documented workflow to manage all of these stages with a single change request.

In case disputes arise over change authorization or rejection, there should be a right of appeal to the higher level. Changes that have been rejected should be formally reviewed and closed.

Coordinate Change Build and Test

Release and deployment management coordinates the packaging of changes into a release, followed by the building and testing of this release. Simple changes may not be packaged into a release, and in that case the coordination will be done by the change management process.

Work orders may be used to request technical teams to build the changes. This helps in tracking the work. Change management also has the responsibility of ensuring that thorough testing is carried out.

Authorize Change Deployment

When the change build and test is complete, the results are assessed to ensure that risks have been minimized and that there is confidence that the predicted and the actual performance match the business requirements. Interim evaluations will be supplied by the change evaluation process where the change is significant; for smaller changes, the change management process itself will carry out the required checks. The change evaluation process is covered in detail in Chapter 13, "Service Validation and Testing and Change Evaluation." The evaluation results will enable the change authority to make an informed decision before it provides the authorization for deployment.

If the change authority has concerns about the change, it may decide not to authorize deployment of the change in its current form but ask for changes to the design instead. It may be concerned about the deployment schedule and request that it be amended. For complex changes, this assessment and request for changes can happen several times until the change authority is satisfied.

Coordinate Change Deployment

The release and deployment management process is responsible for the deployment of a release; some changes will not be part of a release, and, in this case, the change management process will coordinate deployment. The release and deployment management process is covered in detail in Chapter 14, "Release and Deployment Management and Knowledge Management."

Change management coordinates the deployment; the deployment activities themselves will be undertaken by technical, application, and operations management staff as appropriate. As discussed earlier, the procedures to be used in the event of remediation being required are documented in advance so that they will be available if and when required. The change documentation should define who has the authority to decide when a change should be remediated.

Change deployments should be scheduled in line with business requirements—and at times when they will involve minimum disruption to services. There may be occasions when the business is so anxious for a change to take place, they are happy to accept some disruption, rather than wait for a quieter time. Whenever the change is scheduled, it is essential that support staff be available to overcome any issues encountered.

Some changes that require the involvement of the release and deployment management process may have several deployment stages. Each of these deployments must be individually authorized by the appropriate change authority. This can be managed either by raising multiple RFCs or by using a single RFC with multiple authorization stages.

Standard Deployment

After a change has been built and tested, and the deployment procedure has been used successfully one or more times, then it may be appropriate to use a *standard deployment request* change model for future deployments of the same change. This is much simpler than the full change management process flow. You can see an example of a process flow for this kind of standard change in Figure 12.4.

Some very low-risk changes may be delegated to service desk or other service operation staff as a change authority. The change model for this kind of standard change may be very simple, as shown in Figure 12.5.

FIGURE 12.4   Example of a process flow for a standard deployment request

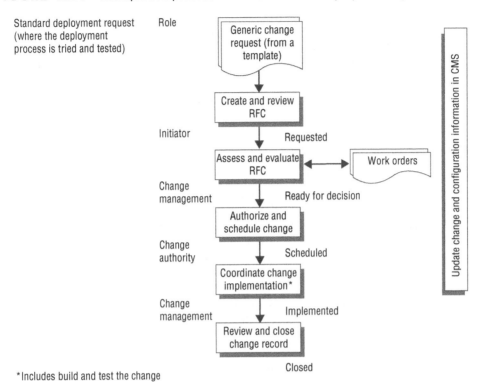

FIGURE 12.5   Example of a process flow for a standard operational change request

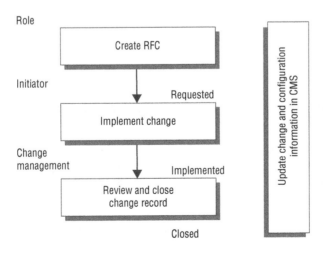

Review and Close Change Record

Following the deployment, the success or otherwise of the change is assessed in terms of performance and remaining risks. As with the evaluation of the build and test stage, a formal evaluation report will be produced by the change evaluation process where required; for smaller changes, the change management process will carry out the evaluation. The evaluation report should include any incidents arising from the change. If the assessment identifies unacceptable risks, the change authority is informed so that it can decide whether any action should be taken.

If the evaluation results in a favorable assessment, the completed change is approved for closure by the appropriate stakeholders. If the change was to resolve problems or known errors, then these records are also closed at this point.

A postimplementation review (PIR) of changes should be carried out to confirm that the change has met its objectives, that the initiator and stakeholders are happy with the results, and that there have been no unexpected side effects. Finally, any possible improvements to the process identified should be submitted for inclusion in the CSI register. Although all changes should be reviewed, smaller organizations may choose to carry out a full PIR on a sample of changes, or only those judged as significant, rather than all changes.

Service changes will be visible to the customer, and the review will usually take place at the next service level management review meeting. Infrastructure changes will often not be visible to customers and will be assessed internally.

Changes should be reviewed after a predefined period has elapsed because the results may not be apparent immediately. If, for example, a change is intended to resolve a problem, this can only be assessed after a period without incidents caused by that problem. If the change is to improve reliability, this can only be assessed after some time has passed. As discussed previously, change reviews are a standard CAB agenda item; if a formal change evaluation has taken place, the evaluation report will be a major input to this review. The review considers whether the change worked as intended without unexpected side effects and whether stakeholders are satisfied. The process itself is also assessed in terms of the accuracy of forecasts of the resources required, timing, and cost. Any issues with the deployment or remediation plans will also be documented. The CAB or change authority members and other involved parties will be notified of any issues, to be addressed as part of process improvement.

If a change is judged as failing to meet its objectives, change management (or the change authority) will decide on any necessary actions; successful changes should be formally closed.

Typical Change Management Activities Performed Day-to-Day during Service Operation

Change management is a key process in the service transition stage of the service lifecycle; there are many day-to-day change management activities, however, that take place during the service operation stage. These include standard changes to action routine operational requirements and raising RFCs to deal with service operation issues. Service operation staff will attend the change advisory board (CAB) or emergency change advisory board (ECAB) meetings to provide an operational perspective on the risk and impact of proposed changes. When changes have been approved, it is often the operational staff who are tasked with the implementation actions. If changes fail, it will be often be operational staff who are responsible for backing out the change. In addition, routine data center equipment moves, which form part of an overall change, will be carried out by operations staff. Service operation staff will receive the change schedule and ensure that they are ready for the changes.

Service operation staff will work with those involved in design and transition to ensure that service operation requirements and concerns are taken into account when new or changed services are being planned or designed.

Managing Organization and Stakeholder Change

Significant changes to the IT services provided will result in changes to how the people in the organization work. The change affects not just the technology but the organization itself. Business change is the responsibility of the business, but it is often the IT service change that puts the business strategy into effect, and this is why IT service changes have to recognize the importance of managing stakeholders when implementing such changes. Examples of such IT service changes that impact how organizations work could include a new IT web commerce service that alters how a retail organization serves its customers or a web portal that changes how IT users interface with the IT service provider.

Failing to understand the importance of organizational and cultural aspects of changes is at the root of the failure of these changes to deliver the planned benefits. A new service may work technically, but if the users are hostile to it, it will never be used properly, and the benefits will never be realized. Staff may be so hostile to the new methods that they actually leave the organization completely.

Effective change has to be led and managed. This means communicating the necessity for the change and the vision of what it will achieve. Those impacted by the change also need to understand the plan of how it is to be achieved, and the managers involved need to ensure that the resources are made available, so that users are not trying to master the new methods while still having to do their "day job." Most of these responsibilities lie with the business, and not IT, but the service transition process owner or manager is a key stakeholder. Issues with implementing the technical aspects, or any impact on operations that will result from the rollout, need to be reported to those leading the change.

Understanding the culture of the organization is important; for example, outsourcing companies brought in to run IT services often struggle to appreciate the very different organizational culture in a public sector or government department. Achieving successful service transition requires staff who understand how to build, test, deploy, and operate the service. Gaps in the required skills should be identified and actions taken to overcome these. Effective knowledge transfer to operational staff is essential and needs to be planned and resourced; too often there is a tendency to assume that operational staff will just "pick up the knowledge as they go along."

Triggers

Let's look at some examples of triggers for the change management process. Remember, changes can be triggered from all stages of the lifecycle.

Strategic Triggers

First we will examine change triggers that are an output of strategy. Strategy may require changes to achieve specific objectives while minimizing costs and risks. There is no such thing as cost-free and risk-free strategic plans or initiatives; we can only try to minimize them. Here are some examples of programs and initiatives that implement strategic changes.

Legal, regulatory, policy, or standards changes may require changes to services, as would organizational changes. Changes may result from an analysis of business, customer, and user activity patterns. Adding new services, or any other updates to the service, customer, or contract portfolios, or a change of sourcing model would also require the service provider to carry out changes. Finally, there are always new advancements in technology; the service provider may want to take advantage of these.

Changes to the services to be offered through the service portfolio and changes to the current services in the service catalog will trigger the change management process. These could include changes to service packages, definitions, or characteristics; utility, warranty, or service levels; or capacity and resource requirements. Any changes to costs, service assets, or acceptance criteria could also trigger the process. Take a minute to consider all these examples of possible triggers and consider the possible impact of each; it is the responsibility of change management to manage the possible impact while ensuring the benefits are realized.

Operational Changes

Many requests from users result in operational changes; these may include requests such as password reset, access request, or a request to move an IT asset. These types of changes will often be managed as standard changes by request fulfillment.

Service operation functions will also implement changes via the normal and standard change procedures. They may be corrective, such as rebooting a server or restarting an application, or preventive, such as applying a service pack that may prevent possible incidents. In either case, these can affect a shared service.

The final trigger comes from CSI and concerns changes to deliver continual improvement. As a result of CSI actions, a requirement for a change may be identified. CSI may identify improvements in technology, processes, documentation, and so forth that are required to deliver an improvement in the service. These changes will be raised as RFCs, and their implementation could have unintended negative effects on service provision and on other CSI initiatives. They therefore need to be managed to minimize the risk.

Inputs

The inputs to the change management process include examples such as these:

- Service charters for new or significantly changed services

- Change requests, change records, and authorized changes

- Business information from the organization's business and IT strategy, plans, and financial plans, and information on their current and future requirements

- Business impact analysis, providing information on the impact, priority, and risk associated with each service or changes to service requirements
- The service portfolio, including the service catalog and the business requirements for new or changed services in terms of service packages and service options
- Governance requirements
- Corporate, legal, and regulatory policies and requirements

Outputs

The process outputs of change management include the following:

- Rejected or approved RFCs
- The change to the services, service, or infrastructure resulting from the approved RFCs
- New, changed, or disposed assets or configuration items, such as baseline, service package, release package
- A revised change schedule and projected service outage, authorized change plans, decisions, and actions
- Change documents, records, and reports

Interfaces

There are several interfaces between change management and other individual processes. Any process may be affected by a change and so a feature of change management is the need for collaboration between diverse areas. It is important to identify clear boundaries, dependencies, and rules on how these interfaces will operate.

Change management works closely with the other transition processes. For example, it works with transition planning and support to ensure that there is a coordinated overall approach to managing service transitions, and with service asset and configuration management, to ensure that all changes to CIs are logged. The process must also be tightly integrated with change evaluation, with clear agreement on which types of change will be subject to formal change evaluation, and the necessary time set aside for this. The evaluation report will be used by the CAB to help their decision making. The implementation of the change may also require an interface with release and deployment management.

When a proposed change could have an impact on other parts of the organization, the change management process must interface with business change processes and business project management. The service portfolio management process will submit change proposals to change management before chartering new or changed services, in order to ensure that potential conflicts for resources or other issues are identified. Any process that could affect, or be affected by, a change must therefore interface with the change management process. The problem management process will be a source of many changes as fixes to faults are implemented. There are several major connections between change management and other processes, including

- Financial management
- Business relationship management
- Strategy management
- Service validation and testing
- Service level management
- Availability, capacity, continuity, and security (the warranty processes)

Each of these can be the source of a change or be affected by a change.

Information Management: The Role of the Configuration Management System

The ability to relate changes to individual CIs and services is essential; a good IT service management tool will enable these relationships to be defined and should also be able to link incidents and problems to CIs and to changes. The aim is to be able to trace the link from the incidents and the affected CIs to the underlying problem and the change being implemented to overcome it; where necessary, the link from a change to a resultant incident should also be traceable.

Change management is dependent on the CMS to understand the potential impact and risk of a proposed change. Other information contained within the SKMS such as the service design package will assist in the planning and management of the changes and will identify the stakeholders involved.

Change Management Process Roles

This section describes a number of roles that need to be performed in support of the change management process. These roles are not job titles; rather they are guidance on the roles that may be needed to successfully run the process, and each organization will have to define appropriate job titles and job descriptions for its needs. Chapter 1, "Introduction to Operational Support and Analysis," explored the generic roles applicable to all processes throughout the service lifecycle. These are relevant to the change management process and to the service asset and configuration management roles we discuss later in this chapter, but once again there are several specific additional requirements that also apply.

Change Management Process Owner

In addition to carrying out the generic process owner role for this process, the change management process owner's responsibilities typically include

- Designing change authority hierarchy and criteria for allocating RFCs to change authorities

- Designing change models and workflows
- Working with other process owners to ensure that there is an integrated approach to the design and implementation of change management, service asset, and configuration management; release and deployment management; and service validation and testing

Change Management Process Manager

In addition to carrying out the generic process manager role for this process, the change management process manager's responsibilities typically include

- Planning and managing support for change management tools and processes
- Maintaining the change schedule and projected service outage
- Coordinating interfaces between change management and other processes—especially service asset and configuration management and release and deployment management

Change Initiator

Each change has a single change initiator; this could be almost anyone in the organization, but it is not usually carried out by people who work in change management. The responsibilities of the role typically include

- Identifying the requirement for a change, and completing and submitting an RFC and a change proposal, if appropriate
- Providing CAB members with additional information if invited
- Reviewing change when requested by change management, and specifically before closure

Change Practitioner

The change practitioner's responsibilities typically include

- Verifying that RFCs are correctly completed and allocating them to the appropriate change authorities
- Submitting requests for evaluation
- Communicating decisions of change authorities
- Ensuring that the building and testing of changes is carried out correctly
- Publishing the change schedule and projected service outage

Change Authority

Each change category will have its own change authority defined. Their responsibilities typically include

- Reviewing specific categories of RFC
- Formally authorizing changes at agreed points

- Helping to review changes before closure
- Attending CAB meetings to discuss and review changes when required

CAB Member

The CAB may be purely advisory, but it is often the change authority for some change categories. Some CAB members may also be change authorities for other specific categories of change. The CAB members' responsibilities typically include

- Participating in CAB meetings, representing a particular group or function
- Communicating RFCs within their group, and gathering feedback, prior to attending the CAB
- Reviewing RFCs and recommending whether they should be authorized
- Reviewing successful, failed, and unauthorized changes
- Contributing to decisions regarding the change schedule so that conflicts or resource issues are avoided
- Providing feedback on the projected service outages

CAB Chair

The CAB is usually chaired by the change manager, unless there are multiple CABs; in this case there may be multiple change managers, each chairing a different CAB.

The CAB chair's responsibilities typically include

- Deciding who should be invited to CAB meetings
- Planning, scheduling, managing, and chairing CAB meetings
- Selecting RFCs for review at CAB meetings, based on the change policy, and circulating them in advance of the meeting
- Convening emergency change advisory board (ECAB) meetings when required
- Selecting successful and failed changes for review at CAB meetings

Critical Success Factors and Key Performance Indicators

The following list includes some sample critical success factors (CSFs) for change management. Each organization should develop key performance indicators (KPIs) that are appropriate for its level of maturity, its CSFs, and its particular circumstances.

Achievement against KPIs should be monitored and used to identify opportunities for improvement, which should be logged in the CSI register for evaluation and possible implementation.

KPIs must be meaningful and SMART (Specific, Measurable, Achievable, Relevant, and Time-bound) and as such should enable management to make timely and accurate actionable decisions. KPIs show whether the CSF is being achieved. For example, the achievement of the CSF of "Responding to business and IT requests for change that will align the services with the business needs while maximizing value" could be measured by KPIs showing an increased percentage of changes that meet the customer's agreed requirements, or delivering benefits of change (measured by the value of improvements made and negative impacts prevented) that exceed the costs of change. Other relevant KPIs would be a reduction in the backlog of change requests, and the average time taken to implement a change falling within SLA targets.

Additional examples are available in the ITIL Service Transition publication.

Challenges

The major challenge for change management is ensuring that all changes are recorded and managed so that no change circumvents the process. The challenge of convincing staff of the importance of the process is helped if senior management support is visibly present. It can also be difficult to persuade staff that change management facilitates changes rather than hampering or delaying them and adds value by helping changes happen faster and with higher success rates. If these challenges in convincing staff of the value of the process are met, the number of unauthorized changes will be reduced.

Another common challenge for organizations is to move away from simple change authorization, when RFCs are only considered just before changes are about to go live, to complete change management where they are assessed and planned from earlier in the lifecycle. Larger organizations may also find it challenging to obtain agreement for the required levels of change authority and to communicate effectively between these levels.

Risks

Risks to change management include, primarily, a lack of commitment to the change management process. This may be a lack of commitment from the business, with a lack of business sponsorship, or from IT management with a lack of IT management sponsorship, or from IT staff, leading to changes circumventing the process.

Other risks include insufficient assessment of changes, with a tick-the-box attitude, which allows changes to go ahead without a full assessment, and unnecessary delays to implementation of changes. This is often due to excessive bureaucracy. These risks, if they occur, encourage the lack of commitment to the process. There may be pressure from the business or projects to cut corners, leading to insufficient time or resources for assessment. Finally the interfaces with other processes may be poorly defined, causing confusion.

Service Asset and Configuration Management

In many ways service asset and configuration management (SACM) is the companion process to change management; each depends on the other for success. Without configuration management, change management would struggle to understand the implications of any change, as it would lack the information regarding the CIs and their interrelationships. Without the discipline of change management, service asset and configuration management would struggle to develop and maintain an accurate CMS, since changes might happen without any notification or documentation.

Purpose

The purpose of the SACM process is to ensure that the assets required to deliver services are properly controlled, and that accurate and reliable information about those assets is available when and where it is needed. This information includes details of how the assets have been configured and the relationships between assets.

Objectives

The objectives of service asset and configuration management are as follows:

- To ensure that IT assets are identified, controlled, and properly cared for throughout their lifecycle by identifying, controlling, recording, reporting, auditing, and verifying all configuration items, including versions, baselines, constituent components, and their attributes and relationships

- To work with change management to ensure that only authorized components are used and only authorized changes are made

- To account for, manage, and protect the integrity of CIs through the service lifecycle

- To ensure the integrity of CIs and configurations required to control the services by establishing and maintaining an accurate and complete configuration management system (CMS)

- To include information regarding the historical, planned, and current state of services and other CIs in the CMS

The existence of an accurate CMS supports the final objective—*to ensure that the other service management processes have accurate configuration information to inform decision making*; for example, to authorize changes and releases, or to resolve incidents and problems. This process helps improve the performance of all the other processes.

Service assets that need to be managed in order to deliver services are known as configuration items (CIs). CIs are service assets that need to be managed in order to deliver services.

Scope

The scope of SACM includes management of the complete lifecycle of every CI. It ensures that changes to all CIs are controlled and releases are authorized. The relationship between items is recorded to build a model of each service. Included within the scope are the interfaces to internal and external service providers where shared assets and CIs need to be controlled.

Configuration management depends on having a close interface with the organization's asset management. Asset management covers the full lifecycle management of IT and service assets and the maintenance of an asset inventory. However, asset management is not about the relationships between CIs and how they work together to deliver a service.

Value to Business

Often the value to the business can be shown by the impact when there is poor configuration management, such as service outages, fines, incorrect license fees, and failed audits. Accurate SACM enables better forecasting by the provision of information to the right people at the right time, which will assist with the management of change. It will also assist in the compliance to governance standards and the ability to assess the cost of services. The process provides visibility of accurate representations of a service, release, or environment that enables better forecasting and planning of changes, enabling better assessment, planning, and delivery of changes and releases. Providing accurate CI information helps ensure that incidents and problems are resolved within the service level targets. By being able to track CIs and their status, the service provider will ensure better adherence to standards or legal and regulatory obligations. Changes can be traced from requirements to implementation and the costs of a service identified from the information showing all the CIs that make up that service. Finally the business benefits from reduced cost and time to discover configuration information when it is needed, and can be assured that the fixed assets that are under the control of the service provider are under proper stewardship too.

Policies and Principles

Modern business functions require complex configurations of items to support business services. For example, a person may use a PC in an office in the United Kingdom, attached to the company network, but may be accessing a financial system running in a completely different part of the world, such as the United States. A change to the network or the financial system may have an impact on this person and the business process they support. Many services may run on different virtual servers hosted on the same physical computer; changes to the physical server could impact all these services.

Policies

Before implementing the SACM process, decisions need to be made regarding the policies that underpin the objectives, scope, and principles and critical success factors (CSFs) for what is to be achieved by the process. These policies are often defined together with those covering the change and release and deployment management processes as they are closely related. Each organization will develop policies that support its own particular business drivers. The policies must also fit any contractual and service management requirements of the business. There may also be a need for specific policies to deal with challenges such as "bring your own device," or policies to ensure compliance with local laws, regulations, and standards as regard intellectual property, software licensing, and other considerations.

Principles

Some of the typical principles for the SACM include ensuring that the costs involved and the resources required are in line with the potential risks to the services. Poor configuration management may be cheap, but failing to document the relationships and dependencies between CIs may hamper the resolution of incidents and lead to downtime that is more costly than an efficient process would have been. There may be a need to deliver governance requirements, such as software asset management, Sarbanes-Oxley, ISO/IEC 20000, ISO/IEC 38500, or COBIT, and the need to deliver the capability, resources, and warranties as defined by SLAs and contracts. Services provided must be available, reliable, and cost-effective. Internal and external stakeholders and other processes may require accurate asset and configuration information to be provided by SACM. Traceability and auditability of CIs must also be supported.

The policies should state clear economic and performance criteria for actions to reduce costs or optimize service delivery. For example, there may be a technical refresh policy that specifies how often PCs should be replaced with newer models and states that any failing in the final year of their designated life should be replaced and not repaired, since it is no longer economically justified to repair them. Other common principles are using CSI to optimize the service levels, assets, and configurations; migrating to a common CMS architecture; and using increased automation to reduce errors and costs.

Basic Concepts

Let's take a few minutes to remind ourselves of some of the basic concepts and definitions for this process. You should remember these from your foundation level studies:

- A service asset is any resource or capability that could contribute to the delivery of a service.

- A configuration item (CI) is a service asset that needs to be managed in order to deliver an IT service.

- All CIs are service assets, but many service assets are not configuration items.

- A configuration record is a set of attributes and relationships about a CI.

- Configuration records are stored in a configuration management database (CMDB) and managed within a configuration management system (CMS).

- The service knowledge management system (SKMS) is a set of tools and databases that are used to manage knowledge, information, and data. We cover the SKMS later in Chapter 14.

Attributes and Relationships

The policies underpinning SACM define which attributes and relationships will be documented for different CI types. Every CI must include the minimum attributes of unique identifier and CI type. Other attributes depend on the CI type. Typical attributes include

- Name/description
- Version (e.g., file, build, baseline, release)
- Supply date
- License details, such as the expiry date
- Status
- Audit trail

Relationship types typically would include

- "Parent–child"—A CI is a part of another CI; for example, a software module is part of a program.
- "Connected to"—For example, a desktop computer is connected to a LAN.
- "Uses"—For example, a program uses a module from another program.
- "Is installed on"—For example, Microsoft Project is installed on a desktop PC.

Other relationships could include links to specific locations, CI owners, suppliers, supported services, related documents, applicable SLAs, and master software copies.

The Configuration Model

Service asset and configuration management delivers a model of the services, assets, and infrastructure by recording the relationships between configuration items, as shown in Figure 12.6.

FIGURE 12.6   Example of a logical configuration model

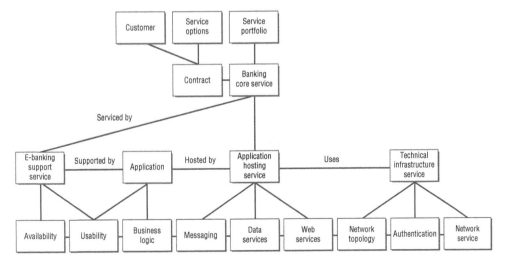

The configuration model enables other processes to access valuable information. Here are examples:

- The information will help when assessing the impact and cause of incidents and problems; assessing the impact of proposed changes; and planning and designing new or changed services.

- The information will help when planning a technology refresh or a software upgrade, or when migrating service assets to different locations and service centers.

- By understanding which CIs make up each service, asset utilization and costs can be optimized and assets reused.

As we said previously, a configuration item (CI) is a service asset that needs to be managed in order to deliver an IT service. Configuration items should hold useful details of the CI attributes. Maintaining such information can require a significant administrative overhead, so care should be taken to include only information where the value provided by the information is greater than the cost of gathering and maintaining it. Configuration items may vary widely in complexity, size, and type, ranging from an entire service or system including all hardware, software, documentation, and support staff to a single software module or a minor hardware component. Configuration items may be grouped and managed together: for example, a set of components may be grouped into a release.

Examples of Different CI Types

We usually think of CIs in terms of hardware, software, and network components, and indeed, the majority of CIs will fit into these categories. Configuration items include anything we want to manage and control, so we may also include other CI types such as the following:

- Service lifecycle CIs, which could include plans, business cases, service design packages, etc.

- Service CIs could describe

  - Capability assets such as management, organization, processes, knowledge, and people

  - Resource assets such as financial capital, systems, applications, information, data, infrastructure and facilities, financial capital, and people

  - Service models and service acceptance criteria could also be service CIs.

- Organization CIs would include items such as business strategy documents or statutory requirements.

- Internal CIs may refer to tangible (data center) and intangible assets (such as software) that are required to deliver and maintain the service and infrastructure.

- External CIs would refer to external customer requirements and agreements, releases from suppliers, and external services.

- An example of an interface CIs could be an escalation document, specifying how two service providers will work together.

Service asset and configuration management uses the configuration management system (CMS) to manage the CI data. The CMS holds all the information about CIs within scope. A service CI will include attributes such as supplier, cost, purchase date, and renewal date for licenses and maintenance contracts; the related documentation such as SLAs and underpinning contracts is held in the SKMS.

Figure 12.7 shows the relationship between configuration records, stored in the CMS, and the actual CIs, which may be stored in the SKMS or may be physical assets outside the SKMS.

FIGURE 12.7   Example of relationships between the CMS and SKMS

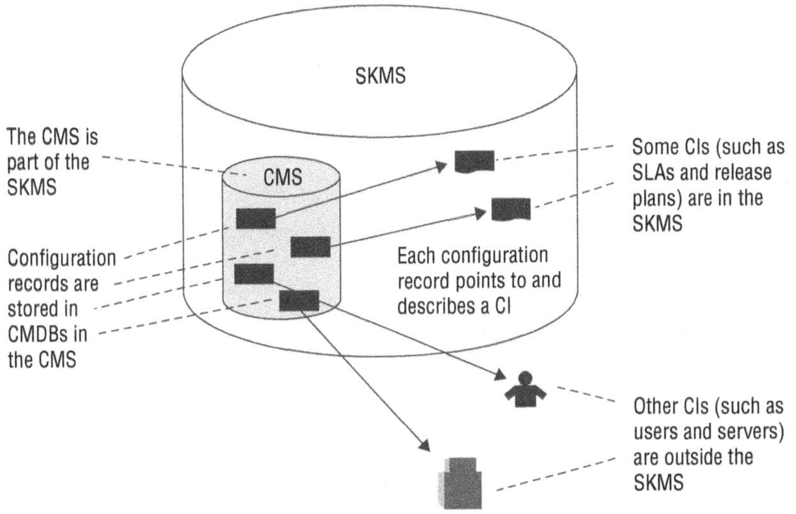

All CI changes must be authorized by change management, and all updates must include updates to the relevant configuration records. The CMS is also used for a wide range of purposes, outside of service asset and configuration management, such as fixed asset financial reporting. It maintains the relationships between all service components and may also include records for related incidents, problems, known errors, changes, and releases. Alternatively, these may be held in the SKMS but show the link to the associated CI. The CMS may either link to corporate data about employees, suppliers, locations and business units, customers, and users or hold copies of this information.

In Figure 12.8 you can see an example of the application of the architectural layers of the CMS. We will look at this in more detail later, when we consider knowledge management in Chapter 14. The CMS may include data from configuration records stored in several physical CMDBs, which come together at the information integration layer to form an integrated CMDB. The integrated CMDB may also incorporate information from external data sources such as an HR database or financial database. The presentation layer of the CMS will contain different views and dashboards to fit the requirements of different groups of people needing access to configuration information. In addition to providing a view suitable for staff responsible for SACM, other views may be provided suitable for those involved in change management and release and deployment management, or staff in technical and application management functions, or the service desk. The CMS will provide access to data in asset inventories wherever possible rather than duplicating data.

FIGURE 12.8   Example of the application of the architectural layers of the CMS

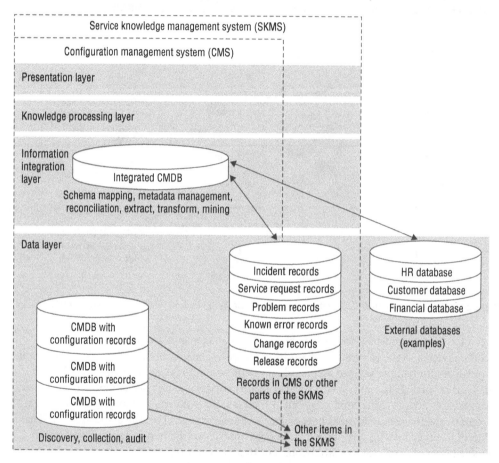

Configuration Baseline

A configuration baseline is a formally reviewed and agreed configuration of a service, product, or infrastructure. It captures the structure, contents, and details of a configuration and represents a set of configuration items that are related to each other. It is used to mark a milestone in the development of a service or to build a service component from a defined set of inputs. It can also be used to change or rebuild a specific version at a later date, to assemble all relevant components in readiness for a change or release, or to provide the basis for a configuration audit and backout.

Snapshot

A snapshot is the current state of a CI, process, or other set of data recorded at a particular point in time. This is useful when problem management needs to analyze evidence about the time incidents actually occurred. It also facilitates system restores and supports security scanning software, since any changes from the previous snapshot are obvious.

Asset Management

Organizations need to manage their fixed assets because they have a financial value. The process includes identifying and naming and labeling each asset and recording its owner. This information would be stored in an asset register, including details of the purchase cost, depreciation, and net book value of each asset. The process has to also safeguard the assets from interference or damage and carry out audits to ensure their integrity. The major difference between asset management and configuration management is that asset management is concerned with the financial aspects of each individual asset, whereas configuration management is concerned with each item's relationship with other items and with the provision of the service. An asset of very low financial value may play a key role in the provision of a service.

Outsourced service providers may manage some of the organization's CI assets and carry out some or all of the same activities—tracking, naming, labeling, protecting, and auditing.

Software Asset Management

Additional risks are involved when managing software assets compared to other asset types. These include too few or too many licenses, loss of evidence of purchase, and inadvertent breaches of terms and conditions. Software asset management manages the software, licenses, and activation codes.

Effective SAM is dependent on use of appropriate tools, including a CMS and a definitive media library (DML). We look at the DML next.

Secure Libraries and Secure Stores

The DML is a secure library holding the definitive authorized versions of all media CIs. It consists of one or more software libraries or file-storage areas, containing the master copies of all controlled software in the organization. This includes purchased software (with the license documents), software developed on site, and master copies of the relevant controlled documentation. The DML will also include a physical store to hold master copies—for example, a fireproof safe. Only authorized media should be accepted into the DML, strictly controlled by SACM. The DML is a foundation for release and deployment management.

An area should also be set aside for the secure storage of definitive hardware spares. Details of these components, their locations, and their respective builds and contents should be comprehensively recorded in the CMS.

Electronic assets in the DML are held within the SKMS, and every item in the DML is a CI. Figure 12.9 shows the relationship between the DML and a CMDB in the CMS.

FIGURE 12.9   The relationship between the definitive media library and the configuration management system

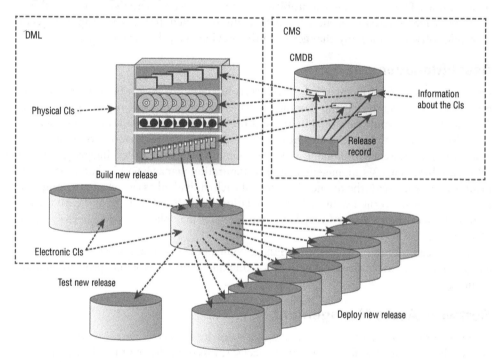

Decommissioning Assets

Assets are decommissioned for a number of reasons, including when a service is retired and the assets used are no longer needed, when a technology refresh replaces old assets, when hardware failure results in components being replaced, or when reduced capacity requirements frees up components.

The detailed steps to be taken when decommissioning assets should be documented in a service design package in the same way as for any other service transition. These steps should include redeploying, reusing, or selling the assets where appropriate to minimize waste and, where this is not possible, ensuring that the disposal meets the required environmental standards. The data stored on decommissioned assets must be removed and managed in accordance with the information security policy. If the equipment is leased it should be returned, and maintenance contracts on decommissioned equipment should be canceled. Finally the asset's status in the CMS should be updated and the fixed asset management process informed so that the asset records can be updated.

Process Activities, Methods, and Techniques

Before we start looking at the service asset and configuration management process activities, let's see how these activities work together. In Figure 12.10 you can see the high-level activities for service asset and configuration management—in this example, of an activity model.

FIGURE 12.10   Typical service asset and configuration management activity model

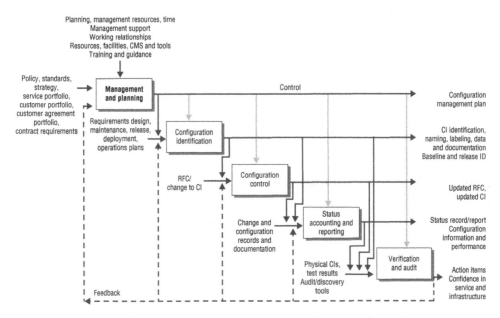

The service asset and configuration management activities include management and planning, configuration identification, configuration control, status accounting and reporting, and verification and audit. We will look at each of them in turn.

Management and Planning

The level of service asset and configuration management required will vary between organizations, so there is no standard template. The management team should decide what level is required for the particular service or project and how this level will be achieved, and then document this in an SACM plan. There may be several SACM plans, for each project, service, or groups of services. These plans define the specific SACM activities within the context of the overarching SACM strategy. Typical contents of a SACM plan would include

- Definition of the scope; which services, locations, environments, and infrastructure elements are to be included

- Definition of the requirements for accountability, traceability, auditability, and for the configuration management system

- Any applicable policies and standards such as ISO/IEC 20000 or ISO/IEC 19770-1

- Relevant internal standards such as agreed hardware standards and desktop standards

- Roles and responsibilities

- Relationship to change management

- The SACM system and tools

- Processes and procedures with regard to configuration identification, version control, supplier management, release and deployment management, builds, and baselines

- Responsibility for the CMS

- How CIs should be procured and retired

- Verification and audit processes

- Relationships and interfaces with other processes and groups, especially with fixed asset management

Configuration Identification

The configuration identification process activities include defining and documenting the criteria for selecting CIs and their components, and then selecting them according to the criteria. Each CI is then assigned a unique identifier and labeled accordingly. The relevant attributes of each CI are specified, including its relationship to other CIs, and the owner responsible for each CI is identified. The date from which each CI is placed under control of SACM process is recorded. Decisions must be made regarding the level at which CIs are to be defined, with top-level CIs broken down into components CIs where this is helpful. A CI can belong to several CI groups at the same time (for instance, a database may be used by many applications).

There is a danger that if too low a level is chosen, the administrative overhead may not be justified. For example, it may be more practical to define a workstation as a single CI, rather than as a collection of CIs—the keyboard, screen, mouse, and base unit. The correct CI level is that which strikes a balance between useful information and the level of control required and the effort required to maintain the information. This will vary between organizations; a secure military facility, for example, may require CIs to be defined and controlled to a low level compared to other organizations. CI information should be gathered and maintained only to the level at which it is useful.

Configuration Control

The configuration control activities ensure that no CI is added, modified, replaced, or removed without an appropriate procedure being followed. The control of the CMS data is dependent on effective change management, which should manage all CI changes and ensure that the CMS is updated after every change. Other SACM procedures would include

- Ensuring that a configuration baseline is taken before a release that can be used for subsequent checking against actual deployment
- Ensuring the integrity of the DML is maintained
- Using license control measures to prevent both the use of software without a valid license and more licenses being purchased than required
- Implementing version and build control
- Implementing physical access control to areas where CIs are stored, particularly the DML

Status Accounting and Reporting

This set of process activities tracks what happens to a CI by means of a number of statuses. Each CI will have one or more states through which it can progress. A simple example of a lifecycle follows:

Development or Draft   Denoting that the CI is under development and that no particular reliance should be placed on it

Approved   Meaning that the CI may be used as a basis for further work

Withdrawn   Meaning that the CI has been withdrawn from use, either because it is no longer fit for its purpose or because there is no further use for it

The method by which CIs move from one state to another should be defined.

Verification and Audit

The activities include a series of reviews or audits to ensure that the configuration records match the actual situation—that CIs and their documentation actually exist as stated in the CMS. The audits aim to verify the existence of CIs and their documentation, and to confirm that they are configured correctly, especially when planning a release. Any unregistered and unauthorized items that are discovered should be investigated and corrective action taken to address possible issues with circumventing of procedures by some staff. All exceptions should be logged and reported, and records of the audit should be created to support future compliance checking.

Configuration audits should be considered at the following times:

- Shortly after changes to the CMS
- Before and after changes to the IT services or infrastructure
- Before a release or installation to ensure that the environment is as expected

- Following recovery from disasters and after a return to normal (this audit should be included in contingency plans)
- At planned intervals (automated audit tools can enable checks to be made at regular intervals, such as weekly)
- At random intervals
- In response to the detection of any unauthorized CIs

Typical SACM Activities Performed on a Daily Basis by Service Operation

As with change management, many day-to-day service asset and configuration management activities take place during the service operation stage. These would include service operation staff identifying any discrepancies between any CIs and the CMS found during their operational activities such as incident resolution and reporting these to SACM. Where authorized by SACM, operational staff may make the necessary amendments to correct these discrepancies. Staff involved in service operation may also be responsible for labeling new equipment as it arrives and logging the details into the CMS. SACM will often use service operation staff to audit and validate the location of CIs. For example, a desktop engineer visiting a remote site may be given a list of all the CIs that are listed in the CMS at that location and asked to confirm that the list is correct.

Although the responsibility for updating the CMS remains with service asset and configuration management, operations staff might be asked, under the direction of service asset and configuration management, to update relationships, or even to add new CIs or mark CIs as "disposed" in the CMS. Operations staff may also report changes in state or status with CIs impacted by incidents to SACM.

Triggers, Inputs and Outputs, and Process Interfaces

Now let's look at the triggers, inputs and outputs, and process interfaces for service asset and configuration management. Let's look first at the triggers for this process.

Triggers

Updates to asset and configuration information are triggered by updates from the change and release and deployment processes. Other triggers include purchase orders, acquisitions, and service requests.

Inputs

Now let's consider the inputs and outputs to this process. Inputs to service asset and configuration management include the designs, plans, and configurations contained in service design packages and the RFCs and work orders from change management. Other inputs are the configuration information collected by discovery tools and audits, and the organization's fixed asset register.

Outputs

Outputs include new and updated configuration records, snapshots and baselines, audit and status reports and updated asset information for inclusion in the fixed asset register. The information output by the process regarding the attributes and relationships of configuration items is used by all the other service management processes.

Interfaces

SACM provides the single virtual repository of configuration data and information for IT service management, so it interfaces with every other process and activity to some extent. Perhaps the most important interface is that with change management where it is used for impact assessment and also ensures that changes to CIs are captured, which is critical if SACM is to work effectively.

Other important interfaces include the interfaces with

- Financial management, where it captures key financial information such as cost, depreciation methods, owner, maintenance, and repair costs
- IT service continuity management, where it provides information regarding critical assets to be protected
- Incident and problem management, where it provides key diagnostic information and data to the service desk and helps identify problem causes
- Availability management, where the information in the configuration management system showing CI relationships helps in the detection of single points of failure

There is also a close relationship with the business process of asset management.

Information Management

Service asset and configuration management is primarily about managing the configuration information held in the CMS. The configuration management system is a crucial resource for many processes, so procedures should be in place to ensure that it is available and accurate. It should be backed up regularly, and the backup copies of the CMS should be stored securely. A current copy of the CMS should be available at a remote location for use in the event the IT service continuity plan is invoked. The information must be accurate and current because it will be used as a basis for making decisions. Where changes to the status or location of CIs happens frequently, the backups should be taken frequently also; it may be enough to just record CIs that have changed, with full backups being made less frequently. Automated discovery tools will help track these changes.

The CMS contains historical information on CIs and archived versions; deleted CIs or CI versions may also be included. The amount of retained information depends on its continuing usefulness to the organization, and the value of the information must be weighed against the cost of retaining it. Some information records must be kept due to regulatory and statutory requirements.

The CMS also includes pointers to knowledge and information assets that are stored in the SKMS. These must be maintained with the same level of control as the CMS.

Service Asset and Configuration Management Process Roles

As we discussed with regard to change management earlier, there are a number of roles that need to be performed in support of the SACM process. These roles are not job titles; rather, they are guidance on the roles that may be needed to successfully run the process, and each organization will have to define appropriate job titles and job descriptions for its needs. Chapter 1 explored the generic roles applicable to all processes throughout the service lifecycle. These are relevant to the SACM process, but once again several specific additional requirements also apply.

SACM Process Owner

The SACM process owner's responsibilities typically include carrying out the generic process owner role for the SACM process. The process owner will also agree and document its scope, including defining the policy specifying which service assets should be treated as configuration items. This individual will also work with other service transition process owners to ensure an integrated approach to the design and implementation of SACM, change management, release and deployment management, and knowledge management.

SACM Process Manager

The SACM process manager's responsibilities typically include carrying out the generic process manager role for the SACM process. The process manager is accountable for stewardship of all IT fixed assets and will assist the process owner in defining and agreeing which service assets will be treated as configuration items.

The process manager will ensure that configuration data is available when and where needed to support other service management processes, and ensure that the necessary support for SACM tools and processes is in place. This individual will also coordinate interfaces between SACM and other transition processes, especially change management, release and deployment management, and knowledge management.

Configuration Analyst

Most organizations combine the roles of configuration analyst and SACM process manager, or the configuration analyst and configuration librarian roles, if the size of the organization does not justify employing staff for each role.

The configuration analyst's responsibilities typically include

- Proposing scope for service asset and configuration management
- Supporting the process owner and process manager in the creation of principles, processes, and procedures

- Defining the structure of the configuration management system, including CI types, naming conventions, and required and optional attributes and relationships
- Training staff in SACM principles, processes, and procedures
- Performing configuration audits

Configuration Librarian

A configuration librarian is the custodian of the assets registered in the configuration management system. Their responsibilities typically include

- Controlling the receipt, identification, storage, and withdrawal of all supported CIs
- Maintaining status information on CIs
- Archiving CIs where no longer required
- Assisting in audit activities
- Identifying, recording, storing, and distributing issues relating to service asset and configuration management

KPIs and CSFs

As with all processes, the performance of SACM should be monitored and reported on and action taken to improve it. As you have seen, SACM plays an essential role in providing many other processes with the information they require, so success or failure in implementing this process will have an indirect impact on customers. As discussed previously, each CSF should have a small number of KPIs that will measure its success, and each organization may choose its own KPIs. The ITIL Service Transition publication lists a number of CSFs and corresponding KPIs. We will just look at a couple of these now.

Example CSF: "Accounting for, managing, and protecting the integrity of CIs throughout the service lifecycle"

This CSF can be measured using the following KPIs:

- Improved accuracy in budgets and charges for the assets utilized by each customer or business unit
- Increase in reuse and redistribution of underutilized resources and assets
- Reduction in the use of unauthorized hardware and software, nonstandard, and variant builds that increase complexity, support costs, and risk to the business services
- Reduced number of exceptions reported during configuration audits

Example CSF: "Establishing and maintaining an accurate and complete configuration management system (CMS)"

This CSF can be measured using the following KPIs:

- Reduction in business impact of outages and incidents caused by poor service asset and configuration management
- Increased quality and accuracy of configuration information

- Improved audit compliance
- Shorter audits, since quality configuration information is easily accessible
- Fewer errors caused by people working with out-of-date information

Challenges

Challenges to SACM include persuading technical support staff to adhere to the process when making changes to CIs. They often regard the process as a hindrance to a fast and responsive support service. Attracting and justifying funding for service asset and configuration management can be difficult because it is invisible to the customer. Another challenge is defining the optimal level of data to be gathered and managed—discovery tools may collect vast quantities of data that is not required but needs to be managed. Finally, due to its invisible nature, management may not appreciate the key support it provides to all other processes, and therefore fail to provide the level of commitment and support required, especially when enforcing the process.

Risks

Risks to successful SACM include regarding it as technically focused and not appreciating what it delivers indirectly to the business. The accuracy of the information may degrade if the processes, and that of change management, are not enforced. Errors found in audits must be not only corrected, but also investigated to identify poor adherence to the processes, which should then be addressed by management. An inaccurate CMS will lead to incorrect decisions, based on faulty data. Too wide a scope will entail cost with little benefit; too narrow will also fail to deliver any real benefit.

Summary

This chapter explored two processes involved in the release, control, and validation activities change management and service asset and configuration management. For each process, we covered

- Purpose
- Objectives
- Scope
- Value
- Policies, principles, and basic concepts
- Process activities, methods, and techniques
- Triggers, inputs, outputs, and interfaces

- Critical success factors and key performance indicators
- Information management
- Roles
- Challenges
- Risks

We examined the importance of these processes to the business and to the IT service provider.

Exam Essentials

Understand the purpose and objectives of change management.   Be able to explain how the change management process controls the lifecycle of all changes, enabling beneficial changes to be made with minimum disruption to IT.

Explain the different types of change and when they would be used.   Understand that not all changes require the same level of oversight, and that even when this is desirable, it may not be possible. Be able to define and explain the differences between normal, standard, and emergency change.

Be able to explain when a change proposal would be required.   A change proposal is only needed if the change has a major impact on the business in terms of risk, cost, or resources.

Be able to explain why the members of the CAB may vary from change to change.   Understand the role of the CAB, and the importance of having the appropriate stakeholders approve each change.

Understand the critical success factors and key performance indicators for each of the processes.   Measurement of each process is an important part of understanding whether it is successful or requires improvement.

Understand the purpose of service asset and configuration management.   Be able to explain that the purpose of the service asset and configuration management process is to capture accurate and reliable information about the assets that make up our services.

Understand the objectives of service asset and configuration management.   SACM objectives are about maintaining accurate information on configuration items and services. It is important to understand that this will enable informed decision making across many processes.

Understand the scope of service asset and configuration management.   SACM covers all service assets and configuration items that make up our services and how these configuration items are identified and recorded as part of the configuration management system (CMS).

Be able to list different types of CIs.   These include hardware CIs, internal and external CIs, service CIs, and service lifecycle CIs. Be able to give examples of each.

Understand the concept of attributes.   Be able to suggest common attributes for different CI types.

Understand the use of configuration models.   These models show the dependencies and relationships between CIs to provide a model of the services, assets, and infrastructure.

Understand how the information held in the configuration management system (CMS) is used by other processes.   Be able to provide examples.

Be able to explain the concept and use of a configuration baseline.   A configuration baseline is used to capture the state of the infrastructure at a specific point to be reviewed and agreed on, and used for trending, comparison, and planning.

Understand the difference between a baseline and a snapshot.   A snapshot is a capture of the infrastructure at a point in time, but it may contain errors and inaccuracies since it is not reviewed and agreed.

Be able to explain the use and contents of the definitive media library (DML).   The DML is a specific secure area set aside for the management of software media. It may consist of physical and electronic stores for master copies of licensed or authorized software in use in the live environment, and the associated documentation.

Be able to list and explain the five main activities of SACM.   These are planning, identification, control, status accounting, and verification and audit.

Review Questions

You can find the answers to the review questions in the appendix.

1. Which of these statements is *not* part of the purpose of the SACM process?
   A. Control of the assets that make up our services
   B. Management of the changes to our service assets
   C. Identification of service assets
   D. Capture accurate information about service assets

2. SACM is a process that supports which of the following stages of the service lifecycle?
   1. Service strategy
   2. Service design
   3. Service transition
   4. Service operation
   5. Continual service improvement
      A. 1, 3, and 5
      B. 2, 3, and 4
      C. 2, 3, 4, and 5
      D. 1, 2, 3, 4, and 5

3. Which of these statements best describes a configuration record?
   A. Any resource or capability that could contribute to the delivery of a service
   B. A service asset that needs to be managed in order to deliver an IT service
   C. A set of attributes and relationships about a CI and stored in a configuration management database
   D. Categorization of the CIs that make up the services

4. Which of the following statements concerning the value of the CMS database to the business is *not* correct?
   A. It helps prevent unnecessary purchases of licenses or equipment by identifying spare items that can be reused.
   B. It ensures that the service desk staff have the knowledge they require to resolve incidents.
   C. It avoids the organization being fined for not being able to prove that all of its software is legal.
   D. It helps prevent failed changes by allowing an accurate impact assessment.

5. Which of the following is *not* a potential danger when implementing SACM?

   A. Examining the related CIs for every change may slow down the process.

   B. Staff may not realize the importance of the process.

   C. The cost of maintaining the level of detail being gathered may not be matched by the benefits from having the information.

   D. Ineffective change management may make maintaining an accurate CMS impossible.

6. The change advisory board (CAB) should contain relevant stakeholders; which of the following stakeholders would be appropriate members of an ECAB?

   1. Customer

   2. Representative of application support team

   3. Senior IT manager

   4. Representative of desktop support team

   5. Senior technical manager

   6. Representative of network support team

   7. Service desk manager

      A. All of the above

      B. 2, 4, and 6 only

      C. 3, 5, and 7 only

      D. 1, 3, and 5 only

7. Which of these would be a valid start point for the change management process?

   1. Request for change

   2. Service desk call

   3. Project initiation document

   4. Change proposal

      A. 1, 2, and 4

      B. 1, 3, and 4

      C. All of the above

      D. 1 and 4 only

8. Which of the following statements about change management is *not* correct?

   A. All changes must be authorized by the CAB or ECAB.

   B. There should be a single CAB for reviewing all changes.

   C. Each change category will have its own change authority defined.

   D. Complex changes may need to be authorized at several points in their lifecycle.

9. Which of these is *not* a valid type of change, according to ITIL?

    A. Emergency

    B. Urgent

    C. Normal

    D. Standard

10. Which of these statements is *not* an example of how the change management process delivers the value to the business?

    A. It enables beneficial changes while protecting existing services.

    B. It ensures that business changes deliver the required strategic benefits.

    C. It ensures that changes meet the business requirements while optimizing the costs of change.

    D. It provides auditable evidence of the adherence of the organization to governance, legal, contractual, and regulatory requirements.

Chapter

13

Service Validation and Testing and Change Evaluation

THE FOLLOWING ITIL RELEASE, CONTROL, AND VALIDATION CAPABILITY INTERMEDIATE EXAM OBJECTIVES ARE DISCUSSED IN THIS CHAPTER:

✓ Service validation and testing and change evaluation are discussed in terms of

- Purpose
- Objectives
- Scope
- Value
- Policies
- Principles and basic concepts
- Test models and testing perspectives (SVT)
- Process activities, methods, and techniques
- Evaluation concepts and reports (CE)
- Triggers, inputs, outputs, and interfaces
- Maintaining test data and models (SVT)
- Process roles and responsibilities
- Information management
- Critical success factors and key performance indicators
- Challenges
- Risks

The syllabus covers the day-to-day operation of each process and the detail of the process activities, methods, and techniques and information management. The managerial and supervisory aspects of service transition processes are covered in the service lifecycle courses.

This chapter covers the day-to-day operation of each process and the detail of the process activities, methods, and techniques and information management. The managerial and supervisory aspects of service transition processes are covered in the *ITIL Intermediate Certificate Companion Study Guide* (Sybex, 2016).

In service validation and testing, we review the concepts of quality assurance, ensuring that the new or changed service will meet the requirements of the business.

Change evaluation is concerned with the choices the business makes relating to the new or changed service. It allows for the organization to decide whether the new or changed service meets the acceptance criteria agreed to as part of the design.

Service Validation and Testing

The underlying concept behind service validation and testing is quality assurance—establishing that the service design and release will deliver a new or changed service or service offering that is fit for its purpose and use.

Purpose

The purpose of the service validation and testing process is to ensure that a new or changed IT service matches its design specification and will meet the needs of the business.

Objective

The objectives of service validation and testing are to ensure that a release will deliver the expected outcomes and value within the projected constraints and to provide quality assurance by validating that a service is "fit for purpose" and "fit for use." Another objective is to confirm that the requirements are correctly defined, remedying any errors or variances early in the service lifecycle. The process aims to provide objective evidence of the release's ability to fulfill its requirements. The final objective is to identify, assess, and address issues, errors, and risks throughout service transition.

Scope

The service provider has a commitment to deliver the required levels of warranty as defined within the service agreement. Throughout the service lifecycle, service validation and testing can be applied to provide assurance that the required capabilities are being delivered and the business needs are met.

The testing activity of service validation and testing directly supports release and deployment by ensuring appropriate testing during the release, build, and deployment activities. It ensures that the service models are fit for its purpose and use before being authorized as live through the service catalog. The output from testing is used by the change evaluation process to judge whether the service is delivering the service performance with an acceptable risk profile.

Value to the Business

The key value to the business and customers from service testing and validation is in terms of the established degree of confidence it delivers that a new or changed service will deliver the value and outcomes required of it and the understanding it provides of the risks.

Successful testing provides a measured degree of confidence rather than guarantees. Service failures can harm the service provider's business and the customer's assets and result in outcomes such as loss of reputation, loss of money, loss of time, injury, and death.

Policies, Principles, and Basic Concepts

Now we'll look at the policies and principles of service validation and testing and the basic concepts behind it. The policies for this process reflect strategy and design requirements. The following list includes typical policy statements:

- All tests must be designed and carried out by people not involved in other design or development activities for the service.
- Test pass/fail criteria must be documented in a service design package before the start of any testing.
- Establish test measurements and monitoring systems to improve the efficiency and effectiveness of service validation and testing.
- Integrate testing into the project lifecycle to help detect and remove defects as soon as possible.
- Test library and reuse policy. Since many of the tests can be repeated, it is valuable to keep a library of test scripts, test models, test cases, and test data that can be reused.
- Engage with customers, stakeholders, users, and service teams to enhance test skills.
- Automate testing wherever possible.

Service validation and testing is affected by policies from other areas of service management. Policies that drive and support service validation and testing include the service quality policy, the risk policy, the security policy, and the service transition, release management, and change management policies.

Service quality will be defined by the senior management, based on customer and stakeholder input. This will drive the adoption and measurement of the basic quality perspectives as listed in the service strategy—level of excellence, value for money, conformance to specifications, and meeting or exceeding expectations. The organization will help to prioritize these, and this will influence the approach taken to service validation and testing.

Risk policies have a direct link to testing. The testing must measure risk according to the appetite for risk in the organization. The testing should include any requirements of risk from the security policy.

The service transition policy sets the working practices for the entire service lifecycle stage. This will include the approach to managing transitions of all scales, and defining the levels of control required during the lifecycle stage. It will cover areas such as governance, use of frameworks, reuse approaches, business alignment and relationship management, knowledge transfer, managing course corrections, early life support, and resource management.

The release policy will define the frequency and type of releases, which in turn will influence the testing approach. The more frequent the releases, the more likely it is to automate and look for reusable test models.

The use of change windows will also influence the testing, so the change management policy will be important in defining the testing approach.

Test Models and Testing Perspectives

Because testing is directly related to the building of the service assets and products that make up services, each one of the assets or products should have an associated acceptance test. This will ensure that the individual components will work effectively prior to use in the new or changed service. Each service model should be supported by a reusable test model that can be used for both release and regression testing in the future. Testing models should be introduced early in the lifecycle to ensure that there is a lifecycle approach to the management of testing and validation.

Test Models

A test model should include a test plan, what is to be tested, and the test scripts that will be used for each element of the service. Making the test model reusable and repeatable ensures that testing remains effective and efficient. This will support traceability back to the design criteria or initial requirements, and the audit of the test execution, evaluation, and reporting. Table 13.1 shows some examples of test models.

TABLE 13.1   Examples of service test models

Test model	Objective/target deliverable	Test conditions based on
Service contract test model	To validate that the customer can use the service to deliver a value proposition	Contract requirements. Fit for purpose, fit for use criteria
Service requirements test model	To validate that the service provider can deliver/has delivered the service required and expected by the customer	Service requirements and service acceptance criteria

Test model	Objective/target deliverable	Test conditions based on
Service level test model	To ensure that the service provider can deliver the service level requirements, and that service level requirements can be met in the live environment, e.g., testing the response and fix time, availability, product delivery times, support services, etc.	Service level requirements, SLA, OLA
Service test model	To ensure that the service provider is capable of delivering, operating and managing the new or changed service using the as-designed service model that includes the resource model, cost model, integrated process model, capacity and performance model, etc.	Service model
Operations test model	To ensure that the service operation functions can operate and support the new or changed service/service component including the service desk, IT operations, application management, technical management. It includes local IT support staff and business representatives responsible for IT service support and operations. There may be different models at different release/test levels, e.g., technology infrastructure, applications, etc.	Service model, service operation standards, processes and plans
Release deployment test model	To verify that the deployment team, tools, and procedures can deploy the release package into a target deployment group or environment within the estimated timeframe. To ensure that the release package contains all the service components required for deployment, e.g., by performing a configuration audit	Release and deployment design and plan
Deployment installation test model	To test that the deployment team, tools, and procedures can install the release package into a target environment within the estimated timeframe	Release and deployment design and plan
Deployment verification test model	To test that a deployment has completed successfully and that all service assets and configurations are in place as planned and meet their quality criteria	Tests and audits of actual service assets and configurations

Testing Perspectives

Service validation and testing should focus on the perspective of those who will use, deliver, deploy, manage, and operate the service. The test entry and exit criteria will have been developed during the development of the service design package. This should cover aspects such as these:

- Service design (functional, management, and operational)
- Technology design
- Process design
- Measurement design
- Documentation
- Skills and knowledge

Service acceptance testing is concerned with the verification of the service requirements. This is verified by the stakeholders, who include business customers or customer representatives, suppliers, and the service provider.

Business Users and Customer Perspective

The business perspective of acceptance testing should consist of a defined and agreed means for measuring the service to ensure that it meets their requirements, and that it has appropriate mechanisms in place to manage the interface to the service provider. This will require the business to provide an appropriate level and capability of resources to take part in the tests.

The service provider requires the interaction of the business to ensure continued engagement in the transition, and to ensure that the overall quality of the new or changed service is meeting expectations.

Use cases can be used to ensure that the testing covers realistic scenarios of interaction between the service provider and the business.

User testing should cover the requirements for applications, systems, and services, and ensure that these meet the functional and quality requirements of the end users. User acceptance testing (UAT) should be as realistic as possible to simulate the live environment. It is important to ensure that the test is viewed appropriately and that the expectation is that not everything will work perfectly.

Service Operations and Continual Service Improvement Perspective

It is important not to forget to test that the new or changed service can be managed and supported successfully. This should include some basic elements:

- Technology
- Staff skills, knowledge, and resources
- Supporting processes and resources
- Business and IT continuity
- Documentation and knowledge management via the SKMS

The engagement of continual service improvement should ensure that the new or changed service is adopted as part of the scope of the overall service management improvement approach.

Levels of Testing

Testing is directly related to the building of the service assets and products, and it is necessary to ensure that each one has an associated acceptance test and activity to verify that it meets requirements.

The diagram in Figure 13.1, sometimes called the service V-model, maps the types of tests to each stage of development. Using the V-model ensures that testing covers business and service requirements, as well as technical ones, so that the delivered service will meet customer expectations for utility and warranty. The left-hand side shows service requirements down to the detailed service design. The right-hand side focuses on the validation activities that are performed against these specifications. At each stage on the left-hand side, there is direct involvement by the equivalent party on the right-hand side. It shows that service validation and acceptance test planning should start with the definition of the service requirements. For example, customers who sign off on the agreed service requirements will also sign off on the service acceptance criteria and test plan.

FIGURE 13.1   Example of service lifecycle configuration levels and baseline points

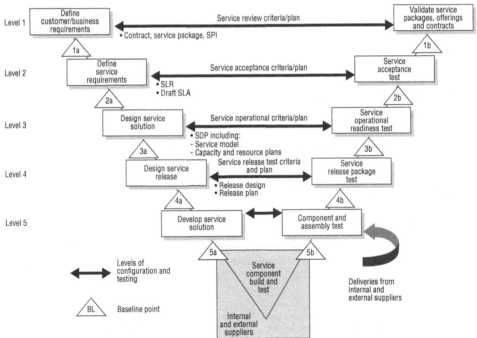

Types of Testing

There are many testing approaches and techniques that can be combined to conduct validation activities and tests. Examples include modeling or simulating situations where the service would be used, limiting testing to the areas of highest risk, testing compliance to the relevant standard, taking the advice of experts on what to test, and using waterfall or agile techniques. Other examples involve conducting a walkthrough or workshop, a dress rehearsal, or a live pilot.

Functional and service tests are used to verify that the service meets the user and customer requirements as well as the service provider's requirements for managing, operating, and supporting the service. Functional testing will depend on the type of service and channel of delivery. Service testing will include many nonfunctional tests. They include testing for usability and accessibility, testing of procedures, and testing knowledge and competence. Testing of the warranty aspects of the service, including capacity, availability, resilience, backup and recovery, and security and continuity, is also included.

Process Activities, Methods, and Techniques

There are seven phases to service validation and testing, shown in Figure 13.2. The basic activities are as follows:

- Validation and test management
- Plan and design tests
- Verify test plan and test design
- Prepare test environment
- Perform tests
- Evaluate exit criteria and report
- Test cleanup and closure

FIGURE 13.2 Example of a validation and testing process

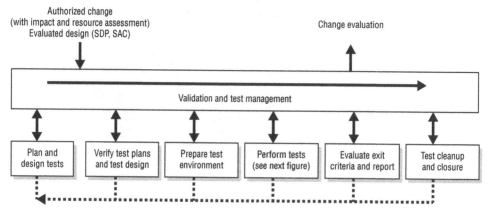

Revise tests to deliver required results

The test activities are not undertaken in a sequence; several may be done in parallel; for example, test execution begins before all the test design is complete. Figure 13.2 shows an example of a validation and testing process; it is described in detail in the following list:

- The first activity is validation and test management, which includes the planning, control, and reporting of activities through the test stages of service transition. Also included are managing issues, mitigating risks, and implementing changes identified from the testing activities because they can impose delays.

- The next step, plan and design tests, starts early in the service lifecycle and covers many of the practical aspects of running tests, such as the resources required; any supporting services (including access, security, catering, and communications services); agreement on the schedule of milestone, handover, and delivery dates; agreement on the time for consideration of reports and other deliverables; specification of the point and time of delivery and acceptance; and any financial requirements.

- The third step is to verify the test plan and test design, ensuring that the testing included in the test model is sufficient and appropriate for the service and covers the key integration points and interfaces. The test scripts should also be checked for accuracy and completeness.

- The next step is to prepare the test environment using the services of the build and test environment staff; use the release and deployment management processes to prepare the test environment where possible. This step also includes capturing a configuration baseline of the initial test environment.

- Next comes the perform tests step. During this stage, the tester carries out the tests using manual or automated techniques and records findings during the tests. In the case of failed tests, the reasons for failures must be fully documented, and testing should continue if at all possible. Should part of a test fail, the incident should be resolved or documented (e.g., as a known error) and the appropriate retests should be performed by the same tester.

- The next step is to evaluate the exit criteria and the report, which has been produced from the test metrics. In this stage, the actual results are compared to what was expected. The service may be considered as having passed or failed, or it may be that the service will work but with higher risk or costs than planned. A decision is made as to whether the exit criteria have been met. The final action of this step is to capture the configuration baselines into the CMS.

- The final step is test cleanup and closure. During this step, the test environments are initialized. The testing process is reviewed, and any possible improvements are passed to CSI.

Next we'll look at the trigger, inputs and outputs, and process interfaces for service validation and testing.

Trigger

This process has only one trigger, a scheduled activity. The scheduled activity could be on a release plan, test plan, or quality assurance plan.

Inputs

A key input to this process is the service design package. This defines the agreed requirements of the service, expressed in terms of the service model and service operation plan. The SDP, as we have discussed previously, contains the service charter, including warranty and utility requirements, definitions of the interface between different service providers, acceptance criteria, and other information. The operation and financial models, capacity plans, and expected test results are further inputs.

The other main input consists of the RFCs that request the required changes to the environment within which the service functions or will function.

Outputs

The direct output from service validation and testing is the report delivered to change evaluation. This sets out the configuration baseline of the testing environment, identifies what testing was carried out, and presents the results. It also includes an analysis of the results (for example, a comparison of actual results with expected results) and any risks identified during testing activities.

Other outputs are the updated data and information and knowledge gained from the testing along with test incidents, problems, and known errors.

Interfaces

Service validation and testing supports all of the release and deployment management steps within service transition. It is important to remember that although release and deployment management is responsible for ensuring that appropriate testing takes place, the actual testing is carried out as part of the service validation and testing. The output from service validation and testing is then a key input to change evaluation. The testing strategy ensures that the process works well with the rest of the service lifecycle—for example, with service design, ensuring that designs are testable, and with CSI, managing improvements identified in testing. Service operation will use maintenance tests to ensure the continued efficacy of services, whereas service strategy provides funding and resources for testing.

Service Validation and Testing Process Roles

In Chapter 1, "Introduction to Operational Support and Analysis," we explored the generic roles applicable to all processes throughout the service lifecycle. These are relevant to the service validation and testing process, but there are specific additional requirements that also apply. Remember that these are not "job titles"; they are guidance on the roles that may be needed to successfully run the process.

Service Validation and Testing Process Owner

The generic process owner role responsibilities described in Chapter 1 apply to this role, and in addition, these specific requirements apply:

- Defining the overall test strategy for the organization
- Ensuring that there is an integrated approach with change management, change evaluation, release, and deployment

Service Validation and Testing Process Manager

It is important to ensure that this role is assigned to a different person from the one who has responsibility for release and deployment management, to avoid conflicts of interest.

The generic process manager role responsibilities described in Chapter 1 apply to this role, and in addition, these specific requirements apply:

- Helping to design and plan testing conditions, test scripts, and test data sets to ensure appropriate and adequate coverage and control
- Allocating and overseeing test resources, ensuring that test policies are adhered to
- Verifying tests conducted by other teams, such as release and deployment
- Managing test environment requirements
- Planning and managing support for appropriate tools and processes
- Providing management reports on test results, issues, risks, and progress

Service Validation and Testing Practitioner

This role typically includes

- Conducting tests as defined in the plans and designs, as documented in the service design package
- Recording, analyzing, diagnosing, reporting, and managing test events, incidents, problems, and retests, dependent on agreed criteria
- Administering test assets and components

Other Roles Contributing to Service Validation and Testing

A number of roles contribute to the service validation and testing process:

- Change management—ensuring that tests are appropriate for the authorized changes
- Developers/suppliers—collaboration between testing staff and development/build/supplier personnel
- Service design personnel—designing tests is an element of overall design
- Customers and users—performance acceptance testing

Information Management

As previously mentioned, the nature of IT service management is repetitive and benefits greatly from reuse of data, scripts, and models during transition. Service management suggests that a test library is maintained. This will also include the use of automated testing tools (computer-aided software testing), which are becoming more and more a part of the service validation and testing process.

Test Data

Data is a requirement for all testing, and its relevance will determine the success of the test. When applied to software this is clearly necessary, but it also applies to other testing environments.

Test Environments

Test environments should be maintained and protected. All changes should be reviewed to see if they have an impact on the test environments. All of these aspects will need to be considered:

- Updating of the test data
- Whether a new separate set of data is required (the existing set will be required for existing services)
- Redundancy of the test data or environment
- Levels of testing

Maintenance of test data should be carried out as part of day-to-day operational activity. It should consider

- Separation from live data
- Data protection regulations
- Backup of test data
- The consequent test database, which can be used as a secure training environment

Critical Success Factors and Key Performance Indicators

As with all processes, the performance of service validation and testing should be monitored and reported, and action should be taken to identify and implement improvements to the process. Each critical success factor (CSF) should have a small number of key performance indicators (KPIs) that will measure its success, and each organization may choose its own KPIs.

The following are two examples of CSFs for service validation and testing and the related KPIs for each.

The success of the CSF "Achieving a balance between cost of testing and effectiveness of testing" can be measured using KPIs that measure

- The reduction in budget variances and in the cost of fixing errors
- The reduced impact on the business due to fewer testing delays and more accurate estimates of customer time required to support testing

The success of the CSF "Providing evidence that the service assets and configurations have been built and implemented correctly in addition to the service delivering what the customer needs" can be measured using KPIs that measure both the improvement in the percentage of service acceptance criteria that have been tested for new and changed services and the improvement in the percentage of services for which build and implementation have been tested separately from any tests of utility or warranty.

Challenges

The most frequent challenges to effective testing are based on other staff's lack of respect and understanding for the role of testing. Traditionally, testing has been starved of funding, and this results in an inability to maintain an adequate test environment and test data that matches the live environment, with not enough staff, skills, and testing tools to deliver adequate testing coverage. Testing is often squeezed due to overruns in other parts of the project so the go-live date can still be met. This impacts the level and quality of testing that can be done. Delays by suppliers in delivering equipment can reduce the time available for testing.

All of these factors can result in inadequate testing, which, once again, feeds the commonly held feeling that it has little real value.

Risks

The most common risks to the success of this process are as follows:

- A lack of clarity regarding expectations or objectives
- A lack of understanding of the risks, resulting in testing that is not targeted at critical elements
- Resource shortages (e.g., users, support staff), which introduce delays and have an impact on other service transitions

Change Evaluation

Before a transition can be closed, it needs to be reviewed to ensure that it has achieved its purpose with no unidentified negative side effects. Successful completion of the change evaluation ensures that the service can be formally closed and handed over to the service operation functions and CSI.

An evaluation report is prepared that lists the deviations from the service charter/SDP and includes a risk profile and recommendations for change management.

Purpose

The purpose of the change evaluation process is to understand the likely performance of a service change and how it might impact the business, the IT infrastructure, and other IT services. The process provides a consistent and standardized means of assessing this impact by assessing the actual performance of a change against its predicted performance. Risks and issues related to the change are identified and managed.

Objectives

The objectives of change evaluation include setting stakeholder expectations correctly and providing accurate information to change management to prevent changes with an adverse impact and changes that introduce risk being transitioned unchecked. Another objective is to evaluate the intended and, as much as possible, the unintended effects of a service change and provide good-quality outputs to enable change management to decide quickly whether a service change is to be authorized.

Scope

Effective change management means that every change must be authorized by a suitable change authority at various points in its lifecycle. Typical authorization points include before build and test starts, before being checked into the DML (if software related), and before deployment to the live environment. The decision on whether to authorize the next step is made based on the evaluation of the change resulting from this process. The evaluation report provides the change authority with advice and guidance. The process describes a formal evaluation suitable for use for significant changes; each organization will decide which changes need formal evaluation and which will be evaluated as part of change management.

Value to the Business

Change evaluation is concerned with value. Effective change evaluation will judge whether the resources used to deliver the benefit that results from the change represent good value. This information will encourage a focus on value in future service development and change management. CSI can benefit enormously from change evaluation regarding possible areas for improvement within the change process itself and the predictions and measurement of service change performance.

Policies, Principles, and Basic Concepts

The following reviews some of the key policies that apply to the change evaluation process. The first is that service designs or service changes will be evaluated before being transitioned. Second, although every change must be evaluated, the formal change evaluation process will be used only on significant changes; this requires, in turn, that criteria be defined to identify which changes are "significant."

Change evaluation will identify risks and issues related to the new or changed service and to any other services or shared infrastructure. Deviation from predicted to actual performance will be managed by the customer accepting the change with the deviation, rejecting the change, or introducing a new change to correct the deviation. These three are the only outcomes of change evaluation allowed.

The principles behind change evaluation include committing to identifying and understanding the consequences of both the unintended and intended effects of a change, as far as possible. Other principles include ensuring that each service change will be fairly, consistently, openly, and, wherever possible, objectively evaluated and ensuring that an evaluation report is provided to change management to facilitate decision making at each authorization point.

The change evaluation process uses the Plan-Do-Check-Act (PDCA) model to ensure consistency across all evaluations. Using this approach, each evaluation is planned and then carried out in multiple stages, the results of the evaluation are checked, and actions are taken to resolve any issues found.

Change Evaluation Terminology

Table 13.2 shows the key terms used by the change evaluation process.

TABLE 13.2 Key terms that apply to the change evaluation process

Term	Meaning
Actual performance	The performance achieved following a service change.
Countermeasure	The mitigation that is implemented to reduce risk.
Deviations report	A report of the difference between predicted and actual performance.
Evaluation report	A report generated by the change evaluation process, which is passed to change management and which consists of A risk profile A deviations report A recommendation A qualification statement
Performance	The utilities and warranties of a service.
Performance model	A representation of a service that is used to help predict performance.
Predicted performance	The expected performance of a service following a service change.
Residual risk	The remaining risk after countermeasures have been deployed.
Service capability	The ability of a service to perform as required.
Service change	A change to an existing service or the introduction of a new service.
Test plan and results	The test plan is a response to an impact assessment of the proposed service change. Typically the plan will specify how the change will be tested; what records will result from testing and where they will be stored; who will authorize the change; and how it will be ensured that the change and the service(s) it affects will remain stable over time. The test plan may include a qualification plan and a validation plan if the change affects a regulated environment. The results represent the actual performance following implementation of the change.

Change Evaluation Process

Figure 13.3 shows the change evaluation process and its key inputs and outputs. You can see the inputs that trigger the evaluation activity and the interim and final evaluation reports that are outputs of the process. Where performance does not meet the requirement, change management is responsible for deciding what to do next.

FIGURE 13.3 Change evaluation process flow

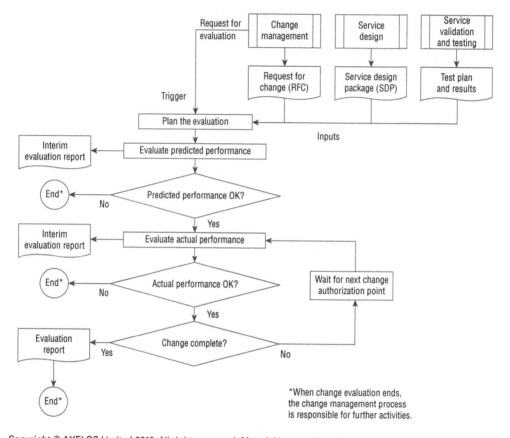

Evaluation Plan

Evaluation of a change should ensure that unintended effects as well as intended effects of the change are understood. Unintended effects will often be negative in terms of impact on other services, customers, and users of the service. Intended effects of a change should match the acceptance criteria. Unintended effects are often not seen until the pilot stage or even until live use; they are difficult to predict or measure.

In Table 13.3 are the factors to be included when considering the effect of a service change.

TABLE 13.3 Factors to consider when assessing the effect of a service change

Factor	Evaluation of service design
S—Service provider capability	The ability of a service provider or service unit to perform as required.
T—Tolerance	The ability or capacity of a service to absorb the service change or release.
O—Organizational setting	The ability of an organization to accept the proposed change. For example, is appropriate access available for the implementation team? Have all existing services that would be affected by the change been updated to ensure smooth transition?
R—Resources	The availability of appropriately skilled and knowledgeable people and sufficient finances, infrastructure, applications, and other resources necessary to run the service following transition.
M—Modeling and measurement	The extent to which the predictions of behavior generated from the model match the actual behavior of the new or changed service.
P—People	The people within a system and the effect of change on them.
U—Use	Will the service be fit for use? Will it be able to deliver the warranties? Is it continuously available? Is there enough capacity? Will it be secure enough?
P—Purpose	Will the new or changed service be fit for purpose? Can the required performance be supported? Will the constraints be removed as planned?

Evaluation of Predicted Performance

Using customer requirements, including the acceptance criteria, the predicted performance, and the performance model, a risk assessment should be carried out. An interim report will be sent to change management.

The report will compare the outcome of the predicted performance to the acceptance criteria and includes the risk assessment. It will include a recommendation as to whether the change should proceed. This will be forwarded to the next authorization point.

Evaluation of Actual Performance

Before change management makes a decision on authorization of a step in a change, change evaluation will evaluate the actual performance. The results will be sent to change management and interim decisions can be made. The decision will rest with the business. If the recommendation is to stop, then the business will have to verify that recommendation.

If the recommendation is to continue, then the next authorization point will be reached for the business to make a decision.

Post implementation, a report on the actual performance, along with a risk assessment, will be compared to the acceptance criteria and predicted performance results. Based on the results of the risk assessment, a decision will be recommended for the business. If it is acceptable, then the decision for acceptance will be made through change management.

Risk Management

Each organization will have its own approach to risk management, and this approach should be used to assess the new or changed service during the change evaluation process. The level of risk should be appropriate for the expected benefits and business appetite for risk. The comparison between actual and predicted will be assessed for risk to the business.

This output is known as a deviation report, and it will be used to support decisions regarding implementation of the new or changed service.

Associated test plans and results from tests will be used in conjunction with the deviation report, and the total evaluation will be presented in an evaluation report.

Evaluation Report

The evaluation report contains the following sections:

- Risk profile, which explains the remaining risk left after a change has been implemented and after countermeasures have been applied

- Deviations report, which describes the difference between predicted and actual performance following the implementation of a change

- Qualification and validation statement (if appropriate), which is a statement of whether the IT infrastructure is appropriate and correctly configured to support the specific application or IT service

- Recommendation, which is a recommendation to change management to accept or reject the change based on the other factors within the evaluation report

Now let's look at the trigger, inputs and outputs, and process interfaces for change evaluation.

Trigger

Let's look first at the trigger for this process. The trigger for change evaluation is receipt of a request for evaluation from change management.

Inputs

Inputs to change evaluation are the service design package (which includes the service charter and service acceptance criteria), a change proposal, an RFC, a change record, and detailed change documentation. Other possible inputs are discussions with stakeholders and the test results and report.

Outputs

The outputs from change evaluation are interim and final evaluation report(s) for change management.

Interfaces

Change evaluation interfaces with a number of other processes. The main interfaces are as follows:

Transition Planning and Support   Change evaluation works with transition planning and support to ensure that appropriate resources are available when needed and that each service transition is well managed.

Change Management   There is a critical interface with change management. The processes of change evaluation and change management must be tightly integrated, with clear agreement on which types of change will be subject to formal evaluation. The time required for this evaluation must be included when planning the change. In addition, it is change management that triggers change evaluation, and change management is dependent on receiving the evaluation report in time for the CAB (or other change authority) to use it to assist in their decision making.

Service Design Coordination   This process provides the information about the service that change evaluation requires in the form of a service design package.

Service Level Management or Business Relationship Management   Change evaluation may need to work with these processes to understand the impact of any issues that arise and to agree on the use of customer resources to perform the evaluation.

Service Validation and Testing   This process provides change evaluation with information; the two processes must coordinate activities to ensure that required inputs are available in sufficient time.

Information Management

Information from testing should be available from the service knowledge management system. Interim and final evaluation reports should be checked into the configuration management system.

Change Evaluation Process Roles

This section explores the process roles relating to the change evaluation process.

Change Evaluation Process Owner

The process owner role will carry out the generic process owner roles as described in Chapter 1. In addition, the process owner will:

- Work with other process owners to ensure an integrated approach across design, change management, change evaluation, release and deployment, and service validation and testing

Change Evaluation Process Manager

In addition to the generic process manager responsibilities, the responsibilities of the process manager also include

- Planning and coordinating resources to evaluate changes
- Ensuring that the change evaluation reports and interim evaluation reports are produced in a timely manner to enable decision making

Change Evaluation Process Practitioner

The practitioner role responsibilities include

- Using the service design package and release package to develop an evaluation plan
- Establishing risks and issues associated with all aspects of the transition
- Creating an evaluation report

Critical Success Factors and Key Performance Indicators

As with the other processes, the performance of change evaluation should be monitored and reported, and action should be taken to improve it. Here are two examples of CSFs for change evaluation and the related KPIs for each.

- Critical success factor: "Stakeholders have a good understanding of the expected performance of new and changed services."
    - KPI: The reduction in incidents reported when a new or changed service fails to deliver the required utility or warranty
    - KPI: Increased customer satisfaction with new or changed services
- Critical success factor: "Change management has good-quality evaluations to help them make correct decisions."
    - KPI: Increased percentage of evaluations delivered within the agreed timeframe
    - KPI: Reduced number of changes that fail or need to be backed out
    - KPI: Increased change management staff satisfaction when surveyed

Challenges

Challenges to change evaluation include developing standard performance measures and measurement methods across projects and suppliers, understanding the different stakeholder perspectives that underpin effective risk management for the change evaluation activities, and understanding (and being able to assess) the balance between managing risk and taking risks because this affects the overall strategy of the organization and service delivery. A further challenge is to measure and demonstrate less variation in predictions during and after transition.

The remaining challenges to change evaluation include taking a pragmatic and measured approach to risk and communicating the organization's attitude toward risk and approach to risk management effectively during risk evaluation. Finally, change evaluation needs to meet the challenges of building a thorough understanding of risks that have impacted or may impact successful service transition of services and releases and encouraging a risk management culture where people share information.

Risks

The most common risks to the success of this process include a lack of clear criteria for when change evaluation should be used and unrealistic expectations of the time required. Another risk is that staff members carrying out the change evaluation have insufficient experience or organizational authority to be able to influence change authorities. Finally, projects and suppliers who fail to deliver on the promised date cause delays in scheduling change evaluation activities.

Summary

This chapter explored two more processes in the service transition stage: service validation and testing and change evaluation. You learned how service validation and testing ensures that the release is fit for use and fit for purpose. We explored the activities relating to the process and the requirements for information management.

We considered the process of change evaluation and the various outputs in the form of interim or final reports.

Finally, we examined how each of these processes supports the other and the importance of these processes to the business and to the IT service provider.

Exam Essentials

Understand and be able to list the objectives of service validation and testing. The objectives of service validation and testing are to ensure that a release will deliver the expected outcomes and value and to provide quality assurance by validating that a service is fit for purpose and fit for use. The process aims to provide objective evidence of the release's ability to fulfill its requirements.

Understand the dependencies between the service transition processes of release and deployment management, service validation and testing, and change evaluation.   Release and deployment management is responsible for ensuring that appropriate testing takes place, but the testing is carried out in service validation and testing. The output from service validation and testing is then a key input to change evaluation.

Be able to list the typical types of testing used in service validation and testing.   The main testing approaches used are as follows:

- Simulation
- Scenario testing
- Role playing
- Prototyping
- Laboratory testing
- Regression testing
- Joint walkthrough/workshops
- Dress/service rehearsal
- Conference room pilot
- Live pilot

Be able to describe the use and contents of a test model.   A test model includes a test plan, what is to be tested, and the test scripts that define how each element will be tested. A test model ensures that testing is executed consistently in a repeatable way that is effective and efficient. It provides traceability back to the requirement or design criteria and an audit trail through test execution, evaluation, and reporting.

Understand the purpose of change evaluation.   Change evaluation enables us to understand the likely performance of a service change and how it might impact the business, the IT infrastructure, and other IT services. It provides a consistent and standardized means of assessing this impact by assessing the actual performance of a change against its predicted performance.

Be able to explain the objectives of change evaluation.   The objectives of change evaluation include setting stakeholder expectations correctly and preventing changes from being accepted into the live environment unless it is known that they will behave as planned. Another objective is to provide good-quality outputs to enable change management to decide quickly whether a service change is to be authorized.

Understand which changes go through the formal change evaluation process and the production of an evaluation report.   Only those changes the organization has deemed important enough or risky enough to require a report will go through the formal change evaluation process; simpler changes will not, except through the change review process.

Be able to list and explain the main process interfaces with change evaluation.   The major interfaces are with the following processes:

Transition Planning and Support   To ensure that appropriate resources are available when needed.

Change Management   There must be agreed criteria for evaluation and time allowed for its completion. Change management is dependent on receiving the evaluation report in time for the CAB (or other change authority) to use it to assist in their decision making.

Service Design Coordination   Provides the service in the service design package.

Service Level Management or Business Relationship Management   To agree on the use of customer resources to perform the evaluation.

Service Validation and Testing   Provides change evaluation with information; the change evaluation and service validation and testing processes must coordinate activities to ensure that required inputs are available in sufficient time.

Review Questions

You can find the answers to the review questions in the appendix.

1. Which of the following is *not* provided as part of a test model?

   A. A test plan

   B. A list of what is to be tested

   C. Test scripts that define how each element will be tested

   D. A test report

2. Which is the correct order of actions when a release is being tested?

   A. Perform tests, design tests, verify test plan, prepare test environment, test cleanup and closure, and evaluate exit criteria and report

   B. Design tests, perform tests, verify test plan, prepare test environment, evaluate exit criteria and report, and test cleanup and closure

   C. Design tests, verify test plan, prepare test environment, perform tests, evaluate exit criteria and report, and test cleanup and closure

   D. Verify test plan, design tests, prepare test environment, evaluate exit criteria and report, perform tests, and test cleanup and closure

3. Where are the entry and exit criteria for testing defined?

   A. The SKMS

   B. The CMS

   C. The KEDB

   D. The SDP

4. The diagram mapping the types of test to each stage of development to ensure that testing covers business and service requirements as well as technical ones is known as what?

   A. DIKW

   B. The service V-model

   C. The test plan

   D. The test strategy

5. Which of the following are valid results of an evaluation of the test report against the exit criteria?

   1. The service will work but with higher risk than planned.

   2. The service passed.

   3. The service failed.

   4. The service will work but with higher costs than planned.

A. 2 and 3 only

B. 2 only

C. All of the above

D. 1, 2, and 4 only

6. Which option is an objective of change evaluation?

   A. Provide assurance that a release is fit for purpose.

   B. Optimize overall business risk.

   C. Provide quality assurance for a release.

   D. Set stakeholder expectations correctly.

7. Which is *not* a factor considered by change evaluation?

   A. Actual performance of a service change

   B. Cost of a service change

   C. Predicted performance of a service change

   D. Likely impact of a service change

8. What may be included in an evaluation report?

   1. A risk profile

   2. A deviations report

   3. A recommendation

   4. A qualification statement

   A. 1 and 2

   B. 2 and 3

   C. 1, 2, and 3

   D. All of the above

9. Which is the *best* description of a performance model?

   A. A performance benchmark

   B. Predefined steps for delivering good performance

   C. A representation of a service used to predict performance

   D. A framework used to manage the performance of a process

10. Which process triggers change evaluation activity?

    A. Change management

    B. Transition planning and support

    C. Release and deployment management

    D. Service validation and testing

Chapter

14

Release and Deployment Management and Knowledge Management

THE FOLLOWING ITIL INTERMEDIATE EXAM OBJECTIVES ARE DISCUSSED IN THIS CHAPTER:

✓ Release and deployment management and knowledge management are discussed in terms of

- Purpose
- Objectives
- Scope
- Value
- Policies
- Principles and basic concepts
- Process activities, methods, and techniques
- Triggers, inputs, outputs, and interfaces
- Process roles and responsibilities
- Critical success factors and key performance indicators
- Challenges
- Risks

This chapter covers the day-to-day operation of each process and the details of the process activities, methods, and techniques as well as its information management. *ITIL Intermediate Certificate Companion Study Guide* (Sybex, 2016) covers the managerial and supervisory aspects of service transition processes. Each process is considered from the perspective of day-to-day activity. That means that at the end of this section of the book, you should understand those aspects that would be required to understand each process, its interfaces, and its implementation, and improve its effectiveness and efficiency.

Release and Deployment Management

A release may include many different types of service assets and involve many people. Release and deployment management ensures that responsibilities for handover and acceptance of a release are defined and understood. It ensures that the requisite planning takes place and controls the release of the new or changed CIs.

Purpose

The purpose of the release and deployment management process is to plan, schedule, and control the build, test, and deployment of releases and to deliver new functionality required by the business while protecting the integrity of existing services. This is an important process because a badly planned deployment can cause disruption to the business and fail to deliver the benefits of the release that is being deployed.

Objectives

The main objective of release and deployment management ensures that the purpose is achieved by delivering plans and managing the release effectively to meet the requirements as defined in the design. It aims to ensure that release packages are built, installed, tested, and deployed efficiently and on schedule and the new or changed service delivers the agreed benefits. An important aspect of release and deployment is that it also seeks to protect the current services by minimizing any adverse impact of the release on the existing services. It aims to satisfy the different needs of customers, users, and service management staff.

The objectives of release and deployment management include defining and agreeing on plans for release and deployment with customers and stakeholders and then creating and testing release packages of compatible CIs. Another objective is to maintain the integrity of the release package and its components throughout transition. All release packages should be stored in and deployed from the DML following an established plan. They should also be recorded accurately in the CMS.

Other objectives of release and deployment management include ensuring that release packages can be tracked, installed, tested, verified, and/or uninstalled or backed out and that organization and stakeholder change is managed. The new or changed service must be able to deliver the agreed utility and warranty.

The process ensures that any deviations, risks, and issues are recorded and managed by taking the necessary corrective action. Customers and users are able to use the service to support their business activities because release and deployment ensures that the necessary knowledge transfer takes place as part of the transition. It also ensures that the required knowledge transfer takes place to enable the service operation functions to deliver, support, and maintain the service according to the required warranties and service levels.

Scope

The scope of release and deployment management includes the processes, systems, and functions to package, build, test, and deploy a release into production and establish the service specified in the service design package before final handover to service operations.

It also includes all the necessary CIs to implement a release. These may be physical, such as a server or network, or virtual, such as a virtual server or virtual storage. Other CIs included within the scope of this process are the applications and software. As we said previously, training for users and IT staff is also included, as are all contracts and agreements related to the service.

You should note that release and deployment is responsible for ensuring that appropriate testing takes place; the actual testing is carried out as part of the service validation and testing process. Release and deployment management also does not authorize changes. At various stages in the lifecycle of a release, it requires authorization from change management to move to the next stage.

Value to the Business

A well-planned approach to the implementation and release and deployment of new or changed services can make a significant difference in the overall costs to the organization. The release and deployment process delivers changes faster and at optimum cost and risk while providing assurance that the new or changed service supports the business goals. It ensures improved consistency in the implementation approach across teams and contributes to meeting audit requirements for traceability.

Poorly designed or managed release deployment may force unnecessary expenditure and waste time.

Policies, Principles, and Basic Concepts

Release and deployment management policies should be in place. The correct policies will help ensure the correct balance between cost of the service, the stability of the service, and its ability to change to meet changing circumstances.

The relative importance of these different elements will vary between organizations. For some services, stability is crucial; for other services, the need to implement releases in order to support rapidly changing business requirements is the most important, and the business is willing to sacrifice some stability to achieve this flexibility. Deciding on the correct balance for an organization is a business decision; release and deployment management policies should therefore support the overall objectives of the business.

These policies can be applicable to all services provided or apply to an individual service, which may have a different desired balance between stability, flexibility, and cost.

Release Unit

The term *release unit* describes the portion of a service or IT infrastructure that is normally released as a single entity according to the organization's release policy. The unit may vary, depending on the different type(s) of service asset or service component being released, such as software or hardware.

In Figure 14.1, you can see a simplified example showing an IT service made up of systems and service assets, which are in turn made up of service components. The actual components to be released on a specific occasion may include one or more release units and are grouped together into a release package for that specific release. Each service asset will have an appropriate release-unit level. The release unit for business-critical applications may be the complete application in order to ensure comprehensive testing, whereas the release unit for a website might be at the page level.

FIGURE 14.1   Simplified example of release units for an IT service

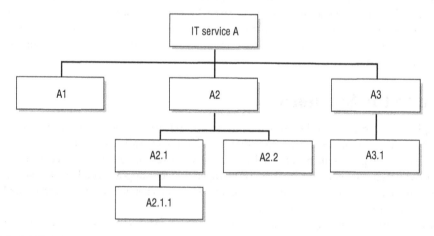

In Figure 14.1 the assets and components might be as follows:

A1 Server

A2 Application

A2.1 Main application, developed within the IT organization

A2.1.1 Commercial off-the-shelf reporting software used by the application

A2.2 Second application, developed within the IT organization

A3 Client software, developed within the IT organization

A3.1 Commercial off-the-shelf library providing supporting routines for the client application.

The general aim is to decide the most appropriate release-unit level for each service asset or component.

Ease of deployment is a major deciding factor when specifying release units. This will depend on the complexity of the interfaces between the release unit and the rest of the services and IT infrastructure.

Releases should be uniquely numbered, and the numbering should be meaningful, referencing the CIs that it represents and a version number—for example, Payroll-System v.1.1.1 or Payroll-System v.2.0. It is common for the first number to change when additional functionality is being released, whereas the later numbers show an update to an existing release.

Release Package

A release package is a set of configuration items that will be built, tested, and deployed together as a single release. It may be a single release unit or a structured set of release units such as the one shown in Figure 14.1. Release packages are useful when there are dependencies between CIs, such as when a new version of an application requires an operating system upgrade, which in turn requires a hardware change. In some cases, the release package may include documentation and procedures.

Figure 14.2 shows how the architectural elements of a service may be changed from the current baseline to the new baseline with releases at each level. The release teams need to understand the relevant architecture to plan, package, build, and test a release to support the new or changed service. For example, the technology infrastructure needs to be ready—with service operation functions prepared to support it with new or changed procedures—before an application is installed.

The example in Figure 14.3 shows an application with its user documentation and a release unit for each technology platform. The customer service asset is supported by two supporting services: SSA for the infrastructure service and SSB for the application service. These release units will contain information about the service, its utilities and warranties, and release documentation.

FIGURE 14.2   Architecture elements to be built and tested

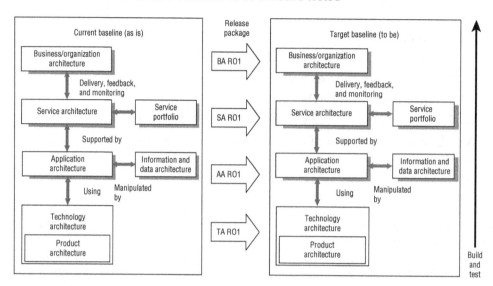

FIGURE 14.3   Example of a release package

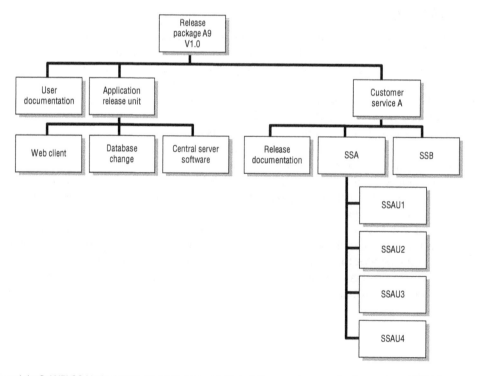

Deployment Options and Considerations

Service design will define the adopted approach to transitioning; it will be documented in the SDP. The choices include a big bang versus a phased approach, using a push or pull deployment method, and automating the deployment or carrying it out manually. We are going to look at each of these now.

A big bang approach deploys a release to all user areas in one operation. This can be useful if it is important that everyone is working on the same version, but it will have a significant impact should the deployment fail. A phased approach deploys the release to different parts of the user base in a scheduled plan. This is less risky but takes longer, and it will mean that there will be more than one version running concurrently.

Using a push mechanism to deploy the release means that the components are deployed from the center and the recipient cannot "opt out" of receiving them. A pull mechanism allows users to choose if and when they want to download the new release.

An automated approach to deployment will help to ensure repeatability and consistency and may be the only practical option if the deployment is to hundreds or thousands of CIs. However, the automated approach requires the distribution tools to be set up, and this may not always be justified. If a manual mechanism is used, the greater risk of errors or inefficiency should be considered.

Release and Deployment Models

As with other processes, the use of predefined models in release and deployment can be a useful way of achieving consistency in approach, no matter how many people are involved. The release and deployment models would contain a series of predefined steps or activities to provide structure and consistency to the delivery of the process. Also included would be the exit and entry criteria for each stage, definitions of roles and responsibilities, controlled build and test environments, and baselines and templates. All the supporting systems and procedures would be defined in the model with the documented handover activities.

Process Activities, Methods, and Techniques

There are four phases to release and deployment management, as shown in Figure 14.4. Let's look at each one in turn in the following sections.

Release and Deployment Planning

The plan release and deployment phase will include plans for all aspects of this phase; the plans will be mostly drawn up during service design and approved by change management. The plans must include not only the release and deployment plans themselves, but also the plans for pilot releases; the plans for building, testing, and packaging the release; and detailed deployment plans. Logistical considerations and financial plans must also be included.

FIGURE 14.4   Phases of release and deployment management

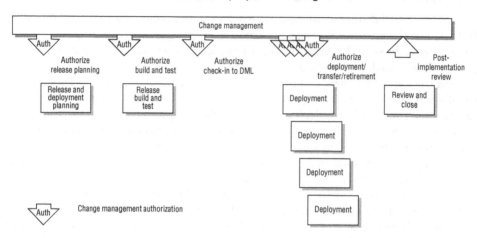

Pass/Fail Criteria

As part of this phase, the criteria for whether an activity has passed or failed to meet the requirements as defined in the design will be decided. It is important to publish these criteria in order to set expectations correctly. Examples might include all tests were successful for a pass, or the service design does not conform to specific operational requirements as defined in the design for a fail.

Build and Test Planning

Next, let's consider the build and test phase. This phase includes writing the release and build documentation, ensuring that the necessary contracts and agreements are in place, and obtaining the necessary configuration items and components. These items will all need to be tested.

Planning Release Packaging and Build

The release packages will then need to be built, and this is an opportunity to make sure build management procedures, methodologies, tools, and checklists are in place to ensure that the release packages are built in a consistent, controlled, and reproducible way. This will help to ensure that the output of this activity matches the solution design defined in the service design package.

Planning Release Build and Test

The test environments must be controlled to ensure that the builds and tests are performed in a consistent, repeatable, and manageable manner. Failure to control the test environments can jeopardize the testing activities and could necessitate significant rework. Dedicated build environments should be established for assembling and building the components to create the controlled test and deployment environments.

The definitive version of the release package (authorized by change management) must be placed in the DML. The release package must always be taken from the DML to deploy to the service operation readiness, service acceptance, and live environments.

Deployment Planning

The entry criteria for the plan and prepare for deployment phase include all stakeholders being confident that they are ready for the deployment and that they accept the deployment costs and the management, organization, and people implications of the release. The deployment includes activities required to deploy, transfer, or decommission/retire services or service assets. It may also include transferring a service or a service unit within an organization or between organizations as well as moving and disposal activities.

Planning of Pilots

There are many different approaches for pilots in the live environment, which may provide significant benefits for the organization in trialing a new or changed service.

A service rehearsal provides a simulation of as much of the service as possible in a practice session. It takes place just before the deployment of the service. The objectives are to confirm that all stakeholders have been identified and their commitment to the deployment. It also allows verification that all stakeholders have the relevant processes and procedures in place to work with the service. It can also be used to check the responses in place to expected user errors. The rehearsal can be run based on the PDCA approach: plan for the day, deliver the rehearsal, document what took place, and act on the outcome of the rehearsal.

Pilots can also be used to detect if the service will work by implementing it in a small controlled and measured environment, using a subset of the organization. It can be used to establish metrics and provide confidence that predicted performance and services levels will be met. A pilot will also demonstrate the actual benefits and costs that will be achieved, and create acceptance of the service with the user base. During a pilot it may also be possible to identify any risks that could affect the final deployment, and provide time to put in place mitigation.

Financial/Commercial Planning

The costs associated with any release will have been considered during the authorization of the release through change management. It is important to ensure that the business is fully aware of and accepts the costs of the release.

This should cover key aspects such as working capital for the release, contracts, and licenses; funding for the supporting services; and any costs associated with intellectual property rights.

Release and Build Documentation

As the release progresses to the next stage, the build and test stage, it is important to ensure that the correct documentation is available. This should include procedures, templates, and guidance for the build and distribution of the assets being used in the release.

The proposed solution should be completely documented to enable knowledge sharing and transfer during the release.

Acquire and Test Input Configuration Items and Components

It is important to ensure that the configuration items and components will meet the required quality levels. There will be a number of verification activities to check the components destined for a release package or build.

This will make sure that the build is created from assets and components that will meet quality standards specified in the design.

Release Packaging

In order to ensure that the release package is built in a controlled, manageable, and reproducible way, the build management procedures, methodologies, tools, and checklists should be applied.

The key activities for building a release package are as follows:

- Assemble and integrate release components in a controlled and repeatable manner.

- Create the build and release documentation.

- Install and verify the release package.

- Baseline the contents of the release package.

- Notify the recipients that the package is ready for installation and use.

If at any step the testing of a release package does not complete successfully, reassessment and rescheduling of the release is managed through change management.

Build and Manage the Test Environments

Effective release management is dependent on the builds and tests being executed in a repeatable and manageable manner. It is important to ensure there is adequate control of the build and test environments.

It is necessary to ensure that any changes to the proposed solutions result in examination of the build and test environments and appropriate alterations be made as part of the implementation of the change.

The environments should always be baselined and verified prior to new services being built or tested.

Service Testing and Pilots

We reviewed the planning requirements for service testing and pilots earlier in this section, and these are some of the considerations for testing prior to live deployment:

Deployment Readiness Test   To ensure that the deployment processes and procedures can successfully deploy the service into the target environment

Service Management Test   To ensure that the service performance can be measured, monitored, and managed in live use

Service Operation Test   To ensure that the service teams will be able to operate the service in live use

User Test   To ensure that the users can access and use the new service

Service Provider Interface Test   To ensure that interfaces to the service are working

Deployment Verification Test   To ensure that the service capability has been correctly deployed

Deployment Phase

The deployment should have been planned as part of the previous phases, but at this point there is an opportunity to prepare the organization for the deployment as well as the support teams.

Plan and Prepare for Deployment

During the actual deployment stage the detailed implementation plan is developed, including assigning individuals to specific activities.

The entry criteria for planning and preparing a target deployment group include the following:

- Deployment stakeholders are sufficiently confident in the service release to carry out the deployment.

- Senior management, customers, business, and service provider teams accept the deployment in all its aspects.

An example of the deployment activities that apply to the deployment for a target group is shown in Figure 14.5. Note the actions taken at each stage, the authorizations obtained from change management at different stages, and the baselines taken at key points.

FIGURE 14.5 Example of a set of deployment activities

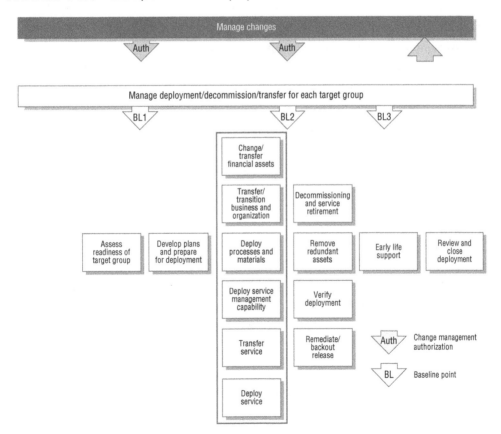

When the deployment activities are complete, it is important to verify that users, service operation functions, other staff, and stakeholders are capable of using or operating the service as planned. This is a good time to gather feedback on the deployment process to feed into future improvements.

Assess Readiness of Target Group

Assessing the readiness of the target group should include

- Issues and risks
- Anticipated impacts
- Gaps to be filled in knowledge transfer
- Financial aspects and assets
- Current capabilities for the business and existing services
- Current service management capabilities
- Organizational readiness
- Information management
- Infrastructure and facilities

Ensuring that all these aspects are covered will not guarantee the success of the deployment but will support the deployment and enable the capture of any issues arising.

Perform Transfer, Deployment, and Retirement

The following activities provide an example of the different aspects that need to be performed during the deployment:

- Change/transfer financial assets.
- Make an organizational change if a new service provider is being introduced.
- Deploy processes and materials.
- Deploy service management capability, including new or changed processes, systems, and tools.
- Transfer service to the new stakeholders.
- Deploy the service at point of receipt.
- Perform decommissioning and service retirement where applicable if the new or changed service is a replacement for existing services.
- Remove redundant assets.
- Verify deployment to ensure that it has met the acceptance criteria.
- Remediate or perform a backout release in the event that the deployment has not succeeded.
- Use early life support that provides the opportunity to maintain contact with the deployment teams to assist with the fix of the initial issues that may arise as the service is deployed. This step also provides the opportunity for the transfer of knowledge and documentation.

Review and Close

When reviewing the deployment, the following activities should be included:

- Capture experience and feedback on satisfaction from customers, users, and support staff.
- Highlight quality criteria that were not met.
- Check that all actions, fixes, and changes are complete.
- Review any open changes to ensure that these are handed over to the production environment.
- Review performance targets and achievements.
- Ensure that issues, problems, and known errors are correctly documented and owned.
- Review the risk register and ensure that ongoing ownership is assigned.
- Confirm that redundant assets have been removed.
- Confirm that the service is ready to move from early life support to service operation.

It is important to remember that a single transition may consist of a number of different deployments. Each will have to be reviewed and closed before the overall transition can be considered complete.

Formal evaluation of the service release will use outputs from the deployment. Change evaluation checks the actual service performance against the predicted performance. Successful completion of the change evaluation ensures that the deployment can be formally closed and handed over to the service operation functions and continual service improvement. Lessons learned and improvement can then be fed into the change management process for a postimplementation review and continual service improvement for future transitions.

Now let's look at the triggers, inputs, outputs, and process interfaces for release and deployment management.

Triggers

We'll look first at the triggers for this process. Release and deployment management is triggered by the receipt of an authorized change to plan, build, and test a production-ready release package. Deployment is triggered by the receipt of an authorized change to deploy a release package to a target deployment group or environment—for example, a business unit, customer group, and/or service unit.

Inputs

The inputs to release and deployment management include the authorized change and the SDP containing a service charter. The charter defines the business requirements, expected utility and warranty, outline budgets and timescales, service models, and service acceptance criteria. Another input is the acquired service assets and components and their documentation and specifications for build, test, release, training, disaster recovery, pilot, and deployment. The release policy and design, release, and deployment models and exit and entry criteria for each stage are the remaining inputs.

Outputs

There are many outputs of this process; the main ones are the new, changed, and retired services; the release and deployment plan; and the updated service catalog. Other outputs include details of the new service capability and documentation, the service transition report, the release package, SLAs, OLAs, contracts, tested continuity plans, CI specifications, and the capacity plan.

Interfaces

The main interfaces are with the other transition processes:

- Design coordination creates the SDP that defines the new service and how it should be created. This is a major input to release and deployment.

- Transition planning and support provides the framework in which release and deployment management will operate, and transition plans provide the context for release and deployment plans.

- Change management is tightly integrated with release and deployment. Change authorizes the release and deployment work. Release and deployment plans form part of the change schedule.

- Service asset and configuration management provides essential data and information from the CMS and provides updates to the CMS.

    Service validation and testing coordinates its actions with release and deployment to ensure that testing is carried out when necessary and that builds are available when required by service validation and testing.

Process Roles and Responsibilities

In Chapter 1, "Introduction to Operational Support and Analysis," we explored the generic roles applicable to all processes throughout the service lifecycle. These are relevant to the release and deployment management process, but there are specific additional requirements that also apply. Remember that these are not "job titles"; they are guidance on the roles that may be needed to successfully run the process.

Release and Deployment Process Owner

In addition to the generic process owner role described in Chapter 1, the process owner role will include the following:

- Designing release models and workflows
- Working with other process owners to ensure an integrated approach to design, change management, service asset and configuration management, release and deployment management, and service validation and testing

Release and Deployment Process Manager

It is important to ensure that this role is not carried out by the same person as the one who is responsible for service validation and testing to avoid conflicts of interest.

In addition to the generic process manager role described in Chapter 1, the process manager role will include

- Planning and coordinating all resources for the process

- Planning and managing support for the tools and process

- Ensuring that change authorization is provided before any activity that requires it

- Coordinating interfaces between processes, especially change management, SACM, and service validation and testing

Release Packaging and Build Practitioner

In smaller organizations it will be necessary to combine roles for release and deployment, with either the manager role or the deployment practitioner role. These are not job descriptions, so this role may be carried out by personnel from the technical or application management functions.

The release packaging and build practitioner will typically include

- Assisting with the design of the release package

- Establishing the final release configuration

- Building the release

- Testing the release

- Establishing and reporting outstanding known errors and workarounds

- Providing input to support change authorization

Deployment Practitioner

In smaller organizations, it will be necessary to combine roles for release and deployment, with either the manager role or the packaging and build practitioner role. These are not job descriptions, so this role may be carried out by personnel from the technical or application management functions.

The deployment practitioner role will typically include

- Assisting with planning the deployment

- Ensuring that the deployment has been authorized by change management

- Carrying out the physical delivery of the deployment

- Coordinating release documentation and communications

- Providing technical and application guidance and support throughout the release process

- Providing feedback on the effectiveness of the release

- Recording and reporting deployment metrics

Early Life Support Practitioner

This role may be carried out by personnel from the technical or application management functions. It may be combined with the packaging and build practitioner or deployment practitioner role.

The early life support practitioner role typically includes

- Providing IT service and business functional support from deployment to final acceptance
- Ensuring delivery of support documentation
- Providing support to the service desk
- Providing release acceptance for provision of initial support
- Adapting and perfecting elements that evolve with final usage, such as user documentation

Build and Test Environment Manager

This role may be carried out by personnel from the technical or application management functions. It may be combined with the deployment practitioner role.

Build and test environment manager responsibilities typically include

- Ensuring that service infrastructure and applications are built to design specification
- Planning the acquisition, build, implementation, and maintenance of ICT infrastructure
- Ensuring that components are from controlled sources
- Developing an integrated application software and infrastructure build
- Delivering appropriate build, operations, and support documentation for the build and test environments
- Building, delivering, and maintaining required test environments

Operational Staff Involvement in Release and Deployment Management

Service operational staff will be involved on a day-to-day basis with the activities of release and deployment. We have already mentioned the engagement of application and technical management with some of the release and deployment management roles. In addition we may find that service operation staff are involved in the following ways:

- Actual implementation actions regarding the deployment of new releases
- Participation in the planning stages of major new releases, by providing advice on service operation issues and risks
- Physical handling of CIs to or from the DML
- Participation in rollback or backout activities for unsuccessful releases

Information Management

Throughout the release and deployment process, appropriate records will be created and maintained. As assets and configuration items are successfully deployed, their records will be updated in the configuration management system.

In addition to the capture of CI information, other data and information for service management will be captured in the service knowledge management system. Examples include release packages in the DML, plans for installation and build, test plans, and training records.

An important part of the deployment cleanup will include deletion or archiving of any redundant information items or records relating to previous services or products.

Critical Success Factors and Key Performance Indicators

As with all processes, the performance of release and deployment management should be monitored and reported, and action should be taken to improve it. And as with the other processes we have discussed, each critical success factor (CSF) should have a small number of key performance indicators (KPIs) that will measure its success, and each organization may choose its own KPIs.

Let's look at two examples of CSFs for release and deployment management and the related KPIs for each.

The success of the CSF "Ensuring integrity of a release package and its constituent components throughout the transition activities" can be measured using KPIs that measure the trends toward increased accuracy of CMS and DML information when audits take place. Other relevant KPIs for this CSF would be the accuracy of the proposed budget and reducing the number of incidents due to incorrect components being deployed.

The success of the CSF "Ensuring that there is appropriate knowledge transfer" can be measured using KPIs that measure a falling number of incidents categorized as "user knowledge," an increase in the percentage of incidents solved by level 1 and level 2 support, and an improved customer satisfaction score when customers are questioned about release and deployment management.

Challenges

Challenges for release and deployment management include developing standard performance measures and measurement methods across projects and suppliers, dealing with projects and suppliers where estimated delivery dates are inaccurate, and understanding the different stakeholder perspectives that underpin effective risk management. The final challenge is encouraging a risk management culture where people share information and take a pragmatic and measured approach to risk.

Risks

The main risks in release and deployment include a poorly defined scope and an incomplete understanding of dependencies, leading to scope creep during release and deployment management. The lack of dedicated staff can cause resource issues. Other risks include the circumvention of the process, insufficient financing, poor controls on software licensing and other areas, ineffective management of organizational and stakeholder change, and poor supplier management. There may also be risks arising from the hostile reaction of staff to the release. Finally, there is a risk that the application or technical infrastructure will be adversely affected, due to an incomplete understanding of the potential impact of the release.

Knowledge Management

The ability to deliver a quality service or process relies to a significant extent on the ability of those involved to respond to circumstances. How effectively they are able to do this depends on their knowledge and experience. Service transition is about change, and change requires new information to be learned if staff are to be effective.

Purpose

The purpose of the knowledge management process is to share perspectives, ideas, experience, and information; to ensure that these are available in the right place at the right time to enable informed decisions; and to improve efficiency by reducing the need to rediscover knowledge.

Objectives

The major objective of knowledge management is to ensure that knowledge, information, and data are gathered, analyzed, stored, shared, used, and maintained throughout the service provider organization. The knowledge is managed through the service knowledge management system (SKMS), which provides controlled access to knowledge, information, and data appropriate for each audience. Having this available will have the following results:

- It will reduce the need to rediscover knowledge, so the service provider can be more efficient—able to deliver improved quality of service and achieve increased satisfaction while reducing cost.

- It will ensure that staff have a clear understanding of the value and benefits realized from the use of those services.

- It will improve management decision making by providing reliable and secure knowledge, information, and data.

Scope

Knowledge management is relevant to all lifecycle sectors, not just service transition. The main scope of the process includes oversight of the management of knowledge and the information and data from which that knowledge derives. Excluded from the process is the capture, maintenance, and use of asset and configuration data, which is the responsibility of the service asset and configuration management process.

Value to the Business

Knowledge management is important for all stages of the lifecycle, for all roles. It is particularly important for the transition of services because there is a strong focus on management of knowledge transfer as part of transition. This will enable the business to use the delivered service effectively.

Effective knowledge management delivers conformance with legal and other requirements, such as company policy and procedures. It provides documented requirements for retention and disposal of each category of data, information, and knowledge and ensures that data, information, and knowledge are current, complete, valid, and available to the people who need it when they need it. It also ensures that procedures are in place for the safe disposal of knowledge that is no longer required.

Policies, Principles, and Basic Concepts

Let's now look at the policies, principles, and basic concepts that underpin knowledge management.

Policies

Knowledge management policies guide staff in the behaviors needed to make knowledge management effective. Policy statements typically include the following items:

- A secure and convenient way of storing and accessing the knowledge should be defined.
- Access should be available to all staff to assist them in supporting the services provided.
- All policies, plans, and processes must be reviewed at least once per year.
- All knowledge and information should be created, reviewed, approved, maintained, controlled, and disposed of following a formal documented process.

Data to Information to Knowledge to Wisdom

Knowledge management is typically displayed within the data, information, knowledge, wisdom (DIKW) model, as shown in Figure 14.6. You should remember this from *ITIL Foundation Exam Study Guide* (Sybex, 2012).

FIGURE 14.6   The flow from data to wisdom

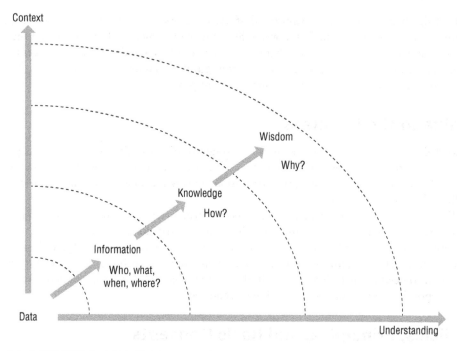

Let's look at the model, and examine what is meant by each of these concepts:

- Data is a set of discrete facts. Most organizations capture significant amounts of data in highly structured databases such as service management and service asset and configuration management tools/systems and databases.

- Information provides context to data. An example of information is the average time to close priority 2 incidents. This information is created by combining data from the start time, end time, and priority of many incidents.

- Knowledge is composed of the tacit experiences, ideas, insights, values, and judgments of individuals. Knowledge puts information into an "ease of use" form, which can facilitate decision making. An example of knowledge is that the average time to close priority 2 incidents has increased by about 10 percent since a new version of the service was released.

- Wisdom makes use of knowledge to create value through correct and well-informed decisions. Wisdom involves having the contextual awareness to provide strong commonsense judgment. An example of wisdom is recognizing that the increase in time to close priority 2 incidents is due to poor-quality documentation for the new version of the service.

The Service Knowledge Management System

The service knowledge management system (SKMS) holds all the knowledge relating to IT service management. This knowledge is underpinned by a large quantity of data gathered by various processes and held in the SKMS. One very important example is the configuration management system (CMS), which forms part of the SKMS. The CMS describes the attributes and relationships of configuration items, many of which are themselves knowledge, information, or data assets stored in the SKMS. We covered the CMS in Chapter 12, "Change Management and Service Asset and Configuration Management."

Figure 14.7 shows a very simplified illustration of the relationship of the three levels, with configuration data being recorded within the CMDB and feeding through the CMS into the SKMS. The knowledge provided by the SKMS supports delivery of the services and informed decision making.

FIGURE 14.7 Relationship of the CMDB, the CMS, and the SKMS

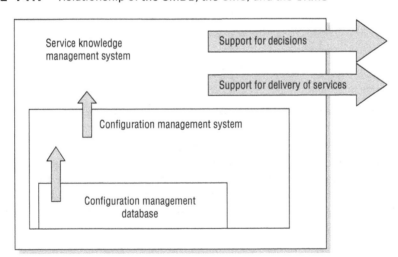

The SKMS will contain many different types of data, information, and knowledge, including the service portfolio, the CMS, the DML, SLAs and OLAs and contracts, the information security policy, the supplier and contract management information system (SCMIS), budgets, and cost models. Many of these knowledge and information assets are configuration items. Changes to CIs must be under the control of the change management process, and details of their attributes and relationships will be documented in the CMS. Figure 14.8 shows examples of information that should be in an SKMS.

FIGURE 14.8   Examples of data and information in the service knowledge management system

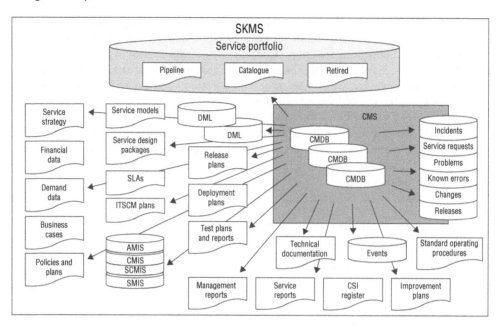

A knowledge management strategy is required. In the absence of an organizational knowledge management approach, action is required to establish the process within transition or IT service management. The strategy will address the governance model, roles and responsibilities, ongoing funding, policies, processes, procedures, methods and technology for knowledge management, performance measures, and how knowledge is to be identified, captured, and maintained.

Process Activities, Methods, and Techniques

In this section we explore the aspects of knowledge management that support the process.

Knowledge Management Strategy

An overall strategy for knowledge management is required. If the organization as a whole has no such strategy, it may be left to those responsible for IT service management as a whole or for service transition to impose knowledge management in their areas. The strategy should ensure that knowledge is shared with as wide a scope as practicable, covering direct IT staff, users, third-party support, and others likely to contribute to or make beneficial use of the knowledge.

If an organization has such a strategy, however, IT service management should be designed to fit within that overall organizational approach.

In either case, the strategy should address the following:

- The governance model, including any applicable legal or regulatory requirements
- Current and future roles and responsibilities
- Funding
- Policies, processes, procedures, and methods for knowledge management
- Technology and other resource requirements
- Performance measures

Knowledge Transfer

Knowledge needs to be transferred to other people and to other parts of the organization at specific points in the lifecycle. For example, knowledge transfer takes place to ensure that the service desk has optimum knowledge when a service is being transitioned into support. This would include information from release and deployment management such as known errors and diagnostic scripts from any of the technical support teams. Links with HR, facilities, and other supporting services need to be set up to facilitate the gathering and sharing of knowledge.

There are many different approaches to knowledge transfer:

- Learning styles—people learn in different ways and vary with age, culture, attitude, and personality. Users may require a different approach to knowledge transfer than the support teams.

- Knowledge visualization aims to improve the transfer of knowledge by using computer- and non-computer-based visuals, such as diagrams, images, photographs, and storyboards. This can include educational animation or gamification.

- Driving behavior can be achieved through provision of scripts or other mechanisms to instruct staff in how to carry out specific tasks.

- Seminars, webinars, and documentation can be used to launch a new or changed service and provide suitable knowledge transfers, which can be repeated and reused as required.

- Journals and newsletters can maintain regular communication channels, and knowledge transfer can be delivered incrementally. These mechanisms can also be easily adapted for specific audiences and provide a message targeted at specific groups.

- Discussion forums and social media can also be used to great effect to communicate with wide audiences, but they must be monitored and maintained to ensure their usefulness and relevance.

Managing Data, Information, and Knowledge

Knowledge rests on the management of the information and data that underpins it. To be efficient, this process requires an understanding of some key process inputs, such as how the data, information, and knowledge will be used, asking questions such as these:

- What knowledge is necessary?
- What do we need to monitor?

- What data is available?
- What is the cost of capturing and maintaining data?
- Does its value justify the cost?

We also need to consider applicable policies, legislation, standards, intellectual property rights, and copyright issues. Using the service knowledge management system reduces the costs of maintaining and managing the services.

Defining the Information Architecture

To make effective use of the data to deliver knowledge, it is important to create and maintain a relevant architecture matched to the organizational structure and needs.

An example of a knowledge, information, and data architecture is shown in Figure 14.9.

FIGURE 14.9   Architectural layers of an SKMS

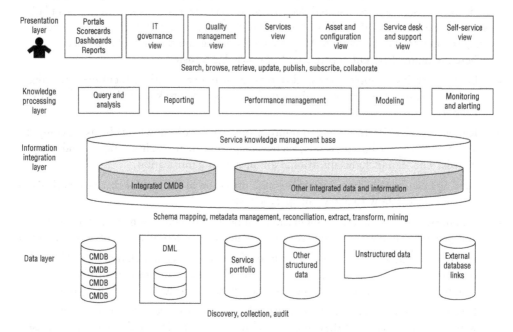

Presentation Layer   This enables searching, browsing, retrieving, updating, subscribing, and collaboration. The different views onto the other layers are suitable for different audiences. Each view should be protected to ensure that only authorized people can see or modify the underlying knowledge, information, and data.

Knowledge Processing Layer   This is where the information is converted into useful knowledge that enables decision making.

Information Integration Layer   This provides integrated information that may be gathered from data in multiple sources in the data layer.

Data Layer   This includes tools for data discovery and data collection, and data items in unstructured and structured forms.

Establishing Data, Information, and Knowledge Management Procedures

The key steps, once the requirements and architecture have been set up, involve setting up the following mechanisms to

- Identify the service lifecycle data and information to be collected
- Define the procedure required to maintain the data and information, and make it available to those requiring it
- Define the activities and transformations that will be used to convert data into information and then to knowledge
- Store and retrieve data
- Establish authority and responsibility for all required items
- Define and publicize rights, obligations, and commitments regarding the retention of, transmission of, and access to knowledge, information, and data items (based on applicable requirements and protecting security, integrity, and consistency)
- Establish adequate backup and recovery of data and information
- Identify the requirements to review, in the light of changing technology, organizational requirements, evolving policy, and legislation changes
- Deal with collection and retention requirements
- Review stored knowledge, information, and data to ensure that it is still relevant and correct
- Update, purge, and archive knowledge, information, and data

These procedures should enable the organization to capture, store, and retrieve the identified data from the relevant sources. In addition, the organization should be able to manage data, information, and knowledge in terms of storage and movement in line with legislative requirements. This will also support the management of archiving according to the organizational, regulatory, and legislative requirements.

As with all processes, knowledge management and the SKMS will be subject to continual service improvement activities.

Using the Service Knowledge Management System

Implementation of a service knowledge management system can support an organization in a number of ways and circumstances:

- A global organization can share information regardless of time zones or locations, as long as a common approach to language is specified.
- An SKMS can assist in the reduction of costs in maintaining and managing the services by increasing the efficiency of operational management procedures.

- The SKMS can assist in the reduction of risks that arise from a lack of, or poorly managed, information.

- Provision of centralized information and knowledge can support functional areas such as the service desk by supporting incident resolutions and problem management information.

- Service knowledge management systems can incorporate self-service portals for use by the customer, providing support knowledge direct to the user and reducing the cost of support.

Triggers

Now let's look at the triggers, inputs and outputs, and process interfaces for knowledge management. Let's look first at the triggers for this process. Knowledge management has many triggers relating to every requirement for storing, maintaining, and using knowledge, information, or data within the organization. For example, any of the following actions could trigger the need to store or retrieve knowledge:

- Business relationship management storing the minutes of a customer meeting

- Updates to the service catalog or service portfolio

- Modification of a service design package

- The creation of a new or updated capacity plan

- The receipt of an updated user manual from a supplier

- The creation of a customer report

- Updates to the CSI register

Inputs

Inputs to knowledge management include all knowledge, information, and data used by the service provider as well as relevant business data.

Outputs

The key output of knowledge management is the knowledge required to make decisions and to manage the IT services; this knowledge is maintained within an SKMS. The success of knowledge management depends in part on the participation of the relevant staff. For example, frontline operations staff will use the information about known errors to help when supporting users; they will also be responsible for gathering a lot of the data that will be stored in the SKMS, such as incident records. Problem management staff will be key users of incident data, whereas transition staff will capture data to be fed back to CSI and design.

Interfaces

Knowledge management has interfaces to every other service management process in every stage of the lifecycle. The SKMS can only be truly effective if all processes and activities use it to store and manage their information and data so that the maximum value can be extracted.

Knowledge Management Roles

In Chapter 1, we explored the generic roles applicable to all processes throughout the service lifecycle. These are relevant to the knowledge management process, but there are specific additional requirements that also apply. Remember that these are not "job titles"; they are guidance on the roles that may be needed to successfully run the process.

Knowledge Management Process Owner

In many organizations this role will be combined with that of the knowledge management process manager role. Other options may include combining the role with service asset and configuration management roles.

In addition to the generic responsibilities for the process owner, the role will typically include

- Creating the overall architecture for identification, capture, and maintenance of knowledge within the organization

Knowledge Management Process Manager

The knowledge management process manager's responsibilities, as well as those of the generic process manager role, include

- Ensuring that all knowledge items are made accessible to those who need them in an efficient and effective manner
- Planning and managing support for knowledge management tools and processes
- Encouraging people throughout the service provider to contribute knowledge to the service knowledge management system (SKMS)
- Acting as an adviser to business and IT personnel on knowledge management matters, including policy decisions on storage, value, worth, and so on

Knowledge Management Process Practitioner

In many organizations this role will be known as a "knowledge librarian." The role typically includes

- Identifying, controlling, and storing any information deemed to be pertinent to the services provided that is not available by other means
- Maintaining controlled knowledge items to ensure that they are current, relevant, and valid
- Monitoring publicity regarding the knowledge information to ensure that information is not duplicated and is recognized as a central source of information

Knowledge Creator

This may be carried out by many different people in an organization since creation and sharing of knowledge is a prerequisite of most roles in an organization, in both business and IT.

Information Management

The creation of a service knowledge management system can involve a significant investment in tools. The SKMS is likely to consist of a number of different but integrated tools and repositories.

The most important aspect of the process is to understand and document, for each item of data, information, or knowledge that the organization needs:

- How does it relate to other data, information and knowledge?

- Where and how is it stored?

- Who is responsible for collecting, updating, and maintaining it?

- What legal, regulatory, or governance considerations apply to it?

- How long is it needed for, and how will it be consolidated, archived, or deleted when it is no longer needed?

- Who should be allowed to access it? Where from? When?

- Who should be allowed to change it?

- Does it need to be audited? If so, how, by whom, and how often?

This can be used to formulate an approach to creation of the SKMS and the associated tools.

Critical Success Factors and Key Performance Indicators

As with the other processes, the performance of knowledge management should be monitored and reported, and action should be taken to improve it. Here are two examples of CSFs for knowledge management and the related KPIs for each.

- Critical success factor: "Availability of knowledge and information that helps to support management decision making"

  - KPI: Increased number of accesses to the SKMS by managers

  - KPI: Increased percentage of SKMS searches by managers that receive a rating of good

- Critical success factor: "Successful implementation and early life support operation of new and changed services with few knowledge-related errors"

  - KPI: Reduction in the number of incidents and problems categorized as knowledge related

  - KPI: The increased percentage of successful service transitions

Challenges

Implementing knowledge management can be challenging. Challenges include justifying the effort needed to create a repository for existing knowledge, information, and data. There may be a perception that knowledge management is interfering in the work of other teams who manage their own information. The final challenge is persuading all the stakeholders of the benefits that a more cooperative and holistic approach to knowledge management can bring.

Risks

The risks to successful knowledge management are as follows:

- The emphasis could be on tools rather than on the creation of value.
- There could be insufficient understanding of what knowledge, information, and data are needed by the organization.
- There may be doubt as to the value of the process, leading to insufficient investment in the tools and people needed to support the SKMS.
- Without a clear knowledge management strategy, effort may be concentrated on knowledge capture with insufficient attention to knowledge transfer and reuse.
- The process may lose credibility if the knowledge and information that is stored and shared is out of date and irrelevant.
- If the benefits are not clear, stakeholders are unlikely to give the support and commitment the process requires.

CSI and Knowledge Management

Knowledge management supports the seven-step improvement process, by enabling the approach to data capture and its generation of information and knowledge. (The seven-step improvement process is covered in the *ITIL Foundation Exam Study Guide* [Sybex, 2012] as part of the ITIL Foundation exam syllabus.) This will be used for decision making, the "wisdom" in the DIKW model.

Summary

This chapter explored two more processes in the service transition stage: release and deployment management and knowledge management. We examined how the release and deployment management process ensures that the required planning for the release is carried out and the release activities are managed to minimize the risk to existing services. We also considered how the knowledge management process ensures that those involved in providing the service have all the information they need to be effective, and to make decisions regarding the service. We examined how each of these processes supports the other and the importance of these processes to the business and to the IT service provider.

Exam Essentials

Understand the purpose of release and deployment management.   Release and deployment management ensures that releases are planned, scheduled, and controlled so the new or changed services are built, tested, and deployed successfully.

Understand and be able to list the objectives of release and deployment management.   The objectives of release and deployment are to ensure successful transition of a new or changed service into production, including the management of issues and risks. It also ensures that knowledge transfer is completed for both recipients and support teams.

Understand the scope of release and deployment management.   The scope of release and deployment management covers all aspects of packaging, building, and testing the release (including managing all CIs that are part of the release) to deploy the release into production.

Be able to explain the contents of a release policy.   The release policy describes the manner in which releases will be carried out, provides definitions for release types, and specifies the activities that should be managed under the control of the process.

Be able to list the four phases of release and deployment management.   The four phases of release and deployment are release and deployment planning, release build and test, deployment, and review and close. All four phases should be triggered by authorization from the change management process.

Understand the purpose of knowledge management.   Knowledge management shares perspectives, ideas, experience, and information in the right place at the right time to enable informed decisions, reducing the need for knowledge rediscovery.

Understand the objectives of knowledge management.   The objectives of knowledge management are to ensure that we have mechanisms for capturing and sharing knowledge to improve the quality of our services and decision making.

Be able to describe the scope of knowledge management.   Knowledge management extends across the whole of the service lifecycle, and included in the scope is the information interaction with customer and users. Excluded is the management of the CIs relating to knowledge.

Be able to describe the DIKW model.   DIKW is data to information to knowledge to wisdom. This ensures that we add context and understanding to the communications we provide to the organization we support.

- Data is a set of discrete facts.

- Information provides context to data.

- Knowledge is composed of the tacit experiences, ideas, insights, values, and judgments of individuals.

- Wisdom makes use of knowledge to create value through correct and well-informed decisions.

Be able to describe the role and purpose of the SKMS.   SKMS is the overarching system for the management of knowledge relating to service management. It integrates all the existing data sources from our service management processes and enables the DIKW structure for knowledge management across the entire service lifecycle.

Review Questions

You can find the answers to the review questions in the appendix.

1. Which of the following is the correct definition of a release package?
   A. A set of configuration items that will be built, tested, and deployed together
   B. A portion of a service or IT infrastructure that is normally released as a single unit
   C. One or more changes to an IT service that are built, tested, and deployed together
   D. A repeatable way of dealing with a particular category of release

2. The release and deployment process covers a concept called early life support. What is meant by early life support?
   A. Early life support refers to the end of the project lifecycle and the management of the postimplementation project review.
   B. Early life support refers to the handover between service transition and service operation, ensuring support for the new or changed service in the initial stages of operation.
   C. Early life support refers to the introduction of new processes into the operational environment, using service transition processes to ensure a complete integration of the new processes.
   D. Early life support refers to the step in the release and deployment process where the project team delivers the documentation of the infrastructure to the service management team.

3. Which of these statements does *not* describe a recommended part of a release policy?
   A. A unique identification structure or naming convention to ensure that releases can be easily identified and tracked
   B. Definitions of the roles and responsibilities required for the management of the release throughout all its stages
   C. Definition of the configuration management system naming convention
   D. Use of the definitive media library for all software asset releases

4. Which of these is *not* one of the phases of the release and deployment process?
   A. Release and deployment planning
   B. Deployment
   C. Review and close
   D. Verification and audit

5. Early life support is an important concept in the release and deployment management process. In which phase of the release and deployment process does early life support happen?
   A. Release build and test
   B. Review and close
   C. Deployment
   D. Release deployment and planning

6. Match each of the DIKW concepts with its definition.

1. Data

2. Information

3. Knowledge

4. Wisdom

   A. Composed of tacit experiences, ideas, insights, values, and judgments

   B. A set of discrete facts

   C. Creates value through correct and well-informed decisions

   D. Gives context to data

7. The knowledge management process maintains and updates a tool used for knowledge management. What is this tool called?

   A. The service management tool

   B. The knowledge base for service management

   C. The service knowledge management system

   D. The service management database

8. An important focus for the service lifecycle is the capture and management of knowledge relating to IT service provision. How does the process of knowledge management work in the service lifecycle?

   A. Knowledge management is solely concerned with the transfer of knowledge when new or changed services are implemented.

   B. Knowledge management is used across the lifecycle stages of continual service improvement and service operation to ensure that improvements are managed effectively.

   C. Knowledge management is used solely in the service operation stage of the lifecycle to ensure that operation issues are managed efficiently.

   D. Knowledge management is used across the whole service lifecycle to ensure that appropriate knowledge is delivered to enable informed decision making.

9. Knowledge management includes a number of different roles. Which of these is an alternative name for a knowledge management practitioner?

   A. Information knowledge analyst

   B. Knowledge librarian

   C. Asset librarian

   D. Asset analyst

10. Which of these is a responsibility of a knowledge management process owner?

   A. Creating the architecture for data, information, and knowledge capture and maintenance across the organization

   B. Updating knowledge records

   C. Creating known error records

   D. Maintaining the known error database

Technology and Implementation Considerations for Release, Control, and Validation

---

THE FOLLOWING ITIL INTERMEDIATE CAPABILITY EXAM OBJECTIVES ARE DISCUSSED IN THIS CHAPTER:

- ✓ Generic requirements for integrated ITSM technology

- ✓ The evaluation criteria for service management tools for process implementation

- ✓ The RCV practices for process implementation including managing change in operations, service operation, and project management and assessing and managing risk in service operation

- ✓ Operational staff in service design and transition

- ✓ The challenges, critical success factors, and risks relating to implementing service transition practices and processes

- ✓ How to plan and implement service management technologies

- ✓ The technology considerations for implementing tools for knowledge management, collaboration, and configuration management

To meet the learning outcomes and examination level of difficulty, you must ensure that you are able to understand, describe, identify, demonstrate, apply, distinguish, produce, decide on, or analyze the concepts described in this chapter.

Generic Requirements for Integrated ITSM Technology

We will begin by considering the generic requirements for IT service management tools. In this section, we look at a number of these requirements, which we would expect any good integrated toolset to offer.

The first two requirements are self-help functionality and a workflow engine.

You should be able to recall from the discussion of the request fulfillment process in Chapter 3, "Event Management, Request Fulfillment, and Access Management," that self-help functionality may be used to automate aspects of that process. This might be restricted to the logging of requests, or it could allow them to be tracked and updated throughout their lifecycle. This functionality may also be used for the incident management process. One major advantage of providing a self-help facility is that requests and incidents can be logged at any time and this process is not dependent on service desk staff being available to answer the phone. This helps the service desk manage high volumes of calls if the less urgent ones are handled via a self-help, self-logging site. Self-help request tools can assist with password resets by, for example, requiring the user to validate their identity by answering previously set questions before the reset takes place. Additionally, a self-help request tool could download approved versions of requested software.

The next generic requirement is for a workflow or a process engine that can automate the steps of the process (assigning, escalating, etc.). It can also release work orders when prerequisite steps have been completed.

Remember, the ITSM toolset is essential for many of the service management processes and functions. As with any essential service, IT service continuity plans need to be put in place to ensure that the service is able to continue despite any major disruptive events.

The third generic requirement is for an integrated configuration management system (CMS). The service management tool should be integrated with the CMS to allow the organization's configuration item (CI) information to be interrogated and linked to incident, problem, known error, and change records as appropriate.

Another generic requirement is for tools to assist in discovery, deployment and licensing; these are extremely helpful in verifying the accuracy of the CMS, especially with regard to license use. It is also very helpful if changes since the last audit can be extracted and reported upon. The same technology can often be used to deploy new software to target locations; this is essential to enable patches and upgrades to be distributed to the correct users. Deployment technology may be used in conjunction with self-help functionality to automate the fulfillment of service requests for software.

Another generic requirement is remote control. This allows the service desk analysts to take control of the user's desktop (under properly controlled security conditions) to conduct investigations and correct settings. Some tools will store diagnostic scripts and other diagnostic utilities to assist with earlier diagnosis of incidents.

Good reporting is a requirement of any ITSM toolset. The tools hold enormous amounts of information about what is happening day to day. This data is helpful in planning ahead and tracking trends, but such reporting has to be flexible if it is to be useful. Standard reports and ad hoc reports should both be easily available.

Another generic requirement to consider is a dashboard facility. Dashboards are useful, for both day-to-day operations and IT and business management to get a clear idea of real-time performance.

To facilitate greater business alignment, business applications and tools need to be able to interface with ITSM support tools to give the required functionality. Examples of integration include event management tools spotting unusual spending patterns on credit cards.

Software as a Service (SaaS) technologies offer hosted service management capabilities over the Internet. The advantages this offers includes lower capital and startup costs, faster implementation, and built-in service continuity.

However, it also means limited customization and changes to functionality, access restricted to vendors' hours of service availability, and licensing schemes that may become restrictive or expensive. There may also be limits on data storage size and possible security and access management constraints or risks. Finally, integration with other service management tools may be difficult or even impossible.

Evaluation Criteria for Service Management Tools

Each organization should review its requirements carefully so that it acquires the most appropriate toolset for its needs. Typical evaluation considerations for service management tools include

- Data structure, data handling, and integration
- Ability to integrate multivendor infrastructure components, now and in the future
- Conformity to open standards

- Flexibility
- Ease of use
- Ability to monitor achievement against service level targets
- Client-server approach
- How easily data from previous tools may be imported
- Data backup capability and security aspects
- Level of vendor support provided
- Scalability

Many service management tools are available, each with its own strengths and weaknesses, which makes choosing the right one difficult. To overcome this, objective selection criteria need to be defined.

One simple method is MoSCoW analysis. This involves creating a detailed list of all requirements and classifying each one as must have, should have, could have, or would like in the future:

- *Must have* requirements are mandatory. Any tool that does not satisfy *all* of those requirements is rejected.
- *Should have* requirements are those that are expected but are not essential.
- *Could have* requirements are useful but not hugely important.
- *Would like in the future* requirements are those that are not needed right now but will be needed in the future. For example, the selection criteria for a tool for incident management may also specify that the tool should have problem management capability for later use.

A scoring system based on this analysis enables alternatives to be ranked.

 Remember, the ITSM toolset is essential, but few if any tools will satisfy every requirement on a wish list. The best fit may be a tool that satisfies 80 percent of requirements with the ability to customize it further.

Release, Control, and Validation Practices for Managing Change in Service Operation

Next we consider how the IT service provider manages changes within service operation. We start by considering the challenges of managing change in operations. The focus in the operational stage of the lifecycle is on protecting the live services, so changes in service operation must be absorbed without impacting stability. We will examine the many different triggers that cause changes to the live environment and consider how the changes are assessed before implementation. Finally, we will look at how changes can be measured to see if they are successful.

Change Triggers

There are many events that can trigger a change in the service operation environment. Changes or upgrades to system software such as operating systems and utilities also need to be handled with care. Some change triggers are external such as those resulting from legislation, the need to conform to an external standard, or new governance rules. For example, a change in legislation that records of transactions need to be kept for a longer period would impact archiving and storage requirements.

Possible triggers for change include the following:

- The need to install or upgrade hardware, network components, or application software.

- Regular updates to software, including patches and bug fixes. These changes need to be carefully managed because they have the potential to have a serious impact on the environment if implemented badly.

- The replacement of obsolete hardware or software. These items may still be functioning correctly but are no longer supported by the supplier and may be incompatible with future releases of other components and therefore need to be replaced. The same is true for any service management tool, whether it is being upgraded or replaced.

- Changes driven by the business, which may need IT to support a new business initiative, such as providing a "reserve and collect" facility through an e-commerce website.

- Changes resulting from continual service improvement of processes and procedures, which need to be implemented without any adverse consequences.

- Staff changes can be potentially disruptive, and care needs to be taken to ensure that the necessary knowledge transfer takes place so the service provided is not affected.

- A requirement for a change in agreed service levels or a change in the sourcing model (outsourcing service provision, changing an outsourcer, or insourcing a service previously outsourced) will need to be planned to ensure that it is implemented smoothly.

Release, control, and validation is responsible for planning these changes; service operation has to be ready to absorb them without disrupting the services provided.

Change Assessment

All changes have a potential impact on operations. This is not always understood by non-operations staff, so it is essential that service operation staff have an opportunity to assess all changes. It is not sufficient to involve operations staff at the CAB stage because it may be too late; fundamental decisions regarding the design of the new or changed service will have been made far earlier. It is unrealistic to think that a redesign could happen at such a late stage. To prevent this, it is essential that operation staff be consulted and informed much earlier, during the initial design stage, and remain involved throughout.

It is good practice for the change manager to inform all affected parties of the changes being assessed so that affected areas (in this case, the service operation area) can prepare a response showing the operational impact of the change and setting out any concerns. This can be distributed prior to the CAB meeting to inform the discussion.

Service operation staff need to be involved throughout the design and implementation of a change with an operational impact. Early involvement is necessary to ensure that the design takes account of operational issues and requirements; involvement in the later stages is necessary to ensure that the change is scheduled to avoid potential disagreements or particularly sensitive periods.

Measurement of Successful Change

The ultimate measure of a successful change made to service operation is that there are no unexpected variations or outages; the only visible effects are the benefits that result from the change, such as enhanced functionality, quality, or financial savings.

Service Operation and Project Management

The use of project management processes to manage changes is commonplace in other lifecycle stages, but there is often a disinclination to use these processes for operational changes. Service operation is generally viewed as "business as usual" and does not include a project approach. In fact, project management processes are both appropriate and helpful for major infrastructure upgrades or the deployment of new or changed procedures; these significant tasks will benefit from the improved control and management of costs and resources delivered by project management. Using project management to manage these types of activity would deliver a number of benefits:

- A clear, agreed statement of the benefits to be delivered by the project.
- Greater visibility of tasks and their management, which enables other IT groups and the business to understand the contributions made by operational teams. This helps in obtaining funding for projects that have traditionally been difficult to cost-justify.
- Greater consistency and improved quality of the deliverables.
- The achievement of objectives, leading to operational groups gaining credibility.

Service Transition Challenges

Challenges for service transition are driven by the complexity of provision because organizations now deal with a large variety of customers, users, programs, projects, suppliers, and partners. This provides a challenge in managing a large stakeholder group because transition affects everybody. The relationships with customers, suppliers, users, and projects are often complicated and need to be managed as a transition moves into operation.

Ensuring that transition processes can integrate with other business processes (for example, finance, HR, and procurement) is also a challenge. There may also be insufficient knowledge of the dependencies on legacy systems, making impact analysis difficult, and this may have a significant effect on the introduction of new systems and services.

A major challenge is to address the balance between maintaining a stable live environment and being responsive to the business needs for changing the services and achieving a balance between pragmatism and bureaucracy. Transition is perfectly placed to support this, and it is one of the reasons that this lifecycle stage is so important and must not be ignored or cut short.

Many of the challenges relate to cultural change, such as creating an environment that fosters standardization, simplification, and knowledge sharing. Service transition must persuade the business that it is an enabler of business change and, therefore, an integral component of the business change programs. It is made easier if the challenge of finding process champions is achieved. This can create a culture that encourages people to collaborate and work effectively together.

Developing standard performance measures across projects and suppliers and ensuring that the quality of delivery and support matches the business use of new technology is a significant challenge for all organizations. Effective use of the service transition processes requires protecting the service transition time and budget from being impacted by events earlier in the service lifecycle.

Risk management is the source of several challenges, including understanding different stakeholder perspectives on risk. This reflects the complexity of managing organizations with varied structures. During transition, it's important to achieve the optimum balance between managing risk and taking risks and to provide effective reporting in relation to risk management and corporate governance.

Some organizations will be driven by the requirements and reporting required by Sarbanes-Oxley, ISO/IEC 20000, ISO/IEC 38500, and COBIT (if applicable). These standards and governance requirements both support and provide challenges to the success of service transition as a lifecycle stage.

Critical Success Factors

Service provision, in all organizations, needs to be matched to current and rapidly changing business demands. The objective is to continually and cost-effectively improve the quality of service while ensuring that it is aligned to the business requirements. To meet this objective, certain critical success factors need to be considered for service transition.

It is necessary to understand and manage the different stakeholder perspectives that underpin effective risk management within an organization. Establishing and maintaining stakeholder buy-in and commitment and having clearly defined relationships and interfaces with program and project management is vital to the success of a transition. Equally important is maintaining these contacts and managing all the relationships during service transition.

Another critical success factor is the integration of service transition with the other service lifecycle stages and the processes and disciplines that impact service transition. It is important to ensure that the dependencies among the legacy systems, new technology, and human elements, and the risks involved in changing any of these areas, are clearly understood. Dependencies between newer and legacy systems are often overlooked but can have a significant impact on the introduction of new services.

Here are some additional critical success factors necessary for successful service transition:

- Automating processes to eliminate errors
- Managing knowledge
- Developing good-quality systems, tools, processes, and procedures
- Exploiting the cultural and political environment
- Understanding the technical configurations and dependencies
- Understanding the processes, procedures, skills, and competencies required for service transition
- Having a workforce with the necessary knowledge and skills, appropriate training, and the right service culture
- Ensuring clear accountabilities, roles, and responsibilities
- Encouraging a knowledge-sharing culture

It is important for service transition to deliver change with less variation in time, cost, and quality predictions during and after transition. This should ensure improved customer and user satisfaction, which is critical for continued successful transitions.

If it cannot be demonstrated that the benefits of establishing and improving the service transition practice and processes outweigh the costs, then there will be a significant impact on the credibility of transition. This should be supported by effective communication of the organization's attitude to risk during service transition activities and by building a thorough understanding of risks that have impacted or may impact successful service transition of services in the service portfolio.

Assessing and Managing Risk in Service Operation

The overriding concern of service operation is to maintain stability; any threat to that stability has to be assessed and acted upon urgently. An obvious example of a situation in which service operation needs to carry out a risk and impact assessment is the risk to stability from a potential change. Service operation staff must assess the possible impact of the change and share this assessment with the CAB.

Risks Resulting from Changes

A change might be implemented despite the existence of known errors that become apparent during testing but were not considered serious enough to delay the change. The existence of such known errors poses a risk to operational stability; until the errors are resolved, incidents resulting from them can recur. The impact of these incidents and the effectiveness of the appropriate workaround for each (including the speed at which it overcomes the fault) must be assessed. The results of this assessment will feed into the prioritization of the problem and the urgency for the change to be implemented.

Other Sources of Risk

There are other risks to operational stability that would require a risk assessment. The first is an environmental risk. Environmental risks would include the sorts of risks that are assessed as part of IT service continuity planning, such as fire and flood. There may also be political and commercial risks and risks related to industrial relations. Examples of these are the risks faced by drug companies that carry out testing on animals and therefore may be subject to sabotage by those opposed to this practice, the risk of strikes affecting operation, or even the risk of a competitor engaging in a price war, which would drive down the income received.

Suppliers may constitute a source of risk also. Their failure to deliver could affect the delivery of the overall service. Their ability to provide a service might also be affected by their own internal risks. This is especially a problem if they are the sole supplier for a particular element of the service. Taking on new suppliers involves some risk also; without a known track record of reliable delivery, there is a risk that their service may not be satisfactory. Another major area of risk involves security; security-related incidents or events may result in either theoretical or actual risks. Finally, every new customer or service to be supported is both an opportunity to be successful and a potential risk for failure.

Implementing new processes for transitioning services can be disruptive, and should not be implemented without recognizing the potential risk to services currently in transition and releases that are planned. A baseline assessment of current transitions and planned projects will help service transition to identify implementation risks.

A source of risk for transition is the potential failure to understand different stakeholder perspectives on risk. This reflects the complexity of managing organizations with varied structures. During transition, it's important to achieve the optimum balance between managing risk and taking risks and to provide effective reporting in relation to risk management and corporate governance.

Particular risks include the reaction of involved staff to changes in accountability and responsibilities that may result from new processes; these may result in the workforce becoming demotivated and key support and operations staff being resentful and hostile to the changes, if they feel that their role has been diminished. This may result in resistance to change and circumvention of the processes due to perceived bureaucracy. Another implementation risk is incurring excessive costs to the business by being overly risk averse.

Uncontrolled knowledge sharing, allowing people to have access to information they should not have, is another implementation risk. A lack of maturity and integration of systems and tools may result in people "blaming" technology for other shortcomings. There may be poor integration between the processes, causing a silo approach to delivering IT service management (ITSM), with no integration between processes. Finally, the loss of productive hours presents a risk, as do higher costs, loss of revenue, and perhaps even business failure as a result of poor service transition processes.

Operational Staff in Design and Transition

All IT groups will be involved during service design and service transition to ensure that new components or services are designed, tested, and implemented to provide the correct levels of functionality, usability, availability, and capacity. Additionally, service operation staff must be involved during the early stages of service design and service transition to ensure that when new services reach the live environment, they are fit for purpose from a service operation perspective and are "supportable" in the future.

In this context, *supportable* means that they will not negatively impact other services, processes, schedules, or operational working practices. They must also be capable of being operated by the current staff, at an understood cost. The support structure, including both the internal support teams and the support provided by third-party suppliers, must be clear and understood. There should be no unexpected costs after the service goes live, and contractual obligations must be clear and straightforward.

Note that change is not just about technology. There is also organizational change to consider. Further details about organizational change are included in the ITIL Service Transition publication, but through awareness and training it is possible to reduce the risk of people resisting change.

Planning and Implementing Service Management Technologies

A good service management tool can be very helpful for implementing processes based on the ITIL framework. Many organizations implement new tools to assist their implementation of new or improved processes. There are a number of factors that these organizations need to consider if the new tool is to be helpful and appropriate.

Licenses

The first factor to be considered is the type of license. There are usually a number of options, at different costs. Where tools are licensed on a modular basis, careful planning is needed to ensure that the right access is obtained to enable people to carry out their work with no unnecessary modules being purchased. Here are some possible options:

Dedicated Licenses   For this option, each named person has his or her own license. Dedicated licenses are suitable for staff members who require frequent and prolonged use of a particular module. For example, service desk staff would need a dedicated license to use an incident management module.

Shared Licenses   These licenses can be shared between individuals; there is, however, a possibility that a staff member may not be able to access the tool because the license is already in use. Shared licenses are suitable for regular users who do not require constant access, such as second-line support staff. Careful calculation is required to ascertain the correct ratio of users to licenses. These licenses are more expensive than dedicated licenses, but fewer are required.

Web Licenses   These allow access via a web browser. Web licenses are usually suitable for staff requiring remote access or only occasional access. They usually cost a lot less than other licenses (they may even be free with other licenses).

On Demand   Access to tools is provided when required (on demand), and the supplier charges for the access based on the time spent using the application. This can be attractive to smaller organizations or if the tools in question are very specialized and used relatively infrequently. A variation to this is the use of a specialist tool as part of a consultancy assignment (e.g., specialist capacity management tools); in such cases, the license fees are likely to be included in the consultancy fee.

Agent/Activity   An alternative licensing method is software that is licensed and charged on an agent/activity basis. An example of this is simulation software (e.g., agent software that can simulate customer paths through a website to assess and report on performance and availability).

In all cases, it is essential that sufficient investigation be done to ensure that the costs are understood and agreed to and that the organization remains legal in respect to having sufficient licenses.

Deployment

Many ITSM tools, particularly discovery and event monitoring tools, will require some client/agent software deploying to all target locations before they can be used. This will need careful planning and execution and should be handled through formal release and deployment management. Some deployment considerations are listed here:

- There should be careful scheduling and testing, and the deployment must be tracked so that it is clear which CIs have the software and which have yet to receive it.
- The CMS should be updated as the deployment progresses.
- It is often necessary to reboot devices for the client software to be recognized; this needs to be arranged in advance to minimize service interruption.

- Special arrangements may be needed for portable equipment, which may not be present on site during deployment.

- The devices receiving the software must be checked in advance to ensure that they have sufficient storage and processing capacity to host and run the new software.

- The network capacity needs to be checked to ensure that it is capable of transmitting everything required.

- Tools should only be deployed when the processes they support are mature. A tool that is deployed too early will shift the focus of the transformation from changing how people work to become simply about the implementation of the tool.

- Training in the tool prior to deployment is necessary if benefits are to be realized.

Remember, a tool is usually not enough to make things work better. However, if it supports processes and the user has been trained to use it, a good tool can help staff carry out new processes. Further aspects of the deployment to be considered include the following:

The Type of Introduction to Be Used   A decision must be made whether a "Big Bang" introduction or some sort of phased approach is to be adopted. Because most organizations will have live services to keep running during the introduction, a phased approach is more likely to be necessary.

Transition between Tools   If an older tool is being replaced, consideration must be given to the best way to transition between the old tool and the new tool. For example, the service desk should not be assigning an incident on a new tool to a team that has yet to transition from the old tool.

Data Migration   A decision needs to be made regarding what data needs to be migrated from the old tool to the new one. This may require reformatting, and so may need to be validated after migration, especially if the data is transferred electronically. A period of parallel running may be implemented instead, with the old tool being available in a read-only mode for an initial period alongside the new one so that historical data can be referenced if needed.

Complete details on the release and deployment management process can be found in Chapter 14, "Release and Deployment Management and Knowledge Management."

Technology Considerations for Implementing Knowledge Management, Collaboration, and the CMS

Technology has a major role to play in service transition, as it does throughout the lifecycle. There are a number of specific tools that support aspects of service transition. Here we examine the use of technology in supporting

- Knowledge management

- Collaboration

- The configuration management system

Knowledge Management Tools

The tools supporting the knowledge management process include tools supporting document management, records management, and content management.

These tools, used in collaboration, provide the structure and functionality of the service knowledge management system (SKMS). Organizations may use a single service management tool that provides the SKMS, but doing so severely limits the capability of the concept. Instead, success should be built on the capability to integrate many different sources to provide a complete approach to the capture and management of knowledge in all its forms.

Knowledge management tools address the requirements of maintaining records and documents electronically. Records are distinguished from documents by the fact that they function as evidence of activities, rather than evidence of intentions. For example, a change record captures the actions that have been carried out during a change.

Documentation, examples of which include policy statements, plans, procedures, service level agreements, and contracts, shows the intent to do something. For example, a service transition policy that states all changes will be managed under the change control process.

Document Management

Document management defines the set of capabilities to support the storage, protection, classification, searching, retrieval, maintenance, archiving, and retirement of documents and information.

Records Management

Records management defines the set of capabilities to support the storage, protection, classification, searching, retrieval, maintenance, archiving, and retirement of records.

Content Management

Content management provides the capability that manages the storage, maintenance, and retrieval of documents and information of a system or website. The result is often a knowledge asset represented in written words, figures, graphics, and other forms of knowledge presentation.

Examples of knowledge services that directly support content management include web-publishing tools, web conferencing, wikis, and blogs. Other examples include word processing, data and financial analysis, presentation tools, flow-charting, and content management systems (codify, organize, version control, document architectures). Of course there are also publication and distribution tools, which support the management of knowledge distribution.

Collaboration

Collaboration is the process of sharing tacit knowledge and working together to accomplish stated goals and objectives. This approach is supported by shared calendars and tasks, and threaded discussions in email. Organizations now find the use of instant messaging, incorporating electronic whiteboards and video, or teleconferencing key parts of the collaboration approach. The introduction of these tools supports a more mobile workforce. It also enables remote working and is valuable in supporting international or global organizations.

Successful transitions rely on the organization having a collaborative approach to information and knowledge. Without this approach, the necessary integration of the many aspects of a transition will be much harder to achieve.

Communities

It is now more common for groups of people spread across time zones and country boundaries to communicate, collaborate, and share knowledge using communities. These communities are typically facilitated through an online medium such as an intranet or extranet, and the community may act as the integration point for all knowledge services provided to its members.

The tools required to support this collaborative approach include community portals, focus groups and online events, and net shows. Other technologies include email alias management. There is a need to be cautious regarding intellectual property, best practice, work examples, and template repository, particularly where the community is engaging third-party organizations as part of the support structure. It is important to remember, though, that communities are a vital part of knowledge sharing in a diverse support model.

Sharing in a collaborative community is often difficult to encourage. To break down the historic view of "knowledge is power," encouragement and reward programs for sharing information may be used.

Workflow Management

Workflow management is another broad area of knowledge services. It provides systemic support for managing knowledge assets through a predefined workflow or process. Workflow applications provide the infrastructure and support necessary to implement a highly efficient process to accomplish specific types of tasks. Many knowledge assets today go through a workflow process that creates, modifies, augments, informs, or approves aspects of the asset.

Typical workflow services provided within this service category include workflow design, routing objects, event services, gatekeeping at authorization checkpoints, and state transition services.

Service management tools include workflow capability that can be configured to support these requirements, and this will be specific to the organizational needs.

Configuration Management

Many organizations have some form of configuration management in operation, but it is often maintained in individual files, in spreadsheets, or even on paper. Although this approach may be manageable on a small scale, for large and complex infrastructures, configuration management will operate more effectively when supported by a software tool that is capable of maintaining a configuration management system (CMS).

The CMS contains details about the attributes and the history of each configuration item (CI) and details of the important relationships between CIs.

It is often a federated system consisting of a number of configuration management databases (CMDB).

In an integrated system, with a number of data sources, ideally these should be connected. This includes sources such as the definitive media library (DML), and the connections between a CMDB and the DML should be captured in the CMS.

The CMS should assist in preventing changes from being made to the IT infrastructure or service configuration baseline without valid authorization via change management. Wherever possible, the authorization record should automatically drive the change. It is important that, as far as possible, all changes be recorded on the CMS at least by the time that the change is implemented. The status (e.g. live, archive, etc.) of each CI affected by a change should be updated automatically if possible. This activity and capture of information should be integrated with the main service management system or the configuration management system where the effort of integration is beneficial. It is tempting to spend time and effort integrating systems so that updates take place automatically, but careful consideration should always be given to the cost of any customization of tools. There are also implications of what will happen in the future when upgrades are needed to the systems in the integrated setup. The integration should always be justified in terms of cost and effort, which can be managed through use of the service lifecycle approach. For example, these questions should be answered: Does it benefit the organization and support the strategy? Has the design been costed and scoped to meet the requirements? Can it be transitioned successfully, and will it be beneficial and effective in operation? Will it support continual improvement and upgrade?

Design of the CMS

When designing a configuration management system, it is important to consider the functionality that will be needed by the organization, such as the ability to integrate multiple data sources, based on open standards or known interfaces and protocols. There will need to be sufficient security controls to limit access on a need-to-know basis, and support for CIs of varying complexity—for example, entire systems, releases, single hardware items, or software modules.

The CMS is all about the relationships between the CIs, and it should be simple to add or delete CIs while automatically maintaining the relationships and history of the items. The more automation there is within the tool, for version controls, data validation, and management of relationships, the more effective the system will be. Ease of use is critical for encouraging accurate updates of records and the management and use of configuration baselines. If the system does not make changes and entries easy for the operators, they are unlikely to keep the information up to date. Use of discovery tools and other automated approaches to populating the information can be very useful. Some software systems will have this as a feature; others will require integration with different tools. This feature is particularly useful when managing software CIs and version controls for patching.

There may be CIs that are not discoverable by tools, and where this is the case manual upload and maintenance will be required. It is necessary to make sure that the CMS supports the integration with other processes. As changes are made (discoverable or not), the database of CIs must be updated accurately for the data to retain its usefulness to the organization. Processes such as incident and problem management are reliant on this accuracy, as are the warranty processes (availability, capacity, security, and continuity) for planning and correct management of the IT estate.

Another extremely important factor in the design of the CMS is the output data. How will it be used, who will be using it, and how data will be captured and managed are all critical issues for the output data. As a result, the reporting capability from the CMS is very important. This should include all forms of reporting, graphical output, standard reports, hierarchy mapping, and the relationships between items to support impact analysis.

Summary

This brings us to the end of this chapter, in which we reviewed the generic requirements for ITSM technology and the evaluation criteria for selecting such tools; we also examined how to plan and implement these technologies.

We considered the relevant release, control, and validation practices for process implementation, including change management in operations, the link between service operation and project management, and the importance of assessing and managing risk in service operation. We also looked at the role of operational staff in service design and transition and the challenges, critical success factors, and risks relating to implementing service transition practices and processes.

Finally we reviewed the technology considerations for implementing specific tools applicable throughout the service transition processes and service lifecycle, including knowledge management tools, collaboration, and the configuration management system.

Exam Essentials

Understand the need to manage changes within service operation so they can be implemented with the minimum adverse impact on the service and its users. Understand the possible triggers for change and how and why changes are assessed and measured.

Explain how project management processes can help in the implementation of changes in service operation. Understand the benefits of using project management processes to implement changes in service operation and the reasons why it might be resisted.

Know the risks that change poses to operational stability. Understand how these risks might be managed.

Understand why service operation staff need to be involved in the design and transition stages. In particular, understand what the concept of a service being supportable means and what is required for this to be the case.

Understand the license options available when implementing a new service management tool. Be able to describe the different options and give examples of when each would be appropriate.

Understand the deployment options available when implementing a new service management tool. Be able to describe the different options and give examples of when each would be appropriate.

Understand the importance of technology in release, control, and validation. Technology is important throughout the lifecycle, and especially when introducing new ideas or concepts in a new service.

Be able to explain and describe the use of technology in release, control and validation. This is important not only for the service provider but also for the customers, users, and all aspects of the business.

Understand the importance of specific toolsets in service transition processes and across the lifecycle. It is important to realize the use of the transition toolsets and how they are used throughout the service lifecycle—for example, how other processes use the configuration management system.

Be able to explain and describe the use of tools relating to service transition. These are tools that are used for testing or software distribution. Know how they relate to the service transition processes such as release and deployment management.

Review Questions

You can find the answers to the review questions in the appendix.

1.   Which of these may be a trigger for changes to service operation?
   1. Changes driven by a business requirement
   2. Process or procedure improvements
   3. Enhancements to service management tools
   4. Staff changes
   5. Changes to required service levels
   6. Changes to the method of service provision
       A.   1, 2, 3, and 4 only
       B.   2, 4, and 6 only
       C.   1, 2, 4, and 6 only
       D.   All of the above

2.   True or False? Service operation personnel should be involved during service design and service transition to ensure that new components or service are correctly designed, tested, and implemented.
       A.   True
       B.   False

3.   Which of these statements is/are correct about the management of change in service operation?
   1. A project management approach is appropriate for larger infrastructure changes.
   2. Changes should be managed in accordance with ITIL best practice guidelines.
   3. Project management should be adopted for all changes.
   4. Project management disciplines are inappropriate for operational changes, which are always "business as usual."
       A.   Statement 2 only
       B.   Statements 2 and 3 only
       C.   Statements 1 and 2 only
       D.   Statements 2 and 4 only

4. Which of the following best describes when service operation staff should be involved in the design and implementation stages?

   A. Early in the design and implementation stages to ensure that the design takes account of operational issues.

   B. Transition hands over design and implementation to service operation staff during the early life support stage; service operation staff are not involved until that point.

   C. Toward the end of the design and implementation stage to ensure that the schedule for implementation does not clash with other operational priorities.

   D. Throughout the design and implementation process.

5. Which of the following is a potential risk in service operation?

   1. Known errors may be introduced into the live environment through changes.

   2. Suppliers may fail to deliver what is required, thus impacting the service being delivered.

   3. Competitors may provide the same service at a lower cost, making your service uncompetitive.

   4. There may be a security breach, causing loss of confidence in the service provider.

   A. 2 only

   B. 2 and 4 only

   C. 1, 2, and 4 only

   D. All of the above

6. Which of the following is *not* a license option for service management tools?

   A. Dedicated

   B. Time limited

   C. Shared

   D. Web based

7. Which of these statements is/are correct?

   1. Service transition is supported by enterprise-wide tools that support the broader systems and processes within which service transition delivers support.

   2. Service transition is supported by tools targeted more specifically at supporting service transition or parts of service transition.

   A. Statement 1 only

   B. Statement 2 only

   C. Both statements

   D. Neither statement

8. What is the main reason for the use of communities in organizations?

   A. Groups of people can be organized effectively.

   B. Communities ensure that teams understand their structures.

   C. Communities create a team-building experience.

   D. Groups of people spread across time zones and country boundaries can communicate, collaborate, and share knowledge.

9. Which of these are included as collaborative knowledge sharing tools?

   1. Definitive media library

   2. Shared calendars and tasks

   3. Threaded discussions

   4. Event management

   5. Video or teleconferencing

   A. 1 and 4 only

   B. 2, 3, and 5 only

   C. 1, 2, 3, and 5 only

   D. 1, 2, 3, 4, and 5

10. What is the relationship between discovery tools and the CMS?

   A. There is no relationship between discovery tools and the CMS.

   B. Discovery tools may be used to populate data in the CMS.

   C. Discovery tools are the only source of data capture for the CMS.

   D. The CMS is used to populate data in discovery tools.

Service Offerings and Agreements

PART IV

Chapter
16

Introduction to Service Offerings and Agreements

THE FOLLOWING ITIL SERVICE OFFERINGS AND AGREEMENTS EXAM OBJECTIVES ARE DISCUSSED IN THIS CHAPTER:

✓ The context in the service lifecycle of the SOA processes from the service strategy stage (service portfolio management, demand management, financial management for IT services and business relationship management) and the reliance of these processes on the existence of a strategy

✓ The purpose, objectives, scope, and value to business of the strategy management for IT services process

✓ The context in the service lifecycle of the SOA processes from the service design stage (service catalog management, service level management, supplier management)

✓ The purpose, objectives, scope, and value to business of the design coordination process

✓ How successful services depend on the customer's perception of utility and warranty and the relevance to the SOA processes

✓ Understanding how the SOA processes are the starting point for understanding and identifying customer requirements

✓ Return on investment (ROI) and the business case and the relevance to the SOA processes

Service offerings and agreements (SOAs) collect together a number of relevant practices from the core guidance related to the creation and management of service offerings and the agreements required to support them. The exam objectives for the SOA intermediate certificate considers SOA processes from the service strategy stage, including service portfolio management, demand management, financial management, and business relationship management, with an overview of the strategy management for IT services process, and from the service design stage, including service catalog management, service level management, and supplier management. It also includes an overview of the design coordination process. This introductory chapter of the SOA section also considers how understanding the customer's perception of utility and warranty is essential if services are to be successful and the relevance of this understanding to the SOA processes. We examine how the SOA processes are the starting point for understanding and identifying customer requirements. We also consider return on investment (ROI) and the business case.

The SOA Processes from Strategy and Design and Their Context in the Service Lifecycle

Service offerings and agreements need to be considered within the context of the service lifecycle—the major relationship is with the service strategy and service design stages. You should be familiar with the concept of the service lifecycle, as shown in Figure 16.1. Each stage addresses a particular set of challenges that need to be addressed for successful service management, and each stage has an impact on all of the others.

Let's now examine the service strategy and service design lifecycle stages and their SOA processes.

Service Strategy

Service strategy is at the core of the service lifecycle. It is the role of strategy to understand the organizational objectives and customer needs. People, processes, and products should support the strategy. ITIL service strategy asks why something is to be done before thinking of how. It helps service providers to set objectives; set expectations of performance serving customers and markets; and identify, select, and prioritize opportunities. Service strategy ensures that providers understand and can handle the costs and risks associated with their service portfolios.

FIGURE 16.1   The ITIL service lifecycle

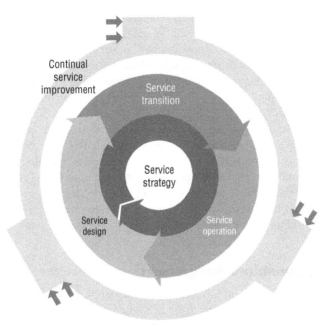

The service strategy processes that we consider as SOA processes include service portfolio management (covered in Chapter 17, "Service Portfolio Management and Service Catalog Management") as well as financial management for IT services and business relationship management, both covered in Chapter 19, "Business Relationship Management and Financial Management for IT." We have already considered demand management in depth in Chapter 9, "IT Service Continuity Management and Demand Management," as part of planning, protection, and optimization. We will be looking at these in more detail in other chapters, so let's summarize them briefly here. In addition to these processes, the strategy management for IT services is considered in more depth later in this chapter.

Service Portfolio Management

This process is intended to ensure that the appropriate mix of services is delivered by the service provider to meet the requirements of the customer. It enables important items of information about services to be tracked, including the investment that has been made and the interaction with other services. It links the services being provided to the business outcomes they support and helps decide which services should be provided, based on an analysis of the potential return that could be generated and acceptable levels of risk. The major output of this service is the service portfolio, which is the definitive list of services, showing the pipeline of planned services, the catalog of current services, and those that have been retired.

Financial Management for IT Services

Organizations have to be able manage their finances—to manage resources and ensure that their objectives are being achieved. Financial management processes and controls will apply across an entire organization. The IT service provider may have a separate process for IT financial management, but this process should follow the overall organizational principles and requirements. The purpose of financial management for IT services is to secure an appropriate level of funding for the design, development, and delivery of the IT services that meet the organizational requirement. At the same time, the process should act as a gatekeeper for the expenditure on IT services and ensure that the service provider is not overextended financially for the services it is required to deliver.

Cost and quality are key factors in the provision of services, and the only way we can allocate and understand the cost of service provision is through sound financial practices. The objectives of the financial management process include identifying, managing, and communicating the actual cost of service delivery and understanding and evaluating the financial impact and implications of any new or changed organizational strategies on the service provider.

Business Relationship Management

Business relationship management has matured from merely providing a named contact within the IT service provider's organization to a role that provides a connection between organizational executives and the strategic management of the service provider. The process has a very important part to play in the alignment of the IT service provider and the customer. The process establishes a relationship between the service provider and the customer and maintains this by a continued review of business and customer needs. This relationship is extremely important for building a business rapport between service provider and customer. It helps to identify customer needs and ensures that the service provider can meet those needs, both now and in the future. Business relationship management is the process that ensures that the service provider is able to understand the changing needs of the business over time and manages the customer's expectations of the services being provided.

Demand Management

Demand management is the process that seeks to understand, anticipate, and influence customer demand for services and the provision of capacity to meet these demands. It is a critical aspect of service management. Poorly managed demand is a source of risk for service providers because of uncertainty in demand. Excess capacity generates cost without creating value.

The purpose of demand management is to understand, anticipate, and influence customer demand for services and to work with capacity management to ensure that the service provider has capacity to meet this demand. Demand seeks to anticipate and prevent or manage situations where demand for a service exceeds the capacity to deliver it, because having insufficient resources affects the achievement of the business objectives. Demand management works at every stage of the lifecycle to ensure that services are designed, tested, and delivered to support the achievement of business outcomes at the appropriate levels of activity. It aims to gear the utilization of resources that deliver services to meet the fluctuating levels of demand for those services.

An Overview of the Strategy Management for IT Services Process

Let's now look in more detail at the remaining strategy SOA process, the strategy management for IT services process. We will consider the purpose, objectives, scope, and value to business of this process.

We start by looking at the definition of this process. Strategy management for IT services is the process of deciding what services are to be offered and how these services will be managed. It is an important process, because it ensures that the service provider defines a strategy and then takes action to ensure that it achieves its purpose. Without this process, a service provider may just "drift" without a clear direction, offering services without evaluating whether they are appropriate, missing opportunities, and so forth.

Purpose

The purpose of a service strategy is to devise and describe how a service provider enables an organization to achieve its business outcomes; it describes how to decide which services to offer and how these services should be managed. Strategy management for IT services ensures that there is such a strategy, and defines, maintains, and periodically evaluates the strategy to ensure that it is achieving its purpose.

Objectives

The objectives of service strategy management include the following:

- To consider the environments (both internal and external) in which the service provider operates. The aim is to identify opportunities that could be of benefit to the organization.

- To identify any constraints that would affect the ability of the business to achieve its desired outcomes or hamper the delivery or management of services, and to identify how those constraints could be removed or their effects reduced.

- To define and agree on the perspective of the service provider and to ensure that it remains relevant so that a clear statement of the vision and mission of the service provider can be defined.

- To understand the position of the service provider relative to its customers and other service providers, enabling the definition of the services to be delivered to each of the market spaces. The service provider will also understand how to maintain a competitive advantage over other providers.

- The final objectives cover the strategic plans. A library of critical documents should be produced, maintained, and distributed to relevant stakeholders. These should include the IT strategy document, the service management strategy document, and strategy plans for each service.

It is essential that these strategic plans be translated into practical tactical and operational guidance for the relevant department or group responsible for delivery. As with all key documents, processes should be in place to ensure that the documents are updated as circumstances change.

Scope

Now let's consider the scope of service strategy management. Strategy management for an organization is the responsibility of the executives who set the objectives of the organization and prioritize the necessary investments to enable these objectives to be met. Large organizations will have a dedicated strategy and planning manager reporting directly into the board of directors responsible for the assessments, the strategy documents, and the execution of the strategy.

It is important to realize that an organization's strategy is not limited to a single document but is more likely to be broken down into a strategy for each unit of the business. You can see an example of how a business strategy might be broken down into strategies for IT and for manufacturing in Figure 16.2. The achievement of each of these enables the overall strategy to be met.

Strategy management for IT services has to ensure that the services and the way they are managed support the overall enterprise strategy.

FIGURE 16.2   Overall business strategy and the strategies of business units

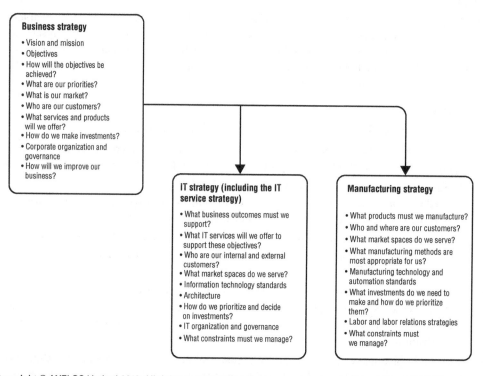

Strategy management can be a generic process that could be applied to the business as a whole or to any of the business units. However, ITIL is specifically concerned with how this process is applied to IT as a service provider. You should note that in an external service provider, the business strategy might be related to IT services delivered to an external customer, and the IT strategy would be related to how those services will be delivered and supported. At the same time, external service providers do not just provide IT services to customers. They are also consumers of their own (and potentially other third-party) IT services. External service providers also have internal IT service requirements that must be met to enable them to survive.

Service Strategy

A service strategy is a subset of the overall strategy for the organization. In the case of an IT organization, the IT strategy will encompass the IT service strategy.

The scope of strategy management in ITIL is shown in Figure 16.3. We can see how a business strategy is used to develop a set of tactics—a set of detailed approaches, processes, and techniques to be used to achieve the strategic objectives—and operations—the specific procedures, technologies, and activities that will be executed by individuals and teams.

FIGURE 16.3 The scope of strategy management

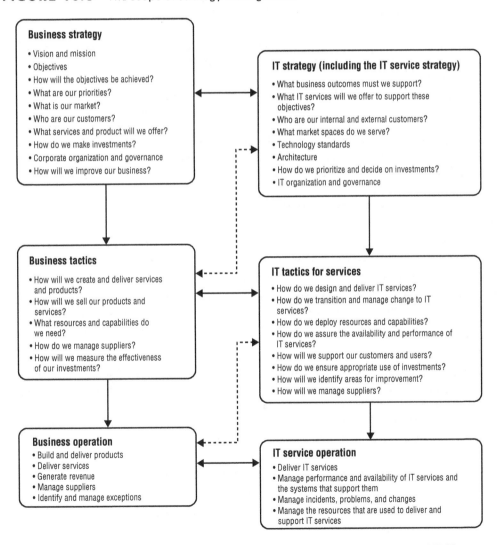

The IT strategy (and therefore also the strategy for IT services) is based on the requirements of the business strategy. The IT strategy can determine whether a strategic objective is technologically possible and the level of investment required so that the business has the information on which to base a decision as to whether the objective should be included and at what priority.

IT tactics are influenced by both IT strategy and the business tactics. If a business tactic requires compliance with a regulation, IT will have to ensure that the IT tactics make this possible, and identify the level of investment required to overcome this if they don't.

IT operations are derived from the IT tactics but also by the requirements of business operations. The way in which the different operational environments are coordinated and how they interact is important to strategy management for IT services.

The dotted line in Figure 16.3 shows the relationship between IT strategy and business tactics. IT must not define a strategy that clashes with the business tactics. The business tactics regarding the use of IT must be compatible with the IT strategy. The business tactics should not make a tactical decision about how IT services are going to be used if the IT strategy does not allow for that type of usage. Similarly, IT tactics need to be valid for business operation.

Strategy management for IT services is intended for managing the strategy of a service provider. It will include a specification of the type of services it will deliver, the customers of those services, and the overall business outcomes to be achieved when the service provider executes the strategy. The IT service strategy is a subset of the IT strategy that, in addition to the IT service strategy, includes strategies for IT architecture, portfolio management (other than services), application management, infrastructure management, project management, technological direction, and so forth.

Remember, a service strategy is not the same as an ITSM strategy, which is really a tactical plan.

- A service strategy is the strategy followed by the service provider to define and execute services that meet a customer's business objectives. For an IT service provider, the service strategy is a subset of the IT strategy.

- A service management (ITSM) strategy is the plan for identifying, implementing, and executing the processes used to manage services identified in a service strategy. In an IT service provider, the ITSM strategy will be a subset of the service strategy.

Value

A well-defined and managed strategy delivers value by ensuring that all stakeholders agree on the objectives and means, resources and capabilities are aligned to achieving business outcomes, and investments match the intended development and growth. As a result, service providers provide the best balance of services, each with a clear business purpose.

Strategy management for IT services encourages appropriate levels of investment, resulting in the following:

- Cost savings; investments and expenditure are matched to achievement of validated business objectives, rather than unsubstantiated demands

- Increased levels of investment for key projects or service improvements

- Shifting investment priorities

Without a strategy there is a real danger that whoever shouts loudest gets to decide what happens, and services (and expenditure) are matched to unproven demand.

Sometimes, what the customer is asking for requires a departure from the service provider's strategy. An external service provider needs to decide whether to change their strategy or to turn down the business. An internal provider does not usually have the second option, and in these cases strategy management for IT services will enable them to work with the business units to make them aware of the impact of their demand on the current strategy. In some cases, customer demands do not change the overall strategy, but they may involve a change in priorities.

Service Design

Service design, which is particularly relevant to service offerings and agreements, turns strategic ideas into deliverables. The design must always consider the strategy, to ensure that services are designed with the business objectives in mind. Design considers the whole IT organization, and how it will deliver and support the services, turning the service strategy into a plan for delivering the business objectives. Remember: Design includes changes to existing services.

The service design processes that we consider as service offerings and agreements processes include service catalog management (covered in Chapter 17, "Service Portfolio Management and Service Catalog Management") and service level management and supplier management, covered in Chapter 18, "Service Level Management and Supplier Management." We will look at these in more detail in other chapters, so let's summarize them briefly here.

In addition to these processes, the design coordination process is considered in a little more depth later in this chapter. The complete list of service design processes includes those that address the warranty aspects of a service. These include availability management, capacity management, and information security management, which are covered in Chapter 8, "Capacity, Availability, and Information Security Management," and IT service continuity management, covered in Chapter 9, as part of planning, protection, and optimization.

Through these processes, design ensures that both the utility and the warranty of the new or changed service is considered in design, covering the continuity of the service, its achievement of the agreed capacity and availability service levels, and its conformance to security standards and regulations.

Service Catalog Management

A *service catalog* is defined in the ITIL glossary as follows:

> A database or structured document with information about all live IT services, including those available for deployment. The service catalog is part of the service portfolio and contains information about two types of IT service: customer-facing services that are visible to the business and supporting services required by the service provider to deliver customer-facing services.

The catalog gathers the service information and presents it in a form that is easy for the business to understand. The catalog contains details of services that are available to the business; in this way, it differs from the other components of the service portfolio (the service pipeline and retired services). Gathering and maintaining that information is the job of service catalog management. The service catalog should be easily available to those who are authorized to access it. The view of the information may vary dependent on the audience—for example, technical support staff need a different perspective on the services than the users.

The process manages the information contained within the service catalog, ensuring that the service catalog is accurate and reflects the current details, status, interfaces, and dependencies of all services that are being run, or being prepared to run, in the live environment.

Service Level Management

ITIL states that the purpose of service level management is to ensure that all current and planned IT services are delivered to agreed achievable targets. Service level management is concerned primarily with the warranty aspects of the service. The response time, capacity, availability, and so on of the new service will be the subject of the SLA.

Service level management is concerned with defining the services, documenting them in an agreement, and then ensuring that the targets are measured and met, identifying where necessary why targets have not been met and wherever possible improving the level of service delivered. These improvements will often be carried out as part of continual service improvement. The process requires a constant cycle of negotiating, agreeing, monitoring, and reporting on and reviewing IT service targets and achievements.

Supplier Management

ITIL defines *supplier management* as the process responsible for obtaining value for money from suppliers, ensuring that all contracts and agreements with suppliers support the needs of the business and that all suppliers meet their contractual commitments.

The supplier management process describes best practices in managing suppliers to ensure that the services they provide meet expectations. The purpose of supplier management is to ensure that suppliers provide value for money. By managing suppliers, the service provider can ensure the best delivery of service to their customer. Managing suppliers ensures that the necessary contracts are in place and enforced. It is important that this aspect is considered while the service is being designed.

An Overview of the Design Coordination Process

Let's now look in more detail at the remaining design SOA process, the design coordination process. We will consider the purpose, objectives, scope, and value to business of this process.

Service design involves many different aspects beyond designing a new application to provide new functionality (utility). Consideration must be given to how the service will operate, both now and in the future; what level of availability, security, continuity, and capacity will need to be provided; and the best approach to this (warranty). Other processes will interface with the service design processes. To ensure a successful outcome, the design activities must be coordinated.

Purpose

The purpose of the *design coordination* process is to carry out the coordination of the many different activities of service design. The many processes and numerous interfaces involved are all potential sources of conflict. By providing a single point, complications and misunderstandings should be avoided.

Objectives

The objectives of design coordination are to ensure that a consistent approach is applied to design across all five aspects of service design. Design is a complex lifecycle stage. Coordination of the design activities is a key objective, since the activities will spread across projects, teams, and suppliers, as well as across the many conflicting demands that need to be managed. This will include time, money, and resources related to day-to-day operational activities.

To make sure the design processes are effective, coordination of the resources and capabilities in use by each process must exist. A common challenge is that there may be overlapping requirements for the same resources, and this is why it is important to have this coordination capability in place. This is a higher-level or strategic objective—for example, in the longer term what skills and how many designers do we need? Design coordination should not be about the individual resource management for specific processes.

The design coordination process is responsible for ensuring the elements of the service design package (SDP) are collated, and the SDP is delivered.

 Remember that the SDP is the "blueprint" for the new or changed service that will capture the requirements and plans for the rest of the lifecycle.

This means that the process is also responsible for managing the interfaces between the service lifecycle stages, ensuring the quality of the inputs and outputs. Design coordination should ensure conformance of designs to policies, architectures, and regulatory, legal, security, and other governance requirements.

Scope

The scope of the design coordination process includes all design activity, particularly all new or changed service solutions that are being designed for transition into (or out of, in the case of a service retirement) the live environment.

The extent of design coordination required will vary, and should only be used when it is required. Some design efforts will be part of a project, whereas others will be managed through the change process alone without a formally defined project. Some design efforts will be extensive and complex whereas others will be simple and swift.

Each organization will need to define the criteria that will be used to determine the level of rigor or attention to be applied in design coordination for each design.

When we consider the further scope of the design coordination process, it should include assisting and supporting each project or other significant or major change. The process will also be responsible for maintaining policies, guidelines, standards, budgets, models, resources, and capabilities for all service design processes and activities. At a strategic level, design coordination will be responsible for the coordinating, prioritizing, and scheduling of service design resources to satisfy conflicting demands from all projects and changes. This is a major challenge for most organizations. It will involve planning and forecasting the resources needed for the future demand for service design activities.

As the process is responsible for ensuring the output from the design lifecycle stage, it will be engaged in reviewing, measuring, and improving the performance of all service design activities and processes. This will also ensure that all requirements are appropriately addressed in service designs, particularly utility and warranty requirements. The final activity for the service design coordination process is ensuring the production of service designs and/or SDPs and their handover to service transition.

It is important to remember that the design coordination process does not include the following:

- Responsibility for any activities or processes outside the design stage of the service lifecycle

- Responsibility for designing the detailed service solutions themselves or the production of the individual parts of the SDPs. These are the responsibility of the individual projects or service management processes that will capture the requirements and plans for the rest of the lifecycle.

Value

The main value of the design coordination process to the business is the production of a set of consistent quality solution designs and service design packages that will provide the desired business outcomes.

Design coordination will improve each of these:

- Achievement of the intended business value of services through ensuring that design takes place within acceptable risk and cost levels

- Minimize the rework and unplanned labor costs associated with reworking design issues during later service lifecycle stages

- Support the achievement of higher customer and user satisfaction and improved confidence in IT and in the services received

- Ensure that all services conform to a consistent architecture, allowing integration and data exchange between services and systems

- Provide improved focus on service value as well as business and customer outcomes

- Develop improved efficiency and effectiveness of all service design activities and processes, supporting higher volumes of successful change delivered in a timely and cost-effective manner

- Achievement of greater agility and better quality in the design of service solutions, within projects and major changes

Utility and Warranty and the Relevance to the SOA Processes

Next, we are going to consider what makes a service valuable in the eyes of the customer and the need for a service provider to adopt a marketing mindset. We'll also look at the concepts of utility and warranty.

Value

The value of a service depends on how well it meets a customer's expectations and what it enables them to do, so its value is determined by the customer using it. The key characteristics of value are as follows:

Value That Is Defined by Customers   Value is not about the cost of provision; a service may be cheap to provide but highly valued by the customer, or the opposite may be true.

Affordable Mix of Features   The customer will always judge the value of a service based on the best mix of features at the price they are willing to pay.

Achievement of Objectives   Services are often judged by the financial return they provide, but many services have other objectives, and their value comes from how well these are achieved. For example, health services will focus on successful outcomes to treatment; the police might focus on reduction in crime. Without an understanding of what the customer objectives are, it is difficult to provide services they will regard as valuable.

Value That Changes with Time and Circumstances   What a customer wants today is different from what they wanted two years ago. For example, just a few years ago, most people just wanted to be able to connect to the Internet from their phone; now they demand high bandwidth so they can stream sports or television. Many retail organizations have failed in recent years because they continued to provide what their customers had valued before and did not adjust to offer what customers want now.

Calculating value can sometimes be a straightforward financial calculation: does the service achieve what is required for an appropriate cost? If the cost does not affect profitability and the price remains competitive, then the service will be valuable. However, to attribute value, the service provider needs to understand three specific inputs:

- What services were provided?
- What did the services achieve?
- What was their cost, or the price that was paid?

The answer to these questions will enable the service provider to demonstrate value to the customer. But the service provider will always be subject to the customer's perception of value.

If we consider value from the perspective of the customer, then three factors make up the understanding of value, as shown in Figure 16.4. As you can see, value is defined in terms of the business outcomes achieved as well as the customer preferences and perception of what was delivered.

FIGURE 16.4   Components of value

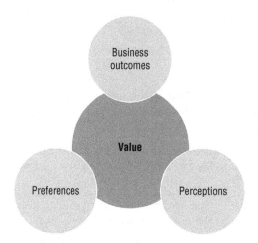

Customers' perceptions are influenced by the attributes of the service, the present or prior experiences of the customer, and the image or market position of the organization. Preferences and perceptions are the basis for selecting one service provider over another, and often, the more intangible the value, the more important the definitions and differentiation of value becomes. This is shown in Figure 16.5, which is based on research completed by Nagle and Holden in 2002. Nagle, T.N. and Holden, R.K., *Strategy and Tactics of Pricing: A Guide to Profitable Decision Making, 3rd edition* (Prentice-Hall, 2002).

Customers perceive value on the understanding that there will be a value on which a customer will base their judgment. This is known as the *reference value*. The reference value is the perception discussed previously, based on present or prior experience. The gains made from utilizing the service are perceived as a positive difference, an addition to the reference value. In an ideal situation, this would form the perception of value for the customer. But utilizing the service is not always perceived as a positive experience. An outage will create a negative difference, which detracts from the existing positive perception. This is shown as the *net difference*.

So in the final analysis, the perception of the economic value of a service will be the original reference value and the net difference. Any negative perception may have a significant impact on the overall perception of the service.

FIGURE 16.5   How customers perceive value

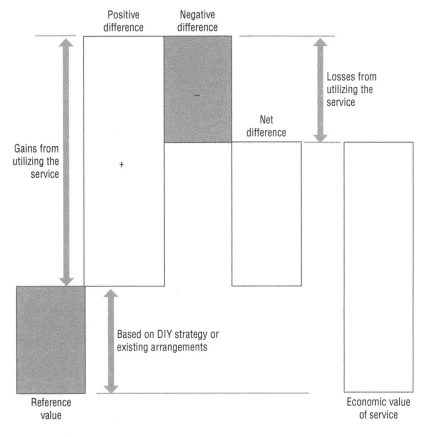

Marketing Mindset

When developing the strategy for an IT service provider, it is useful to have a marketing mindset. This goes further than advertising services to influence customer perception and also includes understanding the customer's context and requirements and ensuring that services are geared to meet the outcomes that are important to the customer. Rather than a focus on the production of services, there is a need to look from the outside in, from the customer's perspective.

A marketing mindset begins with these simple questions:

- What is our business?
- Who is our customer?
- What does the customer value?

- Who depends on our services?

- How do they use our services?

- Why are they valuable to them?

A marketing mindset enables the service provider to understand the components of value from the customer's perspective.

Utility and Warranty

As we discussed earlier, when considering the value of services, the service provider should be concerned with delivering business outcomes and achieving business objectives. Value is created by delivering the two primary elements of a service: *utility* (fit for purpose) and *warranty* (fit for use). These work together to deliver the desired outcomes that allow customers to assess value.

Utility is the functionality offered by a product or a service to meet a specific customer need. Often summarized as "what the service does," this shows if the service is able to meet the required outcomes. This is also commonly known as "fit for purpose." This aspect of service value refers to tasks associated to achieving outcomes.

Warranty provides the assurance that a product or service will meet the agreed-on requirements. This may be captured as part of a formal agreement, such as a service level agreement or contract. It refers to the ability of the service to be available when needed, have sufficient capacity to meet the requirements, and be reliable in terms of both security and continuity. This is often summarized as "how the service is delivered" and is commonly referred to as "fit for use."

Utility is what the service does, and warranty is how it is delivered, as you can see in Figure 16.6. Utility will improve the performance of the tasks used to achieve an outcome or remove constraints that prevent the task from being performed adequately (or both). Warranty ensures the service is available, continuous, and secure and has sufficient capacity so that it can perform at the required level. If the service is both fit for purpose and fit for use, it will create value.

Customers cannot benefit from something that is fit for purpose but not fit for use, and vice versa. Value is only achieved when the required levels of both utility and warranty are delivered. If the focus is on utility only, customers may choose a cheaper option, which will fail to deliver value since it does not deliver the required availability. It is important to realize that increasing utility may not deliver the warranty required without planning and increased investment.

The effect of improving warranty of a service means that the service will continue to do the same things but more reliably. Therefore, a higher probability exists that the desired outcomes will be achieved, along with a decreased risk that the customer will suffer losses due to variations in service performance. However, if the emphasis is too much on warranty, the service may be reliable but fail to deliver the required functionality.

FIGURE 16.6   Services are designed, built, and delivered with both utility and warranty.

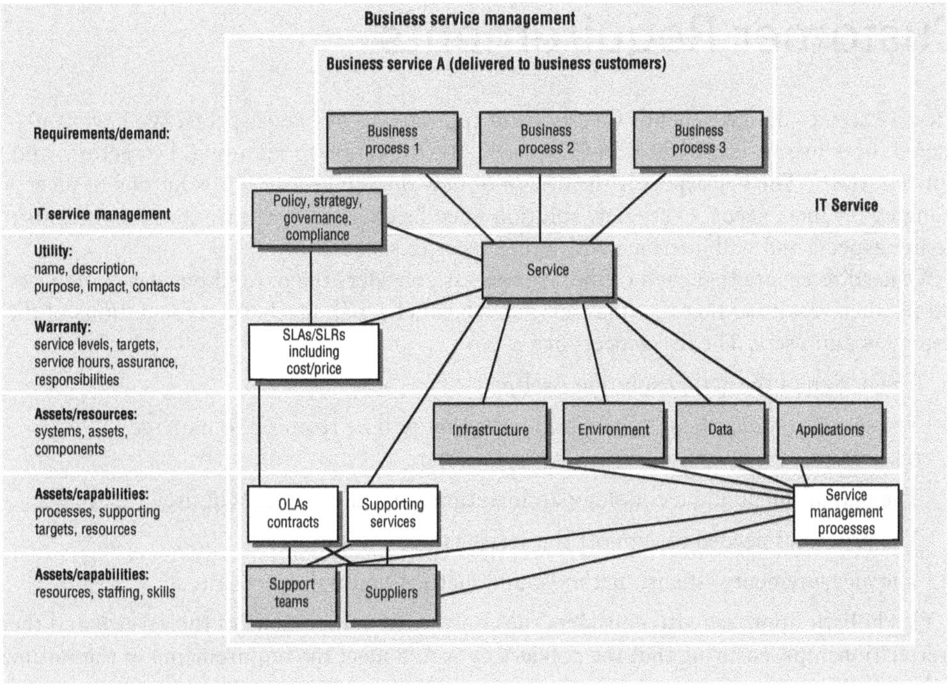

Utility and Warranty Definitions

Utility covers:

- What does the service do?

- The features, inputs, outputs ... is it "fit for purpose"?

- This leads to functional requirements.

Warranty covers:

- How well does the service do it?

- Capacity, performance, availability...is it "fit for use"?

- This leads to nonfunctional requirements.

Understanding and Identifying Customer Requirements

Effective service design depends on a holistic approach to five key aspects. We have considered these five aspects before, in Chapter 7, "Introduction to Planning, Protection, and Optimization." The key aspect is the design of new or changed service solutions to meet changing business needs. Every new solution must be checked to ensure that it conforms to the five aspects and will interface with other services successfully.

We need to ensure that each of the five aspects considers the desired business outcomes and planned results so that the final service, when delivered, meets the expectations of the customers and users. The five aspects are

- The design of the actual solution itself
- The service management system and tools that will be required to manage the service
- The management and technology architectures that the service will use
- The processes needed to support the service in operation
- The measurement systems, methods, and metrics that will be required

This holistic approach also considers the constituent components of the service and their interrelationships, ensuring that the services delivered meet the requirements of the business in the following areas:

- The scalability of the service to meet future requirements
- The business processes and business units supported by the service
- The agreed business requirements for functionality (i.e., utility)
- The service itself and its service level requirements or SLA (addressing warranty)
- The technology components used, including the infrastructure, the environment, the data, and the applications
- The supporting services and components and their associated operational level agreements, if internally supported, or underpinning contracts, if supported by external third parties
- The performance measurements and metrics required
- The required security levels
- Sustainability requirements

The relationships and dependencies between these elements are illustrated in Figure 16.7.

FIGURE 16.7 The service relationships and dependencies

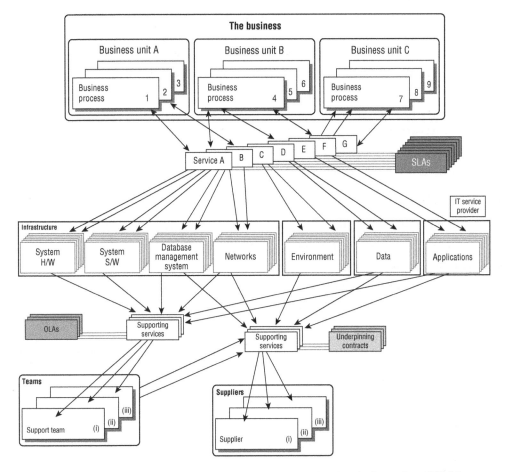

Business Requirements and Drivers

Business drivers are the people, information, and tasks that support the fulfillment of business objectives. The IT service provider must understand business requirements and drivers in order to make sure that it offers appropriate services with an acceptable level of service quality that is aligned to business needs. The business relationship management process, covered in Chapter 19, can be helpful in ensuring that the service provider understands the operational, tactical, and strategic requirements of the business. Business information in three main areas is required to maintain service alignment: the requirements for existing, new, and retiring services.

Existing Services

Examples of information required concerning changes to existing services could include the following:

- New facilities/features and functionality requirements (utility)
- Changes in business processes, dependencies, priorities, criticality, and impact
- Changes in volumes of service transactions
- Increased service levels and service level targets due to new business drivers, or reduced for old services, lowering priority for those due for replacement (warranty)
- Business justification, including the financial and strategic aspects
- Requirements for additional service management information

New Services

Examples of information required for new services could include the following:

- Facilities/features and functionality required (utility)
- Management information required and management needs
- Business processes supported, dependencies, priorities, criticality, and impact
- Business cycles and seasonal variations
- SLRs and service level targets (warranty)
- Business transaction levels, service transaction levels, numbers and types of users, and anticipated future growth
- Business justification, including the financial and strategic aspects
- Predicted level of change—for example, known future business requirements or enhancements
- Level of business capability or support to be provided—for example, local business-based support

Retiring Services

Examples of information required for retiring services could include the following:

- Exact scope of retirement: what facilities/features and functionality are to be retired
- Business justification, including financial and strategic aspects
- What, if anything, will replace the retiring service
- Interfaces and dependencies with other services, components, or configurations
- Disposal and/or reuse requirements for the service assets and configuration items associated with the retiring service
- Business requirements related to the retirement strategy and plan, such as timing of the retirement and the retirement approach to be used (i.e., phased retirement)
- Archiving strategy for any business data and any potential access requirements for archived data related to the retiring service

This information must be accurate and complete, and agreed to and signed off with senior business representatives. Incorrect information will lead to services being delivered that do not match the needs of the business. As requirements change over time, these changes must also be captured while guarding against "scope creep." The information should include the identification of all stakeholders; the prioritization, agreement, and documentation of requirements; outline budgets; and business benefits. Agreement should be reached with the business regarding the balance between the service achievable and cost.

Return on Investment and the Business Case

The final topic of this introductory chapter covers ROI (return on investment) and the business case.

Return on Investment

Return on investment (ROI) is a recognized concept for quantifying the value of an investment. This calculation is normally performed by financial management. The term is not always used consistently and is sometimes used to calculate business performance. In service management, ROI is used as a measure of the ability to use assets to generate additional value.

In the simplest sense, it is the increase in profit resulting from the service divided by the total investment in the service. However, this calculation is overly simplistic—a number of subjective factors need to be considered in service management value for a customer. A project may be intended to deliver qualitative rather than quantitative benefits. Changing the company logo or improving the usability, look, and feel of an organization's website, for example, may result indirectly in increased sales or improved levels of customer loyalty, but this is not a straightforward calculation.

To cover this subjectivity, ITIL covers three main areas in ROI:

- The business case, which is a means to identify business imperatives that depend on service management; we examine this in more detail later.

- Pre-program ROI, which includes techniques for quantitatively analyzing an investment in service management.

- Post-program ROI, which includes techniques for retroactively analyzing an investment in service management.

The dynamics of service economics and the calculation of ROI for external service providers are different from those for internal service providers.

Figure 16.8 illustrates how the external IT service provider supplies a service to an external customer for payment. The service provider measures the total revenue obtained from delivering the service compared to the total investment required to deliver that service.

FIGURE 16.8   Service economic dynamics for external service providers

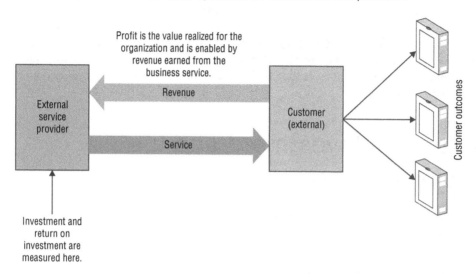

For internal service providers, the investment in the IT service is carried by the business unit and not the service provider. This means that the funding provided to the IT service provider cannot be viewed as a return on investment, because the investment is being made by the business unit. The return has to be calculated based on the profitability generated by the business unit, and the ROI calculation is carried out by the business unit. Figure 16.9 illustrates how the internal IT service provider delivers a service to another business unit, which covers the costs of the IT service.

FIGURE 16.9   Service economic dynamics for internal service providers

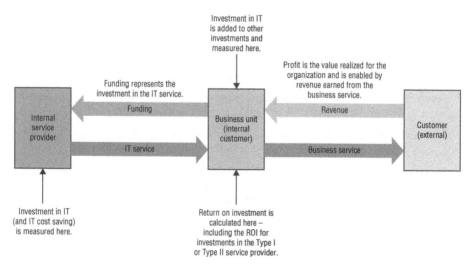

Business Case

A business case is a decision support and planning tool that projects the likely consequences of a business action. The outcome may be assessed on both qualitative and quantitative criteria. A financial analysis is often central to a good business case. Table 16.1 shows a sample business case structure.

TABLE 16.1   Sample business case structure

Heading	Description
A. Introduction	Presents the business objectives addressed by the service.
B. Methods and assumptions	Defines the boundaries of the business case, such as time period, and which organizational context is being used to define costs and benefits.
C. Business impacts	The financial and nonfinancial results anticipated for the service or service management initiative. Please bear in mind that many nonfinancial results can also be expressed in financial terms. For example, an increase in staff morale can result in lower staff turnover, and therefore less expenditure on hiring and training.
D. Risks and contingencies	The probability that alternative results will emerge.
E. Recommendations	Specific actions recommended.

Business objectives are an important part of the business case and will be the justification for the request for funding. There is a difference between the business objectives of a profit and a nonprofit organization. This difference must be part of the consideration of any service provider when constructing a business case.

Business impact is another essential part of the business case, but this is often only based on cost analysis. If there is a nonfinancial business impact, it should be linked to a business objective to provide a value. This often includes expressing nonfinancial results in financial terms, such as translating staff improvements as a reduction in expenditure on training and hiring.

A minimum sample business case structure includes an introduction, presenting the business objectives to be addressed, followed by the methods and assumptions that have been used. This defines the boundaries of the business case, such as the time period and how benefits and costs are being calculated. Risks and contingencies will be important for the decision-making process and must be included in the business case. The final section should cover the recommendations and specific actions.

The term *business case* may imply that only financial aspects of the service or project are included. This is not the case. Financial and nonfinancial impacts of the proposed project or service should be included.

Summary

This chapter introduced service offerings and agreements. It considered the creation and management of service offerings and the agreements required to support them. It introduced relevant processes from service strategy and design, which are covered in more detail in later chapters. We also considered strategy management for IT services and design coordination. We looked at factors when identifying customer requirements and the basic concepts of return on investment and the business case.

Exam Essentials

Understand the importance of a service strategy.   Without a specific strategy to guide the approach to IT, there is serious risk of mismanagement or not providing what the customer requires.

Understand how good design delivers financial and other benefits to the business.   By ensuring that the design fits the business requirement and is adaptable to changing requirements, the need to completely redesign the service is avoided, thus minimizing the total cost of ownership.

Explain service value in the context of the organization.   Recall and explain the use of the terms *utility* and *warranty* in the development of a strategy.

Know the purpose and objectives of design coordination.   It is important for you to be able to explain the purpose and objectives of the design coordination process. The process is there to ensure that the five aspects of design are carried out successfully, and that a service design package is created and published.

Understand that services must be designed to be adaptable to future requirements.   The service should be easily expanded or developed so that it can be easily expanded or developed to meet changing requirements.

Be able to list and explain the five aspects of service design.   Be able to name and describe the five aspects of service design (the solution, management systems, architectures, processes, and metrics) and why they are important.

Review Questions

You can find the answers to the review questions in the appendix.

1. Which of the following service design processes is *not* discussed in relation to service offerings and agreements?
    A. Service level management
    B. Capacity management
    C. Supplier management
    D. Service catalog management

2. What is the purpose of the design coordination process?
    A. Manage the service level management process
    B. Manage the service transition lifecycle stage
    C. Ensure the production of the service design package
    D. Ensure that the strategy is managed throughout the lifecycle

3. Which of the following goals of design coordination responsibilities is incorrect?
    A. To ensure that the goals and objectives of the design stage are met
    B. To design the solution
    C. To provide a single coordination point
    D. To ensure that the design meets the requirements

4. Which of the following is *not* a purpose of strategy management for IT services?
    A. Articulate how a service provider will enable an organization to achieve its business outcomes
    B. Ensure that the service provider is not overextended and so does not commit to services that they are not able to provide
    C. Establish how to decide which services will be best suited to meet the business outcomes
    D. Identify the most effective and efficient way to manage the services

5. Which of the following lists show the aspects of warranty defined in the ITIL guidance?
    A. Integration, capacity, consistency, and continuity
    B. Cost-effectiveness, integration, availability, security
    C. Security, capacity, availability, and consistency
    D. Security, capacity, availability, and continuity

6. True or False? Utility means fit for purpose, and warranty means fit for use.
    A. True
    B. False

7.   Which of these elements constitute the minimum requirements in a business case?

1. Introduction

2. Measurements

3. Methods and assumptions

4. Service targets

5. Business impacts

6. Availability requirements

7. Risks and contingencies

8. Geographic locations

9. Recommendations

    A.   1, 2, 5, 7, 9

    B.   1, 3, 5, 7, 9

    C.   1, 2, 3, 4, 9

    D.   1, 3, 4, 5, 9

8.   What is meant by "holistic" service design?

    A.   The design can be implemented without the users being affected.

    B.   The design has taken into account all five aspects of design.

    C.   The design is balanced between functionality, resources, and the required schedule.

    D.   The design has been costed to show the total cost of ownership.

9.   True or False? Design coordination is responsible for the management of the service operation processes that have design responsibilities.

    A.   True

    B.   False

10.   Which of the following statements about return on investment is false?

    A.   ROI is used as a measure of the ability to use assets to generate additional value.

    B.   ROI is often calculated as the increase in profit resulting from the service divided by the total investment in the service.

    C.   For internal service providers, ROI is calculated based on the profitability generated by the business unit, not the IT department.

    D.   ROI may be an objective or subjective measure.

Chapter

17

Service Portfolio Management and Service Catalog Management

THE FOLLOWING ITIL SERVICE OFFERINGS AND AGREEMENTS EXAM OBJECTIVES ARE DISCUSSED IN THIS CHAPTER:

✓ Service portfolio management and service catalog management

✓ Each process is discussed in terms of

- Purpose
- Objectives
- Scope
- Value
- Policies
- Principles and basic concepts
- Process activities, methods, and techniques
- Triggers, inputs, outputs, and interfaces
- Information management
- Roles and responsibilities
- Critical success factors and key performance indicators
- Challenges
- Risks

This chapter covers the day-to-day operation of each process; the detail of its activities, methods, and techniques; and its information management. Service portfolio management ensures that we have the appropriate mix of services delivered by the service provider to meet the requirements of the customer. Service catalog management manages the production of the service catalog, which is used to display to customers the live operational services, and those about to go live.

Understanding Service Portfolio Management

The following sections look at the service portfolio management process, which provides an important source of information for the management of services across the lifecycle.

Purpose

The purpose of this process is to ensure that the appropriate mix of services is delivered by the service provider to meet the requirements of the customer. The process enables us to track a number of important items of information about our services, including the investment that has been made and the interaction with other services.

The information captured in the service portfolio links the services being provided to the business outcomes they support. This ensures that activities across the whole of the lifecycle are aligned to ensure that value is delivered to customers.

Objectives

The objectives of service portfolio management are as follows:

- Provide a process that allows an organization to manage its overall service provision. Through this process, the service provider develops mechanisms to investigate and decide which services to provide to its customers. This decision is based on the analysis of the potential return that could be generated and acceptable levels of risk.

- Maintain the definitive managed portfolio of services provided by the service provider. Each service should be identified, along with the business need and outcome it supports.

- Provide an information source that allows the organization to understand and evaluate how the IT services provided enable the organization to achieve its desired outcomes. It will also be a mechanism for tracking how IT can respond to organizational changes in the internal or external environments.

- Provide control over which services are offered, to whom, with what level of investment, and under what conditions.

- Track the organizational spend on IT services throughout their lifecycle, allowing for regular reviews of the strategy to ensure that the appropriate investment is being made for the chosen strategic approach.

- Provide information to enable decision making regarding the viability of services and when they should be retired.

Scope

Service portfolio management has a broad scope because it covers all the services a service provider delivers as well as those it is planning to deliver and those that have been retired from live operation.

Because the primary concern of the service portfolio management process is to determine whether the services being provided are delivering value, the process should cover the ability to track investment and expenditure on services. The outcome of the process can then be compared to the desired business outcomes in terms of the value the customer requires.

Internal and external service providers may have a different approach to the way they connect services to business outcomes. For an internal service provider, it will be necessary to work closely with the business units in the organization to compare the outcomes with the investment. External service providers are more likely to have this information captured as part of the agreement or contract that defines the relationship with the business. The services they provide are also more likely to be directly associated with revenue generation or support revenue generation services.

Service portfolio management should be responsible for evaluating the value of the services provided throughout the whole of their lifecycle. It is also important to be able to compare the merits of the existing services against those that are being planned or the benefits they provide in replacing retired services. In this way, we can be certain that the services provided meet the required business needs.

The Service Portfolio

We are now going to review the service portfolio itself, which is the output from the process. Figure 17.1 illustrates the components of the service portfolio: the service pipeline, service catalog, and retired services.

FIGURE 17.1   The service portfolio and its contents

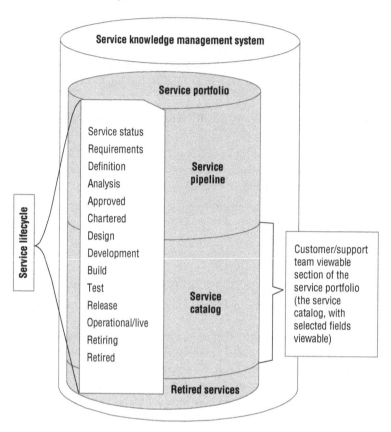

The service portfolio is the complete set of services managed by a service provider. This includes the contractual and financial commitments across internal, external, or third-party providers; new service development activity; and improvement initiatives. All services should be included, whether they are visible, customer-facing services, such as the core or the enhancing services, or the enabling services that support them.

The service portfolio also covers the services that are currently only in a conceptual stage, potentially the services that would be developed if there were no limit on budget, resources, or capabilities. The service portfolio shows the allocation of all the resources in use across the whole service lifecycle. Each stage of the lifecycle will be making demands on the available resources and capabilities, and the service portfolio allows us to see those allocations and resolve any potential conflicts according to the importance of the business outcomes.

Any new project or development should have an approved financial plan and allocated budget demonstrating the cost recovery or return on investment, and this will be captured in the service portfolio. By ensuring that we have the right mix of services across the pipeline and catalog, we can make sure we have the correct funding for all of the IT service provider activities across the service lifecycle.

As you will see later, the service catalog is the only part of the service portfolio that is customer facing, the information it contains may be used as part of customer-facing reports, presentations, and business cases. The live operational services, as captured in the service catalog, are the only services that will recover costs or earn profits.

Value

Service portfolio management helps the business to decide where to invest. Services are implemented not just because they are a good idea or because they are an industry standard, but because there is a good business case. The expected outcomes are compared with the investment required to build and deliver a service. This means that customers understand what will be delivered and under what conditions; they can then decide whether the service is a good or bad investment.

The service provider, through the decisions made as part of service portfolio management, can help its customers achieve their business strategies.

Policies, Principles, and Basic Concepts

The service portfolio represents the commitments and investments made by a service provider across all customers and market spaces. It shows any contractual commitments and which new services are being developed. It will also include current service improvement plans initiated by continual service improvement (CSI). Some services are not provided directly by the service provider but are bought in from suppliers. The service provider remains responsible for these third-party services, since they form an integral part of the customer service offering. An example of such a service would be the wide area networking service. It is important to note, therefore, that the portfolio includes the complete set of services that are managed by a service provider.

Service portfolio management ensures that the service provider understands all the services it provides, the investment that has been made in these services, and the objectives and required returns for each one. This knowledge is necessary before tactical plans for management of the services are made. The process plays a role in strategy generation, ensuring that the agreed strategy is appropriately executed at each stage. This prevents common mistakes such as choosing a new tool before optimizing processes. It also ensures that what is actually done matches what was intended. The service portfolio management approach also helps managers to allocate resources in line with business priorities.

In addition, the service portfolio identifies the services that the organization would provide if it had unlimited resources, capabilities, and funding. This helps identify what can and cannot be done. Every decision to provide a service uses resources that could have been spent on providing a different service, so the choice of what to prioritize and the implications of that choice in terms of the allocation of resources and capabilities are understood. It also ensures that the approval to develop potential services in the pipeline into catalog services is granted only with approved funding and a financial plan for recovering costs where appropriate (internal) or showing profit (external).

The Service Pipeline

The service pipeline lists all services that are being evaluated as potential offerings or are actually being developed. The services in the pipeline are not yet available to customers, and the pipeline is not normally visible to customers. Investment opportunities are assessed in the pipeline. Services enter the pipeline under a number of circumstances:

- As a result of a customer request

- When the service provider identifies an opportunity, such as when a business outcome is underserved by current services

- As a result of new technology becoming available that could create new business opportunities

- When service management processes identify a better solution to the services that are currently offered

- When CSI processes identify a gap in the current service portfolio

The service pipeline ensures that all these opportunities are properly evaluated so that the potential returns can be judged against the investment required.

Service Catalog

The catalog is a database of information regarding the services available to customers—these may be already live or available for deployment. This part of the service portfolio is published to customers, and it includes information about deliverables, prices, contact points, and ordering and request processes. It is essential that due diligence is undertaken before a service is added to the catalog so that the service provider understands how to deliver it successfully, and at the expected cost. The service catalog also contains details about standard service requests, enabling users to request those services using the appropriate channels. These requests may be channeled through a web portal and then routed to the appropriate request fulfillment procedure.

The service catalog also informs service portfolio management decisions. It identifies the linkage between service assets, services, and business outcomes and any potential gaps in the service portfolio.

Take a look at Figure 17.2, which shows linkages between service assets, the services they support, and the business outcomes they facilitate:

- The boxes on the left are service assets used by the service provider to provide services. These could be assets such as servers, databases, applications, and network devices.

- The box in the middle shows the services in the service catalog. There are two layers of services shown. The layer on the left shows supporting services, which are usually not seen by the customer directly, such as application hosting (contained in a view of the service catalog called the technical or supporting service catalog). The second layer of services includes customer-facing services.

- The boxes on the right are business outcomes, which the business achieves when it uses these services.

FIGURE 17.2   The service catalog and linkages between services and outcomes

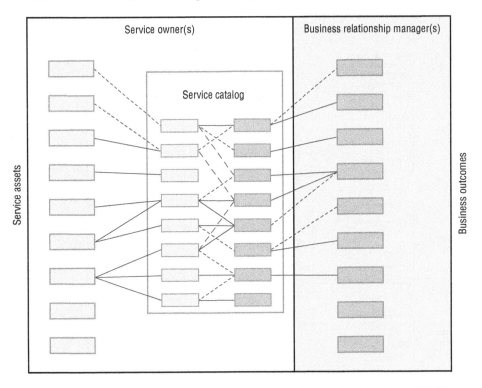

Services that are performing well and are popular are identified. They may be allocated additional resources to ensure that they continue to perform as required and will be able to satisfy increased demand.

Services that are performing in an acceptable manner but could be improved in terms of efficiencies or functionality are deemed viable services. Introducing new attributes, addressing warranty or utility issues, improving how well they match demand, and setting new pricing policies are all approaches that may be used to make the services more popular. Services that are unpopular or that consistently perform badly may be marked for retirement.

A subset of the service catalog may be third-party or outsourced services. These extend the range of the service catalog in terms of customers and market spaces. Figure 17.3 shows how these third-party services may be used as a stopgap to address underserved or unserved demand until items in the service pipeline are phased into operation. They may also be used to replace services being retired from the service catalog.

FIGURE 17.3 Service catalog and demand management

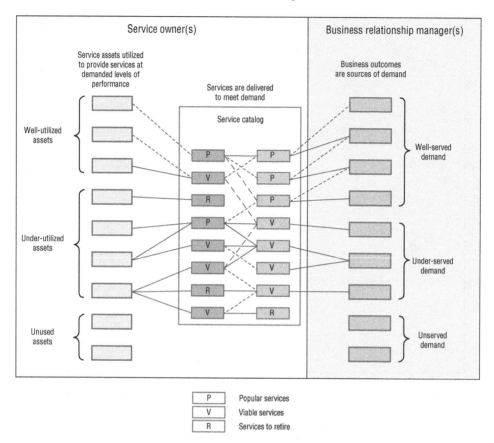

A comparison of the typical content and purpose of the service portfolio and service catalog is illustrated in Figure 17.4.

Retired Services

Some services in the service portfolio are phased out or retired. Each organization should periodically review services to decide when to move a service from the catalog to retired. A decision may be made to phase out the provision of a service by ceasing to offer it to new customers, even though the service is still being delivered to existing customers. Other organizations will wait until there are no users for the service to move the service out of the catalog.

FIGURE 17.4   Service portfolio and service catalogs

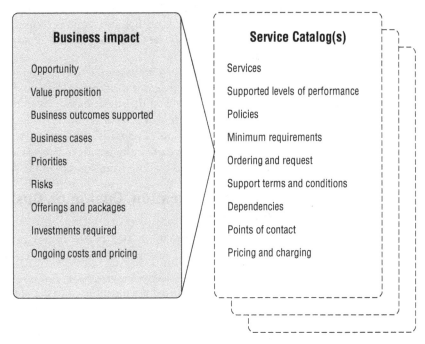

Retired services are maintained in the service portfolio for a number of reasons:

- If the replacement service fails to meet all requirements, it may be necessary to be able to fall back to the previous service.

- When defining a new service, service portfolio management might realize that some functionality is available from a retired service. This could result in the service being reinstated to the service catalog.

- Regulatory requirements to maintain archived data may mean that the service required to access that data needs to remain available. In this case the information is exported to a read-only database for future use.

The retirement of a service should be managed through service transition to ensure that all customer commitments are fulfilled and service assets are released from contracts.

Other Information Sources: The Configuration Management System

The configuration management system (CMS) is a set of tools and databases that are used to manage an IT service provider's configuration data. The CMS is maintained by configuration management and is used by all IT service management processes. It also includes information about incidents, problems, known errors, changes, and releases, and it may contain data about employees, suppliers, locations, business units, customers, and users. The CMS includes tools for collecting, storing, managing, updating, and presenting data about all configuration items and their relationships. The CMS is examined in more detail in the ITIL Service Transition publication.

A configuration management database (CMDB) is a database used to store configuration records throughout their lifecycle. The CMS may include one or more CMDBs, and each database stores attributes of configuration items (CIs) and their relationships with other CIs.

In the context of service portfolio management, the CMS records and controls data about each service, CIs that make up services, the people and tools that support services, and the relationships between all of them. The service portfolio is part of the service knowledge management system (SKMS) and is based on data from sources in the CMS.

Other Information Sources: The Application, Customer, Customer Agreement, and Project Portfolios

Next we cover some other information repositories that are used as part of service portfolio management. They are the application portfolio, the customer portfolio, the customer agreement portfolio, and the project portfolio:

▪ The application portfolio is a database or structured document used to manage applications throughout their lifecycle. It contains key attributes of all applications. Remember: Applications and services are not the same thing. A single service like an online shop might use several applications, or an application might provide a number of services. It is important, therefore, to keep the application portfolio and the service portfolio as two distinct items.

The application portfolio is usually an output from application development, which uses it for tracking investment in the applications. Having the information gathered into the application portfolio helps prevent duplication—when a new request is made, existing applications can be checked to see if they could satisfy the requirement or be amended to do so. It is also helpful when tracking who is responsible for a specific application. It identifies which customers and which services use each application. It plays an important role in service portfolio management for several reasons: First, it links strategic service requirements and requests to specific applications or projects within application development. Second, it enables the organization to track investments in a service at all stages of the service lifecycle. Third, it enables application development and IT operations to coordinate their efforts and facilitates greater cooperation throughout the service lifecycle.

Everything in the application portfolio should have gone through the service portfolio management process, and so every entry in the application portfolio should be linked to one or more entries in the service portfolio.

▪ The customer portfolio is a database or structured document maintained by the business relationship management process; we will look at it in more detail when considering that process in Chapter 19, "Business Relationship Management and Financial Management for IT." It is the business relationship manager's view of the customers who receive services from the IT service provider. Service portfolio management uses the customer portfolio to capture the relationship between business outcomes, customers, and services. The service portfolio shows these linkages and is validated with customers through business relationship management.

- The customer agreement portfolio is another database or structured document. It is used to manage service contracts or agreements between an IT service provider and its customers. Each IT service delivered to a customer should have a contract or other agreement that is listed in the customer agreement portfolio. Even where SLAs are not being used, customer expectations regarding the services provided should be formally documented. The customers should agree to what has been documented.

  - External service providers track the legal contractual requirements using the customer agreement portfolio. The customer agreement portfolio will link the requirements to the service portfolio and customer portfolio.

  - Internal service providers will use the customer agreement portfolio to track SLAs and less formal agreements. They can then ensure that they are able to meet customer expectations. By documenting the customer expectations, any "creep" in requirements can be prevented unless there is a justified (and funded) need.

- The project portfolio is a database or structured document used to manage projects that have been chartered. A charter is a document authorizing the project and stating its scope, terms, and references. The project portfolio is used to coordinate projects, ensuring that objectives are met within time and cost and to specification. It prevents duplication and scope creep, and ensures that resources are available for each project. The project portfolio can be used to manage both single projects and large-scale multiple-project programs. The project portfolio is usually maintained by a project management office (PMO) in larger organizations. Most organizations will use a separate project portfolio for IT projects, but some include both business and IT projects. The project portfolio helps service portfolio management to track the status of these projects, compare expenditure against what was expected, and ensure that the services are being built and designed as intended. The project portfolio will align and coordinate activities where several different projects relate to a single service.

Service Models

Service portfolio management uses service models to analyze the impact of new services or changes to existing services. Service portfolio management will ensure that a service model is defined for every service in the pipeline. Service models are also valuable in assessing which existing service assets can support new services, thus enabling more efficiency through the use of the principle of "create once, use many times."

Service portfolio plays an important role in how assets are allocated, deployed, and managed. As you saw earlier, successful strategy execution depends on effectively aligning service assets to customer outcomes. The service portfolio and configuration management systems document the relationship between service assets, services, and business outcomes; each service in the service portfolio is expressed in the configuration management system as a set of service assets, performance requirements, standard operating procedures, functions, and SLAs.

Service Portfolio Management through the Service Lifecycle

Here we'll look briefly at the role played by service portfolio management across the rest of the service lifecycle. Although service portfolio management is a process within service strategy, it also plays an important part in every stage in the service lifecycle. We start by looking at its role in service design:

- In the service design lifecycle stage, service portfolio management ensures that design work is prioritized according to business needs and clarifies how the service will be measured by the business. It ensures that each service is clearly linked to the agreed-to business outcomes and that the service assets used and performance levels required of the service are documented. Together with demand management information, service portfolio management gives a clear picture of when service will be required and the expected levels of demand. Service portfolio management helps the design team focus on objectives, outcomes, and priorities. It also works with the PMO or project manager, ensuring that the services are built on time, to specification, and to budget.

- Service transition builds and tests the services that will be placed into the service catalog. Change management is used to authorize the move of a service into the service catalog. This authorization ensures that the final product is ready and can be supported, that it is technically feasible and financially viable, and that sufficient operational capability is in place. Before adding items to the catalog, the impact on commitments made to customers must be assessed and sufficient resources and capabilities set aside to provide the service. If resources cannot be made available, the service may be prevented from going live.

- Service operation delivers the service in the service catalog part of the service portfolio. Service portfolio management provides operations with an understanding of the services and how and why they need to be delivered. This is an important input to defining standard operating procedures, event management, incident management priorities, and escalation procedures.

- Continual service improvement evaluates whether the services in the portfolio met the stated objectives, and if not, it identifies ways in which the situation can be rectified. CSI also evaluates the business cases and objectives to ensure that they are still valid and that service portfolio management continues to prioritize services appropriately.

Process Activities, Methods, and Techniques

Service portfolio management consists of four main phases of activity. We are going to examine these one by one:

- The first stage is the Define stage. This phase focuses on documenting and understanding existing services and new services. Each service must have a documented business case. Data for each service, such as which service assets are required and where investments are made, needs to be validated.

- The second stage is the Analyze stage. The analysis of services in the portfolio will indicate whether the service is able to optimize value and how supply and demand can be prioritized and balanced.

- The third stage is the Approve stage. Every service needs to be approved, and the level of investment must be authorized to ensure sufficient resources to deliver the anticipated levels of service.

- The final stage is the Charter stage. A charter is a document authorizing the project and stating its scope, terms, and references. Services are not just built on request from anyone in the organization. They have to be formally chartered, and stakeholders need to be kept up-to-date with information about decisions, resource allocation, and actual investments made.

Before we look at the process in detail, it is important to remember how we define the service portfolio itself. We begin by collecting information from all existing services as well as every proposed service. However, the portfolio is not static, and so the data must be refreshed and validated on a recurring basis. How often this happens will depend on the portfolio itself: does it include stable, legacy systems with few changes or a fast-changing area? A reevaluation of the portfolio may be triggered by external events; for example, a merger with or acquisition of another company would require a thorough reevaluation to spot possible duplications.

New and changed service proposals can be initiated from a number of sources as a result of, for example, changes to plans or the identification of a service improvement plan. They need to be formally assessed and approved. Service portfolio management maintains a central record of all plans, requests, and submissions that are submitted. In some organizations, they are simply called requests, but they are *not* the same as standard service requests submitted for request fulfillment, which could lead to confusion. Inputs to service portfolio management may come from the following processes:

- Strategy management is the primary input to service portfolio management. It presents strategic plans outlining initiatives for business opportunities and outcomes along with the services these require. The plans are evaluated by service portfolio management for technical and financial feasibility and ROI.

- Business relationship management receives requests from customers. These may be dealt with through change management, request fulfillment, or incident management, but some will need to be submitted to service portfolio management. They include requests for new services or added functionality or performance improvements to existing services.

- CSI initiates three types of input to service portfolio management. They may include possible improvements to service levels of existing services. Each will be assessed in terms of the investment and the projected return. CSI may also identify new opportunities or gaps in the current portfolio of services or opportunities for improvements in cost, mitigation of risks, and so on, affecting one or several existing services or even the entire operation of the service provider. Note that any opportunities identified by CSI that would require a change in the organization's strategy are submitted to strategy management.

- Some service management processes involve managing changes to services or modeling warranty and utility options that can be presented to the customer. Many of these would have an impact on investment, so service portfolio management should evaluate these suggested changes before they are initiated.

> The change management process may be sufficient for some requests. Those with a significant impact on the existing levels of investment or achievement of business outcomes should be considered strategic and should be immediately referred to service portfolio management. This requires that service portfolio management and change management define thresholds for what constitutes a strategic issue.

Define the Portfolio

Before we examine the four phases of service portfolio management activity, we will discuss the existing service portfolio. The existing services and new services need to be documented. This provides an initial inventory of services, which will need to be validated on a recurring basis, especially if the business requirements are changing quickly. Each service in the pipeline must have a documented business case and validated information showing which service assets are required and where investments are made. The desired business outcomes should be defined, with opportunities, utility and warranty requirements, and the services themselves as well as the anticipated investment required to achieve the outcomes. If the case for approval is compelling, the proposed service will be approved and moved into the service design stage for design and development.

Changes to the portfolio may result from a new or changed strategy. Service portfolio management should consider the strategy to identify specific service opportunities and identify the stakeholders that will be consulted in defining the services. Another reason for changes to the portfolio may be a request from the business. Business relationship management is responsible for documenting these requests on behalf of the customer. Requests may come in different formats, from detailed proposals to informal ideas that can be formalized into standardized formats later. The requests are registered and customers kept updated on their status.

Another source of change to the service portfolio is a request for service improvement. CSI identifies improvement opportunities and builds service improvement plans (SIPs). These opportunities may concern changes to the services themselves, or the processes, people, and tools that support or deliver the services. They are submitted to service portfolio management because they affect the overall investment in providing services and will need to be allocated to the services at some stage.

Next we'll look at each of the four stages of service portfolio management in more detail.

Define

The Define stage consists of the following:

- Any service suggestions that require significant investment or impact on the agreed utility and the warranty of a service are submitted to service portfolio management. Here are some examples:
    - New technology to improve performance, suggested by capacity management
    - A new recovery plan from IT service continuity management following the identification of a new business impact

- Significant modification to the data center to improve availability
- A suggested resolution to an intermittent problem that requires migration to a new platform
- Changes to third-party services that could affect the service

 Changes to existing services are treated differently from new services. The existence of a service catalog will help determine if this is actually a new service to avoid duplication. When in doubt, the service should be treated as new.

- New services will be defined based on the information provided. At this stage, a detailed architecture or technical design is not necessary. Instead, what is needed are definitions of the service's purpose, customers, consumers, inputs, outputs, and high-level requirements, and the business activity it supports. Other requirements may include regulatory or legal requirements, standards to which it must conform, business outcomes, stakeholders, and the anticipated level of investments and returns. Finally, any constraints that need to be considered will be included.
- The service model will be defined. This is a high-level view of all of the components of the service, both customer assets and service assets, and how they fit together. The impact of a new service is assessed in terms of the current business outcomes, investment levels, service level agreements, existing warranty and utility levels, contractual obligations, patterns of business activity, and levels of demand. The impact of changes to an existing service is similarly assessed, especially the impact on the current service model.

Analyze

Each service is analyzed by linking it to the service strategy. Service portfolio management articulates how the perspective, position, plan, and patterns will be translated into actual services. The analysis to be carried out needs to be defined and understood to ensure that the correct data is collected. It will require input from multiple specialized areas.

Service portfolio management regularly reviews existing services to determine whether they still meet their objectives and the strategy of the organization. The review will also ensure that services in the service pipeline are properly defined, analyzed, approved, and chartered.

The output of this review feeds into the analysis of investments, value, and priorities. Sometimes service portfolio management discovers a new opportunity to be presented during the strategy management cycle as part of the strategy assessment stage. Financial management helps to quantify the investment and value of each service so they can be prioritized. Exact costs require a detailed service design, but the feasibility of the service can be assessed. The investment analysis and prioritization results are documented in the business case, which describes the opportunity, the potential business outcomes, and the investment the organization is prepared to make in the service. This information will be used to calculate ROI. The business case is the justification for pursuing a course of action to meet stated organizational goals; it assesses investment in terms of potential benefits and the resources and capabilities required.

Following the analysis, a decision is made regarding the feasibility of the service and whether it should be approved. This requires authorization for expenditure. (At this stage, this is outline approval only, because without a detailed design, the anticipated level of investment may be inaccurate.) There are six possible decisions:

- Retain/build
- Replace
- Rationalize
- Refactor
- Renew
- Retire

If the customer disagrees with the decision, it may want the service provider to move ahead anyway. Possible responses are likely to include a combination of the following:

- Explaining to the customer why the need cannot be fulfilled
- Explaining what is needed of the customer in terms of commitment, sponsorship, or funding for new service development
- Developing the service if the customer makes the necessary commitment
- Declining the opportunity if the customer cannot commit
- Considering supporting the customer in partnership with third parties

Approve

New services, or changes to existing services judged to be feasible, are submitted to change management for approval in the form of a change proposal. This proposal will allow change management to coordinate the activities of all resources required to investigate the customer and infrastructure requirements before the change is approved or rejected. The change proposal should include the following:

- A high-level description
- Business outcomes
- The utility and warranty to be provided
- A full business case including risks, issues, and alternatives as well as budget and financial expectations
- The expected implementation schedule

The change proposal is submitted to change management, who investigates what the new or changed service will look like and what it will take to design, build, and deploy it. If feasible, the detailed design and deployment begins and service portfolio management drafts a service charter. Following a rejection, service portfolio management notifies all stakeholders and updates the service portfolio with the status.

Charter

The final activity in service portfolio is to charter new services. *Charter* has two meanings:

- The new service (or changes to the existing service) is said to be chartered once it has been commissioned by the customer or business executives.

- A document to authorize work to meet defined objectives, outputs, schedules, and expenditure may be called a charter. In service portfolio management, services are chartered using a service charter.

The service charter ensures that all stakeholders and staff have a common understanding of what will be built, by when, and at what cost. It will be an input into the project management activity and will be entered into the project portfolio. It is important to ensure that stakeholders are kept informed of the progress of the project from charter to deployment; this helps ensure their continued support and informs them of any delays or exceptions. Updates to service portfolio management allow the process to monitor the levels of investment and capability. If cost significantly exceeds the estimate, service portfolio management will escalate the situation to the stakeholders.

Following deployment, the service will be reviewed to confirm that the service has met the requirements of the strategy and is contributing to the achievement of business outcomes as specified by the stakeholders. The services and investments in the portfolio review should be held at least quarterly to ensure that they continue to meet the IT and overall organizational strategies. A disconnect between these may have arisen as a result of the following scenarios:

- Conditions and markets changing, invalidating prior ROI calculations

- Services becoming less optimal due to compliance or regulatory concerns

- Events occurring such as mergers and acquisitions, divestitures, new public legislation, or redeployed missions

Note that not all services need be low risk or high reward; an efficient portfolio with optimal levels of ROI and risk maximizes value.

Triggers

Triggers for service portfolio management are as follows:

- A new or changed strategy—a change to a perspective, position, or pattern of action might impact existing services or service models.

- Business relationship management receives a request for a new or changed service; service portfolio management would help define and formalize this request before submitting it to change management as a change proposal.

- Service improvement opportunities from CSI could involve service portfolio management. Any reported deviation from the specifications, cost, or release time from design, build, and transition teams during the charter stage of the process would involve service portfolio management in estimating the impact and defining corrective action.

- Service level management reviews identify a service failing to deliver its expected outcomes or being used in a different way from how it was intended; service portfolio management would be involved in defining corrective actions.

- Financial management reports that the costs for a service vary significantly from the expectation, thus affecting the potential return on investment for that service; again, service portfolio management would be involved in defining corrective actions.

Inputs

Service portfolio management has the following inputs:

- Strategy plans
- Service improvement opportunities
- Financial reports
- Requests, suggestions, or complaints from the business
- Project updates for services in the charter stage of the process

Outputs

The following list includes the outputs of service portfolio management:

- An up-to-date service portfolio
- Service charters authorizing the work for designing and building new services or changes to existing services
- Reports on the status of new or changed services
- Reports on the investment made in services in the service portfolio and the returns on that investment
- Change proposals to allow change management to assess and schedule the work and resources required to charter services
- Strategic risks that could be added to a central risk register

Interfaces

Interfaces include those with the following processes:

- Service catalog management—service portfolio management determines which services will be placed into the service catalog, whereas service catalog management ensures that this is done.

- Strategy management for IT services defines the overall strategy of services; this strategy determines what type of services should be included in the portfolio. It determines the objectives for investments in terms of anticipated returns and the ideal market spaces that will be targeted.

- Financial management for IT services provides information and tools to enable service portfolio management to perform return on investment calculations; it also helps track the actual costs of services. This information is used to improve the analysis of services and forecasts in the future.

- Demand management provides information about the patterns of business activity that is used to determine the utilization and expected return on investment for the service.

- Business relationship management initiates requests and obtains business information and requirements used in defining services and evaluating whether they would provide a sufficient return on investment. It keeps customers informed about the status of services in service portfolio management.

- Service level management ensures that services are able to achieve the levels of performance defined in service portfolio management and provides feedback when this is not the case.

- Capacity management and availability management ensure that the capacity and availability requirements of chartered services are designed and built.

- IT service continuity management identifies the business impact of risks associated with delivering the service and designs countermeasures and recovery plans to ensure that the service can achieve the objectives defined during service portfolio management.

- Information security management ensures that the confidentiality, integrity, and availability objectives defined during service portfolio management are met.

- The supplier management process identifies situations in which a supplier cannot continue to supply services or a supplier relationship is at risk.

- Change management evaluates the resources required to introduce new services or changes to existing services, thus enabling the service to be chartered. It ensures that all changes involved in designing, building, and releasing the service are controlled and coordinated.

- Service validation and testing ensures that the anticipated functionality and returns of each service can be achieved.

- Knowledge management enables IT managers and architects to make informed decisions about the best service options to meet the organization's objectives.

- Continual service improvement provides feedback about the actual use and return of services against their anticipated use and return. This information is used to improve services and make changes to the mix and availability of services in the service portfolio.

Information Management

This section provides an overview of the main sources of information for the service portfolio:

- The service portfolio, consisting of a service pipeline, a service catalog, and retired services.

- The project portfolio, which manages services that have been chartered and are in the process of design and build.

- The application portfolio, which allows service portfolio management to understand the relationship between applications and services.

- The customer portfolio and customer agreement portfolio, which allow service portfolio management to understand customer requirements, the services that have been designed to meet those services, and the agreements that have been made to deliver the services.

- Service models, which allow service portfolio management to understand the composition and dynamics of a service before it moves into expensive design and build activity, and where a service may leverage existing investments.

- The service strategy, which provides a framework of anticipated opportunities, constraints, objectives, and desired business outcomes. Service portfolio management is expected to define what mix of services can best meet the strategic objectives of the organization.

- The configuration management system provides data and information that supports the development and assessment of service models and the assessment of new services and changes to existing services.

Roles and Responsibilities

This section describes a number of roles that need to be performed in support of the service portfolio management process.

Service Portfolio Management Process Owner

In addition to the generic process owner role described in Chapter 1, "Introduction to Operational Support and Analysis," the service portfolio management process owner works with other process owners to ensure an integrated approach to the design and implementation of service portfolio management.

Service Portfolio Management Process Manager

In addition to the generic responsibilities for a process manager, as described in Chapter 1, the service portfolio management process manager's responsibilities typically include the following:

- Managing and maintaining the organization's service portfolio

- Managing the surrounding processes for keeping the portfolio attractive to customers and up to date

- Marketing the portfolio, and in particular the service catalog, so that customers and potential customers are aware of the services available

- Helping formulate service packages and associated options so that services can be combined in logical groupings to produce products that can be marketed, sold, and consumed to best meet customers' needs

Critical Success Factors and Key Performance Indicators

Finally, we cover the CSFs and KPIs for this process. We will cover some examples, but for the full list, see the ITIL Service Strategy publication:

- Critical success factor: "The existence of a formal process to investigate and decide which services to provide."
    - KPI: A formal service portfolio management process exists under the ownership of the service portfolio management process owner.
    - KPI: The service portfolio management process is audited and reviewed annually and meets its objectives.
- Critical success factor: "The ability to document each service provided, together with the business need it meets and the business outcome it supports."
    - KPI: A service portfolio exists and is used as the basis for deciding which services to offer. An audit shows that every service is documented in the service portfolio.
    - KPI: There is a documented process for defining the business need and business outcome, which is formally owned by the service portfolio management process owner.
    - KPI: Each service in the service portfolio is linked to at least one business outcome. This is verified through a regular review of the service portfolio.

Challenges

Service portfolio management is presented with the following challenges:

- The lack of access to customer business information required to enable service portfolio management to understand the desired business outcomes and strategies
- The absence of a formal project management approach, which makes chartering and tracking services through the design and transition stages more difficult
- The absence of a project portfolio, which makes assessing the impact of new initiatives on new services or proposed changes to services difficult
- Difficulty in identifying objectives, use, and return on investment of services due to the lack of a customer portfolio and customer agreement portfolio
- A service portfolio focusing purely on the service provider aspects of services, which makes it difficult to calculate the value of services, to model future utilization, or to validate the customer requirements for the service
- The lack of a formal change management process to control the introduction of new services and manage changes to existing services

Risks

There are a number of risks to service portfolio management:

- Responding to customer pressure and offering services without validated or complete information and without a full investigation into the risks involved. Service portfolio management is concerned with reducing risks by having a complete understanding of the service being offered; a hurried response negates the whole process.

- Offering services without defining how they will be measured. Without agreeing to this, we cannot calculate the return on investment. A service may be delivering value, but this cannot be proved, making the service vulnerable to being discontinued due to cost cutting.

Service Catalog Management

A *service catalog* is defined in the ITIL glossary as follows:

> A database or structured document with information about all live IT services, including those available for deployment. The service catalog is part of the service portfolio and contains information about two types of IT service: customer-facing services that are visible to the business and supporting services required by the service provider to deliver customer-facing services.

Let's examine this definition in more detail:

A Database or Structured Document   The catalog gathers the service information and presents it in a form that is easy for the business to understand.

Information about All Live IT Services, Including Those Available for Deployment   The catalog contains details of services that are available to the business; in this way, it differs from the other components of the service portfolio (the service pipeline and retired services). Gathering and maintaining that information is the job of service catalog management.

Information about Two Types of IT Service   The catalog provides the details that the customers require about the services available—deliverables, prices, contact points, ordering, and request processes. There is another view of the service catalog—the view that is visible only to IT, showing the supporting services that must be in place if the customer services are to be delivered.

Let's begin by looking at the purpose of the service catalog management process.

Purpose

The purpose of the service catalog management process is to provide and maintain a single source of consistent information on all operational services. It may also include those that are being prepared to be run operationally. The service catalog management process ensures that the service catalog is widely available to those who are authorized to access it.

Objectives

The objectives of the service catalog management process include managing the information contained within the service catalog. This ensures that the service catalog is accurate and reflects the current details, status, interfaces, and dependencies of all services that are being run, or being prepared to run, in the live environment.

Another objective is that this process should ensure that the service catalog is made available to those approved to access it in a manner that supports their effective and efficient use of its information. This may vary depending on the audience; for example, technical support staff members need a different perspective on the services than the users.

Finally, it is important to ensure that the service catalog supports the evolving needs of all other service management processes for service catalog information, including all interface and dependency information.

Scope

The scope of the service catalog management process is to provide and maintain accurate information on all services that are being transitioned or that have been transitioned to the live environment. It is up to the organization to define the point at which it is comfortable having services displayed as part of the service catalog. The services presented in the service catalog may be listed individually, or more typically, some or all of the services may be presented in the form of service packages.

The service catalog management process covers the following items:

- Contribution to the definition of services and service packages
- Development and maintenance of service and service package descriptions appropriate for the service catalog
- Production and maintenance of an accurate service catalog
- Interfaces, dependencies, and consistency between the service catalog and the overall service portfolio
- Interfaces and dependencies between all services and supporting services within the service catalog and the configuration management system (CMS)
- Interfaces and dependencies between all services, and supporting components and configuration items (CIs) within the service catalog and the CMS

The service catalog management process does not include the following:

- Detailed attention to capturing, maintaining, and using service asset and configuration data; this is performed through the service asset and configuration management process
- Detailed attention to capturing, maintaining, and fulfilling service requests; this is performed through the request fulfillment process.

Value

The service catalog provides a central source of information on the IT services delivered by the service provider organization. It includes a customer-facing view (or views) of the IT services in use, how they are intended to be used, the business processes they enable, and the levels and quality of service the customer can expect for each service.

Through the work of service catalog management, organizations can do the following:

- Ensure a common understanding of IT services and improved relationships between the customer and service provider by utilizing the service catalog as a marketing and communication tool

- Improve service provider focus on customer outcomes by correlating internal service provider activities and service assets to business processes and outcomes

- Improve efficiency and effectiveness of other service management processes by leveraging the information contained in or connected to the service catalog

- Improve knowledge, alignment, and focus on the business value of each service throughout the service provider organization and its activities

Policies

Each organization should develop and maintain a policy with regard to both the overall service portfolio and the constituent service catalog, relating to the services recorded within them and what details are recorded (including what statuses are recorded for each of the services).

The policy should also contain details of responsibilities for each section of the overall service portfolio and the scope of each of the constituent sections. This will include policies regarding when a service is published in the service catalog as well as when it will be removed from the service catalog and appear only in the retired services section of the service portfolio.

Principles and Basic Concepts

Different types of service are delivered by a service provider. In Figure 17.5, you can see the types of service described by the framework.

Customer-facing services are IT services that are seen by the customer. They are typically services that support the customer's business units/business processes, directly facilitating some outcome or outcomes desired by the customer.

Supporting services are the IT services that support or "underpin" the customer-facing services. They are typically invisible to the customer but essential to the delivery of customer-facing IT services.

To be most effective, the service catalog views should be tailored to meet the requirements of the audience. The information required from the customer's perspective is different than that required by the technical support teams. In Figure 17.6 you can see the perspective of the service catalog in two views, the business or customer view and the technical view.

FIGURE 17.5   Types of service in a service catalog

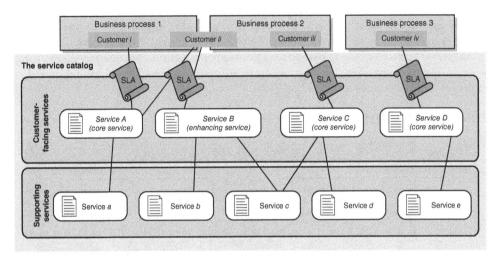

FIGURE 17.6   Two-view service catalog

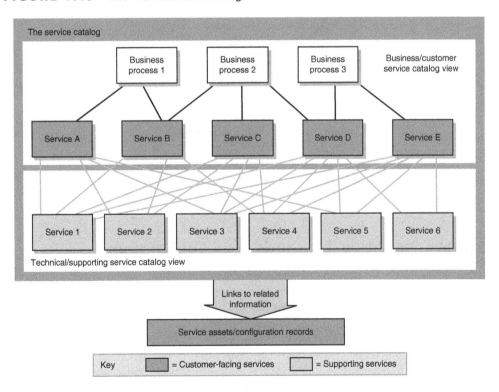

The catalog should form a part of the configuration management system. This should be structured and presented in a manner appropriate to the organization.

In the example in Figure 17.7, the customer-facing catalog has been partitioned such that a business unit has sight of only the services it uses. This might be appropriate for a commercial service provider, where two different customer groups do not need to share visibility across the whole catalog. The two customer groups are generically referred to as either wholesale or retail customers.

FIGURE 17.7 Three-view service catalog

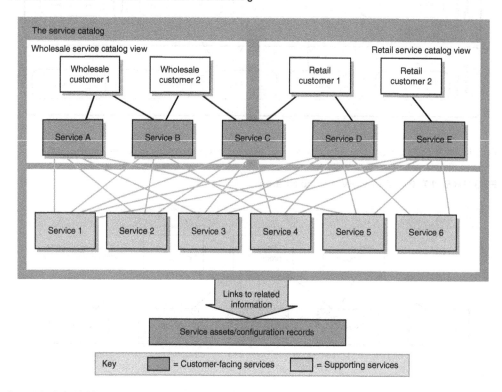

Process Activities, Methods, and Techniques

We will now consider the process activities from a management perspective. There are a number of activities to consider, not least of which is the agreement and documentation of services.

Key activities include ensuring that the services are defined and described appropriately within the documentation.

The service catalog should interface with the service portfolio, so the processes of service catalog management and service portfolio management should be closely linked. This will enable the content of both to remain accurate and up-to-date. The service catalog is a significant information source for the process of IT service continuity and supports business continuity management, ensuring that appropriate services are maintained according to the continuity needs of the business. It also serves to capture the relationships with suppliers and internal service provider teams (such as service asset and configuration management), supporting the understanding of the overall IT estate. The service catalog supports both service level and business relationship management, ensuring alignment to business requirements and processes.

All of these interactions require attention from the service catalog process manager to ensure the continued effective use of the information captured in the catalog.

Triggers, Inputs, Outputs, and Interfaces

First, we will consider the triggers for this process.

Triggers

The triggers for the service catalog management process include changes in the business requirements and services. Among the main triggers are requests for change (RFCs) and the change management process. This includes new services, changes to existing services, and services being retired.

Inputs

A number of sources of information are relevant to the service catalog management process and form the inputs to the catalog:

- Business information from the organization's business and IT strategy, plans and financial plans, and information on its current and future requirements from the service portfolio
- A business impact analysis (BIA) providing information on the impact, priority, and risk associated with each service or changes to service requirements
- Business requirements; details of any agreed, new, or changed business requirements from the service portfolio
- The service portfolio and all related data and documents
- The configuration management system
- Requests for change
- Feedback from all other processes

Outputs

The outputs of the service catalog management process are as follows:

- The documentation and agreement of a definition of the service
- Updates to the service portfolio; should contain the current status of all services and requirements for services
- Updates to requests for change
- The service catalog; should contain the details and the current status of every live service provided by the service provider or every service being transitioned into the live environment, together with the interfaces and dependencies

Interfaces

Every service provider process uses the service catalog, so it could be said that the service catalog management process interfaces with all processes. The following list includes some of the most prominent interfaces:

Service Portfolio Management This process determines which services will be chartered and therefore moved forward for eventual inclusion in the service catalog. It also includes critical information regarding each service or potential service, including any agreed-to service packages and service options.

Business Relationship Management This process ensures that the relationship between the service and the customer(s) who require it is clearly defined in terms of how the service supports the customer(s) needs.

Service Asset and Configuration Management This process works collaboratively with service catalog management to ensure that information in the CMS and information in the service catalog are appropriately linked together to provide a consistent, accurate, and comprehensive view of the interfaces and dependencies between services, customers, business processes, service assets, and configuration items (CIs).

Service Level Management This process negotiates specific levels of service warranty to be delivered, which will be reflected in the service catalog.

Demand Management In conjunction with service portfolio management, this process determines how services will be composed into service packages for provisioning and assists service catalog management in ensuring that these packages are appropriately represented in the service catalog.

Information Management

The key information for this process is that which is contained within the service catalog itself. Because the service catalog is part of the service portfolio, the main input for this information comes from the business via either the business relationship management or service level management process. It is important to verify the information for accuracy before it is recorded within the service catalog. The information and the service catalog itself need to be maintained using the change management process.

There are many different approaches to managing service catalog information:

- Intranet solutions that are built by the service provider organization and leverage technology already in place
- Commercially available solutions designed for service catalog management
- Solutions that are part of a more comprehensive service management suite

The service catalog data may be held in a single repository or multiple repositories. Some service providers may maintain the data that supports different views of the service catalog in different locations or toolsets.

For example, detailed data for supporting services may be stored in the CMS and presented via the same interface used to access other service asset and configuration data, whereas data on customer-facing services may be held for presentation to the customers in a browser-based application via the corporate intranet.

Constructing different views of the service catalog should be based on the perspective and requirements of the intended audience. The service provider should consider which services (rows of data) and which data elements or fields (columns of data) should be included in each view. For example, details of relationships of supporting services may be important to include in a view intended for staff members of the service provider, whereas these details are typically of no interest to customers and are likely to be excluded from a customer-facing view.

Integration with the management of the service portfolio is critical here, as is the ability to access other closely related functionality. Customers should be able to view their service level agreement monitoring reports or access a self-help portal for service requests. Some commercially available service catalog tools are maturing to offer management of the full-service portfolio from proposal to retirement.

Each organization will have to understand the solution that will best serve its current and future needs. It is important, however, not to confuse the toolset used to present the service catalog with the catalog itself. An organization with a paper-based catalog and an organization with a robust technical solution both still have a service catalog.

Roles and Responsibilities

This section describes the roles and responsibilities in addition to the generic roles and responsibilities as described in Chapter 1, associated with the service catalog process.

Service Catalog Management Process Owner

The service catalog management process owner's responsibilities typically include working with other process owners to ensure an integrated approach to the design and implementation of service catalog management, service portfolio management, service level management, and business relationship management.

Service Catalog Management Process Manager

The service catalog management process manager's responsibilities typically include the following:

- Coordinating interfaces between service catalog management and other processes, especially service asset and configuration management, and release and deployment management

- Ensuring that all operational services and all services being prepared for operational running are recorded within the service catalog

- Ensuring that all the information within the service catalog is accurate and up to date

- Ensuring that appropriate views of the service catalog are maintained and made available to those for whom they are targeted

- Ensuring that all the information within the service catalog is consistent with the information within the service portfolio

- Ensuring that the information within the service catalog is adequately protected and backed up

Critical Success Factors and Key Performance Indicators

The following list includes some sample critical success factors and key performance indicators for service catalog management.

- Critical success factor: "An accurate service catalog"

  - KPI: An increase in the number of services recorded and managed within the service catalog as a percentage of those being delivered and transitioned in the live environment

  - KPI: Reduction (measured as a percentage) in the number of variances detected between the information contained within the service catalog and the "real-world" situation

- Critical success factor: "Business users' awareness of the services being provided"

  - KPI: Increase (measured as a percentage) in completeness of the customer-facing views of the service catalog against operational services

  - KPI: Increase (measured as a percentage) in business user survey responses showing knowledge of services listed in the service catalog

  - KPI: Increase in measured business user access to intranet-based service catalog

- Critical success factor: "IT staff awareness of the technology supporting the services"

  - KPI: Increase (measured as a percentage) in completeness of supporting services against the IT components that make up those services

  - KPI: Increase in service desk and other IT staff having access to information to support all live services, measured by the percentage of incidents with the appropriate service-related information

Challenges

The major challenge facing the process of service catalog management is maintaining an accurate service catalog. This should be managed as part of a service portfolio, incorporating all catalog views as part of an overall CMS and SKMS.

For this goal to be achieved, the culture of the organization needs to accept that the catalog and portfolio are essential sources of information. It is then important to ensure that everyone within the IT organization understands that all are responsible for supporting the use and helping maintain its accuracy.

Risks

The risks associated with the provision of an accurate service catalog are as follows:

- Inaccuracy of the data in the catalog and the fact that it is not under rigorous change control.
- Poor acceptance of the service catalog and its usage in all operational processes. The more active the catalog is, the more likely it is to be accurate in its content.
- Inaccuracy of service information received from the business, IT, and the service portfolio.
- Insufficient tools and resources required to maintain the information.
- Poor access to accurate change management information and processes.
- Poor access to and support of an appropriate and up-to-date CMS and SKMS for integration with the service catalog.
- Circumvention of the use of the service portfolio and service catalog.
- Information that is either too detailed to maintain accurately or at too high a level to be of any value. It should be consistent with the level of detail within the CMS and the SKMS.

Summary

In this chapter, we examined the service portfolio management process that supports the decisions on which services should be offered, and to whom, throughout the organization. It includes the pipeline services under development, the live services in operation, and the retired services.

We also explored the service catalog management process, which provides visibility of live operational services to the organization. The central parts of the service portfolio, service catalog management, and service portfolio management are closely associated, although service portfolio management is classified as a strategy process and service catalog management as a design process.

Exam Essentials

Understand the processes of service portfolio management and service catalog management. You need to understand the purpose, objectives, scope, principles, and activities of service portfolio management and service catalog management.

Be able to describe the contents of the service portfolio and their relationship to the lifecycle. It is important to be able to identify the various components of the service portfolio. It consists of the service pipeline, the service catalog, and retired services. Be able to describe how each of these interfaces with the rest of the service lifecycle and the processes from the other lifecycle stages.

Know the business value, challenges, and risks of each process.   Be able to explain the value the business derives from each process and the challenges and risks involved in running the process.

Understand the exclusions from the service catalog.   Service asset and configuration management is concerned with the management of CIs. Fulfillment of service requests is not managed through the service catalog.

Explain the different views of the service catalog.   There are a number of views that can be used to display information in the service catalog. Be able to differentiate between technical and business views and explain the purpose for each. It is also important to understand when to provide multiple views of the service catalog to the organization.

Understand the relationship between the service catalog and the service portfolio.   Be able to explain the relationship between the service portfolio and the service catalog, and understand when a service moves from the service portfolio pipeline into the service catalog.

Explain the role of information management in service catalog management.   Information is critical to the service catalog management process. The output from the process is accurate information and its maintenance.

Review Questions

You can find the answers to the review questions in the appendix.

1. With which stages of the service lifecycle does the service portfolio interact?

    A. Service strategy, service design

    B. Service strategy, service transition, continual service improvement

    C. Service strategy, service design, service operation, continual service improvement

    D. Service strategy, service design, service transition, service operation, continual service improvement

2. Which of these statements reflects the purpose of service portfolio management?

    A. Ensures sufficient capacity for the current and future needs of the business

    B. Ensures that the service delivered by the service providers will align with business requirements

    C. Ensures sufficient availability to meet the current and future needs of the business

    D. Ensures that the service provider has the right mix of services to balance the investment in IT with the ability to meet business outcomes

3. Which description (X, Y, or Z) best matches each catalog type (1, 2, and 3)?

    1. Business/customer catalog

    2. Technical catalog

    3. Multiview catalog

    X. View of all services that are used

    Y. View of the supporting services used to deliver the customer-facing services

    Z. View of the customer-facing services that are directly delivered to the customer

    A. X = 3, Y = 2, Z = 1

    B. X = 1, Y = 2, Z = 3

    C. X = 2, Y = 1, Z = 3

    D. X = 2, Y = 3, Z = 1

4. Which of the following is the correct definition of the service catalog?

    A. A document that describes the IT service, service level targets, and responsibilities of the IT service provider and the customer

    B. The complete set of services managed by a service provider, used to manage the entire lifecycle of all services

    C. A database or document with information about all live IT services

    D. Justification for a particular item of expenditure, including information about costs, benefits, options, and risks

5. Which of the following are included in a service catalog?

    1. Customer-facing services

    2. Strategic services

3. Supporting services

4. Retired services

   A. 1 and 2

   B. 1, 2, 3, and 4

   C. 1 and 3

   D. 2 and 3

6. Which of the following statements is true?

 1. The service catalog forms part of the service portfolio.

 2. The service portfolio forms part of the service catalog.

 3. There is no relationship between the service catalog and the service portfolio.

 4. Customer-facing services appear in the service catalog, and supporting services appear in the service portfolio.

   A. 1 and 3

   B. 1 only

   C. 2 and 4

   D. 4 only

7. Which of the following statements about the service catalog is true?

   A. The service catalog contains information on customer-facing services only.

   B. The service catalog contains information on supporting services only.

   C. The service catalog shows which IT service supports each business process.

   D. The service catalog shows details of services under development.

8. Which of these statements about service catalog management is most correct?

   A. Service catalog management can be connected to the majority of the lifecycle processes.

   B. Service catalog management can be connected to none of the lifecycle processes.

   C. Service catalog management can only be connected to the service portfolio management process.

   D. Service catalog management can only be connected to the service level management process.

9. The service portfolio management process is part of which service lifecycle stage?

   A. Service design

   B. Service transition

   C. Service strategy

   D. Continual service improvement

10. Which role is most likely to be responsible for marketing the service portfolio?

   A. Service portfolio process owner

   B. Service portfolio process manager

   C. Service manager

   D. Service owner

Chapter

18

Service Level Management and Supplier Management

THE FOLLOWING ITIL SERVICE OFFERINGS AND AGREEMENTS EXAM OBJECTIVES ARE DISCUSSED IN THIS CHAPTER:

✓ Service level management and supplier management

✓ Each process is discussed in terms of

- Purpose
- Objectives
- Scope
- Value
- Policies
- Principles and basic concepts
- Process activities, methods, and techniques
- Triggers, inputs, outputs, and interfaces
- Information management
- Roles and responsibilities
- Critical success factors and key performance indicators
- Challenges
- Risks

This chapter covers the day-to-day operation of each process; the detail of its activities, methods, and techniques; and its information management.

Service level management is concerned with defining the services, documenting them in an agreement, and then ensuring that the targets are measured and met, taking action where necessary to improve the level of service delivered.

Supplier management is the process responsible for obtaining value for money from suppliers, ensuring that all contracts and agreements with suppliers support the needs of the business, and verifying that all suppliers meet their contractual commitments.

Service Level Management

The service level management (SLM) process requires a constant cycle of negotiating, agreeing, monitoring, reporting on, and reviewing IT service targets and achievements. Improvements and correction to service levels will be managed as part of continual service improvement and through instigation of actions to correct or improve the level of service delivered.

Purpose of Service Level Management

We will begin by looking at the purpose of the service level management process according to the ITIL framework. ITIL states that the purpose of SLM is to ensure that all current and planned IT services are delivered to agreed achievable targets. The key words here are *agreed* and *targets*. Service level management is about discussing, negotiating, and agreeing with the customer about what IT services should be provided and ensuring that objective measures are used to ascertain whether that service has been provided to the agreed level.

Service level management is therefore concerned with defining the services, documenting them in an agreement, including the commitments on each side, and then ensuring that the targets are measured and met and taking action where necessary to improve the level of service delivered. These improvements will often be carried out as part of continual service improvement.

Note also that the definition of SLM talks about current and planned IT services. Service level management's purpose is to ensure not only that all IT services currently being delivered have a *service level agreement (SLA)* in place, but also that discussion and negotiation takes place regarding the requirements for planned services so that an SLA is agreed on and in place when the service becomes operational. In the initial period following the transition of a new or changed service, the SLA targets are likely to remain provisional, as they are tested in the live environment. They may then be adjusted, if required, before being finalized.

It is for this latter reason that service level management is one of the service design processes; services must be designed to deliver the levels of availability, capacity, and so on that the customer requires and that service level management documents in the SLA. It is a frequent problem that the SLA is not considered until just before (or even after) the go-live date, when it is realized that the customer service level requirements are not met by the design. Service level management is concerned primarily with the warranty aspects of the service. The response time, capacity, availability, and so on of the new service will be the subject of the SLA, and it is essential that the service is designed to meet both utility and warranty requirements.

Objectives of Service Level Management

The objectives of SLM are not restricted to "define, document, agree, monitor, measure, report, and review" (how well the IT service is delivered) and undertaking improvement actions when necessary. It also includes working with business relationship management to build a good working relationship with the business customers. The regular meetings held with the business as part of service level management form the basis of a strong communications channel that strengthens the relationship between the customer and IT.

 The distinction between customer and user is important in service level management. Customers are usually senior people within the organization who specify the level of service required, take part in SLM negotiations, and sign the agreed SLA. Users are provided with the service but have no direct input into the service level to be provided.

It is an essential feature of SLM that the customer and IT agree on what constitutes an acceptable level of service. Therefore, one of the objectives of SLM is to develop appropriate targets for each IT service. These targets must be specific and measurable so that there is no debate whether they were achieved. The temptation to use expressions such as "as soon as possible" or "reasonable endeavors" should be resisted, because the customer and IT may disagree on what constitutes "as soon as possible" or what is "reasonable." By using such expressions in an SLA, it may be impossible for the IT service provider to fail, but this leads to cynicism from the customer and damages the relationship that the SLM aims to build. Where the IT service provider is an external company, the legal department will inevitably seek to reduce the possibility of the provider being sued for breach of contract, and these phrases may therefore be included; for an internal service provider, there is no such excuse. Using objective success criteria is essential if SLM is to achieve another of its objectives: that of ensuring that both the customer and IT have "clear and unambiguous expectations" regarding the level of service.

A further SLM objective is to ascertain the level of customer satisfaction with the service being provided and to take steps to increase it. There are challenges in this objective, because obtaining an accurate assessment of customer satisfaction is not straightforward. Customer satisfaction surveys may be completed only by a self-selecting minority. Those who are unhappy are more likely to complete such a survey than those who are content. Despite this tendency, the service level manager must still attempt to monitor customer satisfaction as accurately as possible, using whatever methods are appropriate. In addition to surveys, focus groups, and individual interviews, other methods can be employed.

The final objective that ITIL lists for SLM is that of improving the level of service, even when the targets are being met. Such improvements must be cost-effective, so an analysis of the return expected for any financial or resource investment must be carried out. SLM actively seeks out opportunities for such cost-effective improvements. Achieving this objective forms part of the continual service improvement that is an essential element in all ITIL processes.

Scope of Service Level Management

The scope of service level management includes the performance of existing services being provided and the definition of required service levels for planned services. It forms a regular communication channel between the business and the IT service provider on all issues concerning the quality of service. SLM therefore has an important role to play in managing customers' expectations to ensure that the level of service they expect and the level of service they perceive they are receiving match. As stated earlier, SLM is concerned with ensuring that the warranty aspects of a service are provided to the expected level. The level of service expected for planned services is detailed in the service level requirements (*SLR*) specification, provided by the customer, and the agreed service levels (following negotiation) are documented in the SLA. SLAs should be written to cover *all* operational services. Through this involvement in the design phase, SLM ensures that the planned services will deliver the warranty levels required by the business.

SLM does *not* include agreeing on the utility aspects. The negotiation and agreement of requirements for service functionality (utility) is not part of the process, except to the degree that the functionality influences a service level requirement or target. Service level agreements typically describe key elements of the service's utility as part of the service description, but service level management activity does not include agreeing what the utility will be.

Service Level Management Value to the Business

Each IT service is composed of a number of elements provided by internal support teams or external third-party suppliers. An essential element of successful service level management is the negotiation and agreement with those who provide each element of the service regarding the level of service that they provide. A failure by these providers will translate to a failure to meet the SLA. We will look at these agreements, called *operational level agreements* (OLAs) in the case of internal teams and *underpinning contracts* in the case of external suppliers, later in this chapter.

Finally, SLM includes measuring and reporting on all service achievements compared to the agreed targets. The frequency, measurement method, and depth of reporting required are agreed on as part of the SLA negotiations.

It is important to understand the relationship between service level management and business relationship management. SLM deals with issues related to the quality of service being provided; a business relationship management's role is more strategic. The business relationship manager works closely with the business, understanding its current and future IT requirements. It is then the responsibility of the business relationship manager (BRM) to ensure that the service provider understands these needs and is able to meet them. SLM is concerned more about how to meet the targets by ensuring that agreements are in place with internal and external suppliers to provide elements of the service to the required standard. Business relationship management is covered in more detail in Chapter 19, "Business Relationship Management and Financial Management for IT."

Service level management cooperates with and complements business relationship management. Similarly, the improvement actions identified by SLM in a *service improvement plan (SIP)* are implemented in conjunction with continual service improvement; they are documented in the CSI register, where they are prioritized and reviewed.

Providers and Suppliers

It is important to understand the difference between providers and suppliers. Suppliers are external organizations that supply an element of the overall service. Customers may have little or no knowledge of the suppliers and the contracts that are held with them. The IT service provider will usually aim to provide a seamless service to the customer.

Providers fall into three categories; they can be embedded in a business unit (Type I), be shared across business units (Type II), or be external to the organization (Type III). Type III service providers will have an SLA with their external customers that will be a legal contract, because they are separate organizations.

The critical difference between suppliers and service providers is that suppliers provide only an element of the service and are not visible to the customer, whereas providers (including Type III providers) provide the whole service. A Type III provider would typically use a number of suppliers to provide elements of the service that they were providing, but the service level agreement is between the provider and the customer; the provider is responsible for ensuring that the supplier fulfills the contract that the provider has with them.

Service Level Management Policies, Principles, and Basic Concepts

Next we consider some of the policies, principles, and basic concepts of service level management.

Policies

The service provider should establish clear policies for the conduct of the service level management process. Policies typically define such things as the minimum required content of service level agreements and operational level agreements; when and how agreements are to be reviewed, renewed, revised, and/or renegotiated; and how frequently service level reporting will be provided and which methods will be used.

Primary importance should be given to the policies that are between SLM and supplier management. The performance of suppliers can be the critical element in the achievement of end-to-end service level commitments.

Principles

Service level management is part of the service design stage of the service lifecycle, although many of its activities take place in the service operation and continual service improvement stages. A fundamental principle of this process is that it includes the capturing of service level requirements (SLRs) and ensures that the new or changed service is designed to meet them. Once the service has been designed, it is the job of service level management to ensure that its delivery satisfies these requirements. SLAs formalize and document what has been agreed to, and they form the basis for managing the relationship between the service provider and the customer.

SLAs should include roles and responsibilities of the different parties involved, including the IT provider, the IT customer, and the actual users. The SLA should be worded as simply and clearly as possible. Agreements covering services provided to internal customers do not require legal language to be used. The emphasis should be on clarity and a shared understanding of the commitments being made. It is helpful to include a glossary of terms; IT terms may be ambiguous to the customer, and business expressions may not be clear to the IT staff.

There may be a temptation to agree to targets that cannot be adequately measured, but only measurable targets should be included in the SLA. Targets such as "Resolution of incidents will be achieved as soon as possible" are subjective and ambiguous.

SLAs should be signed by staff of the appropriate level of seniority on the customer and IT service provider sides. This provides credibility to the commitments made. Once an SLA is agreed to, it should be widely communicated to ensure that customers, users, and IT staff alike are aware of its existence and of the key targets. Where possible, targets should be programmed into the service management tool to facilitate reporting and to automate alerts when a target is likely to be breached so that action can be taken.

Basic Concepts

Service level management terminology is expressed from the point of view of the IT service provider, particularly as it relates to underpinning contracts and agreements. You should be familiar with this terminology from your foundation studies.

Service Level Agreement

The term *SLA* is used to refer to an agreement between the IT service provider and the customer(s) only. It should be a formal, written agreement, defining the key service targets and responsibilities of both parties. It is not sufficient to have an unwritten "understanding" as any disagreements regarding the level of service provided need to be resolved by reference to agreed, defined, and objective targets. The word *agreement* is important—an SLA cannot be imposed by either side since the agreement has to be mutually beneficial. An SLA will typically define targets for the warranty aspects a service should deliver and will also describe the utility of the service.

Underpinning Contract

The term *underpinning contract* is used here to refer to any kind of agreement or contract between an IT service provider and a supplier that supports the delivery of service to the customer. Examples include contracts with Internet service providers or software suppliers describing the service and support provided.

Operational Level Agreement

The term *operational level agreement* is an agreement between an IT service provider and another part of the same organization that assists with the provision of services. It describes agreements made by internal teams regarding the aspects of the service delivered by these teams. Examples include incident response and resolution times and support hours for each second-line support team.

Underpinning Agreements

Underpinning agreements is a generic term used to refer to all OLAs, and contracts or other agreements that underpin the customer SLAs. The term *underpin* means that these agreements support the targets in the SLA. It is essential that all targets contained within these agreements underpin those agreed to by the service provider and its customers. With appropriate underpinning agreements in place, the service provider can be assured that the targets in the SLA can be met. Figure 18.1 shows these service relationships and dependencies.

FIGURE 18.1   The service relationships and dependencies

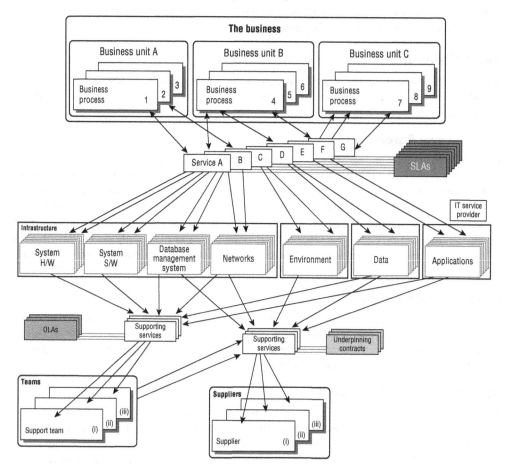

SLA Structures

There are a number of possible structures for SLAs, and the service provider should choose the structure that is most suitable. Each of the potential structures has advantages and disadvantages. Let's examine these structures in turn:

- A service-based SLA structure has an SLA for each service for all the customers of that service. This suits organizations offering a standard service, such as a hardware repair service, where all customers get the same response and repair service targets. It is not suitable where different customers have different requirements for the service, or if different service levels are inevitable. An example might be where customers in remote areas have to accept a slower response time. In such cases, separate targets may be needed within the one agreement. It is important that appropriate signatories to these agreements are identified. In situations where common levels of service are provided across all areas of the business (for example, email or telephony), the service-based SLA can be a suitable structure. To cater to some variation in requirements for these standard services, multiple classes of service (for example, gold, silver, and bronze) can also be used. Customers may not like having to refer to different SLAs for the different services they use.

- A customer-based SLA is an agreement with an individual customer group, covering all the services they use. An example is an SLA with an organization's finance or human resources department covering the IT systems that they use. Customers often like that all of their requirements are covered in a single document. Only one signatory is normally required, which simplifies this issue. The service provider may find it inconvenient that the same service may be referenced in several SLAs.

- Multilevel SLAs are another option and an example of a three-layer structure shown in Figure 18.2. The three layers in this example are corporate, customer, and service. The corporate level describes all the generic SLM issues that apply to every customer throughout the organization. The customer level covers all SLM issues relevant to one particular customer group or business unit, regardless of the service being used. The third level is the service level, which covers all SLM issues relevant to the specific service, in relation to a specific customer group (one for each service covered by the SLA).

FIGURE 18.2   Multilevel SLAs

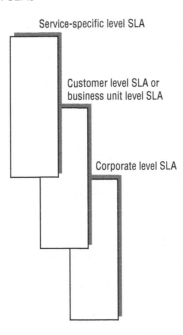

Service-specific level SLA

Customer level SLA or
business unit level SLA

Corporate level SLA

This structure allows SLAs to be kept to a manageable size, avoids unnecessary duplication, and reduces the need for frequent updates. It does involve extra administration to maintain the necessary relationships and links within the service catalog and the CMS.

Service Level Management Process Activities, Methods, and Techniques

Let's now explore the process and its activities in detail. In Figure 18.3, the service level management process, you can see the full scope of the activities in the service level management process.

FIGURE 18.3 The service level management process

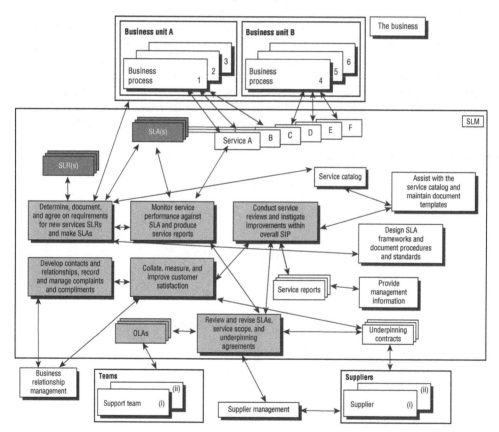

The key activities within the SLM process should include the following; ensure that you can identify each of these steps in the diagram.

Determining, negotiating, documenting, and agreeing on requirements for new or changed services and for existing services   SLAs should be agreed to in advance of the deployment of a new or changed service into the live environment. The targets in the SLA will be the results of the negotiation of service level requirements; for new services these targets will originate from SLRs developed early in the service design stage, and will be developed into a pilot or draft SLA. This document will be refined during the design stage and monitored during early life support. If the targets can be achieved, the SLA will be formally adopted and signed. If the targets are not being achieved, there may need to be improvements implemented to the design so that it can support the required targets, or the targets may need to be renegotiated. When the service meets the specified targets, the draft SLA can be finalized and signed by the service provider and the customer representatives.

As explained earlier, SLRs describe the customer requirement for an aspect of an IT service and are primarily concerned with the warranty aspects such as the availability of the service. These SLRs form the basis for the service level targets. If the requirements exceed the level of service currently supplied by the underpinning agreements, the service level manager will have to either renegotiate these underpinning agreements or negotiate with the customer to agree to a service level that can be supported.

Existing operational services also require service level agreements. If this process is being introduced for the first time, the service level targets for these will also need to be negotiated and agreed on.

Monitoring and measuring achievements of all operational services against targets within SLAs   As stated previously, targets for service performance must be specific, objective, and measurable. A balance must be struck between providing detailed service reporting and overwhelming the customer with numerous graphs. Cynical service providers may believe that providing large numbers of reports may actually obscure the truth about service level achievements. The reporting needs to be simple and clear and reflect the customer experience. It is better to report on a few key metrics, providing detailed analysis of any failures and a plan of action to address them, than to provide dozens of graphs that the customer does not fully understand.

One simple approach is to produce a report with the status of each service each month showing as red, amber, or green. Red signifies a breach or an agreed-to service level target, amber signifies that the target was nearly breached, and green shows that the service performed within target. This "RAG" report can convey a lot of information across all services but draws attention to the areas of concern so that they may be addressed.

Every report produced should follow reporting best practice—it should have a clear purpose, a defined audience, and clearly identified data sources. Reports should be produced to the schedule specified in the SLA.

Conducting service reviews   Some organizations carry out the negotiating, documenting, and agreement stages of service level management, and produce the agreed-to reports, but do not actively manage the level of service being provided. Meeting regularly (on a defined schedule) with customers to discuss achievements or issues and to identify improvement opportunities are important SLM activities. These service reviews build a stronger relationship with the customer and enable issues to be identified and dealt with. It is unfortunately common for organizations to fail to hold regular meetings after the first few. The customer then feels that their concerns are not being addressed.

Collating, measuring, and improving customer satisfaction　Customer satisfaction may be measured in a variety of ways. As with reporting against targets, it is important that issues are identified and actions taken. There is little point in the service desk routinely gathering such information after incident resolution or request fulfillment if no one in the service provider organization is analyzing the results. SLM is also responsible for logging and managing complaints and compliments.

Supporting activities　These other activities within the SLM process support the successful execution of the key activities:

- Designing SLA frameworks as described earlier.
- Periodically reviewing and revising the current SLAs and service scope. Reviewing and revising OLAs and contracts to ensure that they continue to underpin the SLAs (revision of contracts will be done in conjunction with supplier management).
- Developing, maintaining, and operating SLM procedures, including procedures for logging, actioning, and resolving all complaints, and for logging and distributing compliments.
- Making available and maintaining up-to-date SLM document templates and standards, including assisting with the service catalog. These templates are used as a starting point for all SLAs, SLRs, and OLAs and provide a consistent approach and format that will make them easier to maintain and administer.

Service Level Management Triggers, Inputs, and Outputs

Let's consider the triggers, inputs, and outputs for the service level management process. SLM is a process that has many active connections throughout the organization and its processes. It is important that the triggers, inputs, outputs, and interfaces be clearly defined to avoid duplicated effort or gaps in workflow.

Triggers

Many triggers instigate SLM activity:

- Changes in the service portfolio, such as new or changed business requirements or new or changed services
- New or changed agreements, service level requirements, service level agreements, operational level agreements, or contracts
- Service review meetings and actions

- Service breaches or threatened breaches
- Compliments and complaints
- Periodic activities such as reviewing, reporting, and customer satisfaction surveys
- Changes in strategy or policy

Inputs

A number of sources of information are relevant to the service level management process:

- Business information from the organization's business strategy, development plans and financial plans, and information on its current and future requirements
- Business impact analysis, which provides information on the impact, priority, risk, and number of users associated with each service
- Business requirements, which details any agreed-to, new, or changed business requirements
- The strategies, policies, and constraints from service strategy
- The service portfolio and service catalog
- Change information, including RFCs, from the change management process, with a change schedule and a need to assess all changes for their impact on all services
- The configuration management system, which contains information on the relationships between the business services, the supporting services, and the technology
- Customer and user feedback, complaints, and compliments
- Improvement opportunities from the CSI register
- Other inputs, including advice, information, and input from any of the other processes (e.g., incident management, capacity management, and availability management), together with the existing SLAs, SLRs, and OLAs and past service reports on the quality of service delivered

Outputs

The outputs of SLM should include the following:

- Service reports, which provide details of the service levels achieved in relation to the targets contained within SLAs
- Service improvement opportunities for inclusion in the CSI register and for later review and prioritization in conjunction with the CSI manager
- Service improvement plans, which provide an overall program or plan of prioritized improvement actions, encompassing appropriate services and processes, together with associated impacts and risks
- The service quality plan, which should document and plan the overall improvement of service quality
- Document templates for service level requirements capture, service level agreements, operational level agreements, and contracts

- Reports on OLAs and underpinning contracts
- Service review meeting minutes and actions
- SLA review and service scope review meeting minutes
- Updated change information, including updates to RFCs
- Revised requirements for underpinning contracts

Service Level Management Interfaces

SLM interfaces with several other processes to ensure agreed service levels are being met:

- Problem management will address the causes of any failures that impact targets and work to prevent their recurrence, thus improving the delivery of the service against targets.
- Availability management works to remove any single points of failure that could lead to downtime and addresses the causes of such downtime in order to deliver the specified level of availability to the customer.
- Capacity management plans ahead to ensure that sufficient capacity is provided, thus preventing service failures that would otherwise have occurred.
- Incident management focuses on resolving incidents and restoring service as quickly as possible. Performance against targets for incident resolution by identifying agreed-to priorities is usually a major area within an SLA.
- IT service continuity will plan to ensure that service continues to be provided despite major upheavals; where a break in service cannot be prevented, it will work to ensure that the service is restored in line with the business requirements.
- Information security ensures that the customer's data is protected and will work with the service level manager to educate the customers and users regarding their own responsibilities in this area.
- Supplier management ensures that underpinning contracts are in place and are being fulfilled.
- Service catalog management provides information about services to support the SLA.
- Financial management provides cost information.
- Design coordination ensures the design meets the SLR.
- SLM works with CSI in designing and implementing the SIP.
- SLM works with business relationship management (BRM). BRM is more concerned with strategy, identifying customer needs, and ensuring that the objectives are met.

Information Management and Service Level Management

Service level management is a process that provides key information on operational services, their expected targets, and the service achievements and breaches for all operational services. This means it is an important part of information management across the lifecycle. It assists service catalog management with the management of the service catalog and also provides the information and trends on customer satisfaction, including complaints and compliments.

The service provider organization is reliant on the information that service level management provides on the quality of IT service provided to the customer. This includes information on the customer's expectation and perception of that quality of service. This information should be widely available to all areas of the service provider organization.

Service Level Management Process Roles

This section describes a number of roles that need to be performed in support of the service level management process. These roles are not job titles; rather they are guidance on the roles that may be needed to successfully run the process, and each organization will have to define appropriate job titles and job descriptions for its needs. Chapter 1, "Introduction to Operational Support and Analysis," explored the generic roles applicable to all processes throughout the service lifecycle. The roles described there are relevant to the service level management process and to the supplier management roles we discuss later in this chapter, but once again several additional requirements also apply.

Service Level Management Process Owner

The service level management process owner's responsibilities typically include the following:

- Carrying out the generic process owner role for the service level management process
- Liaising with the business relationship management process owner to ensure proper coordination and communication between the two processes
- Working with other process owners to ensure that there is an integrated approach to the design and implementation of service catalog management, service portfolio management, service level management, and business relationship management

Service Level Management Process Manager

The service level management process manager's responsibilities typically include the following:

- Carrying out the generic process manager role for the service level management process
- Coordinating interfaces with other processes, especially service catalog management, service portfolio management, business relationship management, and supplier management
- Keeping aware of changing business needs
- Ensuring that the customers' current and future service level requirements are identified, understood, and documented in SLA and service level requirements documents
- Negotiating and agreeing to levels of service to be delivered with the internal or external customer and formally documenting these levels of service in SLAs
- Negotiating and agreeing to OLAs that underpin the SLAs
- Assisting with the production and maintenance of the service portfolio, service catalog, and application portfolio

- Ensuring that targets agreed to within underpinning contracts are aligned with SLA and SLR targets
- Ensuring that service reports are produced for each customer service
- Investigating breaches of SLA targets and taking action to prevent their recurrence
- Ensuring that service performance reviews take place as planned and are documented with agreed-to actions
- Ensuring that service improvement initiatives are acted on and progress reports are provided to customers
- Reviewing service scope, SLAs, OLAs, and other agreements on a regular basis, ideally at least annually
- Assessing all changes for their impact on service levels, including SLAs, OLAs, and underpinning contracts; this will include attending change advisory board (CAB) meetings if appropriate
- Identifying and building relationships with all customers and other key stakeholders to involve in SLR, SLA, and OLA negotiations
- Managing complaints, ensuring that they are recorded, escalated where necessary, and resolved
- Measuring, recording, analyzing, and improving customer satisfaction

The following two roles are not service level management roles, but they are important for the successful execution of the process.

Service Owner

Service owners' involvement in the service level management process includes the following:

- Ensuring that the ongoing service delivery and support meet agreed-to customer requirements
- Ensuring consistent and appropriate communication with customer(s) for service-related inquiries and issues
- Providing input on service attributes such as performance and availability
- Participating in external service review meetings (with the business)
- Soliciting required data, statistics, and reports for analysis and to facilitate effective service monitoring and performance
- Participating in negotiating SLAs and OLAs relating to the service

Business Relationship Manager

Business relationship managers' involvement in the service level management process includes the following:

- Ensuring high levels of customer satisfaction
- Establishing and maintaining a constructive relationship between the service provider and the customer at a strategic level

- Confirming customer high-level requirements
- Facilitating service level agreement negotiations by ensuring that the correct customer representatives participate
- Identifying opportunities for improvement

Critical Success Factors and Key Performance Indicators for Service Level Management

The term *critical success factor (CSF)* is used for an element that is necessary for an organization or project to achieve its mission. CSFs can be used to identify the important elements of success. These are measured by key performance indicators (KPIs). Understanding the CSFs for each of the SOA processes will provide a strong basis for the KPIs that will be used to demonstrate success.

Key performance indicators can be used to judge the efficiency and effectiveness of service level management activities and the progress of the service improvement plan.

The KPIs should be developed from the service, customer, and business perspective and should cover both subjective (qualitative) and objective (quantitative) measurements.

Objective measures include the following:

- The number or percentage of service targets being met
- The number and severity of service breaches
- The number of services with up-to-date SLAs
- The number of services with timely reports and active service reviews

A subjective measure would be an improvement in customer satisfaction.

The following list includes some sample critical success factors and key performance indicators for SLM:

- CSF: Managing the overall quality of IT services required in both the number and level of services provided and managed.
    - KPI: Percentage reduction in SLA targets threatened
    - KPI: Percentage increase in customer perception and satisfaction of SLA achievements via service reviews and customer satisfaction survey responses
- CSF: Deliver the service as previously agreed at affordable costs.
    - KPI: Total number and percentage increase in fully documented SLAs in place
    - KPI: Percentage reduction in the costs associated with service provision
    - KPI: Frequency of service review meetings
- CSF: Manage the interface with the business and users.
    - KPI: Increased percentage of services covered by SLAs
    - KPI: Documented and agreed-to SLM processes and procedures in place

- KPI: Documentary evidence that issues raised at service and SLA reviews are being followed up and resolved
- KPI: Reduction in the number and severity of SLA breaches
- KPI: Effective review and follow-up of all SLA, OLA, and underpinning contract breaches

Challenges for Service Level Management

You will face numerous challenges when introducing service level management. Doing so requires alignment and engagement across the whole organization.

One challenge faced by service level management is that of identifying suitable customer representatives with whom to negotiate. Who "owns" the service on the customer side?

Another challenge may arise if there has been no previous experience of service level management. In these cases, it is advisable to start with a draft service level agreement. If an organization is just beginning to establish SLM and does not yet have SLAs in place for existing services, the process of defining them may require monitoring, measuring, and reporting on the current levels of service being delivered and using this information to inform negotiations with customers to establish acceptable targets.

One difficulty sometimes encountered is that staff at different levels within the customer community may have different objectives and perceptions.

Risks for Service Level Management

Some of the risks associated with service level management are as follows:

- A lack of accurate input, involvement, and commitment from the business and customers
- Lack of appropriate tools and resources required
- The process becoming a bureaucratic, administrative process
- Insufficient access to and support of appropriate and up-to-date CMS and SKMS
- Bypassing of service level management processes
- High customer expectations and low perception

Supplier Management

ITIL defines *supplier management* as the process responsible for obtaining value for money from suppliers, ensuring that all contracts with external suppliers and agreements with internal suppliers support the needs of the business and that all suppliers meet their contractual commitments.

The supplier management process describes best practices in managing suppliers to ensure that the services they provide meet expectations. It is included in the design phase of the service lifecycle, because it is important that this aspect be considered while the service is being designed. The type of supplier relationship will be part of the strategy phase, and a close relationship with suppliers will be required for a successful service transition. Once the service is operational, the day-to-day delivery against the contract must be monitored and managed, and should any issues arise, the improvement plan will be the responsibility of continual service improvement.

Purpose of Supplier Management

The purpose of supplier management is to ensure that suppliers provide value for money. By managing suppliers, the service provider can ensure the best delivery of service to their customer. Managing suppliers ensures that the necessary contracts are in place and enforced. Some service providers will have a sourcing strategy that ensures that most or all elements of the service are delivered by the service providers themselves, without using third parties, whereas others will use third-party suppliers to provide large parts of the service. Where service provision depends on the performance of suppliers, it is essential that suppliers be appropriately managed to ensure that the service provided is of the required quality.

Objectives of Supplier Management

The main objectives of the supplier management process are to obtain value for money from suppliers and contracts and ensure that contracts with suppliers are aligned to business needs. These contracts should support and align with specified targets in service level requirements and service level agreements, in conjunction with service level management.

Scope of Supplier Management

The supplier management process should include the management of all suppliers and contracts needed to support the provision of IT services to the business. Each service provider should have formal processes for the management of all suppliers and contracts.

The supplier management process should include implementation and enforcement of the supplier policy, including maintenance of a supplier contract management information system (SCMIS). It is important to ensure that suppliers and contracts are categorized and a risk assessment is carried out. Suppliers and contracts need to be evaluated and selected so that the appropriate suppliers are engaged.

A key part of the process is the development, negotiation, and agreement of contracts, including contract review, renewal, and termination. This is part of the management of suppliers and supplier performance.

The process will also identify improvement opportunities for inclusion in the CSI register, as well as the implementation of service and supplier improvement plans.

Supplier management will also manage the maintenance of standard contracts, terms, and conditions; contractual dispute resolution; and, where applicable, the engagement of subcontracted suppliers.

IT supplier management often has to comply with organizational or corporate standards, guidelines, and requirements, particularly those of corporate legal, finance, and purchasing.

Supplier Management Value to the Business

The process will manage relationships with suppliers, and monitor and manage supplier performance. Supplier management is responsible for the negotiation and agreement of contracts with suppliers and managing them through their lifecycle. This process is assisted by the development and maintenance of a supplier policy and a supporting supplier and contract management information system (SCMIS).

The purpose is to ensure the delivery to the business of end-to-end, seamless, quality IT services that are aligned with the business's expectation. The supplier management process should align with all corporate requirements and the requirements of all other IT and service management processes, particularly information security management and IT service continuity management. This ensures that the business obtains value from supporting supplier services and that they are aligned with business needs.

Supplier Management Principles, Policies, and Basic Concepts

The supplier management process seeks to ensure that the service provider receives the level of service from third-party suppliers that is specified in the contracts with them. It ensures that suppliers meet the terms, conditions, and targets of their contracts. The process aims to increase the value for money obtained from suppliers and the services they provide.

Principles

All supplier management process activity should be driven by a supplier strategy and policy from service strategy. The supplier strategy, sometimes called the sourcing strategy, defines the service provider's plan for how it will leverage the contribution of suppliers in the achievement of the overall service strategy. Some organizations might adopt a strategy that dictates the use of suppliers only in very specific and limited circumstances, whereas another organization might choose to make extensive use of suppliers in IT service provision. The greater the contribution the supplier makes to business value, the more effort the service provider should put into the management of the supplier. In Figure 18.4 you can see the engagement of the process with the contracts manager and the various supplier managers in the organization.

FIGURE 18.4   Supplier management: roles and interfaces

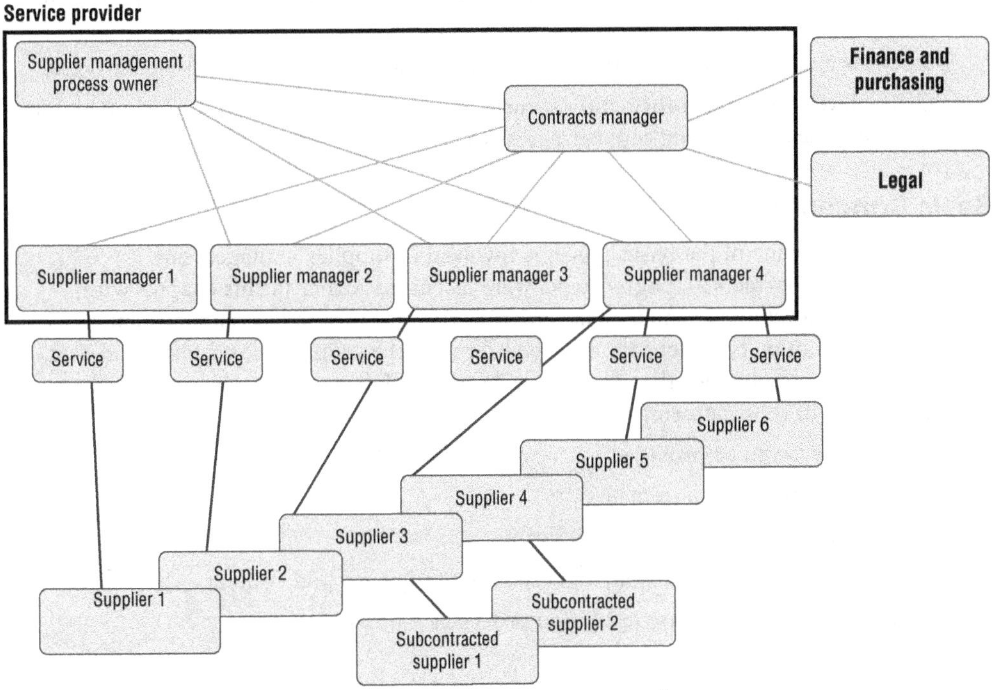

Service provider

You can also see the interaction with finance and purchasing and the legal department, all of which are important when engaging with third parties outside the main organization.

You can see the management of the services provided by or supported by the suppliers, and their subcontracted partners.

Policies

The supplier management policies provide guidance to service provider staff regarding the management of suppliers in accordance with the sourcing strategy. Supplier policies may cover such areas as

- How communications should be conducted with potential suppliers in regard to the solicitation, bidding, and procurement processes to ensure fairness and objectivity.

- Defined responsibilities for interaction with suppliers.

- Rules regarding accepting gifts or promotional items from suppliers to prevent bias in the awarding of contracts.

- Supplier standards—for example, compliance with legislation regarding health and safety, diversity, and minimum wages. This may include standards the supplier in turn imposes on its subcontractors, especially in lower-wage economies. There have been examples when organizations have been embarrassed by press reporting of poor practice in its supply chain.

- Standards and guidelines for various supplier contract types and/or agreement types.
- Policies developed with information security management regarding the ownership of data and policies regarding supplier access to systems.

Basic Concepts

Let's now look at some of the basic concepts involved in supplier management.

Underpinning contracts and agreements were discussed earlier in this chapter with regard to service level management. They are also relevant to supplier management, since the underpinning contracts are managed through the supplier management process. Contracts provide binding legal commitments between IT service provider and supplier. Typical contents of these agreements include

- Scope of services to be provided
- Service performance requirements
- Division and agreement of responsibilities
- Contact points, communication, and reporting frequency and content
- Contract review and dispute resolution processes
- Price structure
- Payment terms
- Commitments to change and investment
- Agreement change process
- Confidentiality and announcements
- Intellectual property rights and copyright
- Liability limitations
- Termination rights of each party
- Obligations at termination and beyond

The procurement and legal departments will input into the wording of these contracts. The contracts may also include a number of other related documents as schedules, including security and business continuity requirements, required technical standards, migration plans, and disclosure agreements.

The supplier and contract management information system is a database or structured document that provides a repository of all the information required to manage supplier contracts throughout their lifecycle. It contains key attributes of all contracts and suppliers together with details of the type of service(s) or product(s) provided by each supplier, and all other information and relationships with other associated CIs. It should be part of the service knowledge management system.

It is important for the organization to appreciate the importance of the suppliers and the impact should they fail to provide the agreed level of service. This requires that the suppliers be categorized according to their value, importance, risk, and impact if the supplier does not perform as contracted, as shown in Figure 18.5.

FIGURE 18.5   Supplier categorization

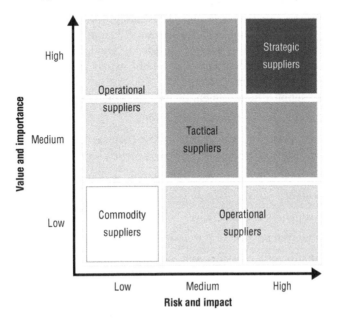

There are four layers of categorization:

Strategic   For significant "partnering" relationships that involve senior managers sharing confidential strategic information to facilitate long-term plans. These relationships would normally be managed and owned at a senior management level within the service provider organization, and would involve regular and frequent contact and performance reviews.

Tactical   For relationships involving significant commercial activity and business interaction. These relationships would normally be managed by middle management and would involve regular contact and performance reviews, often including ongoing improvement programs.

Operational   For suppliers of operational products or services. These relationships would normally be managed by junior operational management and would involve infrequent but regular contact and performance reviews.

Commodity   For suppliers providing low-value and/or readily available products and services, which could be alternatively sourced relatively easily.

Supplier Management Process, Methods, and Techniques

Once the requirements for suppliers have been defined as part of the overall approach to the delivery of a service, the supplier management process needs to evaluate the appropriate suppliers and ensure that the contracts are fit for purpose and use. It is important to establish relationships with new suppliers and ensure that appropriate measures and management are in place to monitor supplier performance. All contracts should have reference to renewal and termination, which should be included in regular views of the contract.

All information, reports, and measures should be stored in the supplier and contract management information system.

The activities of supplier management include the following:

- Define new supplier and contract requirements:

- Identify business needs and preparation of the business case, including options (internal and external), costs, timescales, targets, benefits, and risk assessment

- Produce a statement of requirement (SoR) and/or invitation to tender (ITT)

- Ensure conformance to strategy/policy

- Evaluate new suppliers and contracts

- Identify the preferred method of purchase or procurement

- Establish evaluation criteria—for example, services, capability (both personnel and organization), quality, and cost

- Evaluate alternative options

- Select the best supplier based on the evaluation criteria

- Negotiate contracts, targets, and the terms and conditions, including responsibilities, closure, renewal, extension, dispute, and transfer

- Agree on and award the contract

- Categorize suppliers

- Maintain the SCMIS

- Assess or reassess the supplier and contract

- Ensure that changes progressed through service transition

- Set up the supplier service and contract within the SCMIS and any other associated corporate systems

- Transition the service

- Establish contacts and relationships

- Monitor, report, and manage supplier performance, including implementing improvement plans

- Manage the relationship with the supplier

- Review, at least annually, service scope against business need, targets, and agreements
- Plan for possible closure, renewal, and extension
- Renegotiate and renew or terminate and/or transfer contracts

The process should be subject to the corporate supplier management policy, but an IT supplier strategy should be developed to manage the specific requirements for IT service delivery. Figure 18.6 shows the main activities of the supplier management process.

FIGURE 18.6   Supplier management process

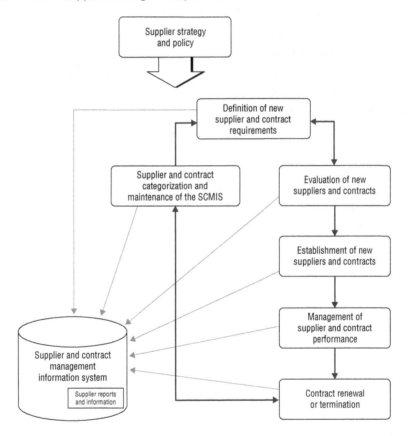

Supplier Management Triggers, Inputs, and Outputs

We will now review the triggers, inputs, and outputs of supplier management.

Triggers

Many events that trigger supplier management activity:

- New or changed corporate governance guidelines
- New or changed business and IT strategies, policies, or plans
- New or changed business needs or new or changed services
- New or changed requirements within agreements, such as service level requirements, service level agreements, operational level agreements, or contracts
- Review and revision of designs and strategies
- Periodic activities such as reviewing, revising, or reporting, including review and revision of supplier management policies, reports, and plans
- Requests from other areas, particularly SLM and information security management, for assistance with supplier issues
- Requirements for new contracts, contract renewal, or contract termination
- Recategorization of suppliers and/or contracts

Inputs

There are numerous inputs to the supplier management process:

- Business information
- Supplier and contracts strategy
- Supplier plans and strategies
- Supplier contracts, agreements, and targets
- Supplier and contract performance information
- IT information
- Performance issues
- Financial information
- Service information
- CMS

Outputs

The outputs of supplier management are used within all other parts of the process, by many other processes, and by other parts of the organization.

The information provided is as follows:

- SCMIS
- Supplier and contract performance information and reports
- Supplier and contract review meeting minutes

- Supplier service improvement plans
- Supplier survey reports

Supplier Management Interfaces

The key interfaces that supplier management has with other processes are as follows:

Service Level Management   Supplier management provides assistance with the determining of targets, requirements, and responsibilities for suppliers. SLM assists supplier management in the investigation of SLA and SLR breaches caused by poor supplier performance. SLM also provides invaluable input into the supplier management review process.

Change Management   Contractual documents should be managed through change control.

Information Security Management   Information security management relies on supplier management for the management of suppliers and their access to services and systems, and their responsibilities with regard to conformance to the service provider's ISM policies and requirements.

Financial Management for IT Services   This process provides adequate funds to finance supplier management requirements and contracts and provides financial advice and guidance on purchase and procurement matters.

Service Portfolio Management   This process looks to supplier management input to ensure that all supporting services and their details and relationships are accurately reflected within the service portfolio.

IT Service Continuity Management   This process works with supplier management with regard to the management of continuity service suppliers.

Information Management

The information required by supplier management should be stored in the supplier contract and management information system (SCMIS) and form part of the CMS or the service knowledge management system (SKMS).

All information relating to suppliers and contracts, as well as all the information relating to the operation of the supporting services provided by suppliers, should be held in the system. Information relating to these supporting services should also be contained within the service portfolio, together with the relationships to all other services and components. This information should be integrated and maintained in alignment with all other IT management information systems, particularly the service portfolio and the CMS.

Supplier Management Process Roles

This section describes a number of roles that need to be performed in support of the supplier management process. As with the service level management roles described earlier in this chapter, these are specific additional requirements to the generic roles applicable to all processes throughout the service lifecycle described in Chapter 1.

Supplier Management Process Owner

The supplier management process owner's responsibilities typically include

- Carrying out the generic process owner role for the supplier management process
- Working with the business to ensure proper coordination and communication between corporate vendor management and/or procurement and supplier management
- Working with other process owners to ensure that there is an integrated approach to the design and implementation of supplier management, service level management, and corporate vendor management and/or procurement processes

Supplier Management Process Manager

The supplier management process manager's responsibilities typically include

- Carrying out the generic process manager role for the process
- Coordinating interfaces between supplier management and other processes, especially service level management and corporate vendor management and/or procurement processes
- Assisting in the development and review of SLAs, contracts, agreements or any other documents for third-party suppliers
- Ensuring that value for money is obtained from all IT suppliers and contracts
- Ensuring that all IT supplier processes are consistent and in line with corporate supplier strategies
- Maintaining the supplier and contract management information system
- Regularly carrying out risk assessments of all suppliers and contracts
- Ensuring that all supporting services are scoped and documented, showing interfaces and dependencies between suppliers
- Ensuring that relationships between lead and subcontracted suppliers are documented and formalized
- Performing contract or SLA reviews at least annually, updating them when required and following the change management process
- Dealing with contractual disputes in an efficient and effective manner
- Dealing with the expected end, early end, or transfer of a service
- Monitoring, reporting, and regularly reviewing supplier performance against targets, identifying improvement actions as appropriate, and ensuring that these actions are implemented
- Assessing changes that impact suppliers, supporting services, and contracts, and attending CAB meetings when appropriate
- Ensuring that each supplier and contract has a nominated owner within the service provider organization

Supplier Management Critical Success Factors and KPIs

The following list includes some sample critical success factors for supplier management.

- CSF: Business protected from poor supplier performance or disruption
    - KPI: Increase in the number of suppliers meeting the targets within the contract
    - KPI: Reduction in the number of breaches of contractual targets
- CSF: Supporting services and their targets align with business needs and targets
    - KPI: Increase in the number of service and contractual reviews held with suppliers
    - KPI: Increase in the number of supplier and contractual targets aligned with SLA and SLR targets
- CSF: Availability of services is not compromised by supplier performance
    - KPI: Reduction in the number of service breaches caused by suppliers
    - KPI: Reduction in the number of threatened service breaches caused by suppliers

Supplier Management Challenges and Risks

We'll begin with looking at the key challenges for the process.

Challenges

Supplier management faces many challenges, which could include

- Continually changing business and IT needs and managing significant change in parallel with delivering existing service
- Working with an imposed nonideal contract, a contract that has poor targets or terms and conditions, or poor or nonexistent definition of service or supplier performance targets, including those that have punitive penalty charges for early exit
- Legacy issues, especially with services recently outsourced
- Insufficient expertise retained within the organization
- Disputes over charges
- Interference by either party in the running of the other's operation
- Being caught in a daily fire-fighting mode, losing the proactive approach
- Poor communication—not interacting often enough or quickly enough or focusing on the right issues, including personality conflicts and/or cultural conflicts
- One party using the contract to the detriment of the other party, resulting in win–lose changes rather than joint win–win changes
- Losing the strategic perspective, focusing solely on operational issues

Risks

The major areas of risk associated with supplier management include

- Lack of commitment from the business and senior management to the supplier management process and procedures

- Lack of appropriate information on future business and IT policies, plans, and strategies

- Lack of resources and/or budget for the supplier management process

- Legacy of badly written and agreed-to contracts that do not underpin or support business needs or SLA and SLR targets

- Supplier personnel or organizational culture that is not aligned with that of the service provider or the business

- Lack of clarity and integration by supplier with service management processes, policies, and procedures of the service provider

- Poor corporate financial processes, such as procurement and purchasing, that do not support good supplier management

Summary

This chapter explored two processes involved in service offerings and agreements: service level management and availability management. It covered the purpose and objectives for the processes, and their scope and value. We reviewed the policies for the processes, and the activities, methods, and techniques.

Lastly we reviewed triggers, inputs, outputs, and interfaces for the processes; the information management associated with the processes; and the roles involved. We also considered the critical success factors and key performance indicators, challenges, and risks for each of the processes.

Exam Essentials

Understand the purpose and objectives of service level management and supplier management. It is important for you to be able to explain the purpose and objectives of the service level management and supplier management processes. Service level management should ensure that the services are delivered to the customer's satisfaction and in line with their requirements. Supplier management should ensure that value for money is obtained from all contractual relationships with external organizations.

Understand the scope of service level management.   SLM does *not* include agreeing on the utility aspects. The negotiation and agreement of requirements for service functionality (utility) is not part of the process, except to the degree that the functionality influences a service level requirement or target.

Explain and differentiate between the different stages of supplier management. Understand the importance of contract negotiation, and the implementation of the supplier policy.

Explain the different categories of service providers.   Providers fall into three categories; they can be embedded in a business unit (Type I Internal services), be shared across business units (Type II Shared services), or be external to the organization (Type III External services). Type III service providers will have an SLA with their external customers that will be a legal contract, because they are separate organizations.

Understand the critical success factors and key performance indicators for the processes. Measurement of the process is an important part of understanding the success. You should be familiar with the CSFs and KPIs for both service level management and supplier management.

Review Questions

You can find the answers to the review questions in the appendix.

1. Which of these statements provides the *best* description of the purpose of service level management?
   A. Ensure that all current and planned IT services are delivered to agreed achievable targets.
   B. Ensure that there is a high-level relationship with customers to capture business demands.
   C. Ensure that users have a single point of contact for all operational issues.
   D. Ensure that there is a smooth transition of services to and from service providers.

2. Which of these is an objective of service level management?
   A. Monitor changes throughout their lifecycle
   B. Define, document, agree, monitor, measure, report, and review services
   C. Respond to service requests and inquiries promptly
   D. Establish the root cause of incidents and problems efficiently and cost effectively

3. Which of the following would *not* be part of a service level agreement?
   A. Description of the service
   B. Service hours
   C. Definition of business strategy
   D. Service continuity arrangements

4. Which of the following agreements commonly supports the achievement of a service level agreement?
   1. Operational-level agreement
   2. Strategic business plan
   3. Underpinning contract
   4. Internal finance agreement
   A. 1, 2, and 3
   B. 1, 2, and 4
   C. 1 and 3
   D. 2 and 4

5. Which of the following is the best description of an underpinning contract?
   A. An agreement between an IT service provider and another part of the same organization assisting in the provision of services
   B. An agreement between an IT service provider and customer relating to the delivery of services
   C. An agreement between different customers about the requirements of the service
   D. A contract between an IT service provider and an external third-party organization assisting in the delivery of services

6. Which of the following is a common color scheme applied to a service level management monitoring chart?

  A. Red, blue, green

  B. Red, amber, green

  C. Blue, green, black

  D. Black, amber, blue

7. Which of the following are responsibilities of supplier management?

  1. Negotiating with internal suppliers

  2. Negotiating with external suppliers

  3. Monitoring delivery against the contract

  4. Ensuring value for money

  A. 1 and 2 only

  B. All of the above

  C. 1, 2, and 3

  D. 2, 3, and 4

8. Which of the following are categories of supplier described in ITIL?

  1. Strategic

  2. Operational

  3. Trusted

  4. Commodity

  A. 1 and 2 only

  B. All of the above

  C. 1, 2, and 4

  D. 2, 3, and 4

9. Suppliers are categorized according to which factors to demonstrate their priority?

  A. Risk and importance/value and impact

  B. Cost and importance/risk and value

  C. Risk and impact/value and importance

  D. Value and cost/risk and probability

10. Which of these statements is/are correct?

  1. Information about supplier policies is held in the SCMIS.

  2. Supplier contracts are held in the SCMIS.

  A. Statement 1 only

  B. Statement 2 only

  C. Both statements

  D. Neither statement

Chapter

19

Business Relationship Management and Financial Management for IT

THE FOLLOWING ITIL SERVICE OFFERINGS AND AGREEMENTS EXAM OBJECTIVES ARE DISCUSSED IN THIS CHAPTER:

✓ Business Relationship Management and Financial Management for IT

✓ Each process is discussed in terms of

- Purpose
- Objectives
- Scope
- Value
- Policies
- Principles and basic concepts
- Process activities, methods, and techniques
- Triggers, inputs, outputs, and interfaces
- Information management
- Roles and responsibilities
- Critical success factors and key performance indicators
- Challenges
- Risks

Business relationship management ensures that the service provider has the necessary information regarding the business's required outcomes, customer needs, and priorities, and serves as the interface with the customer at a strategic level.

Financial management for IT services (FMITS) is the process by which service providers (and other business units) calculate, forecast, and track costs and income related to services.

This chapter covers the day-to-day operation of each process; the detail of its activities, methods, techniques; and its information management.

Business Relationship Management

Business relationship management was originally a role fulfilled to ensure that the business had a named contact within the IT service provider. The process has matured over time to become an essential part of a mature service management approach. BRM is now recognized as a strategic process in its own right, not just as a role supporting service level management at an executive level.

The BRM process provides a connection between organizational executives and the strategic management of the service provider.

Purpose of Business Relationship Management

This process has an important part to play in the alignment of the IT service provider and the customer. The purpose of the process is twofold:

- Establish a relationship between the service provider and the customer, and maintain it with a continued review of business and customer needs. This relationship is extremely important for building a business rapport between service provider and customer.

- Identify customer needs and ensure that the service provider can meet those needs, both now and in the future. BRM is the process that ensures the service provider is able to understand the changing needs of the business over time. The relationship also allows the customer to articulate the value of the services to the service provider.

One of the most important concepts in this relationship is that of expectation—the customer's expectation of the service provider capability and the service provider's expectation of the customer's needs. It is critical that the expectation of the customer does not exceed what they are prepared to pay for, and BRM is instrumental in the management of this communication.

Objectives of Business Relationship Management

The objectives of BRM are as follows:

- Ensure that the service provider has a clear understanding of the customer's perspective of the service so that the service provider is able to prioritize the services and assets accordingly.

- Ensure that customer satisfaction remains high, which will demonstrate that the service is achieving the needs of the customer.

- Establish and maintain a relationship between the customer and service provider that enables understanding of the business drivers and the customer.

- Ensure that the organization and the service provider communicate effectively so that the service provider will be aware of any changes to the customer environment. Changes to the customer environment may have an impact on the services provided.

- Identify technology changes or trends that may have an impact on the type, level, or utilization of the service provided.

- Ensure that the service provider is able to articulate the business requirements for new or changed services and that services continue to meet the needs of the business and continue to deliver value.

- Provide mediation where there is conflict on the use of services between business units. This may be a conflict of resource allocation, or perhaps the requirement to utilize or change functionality differs for specific departments.

- Establish a formal procedure for managing complaints and escalations with the customer.

Scope of Business Relationship Management

The scope of BRM will vary depending on the nature and culture of the organization. If the organization works with an internal service provider, it is likely that BRM will be carried out between senior management representatives in both the IT department and business units. Often in larger organizations, you will be able to find dedicated business relationship managers, but in smaller organizations the role may be combined with other managerial responsibility. The business relationship manager will work with the customer representatives to understand the objectives of the business and ensure that the services provided are in alignment and supportive of those objectives.

If an external service provider supports the organization, you will commonly find that a dedicated account manager carries out the process, with an individual allocated to a customer, or a group of smaller customers with similar requirements. As the external service provider relationship with the business is captured in a contract, the focus will be on maximizing contractual value through customer satisfaction.

One of the major requirements for the business relationship manager is to focus on understanding how the services we provide meet the requirements of our customers. The process must ensure that we can communicate effectively with our customers so that we could understand their needs. Some of the key areas we should consider are as follows:

- We need to consider business outcomes so that we understand what the customer wants to achieve.

- We need to understand how the customer uses our services and which services are being offered to them.

- We need to consider how we manage the services that are being offered, in terms of responsibility for the provision, the service levels we deliver, and the quality of service that is being achieved. We should also consider any changes that may be required in response to business and IT plans.

- As IT service providers, it is vital that we keep track of technology trends and advances, which may impact on our service delivery. All too often, customers will hear about new technologies but not understand the impact of them. It is the responsibility of the business relationship manager to ensure that we communicate and provide advice on the best use of technology to deliver service value.

- We need to measure the levels of customer satisfaction and respond to any drop in satisfaction with suitable action plans. The business relationship manager will be a key figure in the communication and management of any such plans.

- We need to consider how we can optimize the service we provide for the future.

- The BRM process should be concerned with the way that the service provider is represented to the customer. This may mean engaging with the business to ensure that commitments from both sides have been fulfilled.

To successfully carry out the BRM process, and so that all of these factors can be taken into consideration, it is necessary to work with other service management processes and functions. For example, the ability to associate business outcomes with services is part of service portfolio management; service level management provides information about service levels and their achievement; and service asset and configuration management maps customers and service owners to the infrastructure, applications, and services.

Often other activities such as project management will use the business relationship manager when they need someone to communicate with the customer. The communication is done by the business relationship manager, but it remains part of the project. The business relationship manager role is discussed further later in this chapter.

This will require clear boundaries, relationships, and responsibilities to be identified between BRM and other service management processes, since there is a strong potential for confusion. Business relationship management should focus on the relationship between the customer and service provider, and the achievement of customer satisfaction, but the other service management processes should focus on the services themselves and how well they meet the specified requirements.

Business relationship management does not ignore the services, but it should be focused on the high-level perspective of whether the service is meeting the business needs rather than specific targets for delivery. Equally, the other service management processes do not ignore this aspect of customer satisfaction, but they should be focused on the quality of the services and how customer expectations can be met.

An example of this is the difference between the service level management and BRM processes. They both have regular interaction with customers, and both are concerned with the ongoing review and management of service and service quality. But each has a different purpose, and the nature of the interface with the customer differs in content and responsibility. This is clearly shown in Table 19.1, which is an extract from the service strategy publication.

TABLE 19.1   Differences between BRM and service level management

	Business relationship management	Service level management
Purpose	To establish and maintain a business relationship between the service provider and the customer based on understanding the customer and its business needs. To identify customer needs (utility and warranty) and ensure that the service provider is able to meet these needs.	To negotiate service level agreements (warranty terms) with customers and ensure that all service management processes, operational level agreements, and underpinning contracts are appropriate for the service level targets.
Focus	Strategic and tactical—the focus is on the overall relationship between the service provider and their customer, and which services the service provider will deliver to meet customer needs.	Tactical and operational—the focus is on reaching agreement on the level of service that will be delivered for new and existing services, and whether the service provider was able to meet those agreements.
Primary measure	Customer satisfaction, also an improvement in the customer's intention to better use and pay for the service. Another metric is whether customers are willing to recommend the service to other (potential) customers.	Achieving agreed-to levels of service (which leads to customer satisfaction).

Business relationship management is also concerned with the design of services, which makes them the ideal contact for strategic communication with customers for all departments in the service provider. There is a potential connection for BRM with application development, as well as other development and design areas.

There are many connections and similarities between BRM and service level management and other service management processes, and the roles are often combined. But as you can see in Table 19.2 there are distinct differences in the activities for the processes, and there needs to be a clear understanding that when carrying out BRM, an individual needs to be aware when they are working on a strategic business relationship and when they are working tactically.

TABLE 19.2   BRM process and other service management processes

Scenario	Primary process being executed	Other processes involved
Developing high-level customer requirements for a proposed new service	Business relationship management	Service portfolio management
Building a business case for a proposed new service	Business relationship management	Service portfolio management
Confirming customer's detailed functionality requirements for a new service	Design coordination	Business relationship management
Confirming a customer requirement for service availability for a new service	Service level management	Business relationship management, availability management
Establishing patterns of business activity	Demand management	Business relationship management
Evaluating business case for new service request from customer and deciding go/no go	Service portfolio management	Business relationship management, financial management for IT services
Report service performance against service level	SLM	Business relationship management

Make sure you are aware of the differences between BRM and the other service management processes, especially service level management. Remember, BRM is concerned with a strategic relationship with the customer, whereas other processes are more tactically and operationally based.

Value

Business relationship management delivers value by providing structured communication with customers. This enables the service provider to understand the business needs of its customers, now and as they develop. Only through reaching this level of understanding can the service provider ensure that the services it is providing are what the business needs. The customer is also helped to understand the viewpoint of the service provider and what it can realistically deliver. This relationship of mutual understanding and trust helps when difficult issues arise. BRM can act as mediator in these circumstances because it is trusted by the customer and not seen as biased in favor of the service provider. Effective BRM encourages the customer and the service provider to work together as strategic partners.

BRM's focus on customer satisfaction enables the service provider and customer to understand if the business objectives are being met. Although service provision without BRM is possible, BRM helps to ensure that the service understands and continues to provide what the customer needs within the budget they can afford.

Policies, Principles, and Basic Concepts

Next we consider some of the policies, principles, and basic concepts of BRM.

The BRM process is often confused with the business relationship manager role. This is because the role of many business relationship managers is broader than just the BRM process. The business relationship manager often represents other processes when engaged in BRM—for example, when obtaining information about customer requirements and business outcomes for use by service portfolio management, demand, and capacity management.

Among the key concepts are a number of data repositories. You saw these earlier when looking at the service portfolio:

- The customer portfolio is a database or structured document used to record all customers of the IT service provider. It is BRM's view of the customers who receive services from the IT service provider. It is produced by the BRM process and used by several other processes, such as service portfolio management. The customer portfolio documents the service provider's commitments, investments, and risks relative to each customer.

- The customer agreement portfolio is a database or structured document used to manage service contracts or agreements between an IT service provider and its customers. It is an output of the service level management process and contains a contract or other agreement for each IT service provided to a customer. Although produced by SLM, it is an important tool for BRM.

- Contracts or SLAs are negotiated and managed separately for each customer. For internal service providers, SLAs are negotiated and maintained by service level management, involving business relationship managers where these exist, whereas for external service providers the process involves legal specialists, service level management, and dedicated business relationship managers.

BRM works throughout the service lifecycle to understand customer requirements and expectations and ensure that they are being met or exceeded:

- In service strategy, BRM ensures that the service provider understands the customer's objectives and overall requirements.

- In service design, BRM ensures that the service provider has properly understood the customer's detailed requirements and initiates corrective action if this is not the case. In addition, BRM will work with service level management to ensure that the customer's expectations of the new service are set at the appropriate level.

- In service transition, BRM ensures that the customer is involved in change, release, and deployment activities that impact their services, ensuring that their feedback has been taken into due consideration. The business relationship managers may represent the customer on the CAB, or they may arrange for the customer to be at CAB meetings and change evaluation meetings when appropriate.

- In service operation, BRM works with service level management, incident management, and the service desk to ensure that services have been delivered according to the contract or SLA and may well be part of the escalation procedures.

- In continual service improvement, BRM monitors service reports and is given frequent updates about levels of customer satisfaction, exceptions to service levels, or specific requests or complaints from the customer. Working together with other processes and functions, BRM will help identify appropriate remedial action and agree this with the customer.

Business relationship management is involved in defining and clarifying requirements for service. Customers may sometimes request a particular solution, which may not be the most effective solution. BRM needs to focus on the outcome and the value that the customer requires and then work back to defining the service.

Business relationship management enables service providers to be involved in strategic discussions about the customer's business. BRM also ensures that relevant information about the strategic direction of the customer is communicated back into the appropriate processes and people within the service provider organization.

Process Activities, Methods, and Techniques

The BRM process itself consists of activities in every stage of the service lifecycle, rather than a single end-to-end process. The particular activities executed will depend on the situation that has caused the service provider or customer to initiate the process. The process interfaces with a number of other service management processes throughout the service lifecycle. Business relationship management is not a single end-to-end process with a single beginning and end. Rather, it consists of a number of key activities that are linked together. Figure 19.1 shows the process activities.

The BRM process is initiated either by the customer or by service management processes and functions—usually by contacting the business relationship manager. For customers, BRM provides a way for customers to communicate with the service provider about their needs, opportunities, and requirements, and to have these taken care of in a formal, organized manner.

The business relationship manager should document all opportunities, requests, complaints, and compliments to ensure that they are followed through and do not fall between different processes and functions. The service provider is also able to initiate the BRM process if they need input from customers, or if they need to initiate the creation of a new service or changes to an existing service.

Service Strategy

BRM works to apply strategies, policies, and plans to coordinate the service provider's processes with customer requirements and opportunities. Strategy management will have identified the key market spaces and business opportunities. BRM will ensure that these are appropriately defined and executed from a customer perspective.

FIGURE 19.1 BRM activities

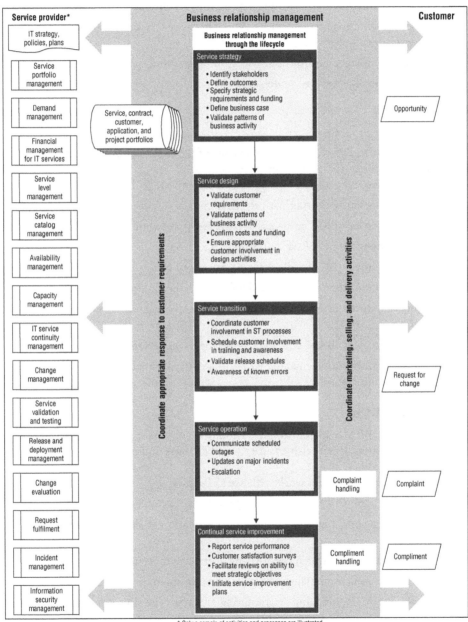

BRM will work with other service strategy processes:

- With IT strategy management, to understand if the request is in line with strategy
- With service portfolio management, to decide if a new service is required or whether existing services can be leveraged
- With financial management for IT services, to understand how it is to be funded
- With demand management, to understand the patterns of business activity

Service Design

In the service design stage, BRM will work to ensure that the detailed design and development of services continue to meet the requirements of the customer and that they are valid for the business outcomes that have been identified.

The main activities and processes BRM will work with are as follows:

- Project management (by liaising with the customer)
- Financial management (BRM ensures that costs are in line with the investment anticipated)
- Service level management (BRM will help define SLAs)
- Demand management (BRM will confirm patterns of business activity)
- Service catalog management (BRM will help define the catalog entry)
- Availability management (BRM will determine exactly when the service needs to be available)
- Capacity management (BRM will identify performance requirements)
- IT service continuity management (BRM will identify business impacts and recovery objectives with the customer)

Service Transition

In service transition, BRM will coordinate customer involvement in the processes active during service transition. It will also ensure that all changes and releases meet the requirements set by the customer.

The main processes BRM will work with are as follows:

- Change management (BRM's role is to represent the customer)
- Knowledge management (ensuring the right information at the right time to the right people)
- Service testing and validation (coordinating user acceptance testing)
- Release and deployment management (ensuring minimum disruption)
- Change evaluation (logging and coordinating any action arising from the evaluation)

Service Operations

In service operations, BRM is still required. First, customers' use of services changes over time. BRM will feed this back to the service provider. Second, although the service desk is able to deal with most incidents and requests, some require a higher level of involvement and communication, which BRM provides.

The main processes the BRM will work with are as follows:

Request Fulfillment   BRM may be the point of contact for requesting some services.

Incident Management   BRM is usually involved during major incidents to provide focused communication to the customer. BRM provides incident management with business information that will help in evaluating the relative priority of incidents.

Continual Service Improvement

In the continual service improvement (CSI) stage, BRM facilitates CSI by identifying improvement opportunities and then coordinating both service provider and customer activities to achieve this improvement. BRM also conducts customer satisfaction surveys, which are instrumental in identifying areas for improvement and new opportunities. BRM measures customer satisfaction and compares service provider performance with customer satisfaction targets and previous scores, usually through a regular survey. BRM surveys are concerned with whether the service achieves its objectives at every level, rather than day-to-day handling of individual incidents.

Significant variations in satisfaction levels or downward trends should be investigated and discussed with customers so that the reasons are understood. Results that appear anomalous should be investigated to identify other possible causes. Any opportunities for improvement should be logged in the CSI register in conjunction with service level management for later review and prioritization.

Triggers

Triggers of BRM include the following:

- A new strategic initiative or a new service, or a change to an existing service, has been initiated.
- A new opportunity has been identified or a service has been chartered by service portfolio management.
- Other triggers could be customer requests, suggestions, or complaints, or the fact that a customer meeting or customer satisfaction survey has been scheduled.

Inputs

Inputs to BRM include the following:

- Customer requirements, requests, complaints, escalations, or compliments
- The service strategy and, where possible, the customer's strategy
- The service and project portfolios, SLAs, and RFCs
- A request to validate patterns of business activity or user profiles defined by demand management

Outputs

Outputs of BRM include the following:

- Stakeholder definitions, defined business outcomes, and an agreement to fund (internal) or pay for (external) services
- The customer portfolio and service requirements for strategy, design, and transition
- Customer satisfaction surveys and their results
- Schedules of customer activity in various service management process activities and of training and awareness events
- Reports on the customer perception of service performance

Interfaces

Major interfaces with BRM include the following:

- Strategy management for IT services works closely with BRM to identify market spaces with information gleaned from customers. BRM also gathers strategic requirements and desired business outcomes and secures funding (internal) or pursues deals (external).
- Service portfolio management works with BRM to identify more detailed requirements and information about the customer environment required to create service models and assess proposed services.
- Financial management for IT services obtains information about the financial objectives of the customer and helps the service provider understand what level of funding or pricing the customer is prepared to accept.
- Demand management works with BRM to identify and validate patterns of business activity and user profiles. BRM will also identify changes to those patterns or the priorities of specific business activities.
- Service level management uses customer information and service requirements gathered by BRM to understand the customer's priorities regarding service performance and deliverables. Actions agreed to during service reviews with the customers will be coordinated and monitored by the BRM, whether the actions apply to customers or the service provider.
- Capacity and availability management rely on information about business outcomes and service requirements gathered through BRM. BRM will also validate whether proposed levels of performance and availability will be acceptable to customers.
- BRM provides information on business priorities and outcomes for IT service continuity management and ensures that countermeasures, recovery plans, and tests accurately represent the world of the customer.

- Service catalog management provides the basis for many discussions, reviews, and requests that are initiated through BRM.

- BRM is often the initiating point for requests for change and will also be involved with assessing the impact and priority of changes.

- BRM ensures the appropriate level of customer involvement in the release and deployment management, and service validation and testing processes.

- BRM has a strong interface with CSI because service improvements and the seven-step improvement process are an important part of BRM. BRM validates, prioritizes, and communicates improvement opportunities and plans with the customer in conjunction with service level management.

Information Management

We have explored some of the documentation and information required for effective BRM, in particular the service portfolio, project portfolio, and application portfolio. These important information sources document current and future services and are used by BRM to facilitate effective communication between the customer and the service provider. BRM ensures that the customer portfolio and customer agreement portfolio are maintained.

Customer satisfaction surveys are another important information source. The BRM process ensures that the surveys cover the relevant aspects of the service and are conducted in a fair, consistent, and objective manner to ensure that the results are an accurate reflection of customer satisfaction. The results will also need to be stored so that trends can be identified and progress against baselines measured.

The service catalog is another important reference used to communicate with customers about the available services.

Business Relationship Management Process Roles

This section describes a number of roles that need to be performed in support of the BRM process. As with the process-specific roles described in other chapters, these are specific additional requirements to the generic roles applicable to all processes throughout the service lifecycle described in Chapter 1, "Introduction to Operational Support and Analysis."

Business Relationship Manager

Many organizations will have a person with the job title *business relationship manager*. This job may combine the roles of BRM process owner and BRM process manager and allocate it to one person.

Business relationship manager may also be used to describe a number of staff working within BRM, each focused on different customer segments or groups. In some organizations, this role may be combined with the role of service level manager.

The role of the business relationship manager and the BRM process can be confused in some organizations. Because business relationship managers interface with the customer, they are often involved in activities from other processes; however, this does not make those activities part of the BRM process.

Business Relationship Management Process Owner

The BRM process owner's responsibilities typically include

- Carrying out the generic process owner role for the BRM process
- Working with other process owners to ensure that there is an integrated approach to the design and implementation of BRM

Business Relationship Management Process Manager

The BRM process manager's responsibilities typically include

- Carrying out the generic process manager role for the BRM process
- Identifying customer needs and ensuring that these needs are met with an appropriate catalog of services
- Working with the customer to balance their expectations with the amount they are willing to pay
- Ensuring that the service provider understands the requirements and is able to deliver the service at the required level before agreeing to deliver the service
- Ensuring high levels of customer satisfaction by ensuring that the service provider meets the customer's requirements
- Building and nourishing a constructive relationship between the service provider and the customer based on understanding the customer and their business drivers
- Understanding the impact of changes to the customer environment on the type, level, or utilization of services provided
- Understanding the impact of technology trends on the type, level, or utilization of services provided
- Establishing and communicating business requirements for new services or changes to existing services
- Mediating in disputes that arise due to conflicting requirements for services from different business units

Customers/Users

The customers and users of the IT services are the other side of BRM. They need to play their part in engaging with BRM to ensure that their needs are understood. A successful relationship requires input from each side, and customer involvement will help ensure that business outcomes are supported.

Critical Success Factors and Key Performance Indicators

Finally we consider the CSFs and KPIs for this process. Here are some examples of CSFs and KPIs for BRM:

- Critical success factor: The ability to document and understand customer requirements of services and the business outcomes they wish to achieve.

  - KPI: That business outcomes and customer requirements are documented and signed off by the customer as input into service portfolio management and service design processes. If this KPI is present and achieved, the CSF will be achieved.

- Critical success factor: The ability to establish and articulate business requirements for new services or changes to existing services.

  - KPI: Every new service has a comprehensive set of requirements defined by business managers and staff, and these have been signed off by both business and IT leadership at the strategy, design, and transition stage.

  - KPI: The reasons for, expected results of, and detailed requirements for changes to services are documented and signed off at the strategy, design, and transition stages.

Challenges

Challenges for BRM include the following:

- Moving beyond using BRM purely as a means of working on levels of customer satisfaction. BRM needs to be involved in defining services and tracking that they are delivered according to the specified levels of service.

- Another challenge can be overcoming a history of poor service, which means BRM struggles to have any credibility. This sometimes results in customers not being willing to share requirements, feedback, and opportunities.

- There may be confusion between the role of business relationship manager and the BRM process. Although business relationship managers are often required to execute activities from other processes simply because of their customer-facing position, this does not make those activities part of the BRM process.

Risks

Business relationship management risks include the following:

- Confusion regarding the boundaries between BRM and other processes. This may lead to duplication of effort, or alternatively, some activities may be neglected. An example of this would be during a major incident the incident manager may receive multiple calls from BRM, service level management, and so forth. It is important that these boundaries be clearly defined.

- A disconnect between the customer-facing processes, such as BRM, and those focusing on technology, such as capacity management. Both are critical for success, and they need to be properly integrated.

Financial Management for IT Services

Organizations have to be able manage their finances, but it is a complex process used across an entire organization. It is normally owned by a very senior executive and managed as a separate business function. It is an extremely important area that allows organizations to manage resources and ensure that their objectives are being achieved.

The IT service provider, as part of the overall organization, must be involved in the financial management process. It is important to make sure that all financial practices are aligned; although a separate process may be used, it should follow the overall organizational principles and requirements.

Purpose of Financial Management for IT Services

To design, develop, and deliver the services that meet the organizational requirements, we must secure an appropriate level of funding. This is the main purpose of financial management for IT services. At the same time, the financial management process should act as a gatekeeper for the expenditure on IT services and ensure that the service provider is not overextended financially for the services they are required to deliver. Obviously this will require a balance between the cost and quality of the service, in line with the balance of supply and demand between the service provider and their customers.

Cost and quality are key factors in the provision of services, and the only way we can allocate and understand the cost of service provision is through sound financial practices.

Objectives of Financial Management for IT Services

The objectives of the financial management process include the following:

- Defining and maintaining a financial framework that allows the service provider to identify, manage, and communicate the actual cost of service delivery.

- Understanding and evaluating the financial impact and implications of any new or changed organizational strategies on the service provider.

- Securing the funding required for the provision of the agreed-to services. This process will require significant input from the business and will depend on the overall approach to financial management and cross-charging within the organization.

- Facilitating good stewardship of service and customer assets to ensure that the organization meets its objectives. This should be done by working with service asset and configuration management and knowledge management.

- Performing basic financial accounting in respect of the relationship between expenses and income, and ensuring that these are balanced according to the overall organizational financial policies.

- Reporting on and managing expenditure for service provision on behalf of the stakeholders.

- Management and execution of the organization's policies and practices relating to financial controls.

- Ensuring that financial controls and accounting practices are applied to the creation, delivery, and support of services.

- Understanding the future financial requirements of the organization; providing financial forecasts for the service commitments and any required compliance for legislative and regulatory controls.

- If appropriate, defining a framework that allows for the recovery of the costs of service provision from the customer.

Scope of Financial Management

Financial management is a well-recognized activity in any organization, but the specific requirement to manage funding related to the provision of IT services may not be so well established.

It is important to understand the strategic approach that is adopted in relation to IT service provision. How will it be managed; is it internally or externally sourced? If internally, is there a requirement to cross-charge for services, or is another mechanism of cost recovery in place?

In the majority of organizations, qualified accountants are in charge of the corporate finances, usually as part of the finance department. They will set the policies, standards, and accounting practices for the business. The strategy relating to IT funding will be part of the overall accounting approach, but the specifics may be managed locally as part of the IT department.

Those engaged in FMITS must ensure that the practices are consistent with the corporate controls, and that reporting and accounting activities meet with the governance standards as defined for the whole organization. Adherence to these standards will also assist with general understanding by the various business units of how IT is funded. Communication and reporting of internal funding practices across an organization is extremely important for enabling a true understanding of the costs of IT services.

Using a service management approach to delivering services should mean that the accounting for IT services is more effective, detailed, and efficient. In an internal service provider, this will enable a translation of the information between service provider and business.

Financial management consists of three main processes:

Budgeting   Budgeting is the process of predicting and controlling the income and expenditure of money within an organization. Budgeting consists of a periodic cycle (usually annually) of negotiation to set budgets, and the monthly monitoring of expenditure against these.

Accounting   Accounting is the process that enables the IT organization to account fully for the way that its money has been spent. It should enable a cost breakdown by customer, service, activity, or other factor to demonstrate the allocation of funds. It will normally require some form of accounting system (ledgers, charts of accounts, journal, etc.) and should be managed and overseen by someone with an accountancy qualification or skills.

Charging Charging is the process required to bill customers for use of the services and will only be applicable where the organizational accounting model requires it to take place. It requires sound accounting practices and supporting systems so that any cross-charging is accurate and traceable.

The cycles associated with financial management are shown in Table 19.3. The two cycles are

- A planning cycle (annual), where cost projections and workload forecasting form a basis for cost calculations and price setting
- An operational cycle (monthly or quarterly), where costs are monitored and checked against budgets, bills are issued, and revenue is collected

TABLE 19.3 Budgeting, IT accounting, and charging cycles

Frequency	Budgeting	IT accounting	Charging
Planning (Annual)	Agree to overall expenditure	Establish standard unit costs for each IT resource	Establish pricing policy and publish price list
Operational (Monthly)	Take actions to manage budget exceptions or changed costs	Monitor expenditure by cost center	Compile and issue bills

Value

Internal IT organizations now realize that they are quite similar to market-facing companies. They share the need to analyze, package, market, and deliver services just as any other business. They also share a common and increasing need to understand and control factors of demand and supply, and to provide services as cost-effectively as possible while maximizing visibility into related cost structures.

Sound FMITS provides the information the service provider needs to achieve the following:

- Enhanced decision making
- Speed of change
- Service portfolio management
- Financial compliance and control
- Operational control
- Value capture and creation

Financial management provides the information needed to generate strategies or to devise new ways of using assets to achieve our goals. It enables the business to understand the financial results of current strategies—for example:

- Has cutting our prices resulted in more business?
- Is that business profitable?
- Which services cost us the most and why?
- How efficient are we compared to alternatives?
- Where could we improve?
- Which areas should we prioritize for CSI?

Good financial management results in a number of specific benefits to the business. It enables the business to comply with regulatory and legislative requirements and generally accepted accounting principles. This compliance ensures that the business is operating legally and is not at risk of being fined for noncompliance. By understanding costs, a realistic budget can be prepared so that the money available is sufficient to cover the cost of service. Finally, the business has the information it needs to make sound business decisions regarding the use of and investment in IT.

Sound financial management also ensures that when it comes to charging for IT services, internal service providers can recover the full cost of service from the business if required. The business units will also have the information regarding the charges they need for preparing their own budgets. External providers can ensure that they charge customers a sufficient amount to cover costs and make a profit. Most fundamentally, linking IT services to business outcomes ensures that all IT spending has a business justification.

Policies, Principles, and Basic Concepts

Financial management for IT services applies the financial management policies of the organization. It must therefore follow the policies and practices of the organization as a whole. Policies that impact an IT service provider might include the following:

- What level of financial expenditure needs to be tracked
- Which configuration items need to be recorded as financial assets and how they should be classified
- How fixed assets are depreciated
- How costs are reported
- How revenue is accounted for (and linked to IT services)
- Whether the cost of services will be accounted for individually, or whether the overall cost of IT will be calculated and allocated back to the business units
- Requirements to comply with legislative or other regulatory requirements

It is a policy decision by the organization's executives whether IT is a profit center or a cost center. A cost center is a business unit or department to which costs are assigned but that does not charge for services provided. It must account for expenditure. A profit center is a business unit that charges for providing services. A profit center can be created with the objective of making a profit, recovering costs, or running at a loss.

Funding

Funding is the sourcing and allocation of money for a specific purpose or project. For IT service management, funding is the means whereby an IT service provider obtains financial resources that pay for the design, transition, operation, and improvement of IT services.

Funding comes from two sources:

- External funding comes from revenue that is received from selling services to external customers.

- Internal funding comes from other business units inside the same organization.

Funding models include the following:

Rolling Plan Funding   A rolling plan is a plan for a fixed number of months, years, or other cycles. At the end of the first cycle, the plan is simply extended by one more cycles.

Trigger-Based Funding   In this model, a plan is initiated and funding is provided when a specific situation or event occurs.

Zero-Based Funding   Most internal service providers are funded using this model, since it is based on ensuring that IT breaks even. IT is allowed to spend up to the specified budget amount, and at the end of the financial period (monthly, quarterly, or annually) the money is recovered from the other business units through cost transfers.

Value

Service economics is about the balance between the cost of providing services, the value of the outcomes achieved, and the returns that the services enable the service provider to achieve. An effective FMITS process is required to calculate, forecast, and track costs and income related to services to be calculated. The value of services can only be calculated with clearly defined and properly executed practices for FMITS. The calculation of value is a joint responsibility of both the service provider and the customer. They need to have a shared understanding of how costs and returns are calculated in order to be able to demonstrate the value of IT services.

Compliance

Compliance relates to the ability to demonstrate that proper and consistent accounting methods and/or practices are being employed. It is essential that enterprise financial management policies clearly outline what legislative and other regulatory requirements apply to the service provider's and customer's organizations. Regulations such as Basel II and Sarbanes-Oxley have had enormous impact on financial audit and compliance activities.

Although this increases costs, regulatory compliance tends to improve data security and quality processes.

Process Activities, Methods, and Techniques

Figure 19.2 shows the financial management process. We are going to examine the high-level steps of accounting, budgeting, and charging.

FIGURE 19.2   Major inputs, outputs, and activities of financial management for IT services

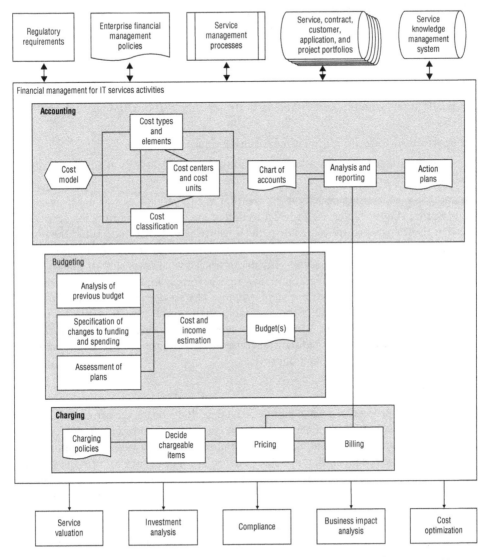

Accounting

First we will look at accounting. This is the process responsible for identifying the actual costs of delivering IT services, comparing these with budgeted costs, and managing variance from the budget. Accounting is also responsible for tracking any income earned by services. Accounting enables the service provider to

- Track actual costs against budget
- Support the development of a sound investment strategy that recognizes and evaluates the options and flexibility available from modern technology
- Provide cost targets for service performance and delivery
- Facilitate prioritization of resource usage
- Make decisions with full understanding of the cost implications and hence the minimum of risk
- Support the introduction, if required, of charging for IT services
- Review the financial consequences of previous strategic decisions to enable the organization to learn and improve

An important accounting activity is the creation of cost models. A cost model is a framework that allows the service provider to determine the costs of providing services and ensure that those costs are allocated correctly. It helps the provider understand the impact of proposed changes to the current service, customer, and customer agreement portfolios.

Accounting also enables the service provider to track actual costs against budget. It helps support the development of a sound investment strategy and enables the provider to set cost targets for service performance and delivery. The service provider is able to make decisions with full understanding of the cost implications and hence the minimum of risk. Accounting also supports the introduction, if required, of charging for IT services. It provides an opportunity to review the financial consequences of previous strategic decisions to enable the organization to learn and improve.

Budgeting

The next high-level process area we look at is budgeting. Budgeting is the activity of predicting and controlling the spending of money. Budgeting consists of a periodic negotiation cycle to set future budgets (usually annual) and the routine monitoring and adjusting of current budgets.

Budgeting is the mechanism that marshals the resources necessary to meet the strategic and tactical objectives of the organization. It answers fundamental business questions such as "Do we have the resources needed to meet the objectives, and where will they come from? What do we need and when?"

A budget is typically documented as a spreadsheet, with rows indicating the items of expenditure columns showing when that expenditure will take place. The steps of the process can be summarized as

- Analyze the previous budget
- Assess current plans

- Make sure you understand any changes to funding and spending
- Estimate expected costs and income
- Draw up the budget

Charging

Finally we'll look at charging. Charging is the activity whereby payment is required for services delivered. Charging is optional for internal service providers—the costs of the service provider may be simply reallocated back to other business units by the central financial function using an internal charging method. This is a decision made by the organization, not by the IT department. External service providers must charge for their services, since this is where the organization obtains the revenue that keeps it in business.

Charging must be seen to be simple, fair, and realistic. There is an argument that customers who pay for services may value them more. They may also question which services they really need. The service provider has to decide which items will be chargeable, as well as how they will be charged—what cost units will be used.

Charging may be calculated in a variety of ways, such as a charge per service, per head, or by processing volume. The prices for the items need to be set, and this is influenced by whether the provider is seeking to make a profit, cover costs, or provide a subsidized service. Finally, the provider issues the bills and collects payment.

Triggers

Triggers of FMITS include the following:

- Mandatory monthly, quarterly, and annual financial reporting cycles such as budgeting
- Outputs from audits suggesting or mandating improvement actions
- Other service management processes, which may request, for example, financial information regarding return on investment data
- An investigation into a new service opportunity
- The introduction of charging for IT services for an internal service provider or the need to determine the price of a service for an external service provider
- A request for change, which will trigger the need for financial information about the cost of making changes and the ongoing financial impact of the change

Inputs

We discussed the process inputs earlier. Typical inputs include the following:

- The policies, standards, and practices established by legislation or regulators and those imposed by the organization's financial managers
- The Generally Accepted Accounting Practices (GAAP) and local variations

- All data sources where financial information is stored, including the supplier database, configuration management system, service portfolio, customer agreement portfolio, application portfolio, and project portfolio

- The service portfolio, which provides the structure of services (these services will be the basis for the accounting system, since all costs and returns will ultimately be expressed in terms of the services provided)

Outputs

Next we'll look at the outputs of financial management. We discussed these earlier, so we'll just briefly recap them here:

Service Valuation   This is the ability to understand the costs of a service relative to its business value.

Service Investment Analysis   Financial management provides the information and history to enable the service provider to determine the value of the investment in a service.

Compliance   Regardless of the location of a service provider, or whether they are internal or external, financial data is subject to regulation and legislation. Financial management for IT services helps implement and enforce policies that ensure that the organization is able to store and archive financial data, secure and control it, and make sure that it is reported to the appropriate people.

Cost Optimization   The goal of cost optimization is to make sure that investments are appropriate for the level of service that the customers demand and the level of returns that are being projected. Business impact analysis (BIA) involves understanding the effect on the business if a service is not available. This enables the business to prioritize investments in services and service continuity.

Planning Confidence   Planning confidence is not a tangible output; it refers to the level of confidence that service stakeholders have in the service provider being able to accurately forecast costs and returns.

Interfaces

All service management processes use financial management to determine the costs and benefits of the process itself. Some also use it to support the execution of their process activities. Major interfaces with financial management for IT services include the following:

- Strategy management works with enterprise financial management to determine the financial objectives for the organization. It defines expected returns on investment, based on information provided by financial management. Financial management will track and report on the achievement of ROI.

- Service portfolio management provides the service structure that will be used to define cost models, accounting, and budgeting systems and the basis for charging.

- Business relationship management provides information to financial management regarding how the business measures the value of services and what they are prepared to pay for services.

- Capacity and availability management are able to provide valuable information to financial management for IT services about the various options of technology and service performance. This in turn will be used to calculate costs.

- Change management uses financial management for IT services to help determine the financial impact or requirements of changes.

- Service asset and configuration management documents financial data about assets and configuration items. This data is used as the basis for financial analysis and reporting. Enterprise financial management also provides the policies that are used as the basis for managing financial assets of the organization (such as depreciation).

- Continual service improvement uses financial management for IT services to determine whether the return of a proposed improvement is worth the investment required to make the improvement.

Information Management

The main sources of documentation and information required for effective financial management include the following:

- Financial management systems, such as accounting, budgeting, and charging systems

- Financial management policies, legislation, and regulations defined by external parties, as well as the internal enterprise finance managers

- Financial reporting structures, templates, and spreadsheets (e.g., budgets), as well as the reports themselves, which are the basis of compliance and also a major output to other service management processes

- The organization's chart of accounts

- The service knowledge management system

Financial Management for IT Process Roles

This section describes a number of roles that need to be performed in support of the financial management process. As with the process-specific roles described in other chapters, these are specific additional requirements to the generic roles applicable to all processes throughout the service lifecycle described in Chapter 1.

Many organizations will have a person with the job title of IT financial manager, which typically combines the roles of FMITS process owner and process manager.

Financial Management for IT Services Process Owner

The financial management for IT services process owner's responsibilities typically include

- Carrying out the generic process owner role for the FMITS process

- Working with other process owners to ensure that there is an integrated approach to the design and implementation of financial management for IT services

Financial Management for IT Services Process Manager

The financial management for IT services process manager's responsibilities typically include

- Carrying out the generic process manager role for the FMITS process
- Compiling the annual IT budgets and submitting them for scrutiny and approval by the IT steering group
- Managing the IT budgets on a daily, monthly, and annual basis, taking action when required to balance income and expenditure in line with the budgets
- Producing regular statements of accounts for management information and allowing relevant managers to manage their own areas of the budgets
- Formulating and managing recharging systems for IT customers
- Reporting on value-for-money of all major activities, projects, and proposed expenditure items within IT

Budget Holders

Various IT managers may have responsibility for the budgets for their own particular area(s). Budget holder responsibilities typically include

- Submitting the annual budget estimate
- Negotiating and agreeing to their annual budget
- Managing their budget on an ongoing basis
- Reporting budget activities and outcomes on a regular basis

Critical Success Factors and Key Performance Indicators

Finally, we will cover the CSFs and KPIs for this process. We will discuss some examples; the full list is available in the FMITS section of the ITIL Service Strategy publication. Examples of CSFs and KPIs for financial management for IT services include the following:

- CSF: The existence of an enterprise-wide framework to identify, manage, and communicate financial information, including the cost and associated return of services
  - KPI: The existence of established standards, policies, and charts of accounts, which enterprise financial management requires all business units to use and comply with. Audits will indicate the extent of compliance.
  - KPI: The financial management for IT services framework specifies how services will be accounted for; regular reports are submitted and used as a basis for measuring the service provider's performance.
  - KPI: The production and submission of timely and accurate financial reports by each organizational unit.

- CSF: The requirement for the service provider to be able to account for the money spent on the creation, delivery, and support of services.

    - KPI: The service provider uses an accounting system, and this is configured to report on its costs by service.

    - KPI: The provision of regular reports on the costs of services in design, transition, and operation.

Challenges

Challenges for FMITS include the following:

- Developing effective financial reporting and cost models that focus on the cost of infrastructure and applications rather than the cost of services, without which it is difficult to communicate the value of services.

- Ensuring that while FMITS must comply with enterprise standards and policies, its chart of accounts and reporting should be appropriate for an IT service provider.

- Resisting an organizational focus on cost saving rather than cost optimization, leading to cost-cutting rather than demonstrating return on investment and value.

- Encountering difficulties in the initial phase in finding where financial data is located and how it is controlled.

- The reliance of the process on planning information provided by other processes, which may be poor or nonexistent.

- Internal service providers experiencing difficulties when introducing charging. This requires a change in culture and in how its success is measured, especially the need to articulate value in relation to alternative service providers. There is a possibility that the users may become more demanding as a result of being charged.

- The need for external service providers to balance the cost of services with the perceived value of those services to ensure the correct pricing models. The correct price must be higher than the cost but must also reflect the value to the customer (what the customer is prepared to pay for the service).

Risk

There are a number of risks to financial management for IT services. These include the following:

- The introduction of dedicated financial management processes for an internal service provider may be viewed as unnecessary, even though the cost of a bad investment decision about the type and level of services offered can far outweigh the costs of implementing the process.

- A lack of adequate financial management processes for IT services may lead to penalties for noncompliance.

- There may be no staff in the organization who understand both IT and finance.

Summary

In this chapter, we completed our examination of the service strategy processes relevant to service offerings and agreements by looking at BRM and financial management for IT. We covered the purpose and objectives for each process in addition to the scope. We looked at the value of the processes; then we reviewed the policies for each process and the activities, methods, and techniques.

Last, we reviewed triggers, inputs, outputs, and interfaces for each process and the information management associated with it. We also considered the critical success factors and key performance indicators and the challenges and risks for the processes.

We examined the importance of these processes to the business and the IT service provider. Business relationship management ensures that the services provided meet the needs of the organization, in both the short and longer terms, by working with senior business management to align the services provided to the business strategic requirements. Financial management plays a crucial role in managing costs, assessing value for money, managing resources, and recovering costs through charging when appropriate.

Exam Essentials

Understand the purpose of financial management for IT services and BRM.   You need to understand the purpose of BRM and financial management for IT services.

Understand the business value of each process.   You should be able to explain the value the business derives from each process.

Know the key activities of financial management.   You will need to be able to identify the purpose, objectives, and scope for financial management. Remember the three main areas: budgeting, IT accounting, and charging. Financial management is crucial for the calculation of value for services.

Understand how BRM works with the senior business management.   Make sure you understand how the business relationship manager works to ensure that the service provider understands the business strategy and provides the services required to further that strategy. Understand that this process also involves explaining to the business what the service provider can and cannot do.

Be able to describe the key differences between BRM and service level management.   You should be able to list and explain the difference in activities and focus between BRM and service level management.

Review Questions

You can find the answers to the review questions in the appendix.

1. What is the definition of *service valuation*?

    A. The process responsible for identifying the actual costs of delivering IT services, comparing them with budgeted costs, and managing variance from the budget

    B. A framework that allows the service provider to determine the costs of providing services

    C. The activity of predicting and controlling the spending of money

    D. The ability to understand the costs of a service relative to its business value

2. Which of the following statements is correct?

    A. IT financial management is quite separate from the enterprise's financial management.

    B. All IT service providers must carry out the three core financial processes of accounting, budgeting, and charging.

    C. The cost of the provision of IT services should always be visible to the customer.

    D. IT spending needs a business justification.

3. Which of the following is an objective of financial management?

    A. Ensuring that customer expectations do not exceed what they are willing to pay for

    B. Helping the business to articulate the value of a service

    C. Ensuring that the service provider does not commit to services that they are not able to provide

    D. Ensuring that the service provider understands and is able to meet customer needs

4. What is the definition of *budgeting*?

    A. The process responsible for identifying the actual costs of delivering IT services, comparing them with budgeted costs, and managing variance from the budget

    B. A framework that allows the service provider to determine the costs of providing services

    C. The activity of predicting and controlling the spending of money

    D. The ability to understand the costs of a service relative to its business value

5. Which of the following responsibilities is *not* a responsibility of BRM?

    A. Identify customer needs (utility and warranty) and ensure that the service provider is able to meet these needs

    B. Strategic focus

    C. Deciding which services the service provider will deliver to meet customer needs

    D. Operational focus

6. Which of the following responsibilities is a responsibility of BRM?

   A. Building a business case for a proposed new service

   B. Agreeing on the level of service that will be delivered for new and existing services

   C. Monitoring whether the service provider is able to meet the agreements

   D. Ensure that all operational level agreements and underpinning contracts are appropriate for the agreed-to service

7. True or false? The customer portfolio is a database or structured document used to record all customers of the IT service provider, and the customer agreement portfolio is a database or structured document used to manage service contracts or agreements between an IT service provider and its customers.

   A. True

   B. False

8. Which of the following is *not* a trigger for BRM?

   A. A new strategic initiative or a new service, or a change to an existing service, has been initiated.

   B. The service provider's ROI is less than predicted in the business case.

   C. A new opportunity has been identified or a service has been chartered by service portfolio management.

   D. Customer complaints have been received.

9. Which of the following is a data repository used by BRM?

   1. The customer portfolio

   2. The configuration management system (CMS)

   3. The customer agreement portfolio

   4. The supplier and contract management information system (SCMIS)

   A. 1 and 2 only

   B. 1 and 3 only

   C. All of the above

   D. 1, 2, and 4 only

10. Which of the following is *not* an output of financial management for IT services?

    A. Service valuation

    B. Service investment analysis

    C. Compliance

    D. Agreement to fund (internal) or pay for (external) services

Chapter

20

Technology Considerations for Service Offerings and Agreements

---

THE FOLLOWING ITIL SERVICE OFFERINGS AND AGREEMENTS EXAM OBJECTIVES ARE DISCUSSED IN THIS CHAPTER:

✓ The generic requirements for technology to assist service design

✓ The evaluation criteria for technology and tooling for process implementation

✓ The good practices for practice and process implementation

✓ The challenges, critical success factors, and risks related to implementing practices and processes

✓ How to plan and implement service management technologies

✓ The consideration for implementing technologies in supporting the processes within planning, protection, and optimization practice, in particular, designing technology architectures

This chapter brings all technology and implementation requirements together to define the overall requirements of an integrated set of service management technology tools to support the processes in service offerings and agreements. The same technology, with some possible additions, should be used for the lifecycle stages of IT service management (ITSM)—service strategy, service design, service transition, service operation, and continual service improvement—to give consistency and allow an effective ITSM lifecycle to be properly managed.

Tools can help the service management processes to work more effectively. They should allow large amounts of repetitive work to be carried out quickly and consistently. Tools also provide a wealth of management information, leading to the identification of weaknesses and opportunities for improvement.

The use of tools will help standardize practices and both centralize and integrate processes.

Often organizations believe that by purchasing or developing a tool, all of their problems will be solved, and it is easy to forget that we are still dependent on the process, the function, and, most important, the people. Remember, "a fool with a tool is still a fool," and therefore training in the process and tool is imperative.

We are going to consider the generic requirements for such tools. It is important that the tool being used should support the processes, not the other way around.

Generic Requirements and Evaluation Criteria for Technology

We will begin by considering the generic requirements for technology to support service design, which for IT service management means IT service management tools. In this section, we will look at a number of these requirements, which you would expect any good integrated toolset to offer.

The first two requirements are self-help functionality and a workflow engine.

You should be able to recall from the discussion of the release fulfillment process that we discussed the option for dealing with requests or simple incidents via self-help functionality.

This might be restricted to the logging of requests and incidents, or it could allow them to be tracked and updated throughout their lifecycle. The advantage to providing a self-help facility is that requests and incidents can be logged at any time, and this process is not dependent on service desk staff being available to answer the phone. This helps the service desk manage high volumes of calls if the less urgent ones are handled via a self-help, self-logging site. Self-help request tools can assist with password resets by, for example, requiring the user to validate their identity by answering previously set questions before the reset takes place. Additionally, a self-help request tool could download approved versions of requested software.

The next generic requirement is for a workflow or a process engine that can automate the steps of the process (assigning, escalating, etc.). It can also release work orders when prerequisite steps have been completed.

 Remember, the ITSM toolset is essential for many of the service management processes and functions and, as such, should be included in the IT service continuity provision.

The next generic requirement is for an integrated configuration management system (CMS).

The service management tool should be integrated with the CMS to allow the organization's configuration item (CI) information to be interrogated and linked to incident, problem, known error, and change records as appropriate.

Another generic requirement is for discovery, deployment, and licensing technology tools. These are extremely helpful in verifying the accuracy of the CMS, especially with regard to license use. It is also helpful if only changes since the last audit can be extracted and reported on. The same technology can often be used to deploy new software to target locations; this is essential to enable patches, upgrades, and so on to be distributed to the correct users.

When implemented in conjunction with the self-help functionality previously mentioned, the service management toolset facilitates the automation of the fulfillment of many service requests for software.

Another generic requirement is remote control. This allows the service desk analysts to take control of the user's desktop (under properly controlled security conditions) to do things such as conduct investigations and correct settings.

Some tools will store diagnostic scripts and other diagnostic utilities to assist with earlier diagnosis of incidents.

Good reporting is a requirement of any ITSM toolset. The tools hold enormous amounts of data about what is happening day to day. This data is helpful in planning ahead and tracking trends, but such reporting has to be flexible if it is to be useful. Standard reports and ad hoc reports should both be easily available.

Another generic requirement to consider is a dashboard facility. Dashboards are useful, both for day-to-day operations and for IT and business management to get a clear idea of real-time performance.

To facilitate greater business alignment, business applications and tools need to be able to interface with ITSM support tools to give the required functionality. An example of integration includes event management tools spotting unusual spending patterns on credit cards.

Software as a Service (SaaS) technologies offer hosted service management capabilities over the Internet. The advantages SaaS offers include lower capital and start-up costs, faster implementation, and built-in service continuity.

However, it also means limited customization and changes to functionality, access restricted to the vendor's hours of service availability, and licensing schemes that may become restrictive or expensive. There may also be limits on data storage size and possible security and access management constraints or risks. Finally, integration with other service management tools may be difficult or even impossible.

Each organization should review its requirements carefully so that it acquires the most appropriate toolset for its needs.

Good Practices for Practice and Process Implementation

In the following sections, we'll consider the basics of implementing good practices and processes. We need to consider the requirements relating to the service offerings and agreements processes, and the approach to implementing service design. This should include

- Where do we start?
- How do we improve?
- How do we know we are making progress?

When looking at the implementation of any service management processes, including those in service design, you must consider the needs and desires of the customer and the business. The activities should be prioritized by

- Business needs and business impacts
- Risks to the services and processes

The activities will also be influenced by the service level requirements and agreements made in service level agreements.

Business Impact Analysis

One of the key inputs for understanding business needs, impacts, and risks is the output from a business impact analysis (BIA). BIA is used in a number of service design processes, particularly IT service continuity management (see Chapter 9, "IT Service Continuity Management and Demand Management"), where it is essential to help define the strategy for risk reduction and service continuity, BIA is normally used to identify the effect a disaster will have on the business, on both individual sections and the business as a whole. It is used to identify the criticality of any particular business process or activity, and will also be used to identify the times when this will particularly affect the business. BIA is also used for other processes—for example, availability management, capacity management, and information security management.

There are two areas of BIA. One is for business management, which involves understanding the impact of loss on a business process or function. The second is to understand the BIA from the perspective of service loss. Both of these should be applied to identify the critical services and determine what constitutes a major incident on the services when a new service is being designed. BIA will also help in defining the acceptable level and duration of service outage, including the important periods to avoid. In addition, BIA can assist with the understanding of financial loss and any security issues.

Service Level Requirements

As part of the service level management process (see Chapter 18, "Service Level Management and Supplier Management"), service level requirements for all services will be identified and the ability to deliver against the requirements will be assessed and defined in the service level agreements. This needs to be part of the approach to the design of services, and all processes in service offerings and agreements will need to be considered as part of the requirements capture.

Risks to the Services and Processes

It is important to ensure that business-as-usual processes are not adversely impacted by the implementation of the service offerings and agreements processes. This factor should be considered as part of the risk assessment during design, and will then be explored more fully during the transition lifecycle stage. Risk assessment and management form a key part of the service offerings and agreements processes—for example, service level management and supplier management. Any solution created during service design must take risks into consideration.

Implementing Service Design

The process, policy, and architecture for the design of IT services will need to be documented and utilized to ensure that the appropriate services are provided to the business.

We recommend that service design follow the continual service improvement approach and base the designs on the business requirements:

- Where do we start?
- How do we improve—the CSI approach:
    - What is the vision?
    - Where are we now?
    - Where do we want to be?

- How do we get there?
- Did we get there?
- How do we keep the momentum going?

Challenges, Critical Success Factors, and Risks

When we consider the relationship between implementing good practices, and service offerings and agreements processes, it is important to be aware of the challenges, CSFs, and risks associated with the implementation.

Challenges

Challenges will take many different forms, depending on the nature of the organization supported. Some common factors are applicable to most organizations in some aspect. These include

- Understanding business requirements and priorities
- Understanding organizational culture
- Effective communication to the business and service management staff
- Collaboration and engagement with all stakeholders
- Gaining commitment from management and staff
- Supplier management and contractual obligations
- Cost and budgetary constraints

These are common to most organizations, and the meeting of these challenges will be critical to the success of implementation of service management processes, including those for service offerings and agreements.

Critical Success Factors

As you are aware, *critical success factor (CSF)* is a term used for an element that is necessary for an organization or project to achieve its mission. CSFs can be used to identify the important elements of success. These are measured by key performance indicators (KPIs) and should be set and measured as part of the service design lifecycle stage. The SOA processes will be critical in establishing the service requirements, and understanding the CSFs for each of the processes will provide a strong basis for the KPIs, which will be used to demonstrate success in the service lifecycle stage.

Risks

As with challenges, some common risks are applicable to most organizations. These need to be appropriately identified and addressed to ensure successful service management implementation. Some examples are

- Meeting the identified CSFs
- Maturity of process
- Unclear business requirements
- Unrealistic business timeframes for service management design, transition, and operation
- Insufficient testing
- Lack of balance in focus on innovation or stability
- Lack of coordination between business, IT, and suppliers
- Insufficient resources, including cost and budget
- Lack of a holistic approach across the whole service management lifecycle

Service Management Tool Choice

Many service management tools are available, each with its own strengths and weaknesses, which makes choosing the right one difficult. To overcome this, you should define some objective selection criteria (see Figure 20.1).

FIGURE 20.1 Service management tool evaluation process

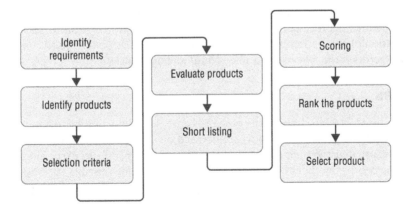

One simple method is MoSCoW analysis. This involves creating a detailed list of all your requirements and classifying each one as must have, should have, could have, or would like in the future.

- *Must have* requirements are mandatory. Any tool that does not satisfy *all* of those requirements is rejected.

- *Should have* requirements are those that we expect but that are not essential.

- *Could have* requirements are useful but not hugely important.

- And *Would like in the future* requirements are those that we don't need right now but will need in the future. For example, we're choosing a tool for incident management right now, but we'd like it to have problem management capability later.

You can then devise a scoring system based on this analysis, which would enable you to rank alternatives. It is possible to weight your decision, making a scoring system to ensure that you are getting the service management tool that delivers against your requirements.

Remember, the ITSM toolset is essential, but you are unlikely to get all of the requirements on your wish list. If you manage to get 80 percent of your requirements and the tool has some ability to be customized to meet your needs, then it probably is the best fit you can find.

Planning and Implementing Service Management Technologies

The final topic of this chapter is service management tools. A good service management tool can be helpful for implementing processes based on the ITIL framework, but the tool should not define the process. Many organizations implement new tools to assist their implementation of new or improved processes. These organizations need to consider a number of factors if the new tool is to be helpful and appropriate.

Licenses

The first factor to be considered is the type of license. Usually a number of options are offered, at different costs. Where tools are licensed on a modular basis, careful planning is needed to ensure that the right access is obtained to enable people to carry out their work with no unnecessary modules being purchased. Here are some possible options:

Dedicated Licenses   For this option, each named person has his or her own license. Dedicated licenses are suitable for staff who require frequent and prolonged use of a particular module. For example, service desk staff would need a dedicated license to use an incident management module.

Shared Licenses   These licenses can be shared between individuals; there is, however, a possibility that a staff member may not be able to access the tool because the license is already in use. Shared licenses are suitable for regular users who do not require constant access, such as second-line support staff. Careful calculation is required to ascertain the correct ratio of users to licenses. These licenses are more expensive than dedicated licenses, but fewer are required.

Web Licenses   These allow access via a web browser. Web licenses are usually suitable for staff requiring remote access or only occasional access. They usually cost a lot less than other licenses (they may even be free with other licenses). It is possible to provide sufficient access for a large number of occasional users by purchasing a small number of such licenses, since the number of concurrent users and therefore the number of licenses required will be low. In this way, overall costs can be reduced further.

On Demand   Access to tools is provided when required (on demand), and the supplier charges for the access based on the time spent using the application. This can be attractive to smaller organizations or if the tools in question are very specialized and used relatively infrequently. A variation to this is the use of a specialist tool as part of a consultancy assignment (e.g., specialist capacity management tools); in such cases, the license fees are likely to be included in the consultancy fee.

Agent/Activity   A further variation in license options is software that is licensed and charged on an agent/activity basis. An example of this is simulation software (e.g., agent software that can simulate customer paths through a website to assess and report on performance and availability).

In all cases, it is essential that sufficient investigation be done to ensure that the costs are understood and agreed to and that the organization remains legal in respect to having sufficient licenses.

Deployment

Many ITSM tools, particularly discovery and event monitoring tools, will require some client/agent software deploying to all target locations before they can be used. This deployment will require careful planning and execution and should be handled through formal release and deployment management. Some deployment considerations are listed here:

- There should be careful scheduling and testing, and the deployment must be tracked so that it is clear which CIs have the software and which have yet to receive it.
- The CMS should be updated as the deployment progresses.
- It is often necessary to reboot devices for the client software to be recognized, and this needs to be arranged in advance to minimize service interruption.
- Special arrangements may be needed for portable equipment, which may not be present on site during deployment.
- The devices receiving the software must be checked in advance to ensure that they have sufficient storage and processing capacity to host and run the new software.
- The network capacity needs to be checked to ensure that it is capable of transmitting everything required.

- The best time to deploy a tool is dependent on the maturity level. A tool that is deployed too early shifts the focus of the improvement initiative away from the requirement to change processes and ways of working, and the whole improvement exercise then becomes merely a tool implementation.

- Training in the tool prior to deployment is necessary if benefits are to be realized.

Remember, a tool is usually not enough to make things work better. However, if it supports processes and the user has been trained to use it, a good tool can help staff carry out new processes.

Here are some further aspects of the deployment that must be considered:

The Type of Introduction to Be Used   A decision must be made whether a "Big Bang" introduction or some sort of phased approach is to be adopted. Because most organizations will have live services to keep running during the introduction, a phased approach is more likely to be necessary.

Transition between Tools   If an older tool is being replaced, consideration must be given to the best way to transition between the old tool and the new tool. For example, the service desk should not be assigning an incident on a new tool to a team that has yet to transition from the old tool.

Data Migration   A decision needs to be made regarding what data needs to be migrated from the old tool to the new one. This may require reformatting, and so may need to be validated after migration, especially if the data is transferred electronically. A period of parallel running may be implemented instead, with the old tool being available in a read-only mode for an initial period alongside the new one so that historical data can be referenced if needed.

Complete details on the release and deployment management process can be found in the ITIL Service Transition publication.

Summary

In this chapter, we examined the key steps to be carried out when choosing and implementing a new integrated service management tool. This included the gathering requirements, considering other factors, assessing tools against requirements, and implementing the tools.

Exam Essentials

Understand the benefits that an integrated service management tool delivers.   This includes understanding how tools can process large amounts of data and deliver consistency and their ability to link different pieces of information together (such as incidents and problems) and to produce reports on service delivery.

Explain the importance of defining the utility and warranty aspects required from a tool. Understand the importance of clearly specifying both what the tool needs to do and the performance it needs to deliver in terms of capacity, availability, and security.

Understand the different types of requirements. Be able to identify the difference between mandatory and desirable requirements.

Explain the selection technique known as MoSCoW. Understand what the acronym stands for (Must/Should/Could/Would) and be able to explain its use in tool selection.

Review Questions

You can find the answers to the review questions in the appendix.

1. Which of the following statements about a statement of requirements is incorrect?
    A. An SoR should always contain business requirements.
    B. An SoR should identify the mandatory facilities.
    C. The SoR should always state the maximum budget available.
    D. The SoR should specify the architecture on which the solution is required to run.

2. Which of the following statements regarding the implementation of a new tool is correct?
    A. Customization will have to be repeated for each upgrade.
    B. Configuration may affect supplier support obligations.
    C. An out-of-the box tool would require customized training.
    D. Following configuration, but before deployment, all the new processes should be defined.

3. The MoSCoW approach is often adopted when preparing a request for a new service management tool. What do the uppercase letters in the term MoSCoW stand for?
    A. Might, Should, Could, Wanted
    B. Mandatory, Should, Costed, Wanted
    C. Must, Should, Could, Would
    D. Mandatory, Should, Customizable, Won't

4. Which of the following shows the correct order of steps to be carried out when selecting a tool?
    A. Agree on selection criteria. Identify requirements. Identify products. Evaluate products. Rank the products. Score each product. Compile a short list of suitable products. Select product.
    B. Identify requirements. Identify products. Agree on selection criteria. Evaluate products. Score each product. Rank the products. Compile a short list of suitable products. Select product.
    C. Identify requirements. Identify products. Agree on selection criteria. Evaluate products. Compile a short list of suitable products. Score the products. Rank the products. Select product.
    D. Identify products. Identify requirements. Agree on selection criteria. Evaluate products. Rank the products. Compile a short list of suitable products. Score each product. Select product.

5. Which of the following is not an advantage of using tools during service design?
    A. They allow large amounts of repetitive work to be carried out quickly and consistently.
    B. They save time because less testing of the solution will be required.

   C. Tools provide a wealth of management information.

   D. The use of tools helps standardize practices and integrates processes.

6. Which of the following statements is untrue?

   A. The tool should be purchased, and then the process should be written to take best advantage of its capabilities.

   B. The process should be written, and then a tool should be found that fits it.

   C. If no tool supports the process, a tool may be chosen that requires the process to be redesigned to some extent as long as it achieves the desired end result.

   D. A tool is deemed to be fit for its purpose if it meets 80 percent or more of the business's operational requirements.

7. Which of the following statements about tool selection is/are correct?

   1. The tool's capabilities and how it matches the process are the only factors to be considered when choosing a tool.

   2. The quality of support offered by the vendor should be assessed; poor support could lead to the product being rejected.

   A. 1 only

   B. 2 only

   C. Both

   D. Neither

8. Which of the following aspects of service design tools should be considered when evaluating different products?

   1. Conformity to international open standards

   2. Flexibility in implementation, usage, and data sharing

   3. Usability—the ease of use permitted by the user interface

   4. Support for monitoring service levels

   5. Conversion requirements for previously tracked data

   6. Data backup, control, and security

   A. 1, 3, 5, and 6 only

   B. 2, 3, 5, and 6 only

   C. All of the above

   D. 3, 4, 5, and 6 only

9. When implementing a new tool, what additional costs should be budgeted for, in addition to the software's purchase costs?

   1. Training of staff in the use of the tool

   2. Cost of time spent setting up web portal

   3. Configuration costs

   4. Cost of time spent setting up reporting

    A. None of the above; these are business-as-usual costs.

    B. 1, 2, and 3 only.

    C. 1, 3, and 4 only.

    D. All of the above.

10. Which of the following are advantages of implementing a new tool under a Software as a Service arrangement?

  1. No extra hardware is required.

  2. No extra software is required.

  3. No extra training is required.

  4. Less management overhead.

    A. All of the above

    B. 1, 2, and 4 only

    C. 1, 2, and 3 only

    D. 1, 3, and 4 only

Appendix

Answers to Review Questions

Chapter 1: Introduction to Operational Support and Analysis

1. D. Testing and rolling out the service are part of the service transition stage, and the decision to retire the service is strategic.

2. D. Design coordination takes place solely within the service design lifecycle stage, whereas the other processes have elements of operational activity.

3. C. This includes the correct list of functions in service operation.

4. B. Defining the infrastructure requirements will be part of service design.

5. B. Option B correctly matches the activities and functions.

6. C. The problem management process is responsible for the prevention of incidents.

7. B. Design coordination is a process of service design, and change management is a process of service transition.

8. D. Service owner is not a role specific to processes; it applies to the overall service.

9. A. Facilities management and operations control are the two elements of operations management, and process roles are applicable to processes, not to an overall service.

10. C. The process practitioner is responsible for carrying out the work instructions for the process. Delivery of service is the responsibility of the service owner, the process owner is responsible for process policies, and the process manager will manage the resources for the process.

Chapter 2: Incident and Problem Management

1. B. Option B is the definition of an incident given in the ITIL framework. Option A refers to an event, and Option C is a diagnosed problem.

2. C. The incident should not be closed until the user confirms that the service has been restored.

3. B. Option B does not restore the service to the agreed level or provide a workaround; the other options do this.

4. C. Option C is the definition of normal service operation given in the ITIL framework. Normal service operation is what the customer should expect because both sides have agreed on it in the SLA.

5. C. These are called incident models. A model is a repeatable way of dealing with a particular item, in this case a particular type of incident. It defines steps to be taken to resolve the incident along with timescales and escalation points. This speeds up logging and improves consistency.

6. D. All incidents should be logged to ensure that a true picture of the customer experience is achieved; this also allows the cumulative impact of minor incidents to be evaluated. It provides evidence as to when these incidents occur, which may be useful in diagnosing the underlying cause. Option B is incorrect because not *all* incidents will come from the user; they could come from event logs, suppliers, technical staff, and so on.

7. B. Priority within ITIL terms is always based on impact (effect on the business) and urgency (how quickly the business needs resolution).

8. B. Hierarchic escalation involves going up the chain of command to inform or gain additional resources. Functional escalation is going across increasing technical skill levels to speed up resolution.

9. C. A problem takes an unknown cause from one or more incidents, diagnoses the cause, and determines a permanent solution, where possible, thus turning an unknown into a known.

10. D. These are all potential outputs of problem management. Known errors and the associated workarounds are documented and passed to the service desk so that new incident occurrences can be resolved. An RFC may need to be raised to implement a permanent resolution.

Chapter 3: Event Management, Request Fulfillment, and Access Management

1. D. Situation 2 would not be helped by using events. Situation 1 would detect an alert that a time threshold or a priority condition existed and would carry out the escalation defined. Situation 3 would similarly respond to a particular event such as an alarm and would automatically notify the police station. Situation 4 could use the events signifying the successful backup of each file to automate the backup of the next file.

2. C. 1, 2, and 4 are all examples of where event management can be used. Heat and moisture content can be monitored through event management, and actions can be taken if they breach acceptable parameters. Licenses can be controlled by monitoring who is signing onto applications and raising an alert if the maximum legal number is breached. Staff rosters do not have changing conditions that could be monitored by the use of events.

3. C. The two types of event monitoring described in the chapter are passive and active. Passive monitoring waits for an error message to be detected, and active monitoring checks periodically on the "health" of the CI. The other two are not recognized by ITIL as event monitoring types.

4.   D. Only common, low-risk requests with a documented fulfillment procedure should be implemented using the request fulfillment process. Other changes require risk assessment through the change advisory board.

5.   A. Service desk staff fulfill many requests, with second-line staff carrying out installations, moves, and so on. Requests do not fall under the responsibilities of the SLM or BRM.

6.   A. Requests do not need CAB approval. If a change is required to fulfill the request, it should usually be preauthorized because the level of risk is low and the fulfillment process known and defined. The usual financial controls still apply, so part of fulfillment may be obtaining the budget holder's agreement to the expenditure. Technical authorization may be required, as mentioned in the chapter.

7.   B. Option A is incorrect because security management does not prevent nonauthorized users from gaining access. Option C is incorrect because security management is responsible for setting security policies. Option D is incorrect because access management carries out the wishes of whoever is responsible for authorizing access (usually a business manager); it does not make the decision.

8.   D. All of the statements except number 3 are correct. Organizations often have a legal requirement to protect data, and failure to do so may damage their reputation and lead to less business. The data belongs to the business, and effective access management is required to ensure that access is based on business reasons, not what IT thinks. Access management does not necessarily reduce costs.

9.   C. The HR department manages changes to users' names; this is not an access management challenge.

10. A. Access management will remove or restrict access for staff on long-term leave because there is no valid reason for them to be accessing data. Any attempt to do so would raise suspicions. Access rights for those who have left the organization should be removed. It is poor practice to keep their access information available for the remaining staff to use; it should be adjusted if required to ensure a proper audit trail.

Chapter 4: The Service Desk

1.   C. The problem management process is responsible for the prevention of incidents, including recurrent. The service desk does not undertake problem management, it provides a first point of contact, resolves as many incidents as possible during the first contact, and updates users regarding the progress of incidents that have been assigned to second-line support teams.

2.   B. Design coordination is a process of service design, and change management is a process of service transition. Neither of these are carried out by the service desk.

3. D. Detailed application knowledge is required for the application management function, not for the service desk. It is sufficient for service desk staff to have enough technical ability and understanding of the infrastructure and applications, to be able to recognize known errors and apply workarounds, or to escalate the incident to the correct support team. A knowledge of the business is required to understand business impact when prioritizing incidents.

4. B. Matrix is not recognized as a service desk structure in the ITIL framework.

5. B. Incident diagnostic scripts are used by the service desk analysts to help in the resolution of incidents at first-line. The known error database will provide workarounds to allow the service desk to restore service. The CMS will provide information regarding the CI experiencing the issue, and show its relationships with other CIs, as faults with other CIs may cause the particular CI to fail (for example, a faulty router may cause a printer to fail to print). Finally, access to the change schedule will highlight if the faulty CI has recently undergone a recent change that may have caused the fault.

6. D. The percentage of incidents closed without escalation to another team will show the first-line resolution rate for the service desk; resolution at the service desk provides the fastest and cheapest solution, and minimizes the impact to the business. The percentage of incidents correctly categorized at logging shows how well the service desk staff understand the issue; incorrect categorization may cause the incident to be escalated to the wrong support team, wasting time and prolonging the impact to the business. Customer satisfaction survey scores will show whether the service being provided meets the business requirement. The percentage of incidents that are judged to be caused by hardware is out of the control of the service desk and does not reflect the level of service provided.

7. B. The service desk resolves simple incidents; this means that these are not escalated to technical staff. The service desk does not document service level requirements or authorize RFCs. Although the service desk staff may help to update the CMS, and thus improve its accuracy, this is an *indirect* benefit as the CMS is the direct responsibility of service asset and configuration management.

8. A. All incidents must be logged, whether by the super user or the service desk; if faults are resolved without being logged, problem management will not be aware of them, so there will be no root cause analysis and permanent resolution to prevent recurrence. Also, if second-line support teams work on incidents without the incident being logged, there will be incomplete management information regarding their workload and productivity. These incidents may also be treated with a higher priority than is warranted.

9. B. Option B describes a virtual service desk structure. Option A describes a local service desk, Option C describes a follow-the-sun structure, and Option D does not describe any of the structures described in the ITIL guidance.

10. B. The senior management of the organization determines what service will be provided and remains accountable for the level of service provided, even if they have employed an outsourcer to deliver it. The outsourcer is responsible for ensuring that the level of service provided matches or exceeds what was agreed in the contract.

Chapter 5: Technical Management, Application Management, and IT Operations Management

1. B. Defining the infrastructure requirements will be part of service design.

2. B. Option B correctly matches the activities and functions.

3. D. Facilities management and operations control are the two elements of operations management.

4. A. Technical management deals with the technical aspects of new or changed services. Option B is carried out by IT operations management, Option C by applications management, and Option D by the service desk.

5. C. All of these are objectives of application management.

6. D. Technical management refers to technical expertise and management of the infrastructure.

7. A. Maintaining status quo of day-to-day operational activity is the objective of IT operations; planning new deployment of applications is the role of application management.

8. D. Application management will take overall responsibility for all application-related issues.

9. C. Technical management includes specialist technical architects, designers, maintenance, and support staff.

10. B. This is a primary objective for IT operations management. Although other functions may be involved in routine tasks, this is not their primary objective.

Chapter 6: Technology and Implementation Considerations for Operational Support and Analysis

1. B. Tools enable processes, not replace them, and although tools are used to support the processes, they should not define them.

2. A. Statement 2 is incorrect; a tool does not need to have a service knowledge management system to be a service management tool. However, having details of all CIs and being able to link incidents, problems, requests, and so on is incredibly useful.

3. B. The first step in selecting a toolset should be requirements gathering; if the requirements are not met, the tool may not function sufficiently to support the needs of the processes and teams.

4. C. All of the options are part of the generic requirements for a service management tool.

5. A. The Must, Should, Could, Would (MoSCoW) technique is used to categorize requirements in the selection of a tool. For example, the tool must have the ability to link incident records to problem records.

6. D. The ability to authorize change requests is unlikely to be part of a self-service portal, but all of the rest are potentially standard capabilities.

7. D. Reporting is essential in service management. A good tool will have a selection of generic reports but should also provide the functionality to support tailored report requirements to support organizational needs.

8. A. Management should provide support and guidance throughout service management, and commitment is apparent if they provide the budget to enable training, obtain tools, and so on.

9. B. Adopting project management does not mean that service operation does not have to fund the change. All other answers are benefits of using project management.

10. B. Time limited is *not* a valid type of license. All the other terms are descriptions of possible licensing options.

Chapter 7: Introduction to Planning, Protection, and Optimization

1. D. The 4 Ps of service design are the four aspects of service design that ensure a robust design that meets the requirement. The first aspect is people—calculating the number of people required to support the new service and ensuring that they have the necessary skill set to do so effectively. The second aspect to be considered is process—the service design processes and any additional processes, such as authorization or procurement processes. The third aspect is partners—ensuring that the best suppliers are chosen, since they provide components of the service. The final aspect is the products—the services being designed and the technology and tools to support the service later.

2. B. A design that is balanced has given the appropriate weight to resources, time, and functionality. This means that if, for example, there is a requirement for a functionally rich product, this product will require either a lot of resources or a lot of time to develop. If, on the other hand, the most important requirement is for a fast delivery, either functionality will need to be sacrificed or extra resources will be required. These three elements should therefore be in balance—the optimal level of functionality, delivered within the optimal timeframe, with a reasonable expenditure of resources.

3. B. A holistic approach ensures that each of the following five aspects is considered:

The design of the actual solution itself

The service management system and tools that will be required to manage the service

The management and technology architectures that the service will use

The processes needed to support the service in operation

The measurement systems, methods, and metrics that will be required

4. C. An inflexible design, late delivery, and insufficient focus on the warranty aspects of capacity, availability, service continuity, and security all pose risks to the success of the design. Option C is incorrect because it wrongly describes warranty as fit for purpose. Warranty describes fitness for use.

5. D. All the aspects listed must be considered if the design is to be successful. The technical components required must be specified, together with the third-party support contracts to ensure that those service components provided by suppliers are delivered to the required quality and cost. If the service is to deliver benefits, it will require properly trained staff to support it in the event of any incidents. Finally, the required reporting and governance controls must be in place to ensure that the service is secure and provides the required information. One such example is ensuring that a finance system provides an audit trail of financial expenditure authorization.

6. B. The service design stage is responsible for researching and evaluating alternative solutions to meet the business requirement, for recommending the best solution, and for procuring it when the best option is to buy a product and further customize it if required. If the best option is to develop the solution in-house, this is also the responsibility of design. The development of the business case is a responsibility of the service strategy stage.

7. A. The purpose of the service design stage of the lifecycle is to design IT services, with the necessary supporting IT practices, processes, and policies, to realize the service provider's strategy. It is important to understand this point—design is not just about the technical design; it also considers the way it will be used and the processes required. Design should also include thinking about how the service will be transitioned; it should facilitate the introduction of the service into the supported environment in such a way as to ensure high-quality service delivery, customer satisfaction, and cost-effective service provision. Evaluating the financial impact of new or changed strategies on the service provider is the purpose of the financial management for IT services process, which is part of service strategy.

8. B. ITIL lists the five aspects of service design as the design of the actual solution; the design of the service management system and tools required to manage the service (missing from the options provided here); the management and technology architectures that the service will use; the processes needed to support the service in operation; and the measurement systems, methods, and metrics that will be required. Risk management is not one of the five aspects.

9. C. Service design plans should cover the approach, timescales, and resource requirements; the organizational and technical impact; risks; commercial aspects; training requirements; and appropriate communication methods. The output from this planning is captured in the service design package (SDP). The SDP should contain everything necessary for the subsequent testing, introduction, and operation of the solution or service. This should also include the production of a set of service acceptance criteria (SAC). All the suggested contents in the question are therefore valid except the change schedule and the CMS.

10. D. The responsibilities of the design coordination process include producing the service design packages based on service charters and change requests and ensuring that these are handed over to service transition as agreed.

Chapter 8: Capacity, Availability, and Information Security Management

1. A. Monitoring and forecasting capacity requirements and dealing with capacity issues and incidents are the responsibility of the capacity management process. Although capacity management would be consulted before capacity requirements would be agreed for inclusion in the SLA, it is the responsibility of the service level management process to negotiate these targets for service level agreements.

2. A. The subprocesses of capacity management described in the ITIL framework are business, service, and component capacity management.

3. C. Business capacity management is concerned with understanding the future business plans and their implications on the IT infrastructure. The detailed planning and management of the technical aspects is covered by the component capacity management subprocess, whereas the service capacity management subprocess is responsible for the service performance achieved in the operational environment.

4. A. There are reactive and proactive elements to the process, to both plan and react to operational needs.

5. B. Risk management is part of information security management but is not a responsibility of capacity management, which plans ahead and includes some contingency in case the expectations for the capacity requirements prove inaccurate. Both processes are cyclic—planning, implementing, monitoring the result, deciding on further actions required and planning them, and so on.

6. A. The purpose of the information security management process is to develop and maintain an information security policy that aligns IT security with business security and ensures that the confidentiality, integrity, and availability of the organization's assets, information, data, and IT services always match the agreed needs of the business. The other purposes listed here are aspects of the implementation of such a policy.

7. C. The elements of the information security management system include plan, implement, evaluate, maintain, and control. Planning incorporates the details and targets in the various agreements and contracts, and the various policies agreed to by the business and IT. Implementation requires awareness of the policies and the systems by all affected by them. Evaluation involves internal and external audits of the security, and maintain captures the lessons learned so that improvements can be planned and implemented. The overall approach is designed to maintain control and establish a framework for managing security throughout the organization.

8. D. The security management information system (SMIS) is an output of the ISM process and is the repository for all the information related to information security management.

9. D. The four key concepts are reliability, resilience, serviceability, and maintainability. Reliability is defined by ITIL as "a measure of how long a service, component, or CI can perform its agreed function without interruption." Resilience is designing the service so that a component failure does not result in downtime. Maintainability is measured as the mean time to restore service (MTRS). Serviceability is defined as the ability of a third-party supplier to meet the terms of its contract.

10. B. VBF stands for vital business function. Availability management works with the business to identify which services or parts of services are the most critical to achieving the required business outcomes. Understanding the VBFs informs decisions regarding where expenditure to protect availability is justified.

Chapter 9: IT Service Continuity Management and Demand Management

1. B. Ensuring that the business has contingency plans in place in case of a disaster is the responsibility of the business, not IT service continuity management.

2. D. BIA stands for business impact analysis.

3. C. BCM and ITSCM are closely linked as described in the option.

4. C. The number of incidents (4) is a KPI for incident management.

5. C. Testing takes place during implementation and ongoing operation.

6. C. Patterns of activity are mechanisms for tracking business activity to deliver business outcomes, which show how the business will need to use business services.

7. B. Demand management is the process that matches business demands to the supply of services by the service provider. The demands will be defined as services through strategy and measured through service level management.

8. A. Demand management will use all of these information sources.

9. A. User profiles allow us to capture information about common roles and responsibilities in the organization to aid with the understanding of demands.

10. D. Demand captures the information about consumption; consumption does not consume it. Patterns of production may or may not be found in highly synchronized patterns.

Chapter 10: Technology and Implementation Considerations for Planning, Protection, and Optimization

1. D. The ability to authorize change requests is unlikely to be part of a self-service portal, but all of the rest are potentially standard capabilities.

2. A. Management should provide support and guidance throughout service management, and commitment is apparent if they provide the budget to enable training, obtain tools, and so on.

3. B. Time limited is *not* a valid type of license. All the other terms are descriptions of possible licensing options.

4. D. Reporting is essential in service management. A good tool will have a selection of generic reports but should also provide the functionality to support tailored report requirements to support organizational needs.

5. B. Adopting project management does not mean that service operation does not have to fund the change. All other answers are benefits of using project management.

6. A. Statement 2 is incorrect; a tool does not need to have a service knowledge management system to be a service management tool. However, having details of all CIs and being able to link incidents, problems, requests, and so on is incredibly useful.

7. C. All of the options are part of the generic requirements for a service management tool.

8. B. Tools enable processes, not replace them, and although tools are used to support the processes, they should not define them.

9. A. The Must, Should, Could, Would (MoSCoW) technique is used to categorize requirements in the selection of a tool. For example, the tool must have the ability to link incident records to problem records.

10. B. The first step in selecting a toolset should be requirements gathering; if the requirements are not met, the tool may not function sufficiently to support the needs of the processes and teams.

Chapter 11: Introduction to Release, Control, and Validation

1. C. Option C is an objective of service strategy, not service transition.

2. C. It is design that turns strategy into deliverables (1), and it is in the service operations stage that the design is used in the real world and the strategy is realized (2).

3. B. Service transition covers the transfer of services, as described in options 1, 3, and 4. Producing a business case is a service strategy task. Terminating a supplier contract would involve a number of transition tasks, such as updating the CMS and supplier and contract management information system, putting an alternative supplier in place, or taking the service in house.

4. B. The purpose of service transition is to ensure seamless transition of designed services to meet the business expectations agreed in strategy.

5. A. Capacity plans are developed as part of service design in the capacity management process.

6. B. Change evaluation focus is strongly related to service transition because evaluation is part of ensuring that the release is fit for delivery into operation.

7. C. Both statements are correct.

8. D. These are all approaches that can be managed under transition.

9. C. Service transition supports the introduction of new services.

10. A. As with all improvement activity across the lifecycle, service transition engages with CSI to ensure that improvements are made and prioritized according to business need.

Chapter 12: Change Management and Service Asset and Configuration Management

1. B. The purpose of the SACM process is to identify and control the assets that make up our services, and to maintain accurate information about these assets.

2. D. SACM is a process that supports all stages of the service lifecycle by providing information about the assets that make up our services.

3. C. A configuration record captures the information about a configuration item and records the attributes and relationships. It is stored in the CMDB. Option A is a service asset, Option B is a configuration item, and Option D is activity carried out in SACM.

4. B. Although it may help provide background information to an incident, the CMS would not normally contain known errors and so forth.

5. A. This information will be easily available in the CMS once the process is implemented, saving time and reducing the risk of changes. Staff members need to understand the criticality of an accurate CMS through an awareness campaign. The level of detail maintained must match the value of such information, and without effective change management, effective SACM is impossible.

6. D. The ECAB decides on emergency changes; it needs to be a small group, because they need to be contacted and make a decision very quickly. The attendees are senior managers, who agree whether the proposed change is workable (using the senior technical manager's assessment) and the risk is acceptable (the senior IT manager and the customer representative would decide on this).

7. C. A call to the service desk may require a change to fulfill the request or resolve the incident. A change proposal defines a major change in principle; this may then lead to several smaller changes being raised. A project initiation document will outline the changes that the project will deliver; each will need to be agreed by change management.

8. B. There may be several CABs, each responsible for dealing with changes for a particular geographic area, business unit, or other category.

9. B. There are three different types of service change:

   Standard changes are low risk and relatively common, and they follow a defined procedure. They are preauthorized.

   Emergency changes must be implemented as soon as possible (for example, to resolve a major incident or implement a security patch). They are normally defined as changes where the risk of not carrying out the change is greater than the risk of implementing it.

   All other changes are defined as normal changes.

10. B. Change management ensures that changes to the IT services and components are delivered with the minimum of risk, within budget and in a controlled manner. Although business changes may involve IT changes, the achievement of the strategic business benefits of business changes is outside the scope of change management as described in ITIL.

Chapter 13: Service Validation and Testing and Change Evaluation

1. D. The test report is not part of a test model. It is produced after testing is complete.

2. C. The correct order is as follows: design tests, verify test plan, prepare test environment, perform tests, evaluate exit criteria and report, test cleanup and closure.

3. D. The exit and entry criteria for testing are defined in the service design package.

4. B. The left-hand side of the service V-model shows service requirements down to the detailed service design. The right-hand side focuses on the validation activities that are performed against these specifications.

5. C. Any of the listed options are valid results.

6. D. The objectives of change evaluation include setting stakeholder expectations correctly and providing accurate information to change management to prevent changes with an adverse impact and changes that introduce risk being transitioned unchecked. It also evaluates the intended and the unintended effects of a service change and provides good-quality outputs to enable change management to decide quickly whether a service change is to be authorized.

7. B. The purpose of the change evaluation process is to understand the likely performance of a service change and how it might impact the business, the IT infrastructure, and other IT services. The process assesses the actual performance of a change against its predicted performance.

8. D. These are the four main sections of the report as described in the change evaluation process.

9. C. A model is a representation of a system, process, IT service, or configuration item that is used to help understand or predict future behavior.

10. A. The trigger for change evaluation is receipt of a request for evaluation from change management.

Chapter 14: Release and Deployment Management and Knowledge Management

1. A. Option B describes a release unit, Option C describes a release, and Option D describes a release model.

2. B. Early life support is the handover that takes place between service transition and service operation during the deployment phase of release and deployment. It ensures that the support of the deployment and development teams is still available as the new or changed service is introduced to the live environment.

3. C. SACM is the process that manages the naming convention for the configuration management system. Release management is concerned with the release controls that are specified in the release policy.

4. D. Verification and audit is a step in the SACM process.

5. C. Early life support takes place in the deployment phase, where the handover to service operation takes place.

6. 1+B, 3+A, 4+C, 2+D. In the DIKW model, Data is a discrete set of facts, Information gives context to data, Knowledge is experiences, ideas, insights, values, and judgments, and Wisdom creates value through correct and well-informed decisions. This progression shows how Data needs to be built on in order to provide a meaningful opportunity for decision making. Data alone will not be sufficient to make a well-informed decision; it must be transformed through greater context and understanding to enable Wisdom.

7. C. The tool is called the service knowledge management system (SKMS), and it's a repository for information, data, and knowledge relating to service management. This has important connections for managing information and knowledge throughout the whole service lifecycle.

8. D. Knowledge management is a process that has influence across the whole of the service lifecycle. It is used to capture and present ideas, perspectives, data, and information to all stages of the lifecycle, ensuring that the appropriate decisions can be made.

9. B. A knowledge librarian is an alternative name for the knowledge management practitioner.

10. A. The process owner is responsible for the creation of the mechanisms for data, information, and knowledge capture throughout the organization.

Chapter 15: Technology and Implementation Considerations for Release, Control, and Validation

1. D. The six items in the question are all triggers for operational change listed in ITIL Service Operation.

2. A. Service operation personnel should be involved in design and transition to ensure that the end result is supportable.

3. C. ITIL and project management can be complementary; however, project management is not required for simple changes. Project management is useful where changes are large or complex. Not all operational changes are business as usual, and simple changes do not require project management.

4. D. Service operation staff need to be involved early in the process to ensure that the design takes into account operational issues, but their involvement is also needed later. Service operation staff need to be involved late in the process to ensure that the schedule for implementation does not clash with other operational priorities, but their involvement is also needed earlier. Therefore, staff involvement is necessary throughout the design and implementation process to ensure that all operational issues and possible impacts are dealt with.

5. D. These are all risks and should be mitigated using ITIL best practice for change, supplier, service strategy, and information security.

6. B. Time limited is not a valid type of license listed in ITIL Service Operation.

7. C. Both answers are correct. Transition is supported by specific process-related tools and enterprise-wide tools such as the configuration management system or service knowledge management system.

8. D. Communities are often used to ensure collaboration across organizations.

9. B. All of these are knowledge sharing tools.

10. B. Discovery tools may be used, but they are not the only source for data entry in the CMS.

Chapter 16: Introduction to Service Offerings and Agreements

1. B. The service design processes discussed in relation to service offerings and agreements include service level management, supplier management, service catalog management, and design coordination. The remaining service design processes of availability, capacity, IT service continuity management, and information security management are out of scope for service offerings and agreements.

2. C. Option A is carried out by the manager of the service level management process. Option B is the responsibility of the transition planning and support process. Option D is completed by the IT steering group and senior management of the department.

3. B. The design coordination process does not design the solution; it coordinates the work of others. It is responsible for ensuring that the design meets the requirements. It is responsible for providing a single coordination point and for ensuring that the objectives of the service design stage are met.

4. B. Strategy management for IT services is responsible for deciding and describing what services the service provider will deliver to enable the organization to achieve its business outcomes, and which services will be the most appropriate to enable this. Ensuring that there are sufficient resources to provide the services to which it is committed is a purpose of the financial management for IT services process, not strategy management.

5. D. Warranty refers to the ability of a service to be available when needed, to provide the required capacity, and to provide the required reliability in terms of continuity and security. Warranty can be summarized as how the service is delivered, and can be used to determine whether a service is fit for use.

6. A. This is the correct definition of utility and warranty.

7. B. These are the basic elements of a business case, as discussed as part of financial management.

8. B. When a design needs to be changed or any of the individual elements of the design need to be amended, consideration must be given to all aspects. This is called having a holistic service design. Holistic service design therefore has taken into account all five aspects of design.

9. B. Design coordination is responsible for the coordination of the service design lifecycle stage, not the service operation stage.

10. D. ROI can be calculated objectively as a straightforward comparison between the profits generated by the new service or the reduced cost in provision compared to the cost of implementing that service. There may also be many other aims for a service that are qualitative, and therefore measurement of these is subjective.

Chapter 17: Service Portfolio Management and Service Catalog Management

1. D. The service portfolio has information that can be used by all stages of the service lifecycle. It is sometimes referred to as the spine of the lifecycle approach.

2. D. The service portfolio allows the IT provider and customer to determine whether the correct services are being provided to meet the business needs by creating a holistic view of all the services under the control of the service provider. This includes services under development and retired services.

3. A. Each of the catalogs is described accurately—customer-facing services are viewed in the business/customer catalog, the technical catalog provides visibility of the supporting services, and the multiview catalog will provide visibility of all services to the appropriate audience.

4. C. A service catalog is a documented information source that details the information relating to all live services.

5. C. Strategic services is not a name used in the ITIL framework, so this can be discounted. Retired services are captured as part of the service portfolio. Customer-facing and supporting services are the descriptions of the services captured in the service catalog.

6. B. The service catalog is the central section of the service portfolio; therefore, it forms a part of the service portfolio.

7. C. Options A and B specify only a part of the catalog each, whereas C correctly states the visibility of services and business processes in the catalog. Services under development will be shown in the service portfolio.

8. A. The service catalog shows details of all live operational services, and these may interact with a number of processes. Therefore, it can be connected to the majority of lifecycle processes.

9. C. The service portfolio is a service strategy process. It supports the decision of what services to offer and to whom, which is a strategic concern.

10. B. The service portfolio manager is responsible for marketing the portfolio so that customers and potential customers are aware of the services available.

Chapter 18: Service Level Management and Supplier Management

1. A. A high-level relationship with the customer is provided through the business relationship management process. The single point of contact for the users is the service desk. Service transition looks after the smooth transition of services.

2. B. Option A is an objective of change management, Option C is an objective of the service desk, and Option D is an objective of problem management.

3. C. You would not find a definition of business strategy in a service level agreement.

4. C. A strategic business plan and an internal finance agreement are not commonly part of the support of an SLA.

5. D. Option A describes an operational level agreement. Option B describes a service level agreement. Option C describes a sort of agreement that is not defined as part of service level management. Option D provides the correct definition of an underpinning contract.

6. B. The service level monitoring chart is also known as a RAG status—red, amber, and green.

7. D. Supplier management is concerned with external suppliers only.

8. C. Tactical is the other category, not trusted.

9. C. ITIL recommends that suppliers are categorized according to the risk and impact to the achievement of business objectives and goals, and the relative value and importance of the supplier in providing the service.

10. C. These are both correct. The SCMIS is a repository for information relating to suppliers, such as supplier policies and contracts.

Chapter 19: Business Relationship Management and Financial Management for IT

1. D. Service valuation is defined as the ability to understand the costs of a service relative to its business value. Accounting is the process responsible for identifying the actual costs of delivering IT services, comparing them with budgeted costs, and managing variance from the budget. The framework that allows the service provider to determine the costs of providing services is the cost model, and the activity of predicting and controlling the spending of money is budgeting.

2.   D. Option A is incorrect because IT finances are a subset of the enterprise's finances, and the same rules and controls apply to it as to any other department. With regard to Option B, internal service providers may not necessarily charge for their services directly. Option C is incorrect because external service providers will not usually share this information, which would show their profit margins, to their customers.

3.   C. Ensuring that the service provider does not commit to services that they are not able to provide is one of the objectives of financial management. The other options are objectives of BRM.

4.   C. Budgeting is defined as the activity of predicting and controlling the spending of money.

5.   D. Business relationship management has a strategic, not an operational focus. It is also responsible for identifying customer needs, deciding which services the service provider will deliver to meet them, and ensuring that the service provider is able to meet them.

6.   A. Business relationship management will work with the business to build a business case for a new service. Service level management is only involved in ensuring that the service can be provided as required, not whether it is the best use of investment funds.

7.   A. Both are true statements, and both portfolios are data repositories used by BRM.

8.   B. Should the service provider's ROI be less than predicted in the business case, this may be a trigger for CSI, but it is not a trigger for BRM.

9.   B. Business relationship management uses the customer portfolio to record all customers of the IT service provider, and it uses the customer agreement portfolio to manage service contracts or agreements between an IT service provider and its customers (although this portfolio is actually managed by service level management). It does not use the supplier and contract management information system or the CMS.

10.   D. Service valuation is the ability to understand the costs of a service relative to its business value, and it is an important output from FMITS, as is service investment analysis, where FMITS provides the information to enable the service provider to determine the value of the investment in a service. The FMITS process ensures compliance to corporate and legislative standards regarding the storage and archiving of financial data. FMITS does not make any agreements about funding or charge for services; this is the responsibility of BRM, although FMITS may be consulted.

Chapter 20: Technology Considerations for Service Offerings and Agreements

1.   C. Stating the budget in advance would hamper negotiation later, which makes Option C the incorrect statement. The other three statements are true.

2. A. Customization (but not configuration) will have to be repeated for each upgrade. Configuration would not affect supplier support obligations (customization might). Out-of-the-box tools would mean standard training could be used. Processes should be defined before tool selection. The tool should follow the process, not vice versa.

3. C. Explanation: *M* stands for *must have* requirements, *S* stands for *should have* requirements, *C* stands for *could have* requirements, and *W* stands for *would like in the future* requirements.

4. C. The steps in Option C are in the right order. Option A suggests selection criteria first, but this cannot be done without understanding requirements. Option B puts shortlisting toward the end of the steps, which would mean a lot of investigation into an unsuitable tool could be done unnecessarily. Option D goes straight to product identification without requirements gathering.

5. B. The use of a service design tool will not reduce testing time. All the other options show actual benefits of using a tool.

6. A. The tool should fit the process, not the other way around. It is acceptable if the tool fails to fit some process areas and some changes are made to the process as long as they are not major.

7. B. It is insufficient to just address the tool's capabilities and how it matches the process; due diligence should be carried out to ensure that the support offered is of the required standard.

8. C. All of the listed aspects should be considered. Excluding any of these may mean the tool does not meet the requirements.

9. D. These costs should all be included. If the tool is implemented but insufficient training or configuration is carried out, the capabilities of the tool will not be realized. Without good reporting, the data held in the tool will not be easily available, and so monitoring achievement against targets, monitoring of KPIs, and so on will be ineffective. Without time spent setting up the web portal, a major advance in terms of efficiency will not be realized because a poorly implemented portal will not be used by the customers. Failure to include these costs explains why so many operation initiatives fail; there is an attempt to deliver too much as business as usual rather than as a costed and funded project.

10. B. Training will still be required, but access to the service across a network to the supplier will simplify implementation and may reduce costs.

Index

Index

Note to the Reader: Throughout this index **boldfaced** page numbers indicate primary discussions of a topic. *Italicized* page numbers indicate illustrations.

C

S

T

Comprehensive Online Learning Environment

Register on Sybex.com to gain access to the comprehensive online interactive learning environment and test bank to help you study for your Intermediate ITIL Service Capability certification.

The online test bank includes:

- **Assessment Test** to help you focus your study to specific objectives
- **Chapter Tests** to reinforce what you learned
- **Digital Flashcards** to reinforce your learning and provide last-minute test prep before the exam
- **Searchable Glossary** gives you instant access to the key terms you'll need to know for the exam

Go to `http://www.wiley.com/go/sybextestprep` to register and gain access to this comprehensive study tool package.

30% off On-Demand IT Video Training from ITProTV

ITProTV and Sybex have partnered to provide 30% off a Premium annual or monthly membership. ITProTV provides a unique, custom learning environment for IT professionals and students alike, looking to validate their skills through vendor certifications. On-demand courses provide over 1,000 hours of video training with new courses being added every month, while labs and practice exams provide additional hands-on experience. For more information on this offer and to start your membership today, visit `http://itpro.tv/sybex30/`.